PHILIP S. FONER

# The Life and Writings of Frederick Douglass

## VOLUME 5

*(Supplementary Volume)*

*1844-1860*

INTERNATIONAL PUBLISHERS   New York

Library of Congress Cataloging in Publication Data   (Revised)

Douglass, Frederick, 1817?-1895.
    The life and writings of Frederick Douglass.
    Includes bibliographical references and index.
    CONTENTS: 1. Early years, 1817-1849. — 2. Pre-Civil War decade, 1850-1860. — 3. The Civil War, 1861-1865. — 4. Reconstruction and after. — 5. Supplementary volume, 1844-1860.
    1. Slavery in the United States — Anti-slavery movements — Collected works. I. Foner, Philip Sheldon, 1910-
E449.D736        322.4'4'0924        50-7654
ISBN 0-7178-0453-4
ISBN 0-7178-0454-2 pbk

# Contents

PART TWO: *From the Founding of the North Star to the Compromise of 1850*

PART FOUR: *From the Kansas-Nebraska Act to the Election
    of Abraham Lincoln*

# INTRODUCTION

In the Foreword to her book, *Speak Out in Thunder Tones: Letters of Black Northerners 1787-1865*, published in 1973, Dorothy Sterling writes: "Fifteen years ago while I was sitting on a beach reading *The Life and Writings of Frederick Douglass*, edited by Philip Foner, a scholarly-looking stranger peered over my shoulder and asked, 'How could he have written enough to fill a *whole book?*' I replied that this was only one of four volumes of Douglass' writings. The man shook his head in disbelief and walked on toward the water."[1]

It would be interesting to speculate on what would have been the reaction of the "scholarly-looking stranger" had he learned that even these four volumes of the writings and speeches of Frederick Douglass were only a portion of the great Black American's literary output. At the time the four volumes of Douglass' writings and speeches were published (1950-1955), the possibilities of incorporating the other unpublished material were remote. No commercial publisher or even university press displayed the slightest interest in making available the letters, editorials, and speeches of this man of towering dimensions. (Indeed, the vast majority of the editors in these publishing houses had never even heard of Frederick Douglass.) The miracle was that even though harassed and financially hard-pressed during these years of McCarthyism—Alexander Trachtenberg, the publisher, even went to prison under the viciously un-American Smith Act—International Publishers undertook the expensive task of publishing the four volumes. These volumes did not include all of Douglass' writings and speeches, but a substantial collection of them along with a full-length biography of the man by myself published originally in four parts, each of which accompanied one of the volumes of the collected writings of Douglass.[2]

Since the four volumes appeared a veritable revolution has occurred in the publishing of books related to the role of Black people in the history of the United States. One sign of the change is the fact that the papers of two important Black Americans, Booker T. Washington and W.E.B. Du Bois, are in the process of being published in multivolume editions.[3] However, the publication of the writings and speeches of Frederick Douglass presents a problem which does not face the editors of the papers of Washington and Du Bois. Both Washington and Du Bois kept copies of nearly all of their writings and speeches, and when they died there existed an almost complete body of their letters, editorials, articles, and speeches. But the ante-bellum papers of Frederick Douglass were destroyed when the Douglass home in Rochester, New York, burned in 1872. Even the only complete file of his three ante-bellum newspapers, *The North Star, Frederick Douglass' Paper,* and *Douglass' Monthly* went up in flames.[4]

For many years whatever remained of Douglass' papers were stored at "Cedar Hill," Frederick Douglass' home in the Anacostia section of Washington, D.C. Included in the collection were more than 5,000 items, predominantly letters received by Douglass, many of them from Black men and women. While manuscripts of Douglass' addresses, speeches, lectures, and articles were amply represented, most of them related to the work of Douglass during and following the Civil War. Moreover, the conditions at "Cedar Hill" when I conducted research in the Douglass papers in preparation of the four-volume edition of Douglass' writings and speeches were anything but conducive to prolonged study, so that it was impossible to include in the collection some valuable material.[5]

In 1964 the papers of Douglass were acquired, along with the home, by the National Park Service. They have since been made available on microfilm by the Library of Congress photoduplication service. On January 17, 1972, the papers of Frederick Douglass were transferred from the National Park Service to the Library of Congress. The greater accessibility to Douglass' papers since my original research will be reflected in the next supplementary volume dealing with the Civil War and post-Civil War period, now in the process of being prepared for publication. For reasons indicated, the papers of Douglass have been of little use in the preparation of the present supplementary volume covering the period 1844 to the eve of the Civil War. To add to the existing body of Douglass' writings and speeches during these years, it has been necessary to correspond with a large number of libraries and historical societies here and abroad.

Jn introducing the first of the four volumes of *The Life and Writings of Frederick Douglass* in 1950, I wrote that the name Frederick Douglass "should be a famous name in American history—placed beside the names of Jefferson and Lincoln. Yet only recently has it been rescued from the oblivion to which it was assigned by our historiography."[6] It is most pleasing, therefore, a quarter of a century later, in introducing this supplementary volume, to be able to observe the high esteem in which Frederick Douglass is held by almost all students of American history. In 1915 Dr. W.E.B. Du Bois was almost alone when he wrote in *The Crisis* that Frederick Douglass was "the greatest of Negro Americans."[7] But today most scholars accept this view, and certainly there is no question that Frederick Douglass was, without even a close rival, the outstanding Black American of the half-century stretching from 1840-1895, a period of profound impact on the condition of Black Americans and on the character of American society. Each year sees the publication of specialized studies dealing with Douglass' place in the history of Black Americans, and it is rare indeed to find a collection of writings of Black Americans which does not include substantial selections from the pen of Douglass.[8] Such expressions as "the towering figure among Negroes in the 1850's,"[9] "the most influential of the former slaves who joined the abolitionist forces,"[10] "the preeminent black leader,"[11] "the most influential black leader,"[12] "one of the greatest men of American Negro history"[13]—are among the characterizations now commonly employed by historians of the antebellum period to describe Frederick Douglass. It is my conviction that the honors to Douglass in recent years will increase as more of his writings become available.[14]

"These writings of a man whom slavery deprived of formal education constitute an important and distinctive contribution to our literature," I wrote in the Preface to the first volume of *The Life and Writings of Frederick Douglass*.[15] The same point was made at the ceremony in the Whitehall Pavilion at the Library of Congress marking the presentation of the transfer of the papers of Frederick Douglass to the Library of Congress. On that occasion, Benjamin Quarles, professor of history at Morgan State College in Baltimore and a biographer of Frederick Douglass, noted: "Douglass' own writings are models of clarity and good literary form. He never wrote an article or gave a speech without careful preparation. . . . Incapable of writing a dull line, Douglass invests his sentences with an almost poetic cadence, compelling the reader to turn the page."[16] Those who are already acquainted with the four volumes of Douglass' writings in print will testify to the accuracy of this description. Further testimony is presented in the pages that follow.

These pages will also furnish the reader with an excellent picture of the Black communities of Cleveland, Cincinnati, Philadelphia, Chicago, Detroit and other northern cities which Douglass visited and from which he sent penetrating dispatches to his paper. They also contain considerable evidence of the ideological debates, sometimes quite bitter, which were part of the life of these Black communities in the ante-bellum years, especially over such issues as emigration. Douglass frequently engaged in such debates with other Black leaders, and in a number of cases I have included both sides of the argument, leaving it to the reader to determine whose agruments—Douglass, Martin R. Delaney, Henry Highland Garnet, Samuel Ringgold Ward, James M. Whitfield and William Wells Brown—were most effective. While there were those in the Black communities who felt that such debates weakened the struggles against racism, Douglass disagreed and emphasized that it was necessary to set forth all sides of an issue so that Black Americans could decide which course to support. On one issue, however, he felt there was no room for debate: the refusal of some Blacks to join the anti-slavery cause and/or yielded to prejudice against Negroes. For these he had only words of contempt, accusing them of having "become tools of their own proscription and degradation."

In presenting this supplementary volume the same procedure is followed as in the original four volumes. All of Douglass' writings and speeches are reproduced with no substantial change whatsoever; misspellings and grammatical errors have been corrected if they appreared in the printed sources and clearly were typographical mistakes. A few passages have been omitted from several of the selections to avoid repetition, but these have been properly indicated. In a few cases the only account of a Douglass speech was in the form of a digest by the reporter, and where these have been included, this has been clearly indicated. The word Negro has been capitalized throughout, and words which are considered scurrilous have not been spelled out. In all of Douglass' editorials and in most of his speeches, the original titles have been retained. The Editor has supplied titles where they were missing. The source of the originals of Douglass' writings and speeches has been placed at the end of each speech or article. The reference notes for the Introduction and for Douglass' writings and speeches have been placed at the end of the volume.

Except for one piece, Douglass, writings and speeches appear chronologically. The exception is "The Heroic Slave," his short story on the slave mutiny on the brig *Creole* in 1841 and the slave rebel who led the uprising, Madison Washington. Since this long piece would have interrupted the flow of events discussed by Douglass in 1853 when it appeared, I decided to place it in an Appendix.

In the preparation of this volume I have had the generous assistance and cooperation of the following: American Philosophical Library; the Library Company of Philadelphia; the Library of Congress; New York Historical Society; New York Public Library; the Schomburg Collection; George Arents Research Library; Syracuse University; Rush Rhees Library; University of Rochester; Trevor Arnett Library; Atlanta University; Moorland Library, Howard University; Boston Public Library; New Hampshire Historical Society; Chicago Historical Society; Maine Historical Society; Cincinnati Historical Society; Houghton Library; Harvard University; Columbia University Library; John Rylands University Library of Manchester, Deansgate, Manchester, England; and Central Library, Paisley, Scotland. I wish to thank Professors Jane H. and William H. Pease of the University of Maine for kindly furnishing me with microfilm copies of issues of *Frederick Douglass' Paper* for 1858-1859, thus enabling me to include material which had long been thought to have ceased to exist. I wish to thank *Ohio History* for permission to reproduce the speech, "Important Truths," published in the Winter 1966 issue. I wish, too, to thank Professor Leslie Goldstein of the University of Delaware, author of a doctoral dissertation dealing with Frederick Douglass' political thought, for having kindly agreed to read this collection of Douglass' writings and for valuable suggestions. Finally, I owe a special debt of gratitude to the staff of the Lincoln University Library, and particularly to Mr. Robert J. Alexander, for assistance in the use of the library's splendid collection of materials relating to Black history and for help in obtaining, through interlibrary loan, materials from many institutions.

Philip S. Foner

Lincoln University, Pennsylvania
July, 1975

THE WRITINGS AND SPEECHES
OF FREDERICK DOUGLASS


1844-1860

The Negro is the test of American civilization, American statesman-ship, American refinement, and American Christianity.

*Frederick Douglass' Paper*, March 25, 1859

## TO J. MILLER McKIM[1]

August 22, 1844

Friend M'Kim:

Though quite unaccustomed to write anything for the public eye, and in many instances quite unwilling to do so, in the present case I cannot content myself to take leave of you and the dear friends of the slave in this part of our anti-slavery vineyard, for home, without dropping you a very hasty, and of course very imperfect, sketch of the Anti-Slavery meetings recently held in Chester county, which, in company with Friend Remond,[2] it was my pleasure to attend.

The first of these was held in West Chester, on Thursday, 25th. In consequence of the Court House and churches of the village being closed against us, our friends there had provided to hold the meeting in a beautiful grove, less than a mile distant from the village. But the falling of a very heavy rain, a few hours before, rendered the woods exceedingly wet, and unfit for our purpose at the hour of meeting. Shut out from Church and from State, our last resort was to the market-house; it, fortunately for us and the slave, was doorless, and could not be shut. The day was extremely damp, and uncomfortably cool; owing to this—coupled with the disgraceful fact that the people of the town have sunken almost inextricably deep into the mire and *Clay*, which in this country, and at the present time everywhere besets the feet of the

3

unsuspecting[3]—we had a very small meeting. Those that came gave very good attention, though I am satisfied that most present came from no higher motive than to gratify an idle curiosity. I am glad, however, they came, from whatever motive; I am willing to be regarded as a curiosity, if I may thereby aid on the high and holy cause of the slaves' emancipation.

Our meeting was very unsatisfactory to ourselves, though not entirely so to our few friends in that place, who are not the sort to be discouraged. They filled me with admiration, as I viewed them occupying their noble position; a few women, almost alone in a community of thousands, asserting truths and living out principles at once hated and feared by almost the entire community; and doing all this with a composure and serenity of soul which would well compare with the most experienced champion and standard bearer of our cause, Friend Garrison himself. Heaven bless them, and continue them strength to withstand all trials through which their principles may call them to pass. From West Chester we were taken by the slave's friend, D. Kent, on to the meeting of the Clarkson Anti-slavery Society, held at Oxford, in Friends' Meeting-house.[4] This Society is very appropriately named; it is certainly one of the most venerable and impressive anti-slavery bodies with which it has been my fortune to meet. It enrolls amongst its members the very salt of anti-slavery wisdom, firmness, and perseverance in Chester county. The names of the Coates, Whitsons, Jacksons, Prestons, Hambletons, and others of the Society, seemed to be anti-slavery watch-words wherever I went in the county. The attendance at the meeting was very large; many had to stand outside, not being able to gain admission into the house. The Society got through their business at an early hour, to give place to addresses of Friend Remond and myself upon the general subject of slavery and anti-slavery. Our remarks were listened to, both within and without the house, with a deep stillness, that indicated an absorbing interest in the subjects we were but feebly attempting to set forth. I took quite too large a part in the meeting myself, to give you a very minute account of it. Suffice it to say, that whatever gloom was cast over my spirits by our meeting at West Chester, was completely dispelled by our meeting at Oxford. At this meeting, friend Remond and I parted; he, I believe, went to Kennett, and I to Fallowfield, being carried thither by our friend James Taylor, in whom the hunted slave has often found a warm friend while groping his way in the dark from slavery to freedom.

According to notice, our next meeting was held on Sunday afternoon at London Grove Meeting-house, *out-doors*. This meeting was a most splendid demonstration. The day was fine, the heavens clear, the sun bright, the air salubrious, and the scenery by which we were surrounded extremely grand; all nature seemed redolent with Anti-Slavery truth.

By many of our anti-slavery friends in Chester county, London Grove, has long been considered as being the very dwelling place of Quaker pro-slavery in the county, and it is the settled opinion of many who have excellent facilities for understanding the views and feelings of voting Quakers in that vicinity, that most of them will vote for Henry Clay, the Slaveholder. *(Query: do Friends bear a faithful testimony against slave-holdings?)* Owing to this opinion the abolitionists in the neighboring towns had long desired to have anti-slavery brought in direct contact with that community. Here was a fine opportunity, and they embraced it gladly; they came from ten, and I believe as far as fifteen miles around to gladden our hearts and cheer us on in the proclamation of Anti-Slavery truth. It was truly delightful, a short time before the commencement of the meeting, to look down the long roads in various directions, and see them almost literally alive with the gathering multitude. The old and young, the men and women on foot, on horseback and in wagons, were all pressing their way amid dust and din, towards the great Quaker meeting house, under the eaves of which, we had to hold our meeting, as it, like the strong hearts of its owners, stood locked and bolted against us. A very large part of the audience seemed to be such as had given no attention to the subject of slavery, and were there to gratify their curiosity, and I thought I discovered at the commencement of the meeting very much to confirm the opinion that I stood in the midst of a pro-slavery neighborhood. I am glad, however, to be able to say, that before the meeting came to a close, a very different aspect was worn by the audience.

Friend Remond first addressed the assemblage. He stood upon a large horse block, and spoke for more than an hour, in a strain of stern rebuke. His text was before him, he did not stray from it, nor it from him. It stood there in the shape of a great *stone Quaker Meeting House*, bolted and barred to the slave; as cold and insensible to the claims of humanity, as Egg Rock seems to be to the surging billows of the Atlantic, when viewed from the banks of old Nahant after a long northwestern storm.

I followed Friend Remond, and spoke for the space of an hour and a half. He had left little for me to do in the way of rebuke, and of consequence I pursued a somewhat different course, and I think reached another class of minds present, as necessary to the cause as any other. Our friends seemed highly gratified at the result of our meeting, and spoke of it as sufficient of itself to make up for all the lost time occasioned by the failure to get a connected series of meetings from the one at Norristown, to the time of our leaving for home.

Our next meeting was that of the Chester County Anti-Slavery Society. My time will not allow me to attempt a description of this meeting, suffice. it to say it held two-days, and was interesting to the last.

I have formed a decidedly favorable opinion of Pennsylvania Anti-Slavery people by recent contact with them. They have not yet quite rid themselves of what seems to me to be prejudice against color; but they are advancing and I trust will soon free themselves from its last vestige. I shall be glad when the time shall come that I shall again meet yourself and the anti-slavery friends of Pennsylvania.

Yours,<br>
Frederick Douglass

*Pennsylvania Freeman*, August 22, 1844

## TO WILLIAM LLOYD GARRISON

Cork, Oct. 28, 1845.

Dear Friend:

I am here, well and hearty, and I trust doing something for the promotion of our holy cause.[5] I have already had several meetings in this city, all of which have been very well attended by highly intelligent and influential people. The abolitionists here are of the true stamp. They look with the deepest interest on all movements for the abolition of slavery in America. When slavery was abolished in the West India Islands,[6] it was proposed to disband their organization, but they nobly resolved never to disband, while the foul blot and bloody stain of slavery disgraced any portion of the globe. And although they have existed in an organized form for many years longer than any of our organizations in America, I find them as warm-hearted, active and energetic, as though they had just commenced operations. For much of the interest manifested toward the Massachusetts A.S. Bazaar by the ladies of the city, the cause is indebted to Charles Lenox Remond. His labors here were abundant, and very effective. He is spoken of here in terms of high approbation; and his name is held in affectionate remembrance by many whose hearts were warmed into life on this question by his soul-stirring eloquence.

My reception here has been truly flattering. Immediately after my arrival, a public breakfast was given to receive myself and friend Buffum[7]—of the details of which, you are already informed. Since then, I have had every kindness shown me that the most ambitious could desire. I am hailed here as a temperance man as well as an abolitionist. My first speech here, as well as in Dublin, was on the temperance question.[8] I have spoken on temperance several times since. On the 21st instant, Father Mathew, the living savior of Ireland from the curse of intemperance, gave a splendid Soiree, as a token of his sympathy and regard for friend Buffum and myself. There were two hundred and fifty persons present. It was decidedly the brightest and happiest company, I think, I ever saw, anywhere. Everyone seemed to be enjoying himself in the fullest manner. It was enough to delight any heart not totally bereft of feeling, to look upon such a company of happy faces. Among them all, I saw no one that seemed to be shocked or disturbed at my dark presence. No one seemed to feel himself contaminated by contact with me. I think it would be difficult to get the same number of persons together in any of our New England cities, without some democratic nose growing deformed at my approach. *But then you know white people in America are whiter, purer, and better than the people here. This accounts for it!* Besides, we are the freest nation on the globe, as well as the most enlightened, and can therefore afford to insult and outrage the colored man with impunity. This is one of the peculiar privileges of our peculiar institution. On the morning after the Soiree, Father Mathew invited us to breakfast with him at his own house—an honor quite unexpected, and one for which I felt myself unprepared. I however accepted his kind invitation, and went. I found him living in a very humble dwelling, and in an obscure street. As I approached, he came out of his house, and took me about thirty yards from his door, and with uplifted hands, in a manner altogether peculiar to himself, and with a face beaming with benevolent expression, he exclaimed—"Welcome! welcome! my dear Sir, to my humble abode";

at the same time taking me cordially by the hand, conducted me through a rough, uncarpeted passage to a green door leading to an uncarpeted stairway, on ascending one flight of which I found myself abruptly ushered into what appeared to be both drawing and dining room. There was no carpet on the floor, and very little furniture of any kind in the room; an old-fashioned side-board, a few chairs, three or four pictures hung carelessly around the walls, comprised nearly the whole furniture and the room. The breakfast table was set when I went In. A large urn stood in the middle, surrounded by cups, saucers, plates, knives and forks, spoons, &c. &c., all of a very plain order.— Rather too plain, I thought, for so great a man.

His greatness, however, was not dependant on outward show; nor was it obscured from me by his plainness. It showed that he could be great without the ordinary attractions with which men of his rank and means are generally anxious to surround themselves. Upon entering the room, Father M. introduced me to Mr. Wm. O'Conner, an invited guest, a gentleman of property and standing, and though not a teetotaler, yet an ardent admirer of Father Mathew. As an evidence of his devoted attachment, honor and esteem, Mr. O'Conner has erected a splendid tower on his own land, about four miles from Cork, in a very conspicuous place, having a commanding view of the harbor of Cork, and a view of the beautiful hills for miles around. The presence of this gentleman at the breakfast afforded me an excellent opportunity of witnessing Father Mathew's faithfulness to his friends. I found him entirely uncompromising. This gentleman complained a little of his severity towards the distillers of Cork, who had large amounts invested in distilleries, and who could not be expected to give their business up to their ruin. To which Father Mathew replied in the natural way, that such men had no right to prosper by the ruin of others. He said he was once met by a rich distiller, who asked him rather imploringly how he could so deliberately plot the ruin of so many good and unoffending people, who had their all invested in distilleries? In reply, Father Mathew then told with good spirit the following excellent anecdote: "A very fat old duck went out early one morning in pursuit of worms, and after being out all day, she succeeded in filling her crop, and on her return home at night, with her crop full of worms, she had the misfortune to be met by a fox, who at once proposed to take her life, to satisfy his hunger. The old duck appealed, argued, implored, and remonstrated. She said to the fox—You cannot be so wicked and hard-hearted as to to take the life of a harmless duck, merely to satisfy your hunger. She exhorted him against the commission of so great a sin, and begged him not to stain his soul with innocent blood. When the fox could stand her cant no longer, he said—'Out upon you, madam, with all your fine feathers; you are a pretty thing, indeed, to lecture me about taking life to satisfy my hunger—is not your own crop now full of worms? You destroy more lives in one day, to satisfy your hunger, than I do in a whole month!" Father Mathew has a fund of anecdotes, which he tells in the happiest manner, always to the point, and with most excellent effect. His whole soul appeared to be wrapped up in the temperance cause. The aim of his life appears to be to spread the blessings of temperance over the whole world. To accomplish this, he spares no pains. His time, strength and money are all freely given to the cause; and his success is truly wonderful. When he is at home, his house is literally surrounded with persons, many of whom have come miles to take the pledge. He seldom takes a meal without being interrupted by some one to take the pledge. He was called away twice while I was there, to dismiss a number who had come to take the pledge. This he did with great delight.

Cork contains one hundred thousand inhabitants. One half of this number have taken the pledge of Father Mathew.[9] The change already wrought in the condition of the whole people of Ireland is almost, through his labors, miraculous; and the cause is still advancing. *Five millions, four hundred eighty-seven thousand, three hundred and ninety-five souls* have received the pledge from him—'and still they come.' So entirely charmed by the goodness of this truly good man was I, that I besought him to administer the pledge to me. He complied with promptness, and gave me a beautiful silver pledge. I now reckon myself with delight the fifth of the last five of Father Mathew's 5,487,395 temperance children.

The papers here leave me little to say about my anti-slavery proceedings. They very readily report any movements.

Friend Buffum left me on the 21st October, to attend the great Anti-Corn-Law Bazaar, now holding at Manchester.[10] We shall meet again in the course of a few weeks in Belfast.

My love to your dear family, and the true that surround you.

Ever and always, Yours for freedom,

Frederick Douglass

*The Liberator*, November 28, 1845

# ADDRESS AT ANTI-SLAVERY MEETING, INDEPENDENT CHAPEL, CORK, IRELAND, NOVEMBER, 1845[11]

The sentiments of gratitude expressed by the meeting are in perfect unison with my own. Never was I held under greater obligations to the press, and to the proprietors of public buildings, than I have been since in Cork, and I express my sincere gratitude for it in behalf of the bondsmen. Particularly am I indebted to the press for their freedom in copying the few feeble words I have been able to say in this city, that they may return to my land, and sound terribly in the ears of the oppressors of my countrymen. Mr. President, the address which has been read, I certainly was not expecting. I expected to go through the length and breadth of your country, preaching to those who are ready to hear the groans of the oppressed. I did not expect the high position that I enjoy during my stay in the city of Cork, and not only here, but in Dublin. The object which we have met to consider is the annexation of Texas to the United States.[12] You have perhaps heard that in America, when an individual has absented himself unaccountably for any time, such a person is said to have gone to Texas, few knowing where it is. Texas is that part of Mexico, bounded on the North by the United States, on the South side by the Gulf of Mexico. The extent of this country is not correctly known. It is as large as France—a most prolific soil—climate most salubrious. The facilities for commercial and agricultural proceedings are unsurpassed anywhere. A Mr. Austin obtained a grant of the Royal Government, to settle three hundred families in Texas, with an understanding that such families should obey the laws then existing, and also, that they should be members of the Roman Catholic religion. He succeeded in introducing 30 families. His son took up the business, and introduced three hundred families. Before he succeeded, the revolution in Mexico severed the Mexican provinces from the Crown, and the contract was rendered void. He made application to the new government, and obtained a similar contract. Other men in the west made similar applications to the Mexican Government. Among the rest were Irishmen, and they were among the few who fulfilled their contracts.

The consequence of making the Catholic religion a necessary qualification to settle in Texas afforded opportunity for hypocrisy. A number of persons not of Catholic persuasion entered the territory, and made complaints. They succeeded in fomenting a revolt against the Mexican Government. Soon after, the Texans managed to lodge complaints of oppression against it. Under these pretenses they declared for religious freedom, applied to the United States for sympathy for religious liberty. After getting the property under conditions of submission, they turn round for sympathy in a revolt in behalf of religious toleration. Mexico came forward nobly and abolished slavery in Texas.[13] In open violation of this, slaves were introduced. Mexico, outraged at this violation of her laws, attempted to compel obedience—this resulted in the revolution. Texas applied to the United States for assistance. Here came the deed that ought to bring down on the United States the *united* execration of the world. She pretended to be in a friendly relation with Mexico. Her Congress looked on with indifference on the raising of troops to aid the slaveholding Texans in wresting from the Mexicans, Texas.—Indeed, they encouraged it. Texans succeeded in holding at bay the Mexican Government. The United States with indecent haste recognized the independence of Texas. This was the preparatory step to the consummation of the annexation to the Union. The object was that of making Texas the market for the surplus slaves of the North American States.

The Middle States of the United States are slave-raising States. In 1837, you might meet in Virginia hundreds of slaves handcuffed and chained together, driving southward to be sold. The Southern States were formerly those where the slaves brought the highest price, but at present they are fully supplied with slaves; and there is a consequent reduction in the price of human flesh and bones. In 1836 slaves brought from 1000 to 1,500 dollars; but a year ago, the price was reduced to 600 dollars.—The slaveholders saw the necessity of opening a new country where there would be a demand for slaves. Americans should be considered a band of plunderers for the worst purposes. Should they go to war with these million of slaves in their bosom, only looking for the first favorable opportunity of lifting their arms in open rebellion? American statesmen are aware of this. The reasons they give for the annexation of Texas not only prove them to be rotten at heart, but a band of dastards. They say that Mexico is not able to go to war, therefore we can take their country. I dare the Americans to reach their arms to Canada. The conduct of America, in this particular, has not been sufficiently dwelt upon by the British press. England should not have stood by and seen a feeble people robbed, without raising a note of remonstrance.

I have done with the question of Texas—let me proceed to the general question. I will read you the laws of a part of the American States, regarding the relation of master and slave, the laws which created the row in the steamship Cambria,[14] not because they are the worst I could select, but because I desire to have them upon your memory. If more then seven slaves are found together without a white person, 20 lashes apiece; for letting loose a boat from where it is moored, 39 lashes, for the first, and for the second offense, the loss of an ear. For having an article for sale without a ticket from his master, 10 lashes. For travelling in the night without a pass, 40 lashes. Found in another person's quarters, 40 lashes. For being on horseback without a written permission, 3 lashes; or riding without leave, a slave may be whipped, cropped or branded with the letter A, in the cheek. The laws may be found in Heywood's manual, and several other works. These laws will be the laws of Texas. How sound these laws, Irishmen and Irish women, in your ears? These laws, as you are aware, are not the worst, for one law in North Carolina makes it a crime punishable with death for the second offense, to teach a slave to read.

My friends, I would wish to allude to another matter in relation to the religious denominations of Cork. My friends, all I have said respecting their brethren in America has been prompted by a regard for the bondman. I know what slavery is by experience. I know what my experience has been at the hands of religionists. The Baptist or Presbyterian that would desire me not to tell the truth, is a man who loves his sect more than he loves his God. To you who have a missionary spirit, I say, there is no better field than America. The slave is on his knees, asking for light; slaves who not only want the Bible, but someone to teach them to read its contents. Their cries come across the Atlantic this evening, appealing to you! Lift up your voices against this giant sin, Mr. President, I am glad to learn that the simple reading of my narrative by a minister in your town, was the cause of his preaching last Sabbath an able anti-slavery discourse. My friends, labor on in this good work, for hearts on the other side of the Atlantic have been cheered by your efforts. When England with one effort wiped from her West Indies the stain of slavery, turning eight hundred thousand *things* to eight hundred thousand human beings, from that time the bondmen in our country looked with more ardent hope to the day when their chains would be broken, and they be permitted to enjoy that liberty in a Republic, which was now enjoyed under the mild rule of a Monarchical Government. This infused amongst us a spirit of hope, of faith, of liberty. Thus you have done much, but *don't feel your power ceases here.* Everyone has an influence. Only speak the true word—breathe the right prayer—trust in the true God—and your influence will be powerful against all wrong!

Your land is now being travelled over by men from our country. Their whole code of justice is based on the changing basis of the color of a man's skin; for in Virginia, there are but three crimes for which a white man is hung, but in the same State, there are seventy-one crimes for which the black suffers death. I want the Americans to know that in the good city of Cork, I ridiculed their nation—I attempted to excite the utter contempt of the people here upon them. O that America were freed from slavery! her brightness would then dazzle the Eastern world. The oppressed of all nations might flock to her as an asylum from monarchical or other despotic rulers. I do believe that America has the elements for becoming a great and glorious nation. Those three millions of foes might be converted into three million of friends—but I am not going to say anything in her favor—I am an outlaw there—and it is time to bid you farewell!

*Cork Examiner* reprinted in *The Liberator*, December 12, 1845

## TO R. D. WEBB[15]

Belfast, Victoria Hotel, 6th December 1845

My dear Friend:

You have already been informed of our success in getting the cause before the people in this place. From all I can see now, I think it will be of the utmost importance that I remain here a much longer time than that allotted in the first instance. The field here is ripe for the harvest; this is the very hotbed of presbyterianism and free churchism, a blow can be struck here more effectually than in any other part of Ireland. One nail drove in a sure place is better than a dozen driven at random, a bird in hand is worth two in the bush, it is better to have a few true friends, than a great many acquaintances, to be known thoroughly by a few is better than being known slightly by many. Well then, the conclusion I draw from this—though it may seem a most lame and impotent one—is, that I had better remain here, and go from here to Scotland than to go to Birmingham on the sixteenth Dec. Will you not, my dear friend, do what you may to have me released? I think you will have little difficulty in doing so, if anything may be learned from the cold letter from Mr. Cadbury, which talks of some-one's paying my expenses for the meeting, &c. &c. You can manage it I know if you think best. So here I leave the matter. Well all my Books went last night at one blow.[16] I want more. I want more. I have everything to hope and nothing to fear. The paper of this morning took a favorable notice of my meeting last night, and a deep interest seems to be excited.

I have written to Short telling him of my success in getting the Methodist meeting house, in the face of letters prejudicial to me both from Cork and Dublin. Short did not like my remarks at the Exchange the other evening. He has written me a long letter giving me his views of the subject there discussed. So you see I am not without counsel.

I found the blanket Thomas gave me of great service to me. Many thanks to him for it. I had a call from Mrs. Webb of this town wishing to ingave [*sic*] me for two days at her house. She is a very good proper looking person. I've engaged for one day only. Well you will want to know how I got on at the Hotel, comfortable, comfortable. The friends have placed me here they say to make me accessible to everyone that wishes to see me. They have gained their purpose thus far. "Still they come." I can thus far truly say, everyone that hears me seems to think he has a special claim on my time to listen to his opinion of me, to tell me just how much he condemned and how much he approved. Very well, let them come, I am ready for them though it is not the most agreeable. In great haste excuse the writing, very truly yours

F. Douglass

*Anti-Slavery Collection, Boston Public Library*

## TO R. D. WEBB

Belfast, 7 Dec. (1845)

Dear friend:

I've read yours of yesterday. I approve of its contents, so I'll say no more of Birmingham. I hardly think fifty copies of the narrative will do. I shall probably sell them all on Tuesday night. Will you send me more immediately? 50 copies more would not be too many. I received a letter this morning from Cork full of affectionate sayings of you of course, it was from your correspondent. Your hint respecting being prompt in replying to letters is useful. I replied to Mr. Smeal as soon as possible. The substance of my letter was to the effect, that I had made the engagement at Birmingham, I felt myself bound by it, I was not at liberty to break it, I would try to get released from it, but if they insisted upon my coming, I should feel myself bound to go. So thus far I am safe. I however think that I ought to go to Glasgow as early as I possibly can. They are certainly anxious to see me and hear me. They ought to be gratified. They have taken every pains to secure me, Thus far to no purpose. I fear they'll grow impatient.

Another letter this morning from Short, by no means a short letter. *What a misnomer?* I bought a watch yesterday, a right down good one, 7L-10 shillings. I swell, but I think I shall not burst. I attend church to day, 'tis not a sin in itself. Everybody I meet with here seems full of religion, drinks wine and prays. Sir John McNeal's letter introducing me here has been of service. Why did not my friend Haughton give me a letter? He is said to have friends here. I wrote to Cork Friday, and to Limerick yesterday. I may lecture on temperance tomorrow. I have had a committee to wait me requesting me to do so. It will all help to prepare me for Birmingham. I have just got an invitation to speak today before a Sabbath School, and to tell how I learned to read. How different from Dublin.

A speedy deliverance of Mrs. Webb and Richy from their cold. If you see Sussanah Fisher tell her to write. In great haste

truly yours<br>F. Douglass

## TO WILLIAM LLOYD GARRISON

Perth (Scotland), 27th Jan. 1846

*To the Editor of the Liberator:*

Dear Friend—For the sake of our righteous cause, I was delighted to see, by an extract copied into the Liberator of 12th Dec. 1845, from the Delaware Republican, that Mr. A.C.C. Thompson, No. 101, Market-street, Wilmington, has undertaken to invalidate my testimony against the slaveholders, whose names I have made prominent in the narrative of my experience while in slavery.[17]

Slaveholders and slave-traders never betray greater indiscretion than when they venture to defend themselves, or their system of plunder, in any other community than a slaveholding one. Slavery has its own standard of morality, humanity, justice, and Christianity. Tried by that standard, it is a system of the greatest kindness to the slave—sanctioned by the purest morality—in perfect agreement with justice—and, of course, not inconsistent with Christianity. But, tried by any other, it is doomed to condemnation. The naked relation of master and slave is one of those monsters of darkness, to whom the light of truth is death! The wise ones among the slaveholders know this, and they studiously avoid doing anything, which, in their judgment, tends to elicit truth. They seem fully to understand, that their safety is in their silence. They may have learned this wisdom from Junius, who counselled his opponent, Sir William Draper, when defending Lord Granby, never to attract attention to a character, which would only pass without condemnation, when it passed without observation.

I am now almost too far away to answer this attempted refutation by Mr. Thompson. I fear his article will be forgotten before you get my reply. I, however, think the whole thing worth reviving, as it is seldom we have so good a case for dissection. In any country but the United States, I might hope to get a hearing through the columns of the paper in which I was attacked. But this would be inconsistent with American usage and magnanimity. It would be folly to expect such a hearing. They might possibly advertise me as a runaway slave, and share the reward of my apprehension; but on no other condition would they allow my reply a place in their columns.

In this, however, I may judge the "Republican" harshly. It may be that, having admitted Mr. Thompson's article, the editor will think it but fair—Negro though I am—to allow my reply for an insertion.

In replying to Mr. Thompson, I shall proceed as I usually do in preaching the slaveholder's sermon—dividing the subject under two general heads, as follows:—

1st. The statement of Mr. Thompson, in confirmation of the truth of my narrative.

2ndly. His denials of its truthfulness.

Under the first, I beg Mr. Thompson to accept my thanks for his full, free and unsolicited testimony, in regard to my identity. There now need be no doubt on that point, however much there may have been before. Your testimony, Mr. Thompson, has settled the question forever. I give you the fullest credit for the deed, saying nothing of the motive. But for you, sir, the pro-slavery people in the North might have persisted, with some show of reason, in representing me as being an imposter—a free Negro who has never been south of Mason & Dixon's line—one whom the abolitionists, acting on the jesuitical principle, that the end justifies the means had educated and sent forth to attract attention to their faltering cause.[18] I am greatly indebted to you, sir, for silencing these truly prejudicial insinuations. I wish I could make you understand the amount of service you have done me. You have completely tripped up the heels of your pro-slavery friends, and laid them flat at my feet. You have done a piece of anti-slavery work, which no anti-slavery man could do. Our cautious and truth-loving people in New England would never have believed this testimony, in proof of my identification, had it been borne by an abolitionist. Not that they really think an abolitionist capable of bearing false witness intentionally; but such persons are thought fanatical, and to look at everything through a distorted medium. They will believe you—they will believe a slaveholder. They have, somehow or other, imbibed (and I confess strangely enough) the idea that persons such as yourself are dispassionate, impartial and disinterested, and therefore capable of giving a fair representation of things connected with slavery. Now, under these circumstances, your testimony is of the utmost importance. It will serve to give effect to my exposures of slavery, both at home and abroad. I hope I shall not administer to your vanity when I tell you that you seem to have been raised up for this purpose! I came to this land with the highest testimonials from some of the most intelligent and distinguished abolitionists in the United States; yet some here have entertained and expressed doubt as to whether I have ever been a slave. You may easily imagine the perplexing and embarrassing nature of my situation, and how anxious I must have been to be relieved from it. You, sir, have relieved me. I now stand before both the American and British public, endorsed by you as being just what I have ever represented myself to be—to wit, an *American Slave.*

You say, 'I knew this recreant slave by the name of Frederick Bailey (instead of Douglass.)' Yes, that was my name; and leaving out the term recreant, which savors a little of bitterness, your testimony is direct and perfect—just what I have long wanted. But you are not yet satisfied. You seem determined to bear the most ample testimony in my favor. You say you knew me when I lived with Mr. Covey—And with most of the persons mentioned in my narrative, 'You are intimately acquainted.' This is excellent. Then Mr. Edward Covey is not a creature of my imagination, but really did, and may yet exist.[19]

You thus brush away the miserable insinuation of my northern pro-slavery enemies, that I have used fictitious not real names. You say—'Col. Lloyd was a wealthy planter. Mr. Gore was once an overseer for Col. Lloyd, but is now living near St. Michael's, is respected and [you] believe he is a member of the Methodist Episcopal Church. Mr. Thomas Auld is an honorable and worthy member of the Methodist Episcopal Church. Mr. Covey, too, is a member of the Methodist church, and all that can be said of him is, that he is a good Christian,' &c. &c. Do allow me, once more to thank you for this triumphant vindication of the truth of my statements; and to show you how highly I value your testimony, I will inform you that I am now publishing a second edition of my narrative in this country, having already disposed of the first. I will insert your article with my reply as an appendix to the edition now in progress. If you find any fault with my frequent thanks, you may find some excuse for me in the fact, that I have serious fears that you will be but poorly thanked by those whose characters you have felt it your duty to defend. I am almost certain they will regard you as running before you were sent, and as having spoken when you should have been silent. Under these trying circumstances, it is evidently the duty of those interested in your welfare to extend to you such words of consolation as may ease, if not remove, the pain of your sad disappointment! But enough of this.

Now, then, to the second part—or your denials. You are confident I did not write the book; and the reason of your confidence is, that when you knew me, I was an unlearned and rather an ordinary Negro. Well, I have to admit I was rather an ordinary Negro when you knew me, and I do not claim to be a very extraordinary one now. But you knew me under very unfavorable circumstances. It was when I lived with Mr. Covey, the Negro-breaker, *and member of the Methodist Church.* I had just been living with master Thomas Auld, where I had been reduced by hunger. Master Thomas did not allow me enough to eat. Well, when I lived with Mr. Covey, I was driven so hard, and whipt so often, that my soul was crushed and my spirits broken. I was a mere wreck. The degradation to which I was then subjected, as I now look back to it, seems more like a dream than a horrible reality. I can scarcely realize how I ever passed through it, without quite losing all my moral and intellectual energies. I can easily understand that you sincerely doubt if I wrote the narrative; for if anyone had told me, seven years ago, I should ever be able to write such an one, I should have doubted as strongly as you now do. You must not judge me now by what I then was—a change of circumstances has made a surprising change in me. Frederick Douglass, the freeman, is a very different person from Frederick Bailey,[20] the *slave.* I feel myself almost a new man—freedom has given me new life. I fancy you would scarcely know me. I think I have altered very much in my general appearance, and know I have in my manners. You remember when I used to meet you on the road to St. Michael's, or near Mr. Covey's lane gate, I hardly dared to lift my head, and look up at you. If I should meet you now, amid the free hills of old Scotland, where the ancient "black Douglass" once met his foe,[21] I presume I might summon sufficient fortitude to look you full in the face; and were you to attempt to make a slave of me, it is possible you might find me almost as disagreeable a subject, as was the Douglass to whom I have just referred. Of one thing, I am certain—you would see a *great change* in me!

I think I have now explained away your reason for thinking I did not write the narrative in question.

You next deny the existence of such cruelty in Maryland as I reveal in my narrative; and ask, with truly marvellous simplicity, "could it be possible that charitable, feeling men could murder human beings with as little remorse as the narrative of this infamous libeller would make us believe, and that the laws of Maryland, which operate alike upon black and white, bond and free, could permit such foul murders to pass unnoticed?" "No," you say, "it is impossible." I am not to determine what charitable, feeling men can do; but, to show what Maryland slaveholders actually do, their charitable feeling is to be determined by their deeds, and their deeds by their charitable feelings. The cowskin makes as deep a gash in my flesh, when wielded by a professed saint, as it does when wielded by an open sinner. The deadly musket does as fatal execution when its trigger is pulled by Austin Gore, the Christian, as when the same is done by Beal Bondly, the infidel. The best way to ascertain what those charitable, feeling men can do, will be to point you to the laws made by them, and which you say operate alike upon the white and the black, the bond and the free. By consulting the statute laws of Maryland, you will find the following: "Any slave for rambling in the night, or riding horses in the day time without leave, or running away, may be punished by whipping, cropping, branding in the cheek, or otherwise—not rendering him unfit for labor."—p. 337.

Then another: "Any slave convicted of petty treason, murder, or wilful burning of dwelling-houses, may be sentenced to have the right hand cut off, to be hanged in the usual way—his head severed from his body—the body divided into four quarters, and the head and quarters set up in the most public place where such act was committed."—Page 190.

Now, Mr. Thompson, when you consider with what ease a slave may be convicted of any one or all of these crimes, how bloody and atrocious do those laws appear! Yet, sir, they are but the breath of these pious and charitable feeling men, whom you would defend. I am sure I have recorded in my narrative, nothing so revoltingly cruel, murderous, and infernal, as may be found in your statute book.

You say that the laws of Maryland operate alike upon the white and black, the bond and free. If you mean by this, that the parties named are all equally protected by law, you perpetrate a falsehood as big as that told by President Polk in his inaugural address.[22] It is a notorious fact, even on this side the Atlantic, that a black man cannot testify against a white in any court in Maryland, or any other slave State. If you do not know this, you are more than ordinarily ignorant, and are to be pitied rather than censured. I will not say "that the detection of this falsehood proves all you have said to be false"—for I wish to avail myself of your testimony, in regard to my identity, but I will say, you have made yourself very liable to suspicion.

I will close these remarks by saying, your positive opposition to slavery is fully explained, and will be well understood by anti-slavery men, when you say the evil of the system does not fall upon the slave but the slaveholder. This is like saying that the evil of being burnt is not felt by the person burnt, but by him who kindles up the fire about him.

Frederick Douglass

*The Liberator,* February 27, 1846

## TO R.D. WEBB

Dundee, 10th Feb. 1846

Dear Friend:

We held a very good meeting here last night, crowded to overflowing with a people whose influence cannot but be felt by the free church. Our faithful dealing with this church has at length had the effect to compel them to a defense of their conduct. They have until a few days since affected to dispise our efforts deeming this the best mode of silencing and defeating our exposures. They now see we are not to be put down by such cunning. Their Newspaper the Dundee "Warder" has attempted to ward off our blows, by attacking us personally, denouncing us as strangers unknown to respectable people in this country, but unfortunately for this purpose they say in the next place we are in the pay of the establishment, sent for and hired by them. Thus they give us a good reputation by associating us with persons against whose moral characters, they dare not utter a single word. The agitation goes nobly on—all this region is in a ferment. The very boys in the street are singing out *"Send back that money."*[23] I am informed this morning by the Dundee "Courier" that the St. Porters session have unanimously recommended the sending back the money. I meet many free church people, who are anxious to have the money sent back. I am certain that the people are right in this point & if the money is not sent back it will be the fault of their leaders. We shall continue with unabated zeal to sound the alarm. the people shall be informed. James and myself leave here at one o'clock today for Arbroath where we hold a meeting this Evening. There too the people are wide awake. This battling is rather unfavorable to the sale of my book, but the cause first, everything else afterwards. My kind regards to Mrs. W and all inquiring Friends.

yours truly

Frederick Douglass

P.S. I have seen the new portrait. It has its faults, but I'll try no more, it must answer.[24] You will probably get it as soon as you get this. You will confer a favor, by sending a copy of the book containing it, as soon as it is bound, to our Friend Miss Jennings, Cork.

*Anti-Slavery Collection, Boston Public Library*

## ADDRESS AT ABBEY CHURCH, ARBROATH, SCOTLAND, FEBRUARY 13, 1846[25]

Ladies and Gentlemen:

I have come hither this evening, in the spirit of candor and fair dealing, to discuss the subject which has now called us together. I am deeply sensible of the prejudice already excited against myself and friends, for daring to call attention to the present connection of the Free Church of Scotland with the slaveholding churches of America. Much of this prejudice is owing to gross misrepresentations of our motives and objects by the Free Church paper at Dundee. The *Warder* having taken one false step, they adopt the common, though not the most Christian, mode of defending the step, by taking a dozen more in the same direction.

In rising to discuss this subject, I wish to be distinctly understood. I have no war with the Free Church, as such. I am not here to offer one word as to the right or wrong of the organization of that body. I am not here to say whether Drs. Chalmers, Cunningham and Candlish, or any of the Free Church leaders, did right or wrong in separating from the establishment. I want no false excuse to be made, or false statements to obtain.

The *Warder* has dared to circulate the story, that myself and friends are in the pay, and under the sanction of, opposing religious denominations. As far as the charge is brought against me, I pronounce it an unblushing falsehood. I am here to speak for those who cannot speak for themselves, to plead the cause of the perishing slave, and to arouse the energies, excite the sympathies, and obtain the aid and co-operation of the good people of old Scotland in behalf of what I believe to be a righteous cause—the breaking of every yoke, the undoing of heavy burdens, and letting the oppressed go free! Thank God! all religious denominations may work in this cause. The anti-slaveholder's platform is as broad as humanity, and as strong as eternal justice; all may stand upon it and work together, without violating any Christian principle. If fewer of the Free than of the Established Church are to be found upon that platform, the fault is theirs, not mine. In a cause like this, he is a mean-spirited bigot who would refuse to labor because another is laboring in the same cause, whose religious opinion happens not to agree with his own. In denouncing the present connection of the Free Church with the slaveholding churches of America, I have distinguished men of different denominations—of the Established Church, Free, and Dissenters—the Rev. John Angell James, of Birmingham, Independent ministers, Dr. Duncan, Dr. Willis, Dr. Ritchie, and thirty-six ministers in Belfast, with a host of others, have nobly come forward and refused Christian fellowship to slaveholders. I am not here alone; I have with me the learned, and wise, and reverend heads of the church, to justify the position I have assumed. But with or without their sanction, I should stand just where I now do, maintaining to the last that man-stealing is incompatible with Christianity—that  slaveholding and true religion are at war with each other—and that a Free Church should have no fellowship with a slave church; that as light can have no union with darkness, Christ has no concord with Beelzebub; as two cannot walk together except they be agreed, and no man can serve two masters; so I maintain that freedom cannot rightfully be blended with slavery. Nay, it cannot, without stabbing liberty to the heart. Now, what is the character of those churches in America with which the Free Church is in full fellowship, and the Christianity of which they endorse in the most unqualified manner? In the language of Isaiah, "Their hands are full of blood." Their hands are full of blood. Allow me to state the case as it really exists.

At this moment, there are three millions of people, for whom Christ died, in the United States, held in the most abject slavery—the most galling and degrading bondage—deprived of every privilege, mental, moral, social, and political—deprived of every right common to humanity—herded together like brutes—denied the institution of marriage—compelled to live in concubinage—left to be devoured by their own lusts—raised like beasts of the field for the market—mere chattels—things—property—deprived of their manhood—they are ranked with beasts—robbed of their identity with the human family—cut off from the race—loaded with chains—galled by fetters—scarred with the whip—burnt with red hot irons.. They are living without a knowledge of God, groping their way from time to eternity in the dark, the heavenly light of religion shut from their minds. A mother may not teach her own child to read our Lord's Prayer, not even to spell the name of the God who made her. For it is a crime punishable with death to teach a slave to read. It is nothing that Christ died, it is nothing that God has revealed his will, for the black as well as the white man. It is nothing that Christ commands us to search the Scriptures; it is a crime punishable with death, by American law, to teach a slave to do it. Good God! what a system! A system of blood and pollution; of infidelity and atheism, of wholesale plunder and murder. Truly did John Wesley denounce it as the sum of all villainies, and the compendium of all crime. This, Christian friends, is but a faint picture of American slavery, and this is the system upheld and sustained by the entire church in the Southern States of the American Union. It is with such a church that the Free Church of Scotland is linked, and interlinked in Christian fellowship. It is such a church that the Free Church of Scotland are trying to palm off upon the world as being a Christian Church. Thus making Christianity and slaveholding compatible, thus saying that man-stealing ought not to be a barrier to Christian communion, and lowering the standard of Christianity, so that the vilest thief, the foulest murderer, the most abandoned profligate may claim to be a Christian, and to be recognized as such. The Free Church, in vindicationg their fellowship of slaveholders, have acted upon the damning heresy that a man may be a Christian, whatever may be his practice, so his creed be right. So he pays tithes of mint, anise and cummin, he may be a Christian, though he totally neglect judgment and mercy. It is this heresy that now holds in chains three millions of men, women and children in the United States. The slaveholder's conscience is put at ease by those ministers and churches. They tell him that slaveholding is quite consistent with a profession of religion, and thus sing his conscience to sleep. Now, let us look at the circumstances under which this deed of Christian fellowship was con-

*[margin note, handwritten]: heresy: deed of creed*

summated. The Free Church had just broken off from the Established Church, as they say, in defense of Christian liberty. They professed to bring off with them nearly all that was good, pure, and holy, from the Establishment. They proclaimed themselves the true exponents of the moral and religious sentiment of Scotland. Taking their word, they are the life, the soul, the embodiment of Christianity in this country. So good, pure, and holy are they, that they would almost feel themselves contaminated by a touch of a member of the Establishment. And so *free* are they, that they look upon those who remain in the church as mere slaves.

With all this profession of freedom and purity, they appointed a delegation to visit the slave-holding Churches in the United States, to beg money to build churches, and pay their ministers. The delegation went over three thousand miles of perilous deep. On their arrival at New York, they were besought, in the name of the perishing slave, not to go to the slave-holding Churches of the South; that as sure as they went, they would contaminate their own church, as well as stab the cause of the slave. But reason gave way to avarice, purity yielded to temptation, and the result is, the Free Church is now wallowing in the filth and mire of slavery, possessing the bad pre-eminence at this time of being the only church in Scotland that makes it a religious duty to fellowship men-stealers as the followers of Jesus Christ. Now, you have the case before you. The Free Church stands charged with fellowshipping slave-holders as followers of Christ, and of taking the wages of unrighteousness to build her churches, and pay her ministers. Are those charges true, or are they false? The Free Church admits these truths, but denies that she has done wrong. Then the question between us is as to the rightfulness of holding Christian fellowship with slaveholders, and taking the results of slave-holding to build churches and pay ministers. The Free Church says it is right; I say it is wrong; and you shall judge between us. My first position is that slavery is a sin, the vilest that ever saw the sun, and thus far the Free Church and myself are at agreement. If, then, slavery is a sin, those who hold slaves must be sinners. This seems to me to be the only rational and natural result to which we can come from such a premise. If lying, swearing, murder, adultery, and stealing be sin, then it is clear that the liars, swearers, murderers, and adulterers, and thieves must be sinners. The argument in opposition to this is, that although lying, swearing, murder, adultery, and slave-holding be sin, yet liars, swearers, murderers, and slaveholders may be, and are, followers of the meek and lowly Savior; for says Dr. Chalmers on this point,[26] "Distinction *ought to be made between the character of a system and the character of the person whom* circumstances *have implicated therewith.*" The Doctor would denounce slaveholding, robbery, and murder as sin, but would not denounce the slaveholder, robber, and murderer as a sinner. He would make a *distinction* between sins and the persons whom *circumstances* have implicated therewith. He would denounce the dice, but spare the sharper; he would denounce the murder, but spare the murderer; he would denounce the adultery, but spare the adulterer; for, says the Doctor, "distinction ought to be made between the character of a system and the persons whom circumstances have implicated therewith." "Oh! the artful Dodger." What an excellent outlet for all sinners! Let slaveholders rejoice! Let a fiendish glee run round and round through hell! Dr. Chalmers, the eloquent Scotch divine, has, by long study and deep research found that distinction should be made between sin and the sinner, so that while slavery may be a heinous sin, the slaveholder may be a good Christian, the representative of the blessed Savior on earth, and heir of heaven and eternal glory, for such is what is implied by Christian fellowship. When a man is received into the Church, those who receive him say to the world, "we believe this man to be a Christian, a representative of Christ, a member of his blessed body." This is most horrible doctrine, glossing over the awful sin. But there is another point in this one sentence, the key to the entire defense which the Free Church have made in the fellowshipping slaveholders as Christians. But to the point. He says that distinction should be made between the character of a system and the character of the persons whom circumstances have implicated therewith. Yes, circumstances—the doctrine of circumstances. Who proclaims it? Dr. Chalmers. Yes, this doctrine, which has justly brought down upon the head of the infidel, Robert Owen, the execrations of Christendom, is now proclaimed by the eloquent Scotch divine. The Doctor has been driven to this hateful dilemma by taking a false step, in fellowshipping slaveholders as Christians. This doctrine, carried out, does away with moral responsibility. All that a thief has to do in justification of his theft is to plead that circumstances have implicated him in the theft, and he has Dr. Chalmers to apologize for him, and recognize him as a Christian. A man-thief, the worst of all thieves has but to make this plea; nay, the Doctor makes the plea for him, and receives him to the bosom of the Church as a Christian. Christ says, "By their fruits shall ye know them." Dr. Chalmers says, "no; distinction is to be made between the character of the individual and the character of his deeds." Now, my friends, I wish to ask, do Dr. Chalmers and the Free Church represent your sentiments on this subject?—(here the audience loudly shouted, No!)—I am glad you speak out. I regret to find that such is the power of the Free Church in some parts of this country, and even here in Arbroath, that the Dissenters, who know the Free Church to be wrong, yet do not dare to speak out, for fear of the displeasure of that Church. I am ashamed of such abolitionists; they are unworthy the name, being destitute of the spirit. They have not yet learned to value their principles. But the people will speak, they will speak in tones not to be misunderstood. They have already spoken, and I trust will continue to speak, until they silence the arrogant pretensions of the Free Church, and cause her to send back that blood-stained money. I now propose three cheers, which shall be given in the following words: *Send back that money!* (Here the audience joined with Mr. Douglass, making the welkin ring with 'Send back that money,' repeating it three times.) Mr. Douglass read a compliment to Dr. Chalmers, from the *New Orleans Picayune,* and also two advertisements of runaway slaves from the same paper, showing that the slaveholders were highly pleased with the Doctor's position on the slave question. And after commenting on the character of the paper by which the Doctor was eulogized, he closed with an eloquent appeal to the Christian people of Scotland to agitate the question of holding Christian fellowship with slaveholders, and to proclaim in the ears of the Free Church, "Send back that money." Oh! that the Free Church would send it back, and confess that they did wrong in taking it. Such a course would send slavery reeling towards its grave as if struck by a bolt from heaven.

*Arbroath Guide,* February 14, 1846, reprinted in *The Liberator,* April 3, 1846.

## AMERICAN SLAVERY

ADDRESS in Pailsey, Scotland, March 18, 1846

On Tuesday evening last week the eloquent American fugitive slave, Mr. Frederick Douglass, and his friend Mr. James N. Buffum, addressed a large meeting in the Rev. Mr. Nisbet's church on slavery.

Mr. Douglas on rising said: — "I experience great pleasure in addressing such a large audience, assembled for the purpose of hearing the wrongs inflicted upon my brethren across the Atlantic. The audience cannot be too small to interest me in speaking on such a subject, and if I had but one dozen of an audience I would feel pleasure in addressing them. I am anxious that all people should understand, and I am come here to impart accurate information respecting the workings of American slavery. I am one of those who believe that slavery is to be abolished by revealing its outrages upon its victims, by exposing it to the gaze and indignation of the Christian world. In order to accomplish this, it is necessary for us to leave our homes that correct information may be spread regarding this system of gross fraud, so that it may be swept from off the land. And will any person dispute my right of being here? I have been asked, why not employ my talents to burst asunder the strong fetters by which you, the people of England, are bound? I am not the man to speak lightly of any wrongs existing in England, but the evils stalking abroad in this land are nothing like American slavery.[27] If you have the slightest approach to slavery, I will do all in my power to crush it, but I utterly deny you have the least shadow of it. What is slavery? There seems to be a great want of information regarding it. It is not a system whereby a man is compelled to work, it is not slavery to have one peculiar right struck down; if it is, all women, all minors, are slaves. I protest against the use of the term slavery being applied in such a manner — it is an awful misnomer. Slavery must be regarded as something different; it must be regarded as one man holding property in another, subjected to the destroying of all the higher qualities of his nature, deprived of his own body, his own soul. A slave is one who is to all intents and purposes a marketable commodity — common goods and chattels. There are three millions such as I, within two weeks sail of your own shores, deprived of every right, sunk from the rank of humanity to the common level of the trade. God has given them powers of mind to glorify him, slavery flies in the face of God to supplant his place, and claims that homage which is due to Him alone. Slaveholders determine when a man shall marry, how long he shall continue married; they also claim the right of tearing the babe from the arms of the frantic mother. Conscience, which God has planted in the heart of man, all his religious aspirations, all his hopes, are subject to the will of him who dares to claim man as his property. They are forced to resort to all the unnatural means we have associated with slavery as its necessary concomitants; they are constantly devising new means to keep their slaves in subjection for no one will willingly submit to deliver up his conscience, his body, his soul, his all, to any man. Three millions of people are at this moment working [under] the tortures of the lash, weeping in bondage, clanking their chains, and calling upon Britons to aid them in their emancipation. I have come here because slavery is such a gigantic system that one nation is not fit to cope with it — a system so deeply imbedded in the Constitution of America, so firmly rooted in her churches, so entwined about the hearts of the whole people that it requires a moral force from without as well as within. I am anxious to have a remonstrance from Britain. America may boast of her abilities to build forts to stand the fire of the enemy, but she shall never be able to drive back that moral force which shall send slavery to its grave. I know you have done a great deal toward emancipation. I thank you most heartily. What you have done has had a good and glorious effect in rousing our people, in nerving the minds of the broken-hearted bondsmen, in calling attention to slavery, and causing the slaveholder to tremble. But there is a great deal more to be done; speak out with a loud voice, such as ye never spake before; let them know that they live by plunder, that the term slaveholder is synonymous with murderer and robber — that they are committing robberies which tower above all others, robberies of the deepest die." He now began to give a brief sketch of his life. He stated, it was now seven years since he escaped from bondage. "Seven years since, a man claimed these hands as his own, but I thought they belonged to me, so I took leg-bail and gave him the distance for security. I was an abolitionist, of course, born one, a friend to freedom, my own freedom; and while working on the wharfs after my escape, I thought these were the sweetest moments in all my life. Why? Because I was free, and got a dollar a day. Before, my master used to get my dollar — he thought I could not use it, he kept it for me, and used it for me, he did anything he pleased with it. I not only got free, but I got a wife free — the first matter a free man thinks of. Previously, I had always looked upon the white people as enemies, taught to look upon them as masters. I was obliged to retreat from America after publishing my narrative, for there is no part of that boasted land of freedom and independence where a slave can be safe — the American eagle may pursue him on expanded wings to the far north, and clutch him with his talons, and carry him back in triumph to his blood-thirsty oppressors. Let me tell you here, it does not cost much to be a respectable man in America; they make presidents, grave senators, holy divines, &c, robbers, murderers, and the greatest of all thieves, human-thieves. And now, since I am among the free-hills of old Scotland, treading upon British soil, I can appreciate and perceive the grandeur of the noble, the patriotic sentiments, uttered by Curran on universal emancipation. Liberty is commensurate with and insepa-rable from British soil. British law proclaims even to the stranger and sojourner the moment he sets his feet upon British earth, that the ground on which he treads is holy, and consecrated by the genius of universal emancipation. No matter in what language his doom may have been pronounced; no matter what complexion incompatible with freedom an Indian or an African sun may have burnt upon him; no matter in what disastrous battle his liberties may have been cloven down; — no matter with what solemnities he may have been devoted upon the altar of slavery; the first moment he touches the sacred soil of Britain, the altar and the god sink together in the dust;[28] his soul walks abroad in her own majesty, his body swells beyond the measure of his chains that burst from around him, and he stands redeemed, regenerated, and disenthralled, by the irresistible genius of Universal Emancipation." He concluded an interesting and most eloquent ad-dress, by introducing his friend and companion, Mr. Buffum.

Mr. Douglas again addressed a crowded meeting on Thursday evening, in the Rev. Mr. Nisbet's church, on the responsibility of the free states for the existence of slavery, morally, physically, and reli-giously, and on the sin committed by the Free Church of Scotland in accepting the blood-stained dollars. He said, "Although there are no slaves in the free states, these states have constitutions of their own, but there is one Constitution over all, the federal Constitution, and there are certain provisions in that Constitution which compel the free states to lend their political aid, their moral aid, and their religious aid, in upholding and sustaining the existence of slavery — therefore, the free states are responsible for the existence of slavery in the slave states. But, my friends, there are no free states, they are linked and interlinked together in the bloody traffic. There are 3000 (sic) slaveholders in the United States, men who hold, in their own right, men as property — there are about ten slaves to each slaveholder; you may probably ask how can one man hold ten in bondage — no man could make me his slave — he has not the power. How is this that the slaves are held? It is by an extraneous influence from without. Why don't the slaves rise? Because they would have no chance, the arms of the whole nation would be directed against them; it would be like the struggle of the poor Poles, whose struggles you have just heard of — they are falling beneath the swords and bayonets of the bloody and despotic power of Russia. But if a foreign enemy were to land in America and plant the standard of freedom, the slaves would rise to a man, they would rally round that standard; a strong fire would be kindled within their breasts, which would remind them that their fathers and mothers had been tortured by the oppressors, that the white face had been guilty of grinding the poor blacks — they would not spare the guilty traders in human blood. But you are not to infer from this that I am an advocate for war, no, I hate war, I have no weapon but that which is consistent with morality, I am engaged in a holy war; I ask not the aid of the sword, I appeal to the understanding and the hearts of men — we use these weapons, and hope that God will give us the victory. The free states have it in their power to abolish slavery; they have the moral power, they have the religious power, they have the press, they have the ear of the people, into which they could pour arguments which would be too strong for them to repel, and if they do not use that power they are morally and religiously responsible. We call upon them as Christians, philanthropists, and in the awful name of God, to abolish this horrid system. Let us take a view of the Constitution of America — it is based upon the broad principle of equality. It holds this truth to be self-evident — that all men are equal. It pretends to establish justice, and to secure the blessings of liberty to the present generation and to posterity. The Americans are political hypocrites. They declare by lip these truths, but fail in practice; and, if you want a sample of lies, just read the last message of the man-thief President. He declares that the people of America are a free people — a religious people. No such thing. We have churches — they belong to the same people as the slaves; we have all the forms, all the ceremonies, all the appearance of religion; we profess to be the followers of the meek and lowly Christ the same as here, but right under the droppings of the church, slavery has existed for two hundred years; those who love the heathen on the other side of the globe hate the heathen at their own doors. We have the Bible and slave-trade, the church and the prison, the gates of heaven and hell in the same street; the church bell and the auctioneer's bell opposite to each other; we have devils dressed in angel's robes who leave off flogging their slaves to go and preach in the pulpit, taking for their text "Thou shalt not steal." Children are sold, that the price of their blood may purchase communion service; to prove which, let me read you an advertisement: — "A prime gang of Negroes to be sold, belonging to the Independent Church, in Christ Church Parish — proceeds to go to the funds of the Independent Church." I have seen my own master, who was a Methodist reader, tie up a young woman, a cousin of my own, and flog her till the blood flowed in streams at her feet, and quote Scripture in vindication of it. "He that knoweth his master's will, and doeth it not, shall be beaten with many stripes." But I am glad that some of the churches in America are beginning to throw off slavery. The slaveholder is forbid to enter lest he drink damnation to his soul. This is beginning to be the feeling of some of the churches, and when we are swelling a religious chorus against it, what voice is it that breaks in upon the harmonious concord to palliate slavery? 'Tis the *Free* Church of Scotland; [but] free church and slave church [are] opposites! — light and darkness, liberty and slavery, freedom and oppression, bibles and thumbscrews, exhortations and horsewhips, all linked and interlinked. I have come here for the purpose of calling upon the Free Church of Scotland to send back the blood-stained dollars. I will give them no rest till they send back that money, for as long as they retain that money they are liberty's deadliest enemy. I feel I have a right to come to Scotland. They wish I had not come, but I mean to stay and talk. We want them to go along with us in that glorious enterprise; but so long as they keep that money, they cannot share in the glory — they cannot go along with us, while they hold fellowship with slaveholders. Had Andrew Thomson lived— he whose words burst asunder the chains of the Indian bondsmen— he would have shattered the connexion into a thousand fragments. If they would return that money, it would turn the religious tide against slavery. It is already being hemmed in by a broad and mighty force; and they are whispering to themselves that nobody in our old country has any regard for us but the Free Church, and we sometimes think she does not care so much for us as for our dollars." He concluded an eloquent and powerful address, by calling upon the Free Church, in name of the slaves, appealing to them, as Christians and the sons of God, to return the bloody gold.

*Glasgow Saturday Post & Paisley & Renfrewshire Reformer,* March 21-30, 1846, *cuttings in Anti-Slavery Cuttings, Paisley, Central Library Scotland*


## REMARKS AT SOIREE IN HONOR OF MESSRS DOUGLASS AND BUFFUM, PAISLEY, SCOTLAND, MARCH, 1846[29]

Mr. Douglass, who was received with loud cheering, then came forward and said: "Ladies and Gentlemen I have seldom stepped on a platform where I desire more to do justice to the cause of which I am an humble advocate, then on the present occasion. Yet I have seldom appeared before an audience less qualified to discharge that duty. I will not, however, apologize further than to say, that previous to coming to this gathering, I felt indisposed to be present at all; but since entering and looking on the right, on the left, in front, and in the rear — I really feel my health has come again. I confess, however, that this gathering is one for which I was not prepared. I had not supposed that such a congregation of intelligence and respectability would gather around a poor fugitive slave, to hear what he might have to say, and even to do him honor. If I am not able to do justice to the sentiments in the address, attribute it to the extraordinary character of my position. This is not an evening for entering into any argument on the subject of slavery. You have all signified your abhorrence of slavery, by the adoption of the address now read in your hearing, and it would therefore be like carrying coals to Newcastle to give you a discourse on American slavery. Our language must be that of happy triumph and glory, and it would not become me to enter into any lengthened details respecting the horrors of slavery. I will call your attention to that brighter aspect of our cause—its progress in the world. More than 300 years ago, the slave-trade was not only made legal, but it was also sanctioned and sanctified by the church. For 200 years the traffic in human flesh was carried on by the Christian world unchecked, undisturbed, unquestioned, by any considerable number of the human family. There were, to be sure, occasionally found foes aroused— such as Granville Sharp in this country.[30] It was not till 70 years ago that any stand was taken against the slave-trade, when a number of Quakers resolved to form themselves into an alliance, and to seek its overthrow. At this time the whole Christian world was engaged in the trade. It was regarded as a species of commerce as legitimate as any other that then existed. The legislatures of various countries legalized it, protecting it by their arms, and defending it in various ways. These Quakers gathered themselves together from time to time, contemplating the horrors of the middle passage and resolved to contribute their means to the publishing of tracts, and circulating information throughout the country on the subject. They told their neighbors they were going to work out under God the overthrow of the slave-trade. This was regarded by the multitude as an idle tale— as one of the most foolish attempts ever undertaken by any class of people. They met from time to time, devising and discussing matters. With hearts devoted to the sacred cause, they went on, believing that God would eventually crown their efforts with complete success. There soon sprung up a Clarkson and a Wilberforce,[31] to mention whom ought to produce three pounds of applause. When Wilberforce came forward, public attention became directed to the matter. Ten times did he introduce a bill for the abolition of the slave-trade, and ten times was it doomed to defeat— Parliament sometimes laying the matter on the table, and at other times giving it an indefinite postponement. Convinced that justice, that humanity, that all nature was on his side, believing that by perseverance he would succeed, he went on with his good work. And what do we see take place within half a century? We see the slave trade, which was sanctioned by all Christians, is now nearly regarded as not only improper, but as piracy, and the men caught at it are hung up at the yard-arm. The cause rolled on till slavery was considered wrong— not only wrong, but sin—a great, a grave, an overwhelming sin—and those sons of sires who had carried it on, now sprung up and sought its abolition. I need only remind you of the means adopted to ensure success—of the nature of the anti-slavery conflict in this country, and I may say that success will follow the use of the same means in the United States as those which were employed here. Some who hear me

this evening remember the debates on the subject of West India slavery. George Thompson went over the length and breadth of Scotland,
proclaiming the damning influence of West India slavery. In this way
he did much to remove that foul blot from the character of Britain.[32]
Borthwick and others who opposed the success of the glorious cause,
are familiar to many who now hear me. But although the cause had to
contend against the most adroit talent, against the supineness of the
church, and against the indifference of the state, the cause rolled on
until, in 1838, eight hundred thousand of British slaves were turned
into men. I have been asked if I supposed the slavery of the United
States would ever by abolished? It might as well be asked of me if God
sat on his throne in heaven. So sure as truth is stronger than error, so
sure as right is better than wrong, so sure as religion is better than
infidelity, so sure must slavery of every form in every land become
extinct. Anti-slavery must triumph. God has decreed its triumph. So
sure as the tears of the slaves are falling, so sure as the groans of the
oppressed rend the air with the cry of "How long, O Lord God of
Sabaoth," &c., so sure shall these things come to an end—not by a
miracle, but by the force of truth. Who can calculate the great good
that may result even from the present meeting? Who can calculate the
power which such meetings exert in the United States? No slaveholder
who may be acquainted with it, but will be struck in conscience with a
certain feeling, which must ever accompany a man with a wrong cause.
When meetings of this kind are held in this country, they confess they
feel that the effect is to awaken, to arouse the energies of the humane in
the anti-slavery cause in the United States. I believe that slavery is such
an enormous system of fraud and wrong, that if once we get the people
to see it they will exert themselves for its removal. It would have been
long since removed if the honest people had been prevailed on to
discuss the matter. I trust we shall now soon succeed in awakening
them from their indolence—in rousing them to get the weight off
which bears down their moral energies. We have not yet been able to
get them to see it—to get them to concentrate their attention upon it.
We must get the people to speak about it, preach about it, and pray
about it. In this way we shall get them heartily enlisted in the cause.
Some there are in the United States who lay great weight on the public
opinion of this country; for you know distance sometimes lends en-
chantment. It is so, at all events, in this particular instance. If we wish
to call attention to anything we may point at Britain. We learn what is

the mind of Britain by reading the writings of such men as Dickens, as well as by the public press. I believe that the notice of Dickens had more effect in calling attention to the subject, than all the books published in America for ten years. This is because they have same deference for the opinions of those out of the country. Americans are very peculiar in this respect—for like the beggar, they like to know what others think of them. This good or bad trait in Brother Jonathan's character, must be made available to anti-slavery. We want to tell them in what light their religion and their institutions are viewed in other lands; and as they look to others we will take advantage of this disposition in effecting the overthrow of slavery in the United States. Since I came to this country I have been the means of calling more attention to the subject in America, than I could have done had I remained there twelve years. I have been travelling up and down, showing them up in their true colors. I see that the *New York Herald* is abusing me. The *Express*, a democratic paper, is denouncing me—all are denouncing me as a glib-tongued scoundrel. They say I am speaking against American institutions, and am stirring up a warlike spirit against them.[33] Never, in any instance, have I done this although, if I were a war man, I might with some degree of pride call your attention to slavery, and urge you, as friends of freedom, in the event of a war, to take advantage of it for abolishing slavery. I have never, in any instance, attempted to stir up their bloody feelings, never advocated the use of means inconsistent with the doctrines of Christianity. I wish to act by the power of truth, to apply undisguised truth to the hearts and consciences of the slaveholders. Slavery is as abhorrent to God, as revolting to humanity, as it is inconsistent with American institutions. So far from my efforts having the effect of stirring up war amongst the British, they will have the effect of cementing the two nations in the bonds of peace. What are the abolitionists of the United States? Almost all—universally peacemen—as opposed to war as they are to slavery. They are men who cancel the existence of the spirit of war, and who labor to supplant it with the spirit of peace and its attendant blessings. So far from there being any tendency in our proceedings to war, the very opposite is the effect. I do speak against an American institution—that institution is American slavery. But I love the Declaration of Independence, I believe it contains a true doctrine—"that all men are born equal." It is, however, because they do not carry out these principles that I am here to speak. I have a right to appeal to the people of Britain—to people everywhere—I would draw all men's attention to slavery. I would fix the indignant eye of the world on slavery be swept from off the face of the earth. I believe I have a right to do this, God has not built up such walls between nations as that they may not be brethern to each other. I am a man before I am an American. To be a man is above all the claims of nationality. But I have no nation. America only welcomes me to her shores as a brute. She spurns the idea of treating me in any other way than as a brute—she would not receive me as a man The last steamer from America brings word that my old master, Mr Auld, has transferred his right of property in me to his brother Hugh. Oh! what poor property—and if I ever step on American soil he will have me. In case Frederick returns to America, he will spare no pains or expense to regain possession. This reminds me of the man who told his wife that he saw a rainbow running round. His wife, however, could not see it. It was running round and round, and the man said always he would catch it next time it came round. Mr Auld will catch me the next time I go round.[34]

*Glasgow Saturday Post & Paisley & Renfrewshire Reformer*, March 21-30, 1846, *cuttings in Anti-Slavery Cuttings, Central Library, Paisley, Scotland.*


# ADDRESS AT TEMPERANCE MEETING, PAISLEY, SCOTLAND, MARCH, 1846

On Monday evening last, a public meeting of the inhabitants of Paisley was held in the secession church, Abbey close, for the purpose of discussing the subject of Temperance. Mr. Wm. Melvin occupied the chair, Mr. Frederick Douglass then came forward and said: "Ladies and Gentleman, I am proud to stand on this platform; I regard it a pleasure and a privilege—one which I am not very frequently permitted to enjoy in the United States, such is the prejudice against the colored man, such the contempt in which he is held, that no temperance society in the land would so far jeopardize its popularity as to invite a colored man to stand before them. He might be a Webster in intellect, a Channing in literature, or a Howard in philanthropy, yet the bare fact of his being a man of color, would prevent him from being welcomed on a temperance platform in the United States. This is my apology. I have been excluded from the temperance movement in the United States, because God has given me a skin not colored like yours. I can speak, however, in regard to the facts concerning ardent spirits, for the same spirit which makes a white man makes a black man drunk too. Indeed, in this I can find proof of my identity with the family of man. The colored man in the United States has great difficulties in the way of his moral, social, and religious advancement. Almost every step he takes toward mental, moral, or social improvement is repulsed by the cold indifference or the active mob of the white. He is compelled to live an outcast from society; he is as it were, a border or selvage on the great cloth of humanity, and the very fact of his degradation is given as a reason why he should be continued in the condition of a slave. The blacks are to a considerable extent intemperate and of course vicious in other respects and this is counted against them as a reason why their emancipation from intemperance, because I believe it would be the means—a great and glorious means—towards helping to break their physical chains, and letting them go free. To give you some idea of the strength of this prejudice and passion against the colored people, I may state that they formed themselves into a temperance procession in Philadelphia, on the day on which the legislature in this country had by a benevolent act awarded freedom to the Negroes in the West Indian islands.[35] They formed themselves into a procession with appropriate banners, but they had not proceeded up two streets before they were attacked by a reckless mob, their procession broken up, their banners destroyed, their houses and churches burned, and all because they had dared to have a temperance procession on the 1st of August. They had saved enough to build a hall, besides their churches. These were not saved, they were burned down, and the mob was backed out by the most respectable people in Philadelphia. These are the difficulties which beset their path. And yet the Americans, those demons in human shape, they speak to us, and say that we are morally and religiously incapacitated for enjoying liberty with themselves. I am afraid I am making this an anti-slavery meeting. I want to state another fact. The black population pay sufficient tax to government to support their own poor, besides 300 dollars over and above. This is a fact which no American pale-face can deny. I, however, love white people when they are good; but this is precious seldom. I have had some experience of intemperance as well as of slavery. In the Southern States, masters induce their slaves to drink whisky, in order to keep them from devising ways and means by which to obtain their freedom. In order to make a man a slave, it is necessary to silence or drown his mind. It is not the flesh that objects to being bound—it is the spirit. It is not the mere animal part—it is the immortal mind which distinguishes man from the brute creation. To blind his affections, it is necessary to bedim and bedizzy his understanding. In no other way can this be so well accomplished as using ardent spirits. On Saturday evening, it is the custom of the slaveholder to give his slaves drink, and why? Because if they had time to think, if left to reflection on the Sabbath day, they might devise means by which to obtain their liberty. I knew once what it was to drink with all the ardor of *old soker*. I lived with a Mr. Freeland who used to give his slaves apple brandy. Some of the slaves were not able to drink their own share, but I was able to drink my own and theirs too. I took it because it made me feel I was a great man. I used to think I was a president. And this puts me in mind of a man who once thought himself a president. He was coming across a field pretty tipsy. Happening to lay himself down near a pig-sty, and the pig being out at the time, he crawled into it. After a little, in came the old sow and her company of pigs. They commenced *posing* at the intruder. An individual happening to pass at the time, heard a voice demanding order, order. He went forward and looked, when he saw a fellow surrounded by the pigs calling for order, order. He had imagined he was the president of a meeting, and was calling for order. There are certain objections urged against the temperance reform. One very frequently urged, runs thus:—The gospel of Jesus Christ was given for the purpose of removing all the ills that ought to be removed from society; therefore we can have no union with teetotalism because it is out of the church. It is treason to go out of her borders and join a teetotal society. There is as much truth in this as you can hang a few falsehoods upon. There is a truth at the beginning. It will remove slavery, it will remove war, it will remove licentiousness, it will remove fraud, it will remove adultery. All the ills to which flesh is heir will be removed by an application to them of the truths of the gospel. What we want is to adopt the most efficacious means of applying gospel truth. I dined the other day with six ministers in Perth. With the exception of one, they all drank whisky, and that one drank wine. So disgusted was I that I left, and that night I delivered a temperance lecture. I need not tell you that I was never again invited to dine at that house. I told the people at Perth that the ministers were responsible for a great part of the drinking habits among the people. The ministers have the influence to aid in removing this curse from the community; 1st, by abandoning drinking habits themselves; and, 2d, by doing what they can to make others follow their example. If the ministers used their moral influence, Scotland might soon be redeemed from this curse; and why? Because the ministers had done it in the United States. A man would not be allowed to stand in an American pulpit if it was known that he tippled the whisky. We feel that it is not proper that a minister of the gospel in the nineteenth century should be a man to mar the advancement of this cause, by using these intoxicating beverages. Our success has been glorious, for in Lynn I never saw a barefooted child in winter—I never saw a beggar in the streets in winter—I never saw a family without fuel in winter. And why have we this glorious result? Because no money is spent for whisky.

I am a temperance man because I am an anti-slavery man; and I am an anti-slavery man because I love my fellow men. There is no other cure for intemperance but total abstinence. Will not temperance do, says one? No. Temperance was tried in America, but it would not do. The total abstinence principle came and made clean work of it. It is now seen spreading its balmy influence over the whole of that land. It is seen in making peace where there was war. It has planted light and education where there was nothing but degradation, and darkness, and misery. It is your duty to plant—you cannot do all, but if you plant, God has promised, and will give the increase. We shall see most gloriously this cause yet triumph in Scotland. Is there a man within the sound of my voice who does not know that nine-tenths of the crime, misery, disease, and death, of these lands is occasioned by intemperance? You may talk of the charter and the corn-laws, but until you have banished the demon intemperance, you cannot expect one day of prosperity in your land. In the name of humanity then I call upon you to abandon your bowl. To those who would feel it no sacrifice, I say give it up. To those who would consider it a sacrifice, I say it is time you had given it up, and then we shall see our cause progressing gloriously. Were this meeting all teetotally and to pledge themselves to work in the cause, twelve months would see a most miraculous change in Paisley. Many thanks now for your kind patience; pardon me if I have said anything amiss, anything inconsistent with truth." Mr. Douglass resumed his seat amid much applause.

Mr. Buffum intimated, that next week they would likely have another meeting on the subject of slavery.

The chairman stated that it was in contemplation to invite their American friends, Messrs. Buffum and Douglass, to a soiree, in the course of a week or two, and that it was expected Mr. George Thompson, the celebrated anti-slavery lecturer, would be present on the occasion.

The church was literally packed in all corners, and the meeting broke up about eleven o'clock.

*Glasgow Saturday Post & Paisley & Renfrewshire Reformer*, March 21-30, 1846, *cuttings in Anti-Slavery Cuttings, Central Library, Paisley, Scotland*

## TO R.D. WEBB

Wilmanock (Scotland), 29 March 1846

My Dear Friend Webb:

It struck me today that it had been a long time since I wrote to you, some three or four weeks I believe. I fear you will begin to think I have forgotten you. I have therefore resolved to write although I have nothing of importance to communicate. I should have done so before but I knew you were a business man and like to get letters written for some purpose more than stating the good health of the writer. I have received the books and am pleased with them. I got the liberty bell with a note from Mrs. Chapman which you sent. I got the letters from home, for all which I thank you, until you are better paid. I did not expect a liberty bell from Mrs. Chapman since she is so fearful that I may be bought up by the London committee.[36] It may be pleasant to her to learn that I am not yet bought up by the London committee. I am still an old organized Garrison abolitionist. And shall probably remain such. At any rate poverty shall not drive me nor money allure me from my present position.

Yours in haste,<br>Frederick Douglass

*Anti-Slavery Collection, Boston Public Library*

## TO RICHARD D. WEBB

Glasgow, April 16(?) 1846

My Dear Friend:

I have received the Books, and your letter of 10th ultimo. I have adopted your advice how I might correct and amend the Narrative. You asked my opinion of the portrait. I gave it and still adhere to it, though I hope not without deference to yourself and those who think like you, that the picture does not suit. I am displeased with it not because I wish to be, but because I can't help it. I am certain the engraving is as good as the original portrait. I don't like it, and I have said so without heat or thunder. Pardon me if I venture to say you have trifled with me in regard to getting letters from your countrymen. You were the first to suggest and approve it, and now that I have taken the advice you are the first to condemn and oppose it. You ought to have thought of your prejudice against priests sooner. If clergymen read my narrative and approve of it, prejudice against their office would be but a poor reason for rejecting benefit of such approval. The enclosed is from Mr. Jackson, the Presbyterian Minister. I wish both it, and that of Dr. Drew, to be inserted in the second edition. To leave them out because they are ministers would be to show oneself as much and more sectarian than themselves. It would be virtually like their casting out devils because they follow us, the spirit of bigotry and sectarianism may exist, and be as deeply rooted among those who damn sects, and those who adhere to them. I have no time to discuss the question, nor is it necessary. Be so kind as to send me at once, three hundred copies of the Narrative to the care of Wm. Smeal,[37] 161 Gallow gate. They will come safest by sending them in a strong box.

Let me have the second edition as soon as possible, making it shorter and thicker, agreeable to your suggestion, in your former letter. Get as good, and if you can get better paper than that used in the first edition.

My first meeting here will be held tomorrow in the City Hall, a very large building. You shall here from me again soon. Please make my regards to Mrs. Webb and children.

As ever,
F. Douglass

*Anti-Slavery Collection, Boston Public Library*


## ADDRESS AT LONDON PEACE CONVENTION, MAY, 1846[38]

I experience great pleasure in rising to support the resolution which has been so ably advocated by the gentleman preceding me. You may think it somewhat singular, that I, a slave, an American slave, should stand forth at this time as an advocate of peace between two countries situated as this and the United States are, when it is universally believed that a war between them would eventuate in the emancipation of three millions of my brethren who are now held in most cruel bonds in that country. I believe this would be the result; but such is my regard for the principle of peace—such is my deep, firm conviction that nothing can be attained for liberty universally by war, that were I to be asked the question as to whether I would have my emancipation by the shedding of one single drop of blood, my answer would be in the negative. I am opposed to war, because I am a lover of my race. The first gleam of Christian truth that beamed upon my dark mind, after having escaped the clutches of those who held me in slavery, was accompanied by the spirit of love. I felt in that moment as if I were embracing the whole world in the arms of love and affection. I could not have injured one hair of the head of my worst enemy, although that enemy might have been at that very time imbruing his hands in the blood of a brother or a sister. I believe all who have experienced this love, who are living in the enjoyment of this love, feel this same spirit, this same abhorrence of injuring a single individual, no matter what his conduct happens to be. One of my reasons for hating war, and by which my attention was first attracted to its many evils, was a circumstance which occurred a few years since in the city of New York.

During the revolutionary war, an attempt was made to bombard many of our cities on the coast. Some of the bomb-shells had been recently found that were thrown during that war. One was taken from the shores of New Jersey, and sent to an iron-monger in the city of New York. When in the shop, one of the workmen took it out of doors, and finding it had not been discharged, he commenced with a hammer and chisel to take out its contents; and in so doing, by one stroke with the hammer, a spark was emitted, and at once the shell exploded, blowing the poor man to atoms—his legs one way, his arms another, his skull, his whole person was shattered by the single bomb. Pieces passed into several dwellings and three or four women and one or two children were killed in consequence of that single bomb-shell. The thought struck me, what must be the state of things when hundreds of these are thrown into innocent families, not among the hostile parties, not among those on the field of battle, armed and equipped, infuriated with the spirit of war, but into the domestic circle, among children some of whom may have been intended by the Creator to fill a prominent place in the reformation and purification of the world—these all destroyed by the demon, war. On reading an account of this, I thought if I had power within me, it should be used, whenever it could, in opposition to the demoniacal spirit of war. Some people contend that they can fight in love. I have heard individuals say they could go to war in love. Yes, this foul reproach has been brought upon Christianity, and ministers have been heard to say that they could go to war in love. This was answered very well by an advocate of peace in the United States, and I am happy to inform the good people here that advocates of peace are multiplying in the United States. An advocate of peace was arguing this question with a brother who was a minister of the gospel. The minister was against it; in fact, they were both ministers. He was asked, "If he believed Christianity was a religion of love? If the spirit of Christ breathed love"; He admitted it—he said, "God is love." "Then," said the other, "all that dwell in him, should dwell in love." This he admitted at once. "Then we should do nothing but what can be done in entire consistency with love?" "Of course this must be granted." "Well," said he, "can you go to war in love?" "Oh! yes." "Can you kill an enemy in love?" "Oh! Yes. I can conceive of circumstances when I should be bound by love to kill him." "What, throw bomb-shells, shoot cannon, use the sword in love?" "Yes." "Well," said my good friend, "if you can do all these things in love, what can you do in hate?" I believe, if there is one thing more than another that has brought reproach upon the Christian religion, it is the spirit of war. Why, a little while ago, in the Congress of the United States, a member arose and proposed the appropriation of a large sum to the support of the chaplaincy in the navy. Our Congress is made up of various materials; among the number there is an infidel, the son of Robert Owen.[39] That infidel, Mr. Owen, rose in his place at once, and opposed the proposition to support the chaplaincy; and on what ground, do you suppose? He did it, he said, on patriotic grounds. He was opposed to the introduction of the Scriptures in the navy, for, he said, "if the principles of Christianity, if the doctrines inculcated in the New Testament are carried out in the lives of our soldiers, they would do the very opposite to that for which we enlist them in the service. Instead of shooting their enemies, they would love them; instead of butchering them into atoms, they would seek to preserve their lives." He added, "I am utterly and unequivocally opposed to any support being given to the chaplaincy—they would preach the doctrines of the New Testament." What a stain, what a blot; an infidel rising up and rebuking ministers claiming to be ministers of the God of love; rebuking them for their delinquency, and preaching a higher Christianity than those to whom he has been accustomed to look!

*The Liberator*, July 3, 1846

## TO ISABEL JENNINGS

Edinburgh, 30 July 1846

My Dear Isa:

This is my first opportunity of addressing you since I received your last note. What shall I say to avert your displeasure? I can say with truth that I regret having made you angry, and regret having wrote the letter at which you took offense. You rightly account for its seeming harshness. Let Dr. Smyth bear the blame. I should never have written such a letter had I not been irritated by the foul slanders of this Revd manstealer. Still, Dear Isa, I cannot be as kind to myself as you have been to me. I cannot throw all the blame so far from home, I must take a share of it myself. I will not take much of it however. I will throw it off upon poor human nature. No man hath power over the spirit. He must submit to its magic sway with the same resignation that the weather-beaten Mariner does when dashed upon the waves of the storm tossed ocean. I would be always pleasant and agreeable if I could be, but so I can not always be. I cannot be always upon the mountain top, no more than I can be always in the tranquil shade of the valley. I have my times and seasons like everybody else. You told me nothing new, when you told me that I was imperfect. It was known here three weeks before your letter came to hand. I am sorry that Mr. Garrison or Phillips led you astray in regard to my character. But enough of this. I an indeed a very imperfect being, and that should have been my submissive reply to your *kind* note instead of the naughty letter which made you so angry. Please make my love to all at Brown street and believe as ever your sincere friend.

F. Douglass

*Douglass Ms., Frederick Douglass Papers, Library of Congress*

TO——————

Edinburgh, 30 July 1846

Dear Friend:

I shall leave here for New Castle upon Tyne Saturday. I write now to request that you will send any communication you may have for me between this and the 4th Aug to that place as I shall not leave there before the 5th. I have now on satisfactory terms agreed with the Scottish Antislavery Society to become their agent, and to labor in Scotland for a while. It is deemed very important to continue the agitation. My refusal to serve as an agent threw the committee here into some confusion as they had relied upon me for that office. I shall speak here tomorrow evening in commemoration of West India emancipation. In haste, yours Sincerely

F. Douglass

*Douglass Ms., Frederick Douglass Papers, Library of Congress*

## TO ELIZA NICHOLSON

New Castle, 1st Aug. 1846

Dear Friend:

I arrived here safely about 10 tonight. Had a pleasant journey for the most part, the day being clear, bright and beautiful until about 4 o'clk in afternoon, when were plunged head and ears into a heavy mist, or what would be called in America a dense fog. It seemed to be the South wing of that I left this morning in Edinburgh. They are disagreeable customers to those accustomed to a dry climate. Our passengers seemed to be [a] stupid set, giving little or no sign of life, except when the coach changed horses and then only when they stood in the inspiring presence of "John Barleycorn." I felt sorry to see them tippling the whisky. But for one to lecture on such occasions is like casting one's pearls before swine. So I looked on in silence, speaking only by example. I am deeply convinced that the great sin of Scotland is the use of ardent spirits as a beverage. Our Garind, a kind hearted and well disposed person, seemed quite intoxicated by the time we reached New Castle. This drinking at every stage is a dangerous practice and travellers ought to protest against it. But alas, they are often to blame, since they furnish the drink, that is, pay for it.

I have just received a letter from George Thompson inviting me to make his house my home during my stay in London. I shall accept his invitation. I write this in great haste upon my manifold which will account to you for the singularity of the hand. A meeting is advertised here for me. In haste Sincere,

F. Douglass

*Douglass Ms., Frederick Douglass Papers, Library of Congress*

## TO—————

(August, 1846)

My Dear Abner:

It is just one year ago this morning since I took farewell with yourself and dear companion at Buffalo. I am now about four thousand miles from you & have been going with the greatest rapidity ever since. Where I shall stop or when I shall stop our Father in heaven can only determine. I have resolved to labor on while He lends me ability, never to stop while the chain lays unbroken on the limbs of my beloved Brethren in the United States. I wish I could see you this morning, could press your generous hand, and hear your friendly voice.

*Frederick Douglass Ms., Frederick Douglass Papers, Library of Congress*


## TO ISABEL JENNINGS

Glasgow, 22d Sept 1846

My Dear Friend:

May I hope to be forgiven for this long silence. I know if you were acquainted with my movements for a few weeks past I should readily receive your forgiveness. I have been very closely engaged so much so that I have hardly had time to attend to my business correspondence. I have time now to do little more than to inform you where I am, and where I am likely to be the coming fortnight. I came to this city yesterday expecting to assist friend Garrison in holding a meeting here last night, but owing to the shortness of the notice given to the friends here of his coming there was no meeting appointed, and hence my labor in coming is for the present lost. We have a meeting in Greenock tonight and another in Paisley tomorrow night, and Thursday night and Friday night we hold meetings in Edinburgh, and on Tuesday night and Wednesday night probably at Dundee. Mr Garrison will then proceed to Belfast stopping however in this city long enough to hold two meetings. I shall not accompany him to Belfast or in any part of Ireland. He will have the field to himself. I could wish to be with him at Cork, but it will not be in my power.

I am now about to tell you something which will make you think me the most fickle of men. I have decided to stay in this country six months longer and I should not wonder if Mr Wright should do the same though I am sure with far less reason than I have to justify me in staying. I have decided to stay in consequence of the advice both of Mr. Garrison and Mr. Thompson. Both think the present a most favorable opportunity for remodelling the Antislavery feeling of this country and bringing it to the aid of the true anti-slavery society in America,[40] and each think it would be wrong for me to miss it. I have therefore decided to stay. You may easily suppose the conclusion came reluctantly when I tell you I had already written to my Anna[41] telling her to expect me home on the 20th Nov. It will cost her some pain. Disappointment is the common lot of all. This may afford slight relief till I come.

In haste Dear Isa
Sincerely yours
Frederick Douglass

*Douglass Ms., Frederick Douglass Papers, Library of Congress*

# TO——————

Lynn, April 21, 1847

My Dear Friend:

I hasten to inform you of my safe arrival at home. I left Liverpool per steamship Cambria, at 12 o'clock, on Sunday, April 4th, and reached Halifax on Sunday evening, the 18th, and here on Tuesday afternoon, about six—thus performing the voyage in sixteen days and six hours.

My passage was not the most agreeable; for aside from the head winds, a rough sea, and the innumerable perils of the deep, I had the cruel, and almost omnipotent and omnipresent spirit of American Slavery with which to contend.

After an interesting tour of twenty months through the British isles—during which, I made use of all the various means of conveyance, by land and sea, from town to town, and city to city, my feeling as a man, and my rights as a passenger, sacredly regarded, and never being able to detect the slightest dislike to me on account of my color—I bid farewell to monarchical England, and looked toward democratic America; and while yet three thousand miles away from her shores, at the first step, I am smitten with the pestilential breath of her slave system! I came home a proscribed man, and this, solely to propitiate American pro-slavery hate. The American public demanded my exclusion from the saloon of the steamship, and the company owning the steamer, had not the virtue to resist the demand. The dominion of Slavery is no longer confined under the star-spangled banner, but extends itself, and bears sway, even under that of Great Britain. But, without farther preface, I will at once put you in possession of the facts in the case.

On the 4th of last March, in company with my friend, Mr. George Moxhay, of the Hall of Commerce, London, I called upon the agent of the Cunard line of steamers, for the purpose of securing a berth in one of the company's vessels, to sail for the United States on the 4th of April. I was informed by the agent, that there was but one berth unsold, and that was berth 72, in the Cambria. This berth I took, and paid for—paying first-class price. I then asked the agent, whether there would be any difficulty in my enjoying any of the rights and privileges on board the ship, granted to white passengers. "Certainly not," was the reply. On hearing this, I left the office.

Reposing on the honor and the integrity of the company, and never dreaming of the possibility of a contingency to deprive me of my berth, I made myself perfectly easy till the afternoon of the 3rd of April, the day previous to our contemplated departure from Liverpool to Boston. I then went on board with my baggage; and here, to my surprise, disappointment, and mortification, I learned that my berth was given to another—that on account of the color of my skin, it had been decided that I should not have the berth for which I had paid and to which I was justly entitled! Confused and confounded by this intelligence, I went to the office of the agent in Liverpool, for an explanation of what I had heard on board the steamer, which was now lying in the Mersey, about two miles from the shore. The agent, Mr. McIver, with the harshness of an American slaveholder, told me that the agent from whom I had purchased my ticket, had no right to sell it to me. I replied that I knew nothing more of the authority of the agent to sell tickets, than what I learned from the public press. He was there advertised as the authorized agent of the company, and persons wishing to secure passage in the company's ships were requested to call upon him. I had as much right to regard Mr. Ford as the agent in London, as to regard Mr. McIver the agent in Liverpool. They were both the advertising agents of the company. But here was not the difficulty, as I afterwards compelled him to confess. This was a deceitful stratagem, (I will say nothing of its meanness,) to deprive me of my berth, without openly incurring the responsibility of trampling upon, and robbing a traveller of his rights, on account of the color of his skin.

The agent said, that great dissatisfaction had been given to the

*American* travelling public, by my having been permitted on the quarter-deck, when crossing the Atlantic in the summer of 1845, and that much ill-feeling had been created against the line in America by what I said against American Slavery during the voyage; and that while he would not undertake to defend American prejudices, he must, nevertheless, prevent the recurrence of any such event again; and that, if I went home in the ship, I must go in an apartment wholly separate from the white passengers; but that I should have every accommodation in the way of attention, and apartments enjoyed by other passengers. Subject to this restriction, I must never enter the saloon,—the part of the ship the most commodious, and where other passengers took their meals. I must eat alone—sleep alone—*be alone.* These were my limits on board the British steamship Cambria. By this regulation, I was not only deprived of the privilege of eating in the saloon, but also shut out from religious worship. We had two Sundays during the voyage, and, in conformity to the religious ideas of the company, as well as of the British public, had regular religious services performed on board. They called upon *"Our Father,"* the Creator of the heavens and the earth—the God who has made of one blood all nations, *the black as well as the white*—to bless them—while they cursed and excluded me on account of the color of my skin. This, I thought, was American slaveholding religion, *under British colors*, and I felt myself no great loser by being excluded from its benefits.

Aside from this proscription, I was as well provided for as any other passenger. Indeed, my apartments were much to be preferred to many which I saw on board. I was treated with the utmost politeness by every officer on board, and received every attention from the servants during the whole voyage. It may be asked, then, why do I complain? The answer is, that my position was one of coercion, when it ought to have been that of option. The difference is as wide as that of freedom and Slavery; and the man who cannot see the one, cannot see the other.[42]

In haste, yours, sincerely,

Frederick Douglass

*National Anti-Slavery Standard,* May, 6, 1847

TO————————

Lynn, (Mass.), 29th Apr., 1847

My Dear Friends:

I am at home— in the warm bosom of my family, caressed and administered to, by the beloved ones of my heart. It is good to be here—Thanks be to God, the giver of every good and perfect gift, whose tender mercies are over all, and without the notice of whose eye, even a sparrow may not fall to the ground, I have been preserved. After more than sixteen days of fierce conflict with head winds, adverse waves, and the innumerable hardships and perils of a spring voyage across the Atlantic, I am surrounded by the calm, soothing, and tranquilizing influences of home. You will be glad to know that I found my family all well. . . . You have heard ere this, that an attempt was made to degrade me by proscribing and placing me beyond the circle of my fellow-passengers during the voyage. This was done to conciliate the *democratic slaveholders* on board, who would have felt degraded by my presence at the table with them; these men would have been glad to have owned me for their slave, but they could not tolerate me as a *free man.* The proscription, though an early and at first a bitter foretaste of what then awaited me in this land, proved a blessing rather than a curse, since by compelling me to go into separate apartments, I was placed beyond the social influence of a set of persons who proved to be a band of wild, uproarious, gambling tipplers, whose foul-mouthed utterances interposed an impassable gulf between us.

The first few days of the voyage, I felt the degradation of my position, and felt a degree of loneliness. I was on a British steamer, a British flag waving over me; on her deck were a hundred and twenty passengers, not one of all of them had paid more for their passage than I had, yet while I was confined like a criminal to a certain part of the ship because of my color, they enjoyed the privilege of going at large, and in the spacious saloon, from which I was excluded. These superior privileges naturally enough induced in some a feeling of superiority over me; so while among men, children of one common Father, I was without society, I stood isolated and alone, with none to extend to me the hand of civility or pass a friendly smile in common, on the frowning waves of the deep—thus solitary and alone, my heart could dwell on the many beloved friends whose homes and hearts were ever open to me when I sojourned among you. . . .

After the first few days of our voyage, my proscription and the cause of it became generally known, and was at once the topic of common conversation among the passengers. A few persons, either from curiosity or humanity, spoke to me in my loneliness, and extended to me the common civilities of the day; they were of the more respectable part of our number, and this continued during the voyage. Thus was the attempt to degrade me made unavailing. I landed at Boston on Tuesday night, the 29th April, and a reception meeting was given me in Lynn, on Friday night, the 23d,[43] and the colored people of Boston intend giving me one on the 3d of May. Invitations are pressing in upon me from all quarters. I cannot attend one half of the meetings that parties are anxious to get up for me. My old friends receive me gladly, and new ones flock around to encourage me in my work, still I see before me a life of toil and trial. The war with Mexico, undertaken and carried on for the infamously wicked purpose of extending and perpetuating the enslavement of my race, is becoming more and more popular every day, and such is the feeling here that to denounce this war in the terms which its atrocious character merits, is at once to be branded as a traitor; but justice must be done, the truth must be told, the wicked must be be exposed, freedom and righteousness must be vindicated, and with the help of the God of peace and the oppressed, I will not be silent.[44] I am still strongly determined to devote myself to *printing* as well as speaking of my race. . . .

In kind remembrance to all my friends,

Yours truly &c. &c.

Frederick Douglass

*British Friend*, reprinted in *National Anti-Slavery Standard*, July 8, 1847

# TO SIDNEY HOWARD GAY[45]

Pittsburgh Pa. 13 Aug. 1847

My Dear Gay:

Pardon my neglect in not having written to you before now respecting my proposed alliance with the *Ram's Horn*[46]—I wish you carefully to examine the Books of the establishment—and if you find that the publication of the paper be not likely to involve me in monetary obligations and the payment of debts—already contracted by the publishers of that paper—You may draw up an agreement with Mr. Van Rensselaer in writing, making me a third party to concern for six months after the agreement shall be mutually signed. But should you find that the concern is in debt I beg you will make no arrangement whatever—further than that I will act as a corresponding Editor of that paper without compensation as long as I may find it convenient so to do—and that I will not take upon me any pecuniary responsibility—except to make the concern a donation of $25—if such a donation may be needed by the publishers.

Yours in great haste<br>Sincerely—F. Douglass

*Sidney Howard Gay Collection, Columbia University Library, Rare Book Division, Special Collections*

# FIRST OF AUGUST ADDRESS, AT CANANDAIGUA, NEW YORK, AUGUST 1, 1847[47]

We have assembled here to-day to celebrate the anniversary of West India Emancipation; an event which may be justly regarded the greatest and grandest of the nineteenth century. We meet here in the fulness of grateful sincerity, joyfully to commemorate that glad day, the bright sun of whose morning beamed light and Liberty upon the Western Isles. We are to direct our attention with joyous admiration to a splendid achievement, a glorious triumph of justice, love, and mercy, over avarice, pride, and cruelty. In a word, we meet here on this occasion to revive the fire of Freedom, to rekindle its holy flame upon the altar of our hearts, and to renew the impression made nine years ago upon the tablets of our memory by that magnanimous act of British legislation, descending like a voice from the celestial throne of God, scattering the infernal altars of Slavery, proclaiming deliverance from thraldom to eight hundred thousand of our fellow-men.

In view of the majestic grandeur and moral sublimity of the subject I might well pause, and apologize for consenting to occupy the prominent position which the Committee of arrangements have, in their kindness, seen fit to assign me. It is without the slightest affectation of humility that I confess the theme worthy of more eloquent lips, and of a more comprehensive mind. I would prefer to be the last, rather than the first on this platform. I have, however, one consolation in my present somewhat unaccustomed position, and that is, I am to be followed by gentlemen, distinguished alike for philanthropy and ability, who I am sure, will make good any defects which may appear in my humble address.

Friends and countrymen! I rejoice to meet you here. I am proud to assemble with you. The vastness of your numbers is delightful to my heart; your holy enthusiasm carries gladness through my heart; your presence here is a mighty argument—a powerful demonstration, which must act advantageously wherever known and heard of. The sentiment that leads us to celebrate noble deeds, to mark and commemorate great events in the world's progress, is natural and universal. The existence of this sentiment, like that of religion, is a grand proof of the superiority of mankind over brute creation. This sentiment is useful as it is universal. It is the power which makes the present generation the proprietors of the wisdom and experience of bygone ages. It makes the good of the past, the property of the present. It seems to keep alive that sense of gratitude to God, essential to the faith, without which it is impossible to succeed against present ills. It is the golden chain extending from earth to heaven, and to it we may summon the millions in eternity to aid us in pulling down the giant crimes of our age.

In coming together this day, to celebrate this glorious anniversary, we but act out one of the noblest sentiments of human nature and vindicate our just claim to an equal place in the ranks of human brotherhood.

It is just possible, however, that some may doubt the propriety of people of one nation celebrating the deeds of another. On this point I have no scruples. Neither geographical boundaries, nor national restrictions, ought, or shall prevent me from rejoicing over the triumphs of freedom, no matter where or by whom achieved. We are not only Americans, but men—colored men. Many of us have borne the yoke of bondage. We have dragged its heavy chains; the chambers of our souls have been made dark with its infernal gloom; our spirit has been crushed beneath its ponderous weight; our lacerated hearts have swollen with bitter anguish, while we sighed for the inestimable boon of liberty; and having now, by the blessing of God, escaped the galling chain, and being in the enjoyment of personal liberty, we should be unworthy of the name of men, and our own freedom if we did not remember, with gratitude and rejoicing, the day of deliverance to so many of our long-abused race.

On this question, we are strangers to nationality. Our platform is as broad as humanity. We repudiate, with unutterable loathing and disgust, that narrow spirit which would confine our duties to one quarter of the globe, to the exclusion of another, that can see nothing good or great in any land but our own, and which makes

> Lands intersected by a narrow faith
> Abhor each other. Mountains interposed,
> Make enemies of nations—who had else
> Like kindred drops, been mingled into one.

In celebrating this day, we place ourselves beneath the broad aegis of human brotherhood, and adopt the motto of our illustrious pioneer, "Our country is the world, and all mankind are our countrymen," and maintain the right and propriety of commemorating the victories of liberty over tyranny throughout the world. And, Sir, where is the man, of high or low standing, white or black, who would lift his arm, or raise his voice, to remove us from this place, or to silence our joyous exultations? It is true that but a few years ago, our brethren in Philadelphia undertook to do just what we are now doing. They undertook to celebrate the anniversary of West India Emancipation. They formed their procession with the utmost order and decorum.—They neither assaulted nor insulted any man. Their banners were raised in honor of Liberty; and in order to avoid offense to their white brethren, as well as a desire to advance the cause of righteousness, they inscribed Temperance as well as Freedom on their banners. But, Sir, with all these virtuous precautions, they did not avoid giving offense; nor did they escape brutal chastisement. They had not passed through two streets of that city before they were cruelly assaulted by the populace.—The ranks of their procession were broken up, their banners were torn into fragments, and many of themselves were trampled in the dust, and left horribly bruised and mangled in the streets. Mob violence, stimulated by the cheers of a profligate press, and an inefficient police, reigned supreme in that city.—They marched in the very presence of the city Government, and with the ferocity of wildbeasts, rushed into the houses of colored people, sparing neither men, women, nor children, but dealing heavy blows with sticks, stones, and clubs, upon the defenseless heads of their victims. From the private dwellings, they passed to the colored churches. —They burned the colored Presbyterian Church—threatened the Methodist, and destroyed their Temperance Hall; and all this, fellow-countrymen, for doing just what we are now doing.[48] I mention this in sorrow rather than anger, and I thank God, we are not subjected to such outrages here to-day; and it is peculiarly gratifying to see so many of our white fellow-countrymen present to participate with us in these joyous proceedings. We are worshipping at the same shrine, with the same heart and spirit, and I trust, we shall be mutually refreshed and blessed in the deed.

Sir, rightly to comprehend the grandeur of West India Emancipation, we must do more than fix our attention upon the simple act of manumission. To know the value of a result, we must know something of the labor and toil of bringing it about. Properly to appreciate the value of deliverance, we must adequately comprehend the greatness of the evil or enormity from which deliverance has been wrought out. The importance of this glorious event must be determined, by considering its connection with the past, its bearing on the present, and its influence on the future.

I shall not be able to enter fully or partially into all the branches of this great subject, but will confine myself to one or more, and leave the field to other and abler hands.

From the earliest periods of man's history, we are able to trace manifestations of that spirit of selfishness, which leads one man to prey upon the rights and interests of his fellow-men. Love of ease, love of power, a strong human heart. These elements of character, over-riding all the better promptings of human nature, has cursed the world with Slavery and kindred crimes. Weakness has ever been the prey of power, and ignorance of intelligence. Joseph was sold into Egyptian bondage by his own brethren, at a time when he ought to have been most dear unto them. The famine-stricken Israelites were reduced to bondage, when their sufferings ought to have aroused the most benevolent energies of the human heart. The Helots were consigned to serfdom or Slavery, while yet smarting under wounds received in battle for their country.—The proud Anglo-Saxons, overpowered in war, had their property confiscated by their haughty Norman superiors, and enslaved upon their own sacred soil. There are, at this moment, not fewer than forty million white slaves in Russia, a number far exceeding the present number of black slaves.

However much we may deplore the wickedness of such wholesale Slavery, it is somewhat consoling, that all nations have had a share of it, and that it cannot be said to be the peculiar condition of our race, any more than others. "He that leadeth into captivity, shall go into captivity," is a truth confirmed by all history, and will remain immutably true.

Who were the fathers of our present haughty oppressors in this land? They were, until within the last four centuries, the miserable, slaves, the degraded serfs, of Norman nobles. They were subjected to every species of brutality which their fiendish oppressors could invent. They were regarded as an inferior race—unfit to be trusted with their own rights. They were not even allowed to walk on the public highway, and travel from town without written permission from their owners. They could not hold any property whatever, but were themselves property, bought and sold. They were not permitted to give testimony in courts of law. They were punished for crimes, which, if committed by their haughty masters, were not deemed worthy of punishment at all. They were not allowed to marry without the consent of their owners. They were subjected to the lash, and might even be murdered with impunity by their cruel masters. But, Sir, I must not dwell here, though a profitable comparison might be drawn between the condition of the colored slaves of our land, and the ancient Anglo-Saxon slaves of England.

I come at once to the history of the enslavement of that race, whose deliverance from thraldom we have met to celebrate. The Slave-Trade by which Slavery was introduced, and established in the British West Indies, was commenced in the reign of Elizabeth, 1562. Spain and Italy had long been engaged in the traffic,[49] and England, no doubt tempted by their success, was induced, reluctantly, to follow in their footsteps. I say reluctantly, because from the first, the great Princess, Elizabeth, seems to have entertained religious scruples concerning it, and to have revolted at the thought of it. This is inferred from a conversation which the Queen had with Sir John Hawkins, on his return from his first slave-trading voyage. At this interview, she expressed her concern lest any of the Africans should be carried off without their consent, declaring it would be detestable, and would call down the vengeance of Heaven upon the undertakers![50] This pious outburst, though monstrous and absurd, as coming from one who had just given her royal assent to this infernal traffic, was the natural result of her wicked position, and is not without its parallel in our land. It was like Pilate delivering the Lamb of Calvary to the iron-hearted murderers, and—washing his hands of his blood. Of course, the declarations of the Queen were disregarded. It could not be otherwise. To make merchandise of man, and treat him kindly, and respect his will, is morally impossible. The expression of the Queen, if sincere, may be creditable to her humanity, but it is a dark reflection on her sagacity. The will of a victim is never respected. The lamb committed to the wolf may expect no quarter. The injustice, cruelty, and barbarity of this inhuman traffic can never be told, or conceived. They are known only to God. He alone can fully comprehend them. We mortal, and finite beings, can only receive a partial view of them. To assist in this, let us imagine, what must be far less than the whole truth. Let us go to that little village on the West Coast of Africa. The inhabitants are quiet, simple, peaceful, and happy. It is evening.—Through the rents and crevices of their fragile dwellings, a bright moon pours her soft and tranquil rays. The day's work is done, and the profound stillness is only relieved by the melodious hum of tropical insects. How sweet the scene. The husband, and wife, the parent and child, the sister and brother, and "friends of the kindred tie," have met to while away the evening hour in simple talk, and innocent song, and how sweet the moments glide. At the hour appointed, the mother clasps her innocent babe to her bosom, and with looks and words of love and admonition, she retires. Soon all follow, and our hut and village is still. The unsuspecting inhabitants are in the arms of "Nature's soft nurse," "and lulled with sounds of sweetest melody."—They sleep on the brink of destruction. Let us leave for a moment this happy village, and go to the shore. A slave-ship is anchored off the Coast. On her deck, dim lights are seen in motion. A boat is now lowered from the side, and softly rowed ashore. Twelve armed men land. Their swords, guns, and cutlasses, reflect the moonlight. When ready for their infernal work, they move off stealthily toward the doomed village. They are met by some wretch calling himself a Prince, who, bribed by this wicked crew, becomes the treacherous instrument of destruction to this abode of happiness, and the enslavement of its unoffending people. A few moments, and the village is in flames. The fear-smitten people start forth from the devouring fire, and in the hour of surprise, and consternation, its people have become the prey of the spoiler. Grim death, and desolation reigns, where before was life, peace, and joy.

Let us follow those despoiled people a short distance on their voyage to West Indian bondage.—Chained and hand-cuffed, they are driven before cutlasses, and pistols, to the ship. Their path is marked with blood. Torn from home, despoiled of their freedom, they go to drag out a miserable existence in Colonial Slavery. What pain, what anguish, what agony of soul, struggles beneath the hatchway of that pirate ship. They are stowed away, with as little regard to health, as to decency. Breathing the putrid air inseparable from being so closely packed, disease and death soon reign in their infernal dungeon. Many of them become food for the hungry shark, who reddens the wake of a slave-ship with their blood. And by the time they land at their point of destination, one-third of all taken on board, have been thrown overboard during the voyage, and more horrible still, many have been thrown overboard alive, lest they should spread the death-dealing contagion among the rest. Those who reach the shore, are sick, emaciated, and covered with sores. Landed on English soil, strangers to the English tongue, their only language is that of the lash. Before the bloody lash, they are driven to market, and under the cry of the auctioneer, they are sold, and separated from each other. All is lost! They are, they know not where. Such is but a faint picture of that trade, which is even now plied, and which peopled with slaves the Western Isles, and made Liverpool, Glasgow, and Bristol rich, on the blood, bones, and sinews of men. A view of this God-defying trade, led the great Anti-Slavery poet of England, to cry out in the agony of his mighty soul:

> Is there not some chosen curse,
>      Hid in the stores of Heaven,
>           red with uncommon wrath,
> To blast the man, who gains his fortune
>      By the blood of souls.[51]

In view of the cruel inhumanity of this trade, it is matter of astonishment that it was carried on for nearly two centuries, under the very eye of the British Government, and under the very droppings of British pulpits, without interruption, or opposition. For two hundred years did this trade go on, despoiling Africa of her children, bearing them away into a worse than Egyptian bondage, consigning them to the cruel lash, and hurrying them into eternity, uninformed and unprepared. Yet scarce a voice was heard against it during this long and dreary period. Silence prevailed. The Slave-Trade, with its train of evils, increased. Every year added to its strength, and augmented its influence, both upon the Government, and the Church. The first merchants of England were engaged in it, and it became so interwoven with the interests of various classes, as when attacked, to bring the powers of Church and State to its defense. The ministers of religion pleaded the Bible in its favor, and the minister of the crown pleaded national prosperity in its behalf. Thus bulwarked and protected, it became a giant in the land, threatening to cast down at a blow, any who might venture to attack it. Giant, however, though it was, and greatly to be dreaded, thank Heaven, there were found a chosen few, who did not shrink from the attack. I should be most happy, did my brief hour permit, to give you the names, and the history of those who had the humanity and intrepidity to stand forth as pioneers in this holy cause. But this I cannot do; I may only in reverence repeat their names, and bestow a tear of gratitude upon each. They have gone from this stage of life and activity, into the boundless realm of eternity.—They rest from their labor, and their good works do follow them. Yea, we are at this moment reaping the rich reward of their labors.

Among the most distinguished of those who early struggled in this glorious cause, history has handed down the names of Richard Baxter,[52] Addison,[53] Montesquieu,[54] Godwin,[55] Steele,[56] Shenstone,[57] Sterne,[58] Warburton,[59] Wesley,[60] Whitfield,[61] Dr. Hartley,[62] Granville Sharpe, Dr. Robertson, Abbe Raynal,[63] Thomas Day, [64] Bishop Portius, Necker,[65] Thomson, Adam Smith,[66] Gilbert Wakefield, and George Fox.[67]

Brave men; let their names be remembered, and their memory cherished.[68] Let us thank God that such men were raised up. Let us hand down their names to our children, and commend their conduct . . .[69] their imitation. These holy men laid the foundation upon which the noble Wilberforce[70] and Clarkson erected the temple of West Indian freedom. What confidence in truth, what faith in God, what a self-sacrificing spirit, must have animated the bosoms of those forerunners in the cause of emancipation. They arrayed themselves against powers and principalities. The nation was against them, a large part of the Church was against them, the wealth of England was against them, practice and the press was against them. So universal was Slavery in that land, it was common to see advertisements in respectable London journals, for runaway slaves. Slaveholders from "Jamaica," hunted and apprehended their slaves in London with as much impunity as American slaveholders do in our own land, and this practice continued until the sainted Sharpe, in 1769, obtained the decision in the famous Sommerset case, by which England was redeemed from the disgrace of being slave-hunting ground.[71]

The Slave-Trade was regarded by the friends of freedom, the life-blood of Slavery. Hence the first object of attack. It is a remarkable circumstance, "that men so sagacious and disinterested as Clarkson and Wilberforce, should have labored so long, and so hard, for the accomplishment of a half-way measure; and their experience ought to be a lesson for us, for with all their caution against asking too much they neither appeased the wrath of slave-traders, nor gained the good will of slaveholders." They were called wild enthusiasts, fanatical dreamers, and humanity mongers. The now sainted Clarkson was once burnt in effigy in Bristol, and came near being thrown overboard and drowned, at Liverpool. It was with the utmost difficulty, that these men could be heard against the giant crime. Ten times did the noble-hearted Wilberforce move a bill to abolish this infernal traffic, and ten times was he doomed to defeat. The slave-power in Parliament, like the slave-power in Congress, maintained a united and bold front. The arguments used by these defendants of the Slave-Trade, were quite similar to those used now in this country, in behalf of Slavery. It was said, that if the Slave-Trade were abolished, prisoners taken in war, in Africa, would be murdered. That it was merciful to bring them into Slavery; they were better off than the laborers in England. It was a source of revenue to the country. It was a religious duty to bring the heathen where they could be brought under the influence of the Christian religion, and it was contended the Scriptures sanctioned it. However, as the cause prospered, some more prudent, just, and magnanimous than the rest, were for *regulating* the trade. And this was deemed a great concession. It was confession that something ought to be done.

But what an idea to talk of regulating a system of wholesale plunder. Mr. Fox replied to this argument in a most powerful manner. He said that it was impossible to regulate robbery and murder. After twenty-four years of anxious conflict with this great crime, the friends of humanity triumphed. The bill to abolish the Slave-Trade, was carried through the British Parliament, and obtained the royal consent in 1807.[72] This was regarded a great victory, and such it truly was at that time.

Immediately after this, and in the same year, a society was formed, called the "African Institution." Mr. Clarkson was identified, and took an active part in its proceedings. The object of the institution, was the ultimate abolition of Slavery in the West Indies. All this time, no one thought of immediate emancipation as practicable, or desirable. Gradual emancipation was the most ultra idea then broached, and though tame, insipid, and stale, it was at the first a terrible note to the slaveholder, as well as their abettors. It, however, lost its power to stir the souls of its friends, or disturb the fears of its foes. The cause languished, Everybody was in favor of gradual abolition, but no one was ready for action, now. After twenty years of toil to promote gradual abolition—the cause dragging heavily along—while those noble men were hesitating about what they should do to infuse spirit into the Anti-Slavery ranks, and to accomplish their noble purpose—a woman, with the head of a prophetess, and the heart of an angel, came to instruct and strengthen their faltering ranks. She taught that what is right, is reasonable, and what ought to be done, can be done, and that immediate emancipation was the right of the slave, and the duty of the master. Her heavenly counsel was heeded.[73] Wilberforce was converted. The agitation now went on with vigor. They organized committees, appointed agents, and sent forth lecturers in all parts of the country. They printed tracts, and circulated their views through the press in various ways, till they succeeded in impressing the public mind favorably to their objects, and created that tide of public opinion which demanded immediate and unconditional freedom to the West Indian slave.

The Anti-Slavery cause in England received but little support from the Government Church, yet it was ever regarded as a religious movement, and was early espoused by dissenting churches and ministers in that land. In this honorable work, the Baptist and Congregational denominations stood foremost. It was the noble Knibb, and Purchell, Baptist ministers, who gave the last and most powerful blows towards the overthrow of this foul crime, and which ended its existence in the West Indies.[74]

In perusing this history, one is struck with the contrast between the churches and ministers of our own country, and those of England. Slavery found no support in the Baptist, Methodist, or Congregational churches, in England, Ireland, or Scotland. But how different with us today. The slave-system finds no such palliators and defenders, as emanate from those bodies, in our own land. Our churches are directly implicated in the crime. In the slave States of the Union, we have Slavery openly defended from the Bible. Corrupt and corrupting as are our political parties, they send no champions to the field to battle for Slavery, equal to these. They speak in the name of God, and are clothed with divine authority. They brand all movements for the abolition of Slavery, with the charge of infidelity. They are the choice friends of Slavery. When we attack it, it runs to them for protection. Religion is prostituted to the support of robbery. The Gospel of Liberty is tortured to maintain Slavery. Piety is pressed into the service of cruelty; and slaveholding, slave-buying, and slave-trading, is deliberately carried on in this land by all the leading Christian denominations. We have men sold to build churches, and babes sold to buy Bibles, and women sold to support missionaries. It was not thus in England. Slavery was the deadly foe of religion. It hated the missionary. It robbed their chapels, assaulted their ministers; and for the best of all reasons, the minister was faithful to his charge, denounced Slavery as being from the infernal, and not from the celestial regions.

But, Sir, I must hasten to a close—others are to follow me, who will do ample justice to the subject. I will just say, in conclusion, that I am not disheartened—I am not discouraged. The cause is in good hands. God, truth, and humanity are with us, and are working for our good. I see cause of[75]—in the movements of our enemies than in those of our friends. The wrath . . . God. He has declared that he will confound the wisdom of the crafty, and bring to naught the counsels of the ungodly. In the spirit of the age, in the voice of civilization, in the improvements of steam navigation, in every bar of railroad iron, I read the approach of that happy period, when, instead of being called upon to celebrate the emancipation of eight hundred thousand persons in the West Indies, we shall be summoned to rejoice over the downfall of Slavery in our own land.

*National Anti-Slavery Standard,* August 19, 1847

## TO SIDNEY HOWARD GAY

Albany, 4th October, 1847

My Dear Friend:

I have just completed a course of four lectures in this city—and on the score of order and respectability, I have never seen my audience excelled. One of the most encouraging and gratifying circumstances connected with the meetings relates to the place in which they were held. The State street Baptist Church, a large and commodious building, was readily and gratuitously thrown open to our use, and everything done by the officers of the church, from the minister down, to make the meetings beneficial to our sacred cause. This treatment, in such a place, may very properly be regarded as a hopeful sign of the times.

Like most other metropolitan towns and cities, Albany is by no means remarkable for either the depth or intensity of its interest in reform. No great cause was ever much indebted to Albany for assistance. Many reasons might be given, accounting for the tardiness of its people in matters of reform in general, and Anti-Slavery reform in particular. I believe that many of its wealthiest and most influential families have either been slaveholders, or are connected with slaveholders by family ties, and it is not too much to presume that they have not been entirely purified and cleansed of the old leaven. Their influence is yet visible on the face of this community.

"The evil that man do lives after them." Thirty years ago, and slaves were held, bought and sold in this same goodly city; and in the darkness of midnight, the panting fugitive, running from the steeples and domes, swam the cold waters of the Hudson, and sought a refuge from Albany man-hunters, in the old Bay State. The beautiful Hudson was then to the slaves of this State, what the Ohio is to slaves in Virginia and Kentucky. The foul upas has been cut down for nearly thirty years, and yet its roots of poison and bitterness may be felt in the moral soil of this community, obstructing the plough of reform, and disheartening the humble laborer. Many efforts have been made to awaken the sympathies, quicken the moral sense, and rouse the energies of this community in the Anti-Slavery cause—but to very little purpose. Many of the best and ablest advocates of the slave, including George Thompson, of London, have wrought here, but *apparently* in vain. So hard and so dead are its community considered to be, our lecturers pass through it from year to year without dreaming of the utility of holding a meeting in it; all are disposed to think Slavery may be abolished in the United States without the aid of Albany. Like Webster, of New Hampshire, they think this is a good place to emigrate from.

Situated on the banks of the noble Hudson, near the heart of navigation, Albany is the grand junction of eastern and western travel. Its people have a restless, unstable, and irresponsible appearance, altogether unfavorable to reform. A flood of immorality is poured into the city through the great Erie Canal, and the very cheap travel on the Hudson facilitates the egress of a swarm of loafers and rum-suckers from New York. I have received more of insult, and encountered more of low blackguardism in the streets of this city in one day than I should meet with in Boston during a whole month.

The general character of a community may be ascertained by the tone and spirit of its press. A virtuous community will not support a vicious press. Albany is not without respectable newspapers, some of them are justly to be regarded among the best in this country; and yet I undertake to affirm that there is not to be found in the whole North, a city of equal population supporting half the vile trash in prints and newspapers, pandering to the mean and general prejudice against persons of color. We are almost without the protection of Law or Gospel here, and we are constantly made the object of attack by the dastardly conductors of these villainous papers.

Mean and corrupt as those conductors are, one would think the honor even of a blackguard and a bully, would forbid his selecting persons so helpless as ourselves. His ambition is low indeed, who is satisfied by trampling upon those who are already weak and defenseless. There is something that commands the respect if not the admiration in two equals arrayed against each other—but to see a big-fisted wretch smiting a sick and emaciated man, is a sight so cruel and disgusting that I wonder that the dastard himself is not ashamed of his cowardice. The colored people are defenseless. They are outlawed from political rights and social respectability. In these circumstances is it generous? is it fair? is it witty?—or bold to make them the special objects of newspaper attack? Magnanimous Albanians judge! In this city, the religious and irreligious, the rude and the refined, are equally opposed to our holy cause. Diverse in all things else, they are agreed in this. The rude and irreligious base their opposition on their hatred of the Negroes. The refined and religious talk learnedly and piously of time-honored and time-hallowed institutions. This is the headquarters of New York law and politics, and the community is accustomed to give importance to political precedents rather than to moral principle. And to make the sage inquiry, as to what saith the Law, rather than what saith the Lord. I know not how it is, nor will I attempt to explain—but it does seem that State-houses, Law Schools, and Theological Seminaries, are all unfavorable to a healthy development of the moral sentiment, and of the spirit of progress, in the community where they may exist. Like huge trees that cumber the ground, they seem to extract so much strength from the soil, that more useful though less powerful plants may not grow in their vicinity. Under the dark shadow of the State-house, reform withers, droops, and dies. Its cold stone walls and moldy parchments are too stiff and gloomy for the warm heart and elastic spirit of philanthropic reform. Deliver me from cities; a country audience forever, before whom to advocate the cause of liberty and humanity. And yet it must be confessed that some of the noblest of mankind, and the most determined and fearless reformers are to be found in cities; and in this, Albany is not altogether unlike many others.

There is a man in this city whose voice is seldom heard or his person seen in the street, who lives unobserved by the community, who never attends a public meeting or makes any public demonstration; but whose heart, hand, and home, is ever ready to cheer on the advocates of every righteous cause. He is the only man with whom I have ever met in this country who seems familiar with the benevolent works of what in England is known as the Animals' Friend's Society. To this man the cause of the slave is indebted more than to any other in this place. It is needless to mention his name—among so few he will easily be selected.

On one evening during the meetings I had the assistance of that venerable patriarch in the cause of liberty and humanity, Isaac T. Hopper.[76] His presence, in plain dress, with hat on, made some sensation in the audience. He opened the meeting with a few appropriate remarks, which were very well received. He expressed his great gratification at meeting with persons of different religious persuasions, and political opinions, on the Anti-Slavery platform;—gave some interesting anecdotes from his almost inexhaustible fund of such illustrations, and exhorted the colored persons in the audience to civility and Christian forbearance, under the embarrassments and hardships which it is their present lot to endure. He administered a short, but pointed, rebuke to the Society of Friends, for their cold indifference to the cause of the slave, and gave us a word of encouragement to persevere in our noble work, by alluding to the progress the cause has already made. Long may the good man live. Long will his good deeds be remembered, especially by the hundreds whom he has been instrumental in delivering out of the hand of the spoiler.

I am glad to inform you that there is one minister in this city whose influence will I am sure do much to advance our righteous cause in this place. It is Mr. Warren, of the church in which I lectured, who, though not agreeing with me on several points connected with this question, was nevertheless highly pleased to allow me a fair hearing before his congregation, and to do everything he could to make my meetings here successful. All our meetings were well attended. Many of the members of the Legislature were present, and many of them probably heard an Anti-Slavery lecture for the first time.

Since my lectures here I have held a meeting in Poughkeepsie. Here I was welcomed by that friend of universal Liberty, *Charles Vanloon*, who, you will remember a few weeks ago was called to account by the junior editor of the Albany Patriot for being found in company with "vipers" such as Remond, Hathaway, and myself. Though sternly reproved and faithfully admonished he does not seem to have repented of his sin, if sin there was in being found in our company. He is one of the few noble spirits whose energies are not to be bound or his sympathies narrowed down to the narrow limits of a sect, either in religion or politics. My meeting in Poughkeepsie was held in the Congregational Church. It was crowded to overflowing, and I have no doubt that a good impression was made upon the audience.

I have also been attending the Colored National Convention which has just closed its sittings in Troy. It continued four days. I may give you some account of it next week.

Yours,

F.D.

*National Anti-Slavery Standard*, Oct. 12, 1847

## PROSPECTUS FOR AN ANTI-SLAVERY PAPER
## TO BE ENTITLED NORTH STAR.

FREDERICK DOUGLASS proposes to publish, in Rochester, N. Y., a WEEKLY ANTI-SLAVERY PAPER, with the above title.

The object of the NORTH STAR will be to attack *Slavery* in all its forms and aspects; advocate *Universal Emancipation;* exalt the standard of *Public Morality;* promote the Moral and Intellectual Improvement of the COLORED PEOPLE; and hasten the day of FREEDOM to the Three Millions of our *Enslaved Fellow Countrymen.*

The Paper will be printed upon a double medium sheet, at $2.00 per annum, if paid in advance, or $2.50, if payment be delayed over six months.

The names of Subscribers may be sent to the following named persons, and should be forwarded, as far as practicable, by the first of November, proximo.

FREDERICK DOUGLASS, Lynn, Mass.
SAMUEL BROOKS, Salem, Ohio
M. R. DELANY, Pittsburgh, Pa.
VALENTINE NICHOLSON, Harveysburgh, Warren Co., O.
Mr.. WALCOTT, 21 Cornhill, Boston
JOEL P. DAVIS, Economy, Wayne County, Ind.
CHRISTIAN DONALDSON, Cincinnati, Ohio
J. M. M'KIM, Philadelphia, Pa.

AMARANCY PAINE, Providence, R. I.
Mr. GAY, 142 Nassau Street, New York

*Sidney Howard Gay Collection, Columbia University Library, Rare Book Division, Special Collections*

## TO SIDNEY HOWARD GAY[1]

8, Jan. 1848

My Dear Gay:

I thank you for the several subscribers you have sent me—and the interest you take in my hazardous enterprise. Your good wishes are highly appreciated. One of the most discouraging forms of opposition which I meet is the fears of my friends—some of whom draw gaunt pictures of starvation—and predict that I am soon to be victimized.[2] It may be even so.

Yours Ever,
Frederick Douglass

*Sidney Howard Gay Collection, Columbia University Library, Rare Book Division, Special Collections*

## TO MARTIN R. DELANY

Rochester, 12, Jan. 1848

My Dear Delany:

We must go to press again much to my regret without a single line from your pen or the ability to tell our readers where you are or what you are doing.[3] I wish you attached as much importance to writing as we do to hearing from you. Do my Dear fellow, do write let us know what you are doing and how you are getting on. We hope to give our readers a good sheet this week. I have said a few words to our brethren who are interested in getting up what they dignify with the title of a national press. I hope what I have said will meet your approval. Subscribers come in slowly, and I am doing all I can by lectures and letters to keep our heads above the water. Ohio does not respond in anything like the numbers which I had a right to expect. Do all you can for us in Pittsburgh. Our list does not yet reach more than seven hundred subscribers, and our expenses are all of fifty five dollars per week. Send on subscribers and money. Nell is doing his duty nobly,[4] and the men are at work manfully.

In haste yours always,
Frederick Douglass

*Douglass Ms., Frederick Douglass Papers, Library of Congress*

## TO MARTIN R. DELANY

Rochester, 19, Jan. 1848

My Dear Delany:

Yours of 10 Jan. including 20 Dollars came safely to hand. It afforded both myself and Mr. Nell great pleasure to hear from you, and we mutually regret to learn the illness of your Dear child, and hope ere this its health has been restored. How strangely your old friends are behaving toward you. What can it mean? We shall publish in this week's paper your valedictory to the readers of the Mystery.[5] I have been very busy this week in lecturing and trying to obtain subscribers, but have not done much. The work is uphill just now, but I hope there is a good time coming. I am now boarding with Mr. Joines, whose family is well and desire love to you. Mr. Nell will finish this letter. I shall leave here Thursday for Penn Yan, where I hope to get some subscribers. Everything will depend upon our getting subscribers. I am out on the Mexican war this week.[6] My best love to your family.

Yours always,
Frederick Douglass

*Douglass Ms., Frederick Douglass Papers, Library of Congress*

## TO ISAAC POST

Lynn, Mass., 3d Feb. 1848

My Dear Isaac:

I have now fully resolved to bring my family to Rochester with me, and shall probably reach there as early as one week from tomorrow which is Friday. I write to request that you will secure me a tenement, the rent of which will not exceed one hundred dollars per annum. I arrived here yesterday, having held meetings in Richfield, Troy and Springfield, since I left West Winfield. I saw Friend Garrison yesterday, he was well and made affectionate enquiries for the health of your family. I regret to be absent from Rochester so long, as I shall have to be this time, but the length of time now may prevent a longer period in future. I am getting subscribers, which is no unimportant item. With love to all the members of your Dear family, I am yours ever, In great haste,

Frederick Douglass

*Phoebe Post Willis Papers, Rush Rhees Library, University of Rochester*

## COLORED CHURCHES.—No. III

One of the greatest evils resulting from separate religious organizations for the exclusive use of colored persons, is the countenance and support which they give to exclusive colored schools. The very existence of the former is an argument in favor of the latter. If there be any good reason for a colored church, the same will hold good in regard to a colored school, and indeed to every other institution founded on complexion. Negro pews in the church; Negro boxes in the theatre; Negro cars on the railroad; Negro berths in the steamboat; Negro churches and Negro schools in the community, are all the pernicious fruit of a wicked, unnatural, and blasphemous prejudice against our God-given complexion; and as such stand directly in the way of our progress and equality. The axe must be laid at the root of the tree. This whole system of things is false, foul, and infernal, and should receive our most earnest and unceasing reprobation. The evils of separate colored schools are obvious to the common sense of all. Their very tendency is to produce feelings of superiority in the minds of white children, and a sense of inferiority in those of colored children; thus producing pride on the one hand, and servility on the other, and making those who would be the best of friends the worst of enemies. As we have frequently urged on the platform and elsewhere, prejudice is not the creature of birth, but of education. When a boy in the streets of Baltimore, we were never objected to by our white playfellows on account of our color. When the hat was tossed up for a choice of partners in the play, we were selected as readily as any other boy, and were esteemed as highly as any. No one ever objected to our complexion. We could run as fast, jump as far, throw the ball as direct and true, and catch it with as much dexterity and skill as the white boys; and were esteemed for what we could do. And such, in our judgment, would be the case here at the North, but for the many influences tending to a separation of white from colored children. We shall, however, have more to say on this subject at another time; for it is one which ought to receive speedy and thorough attention, not only in this community, but throughout the Union.

Another reason against colored churches originates in the character and qualifications of the men almost universally and necessarily employed as their teachers and pastors. With few exceptions, colored ministers have not the mental qualifications to instruct and improve their congregations; and instead of advancing, they retard the intellectual progress of the people. Some of the most popular colored preachers in this country are men unable to write their own names; and many of them are unable to read without spelling half their words. Colored churches form a field for this class of "would-be ministers;" and their existence is one great reason of the ignorance and mental inactivity, and general want of enterprise among us as a class. We have heard them denounce what they called "letter killeth, but the spirit giveth life: and that all we should care about is to get to heaven when we die." Of course the effect of such teachers and teaching is to establish the conviction, that "ignorance is bliss, and it is folly to be wise." A virtue is made of ignorance, and sound is preferred to sense. In point of elevation and improvement, wicked as are the white churches, and corrupt as are their white ministers, colored persons would have gained much more by remaining in them, than they have done by coming out from them; and they might ere this, in the northern States, at least have obtained equal rights in every department of the church, had they remained in them and contended for their rights. The example set by a few colored men in New England, with respect to the unjust and odious distinctions formerly practised there in the use of railroad cars, is worthy of imitation in the churches. We have frequently gone into cars intended only for white passengers, and allowed ourself to be beaten and dragged out by the servants and conductors, as a means of distinctly asserting the equal rights of colored persons in the use of those cars. And what has been the result of such conduct on our part! Why this—the whole system of compelling colored persons to ride in separate cars from others has been totally abolished.[7] The railroad companies became ashamed of their proscription, and abandoned it. Colored men are now treated with the utmost kindness and equality on the same roads where five years ago, they were insulted and degraded. We should like to see the same course pursued toward white churches. Colored members should go in and take seats, without regard to their complexion, and allow themselves to be dragged out by the ministers, elders, and deacons. Such a course would very soon settle the question, and in the right way. It would compel the church to develop her character in such a manner as either to secure the rights of her colored members, or to secure her own destruction. We shall practice on this principle, and in every instance give white religious worshippers the trouble of removing us from among them, or the pain of enduring our dark appearance.

Another evil of colored churches is their expensiveness. Colored people are scattered over the country in small numbers, and are generally poor; and to be compelled to build churches for themselves, and hire their own minister, is by no means a trifling hardship. The minister and his family must be supported, though the members have scarcely the means of living, to say nothing of the means of educating and improving the minds of their children. We have known of churches composed of a dozen good colored women and as many men; the former gaining their living over the washtub, and the latter obtaining theirs by daily toil; at the same time supporting a minister and his family at an expense of from two to three hundred dollars a year.

*The North Star,* March 10, 1848

# THE DOUGLASS TESTIMONIAL

*The absence of Mr. Douglass suggests the publication of an extract from his letter to English friends, relative to the testimonial of a printing press and materials. The letter was inserted in Howitt's Journal.*

The tone of the British press, on the subject of my exclusion from the saloon of the steam ship Cambria, during her April voyage from Liverpool to Boston, has been all and more than all, I had ventured to hope or expect. How nobly and successfully has the press performed its duty—that of vindicating the right, denouncing the wrong and throwing its broad shield of protection around humanity in its humblest and most defenseless form. Their promptness in this instance has done more to impress me with a sense of your nation's honor, than all the other incidents connected with my visit to your land. I feel that my mission would have been incomplete without this crowning chapter in its history. It is a nation's press defining a nation's position in a question of the greatest importance to my downtrodden and long-abused race. I will point Americans to that definition, and with its testimony I will confound those who slander your country (as many here are wont to do) by the charge of prejudice against color in England.

You speak of the printing press, and ask, shall I like to have it? I answer, yes, yes.[8] The very best instrumentalities are not too good for this cause. I should feel it quite improper to express myself thus, if the proposed present were merely an expression of personal consideration. I look upon it as an aid to a great cause, and I cannot but accept of the best gifts which may be offered to it.

I hope to be able to do a good work in behalf of my race with it.

Yours respectfully,

F. Douglass

*The North Star*, April 14, 1848

# "PREJUDICE AGAINST COLOR"

Prejudice against color! Pray tell us *what* color? Black? brown? copper color? yellow? tawny? or olive? Native Americans of all these colors everywhere experience hourly indignities at the hands of persons claiming to be white. Now, is all this for *color's* sake? If so, which of these colors excites such commotion in those sallow-skinned Americans who call themselves white? Is it black? When did they begin to be so horrified at black? Was it before black stocks came into fashion? Black coats? black hats? black walking canes? black reticules? black umbrellas? black-walnut tables? black ebony picture frames and sculptural decorations? black eyes, hair and whiskers? bright black shoes, and glossy black horses? How this American colorphobia would have lashed itself into a foam at the sight of the celebrated *black* goddess Diana, of Ephesus! How it would have gnashed upon the old statue and hacked away at it out of sheer spite at its color! What exemplary havoc it would have made of the most celebrated statues of antiquity. Forsooth they were *black*! Their color would have been their doom. These half-white Americans owe the genius of sculpture a great grudge. She has so often crossed their path in the hated color, it would fare hard with her if she were to fall into their clutches. By the way, it would be well for Marshall and other European sculptors to keep a keen lookout upon all Americans visiting their collections. American colorphobia would be untrue to itself if it did not pitch battle with every black statue and bust that came in its way in going the rounds. A black Apollo, whatever the symmetry of his proportions, the majesty of his attitude, or the divinity of his air, would meet with great good fortune if it escaped mutilation at its hands, or at least defilement from its spittle. If all foreign artists, whose collections are visited by Americans, would fence off a corner of their galleries for a "Negro pew," and staightway colonize in thither every specimen of ancient and modern art that is chiselled or cast in *black*, it would be wise precaution. The only tolerable substitute for such colonization would be plenty of *whitewash*, which would avail little as a peace-offering to brother Jonathan unless *freshly* put on: in that case a thick coat of it might sufficiently placate his outraged sense of propriety to rescue the finest models of art from American Lynch-law: but it would not be best to presume too far, for colorphobia has no lucid intervals, *the fit is on all the time.* The anti-black feeling, being "a law of nature," must have vent; and unless it be provided, wherever it goes, with a sort of portable Liberia to scrape the offensive color into it twitches and jerks in convulsions directly. But stop—this anti-black passion is, we are told, "a law of nature," and not to be trifled with! "Prejudice against color" "a law of nature!" Forsooth! What a sinner against *nature* old Homer was! He goes off in ecstasies in his description, of the *black* Ethiopians, praises their beauty, calls them the favorites of the gods, and represents all the ancient divinities as selecting them from all the nations of the world as their intimate companions, the objects of their peculiar complacency. If Homer had only been indoctrinated into this "law of nature," he would have insulted his deities by representing them as making Negroes their chosen associates. What impious trifling with this sacred "law," was perpetrated by the old Greeks, who represented Minerva their favorite goddess of Wisdom as an *African* princess. Herodotus pronounces the Ethiopians the most majestic and beautiful of men. The great father of history was fated to live and die in the dark, as to this great "law of nature!" Why do so many Greek and Latin authors adorn with eulogy the beauty and graces of the black Memnon who served at the siege of Troy, styling him, in their eulogiums, the son of Aurora? Ignoramuses! They knew nothing of this great "law of nature." How little reverence for this sublime "law" had Solon, Pythagoras, Plato, and those other master spirits of ancient Greece, who, in their pilgrimage after knowledge, went to Ethiopia and Egypt, and sat at the feet of black philosophers, to drink in wisdom. Alas for the multitudes who flocked from all parts of the world to the instructions of that Negro, Euclid, who three hundred years before Christ, was at the head of the most celebrated mathematical school in the world. However learned in the mathematics, they were plainly numbskulls in the "law of nature!"

How little had Antiochus the Great the fear of this "law of nature" before his eyes, when he welcomed to his court, with the most signal honors, the black African Hannibal; and what an impious perverter of this same law was the great conqueror of Hannibal, since he made the *black* poet Terence one of his most intimate associates and confidants. What heathenish darkness brooded over the early ages of Christianity respecting this "law of nature." What a sin of ignorance! The most celebrated fathers of the church, Origen, Cyprian, Tertullian, Augustine, Clemens, Alexandrinus, and Cyril—why were not these black African bishops colonized into a "Negro pew," when attending the ecclesiastical councils of their day? Alas, though the sun of righteousness had risen on primitive Christians, this great "law of nature" had not! This leads us reverently to ask the age of this law. A law of nature, being a part of nature, must be as old as nature: but perhaps human nature was created by piecemeal, and this part was overlooked in the early editions, but supplied in a later revisal. Well, what is the date of the revised edition? We will save our readers the trouble of fumbling for it, by just saying that this "law of nature" was never heard of till long after the commencement of the African slave trade; and that the feeling called "prejudice against color," has never existed in Great Britain, France, Spain, Portugal, the Italian States, Prussia, Austria, Russia, or in any part of the world where colored persons have not been held as slaves. Indeed, in many countries, where multitudes of Africans and their descendants have been long held slaves, no prejudice against color has ever existed. This is the case in Turkey, Brazil, and Persia. In Brazil there are more than two millions of slaves. Yet some of the highest offices of state are filled by black men. Some of the most distinguished officers in the Brazilian army are blacks and mulattoes. Colored lawyers and physicians are found in all parts of the country. Besides this, hundreds of the Roman Catholic clergy are black and colored men, these minister to congregations made up indiscriminately of blacks and whites.

*The North Star,* May 5, 1848

# SPEECH AT AMERICAN ANTI-SLAVERY SOCIETY, MAY, 1848

*Frederick Douglass, of Rochester, ascended the platform when Mr. Phillips*[9] *had finished, and said:*
Mr. Chairman and Ladies and Gentlemen:

It is with great hestiation that I consent to rise here to speak, after the able speech to which you have just listened. I had far rather remain a listener to others, than to become myself a speaker at this stage of the proceedings of this meeting. I do not hope to be able, in the few remarks I have to make, to say anything new or eloquent, if, indeed, anything new were needed, for it will be time enough to discuss new truths when old ones shall have been recognized and adopted.

For seventeen years, Mr. Chairman, the Abolitionists of the United States have been encountering obloquy, scorn, and opposition of the most furious character, for uttering—what? Their conviction that a *Man is a man*; that a man belongs to himself and to noone else. In propaganding this idea, this simple proposition, we have met with all sorts of opposition, and with all sorts of arguments, drawn from the

Bible, from the Constitution, and from philosophy, till at length many have arrived at the sage conclusion that a man is something else than a man, and that he has not the rights of a man. An event has just occurred in the District of Columbia, the capital of the country, known to you all, which furnishes the proof of this assertion. Some seventy-seven men, women, and children, took it into their heads, contrary to the Constitution, that they were *Men*—not *three-fifths* of *men*—that they would leave the refined avocation of blacking boots for nothing for members of Congress and seek an asylum from oppression and tyranny in some of the Northern States, or under the protection of the British Lion in Canada. The sequel is well known; they were pursued by a band of armed men, overtaken, and brought back in chains, and the men who aided them in their flight are in a dungeon, and there they will probably end their lives.[10]

Very little is thought about this affair—very little noise is made about it. It excites about as much remark, and about as much sympathy, as if as many horses had broken away from the halters of their owners, and again been recovered.

Sir, we have, in this country, no adequate idea of humanity yet; the nation does not feel that these are men; it cannot see, through the dark skin and curly hair of the black man, anything like humanity, or that has claims to human rights. Had they been white men and women, or were they regarded as human beings, this nation would have been agitated to its centre, and rocked as with an earthquake, and like the nations of the old world, would have rung with the thunders of freedom against tyranny, at such an event as this. We do not regard these men as formed in the image of God. We do not see that in the persons of these men and women whose rights have been stricken down, whose virtuous attempt to gain their freedom has been defeated, the violation of the common rights of man. Even the gallant Hale, of the Liberty Party, does not dare speak of the men who aided their escape, as having done a noble deed. To be sure, he can bring in a propsition for the better protection of property in the District of Columbia, but he makes no allusion whatever to the rights of black men.[11] This proposition in relation to the rights of property, is regarded by his adherents as a noble act; as a timely measure; as indicating great courage and heroism. Nor do I care to deny it. But what is the inference? If it be a noble act, a courageous act, to move in the Capitol of the nation; in the Senate of the United States, a bill to protect property from the assaults of a brutal and ferocious mob—if that be bold, of course it would be no less daring and fanatical to move in that District that the rights of man be protected.

I do not propose to make a lengthy speech, but I would like to say a few words about how these things look to others.

> "O wad some power the giftie gie us,
> To see our selves as others see us."

I would like to hold up to you a picture; not drawn by an American pen or pencil, but by a foreigner. I want to show you how you look abroad in the delectable business of kidnapping and slavedriving. Some time since—I think it was in the December number of "Punch"—I saw an excellent pictorial description of America. What think you it was? It was entitled, "Brother Jonathan." It was a long, lean, gaunt, shrivelled-looking creature, stretched out on two chairs, and his legs resting on the prostrate bust of Washington: projecting from behind was a cat o' nine tails knotted at the ends; around his person he wore a belt, in which were stuck those truly American implements, a bowie-knife, dirk, and revolving pistol: behind him was a whipping-post, with a naked woman tied to it, and a strong-armed American citizen in the act of scourging her livid flesh with a cowskin. At his feet was another group;—a sale going on of human cattle, and around the auctioneer's table were gathered the *respectability*—the religion represented in the person of the clergy—of America, buying them for export to the goodly city of New Orleans. Little further on, there was a scene of branding—a small group of slaves tied hand and foot, while their patriotic and philanthropic masters were burning their name into their quivering flesh. Further on, there was a drove of slaves, driven before the lash to a ship moored out in the stream, bound for New Orleans. Above these and several other scenes illustrative of the character of our institutions, waved the star-spangled banner.—Still further back in the distance was the picture of the achievements of our gallant army in Mexico, shooting, stabbing, hanging, destroying property, and massacreing the innocent with the innocent, not with the guilty, and over all this was a picture of the devil himself, looking down with satanic satisfaction on passing events. Here I conceive to be a true picture of America, and I hesitate not to say but this description falls far short of the real facts and of the aspect we bear to the world around us.

Sir, although we have heard conflicting views uttered here today, of hopeful and desponding aspect, (if, indeed, we have any desponding aspects brought to us,) still, I think much more may be said in behalf of the hopeful aspects. The signs of the times have already been alluded to; we have very properly gone beyond the limits of the United States.

I see some of the audience are going out, which, makes me think I have spoken long enough: some plants thrive better by being cut off here; not because there is not more to be said, but because your energies have been taxed quite enough already. Since then, you wished me to proceed, and, as Henry Clay says, "I am always subject to the will of the people," there may yet be room for something of a speech.

As I was proceeding to remark concerning the hopeful aspects of the times, I wish to bring with more distinctness before your minds the news which comes from abroad—the action of the Provisional Government of France. We have been accustomed, in this country, to hear much talk about "Christian America and Infidel France." I want to say in behalf of France, that I go for that infidelity, no matter how heinous it may be in the estimation of the American people, which strikes the chains from the limbs of our brethren: and against that Christianity which puts them on; for that infidelity, which, in the person of Cremeaux, one of the members of the Provisional Government of France, speaks to the black and mulatto men that come to congratulate them, and express their sentiments upon the immediate emancipation of their brethren in the French islands.[12] I sympathize with that infidelity that speaks to them in language like this—friends! brothers! men! In France, the Negro is a man, while you are throwing up your caps, waving your banners, and making beautiful speeches in behalf of liberty, deny us our humanity, and traffic in our flesh. Sir, I would like to bring more vividly before this audience, the wrongs of my downtrodden countrymen. I have no disposition to look at this matter in any sentimental light, but to bring before you stern facts, and keep forever before the American people the damning and disgraceful fact that three millions of people are in chains to-day; that while we are here speaking in their behalf, saying noble words and doing noble deeds, they are under the yoke, smarting beneath the lash, sundered from each other, trafficked in and brutally treated; and that the American nation, to keep them in their present condition, stands ready with its ten thousand bayonets, to plunge them into their hearts, if they attempt to strike for their freedom. I want every man north of Mason and Dixon's line, whenever they attend an antislavery meeting, to remember that it is the Northern arm that does this; that you are not only guilty of withholding your influence, but that you are the positive enemies of the slave, the positive holders of the slave, and that in your right arm rests the physical power that keeps him under the yoke. I want you to feel that I am addressing slaveholders, speaking to men who have entered into a solemn league and covenant with the slaveholders of the country, that in any emergency, if at any time the spirit of freedom finds a lodgment in the bosom of the American slave, and they shall be moved to throw up barricades against their tyrants, as the French did in the streets of Paris, that you, every man of you that swears to support the Constitution, is sworn to pour leaden death in their hearts. I am speaking to slaveholders; and if I speak plainly, set it not down to impudence, but to oppression, to slavery. For God's sake, let a man speak when he cannot do anything else; when fetters are on his limbs, let him have this small right of making his wrongs known; at least, let it be done in New York. I am glad to see there is a disposition to let it be done here—to allow him to tell what is in him, with regard to his own personal wrongs at any rate.

Sir, I have been frequently denounced because I have dared to speak against the American nation, against the church, the northern churches, especially, charging them with being the slaveholders of the country. I desire to say here as elsewhere, that I am not at all ambitious of the ill opinions of my countrymen, nor do I desire their hatred; but I must say, as I have said, that I want no man's friendship, no matter how high he may stand in church or state, I want no man's sympathies or approbation who is not ready to strike the chains from the limbs of my brethren. I do not ask the esteem and friendship of any minister or any man, no matter how high his standing, nor do I wish to shake any man's hand who stands indifferent to the wrongs of any brethren. Some have boasted that when Fred. Douglass has been at their houses, he has been treated kindly, but as soon as he got into their pulpits he began to abuse them—that as soon as the advantage is given to him, he takes it to stab those who befriend him.—Friends, I wish to stab no man, but if you stand on the side of the slaveholder, and cry out "the Union as it is," "the Constitution as it is," "the Church as it is," you may expect that the heart that throbs beneath this bosom, will give utterance against you. I am bound to speak, and whenever there is an opportunity to do so, I *will* speak against slavery.

I meant to have said a word about Colonization,[13] as I observed there was a *very dark looking* individual here, (Gov. Pinney, of Liberia,) for whose special benefit I wished to say something on that subject. But as I do not see him here now, there is no necessity to discuss this subject for his benefit. When he was pointed out to me, I thought it quite remarkable that so dark a man should be in favor of colonization; but there are some simple minded men even among colored people! I will just say, however, that we have had some advice given us lately, from very high authority, I allude to Henry Clay, who, in his last speech before the Colonization Society, at Washington, advised the free colored people of the United States that they had better go to Africa.

He says he does not wish to coerce us, but thinks we had better go! What right has he to tell us to go? We have as much right to stay here as he has. I don't care if you did throw up your caps for him when he came to this city—I don't care if he did give you "his heart on the outside of the City Hall and his hand on the inside." I have as much right to stay here as he has! And I want to say to our white friends that we, colored folks, have had the subject under careful consideration, and have decided to stay! I want to say to any colonization friends here, that they may give their minds no further uneasiness on our account, for our minds are made up. I think this is about the best argument on that subject.

Now there is one thing about us colored folks; it is this, that under all these most adverse circumstances, we live, and move and have our being, and that too in peace, and we are almost persuaded that there is a providence in our staying here. I do not know but the United States would rot in this tyranny if there were not some Negroes in this land—some to clink their chains in the ear of listening humanity, and from whose prostrate forms the lessons of liberty can be taught to the whites. It is through us now that you are learning that your own rights are stricken down. At this time it is the abolitionist that holds up the lamp that shows the political parties of the north their fetters and chains. A little while ago, and the northern men were bound in the strange fanatic delusion that they had something to do with making of presidents of the U. States; that is about given up now. No one now of common sense, or common reading, imagines for a moment that New York has anything to do with deciding who the President shall be. They are allowed to vote, but what is the amount of this privilege? It is to vote for the slaveholder, or whom the slaveholders select? No men that are now accounted sane think of any other than of a slaveholder or assassin, or both, who shall hold the destinies of the nation, and the reason is because the people are convinced that they belong—as they used to say—to the colored boys of the south, to the party. They used sometimes to ask me, "Boy, who do you belong to?" and I used to answer, "to Captain Thomas Auld, of St. Michael's, a classleader in the Methodist Episcopal church; and now," I would ask, "who do you belong to?" I will tell you. You belong to the Democratic party, to the Whig party, and these parties belong to the slaveholder, and the slaveholder rules the country. As the boy said about ruling England— "I rule mamma, and mamma rules papa, and papa rules the people, and the people rule England." To be sure you have the right to vote, which is like what I once heard of a certain boy, who said he was going to live with his Uncle Robert, and when I go there, said he, I am going to do just as I please—if Uncle Robert will let me! The Northern people are going to do just as they please—if the slaveholders will let them! The little bit of oppostion that has manifested itself in that little protuberance on American politics—the Wilmot Proviso[14]—which our friend Clay has fully described as a tempest in a teapot, has now quite flattened down. The Whigs, who said, We will stand by it at all hazards, have fairly backed out; they got afraid of the Union. In Ohio, I heard men, striking their fists together, saying they would stand by at all hazards; and after a little while the Ohio State Legislature came to the conclusion, after having carefully considered the matter, that "to press the question of no more slave territory, must be disastrous to our American Union." New York came out expressly in favor of the Proviso, and it has since seen that the Union will be periled by adherence to that principle. And all over the North there is this fainting away before that power which was before undefined, as has been so eloquently touched upon by my friend Phillips; for while men hold up their hands in favor of the Union and the Constitution, there is a moral conflict in their hearts, for, as was so beautifully expressed by Mr. Parker, of Boston,[15] men cannot fight slavery under the Constitution; the Constitution soils the armor about them: we cannot strike slavery while we have it on us: there is not other way but to throw it off.

I have no prepared speech, and I will not weary you any longer. I have sometimes thought since the late occurrence in France, there may be an under current in Men's hearts here as there were in Paris; Louis

Philippe thought himself perfectly secure surrounded by his 300,000 soldiers who, with fixed bayonets, were ready to support him in the suppression of the riots, but the troops were found to fraternize with the people; the soldier joined the civilian to assert and defend his rights. So I believe here, after all we have said against the American people, there is yet an undercurrent pervading the mass of this country, uniting Democrat and Whig, and men of no party, taking hold in quarters we know not of, which shall one day rise up in one glorious fraternity for freedom, uniting into one mighty phalanx of freedom to bring down the haughty citadel of slavery with all its bloody towers and turrets.

> "There's a good time coming, boys,
> A good time coming,
>     Wait a little longer.
> We may not live to see the day,
> But earth shall glisten in the ray
>     Of the good time coming;
> Cannon balls may aid the truth,
> But thought's a weapon stronger,
> We'll win the battle by its aid,
>     Wait a little longer."

*The North Star*, June 2, 1848

# FRANCE

We gave in our last number telegraphic accounts of the recent appalling insurrection in Paris, as early as they could have received them in the eastern papers. The deep interest which is taken in the affairs of France by reformers in this country, and throughout the world, has induced us to publish this week a more detailed account of this fearful strife. Coutd the prayers of the friends of freedom and humanity have availed, France might have escaped this most terrific and bloody baptism. But he that taketh the sword shall perish by the sword, remains the law of the living God, and is sure to execute itself. For the sake of Freedom and Progress, we lament this sad result.

Superficial men will charge its evils upon Liberty and Democracy, just as the malpractices of churches and professed ministers of the gospel are too often charged upon Christianity; and for a time the cause of righteous Liberty, must bear up under a heavy load of reproach and infamy. Calhoun, and the whole group of American mansteelers, will undoubtedly regard it as the consequence of a too broad assertion of human equality, and as the folly of attempting to erect a Republican edifice without having slavery for its corner-stone. But in answer, we say, God reigns, and will yet vindicate the right. He is now teaching the world, by French example, the folly of injustice, oppression and wrong, and of the foolishness of relying upon the sword for that which can only be accomplished by preaching.[16]

Respecting the immediate cause of the insurrection, there seems to be considerable doubt. Some in France think it the work of foreign emissaries, who sought to overthrow order and the Government by corrupting the people with gold. This might be, to a certain extent, true; but the real cause must be deeper down than this supposition implies. Wretched must be the lot, and dark the minds of those who could be bought for paltry gold to involve their country in a common anarchy and ruin. That designing and disappointed politicians have had a hand in this bloody work, we have no doubt. Men who, foiled of their ambition by honorable means, have resorted to this as the last expedient to accomplish those purposes—deeming it "better to rule in hell than serve in heaven," they have sought to gain their preference through the wild and wicked means of anarchy and bloodshed. It appears from highly intelligent sources, that this whole plot of horrid destruction had been maturing for weeks in the national work-shops,[17] and that the leaders and chiefs on the side of the insurrection, exercised as complete authority over their men as that exercised by the officers over the regular troops. This fact shows plainly that the event has been the result of no mere accident, but a long-determined, regularly-organized and skillfully-contrived plan to subvert all order—that out of the wild chaos and fury, its projectors might snatch the bloody reins of government.

But while this may have been true to a certain extent, if the war-cry of the revolutionists means anything, the communists of Paris are chiefly responsible for this last confused scene of human slaughter. They have been the agents, if not the principals, in the concern, and to them must attach the glory or shame of the foul undertaking. Dark and gloomy as is the prospect, we will not despair of society in France. Even amid the wildest elements of revolution, and what are called the baser and more profligate sort, the prophet may scan certain rays of character which may kindle in his bosom a blaze of hope. The people, however mistaken and deluded, evidently felt that they were fighting for their just rights. They regarded themselves deceived and defrauded by the government, and whether correct or incorrect, they acted upon their belief. Two important lessons are here taught the statesmen: first, that the people will not endure oppression and injustice when they believe the means in their power to throw it off; second, that however just and impartial may be the laws and institutions of a country, there is absolutely no safety while the great mass of the people are ignorant and uneducated. Educate the people—educate the people, for therein is the safety of society.

*The North Star*, July 21, 1848

# MR. S. R. WARD[18]

The address of this gentleman to the four thousand colored voters of this State, will be found on the first page of this week's paper.[19] The deep interest which is just now felt on the subject which it discusses, as well as the source from which it emanates, will ensure for it an attentive reading. Mr. Ward has certainly made out as strong a case against supporting the Buffalo nominees for President and Vice President, as the facts upon which his argument is based will admit of. The past transgressions of Mr. Van Buren, and the sins of omission on the part of the Buffalo Convention,[20] are very distinctly and forcibly brought out. The whole argument, it strikes us, would have answered very well a few years ago; but considering present circumstances, we regard it as quite inconclusive, and to some extent uncharitable. The address complains,

"*1st. Because the Platform of the Buffalo Convention does not include the Equal and Inalienable Rights of all men.*"

Mr. Ward thinks this omission has the appearance of design. We think otherwise.—The times create their own watch-words; and the watch-words of one generation may not always be appropriate to another. We would as willingly fight the battle of liberty and equality under the banner of "Free Sons and Free Men," as that of the Declaration of American Independence. "Deeds, not words," is our motto. The only question which we should be disposed to ask, as a preliminary to giving our influence in favor of a political party, would relate to what that party proposed to do, rather than the doctrines they proposed to teach, and if these deeds commended themselves to our judgment as perfectly right in themselves, and involved no departure from moral principle in the means of accomplishing them, we should not hesitate to give our aid and vote to such a party. The address condemns the "Free Soil Party," because some of its leading men—such as Senator Dix[21]—entertain wrong views and prejudices against the colored people, and voted against Mr. Hale's motion for the abolition of slavery in the District of Columbia. These objections would be quite pertinent if Senator Dix were a candidate, and the party called upon to vote for him.—The views of Senator Dix, if we understand them, are quite similar to those of Senator Morns, of Ohio, who was Mr. Ward's candidate for the Vice-Presidency up to 1844.—That gentleman was far from regarding the colored man as equally entitled to suffrage in this country with the whites; and we know of but few, even among professed abolitionists, who have entirely triumphed over their long-cherished prejudices against us. But should we refuse to co-operate with them in securing a great good, because they may possess these prejudices? Certainly not. One of the most successful modes of removing prejudices, is to act with such men just so far as we can without a compromise of fundamental truths.—The presence of such a man as Mr. Ward as a delegate to the Buffalo Convention and the several able speeches which he made there, was one of the most powerful blows ever dealt upon the thick skull of Americans' prejudice against colored persons. Thousands had an opportunity afforded them on that occasion of learning, for the first time in their lives, something of the manly energy of the black man's mind. We saw thousands listening to his eloquent words with astonishment, mingled with admiration, and all probably went home with a higher and more truthful estimate of our race than they ever entertained before. We think that, so far from prejudice and false views of our equality being a valid reason for not acting with a party, it is sometimes the most valid reason which can be given for such action.

Mr. Ward's next objection to the Buffalo *nominees*, is stated as follows:

In 1841, a bill passed Congress having for its object the adjustment of the Pre-emption Rights of new settlers upon lands belonging to the General Government.[22] Among its provisions, is one allowing the privilege of preemption to free white male citizens, and to such only. If, therefore, black men settle in any of that territory which is now or shall hereafter become the property of the Government, white settlers can buy the lands upon which such blacks have settled at Government price, and the blacks be ejected, because the latter are not free white male citizens. No alteration of this abominable law is sought or desired by the new Free Soil Party.

To us, all this appears far-fetched, and unjust. It would be easy to condemn any party, if the justice of such reasoning be allowed.—We think the statement, that "No alteration of this abominable law is sought or desired by the new Free Soil Party," is far from being justified by the history, character, and composition of that party. From all that we have observed of the spirit of the Free Soil Party, we should come to any other conclusion with respect to their future conduct and desires, than that at which Mr. Ward has arrived.—We believe that the present Free Soil Party would repeal with delight the infamous law in question. Not to believe this, is to regard as false and hypocritical nearly all the declarations made at the recent Buffalo Convention. The very idea of "free soil" would forbid their tolerating any such odious and unjust distinction as the one in question; and we fear that prejudice, rather than candor, dictated the assertion that the Free Soil party neither sought nor desired the repeal of that wicked law. We should render to every party, however good that party may be, to the injury of another.

Again Mr. Ward says:

To vote for Mr. Van Buren, therefore, is to vote for the continuance of Slavery in the District of Columbia, inasmuch as that is one of Mr. Van Buren's Democratic Free Soil principles.

This was penned before Mr. Van Buren's letter accepting his nomination was published, which affords some excuse for its palpable unfairness. Mr. Van Buren has declared his willingness to sign a bill for the abolition of slavery in the District of Columbia. We think the party should have been judged of in the light of its platform, at least until the candidates accepted or refused their nomination. So judged, friend Ward would never have supposed that voting for Van Buren could possibly be voting for slavery in the District of Columbia.

The next and last objection which Mr. Ward urges against voting for the Free Soil nominees, relates to the action of the Barn-burner Democrats[23] of this State with respect to the Right of Suffrage. It is alleged that since they did not, *some time ago*, maintain the black man's right to vote, they cannot now be voted for without an abandonment of self-respect on our part. To give this argument any force, it must be shown that the Free Soil party stand just now on this question where the Barnburners then stood, otherwise the logic is just about as good as this—Gerrit Smith, in 1830, was in favor of sending black men out of this country to Africa;[24] therefore, black men cannot vote for Gerrit Smith, in 1848, without an abandonment of self-respect.

With all deference to Mr. Ward, we see no force whatever in this reasoning. To reproach Free Soil men for what they once were, is as bad as to reproach the Apostle Paul for sins committed before his conversion. The Free Soil party are not now what they once were. They have undergone a great change of mind; if not in respect to abstract right, they certainly have in regard to expediency, and it does seem to us that we are not accountable for the motives of men, and that it is unfair and uncharitable to be thus forward to attach sinister motives to the good deeds of those with whom we differ. To make this case plain: There is a man overboard, and needs our help to save him from a watery grave. Is it our duty to refuse, because some with whom we may be called upon to act, are animated in what they do by an improper or sinful motive? Certainly not. You will say, and all other reasonable men would say in such a case, Save the man! though the motives of all your associates should be wrong except your own. If the act be good, do it, and leave the motives of your fellows to be disposed of by the Searcher of all hearts.

It is certainly to be regretted that Mr. Ward should have adopted his present policy. We know him too well to suspect him of any desire to play into the hands of the Cass and Taylor parties; but we know just as well that such will be the inevitable and almost only effect of his position. Indeed, such has already been the effect of his speeches on this subject. The old slaveholding, Negro-hating, and slavery-extending parties have almost ceased to fight each other, and are rallying all their forces to defeat their common enemy—the Free Soil party; and they hail with much pleasure the slightest aid which Mr. Ward, or any other man possessing an anti-slavery character, can render them. In proof of this, we cut the following extract from a letter published in the *Albany Evening Journal* of last week, written in Cortland, giving an account of Mr. Ward's meeting on his return from the late Buffalo Convention. The writer says:

"It had been whispered around, since the return of Mr. Ward, that he intended to take ground against the Buffalo nominations, and rumor had not disappointed us. After giving us a history of the proceedings of that body, he was requested by some of the audience to define his own position in reference to the nominations. This he did at considerable length, declaring his hostility to the nomination of Martin Van Buren, and his determination to take the stump, and advise his abolition friends not to give the Ex-President their votes. He avowed himself in favor of the election of Gerrit Smith, and declared that he was the only Liberty party candidate who was or had been in the field. As for John P. Hale, he stated that he obtained a nomination from a Liberty party convention with the intention of selling out to some other candidate, and that by his letter to the Buffalo Convention he had accomplished his purpose, and had endeavored to hand over the Liberty party to Martin Van Buren. He quoted largely from the letters, speeches and inaugural address of Mr. Van Buren, and claimed that in none of his recent letters on the subject of Free Soil, had he given any evidence of a change of heart, nor of sorrow and contrition for the past. Mr. Ward stated that in a few days he should address a letter to his colored brethren who were voters, and who numbered some four or five thousand in this State, advising them to withhold their votes from Mr. Van Buren.

"On the whole the meeting had a good effect. A few Whigs who had remained undecided whether to support General Taylor, came away from the meeting fully satisfied with the claims of Martin Van Buren to the support of Northern men on the score of his anti-slavery opinions! They will now give "Old Zack" their hearty support, convinced, although he lives in the South, that the reins of Government will be safer in his hands, than in those of either Cass or Van Buren, the two Northern 'dough-faces.' "[25]

Now, if the only effect of Mr. Ward's address was to drive men from the Van Buren ranks into those of Gen. Taylor, we think it becomes him to reconsider and abandon his course. Certainly he cannot feel very comfortable in such companionship. The course of the colored voters should not be determined by the past transgressions of the members of the "Free Soil" party but by what they now are, and what they are now aiming to accomplish.

Our course is clear. We shall vote for neither of the candidates. With our views of the pro-slavery character of the American Constitution, and the criminality of executing its infernal provisions against the slave, we could as soon run our hands into a fiery furnace, as into the American ballot-box, if thereby a man was to be elected who would swear to support that accursed bond of Union. We desire to see this Union broken up, and a Free Republic established in the North, and to this end we shall lend our energies, now and always, unless reasons stronger than those which have yet been presented shall determine us otherwise.[26] The slave power can never be fully grappled with by Northern men while they are under their present delusion about the advantages of this Union.—They must be made to count it a curse before they can meet this hoary-headed monster.—The Free Soil men have followed slavery up to the ramparts of the Constitution, and there they stop. They will do some good by thus hemming slavery in, but the bloody ramparts of the Constitution must be scaled and battered down before the millions within its compass can gain their freedom. We shall never rest while the Northern people are sworn to return the fugitive slave to bondage, and to put down the slave, should he rise to strike for freedom. These compromises make it impossible for us to vote under the American Constitution. It would be a violation of anti-slavery principle for us to vote.

But here it may be asked, If those be your views, are you not inconsistent in advising men to vote for Mr. Van Buren? We may be, but we think not. Our advice, properly speaking, does not extend to the voting.—That is a matter already settled in the minds which we address. Our advice only extends to the party to be preferred by men who are already voters, had meant still to vote. We say to the multitude who are rushing to the ballot-box, See to it that you do not add to the sin of voting at all, the great sin of slave-rule, slavery-extension, and the perpetuity of slavery in the District of Columbia. To deny that we have this right, would be equal to saying that a man has not the right to pray the robber to spare his life after he has taken his purse.

We have now extended these comments beyond the length which we had allotted to this subject, and will therefore at once conclude by saying, that while we would not be the means of diverting a single vote from Mr. Gerrit Smith, we would not as we desire the slave power overthrown—the old slaveholding parties broken up—the slave-trade between the States discontinued—slave territory kept out of the Union—slavery in the District of Columbia abolished—slavery limited, circumscribed, and humbled—be instrumental, directly or indirectly, in leading a single voter to cast his vote for the servile doughface, Gen. Cass, or the bloodhound candidate, Gen. Taylor, each of whom we regard as among the most unscrupulous robbers in the world.

*The North Star,* September 1, 1848

# STEAMBOAT OREGON

Lake Erie, September 9th, 1848

. . . I am now on the steamboat bound to Buffalo, and for the first time during the last few years find myself almost entirely among strangers, and therefore enjoy the happiness of a temporary repose. The deportment of officers and men is respectful and polite, subjecting me to no deeper degradation than prohibiting me from eating with the hungry herd of whites who generally swarm the first table—no great degradation after all, but still not exactly as it ought to be. My Dear Mr. Francis, who is on board in company with Mrs. Francis, has just told a gentleman who I am; and they insist upon me to give them an Anti-slavery speech. A vote is taken, by which I am unanimously invited to speak, the Captain himself consenting. I am told that this is the first trip of the "Oregon" when a colored man has been allowed a cabin passage. Another "Oregon" free soil victory.[27] Oh! the cause is rolling on; believing that this was a favorable opportunity for influencing the popular mind, I accepted the invitation to make a speech. The audience listened to me without the slightest manifestation of approval on the one hand and dissent on the other. The passengers were evidently strangers to each other's views, and the political excitement now abroad and the breaking up of the old parties made it still more difficult to applaud or condemn, for you know our Northern people *are very independent* and are peculiarly careless of public opinion. During my remarks, I convicted the slaveholder of theft and robbery, and considering myself among strangers to the anti-slavery subject, I fortified myself on every hand and hemmed the slaveholder in beyond the possibility of escape. At the close of my remarks, I invited any persons who might feel disposed to question any of my positions, to avail themselves of the opportunity of doing so, for I was ready to submit my speech to the closest examination. Here a scene transpired which would require the pen of a Jerrold to describe. A man rose with the most contemptuous sneer on his face and said, "If there are any slaveholders on board, he supposed that they were white gentlemen and it was not to be supposed that any white man would condescend to discuss this question with a n----r." He was himself a slaveholder, and I had called him a robber, &c. At the end of this little speech, finding the passengers pleased with the *verdancy* of the slaveholding gentleman, I replied to his speech in a somewhat facetious account of my genealogy. I informed the gentleman that he was much mistaken in supposing me to be a n----r, that I was but a half Negro—that my *Dear father* was as white as himself,[28] and if he could not condescend to reply to Negro blood, to reply to the European blood. Here the "grin" was completely on the poor slaveholder. I then went on to show that he had assumed a little too much in presuming all slaveholders to be white and cited cases of black men, who were slaveholders—showing that though we may differ widely in the complexion of our skins, we are identical in the color of our morals. It was easy to see that the slaveholder felt himself losing favor with the passengers. When I sat down, he rose again as if in utter desperation, he stamped upon the deck and said that he had travelled in various parts of this country, that he thought he knew something of the public sentiment of the country, and that nothing but the actual knowledge which he had that night acquired, could have made him believe that such sentiments and impudence as he had heard from my lips could be tolerated and applauded by white men in any part of this Union. The only effect produced by this exclamation of astonishment and chagrin, was, to bring to his feet a Northern man who whined out an apology for the slaveholder, on the ground that abolitionists had not been sufficiently careful of the feelings of slaveholders.—That bad as was the condition of the slave, the poor slaveholder was in the most *unfortunate* condition of the two. This opened up another view of the subject and induced a comparison of the relative condition of the slave and the slaveholder, and led to an interesting discussion in which a number of the passengers participated. The meeting continued from about eight in the evening to ten o'clock, and the meeting adjourned. The whole affair showed the great change going on in the public mind on the subject of slavery.

Yours for Freedom,
Frederick Douglass

*The North Star*, September 15, 1848

# COLORED NATIONAL CONVENTION AT CLEVELAND

We return from this Convention[29] with a higher sense of the excellence of character and mental ability of our people, than we have ever entertained before. Cut off from them for seven years past by the duties of our vocation as a lecturer, and seldom meeting them when their characters and sentiments could be well determined, we had almost come to think that they cared very little about the fettered bondman, and less about their own elevation and improvement. No man with such impressions could have gone to a better place than the Colored National Convention at Cleveland, during the last week, to have such impressions entirely removed. He would have witnessed an elevation of sentiment, a warm philanthropy, an ardent love of freedom, and earnestness of purpose, a brilliance of talent, and a dignity of deportment, which would have done discredit to no deliberative assembly ever held in this country. We feel proud to be associated and identified with these, our maligned and despised fellow-countrymen. The Convention, taken as a whole, was the most satisfactory and unexceptionable of any colored convention which we ever attended. Whilst there was manifested a variety of views, warmly set forth and insisted upon by the various speakers, there was a commendable toleration and forbearance towards each other, as well as an absence of party or sectional feeling, quite surpassing any convention which we ever attended. There appeared to be but one heart and one soul in the Convention and that pervaded by one spirit. Everyone seemed to be deeply desirous of getting at the best means for improving our condition at the North, and removing every hindrance to the emancipation of our brethren at the South.

Having but just returned from this Convention, and withal quite jaded out with our labors during the past week, we shall not be able to give our readers that detailed account of its proceedings which they might have expected in this number of the North Star.—They will, however, be content to wait a "little longer," when we assure them that an authenticated and carefully drawn up account of those proceedings will be speedily published by the industrious and talented Secretaries, whose able and accurate discharge of the duties incumbent upon them, commanded the high respect and the warm gratitude of the Convention that appointed them.

There was no feature of the Convention more gratifying than the spirit with which it was regarded by the white citizens of Cleveland. On these, the Convention exerted a most cheering influence. Our day meetings were all largely attended by white persons, while our evening meetings were literally thronged,many being compelled to leave the Court House and the Tabernacle (large rooms where the Convention was alternately held,) unable to gain admission. As an indication of the change which has taken place in the public mind in reference to our people, we may state that the Court actually adjourned several hours earlier in consequence of the Court House having been previously engaged to the Convention. This change in public opinion, and its superiority to the law, was frequently referred to during the interesting discussions of the Convention. It will be remembered that Ohio is disgraced by what are called *black laws*,[30] (and such they are.) One of those laws forbids colored men to come into her borders without giving bonds that they will not become paupers and a public expense, and all such persons are liable to arrest if found in the State. But here such is the change of public opinion, that we are not only welcomed within her borders, but her law administrators throw open the doors of her public buildings for our accommodation.—We call upon slaveholders and their abettors to mark this fact, and we also call upon our colored brethren to mark it, and hail it, as a sign of the good time coming, when worth, not complexion, shall be the test of respectability and excellence. During the whole three days of the Convention, we did not hear of a single indignity offered by a white citizen of Cleveland to a colored man. It is true, when we entered the city and went to the New

England Hotel, there was manifested on the part of the bar-keepers of that house, a slight want of courtesy when questioned to know if he could accommodate us; but this treatment stopped at that hotel. The delegates who went to the American Hotel, and also those who put up at the "Dunham House," were treated with the respect and attention commonly paid to other travellers, and we have not heard of any of the white inmates or boarders who raised the slightest objection to this treatment of colored persons. The Dunham House, one of the most orderly and elegantly conducted hotels in the city, was peculiarly free from skin aristocracy, and we would especially recommend that house to the attention of all the travelling friends of "free soil, free men, and free speech," who may chance to pass through or stop any length of time in Cleveland. We are sure that they will find in that house a rare combination of those excellencies of character in the proprietor, and all connected with its management, which make a temporary home in a hotel pleasant and agreeable.

We feel sure that the Convention, if its influence shall not extend even beyond the limits of Cleveland, has done a sufficient amount of good to justify the holding of it; but its influence will not stop here. The delegates in attendance from Illinois, Michigan, Ohio, and New York, will return to the various circles who sent them, and carry to them new zeal and increased knowledge, a firm determination to dedicate their energies to higher and holier objects than those to which we, as a people, have been too long and too deeply devoted. They will tell them that they can only be free where the truth makes free; that in order to be elevated, their lives must be in harmony with the truth; that they must "add to their faith, virtue, knowledge, brotherly kindness and charity;" that earth and perdition cannot prevail against a character made up of such heaven-descended qualities. —F.D.

*The North Star,* September 15, 1848

## VISIT TO PHILADELPHIA

We have seldom spent two weeks more agreeably, or usefully, than those which we have just passed in the City of Brotherly Love. At the urgent request of several devoted friends of the cause in that place we were reluctantly induced to leave our editorial post, for the purpose of holding a series of meetings in that city among the colored people, and thereby extend the circulation of the *North Star*. In the pleasure which the visit afforded, the numerous friends and acquaintances made, the increased knowledge of the social condition of our people acquired, subscriptions to the *North Star* obtained, and the general and we trust praiseworthy good done, we feel abundantly compensated for the toil and inconvenience to which absence from our editorial duties invariably subject us. Of the meetings of the first week, our co-editor, Delany, has already informed you.[31] They were such as would have cheered the hearts of freedom's friends, and chilled the blood of tyrants to have witnessed. They were large, generous, enthusiastic and unanimous. There was never so general an interest excited among the colored people of that city before. The whole population seemed moved by a general impulse from Lombard street to West Philadelphia, and from thence to the Northern Liberties, the cause of freedom rolled, sweeping all before it. For much of the interest excited, the cause is largely indebted to the well-directed efforts of Charles Leonx Remond. He had, in company with Dr. Bias, George W. Goines, Rev. Messrs. Galbreath, and Catto, and other devoted friends of freedom, kept up a constant fire upon the pro-slavery churches and ministry of Philadelphia. When nearly exhausted, the appearance of M. R. Delany refreshed and invigorated them for a renewal of the contest, and they were in full blast when we arrived. Many of the colored churches have been closed against the discussion. Little Wesley, presided over by Rev. Mr. Catto, was for a time almost the only house where the cause of the slave could be freely pleaded. Brick Wesley, a large and commodious building, presided over by Rev. Mr. Galbreath, came open; next Shiloh Baptist Church, presided over by Rev. S. Serrington, threw open its doors; and last, though not least, the Union and Zoar Churches, in the Northern Liberties, were opened to the causes next. The churches most hostile to the Anti-Slavery movement, and bitterly opposed to opening their doors, are Stephen Gloucester's, St. Thomas's, and Large Bethel. These three men are close against discussion, and for various reasons. The first of this pro-slavery trio is presided over by one of the vilest traitors to his race that ever lived. When the mob spirit raged in Philadelphia in 1842, and the persons and property of colored citizens had been attacked, some killed, and much property destroyed, this miserable traitor came out in a card in the Philadelphia Ledger, and attempted to propitiate the pro-slavery demon, by declaring that *his church had never been opened for Anti-Slavery meetings*, thus, dastard-like, making a merit of his meanness, and claiming protection from the oppressor because he had basely turned his back upon the oppressed. He is the same Gloucester who was the pet of the misnamed Free Church of Scotland, which sent a deputation to this country four years ago to solicit donations for the purpose of building Free Churches, and paying Free Church ministers in Scotland, which deputation went into the slave States, saw the slaves in their horrible condition, divested of all rights, herded with the beast of the field, bound with chains, maimed with irons, scarred by the lash, locked up in midnight ignorance, denied the opportunity of learning to read the name and will of God; and with this giant crime before them, they fellowshipped the slaveholder, called him Dear Christian brother, solicited and obtained his blood-stained gold, saying nothing of his crimes, or whispering a word of sympathy with the perished slaves. They left our shores, placed their stolen treasures in the sustention fund, and when rebuked for it by Henry C. Wright, George Thompson, Wm. Lloyd Garrison, and ourselves, they immediately pressed the Bible into the service of slavery, and in defense of their conduct, to their communion and fellowship the guilty wretch who perpetuates the fiendish outrage! We know that colored Episcopalians, as well as white ones, excuse themselves for not opening their churches to Anti-slavery meetings, on the ground that those churches are dedicated to the worship of God, and that it would therefore be using the house of God improperly, misappropriating it, to throw it open for such purposes. We are willing to give this doctrine all the weight it deserves. It may be conscientiously believed, and so far deserves some respect. But the fact that such a superstitious doctrine is held by any colored man in this country, shows the necessity for a more radical reform than we have hitherto attempted. The Jewish religion sanctified times and places, and set them apart for certain forms and ceremonies. Christ found them all in existence, and left them destroyed after him. He placed mercy above sacrifice, man above the Sabbath, and worship above time or place. We claim to be complete in him. Regarding the old law as a school-master, we approach the true Prophet, whom we are to hear in all things. Now, what does Christ say on the subject of worship? "But the hour cometh, and now is when the true worshippers shall worship the Father in spirit and in truth; for the Father seeketh such to worship him. God is a spirit, and they that worship him, must worship him in spirit and in truth." The idea of temple worship here is clearly disclaimed. To build a house of God, and regard it as being too holy in which to plead the cause of injured man, is like "tithing mint, annise and cummin, and omitting the weightier matters of the law." It is to make clean the outside of the cups and the platter, whilst disregarding the uncleanness within.—It is not holiness of timber, but holiness of heart, that God enjoins. It is not churches of bricks and mortar, of wood and paint, of brass and iron. The house which God requires is a spiritual one. "Ye also, as lively stones, are built up a *spiritual house*—a holy priesthood to offer up spiritual sacrifices unto God, by Jesus Christ." Now, the notion—for such we must call it—of regarding houses with peculiar reverence and thinking that the Almighty regards them with any special favor, is diametrically opposed to the very genius of Christianity, and has no sanction in the New Testament Scriptures. Houses are for men; they need them—God does not;—He fills immensity of space with his presence, and may well ask, "Where is the house ye build unto me?" We need houses—meeting houses if you please; but we need for man—for his improvement, elevation, and freedom; and any worship which does not contemplate this, in the most enlarged and comprehensive sense, is blind, superstitious, and Anti-Christian. Yet we are bound to say that this worship is almost the only visible worship that the world presents. Our worship abounds with honor for God, and contempt for man. Away with all such worship, the sooner the world is rid of it, the better.—It is perfectly unmeaning, and may be performed by the bad as well as the good—slaveholders, slavetraders, thieves and liars, may engage in it with all the outward solemnity of saints, and it leaves them as wicked as ever, as much devoted to their sins as ever. To worship God, is to worship goodness, to be wholly devoted to good, to imitate Christ, who went about doing good, to love and adore God for his goodness, and to strive to be like God in doing good, is the true worship. Let us ask our friends of St. Thomas's Church, Philadelphia, if they think slavery contrary to goodness and if so, how they can close their doors against those who are laboring to remove it. They will answer us that they have a *canon* against allowing any person who has not been ordained occupying their church. Here again they exalt the form, regardless of the power of godliness. The devil, in holy orders would be received, while Christ, unordained, would be rejected. Such a religion will do very well by the oppressors, but is by no means suited to the oppressed. We call upon William Douglass, the minister of that church, to break his chains and those of his church, and be no longer hampered and enslaved by those powers of darkness. He has the head, and we believe the heart, (had he but the independence to break his fetters,) to make himself very useful to his race in their times of need.

The next church which remained closed to the hour of our leaving was large Bethel.—We have several times pleaded the cause of the slave within her walls, and why she is closed at this time is a mystery. We were informed that the minister and people were willing to have the house opened, but that the trustees were divided, and that the church was in great difficulty about matters of their own concern. This, however is no excuse for them. At the very mention of the bondman's name, and the slightest chance of striking a blow for the overthrow of oppression, they ought to have forgotten minor differences and rallied as one man to the rescue. But such was far from being the case. They saw the people, eager to hear the truth, blocking up the street in front of Little Wesley, unable to gain admission within its narrow walls and ourselves begging the use of their house, and they closed it against us. We say to these churches, one and all, You are standing in your own light—you are playing into the hands of your enemies and sealing your own degradation.

We have given the foregoing notice of the churches named, with no desire to reflect unjustly upon the Anti-Slavery members of them, of whom, we are glad to say, there are many; but to record instructive facts, to which our children and coming generations may turn and ascertain some of the difficulties with which those who labored for their rights and liberties had to grapple, even among our own brethren. It will be a painful and deeply mortifying fact for those who come after us, to look back upon that, in the year one thousand eight hundred and forty-eight, when the whole world seemed moved on the question of human rights, and our own land was agitated by movements designed to promote our happiness as a people, the very churches and ministers of our own complexion, and suffering many of the hardships and grievances sought to be removed, stood side by side with the oppressors, and instead of aiding the cause of their own redemption, opposed the efforts to gain it with all the means in their power. We call upon those churches to throw open their doors to the discussion of slavery and the means necessary to our improvement and elevation. This they must do, or be execrated by coming generations, as the worst enemies of their own variety of the human family. It is plain that whatever improvement has taken place in our condition during the last fifteen years, has been chiefly the result of the Anti-Slavery sentiments, given to the public by abolitionists. Now to shut the doors of the churches against those emancipating truths and sentiments, is thus far to shut the public ear and darken the public heart on the subject. It is to do our best to silence free discussion, to smoother freedom of speech and to allow all things to remain as they are. We have no hesitancy in saying that if those colored churches which shut their doors against the cause of the slave had the power they would shut every church in the land against the discussion of slavery; they would silence every lecturer, and banish every press favorable to the discussion of human rights. They would play the tyrant as readily and as bitterly as do our white oppressors. We leave these churches to their intelligent members, whom we are sure will give them no peace while they remain in their present slaveholding position.

We now turn to the signs of encouragement and cheer which greeted us among the colored people of Philadelphia; and not the least among these was the interest taken in the cause by some of the most influential ladies in that city. At the first meeting which we attended, a desire was expressed that some ladies volunteer to obtain subscribers to the *North Star*, and in a very few moments we had nearly a dozen ladies volunteering to do their best in this department. Among these, we may mention the names of Mrs. James Foster, Mrs. Bias, Mrs. Joseph Cassey, Mrs. Stephen Smith, Miss Bustell, and some young ladies who might shrink from having their names made thus public. To these ladies we are indebted for a considerable accession to our subscription list, for which they have our sincere thanks. If these lend their aid, we defy opposition. Mainly through the help of these ladies, a society, called the Philadelphia North Star Association, intended especially to aid the *North Star*, and to promote the circulation of truth by assisting Anti-Slavery agents, was formed and put in operation. From the formation of this society, we anticipate much good to our cause, through the country at large.—Another encouraging fact is, that a Convention was held during three days in Brick Wesley, crowded to overflowing with a deeply interested audience, before whom the subject of our duties to the slave and ourselves was thoroughly canvassed. The Convention was mainly addressed by Dr. Bias, Mivlin Gibbs, Robert Purvis,[32] of Byberry, Charles Lenox Remond, Henry Highland Garnet,[33] Stephen Smith, George Goines, William Whipper,[34] Rev. Mr. Galbrath, Rev. Mr. Catto, and many others, who displayed a zeal and devotion to the cause, not less worthy than those whose names we have just mentioned. The Convention was such as was never held in that city before, and long will it be remembered as the commencement of better days in that place. It was a free Convention—as free to our foes as to our friends and there were not wanting men to oppose us. Some of them had evidently learned their lesson well. It sounded rather strange, however, to have colored men preferring the old man-dog charge of *Infidelity, Anti-Slavery, Anti-Church, Anti-Ministry*, &c., against the abolitionists.—These stale charges, caught from the lips of their evangelical oppressors were blown into our ears by a Mr. Wears and Bowers with all the enthusiasm of newly discovered truth. Poor fellows, they were merely echoing the stale slang of slaveholders, put forth to prolong their infernal reign over their heart-broken bondmen. They little know that it is the religion of our enslavers which must be repudiated before the colored men can be free. In accepting the white man's Christianity for our souls, we accept his chains for our limbs.—We spurn both. Our God is opposed to slavery; the slaveholder's God sanctions slavery. Our church is opposed to slavery; the white man's church is in favor of slavery.—Our Christ loves the slave; the white man's Christ has no sympathy with the slave, but is on the side of the oppressor. We must repudiate the one, and cling to the other.

Among the number of our white friends who aided us in the objects of the Convention—we gratefully name Lucretia Mott,[35] and Hannah Moore, two of the purest and best benefactors of our people in that city. It was gratifying to see the respect and deference paid to the words of truth and wisdom which fell from the lips of those noble women.—Long may they live to soothe the sorrows of the poor—enlighten the minds of the uninformed—and to bless the plundered slave.—With one hundred such abolitionists as these, Philadelphia would soon be redeemed, prejudice against color would soon be unknown, and the colored man's rights would be fully respected in the city. We have given this somewhat lengthy, though very imperfect letter respecting our visit to Philadelphia—because we attach great importance to that point as a place, which more than almost any other in our land, holds the destiny of our people.—The colored population there is large—numbering from twenty-five to thirty thousand souls—and these are variously conditioned.—Among them we are proud to say, there are many who are well informed—many who take a warm and intelligent interest in the subject of our elevation from degradation to respectability. Some of these are not only educated, but persons of wealth and standing in the community, commanding the respect of all who know them. Candor, however, compels us to confess, that this description of persons forms a minority of the people of that city. Unfortunately for us, as with all oppressed people—oppression not only begets a character in the oppressor favorable to the continuance of his oppression, but also begets a corresponding character in his victim. There are a large portion of our people in that city, whose conduct is greatly to the prejudice of our cause, as it puts arguments into the mouths of our oppressors, and gives to them at least the shadow of a reason for keeping us just where we are. To arouse this class of persons to a sense of their manhood, to insert into their minds higher ideas of truth and duty—to awaken them to their social degradation, and to inspire them with higher aims than those which have hitherto distinguished them is a work of great practical importance. Their numerical greatness, and geographical proximity to slavery, gives them a mighty lever of influence on this question. Make the colored people in Philadelphia what they ought to be, and there is no power in the land which can long oppress and degrade us.—F. D.

*The North Star*, October 13, 1848

# PROPERTY IN SOIL AND PROPERTY IN MAN

Northampton, Nov. 18, 1848

Since leaving Rochester on the 27th of October, I have spoken once in Springfield, once in Lynn, three times in New Bedford, once in Abington, once in Plymouth, and attended the Annual Meeting of the Rhode Island Anti-Slavery Society. . . .

On Thursday evening last I attended the meeting of the Rhode Island State Anti-Slavery Society. . . . On this evening there were no resolutions before the meeting, and everyone spoke just what he was disposed to speak. The first speaker who came upon the stand was Mr. Inglis, I believe, the editor of Young America.[36] I should be glad to give his remarks in full, and reply to them at length, did time and space permit; but in the circumstances can only glance at the subject. He commenced by stating his high regard for the slave, and his deep interest in the Anti-Slavery movement; but strangely enough went on in an effort to show that wages slavery is as bad as chattel slavery, and that if the slaves were emancipated , they would soon be as badly off as the paupers of Ireland. He recommended an enlargement of our objects as a means of bringing into our ranks the white working people, and stated as a reason why they did not care anything about the Anti-Slavery movement, that they saw the abolitionists taking an interest in the cause of the black, while they neglected and opposed the white laborer. These and many other views of the same stamp, were put forth by the speaker. It was difficult to think the speaker honest, yet he seemed to be perfectly so. He appeared to be full of his cause, and to give it his best energies. So far so good. There was, however, one great falsehood running through the whole speech, which even the dullest could not fail to perceive.

The attempts to place holding property in the soil—on the same footing as holding property in man, was most lame and impotent—and the wonder is, that anyone, could listen with patience to such arrant nonsense. That land monopoly is a great evil there is no question—but to speak of it in the same age with chattel slavery, is to lose sight of all the mortal distinctions most obvious to common sense. I would be ashamed to argue with a person such a question—but that I believe there are some good men who honestly believe it. To own the soil is no harm in itself. It was given to man. It is right that he should own it. It is his duty to possess it—and to possess it in that way in which its energies and properties can be made the most useful to the human family—now and always. There is therefore no wrong in the fact of holding property in the soil itself. And the question raised must therefore relate to the mode of holding and the amount held—and not to the act of holding. The question them, as to the manner, and the amount, with respect to these various opinions may be honestly entertained. What manner of holding property in the soil is the best, which best secures the happiness of the whole human family? The Land Reformers, have one view—but other men have views directly opposite—and as honestly entertained. It is not therefore for either to denounce the other

as criminals. The question is one of expediency—about which it is easy
to err. Not so with slavery. It is to sin against self-evident truth to
enslave a fellow man. . . .

Yours for Righteous Freedom,

Frederick Douglass

*The North Star*, November 24, 1848


# AWAY WITH WAR!


Did you ever think of the evils of War? Did you ever realize that it
was one of the greatest curses of mankind? Did you ever see that the
practice of war filled the world with Blood, with Slavery, with Barbarism and every species of Misery; Yet this is the case; and, reader, are
you not a military man, or guilty in some way of promoting War? If
so, complain not of want, suffering, ignorance, or degradation. Oppressed Laboring man or Factory girl, don't murmur at your hard lot; if
your politics, religion or social influence upholds war, the reproach
falls upon your own head. You foolishly empty your own pockets and
cause your own sufferings. Benevolent man, Philanthropist—do you
favor armies, navies, and military governments? Wonder not, then at
the depravity of man and the slow progress of truth and righteousness.
Your self-contradiction and inconsistency in sustaining the custom of
war, swells the current of wickedness more than your good efforts can
that of righteousness.

*What has War done?*–Evil, evil! It has done nothing but evil! It
has destroyed human life, property, virtue and happiness. Nothing else
has it aimed to do. Drunkenness, profanity and licentiousness have
been its legitimate products. Widows, orphans, paupers, beggars it
has multiplied. Dr. Dick estimates that *fourteen thousand millions* of
human beings have been slaughtered by war—inhabitants enough to
people 18 worlds like the Earth! Think of this. What greater curse
could wickedness invent? Plague, Pestilence and Famine have followed
in its track; but these of themselves have not begun to equal war in
their number of victims. Had Hyenas, Tigers, Panthers and Serpents
been the world's only inhabitants, they would not have equaled Man in
the destruction of life. What a field of human bones! What a sea of
human blood!

*What has War cost?*—The mere money cost of war has been enough to pauperize the world. According to reliable estimate the present unpaid War Debt of Europe and the United States, incurred within the last 160 years, is about *Seven Thousand Million Dollars!* The annual interest of this debt, including the expenses of the Army and Navy, is nearly *Four Hundred Million Dollars,* The specie circulation of the world does not equal this amount, and, according to Humboldt,[37] the mines of South America and Mexico have not yielded this sum since the discovery of the New World by Columbus! 50 per cent of the annual expenditures of European governments goes for military purposes. No wonder the people are crushed beneath such a load, on top of the expenses of royalty, nobility and aristocracy. No wonder the people are taxed for all they eat, drink and wear, for sunshine, air and water— taxed for being born, taxed for breathing, taxed for dying.

In the United States, the Executive, Legislative and Judicial departments of government are not poorly paid at all. But for every 21 cents they receive $1 is paid for purposes of war. 80 per cent, of the government expenses are for war! Within the borders of Massachusetts scarcely a cent has been expended for schools, colleges and charitable asylums where dollars have been lavished upon war-ships, the Navy-Yard and the Arsenal. In addition to all this, the annual cost, in time and money of training the militia of the United States is calculated to be *Fifty Million Dollars.* Why should not there be poverty and hard times in this country?                                      —F.D.

*The North Star,* December 22, 1848

# PHILADELPHIA

Our Anti-Slavery friends and coadjutors in Philadelphia seem to have had an excellent protracted meeting during the holding of their annual Bazaar in aid of the cause. From the proceedings, as published in the last number of the *Pennsylvania Freeman,* we learn that an earnest debate took place with respect to the Free Soil party, in which Lucretia Mott, H.C. Wright, C.C. Burleigh, Charles I. Remond, Robert Purvis, Mary Grew, E.M. Davis, and Dr. Bias participated. In this discussion, friend Remond defined his present position, both with respect to the Free Soil party and his old anti-slavery friends, as follows. What does it mean?

"C.L. Remond thought there was danger of our exacting more than men can perform. We cannot expect the people to abolish the government, however we may theorize about it.

"I know of no man who thoroughly carries out the simplest anti-slavery principles, much less the most radical. We are told that the Free Soil party carries a lie on its face. It is doing anti-slavery work; and if it does not profess to arm to abolish slavery, I had rather see a party which performs without profession, than one which professes without performing. The colored people lack confidence in the anti-slavery society, because they see so much more profession than practice. If the Free Soil party will give them their rights, they will not ask under what name it is done. I have never voted but twice, and once was for the Free Soil State ticket at the last election, in Massachusetts.

"My confidence in the system of the no-voters is lessening; and I bid God-speed to any party which will abolish slavery. If it cannot be done in H.C. Wright's way, then let it be done in Martin Van Buren's way. I am out of patience with theories which we can never carry into practice, and welcome *any* means that will abolish slavery."

Remond was replied to by several speakers, and among others, that excellent woman and devoted abolitionist, Mary Grew. We scarce need say that we think her views of the relations of the colored people to the anti-slavery cause the correct one. Her reply is as follows:

"Mary Grew said that many of the colored people do sympathize and co-operate with the Anti-Slavery Society, and so far as they do not, it is for the same reasons that white men do not—because they love their ease, their sect, or their money, better than the cause of the slave."

The debate was continued by Dr. Bias.—His remarks are not reported, but he was understood to insinuate that the abolitionists, with all their professions, were not so superior to the rest of the community in their treatment of the people of color as might be imagined.

The Doctor was replied to by Robert Purvis, who "Thought the accusation and insinuations made aginst the abolitionists for their course toward the people of color were neither just nor kind, however they might be intended. The abolitionists had been the fast friends of the colored people from the beginning. In our darkest hour of trial, when hunted by the mob, and forsaken by the civil authorities, and through all our persecutions, we have ever found them true to us. Men who have risked reputation, property, and life even, in our cause, have given too good proof of friendship for insinuations or unsustained charges to disprove it. Such accusations should not be made without proofs."

We shall deeply regret to see the day when the oppressed shall become the accusers of the abolitionists. With all the imperfections of the latter, and they are many, we are under God, indebted to them for all the improvements which have thus far taken place in our condition as a people. This murmuring against the abolitionists, is like the murmurings of the Israelites against Moses. Brethren, cease your assaults upon the abolitionists, and turn your arms against your foes.                                                    F.D.

*The North Star,* January 5, 1849


## OUR FEMALE CORRESPONDENT

We may have sinned somewhat in admitting the letter of "Irwin" into the columns of the *North Star.* It is a tart, sharp letter, and written with some ability, though it lacks all appreciation of Reforms, or the means of accomplishing them, and want of charity for the foibles of those engaged in them. Her attention has been attracted by the cry of Reform! Reform! and startled by the cry, she exclaims, Where? what? as though the cry were altogether new, and the need of it a mystery! Like Rip Van Winkle, she has just come out of an age of sleep, just from "the fair and sunny South,"[38] and is utterly amazed to see the state of things around her. This is all very natural, and we are disposed to make every allowance for our astonished correspondent, and proceed at once to remove some causes of her astonishment. She has lived in a dark though sunny region, where meeting-houses are thought more sacred than men—where men are sold to build churches, and women sold to furnish what she is accustomed to regard as the house of God—where revivals of religion and revivals of the slave-trade go hand in hand—where worship is performed by menstealers, and ministers traffic in human flesh, and where to oppose slavery as a great sin, is, in the popular estimation, to fight against the purposes of a merciful God.

It is therefore not strange that our correspondent feels amazed when she finds herself among a people who believe slavery to be from the infernal, and not the celestial regions. She is shocked at the terms "infernal" and "hellish," and thinks that the use of them in the house of God is desecration; and yet we suppose that these words would not be offensive to her, if they dropped from the lips of a minister, or were read from the Bible in the pulpit. They are strong words, we confess; but their propriety or impropriety depends wholly upon the application made of them. If they are applied to good and holy things, the person so using them deserves to be shunned as a foul-mouthed person. But if the things or persons to whom those epithets are applied be really devilish, manifesting a wicked and malignant spirit, it may be perfectly proper thus to characterize them, and to do so anywhere on earth; for there is no place where the command to be holy is more binding than another. To think otherwise, is to think that right and wrong, virtue and vice, depend upon time and place, and denies the everywhere present God.

The unwillingness of our correspondent to have the Church rebuked, is a true index of the state of her mind upon the whole subject of reform. She would have the church rebuked, but it must be by men who love God; but it so turns out, that the persons who in her judgment are fit, are the very persons who utterly refuse to have anything to do with the discharge of that duty, and leave it for what she terms sinners.

We are glad that Irwin has spoken, and hope her attention may dwell longer upon this subject. A further investigation may lead her to see as we do. The persons upon whose course she has commented are abundantly able to take care of themselves; and we leave it to them to say how far she has misrepresented their conduct. —F. D.

*The North Star*, February 2, 1849

# NATIONAL REFORMER

It is with unaffected regret that we announce the discontinuance of the *National Reformer*, published in this city. It has ceased for the want of support, a sad commentary upon the amount of interest felt in the great cause to which it was mainly and ably devoted. The *National Reformer* was a Land Reform paper; but unlike "Young America" and the "Land-Mark," it never sought to promote its great purpose by decrying other reforms and reformers. It was the poor man's friend, and every man's friend. We differed with it on some points, but agreed with it in many others; and whether agreeing or disagreeing, we cherish for its conductors the highest respect. It is to be hoped that Rochester will not be long without such a paper as the *National Reformer*. —F. D.

*The North Star*, March 16, 1849

# SPEECHES AT GREAT ANTI-COLONIZATION MASS MEETING OF THE COLORED CITIZENS OF THE CITY OF NEW YORK, APRIL 23, 1849[39]

Mr. Frederick Douglass:

Mr. Chairman, there is no end to the devices of our enemies. The failure of one only makes room for another. One is scarcely defeated when another is invented. When driven from one point, they plant themselves at another. They are as prolific of schemes as Egypt was of frogs. In these circumstances we ought to be always on the lookout— armed at all points, and ready to march in any direction, and to meet the enemy whether in this or any other country.

Of all the assaults which we have experienced during the last twenty years, none have been more subtle and plausible than those emanating from the American Colonization Society.

Under the garb of philanthropy and religion its efforts to degrade us have been as various as they have been grievous. Of the history of that Society you have already been well informed, and with its origin you are equally familiar. It is, as you are aware, the joint product of slaveholders of the South and Negro-haters of the North, and fitly bears the image of both parents. Embodying all the malignity of the slaveholder, and all the Negro-hating spirit of the Northerner, it is our ever vigilant and bitter adversary. It has often changed its position, and assumed by turns all the colors of the rainbow, but has never changed its essential character. It is now, as it ever has been, a most deceitful and cunning scheme against the peace and freedom of the colored people of the land.

Sir, we are here to expose and denounce this Janus-faced enemy. And I am glad to bear a humble share in this work. The special duty of this meeting has already been well and honourably discharged, and I for one have no fear of the result. Our humble words on the strong wings of the winds will be speedily wafted to the shores of England. They will strengthen the hands of our faithful and able representative there, and defeat the schemes of our subtle foe, What I have to say must be only by way of amplification.

Is it not strange, sir, that a system which has been condemned by the noble Wilberforce, exposed by the good and great Clarkson, and shattered by the thunder-bolts of O'Connell[40]—whose honored graves are yet scarcely green with the verdure of two summers—should so soon make its appearance on the shores of old England? The audacity of this Society is only equalled by its malignity. Scourged and driven from the shores of England by Wilberforce, Clarkson and O'Connell, it seems to have waited impatiently for their removal to the land of spirits, to return again to its work of meanness and deception. As usual, it has gone abroad with a smile on its cheek, and a lie in its mouth. In the semblance of angel, and the reality of a demon professing sympathy for the colored people of America—it labors to drive us from our home and country.

Sir, it does not seek to do this by open and fair means. If such were true, we should have less fault to find. It does not propose to compel us to leave this country by force and arms, but seeks to bring about a state of things unfavorable to our remaining in this country. It does not tell us to go—*but tells us we had better go*—that we can never enjoy equal rights or peace in this country—that we are a doomed people, and that no efforts can save us while we remain here; and sometimes goes so far as to intimate that if we do not go now, the time is not far distant when we may be compelled to go.

Such, sir, are the sentiments of that Society; and it is these discouraging, insulting and menacing sentiments which have strengthened prejudice, and supported Slavery in this country. But for the efforts of this Society, I believe there would, long before this, have been a united and determined effort on the part of the whole North against Slavery. It has kept alive this prejudice. The agents, and presses, and reports of that Society carefully kept out of sight all the evidence of our improvement and only represented us as degraded, ignorant and besotted.

Mr. Chairman, the fundamental, and—as Daniel Webster would say—the everlasting objection to Colonization is this; that it assumes that the colored people, while they remain in this country, can never stand on an equal footing with the white population of the United States. This objection, I say, is a fundamental one; it lies at the very basis of this enterprise, and, as such, I am opposed to it, have ever been opposed to it, and shall, I presume, ever continue to oppose it. It takes the ground that the colored people of this country can never be free, can never improve here; and it is spreading throughout the country this hope-destroying, this misanthropic doctrine, chilling the aspirations of the colored people themselves, and leading them to feel that they cannot, indeed, ever be free in this land. In this respect the influence of the Colonization scheme has been most disastrous to us. It has advocated the most stringent persecution in some instances towards colored men. But let me, sir, read a resolution:

Resolved, That if it be left optional with a slave to go to Africa or not, we advise him not to go, but rather to remain here and add to the number of those who may yet imitate the example of our fathers of '76.

I do not mean to say here my friends, that this result is a desirable one—the result to which I look—but I look to it as an inevitable one, if the nation shall persevere in the enslavement of the colored people. I have not the slightest doubt but that at this moment, in the Southern States, there are skillfully-contrived and deeply-laid schemes in the minds at least of the leading thinkers there, for the accomplishment of this very result. The slaveholders are sleeping on slumbering volcanoes, if they did but know it; and I want every colored man in the South to remain there and cry in the ears of the oppressors, "Liberty for all or chains for all." I want them to stay there with the understanding that the day may come—I do not say it *will* come, I do not say that I would hasten it, I do not say that I would advocate the result or aim to accomplish or bring it about,—but I say it *may* come; and in so saying, I only base myself upon the doctrine of the Scriptures, and upon human nature, and speaking out through all history. "Those that lead into captivity shall go into captivity." "Those that take the sword shall perish by the sword." Those who have trampled upon us for the last two hundred years, who have used their utmost endeavors to crush every noble sentiment in our bosom, and destroy our manly aspirations; those who have given us blood to drink for wages, may expect that their turn will come one day. It was in view of this fact that Thomas Jefferson, looking down through the vista of the future, exclaimed: "I tremble for my country when I reflect that God is just, and that his justice cannot sleep forever." He saw even through the distance of time through which he looked, down beyond the present to a future period, when the spirit of liberty and manhood would lead the slave to bare his bosom and struggle in his claims for Freedom, as was illustrated by the fathers of '76; and seeing this he said "I tremble for my country."

The Colonization scheme aims, they say, to prevent or avert this disastrous consequence. Sir, such an effort is unscriptural, it is unchristian. There is no other way whereby men can escape the penalty of their crimes but by repentance. But instead of preaching the repentance to slaveholders, these Colonizationists are proposing to remove away from them the object of their hatred without dislocating the hatred itself. I say then, that it is unchristian and unscriptural. Those slaveholders must take the consequence of their crime. Man loves liberty and will ever try to regain it.

> "O, tell me not that I am blest,
> Nor bid me glory in my lot—
> That plebeian freemen are opprest
> With wants and woes that you are not.
> Out of such kindness, I would be
> The wreck of fortune to be free.
> Go, let a cage with grates of gold,
> And pearly roof, the eagle hold;
> Let dainty viands be his fare,
> And give the Captive tenderest care;
> But say, in luxury's limits pent,
> Find you the king of birds *content?*
> No, oft he'll sound the startling shriek.
> And dash the grates with angry beak.

Precarious freedom's far more dear,
Than all the prison's pamp'ring cheer!
He longs to see his Eyrie's seat,
Some cliff on ocean's lonely shore,
Whose old bare tops the tempests beat
And round whose base the billows roar,
When tossed by gales they yawn like graves, —
He longs for joys to skim those waves;
Or rise through tempest-shrouded air,
All thick and dark with wild winds swelling,
To brave the lightning's lurid glare,
And talk with thunders in their dwelling."

The cry of the slave goes up to heaven, to God, and unless the American people shall break every yoke, and let the oppressed go free, that spirit in man which abhors chains, and will not be restrained by them, will lead those sable arms that have long been engaged in cultivating, beautifying and adorning the South, to spread death and devastation there.[41] Some men go for the abolition of Slavery by peaceable means. So do I; I am a peace man; but I recognize in the Southern States at this moment, as has been remarked here, a *state of war*. Sir, I know that I am speaking now, not to this audience alone, for I see reporters here, and I learn that what is spoken here is to be published, and will be read by Colonizationists and perhaps by slaveholders. I want them to know that at least one colored man in the Union, peace man though he is, would greet with joy the glad news should it come here to-morrow, that an insurrection had broken out in the Southern States. I want them to know that a *black man* cherishes that sentiment—that one of the fugitive slaves holds it, and that it is not impossible that some other black men may have occasion at some time or other, to put this theory into practice. Sir, I want to alarm the slaveholders, and not to alarm them by mere declamation or by mere bold assertions, but to show them that there is really danger in persisting in the crime of continuing Slavery in this land. I want them to know that there are some Madison Washingtons in this country.[42] The Colonization Society has told them that we are inferior beings, and that in consequence of our calm and tame submission to the yoke which they have imposed upon us; to their chains, fetters, gags, lashes, whipping-posts, dungeons and bloodhounds, we must be regarded as inferior—that there is not fight in us—and that is evidence enough to prove that God intended us to retain the position which we now occupy. I want to prevent them from laying this flattering unction to their souls. There are colored persons who hold other views, who entertain other feelings, with respect to this matter.

As an illustration of the spirit that is in the black man, let me refer to the story of Madison Washington. The treatment of that man by this Government was such as to disgrace it in the eyes of the civilized world. He escaped some years ago from Virginia, and succeeded in reaching Canada, where, nestled in the mane of the British Lion, the American Eagle might scream in vain above him, for from his bloody beak and talons he was free. There he could repose in quiet and peace. But he remembered that he had left in bondage a wife, and in the true spirit of a noble minded and noble hearted man, he said: while my wife is a slave I cannot be free. I will leave the shores of Canada, and God being my helper, I will go to Virginia, and snatch my wife from the bloody hands of the oppressor. He went to Virginia, against the entreaties of friends, against the advice of my friend Gurney, whom to name here ought to secure a round of applause. He went, contrary to the advice of another—I was going to say, a nobler hero, but I can scarcely recognize a nobler one than Gurney: Robert Purvis was the man: he advised him not to go, and for a time he was inclined to listen to his counsel. He told him it would be of no use for him to go, for that as sure as he went he would only be himself enslaved, and could of course do nothing towards freeing his wife. Under the influence of his counsel he consented not to go; but when he left the house of Purvis, the thoughts of his wife in Slavery came back to his mind to trouble his peace and disturb his slumbers. So he resolved again to take no counsel either on the one hand or the other, but to go back to Virginia and rescue his wife if possible. That was a noble resolve and the result was still more noble. On reaching there he was unfortunately arrested and thrown into prison and put under heavy irons. At the appointed time he was brought manacled upon the auctioneer's block, and sold to a New Orleans trader. We see nothing more of Madison Washington, until we see him at the head of a gang of one hundred slaves destined for the Southern market. He, together with the rest of the gang, were driven on board the brig *Creole*, at Richmond, and placed beneath the hatchway, in irons; the slave-dealer—I sometimes think I see him—walking the deck of that ship freighted with human misery, quietly smoking his segar, calmly and coolly calculating the value of human flesh beneath the hatchway. The first day passed away—the second, third, fourth, fifth, sixth and seventh passed, and there was nothing on board to disturb the repose of this iron-hearted monster. He was quietly hoping for a pleasant breeze to waft him to the New Orleans market before it should be glutted with human flesh. On the 8th day it seems that Madison Washington succeeded in getting off one of his irons, for he had been at work all the while. The same day he succeeded in getting the irons off the hands of some seventeen or eighteen others. When the slaveholders came down below they found their human chattels apparently all with their irons on, but they were broken. About twilight on the ninth day, Madison, it seems, reached his head above the hatchway, looked out on the swelling billows of the Atlantic, and feeling the breeze that coursed over its surface, was inspired with the spirit of freedom. He leapt from beneath the hatchway, gave a cry like an eagle to his comrades beneath, saying, *we must go through.* Suiting the action to the word, in an instant his guilty master was prostrate on the deck, and in a very few minutes Madison Washington, a black man, with woolly head, high cheek bones, protruding lip, distended nostril, and retreating forehead, had the mastery of that ship, and under his direction, that brig was brought safely into the port of Nassau, New Providence.

There are more Madison Washingtons in the South, and the time may not be distant when the whole South will present again a scene something similar to the deck of the *Creole.*

But what was the result. The moment they found themselves in the waters of England, under British rule, the slave-sellers went to the American consul for the purpose of obtaining assistance to keep the slaves on board. But they had applied to the wrong source—they were in the wrong pew. The Government sent them assistance, but in that most questionable shape that they knew not whether their intents were charitable or wicked. The assistance came in the shape of a platoon of black soldiers. Down they came, and it seems that they came not so much after all to protect the passengers, (for it was supposed that they could protect themselves) as to protect the vessel. And they speedily communicated the idea that these colored passengers were at liberty to go where they pleased. They had reached the British soil, of which Curran has so eloquently spoken, and which I will here repeat.

"I speak in the spirit of British law, which makes liberty commensurate with, and inseparable from British soil; [43] which proclaims liberty even to the stranger and sojourner. The moment he sets his foot on British earth, the ground on which he treads is holy. No matter in what language his doom may have been pronounced; no matter in what disastrous battle his liberty may have been cloven down; no matter what obligation incompatible with freedom may have borne upon him; no matter with what solemnity he has been devoted on the altar of Slavery; the moment he stands on British earth the altar and the god tumble to the dust; his spirit walks forth in its majesty, his body swells beyond the measure of his chains that burst from round him, and he stands redeemed, regenerated, disenthralled by the irresistible genius of universal emancipation."

That eloquent outburst of Curran was perfectly true as applied to the case of these slaves. They went ashore and walked about their business. Of course the transaction created some sensation in this *free, democratic* republic. The news came across the Atlantic with electrical effect, and fell into the midst of our Congress like a bombshell. The greatest amount of consternation and alarm abounded there. Henry Clay rose in his place with tears in his eyes, and said it was time that the American people in all sections of the country should lay aside all sectional difficulties, and present an unbroken front to the English. Mr. Calhoun said that American ships were American territories: they constituted a part of the national domain, and that wherever the American star spangled banner waved, of course the right of slaveholders to hold their property was to be sacredly guarded. England had violated her treaties and stipulations. England had violated the comity of nations. Mr. Rives thought that this event presented a crisis in the history of our diplomacy with England. Mr. Preston thought that immediate energetic measures should be adopted for the reclamation of these slaves to bring them back to the United States. Daniel Webster, the God-like, the man of "October Sun" memory, was then Secretary of State, under the long nose of—I had almost forgotten the name—John Tyler; or rather Captain Tyler, that's the name. And what did Webster do? Why the first thing he did was to write a letter to Edward Everett, [44] who was then our Minister at the Court of St. James, directing him at once to commence negotiations for the return of these men who had gained their freedom; at any rate for the return of Madison Washington and the brave eighteen who had so nobly achieved their freedom on the deck of the *Creole*, and demanding payment for the remainder. It resulted just as you might have expected. The British Government treated it with the utmost deference—for they are a very deferential people. They talked about honorable and right honorable, lords, dukes, and going through all their Parliamentary titles, and sent Lord Ashburton over to this country to tell us of course, that that very deferential people could not send back the "n-----s." So Uncle Sam could not get them and he has not got them yet.

Sir, I thank God that there is some part of his footstool upon which the blood statutes of Slavery cannot be written. They cannot be written on the proud, towering billows of the Atlantic. The restless waves will not permit those bloody statutes to be recorded there; those foaming billows forbid it; old ocean gnawing with its hungry surges upon our rockbound coast preaches a lesson to American soil: "You may bind chains upon the limbs of your people if you will; you may place the yoke upon them if you will; you may brand them with irons; you may write out your statutes and preserve them in the archives of your nation if you will; but the moment they mount the surface of our unsteady waves, those statutes are obliterated, and the slave stands redemmed, disenthralled." This part of God's domain then is free, and I hope that ere long our own soil will also be free.

Mr. Frederick Douglass then proceeded to address the meeting on the subject of the resolution, as follows:

Mr. Chairman, ladies and gentlemen: The resolution which I have been called upon to second[45] is an appeal to the people of Great Britain from us, not to unite with our enemies against us, but to set their faces against our enemies and thereby help us. I shall return to this resolution after I shall have said a few things in favor of Colonization and against ourselves.

I think sir, to begin with, that we shall be regarded as a very unthankful people—a very unthankful people indeed; strangers to the sentiment of virtue and gratitude. Why here is a society which springs up in our midst, organized and aided by some of the greatest men in church and state—a society which raises vast sums of money, going not only to and fro in our own land but braving the dangers and perils of the deep, crossing the Atlantic ocean to gather money for the purpose of sending us to the land where we are confidently assured that if we shall go, we shall become Presidents, Vice Presidents, Secretaries, Treasurers; where we shall become grave Senators, Representatives, diplomatic agents, Ministers Plenopotentiary, judges of the Supreme Court; and yet we are so ungrateful, so unthankful that we meet here to denounce this very class of men who are going to shower upon us those offices of honor and profit! Now are we not an ungrateful class of people?—that after all the trouble that our friends have been to bring us from Africa and then to get up a scheme to send us back again, having done it Caudle-like, for our own good and never consulting their own, that we should be so ungrateful as to meet here for the purpose of denouncing that movement! Well we are unthankful—ain't we?

But Mr. Chairman, to the resolution—This meeting is held more with a view to affect this question in England than in our own land. The fact is renegade colored men, who will consent to make themselves the tools of this Colonization Society in this matter, are easily disposed of; but there is a skillful, an adroit, a subtile son of a Dr. of Divinity now perambulating England and portions of Ireland and Scotland, representing to the British public the desireableness of this emigration scheme, and soliciting funds from the humane and benevolent of that land to enable this Colonization Society to transport us from this land of our birth to Liberia, or to some part of Africa. It is with this agent that we have to deal. But I have no fears for the result of our dealing. The statistics adduced by our eloquent friend Mr. Reason, the arguments produced from other sources and the extracts from the report of the American Colonization Society, together with the various speeches that have been made here during these two evenings past, will be gathered up with the resolutions under consideration and sent to England. I have no doubt then I say as to the effect which they will produce upon the public mind of that country.

Sir, it is not the first time that our enemies have sent to England men for the purpose of degrading us. I recollect that about two years ago there were some seventy ministers sent from the United States to attend the Evangelical Alliance at London, and that one of the main purposes of that body of evangelical divines from this land, was to misrepresent and slander the colored people of this country, and their friends. And I remember well the generous and unsophisticated manner in which the British people were disposed to listen to arguments pro and con, both from these ministers themselves and from the humble individual now addressing you. I remember that their adroit and cunning statements produced upon the public mind of England quite a sensation—quite an impression in favor of their views with respect to us, and but for the presence in the midst of them of one of this despised race and one of the "fanatical Abolitionists" to expose their doings the probability is that the churches of England would have been linked to the churches of America, and would have thrown round the guilty slaveholder, who gains his fortune by the blood of souls, all the sanction of the religion of England; that effort failed. This best effort of the Colonization Society will fail likewise; and it will fail by the same means. I was glad at that time to be present in that country when these divines were slandering colored people in this country. I am equally thankful that one Alexander Crummell, whom you all know, is on the ground at this moment doing battle against the equally subtile foe in the person of the son of this Dr. of Divinity. I say I have no fear of the result of this meeting uopn the English people. They are naturally jealous and they ought to be jealous of propositions coming from the white people of this country, affecting the character or condition of the colored people. John Bull is honest, strictly honest, in comparison with other nations, especially with our own Democratic Republic, and would be liable to be led astray, but that he is jealous with respect to propositions coming from white people in this country affecting the condition or character of the colored people. He has seen the efforts made on the part of this country to degrade us. They have seen the various subterfuges and refuges of lies to which they have resorted to sustain their system of Slavery and to keep up the abominable prejudice and proscription that prevails against us. Therefore the people of England are more ready to listen to what comes from us than to what comes from them.

I do think the Colonization Society is one of the most impudent Societies in the world. I never saw its equal. Once upon a time the immortal Shakespeare said that a thing would die when its brains were out. But it is not so with this Colonization Society. It seems to have nine or ten lives . Why, sir, it was exposed and rebuked by the noble Clarkson. It was denounced by the benevolent and eloquent Wilberforce. It was thundered at by the eloquent O'Connell, and two or three years ago it was attacked by the ever-to-be-remembered George Thompson. Scarcely have the graves of the philanthropic Wilberforce and the illustrious O'Connell become green, ere this same saucy, impudent Colonization Society appears again on the shores of old England to deceive the public and mislead them. It seems to have been sitting cat-like on the borders of the Atlantic, watching to see this noble man expire, and as soon as the breath is out of his body, this same insidious deceiver, "full of deceivableness and unrighteousness," walks abroad again on its mission of Negro-hatred. But it will not succeed; it cannot succeed. Crummell is there. The spirit that warmed the bosom of Clarkson and Wilberforce and O'Connell is there. Thompson and Sturge are there. They will meet this man, disrobe him of his mask, and send him home to be cheered and pampered by his brother Colonizationists, while he shall quiver under the detestation of the colored people of the United States.

I want to say a word about John Bull. I have a peculiar affection for Englishmen, and a respect for the English character. They were among the first to do us injury and the first to try to right that injury. I respect them—for I forgive them for what they did in days of yore. I respect them for what they have already done, and what they are still doing in our behalf. Englishmen hate American Slavery; they hate American prejudice, and from my experience among them, I can safely say that they do not appreciate the spirit in this Colonization movement originates. They do not understand what the Americans call prejudice. I have travelled England, Ireland, Scotland, and Wales for nearly a year; and during my sojourn in that land, riding on railways, stage-coaches, omnibuses, steamboats, and putting up at hotels, I have yet to see the first look or the first act, or to hear the first word from any Englishman indicating a dislike to me on account of my complexion. I have had illustration also of the generosity of Englishmen, and of their freedom from all this matter of prejudice in this country. I had occasion, a few days since, to enter one of the hotels of this city for the purpose of seeing one of the chief waiters. I had not been in the hotel two minutes, before a couple of English gentlemen, sitting at the dining-table, and hearing my name mentioned, called for me immediately to come into the dining-room and unite with them around the festive board—to sit down to the table with them and *take a glass of wine* which I respectfully declined. They assured me that they felt a deep interest in this matter of Anti-Slavery, and that the people of England were, to a man, Anti-Slavery at heart. I mention this fact to show you that intelligent and respectable English gentlemen when they come to this country, if they have only been here but a few days are entirely unsophisticated—are such strangers to American taste and *democratic* aristocracy that they can welcome not only myself, but other colored gentlemen at the dining-table with themselves. Of course, my friends, I did not look upon it as any distinguished honor, to sit at the table with white men; why, bless my soul! I have often been too near the tables where white men are, (great laughter), and I have not the slightest aspiration that way. I only mention the fact to illustrate the character of the English people generally. How different is the case with our American gentlemen. They, so far from being willing to sit at the table with the colored man, will scarcely allow a colored man to sit in the same pew with them in church. And they would feel themselves degraded to walk through the streets of New York in company with a colored gentleman, though he were far superior to themselves—a Webster in intellect or a Wesley in piety.

There is one class, however, of transatlantic men who come to this country, to which I wish to call special attention. It is the Irish. Now I am far from finding fault with the Irish for coming to this country, for they have a right to come here or go anywhere else they please; but I met with an Irishman a few weeks ago in the town of Bath in the State of New York. He conversed with me on the subject of Slavery. He had scarcely shed the first feathers of "ould Ireland," and had the brogue still on his lip. And that man, newly imported to this country, gravely told me that it was his deliberate opinion that the colored people in this country could never rise here, and ought to go to Africa. What I have to say to Ireland is,—send no more such children here. We do not want any such specimens among us. I told the gentleman that I hoped I should give him no offense, but that I was an American-born citizen, and hoped he would not take any pride in what I was about to tell him, which was, that I intended to stay in this country.

Sir, these foreigners who come to this country, (I use the term foreigner not invidiously) ought to know that the black people of this country are in fact the rightful owners of the soil of this country—at least in one half the States of the Union. Why the theory of property in the soil runs thus:—that man has a right to as much soil as is necessary for his existence; and when a human being has incorporated a portion of his own strength and that which belongs to his personality into that soil he therefore has a right to that soil against the universe. What is the fact with regard to us? In the language of James Forten[46]—whose name I never mention but my heart swells within me—"We have watered the soil of America with our tears, we have enriched it with our blood, we have tilled it with our hard hands; we only ask to be treated as well as you treat ordinary paupers. We are American born citizens; we only ask to be treated as well as you treat your aliens. We have fought for this country; we only ask to be treated and respected as well as you respect those who have fought against it. We are the lovers of our country; we only ask to be treated and respected as you treat and respect those who are haters of it." These sentiments are attributed to the venerated and departed James Forten, a colored man, who, I believe, stood side by side with American freemen and who bared his bosom in defense of this country.

And in this connection I wish to refer to others who fought in defense of our country. We are credibly informed that among the first blood spilt on Bunker's mound was that which spurted from the bosom of a black man. We have it also on the page of history that those who stood foremost, who fought bravest, who presented most undoubted valor on the banks of the Mobile were the black men of Louisiana and Alabama. General Jackson, stern and iron-hearted as he was, stained with crime of Slavery, was compelled to confess that, to black men he was as much indebted as to any other class for his cotton bale victory.[47] Why, sir, these foreigners, some of them from Ireland and some of them from elsewhere, come here after we have fought and bled for our country and gravely propose our removal from this to our *native* land, Africa.

Let me inform my audience and the good people abroad what sort of missionaries are yearly sent off to Liberia. I am a Baltimorean, and that is the very hotbed of Colonization.[48] I have been on the wharf to hear those men who go about the South for the purpose of teaching and evangelizing the colored people. I hope it will not be deemed profane in me to give you a specimen of the class of preachers that are found there. You know that we are not as a people very distinguished for the elegance of our use of the Queen's English. I mean, we are not very distinguished among our white friends for elegance of language or theological knowledge. Now these colonizationists fail to get the right sort of men to go to Liberia, even if evangelization was their object. I will tell you what kind they take. They take those old exhorters from among the licensed preachers on the Southern stations who have got their freedom in order to be there. And what is the amount of their preaching? Why, I heard one of them one day exhorting thus: "I take my text from de Rebelations ob Saint John. John you know was cast away on de island of Patmos." Well he went on in this style until he worked himself up into a paroxysm, and there was no telling head, front, side, end, or beginning of his sermon. *He* was one of those evangelists to Africa. Now I think the Colonization Society had much better keep such specimens here until they can be instructed and improved before they are sent to Africa.

Friends, in conclusion, I wish to say that I shall return to Rochester, with my hands strengthened and energies increased by the intercourse I have had with free hearts and free spirits in this city. I want to feel that this is no effervescent thing—that the feeling got up against Colonization, and in behalf of freedom is not to disappear and die out the next week, but that the fire kindled here is to continue to burn until slave prejudice, and last, though not least, Colonization, with all its deceptive acts, shall be utterly consumed. Friends, let us unite in a league against the oppressor; all those who are in favor of doing so, say aye!

[The audience responded in a most decisive manner. The resolution was then unanimously adopted.]

*National Anti-Slavery Standard,* May 3, 1849

# NEW YORK COLORED SCHOOL, No. 2.

While here, I have done myself the pleasure of visiting this somewhat noted school. It is under the superintendence of Mr. Charles L. Reason, one of the most accomplished and gentlemanly teachers in this country, of any color. He has recently been called to a Professorship, in the new Free College, now in progress in Central New York;[49] and will doubtless do honor to himself and the colored people of this country generally, by his services in that capacity. The school now under consideration, is the largest, I believe in this city. The female department is under the care of Mrs. Jane Forten, a lady of large attainments and I should think well qualified for her station. The children were neat in their attire, and orderly in their conduct. Mr. Reason carried them through a few exercises in Geography, Astronomy, Grammar, and Arithmetic. The questions were put in a familiar way, without any routine formality, and were answered in a manner that led me to believe that they were not only taught to remember the thoughts of others, but to think for themselves. The examination was deeply gratifying to me, although I found boys of twelve, answering correctly questions in geography, astronomy, arithmetic and grammar, which I could not answer. I am not the less proud and joyful on this account. I rejoice that such colored lads are on their road to manhood. They will grow up, I trust, and occupy a higher position, than that to which the present uneducated fugitive has yet attained.

While looking out upon this multitude of sable, yet bright faces, I felt a deep wish that J. C. Calhoun and all his guilty companions on the crime of man-stealing and libelling my humble race, could share with me the soul-cheering scene. A better or more impressive condemnation of slavery; or a more forcible and conclusive refutation of the miserable calumnies against the colored people cannot be found, than is presented in this school. I am glad Mr. Reason is called to the honorable station of Professor—but sorry that New York City is about to lose the benefit of such a gentleman and scholar.—F. D.

*The North Star*, May 11, 1849

# SPEECHES DELIVERED AT THE FIFTEENTH ANNUAL MEETING OF THE AMERICAN ANTI-SLAVERY SOCIETY, MAY, 1849

Mr. Chairman: I think, we, as Abolitionists, are apt to overrate the intelligence of our audience with respect to their knowledge of Slavery, and also with respect to their knowledge of the guilt of the churches. I think there are few people out of the ranks of the Abolitionists, who really know anything of the real position of the American Church in regard to Slavery. We meet in this city from year to year and denounce the pro-slavery position of the American Church and Clergy, but we seldom have time to lay before our meetings any facts connected with the proceedings of the Church in regard to Slavery. I propose in the few remarks that I shall make this evening to say a word with respect to this sort of evidence, and to give a few facts which are familiar enough to the Abolitionist, but which are quite unknown, I have reason to believe, even to the very church members themselves. The ministers know what action they have taken on the subject of Slavery, but the people know very little about it.

Take for instance, the Methodist Episcopal Church.—That Church probably wields an influence second to no other in the land. In the year 1836, when the question of Slavery was rocking the country from center to circumference, and when the lives of Abolitionists were scarcely safe at times from the fury of mobs, that were howling around their persons and their houses, this subject came up before the General Conference of the Methodist Episcopal Church. It seems that two ministers of that denomination ventured to lecture upon, and in favor of emancipation in the city of Cincinnati. The very next day after these lectures were given, the Rev. Stephen G. Roszell, a distinguished minister in that Church, brought forward two or three distinct resolutions setting forth the views of the General Conference with respect to Slavery. What were these views? They declared in their first resolution, in Annual Conference assembled, "that they were wholly opposed to modern Abolitionism, and, that they wholly disapproved of the conduct of the two ministers who were reported to have lectured upon and in favor of this agitated topic." They went further, and in another resolution declared, "that they were not only opposed to modern Abolitionists, but they had no right, no wish, no intention to interfere with the relations existing between masters and slaves in the Southern States of our Union." These resolutions were adopted by that large conference, with only eleven voting against them. An overwhelming concourse of divines professing to be called of God to preach the Gospel, to deliverance to the captive and the opening of the prison doors to those that were bound, declared before the world that they had "no right, no wish, no intention to interfere with the relations of masters and slaves." The slaveholders rejoiced in that action. They could smoke their pipes in comfort when they got a knowledge of the proceedings of that body of divines.—They could hear of revivals of religion going on in the Church with the utmost complacency. They felt in no wise alarmed, but rather strenghtened by the members, added to that Church, which, so far from being an abolition Church, had "no right, no wish, no intention to interfere with the relation of master and slave." That is the religion for me, says the slaveholder. There sat the bondman before the body of Methodist divines in his chains, calling upon them in the name of God and humanity to give him his freedom and deliver him from his bonds. Deliver me from my chains! was the cry that came up from the lips of three millions of bondmen, and yet these Methodist clergymen responded, "we have no right, no wish, no intention to give you freedom."

How is it with the Presbyterian Christian? You know that a few years ago, through the agency of the Abolitionists in New England, a large number of petitions and memorials were sent to the general Assembly of the Presbyterian Church, calling upon that body to pass resolutions declaring Slavery to be a moral evil. They stated that body had already denounced dancing, declaring it to be incompatible with church membership to move the feet at the sound of music, and they believed their consciences were now becoming alive to the sin of dancing. They were encouraged therefore to send petitions asking these divines merely to consider Slavery to be a moral evil. So the General Assembly passed this resolution in answer to their memorials.

"Resolved, That it is inexpedient and not for the edification of the Church, to pass any judgement in respect to Slavery."

It is the boast of the Protestant Episcopal Church of this country that it never has anything to do with such sins as Slavery. It is their boast that their Church has not been distracted or disturbed by this agitating topic.—To be sure it has had some other topics that have agitated the public mind to some extent, which I need not mention here. If I were in a Moral Reform meeting, I might speak of them. But as to the question of American Slavery, it is their boast that they are not disturbed by it. The groans of heart-broken millions come up on every breeze, but they do not hear them, they are indifferent about them, "we are worshipping the Lord," say they, "we are engaged in giving honor to God; that is our business."

Now I have taken these three Christian Churches, and they are samples of the rest. The Baptists are no better than the Methodists and Presbyterians, and the Episcopalians are as bad as either. They are all as pro-slavery as can be. It is because these churches have passed resolutions favoring Slavery, and have in other cases resolved to have nothing to do with the matter, that we are compelled to attack them if we would be faithful to [Anti-] Slavery. And if there is one thing that leads me to identify myself with the American Anti-Slavery Society it is their Anti-Slavery test of all institutions. I have been into various Anti-Slavery meetings since I came to this city, and I have heard speeches of various branches of the Anti-Slavery topic; but the most earnest, the most sincere, the most radical tone in sentiment from any quarter has been from the platform of the old fashioned Garrisonian Abolitionists. I mention this for the benefit of some I see before me who attend these other meetings, and who think that because everything went on orderly at them, it indicates great progress.

Why the other day I went into the meeting of the American and Foreign Anti-Slavery Society, and after a long abstract of the report was read and my soul was fired up with the expectation of hearing Slavery denounced and its supporters held up to the detestation of all those who loved the slave, while I was waiting to get my spiritual strength renewed, a grave gentleman arose and said "the next thing in order will be music." Now Anti-Slavery meetings, according to my notion, should not be very orderly. I like the wild disorder of our free-discussion meetings. I like to hear the earnest voice of Anti-Slavery, so far forgetting the character of its speech, and the manner of its delivery, that almost any person may be able to take exception to the remark made. I always feel glad when I have a thousand explanations to make after I go away from Anti-Slavery meetings. When I have spoken in such a way as to make people think that I am a despiser of religion, or that I hate the very name of a clergyman, or that I am myself an infidel, then I feel that I have done something towards leading the people to think of their responsibility in regard to Slavery.

I believe the grand reason why we have Slavery in this land at the present moment is that we are too religious as a nation, in other words, that we have substituted religion for humanity—we have substituted a form of Godliness, an outside show for the real thing itself. We have houses built for the worship of God, which are regarded as too sacred to plead the cause of the down-trodden millions in them. They will tell you in these churches that they are willing to receive you to talk to them about the sins of the Scribes and Pharisees, or on the subject of heathenism of the South Sea Islands, or on any of the subjects connected with missions, the Tract Society, the Bible Society, and other Societies connected with the Church, but the very moment you ask them to open their mouths for the liberation of the Southern slaves, they will tell you, that it is a subject with which they have nothing to do, and which they do not wish to have introduced into their Church;

it is foreign to the object for which churches in this country were formed, and houses built.

The American and Foreign Anti-Slavery Society seems to have fallen into the error of supposing that the distribution of the Bible among the slaves will be the means of their ultimate liberation.[50] I should not wonder, if the slaves could be allowed to make known to that Society its view of their efforts to give them liberty, if they should, say "First give us ourselves, and then we will get Bibles." What the slave begs for is his freedom and the American and Foreign Anti-Slavery Society comes forward and says "Here is a Bible." To be sure, they say they would be glad to have the slave free, but I ask any of you who were present in their meeting yesterday and heard the speech made by Mr. Henry Bibb[51] if the chief design of that Society did not seem to be, to give the slave the Bible, which, when it is given him he cannot read. For my part I am not for giving the slave the Bible or anything else this side of his freedom. Give him that first and then you need not give him anything else. He can then get what he needs. I know that the inference was left in the minds of some who attended that meeting that the Old Organization were not in favor of giving the Bible to the slaves, for the Society arrogated to itself a great amount of piety in that it was said by their speaker, I believe, that if the old Abolitionists had gone to work and and tried to distribute the Bible among the slaves, ere this, Slavery would have been abolished. Now what we want is first to give the slave himself. It is but another attempt to mend old garments with new cloth—to put new wine into old bottles, to think of giving the slave the Bible without first giving him himself. God did not say to Moses "Tell my people to serve me that they may go free," but "Go and tell Pharoah to let my people go that they may serve me." The first thing is freedom. It is the all important thing. There can be no virtue without freedom—there can be no obedience to the Bible without freedom. When the slave is free he can own a Bible; but suppose we carry it to him now, what is the law of slavery? It is that the slave shall be taken, deemed, reputed and judged in law to be property to all intents and purposes whatsoever. Now how can property own property—how can property own the Bible? It takes persons to own property, but the personality of the slave is annihilated. He is not looked or treated in any way as a person except when he is to be punished.

I throw out these remarks because I think there is danger of confounding our Anti-Slavery duties with what are not our Anti-Slavery duties. There is an attempt on the part of some professedly Anti-Slavery advocates, to make themselves out as religious advocates of Anti-Slavery and all others as irreligious advocates of the cause.

## MR. FOSTER:

Now to test the honor and integrity of those men, I will state here publicly, and any gentleman present may carry the intelligence to the leaders of that party, that to save them the trouble of raising funds, I will furnish them with *one thousand Bibles*, if Mr. Bibb or any other prominent man among them will go, openly and in person, and carry them to the slaves. I will have nothing to do with any underhand movement to steal Bibles in the South. Thieving is bad enough when connected with getting property, but when connected with the glory of God it is utterly detestable, I will have nothing to do with it. And I can do more; I think I can pledge that individual one thousand more after he has distributed the first thousand; but I will keep within my means. Let them spare themselves the trouble to go through this city to collect funds for that purpose, for I am ready to fulfill my pledge.

## MR. DOUGLASS:

I wish to make a single remark further about giving the Bible to the slaves. Here are three or four facts connected with the matter which makes the thing impossible. In the first place the slaveholder's consent must be obtained before any Bibles can be given to the slaves, and the slaveholder will never give his consent to let the slave have anything which may open his mind to the wrong of holding him as his property. If his consent is had at all, it is purchased at the expense of the silence of the person giving the Bible to his slave, as to its being presented for the purpose of opening his mind to the sin of Slavery.

In the next place, if the Bible is given to the slave he cannot read it. So it is absolutely not given at all; for you might as well give him a block with no letters upon it as the Bible with letters in it; because he cannot read it. Now if this Society would only ask for money to educate the slaves whether the masters would or not, and some good volunteer like my friend in the distance, should go there professing that his object is to educate the slave whether with or without the consent of the slaveholders, I should think the movement however impracticable, was in the hands of honest and sincere men at any rate. The fact is they cannot give the Bible to the Slave. It is idle to make the Bible and Slavery go hand in hand; they are at war with each other, and the slaveholder knows this as well as any man. The moment they begin to read, that moment they begin to be restless in their chains. There are only three or four passages of Scripture that the slaveholder wants them to read, and these can be read to them. They are the passages which relate to servants being obedient &c., which they torture to a sort of sanction of Slavery. These they like to have the slaves know, but as to knowing about the Golden Rule, "All things whatsoever ye would that others should do unto you do ye also to them," or anything of the doctrines of love to man, they do not want them to know anything about it. The more ignorant he is, the better slave he makes, and hence the most stringent laws are enacted throughout the South to prevent the slaves from learning to read.

Now I suppose that those who hiss think that I have stated what is not true, but what is the act! There is Zachary Taylor in the Presidential Chair. You knew nothing about Taylor, until you heard of his blowing out the brains of the Mexicans.[53] No minister of the Gospel ever came out and endorsed the Christian character of General Taylor before he succeeded in taking Monterey. No minister of the Gospel ever made him a member of the Home Missionary Society until he heard that he had fought his battles in Mexico. No one thought of saying aught in favor of that man for the Presidency until the Christianity of this country learned that he had favored the importation of bloodhounds from Cuba to hunt down the Florida Indians.

I mentioned yesterday in another place, that the great men of the nation might always be taken as fair examples of the moral sentiment of the people. I have taken Zachary Taylor who I believe is just as good as those who voted for him; I do not think he is in any degree worse at heart than those who had no objections to him as their candidate on moral grounds. I am not at all lowering him that you need come to his defense. In him I see yourselves reflected who have no moral objections to Slavery. You only need a geographical change. You need only to be transported from New York to New Orleans to become as much a slaveholder as General Taylor at Baton Rouge. Sir, if the American pulpit had been what it ought to have been, and what I trust it will yet be, no party in this country could have been found base enough to have brought forward the name of such a candidate for the suffrages of the American people. NO! had the American pulpit uttered its voice in righteous denunciation against Slavery and War and kindred crimes, we should never have heard of such a being as a legalized cut-throat presiding over the destinies of this nation.

But I will touch no longer your idol, friends. I will leave him and pass to another who is perhaps less an idol now, because he has no office to give to those who may be disposed to hiss in his favor. I allude to Henry Clay. I never was more forcibly struck with the truth of Garrison's remark, that he never looked upon the slave but as upon a member of his own family, than when I heard the various eulogies showered down upon this man by the North on account of his letter on Emancipation, or rather Expatriation. You are aware of the character of that letter. It sets out with a sort of argument against Slavery, declares that the arguments that are put forth by Calhoun and that class of politicians at the South in favor of eternising Slavery are erroneous, and he goes on to say, granting that the whites are superior to the blacks, that it is the duty of the whites to instruct, improve, and enlighten the blacks. For so much I thank him but take this out and the remainder is full of all manner of sin and injustice. With the exception of these few sentiments, it is one of the most skillfully-contrived schemes for oppressing the slave and perpetuating Slavery that I ever read. Mr. Clay, after having laid down his platform of principles, that the slaves should be enlightened and instructed by the superior classes, goes on to fix a day when the slaves should be emancipated, and that day is set in this wise: All children born of slave parents after the year 1860, shall be free at 25. And how free? Free to stay where they are, and work for a living? No. Free to be expelled, free to be driven away from Kentucky and transported to Africa, on the ground that is their native land. But they are not free even then for he has another proviso, and it is this; That after having arrived at the age of 25, they shall be hired out under an officer of the State for three years, in order to raise $150 to pay for their own exportation from their homes and their families. Yet the people read this letter and say, O how just, how merciful, how humane, how philanthropic is Henry Clay.

There is another point about this letter to which I object strongly; it is this: You are aware that at the age of 28 almost all the slaves have families. Mr. Clay proposed that the slaves having families and children of 3, 4 and 5 years of age, shall be snatched from those children and hurried off to Africa, leaving those children parentless, guardianless, with no one to care for them. Those children are to live 25 years longer in Slavery, and then to be hired out until they are 28 years of age, and afterward to be hurried out of the country. And yet young men and women, old men and old women, mothers, sisters, and daughters read the cold-blooded proposition from which, if it were to be applied to white persons, they would shrink in horror, and they say how good, how kind, how philanthropic is Mr. Clay! Such is the man in whose pathway they will strew flowers when he comes to the North—a man who boldly proposes to sunder parents from their children, and compel them to leave the country on pain of being again reduced to Slavery.

In another part of that letter he says that the trifling loss that would result from Emancipation may be prevented by leaving the rights of the owners undisturbed during the next 25 years. What is the meaning of this? It is just this: That Henry Clay would leave the slaveholder after the year 1860 until the year 1885, in full possession of the right to sell slaves from Kentucky into Louisiana, or any of the more Southern States. The proposition is not, after all, that they shall emancipate their slaves at the end of 25 years, but it allows them 25 years in which to watch the New Orleans and Mobile markets, and if they do not see fit to sell them during the course of 10, 15 or 20 years, just in the last of the 25 years, when the slave is about to grasp hold of Freedom, their masters can put them upon the block and sell them to the highest bidder; thus Kentucky will only be getting rid of Slavery to send their slaves to clank their chains on Southern plantations.

Oh, the blinded moral sense of the American people! how lost to all principle! how lost to all sense of justice! We can eulogize the man who with iron heart would revive the horrors of the Slave trade, under the delusive idea of advancing the cause of Freedom.

Friends, I have not used the name of General Taylor or Henry Clay because I have any personal pique towards them, or any difference of political opinion with them, or political ends to serve. You have denied me the right of citizenship, you have trampled on my rights as a man. I have no voice in your politics, I only speak as one of the three millions of slaves in your land. I speak as one of the injured party. I speak in the name of four sisters and one brother who now live, if indeed they live at all, under the burning sun and the biting lash of the slave-driver. I speak in behalf of those whom I have left behind me. How would you speak if you yourselves had relatives and friends in the condition of Slavery? Would you speak soft words of the Church and clergy who

could live indifferent to the condition of your sisters and brothers?
Think not because I am black that I love not my kindred and friends.

> "Fleecy locks and black complexion
> Do not alter nature's claims,
> Skins may differ, but affection
> Dwells in white and black the same."

My sisters are as dear to me as yours can be to you. My brother lies
as near my heart as your brother can lie to yours. My mother, my
family, my friends are all as dear to me as yours can possibly be to you.
O! if you could put yourselves in the place of the slave, the question
would be carried; there would be no differences at all; you would feel
that we were your brothers and sisters and Slavery would soon be at an
end.

*The North Star*, June 1, 1849


# THE MEETING AT ZION CHURCH

FROM the *Impartial Citizen*[54]

"But the most extraordinary meeting of the series I attended, was
that at Zion Church, on Thursday evening the 10th. That meeting was
called and the house obtained, by and for Mr. Garnet and myself, in
connection with Mr. Bibb. By our arrangements, Mr. B. was first to
speak, and Garnet and I to follow. Bibb having heard his remarks,
position and motives attacked on Tuesday evening, felt himself called
upon to defend himself against Mr. Douglass' opposition and imputations. Immediately upon Mr. B's taking his seat, Douglass arose,
claimed the floor, and seemed determined to speak, irrespective of the
rights and wishes of the callers and holders of the meeting. After
declaring any public and open resistance to Mr. Douglass' claims, in
the matter, and after speaking out my own views, by courtesy Mr.
Douglass was permitted to speak, and in his speech he opposed again
the giving of the Bible to the enslaved. Mr. Garnet rose to speak
afterwards, and upon asking Mr. Douglass a question, though not

yielding the floor, Mr. Douglass, after answering the question, insisted upon having the floor, for an extended reply. Mr. Garnet did not give up the floor, knowing that all law of Parlimentary usage, and gentlemanly intercourse, entitled him to the undisturbed use of the floor, and though Mr. Douglass, who had boasted that he was no obscure man, in the anti-slavery cause, being well known in this country, and in England must have known what Mr. Garnet's rights were, he persisted in claiming the floor until midnight, when the meeting broke up in confusion."

The meeting of which the above purports to be a description, has not been before referred to by me in the columns of *The North Star*. A feeling of delicacy prevented my taking advantage of my position as Editor to vindicate my course at a public meeting, where I had an opportunity to do so on the spot; and I should not now refer to the matter but for the uncandid and one-sided statement made by Mr. [Samuel Ringgold] Ward in the foregoing article.

I can scarcely conceive how an honest man, witnessing the facts as they there transpired, could open such an article as the one in question. It is a misrepresentation from beginning to end; and duty to myself, not less than to the cause, demands at my hands a correct statement of the whole affair.

I attended the meeting on Thursday evening, the tenth of May, just as I would attend any other anti-slavery meeting; and, although Mr. Garnet, Mr. Bibb and Mr. Ward, had been advertised to speak, I did not suppose that the act of such an advertisement necessarily excluded all others from participating in the deliberations of the meeting. Had I supposed so I would as readily have been found in a Whig caucus as in such a meeting—having long since resolved to countenance no meeting of a pretended anti-slavery character where the right of speech is denied to the humblest advocate of the slave. Mr. Ward represents me as having at a previous meeting attacked the motives of Mr. Bibb. I deny it, and so I declared at the very meeting Mr. Ward had undertaken to describe. Had he desired to represent me as I represented myself no man could have done it better; but having a cause to serve, he conveniently forgets my statement, and puts words in mouth, as men will often do "when the wish is father to the thought." Mr. Ward declares that I rose to speak "irrespective of the rights and wishes of the callers and holders of the meeting." This statement is totally incorrect. So far from rising in opposition to their wishes, I briefly requested the privilege to be heard and waited patiently on my legs, for several minutes; and did not attempt to speak until informed by the Chairman that to proceed with my remarks would be in order. This, Mr. Ward knows very well. According to Mr. Ward's statement, the reader would imagine that I was treated in the most courteous manner by himself and Mr. Garnet I confess I never was treated more rudely. The moment I arose to reply to the mis-statements and insinuations thrown out by Mr. Bibb, impeaching my religious character, misrepresenting my religious faith, making me out an enemy to the Bible, and giving that as a reason for my opposition to the impracticable scheme of sending Bibles to the slave, Mr. Garnet rose and proposed to take up a collection for defraying the expense of the meeting—remaining on his feet the while, giving the audience to understand that they were now to witness an engagement, and that it was dangerous to defer the collection until the skirmish was over. At the close of the collection I again rose to speak, whereupon I was screamed down by Mr. Garnet, who proposed to sing a *favorite song,* of which he is the author. After singing about twelve verses, I again rose to speak, at the call of the meeting; but was again silenced by the superior vocal powers of Mr. Ward, who insisted that I had no right to speak in that meeting, and went on with a long speech, presenting the claims of "the Impartial Citizen" to the support of the colored people. After which, he, and a number of others waited on the congregation, with "slips" of paper and pencils in hand, to record their names and to receive their cash. This continued until nearly half past ten o'clock, and before which time I had done nothing more than to ask the small privilege of speaking. Having secured their collection, *sung Mr. Garnet's song,* obtained all the subscribers that they could hope to do, and completed their speeches—the audience appearing tired out and desirous to depart— the Chairman very graciously informed me that I now would be allowed to speak. Availing myself of this opportunity, I rose, and occupied the attention of the audience for about thirty minutes— concluding my remarks by submitting the question as to the correctness of my views which resulted in a general response on their part of "Right—right—right." I then sat down, when Mr. Bibb commenced a reply; but, from some cause or other, the audience appeared unwilling to *hear him;*—whereupon Mr. Garnet again took the floor—the fourth time during the evening. At this point I was about leaving the house, (it being near 11 o'clock); but, while in the act of doing so, Mr. Garnet requested me to answer a question, to which I responded. When in the middle of the sentence he insisted that I had said enough, and shouted, with the wildest apparent excitement, "I have the floor—I have the floor—I have the floor." Perceiving that Mr. Garnet had resolved to misrepresent me, and, by garbling my sentence make me say the very opposite of what I intended to be understood, I insisted that, inasmuch as I had been called by name to answer the question, and that as the Chairman had allowed me thus to be called, my right to answer on parliamentary (as well as moral) grounds, was indisputable.

I, therefore held my right to the floor; but repeatedly declared not only my willingness, but my happiness, to yield it at any moment after I should be allowed to answer the question proposed. This was refused me; and I was compelled whether to pursue the course I did, or to allow the audience to be grossly deceived as to what I really did say. In face of these facts Mr. Ward declared that I insisted "on having the floor for an extended reply." The only answer I make to this is—the statement is wholly destitute of truth, as I never desired anything more than to finish the sentence, in the midst of which Mr. Garnet broke in upon me.

I shall only refer to one other point—the unkind and untruthful statement of Mr. Ward. He affirms that I opposed the giving of the Bible to the enslaved. This assertion is false. *I never have been guilty—I never expect to be guilty of opposing the giving of Bibles to any portion of the human family;* and this I affirmed in the presence of Mr. Ward. What I opposed (whether erroneously or otherwise is not material) is the impracticable and delusive scheme, advocated by Messrs. Bibb, Ward, and Garnet. Upon this issue I am prepared to meet any or all of these gentlemen in the columns of the *North Star,* or in their own papers. I am heartily ashamed, that such men should find no better employment than that of imputing to me deeds which I never performed; words which I never said; opinions which I never held; and then display their skill in attacking such deeds words and opinions.

In searching for a motive for such singular conduct, I am unable to find any better one than a contemptible desire to build up their own fame by meanly traducing and defaming others.—F.D.

*The North Star,* June 15, 1849

# FREDERICK DOUGLASS vs. HENRY BIBB

A copy of the *True Wesleyan* has been handed to us, containing an article with the above caption, animadverting upon the remarks in reference to the speech of Mr. Bibb, made at the anniversary of the American and Foreign Anti-Slavery Society. The remarks upon him were as follows:

"Mr. Bibb took the platform to second a resolution proposing to give Bibles to the slave, and made a long speech in favor of this most absurd and extraordinary proposition. The speech was as absurd as the proposition it was intended to support. When he confines himself to a narrative of his own sufferings, and those of his wife, who is yet in slavery, Mr. Bibb is always interesting, touching, and powerful. Beyond that he is weak, insipid and powerless.

"His address on the present occasion was made up of a most illogical display of cant phrases about the Bible, its power to abolish slavery if given to the slave, etc. It was a poor thing, which would do very well for that namby-pamby class of persons in our country who care a great deal about the souls of men, but care nothing for their bodies."

The *True Wesleyan* terms this "an uncalled for and low attack on Mr. Bibb;" and its Editor says he was "present, and listened to the speech with great pleasure, and regarded his speech as an able argument—logical, impressive and animated." Many men have many minds. We will give a few specimens from the speech of Mr. Bibb, in order to show upon what grounds we pronounced the speech "weak, insipid, and powerless." The aim of the speech was in the language of the resolution, "a recommendation to all the friends of the anti-slavery cause to aid the American Missionary Association to distribute the Bible among the slaves." The speech, in order to have been to the purpose, should have demonstrated not merely the right of the slave to the Bible, or his destitution of it, but the practicability of the meas-ure; for about the first there is no question and words upon it are mis-spent—unless it can be shown that the scheme proposed will accomplish the end aimed at. The latter not being shown, the speech was *inconclusive, weak and illogical.*

It seems to us that no scheme of giving Bibles to the slave, can succeed without the cooperation of the slave holders themselves; and this cooperation, Mr. Bibb, in the speech in question virtually told the audience could never be obtained—thus involving himself in a contradiction. He said, on that occasion—"As well might they expect the fox to guard the geese or the wolf to protect the lamb, as to think the slaveholders would circulate the Word of God among their slaves." On this assertion, though it is diametrically opposed to Mr. Bibb's scheme we most fully unite and conclude from it, that the first thing to be done, is to break the power of the slaveholder, as the first means of giving the Bible to the slave. Mr. Bibb, contrary to our experience, and the experience of many others whom we have consulted, said, "there was no plantation on which was a considerable number of slaves where one or more could not be found able to read," and he added— "there are many slaves at the South who could read the Bible if they had *the chance.*" What "the chance" required is, or how to give the slave that "chance," is a part of the story Mr. Bibb left untold, though this is the only thing material. It is quite easy to speculate upon the inhabitants of the moon—to draw beautiful pictures of the happiness to be enjoyed there—and even to propose a journey to that orb; but common sense will inquire, before starting thither by what road and by what conveyance one is to get there. It is all well enough to assert the slave's right to the Bible and it is equally so to assert his right to spellingbook, since the former would be useless without a knowledge of the latter; but neither the one nor the other should take precedence of the great and comprehensive assertion of his right to personality as the foundation of all other rights. In the language of Theodore D. Weld[55]—"This is the post in the center, by which all other rights are upheld, and without which no other rights can exist."—F.D.

*The North Star,* June 22, 1849


# THE NORTH STAR

After the present number, by a mutual understanding with our esteemed friend and coadjutor, M. R. Delany, the whole responsibility of editing and publishing the *North Star,* will devolve upon myself.[56] After a full consultation, and a consideration of all the circumstances, it has been deemed best that the paper should be left under my exclusive control. The pecuniary burdens of the concern will therefore, in future, fall entirely upon me. In connexion with this arrangement, I am happy to state, that while the copartnership which has subsisted between myself and M. R. Delany, is now terminated, his interest in the success of the enterprise remains unabated; and he will continue to contribute by his pen, as formerly, to the columns on the *North Star*: and do all, consistently with his other duties, towards making the paper prosperous to its editor, and valuable to its readers. It is proper for me to state that this far, Mr. Delany has been a loser, (as well as myself) by the enterprise; and that he is still willing to make sacrifices that our favorite sheet may be sustained.

Frederick Douglass

*The North Star,* June 29, 1849

## GAVITT'S ORIGINAL ETHIOPIAN SERENADERS

Partly from a love of music, and partly from curiosity to see persons of color exaggerating the peculiarities of their race, we were induced last evening to hear these Serenaders. The Company is said to be composed entirely of colored people; and it may be so. We observed, however, that they, too had recourse to the burnt cork and lamp black, the better to express their characters, and to produce uniformity of complexion. Their lips, too, were evidently painted, and otherwise exaggerated. Their singing generally was but an imitation of white performers, and not even a tolerable representation of the character of colored people. Their attempts at it showed them to possess a plentiful lack of it, and gave their audience a very low idea of the sharpness and shrewdness of the race to which they belong. With two or three exceptions, they were a poor set, and will make themselves ridiculous wherever they may go. We heard but one really fine voice among the whole, and that was Cooper's who is truly an excellent singer; and a company possessing equal ability with himself, would no doubt, be very successful in commanding the respect and patronage of the public generally. Davis (the *Bones)* too, is certainly a master player; but the *Tambourine* is an utter failure. B. Richardson is an extraordinary character. His Virginia Breakdown excelled anything which we have ever seen of that description of dancing. He is certainly far before the dancer in the Company of Campbells. We are not sure that our readers will approve of our mention of those persons, so strong must be their dislike of everything that seems to feed the flame of American prejudice against colored people; and in this they might be right; but we think otherwise. It is something gained, when the colored man in any form can appear before a white audience; and we think that even this company, with industry, application, and a proper cultivation of their taste, may yet be instrumental in removing the prejudice against our race. But they must cease to exaggerate the exaggerations of our enemies; and represent the colored man rather as he is, than as Ethiopian Minstrels usually represent him to be. They will *then* command the respect of both races; whereas *now* they only shock the taste of the one, and provoke the disgust of the other. Let Cooper, Davis, and Richardson bring around themselves persons of equal skill, and seek to improve, relying more upon the refinement of the public, than its vulgarity, let them strive to conform to it, rather than to cater to the lower elements of the baser sort, and they may do much to elevate themselves and their race in popular estimation.—F.D.

*The North Star,* June 29, 1849

## REV. HENRY HIGHLAND GARNET

This individual, we understand, is to leave the United States for England during the approaching autumn. The particular object of his mission to that country is not positively known—but from the well known views of the party by whom he has been invited and by whom he is to be supported while there, it is probable, that he goes out as the Champion of the "Free Produce Cause."[57] Mr. Garnet is a man of talents and address. As a speaker he ranks deservedly amongst the first and most eloquent of his race, in this country. To an English audience, he will doubtless prove a most acceptable speaker, and will excite much interest wherever he may go. His complexion will be a help, rather than a hindrance to his success. He will find that the warm right hand of human brotherhood, will be extended as freely to him in old England, as to any other man—of whatever color, caste, or clime. He will look around in vain among the crowds of white persons whom he may meet to observe a single averted eye, or the slightest manifestation of the bitter and malignant hatred with which the colored man is haunted in this boasted land of Liberty. He will find to his entire satisfaction that color is no crime in England. We predict therefore that personally the visit of Mr. Garnet to England will be a very pleasant one.

As to the actual good that the cause of the slave will receive from his labor in that country, doubt may be very innocently entertained. On this point, duty requires us to be plain, and while we would neither detract from the talents not the zeal of Mr. Garnet, but freely give him the full benefit of our testimony to both—we deem it due to ourselves, as a friend of the cause of Emancipation, and the elevation of the oppressed—as well as to fair dealing, to give the public on either side of the Atlantic, in the most explicit manner, both views of the man and his mission. In the first place, Mr. Garnet has again and again declared that he had no faith in moral means for the overthrow of American Slavery. That his hope for success was in the sword.[58] He has held up moral suasion repeatedly, to the scorn and contempt of the colored people in our presence, and made many speeches in favor of insurrection among themselves, and these sentiments have never to our knowledge been recalled nor repented of. Now for such a man to appeal to the moral sense of England, and ask the moral aid of England for the abolition of slavery is the veriest hypocrisy and hollowness. The man whose convictions do not go with his words, is not fit to plead this cause—and his eloquence will merely be sound and fury signifying nothing.

Another reason which leads us to suspect no good from the visit of Mr. Garnet to England—is, that he goes there to espouse a cause which we believe he has never advocated here, either by precept or example. Now a man who will advocate a cause abroad with respect to which he is silent at home, does not give the best evidence of sincerity, and leaves the impression that his motives are at least questionable. When and where has Mr. Garnet written or spoken a word in this country in favor of abstinence from slave produce? We have attended with him many conventions where he has taken an active and even a leading part, but we remember yet to have seen the first line from his pen, or heard the first word from his lips, stating him to be an advocate of the use of free produce. He may have become converted recently, but if so, one would suppose that he would have made his conversion public at home, at least as soon as he published it abroad. But no such profession has been made here, and the natural inference from the fact is, that this profession of faith is intended for a foreign market rather than for home consumption. The party who has invited him to England, hires him to advocate a given movement, and Mr. Garnet like a practical man, prepares himself for his office. We do not hesitate to say, that no reliance may be placed upon any statements which he may make respecting the *North Star* or its editor, should he condescend to notice either while in England. His feeling towards us so far as we have been able to learn them, are those of bitter hostility. His course here has been that of an enemy, and we have no reason to believe that his course abroad will be that of a friend. We now take leave of Mr. Garnet, having honestly given our opinion of him. He is at full liberty to slander and misrepresent us in England or elsewhere, as he has done most liberally in various parts of the United States. We prefer an open enemy, to one in disguise; we therefore without any cowardly disclaimer of any kind, wish it to be understood that Mr. Garnet and ourselves are on any other terms than those of good fellowship. —F.D.

*The North Star,* July 27, 1849

# REV. HENRY H. GARNET

When we penned our portrait of this gentleman three weeks since, we had no idea of administering to his vanity, and are not surprised that he should seize on the first opportunity to manifest his spleen towards us on account of it. The only part of his speech delivered at the Auburn celebration, which Mr. Ward has allowed to see the light, or perhaps thought worth reporting, is a denunciation of us and our esteemed friend, C. L. Remond. Mr. Garnet begins with the following solemn warning to his hearers: "Beware of the baneful and hell-born doctrines which are cunningly scattered among you, and that, too, with an industry worthy of a better cause. I speak plainly and pointedly, because the poison which I am about to analyze emanates from a high and respectable source, so far as talents and influence are concerned. Mr. Frederick Douglass tells us we have no country."[59] In one sense, and in the sense in which this sentiment was uttered, this is perfectly true—"we have no country." In making the declaration, we meant only to exhibit forcibly the glaring fact that the colored man is denied the rights and privileges of an American citizen, by the American government; and that, in this respect, he is an outlaw in the land. This was the meaning which we attached to that declaration when we uttered it, and *no man knew better at the time that such was our meaning than Mr. Garnet,* yet he has the unfairness to affirm that the view we take of it is the same taken by John C. Calhoun! Nothing can more clearly indicate Mr. Garnet's own sense of the utter weakness of his cause, than a resort to palpable falsehood in his defense. If any colored man wants to know whether he has a country, let him go to Charleston, South Carolina, under the protection of the American Constitution, and his country will be limited to a prison. That the colored people have a right to a country here, we have ever affirmed; and Mr. Garnet will never succeed in trying to make the colored people, nor any other enlightened people, believe the contrary.

Charge 2d.—We have spoken lightly and contemptuously of the religious conviction of the colored people, and of their "religious hope." We deny the charge, and demand the proof; and if the former be not withdrawn, or proved, its author must rest under the infamous discharge of being a Reverend false-witness.

Charge 3d.—We were once a preacher in the Methodist Church, and deserted it.[60] This is very true. Those who are acquainted with the character of the Methodist Church, and have a spark of self-respect, or feel a single pulsation of sympathy for the downtrodden slave, will commend us for our course.

Charge 4th.—We "deny the inspiration of the Bible." This is a broad charge, and if well founded, Mr. Garnet will, of course, produce the proof; meanwhile, we utterly disavow that we have made such a denial.

Charge 5th.—We are "unstable." It might perhaps be better for him if we were so; he might then expect at some future time he would be able to deceive us into the belief that Mr. Garnet is a man of veracity and honor; no such hopes nor expectations need ever be cherished. "Unstable" though we may be, we shall ever maintain a consistent view of his character, and shape our conduct towards him accordingly.

Charge 6th. is, that we ask the colored people to bow down to "the unreasonable and unnatural dogmas of non-resistance." What Mr. Garnet terms, "unreasonable and unnatural dogmas," (though we have never insisted upon them before any congregation of our people,) may be found in that said volume which HE affects to honor, and which WE are presumed to slight. We should like to hear a sermon from this

Reverend man of blood and pretended disciple of the Lord Jesus Christ, on the following passages of scripture: "Ye have heard that it hath been said, an eye for an eye, and a tooth for a tooth; *But I say onto you, that ye resist not evil; but whosoever shall smite thee on the right cheek, turn to him the other also;* and if any man will sue thee at the law, and take away thy coat, let him have thy cloak also; and whosoever shall compel thee to go a mile, go with him twain." Will Mr Garnet denounce these as "unnatural and unreasonable dogmas"? and if so, how much respect has he for Christ or the Bible? We believe that he has no more regard for the Bible than had Abner Kneeland or any other infidel; and he merely follows that part of it which he deems most in accordance with his bloodthirsty disposition, and as a means of putting money in his purse. This Reverend gentleman bound himself under the most solemn obligations to be present at Buffalo at the appointed time." He was not there! but was pouring out the vials of his wrath upon us, at Auburn!! adding to the sin his breach of faith with his Buffalo brethren, by fabricating falsehoods against us! From *such* teachers of morality and religion, we say, in the language of "the Book of Common Prayer," *"Good Lord deliver us."* The whole phillippic of Mr. Garnet, delivered against us at Auburn, is a tissue of dishonesty and falsehood, from beginning to end. He tells his hearers that we are opposed to giving the slave the Bible, but has not the honesty to say that we are in favor of giving Bibles to free men. He says we ridicule religion; but has too much contempt for truth to say it is the *slaveholder's religion.* He condemns us as a non-resistant, and in the same speech charges us with holding to the right of self-defense. He charges us with saying that the Bible would make the slave wretched, and basely leaves the inference to be drawn that we think it a pernicious book, when our assailant knows that the remark was made as an argument in favor of *giving the slave himself, as the only condition upon which he could really own a Bible.*

Mr. Garnet next tries his venomous tooth on our esteemed friend and co-laborer, Charles Lenox Remond. He charges him with "draining the wine cup"—with "descending from the consecrated desk, and repairing to the ball chamber"—denounces him as a sportsman, and warns the people against him, as a "dangerous" teacher. Mr. Remond is well known. He makes no high pretensions to religion. He does not profess to believe that dancing is a sin, and then contradict his profession by dancing at a ball. As to his draining the wine cup, we might be disposed to believe the charge, if the man who brings it did not stand openly convicted of gross dereliction of moral principle, and of a series of deliberate falsehoods. We shall, however, leave Mr. Remond to speak for himself—"He is of age," and we are sure that he is fully equal to the task.—F. D.

*The North Star,* August 17, 1849


# FATHER MATHEW AND SLAVERY[61]

Nothing reveals more completely and mournfully the all-prevailing presence and power of the spirit of slavery in this land, than the sad fact, that scarcely a single foreigner that ventures on our soil is found able to withstand its pernicious and seductive influence. Man after man has appeared in our midst, from whom, in view of his previous history, we had reason to expect a bold and uncompromising stand against this giant wrong, has fallen before it, and drifted away in the pro-slavery tide of public opinion.—Many names might be mentioned—especially those of divines—from England, Ireland and Scotland, known and distinguished at home as the friends of the anti-slavery cause, who have almost, immediately on landing, deserted their principles, abandoned the cause, and linked themselves with the oppressors and haters of liberty, finding it much easier to sail with the popular breeze than to maintain their integrity. It would seem that the foul demon stands ready, upon all our borders, to reduce or overwhelm every man who comes within his reach.

From our acquaintance with Father Mathew, we had fondly hoped that his would be a better fate; that he would not change his morality by changing his locality; but that he would nobly avow and stand hard by the principles he professed to cherish in his own land. We are, however grieved, humbled and mortified to know that he too has fallen in the wake of his predecessors, and forsaken the cause of the oppressed, by pledging himself to the oppressor that he will remain dumb on the subject of slavery during his sojourn in this country. A more melancholy spectacle cannot well be imagined; and though most painful to us, we should be false to our high obligations to liberty did we not expose this disgraceful apostasy.

In the year 1842, Theobald Mathew signed an address from the people of Ireland to their countrymen and countrywomen in America, calling their attention to the subject of American slavery, denouncing the system as "a foul blot", declaring that our land never "could be glorious so long as its soil is polluted by the footstep of a single slave"; affirming slavery to be the most tremendous invasion of the natural, inalienable rights of man, and of some of the noblest gifts of God; and says, "What a spectacle does America present to the people of the earth—a land of professing Christian republicans uniting their energies for the oppression and degradation of three millions of innocent human beings, the children of one common father, who suffer the most grievous wrongs and the utmost degradation, for no crime of their own, nor of their ancestors! Slavery is a sin against God and man. All who are not for it must be against it; none can be neutral. We entreat you to take the part of justice, religion and liberty. We call upon you to unite with the abolitionists."

Such was Father Mathew's advice to his countrymen in America, when he stood under the shadow of the British monarchy; but oh! how different, how changed is his tune, when he treads the soil of this Republic? Within a few days, a train of circumstances has compelled him to define his position; and, sadly enough, he has sought to find for himself a refuge, of which, seven years since, he denied the existence.—*"None can be neutral,"* he *then* said: upon this point his mind has undergone a change. He *now* thinks he has found *neutral* ground. The circumstances leading to this development are briefly these: The committee of arrangements appointed by the American Anti-Slavery Society to make preparations for celebrating the anniversary of West India Emancipation, addressed to Father Mathew a letter, respectfully inviting him to be present, and to participate in the celebration. "To make assurance doubly sure," a committee was appointed, consisting of W. L. Garrison and Dr. H. I. Bowditch, to see that Father Mathew received the said letter; and at this interview, Father Mathew declared what it appears to us will be his policy during his sojourn in this country. He said on that occasion, "I have as much as I can do to save men from the slavery of intemperance, without attempting the overthrow of any other kind of slavery. Besides it would not be proper for me to commit myself on a question like this, under present circumstances. I am a Catholic priest; but being here to promote the cause of temperance, I should not be justified in turning aside from my mission for the purpose of subserving the cause of catholicism." He further said, "I am not in favor of slavery. I should never think of advocating it, though I don't know as we can say that there is any specific injunction against it in the scriptures." Such seems to be the present position of Father Mathew; and it is one of which, we have no doubt, his countrymen at home will be heartily ashamed. It is needless for us to expose the sophistry by which Father Mathew seeks to defend his position. The case which he puts of being a Catholic priest, is the last which he should have taken to illustrate the relation he shall maintain to the anti-slavery cause in this country. He was a Catholic priest in Ireland, and a temperance man in Ireland; and though pressed on all sides with engagements, he found time to express himselk fully and clearly in behalf of the anti-slavery cause; and it is not to be believed that what he then said against American slavery in any degree lessened his power against the slavery of intemperance. His assumed unwillingness to "turn aside" from the temperance cause, to promote catholicism, would wear the appearance of impartiality, if the cases were alike—which they are not. Everyone knows Father Mathew to be an abolitionist. On the one question he is openly committed, and is willing to stand committed; *on the other, he is entirely opposed to committing himself.* He has no occasion to "turn aside" to promote catholicism. *He does promote it*, and cannot help promoting it. In every good word that he speaks, and in every good deed that he performs, he promotes the cause of Roman Catholicism, while he is openly identified with that system of religion. But it is not so on the subject of slavery. The anti-slavery cause derives no influence in its favor from a man who declares himself unwilling to "commit himself" in its behalf. The reader must remember that our Boston friends made no exorbitant or unreasonable demand upon Father Mathew's time. They assured him of their unwillingness to divert him from the great purpose of his mission to this country, and they simply wished him to attend this celebration as an appropriate opportunity in which to make known his sympathy with the cause of the oppressed. The length of time required for this could not exceed one day so that, on this score, Father Mathew is without excuse.

It is obvious to common sense, that, the policy of Father Mathew will fail in its object. Thank God that it is within the power of the anti-slavery press of the country (feeble as it is ) to make his treachery to liberty known throughout the land; and although he may luxuriate for awhile in the smiles of American fleshmongers, and eat the bread wrung out from the sweat and blood of the bondman, *the time will come* when his treachery must recoil upon him. God will "confound the wisdom of the crafty," and "Bring to nought the counsels of the ungodly."—But we will not be too severe. We hope that Father Mathew may yet see his error, confess his fault, and nobly indentify himself with the cause of the long-degraded and deeply-injured bondman, before he leaves this country.—F. D.

*The North Star,* August 17, 1849

## CALLING HIM OUT!

Mr. Ward, in a letter addressed to the Rev. Henry Highland Garnet, calls upon that gentleman to state whether he holds the views we attributed to him, (on our remarks upon his mission to England) or not.

We shall be as happy as Mr. Ward to have Mr. Garnet's affirmation or denial of any part of the article in question. We aim at all times to give a fair and candid statement of the views of an opponent; and if we have misstated him, the columns of the *North Star* are open to him. The impeachment of Mr. Garnet's motives was derived legitimately from well defined premises; and the latter must be overthrown before he can escapt the charge of hollowness and hypocrisy.—F.D.

*The North Star,* August 31, 1849

## "CALLING HIM OUT," AND HE COMES

Mr. Douglass:

In the last number of the *North Star,* you offer me an opportunity, to speak for myself, through the same medium through which you have slandered and traduced me. I thank you for it, and at the same time I assure you, that whenever you lay aside low and vulgar personalities, and call me out as a gentleman I will answer and not otherwise. I had two reasons for not resorting to your paper in order to make a reply.

First, because I addressed a letter to you last winter for publication, expressive of my gratitude to some of my anti-slavery friends in Penn Yan, and you did not suffer it to see the light, because it contained some views which were unpalatable to you. And in the second place, because I thought it unlikely that after having willfully misrepresented me, you could not even "for a pretense" show so much liberality.

You heard that my friends, and the friends of universal freedom in England, had invited me to visit that country, and immediately you became very much alarmed, and your friends also. The reason for this trouble of mind on your part I have not been able to determine, unless it is, that you have the spirit of the Old Roman, and believe that "the world was made for Caesar." You did not even want to know whether I was going to that country, before you labored like a Hercules to blacken my character in the eyes of a people who may never see me. I knew sir, that in your hot pursuit after a worthless, and a transient fame, you would sometimes stoop to mean things, but I never dreamed that you would ever sink so low, that you would have to reach up, standing on tip-toe, to find that level of meanness where common knaves are inclined to pause. Ah, sir, the geeen-eyed monster has made you mad. Pardon me, when I tell you that you never imbibed a spirit so narrow from any dark son of our native Maryland, living or dead. But why should I marvel? When did you ever manifest friendship to any colored man who differed with you in sentiment? You design not to mention the name of the noble Alexander Crummell; you have stabbed at J.W.C. Pennington, you have tried to ruin that eloquent fugitive Henry Bibb; and you have vainly attempted to crush that intellectual giant Samuel R. Ward. But you are at home in the company of Thomas Van Rennselaer, editor of the *Ram's Horn*, whom you have accused of falsehood. What think you of the old adage, Show me a man's company, and I will tell you what he is?

In your assassin-like article, which you desired to take effect in England, you say that I am a man and may stand among my brethren. Why was all that necessary? Why raise a mortal to the sky? You talk of *my race*, pray sir, how many races of men are there? Certainly if you do not belong to *my race*, you must belong to that of Haman.

You make *four* charges against me, everyone of which is *generally* and *particularly* false; and you knew them to be such when you made them.

1. You say that I go to England to advocate a cause which I have

not espoused at home—the Free Produce cause. This is untrue in two particulars. I go not for that purpose alone—I am requested to advocate the cause of freedom generally. I am a friend of Free Produce, and have humbly commenced practicing it.

2. You publish that I have no faith in the use of moral means for the extinction of American Slavery. *I believe with all my heart in such means—and I believe that political power ought to be used for that end, and that when rightly used, it is strictly moral.* I also believe that the slave has a moral right to use his physical power to obtain his liberty—my motto is, give me liberty, or give me death. Dare you, Frederick Douglass, say otherwise! Speak plainly—I am "calling you out."

3. You accuse me of being your enemy. I am not. I stand in that relation to no man. You hate me because I tell you the truth. May you seek speedy repentance.

4. You, and the *Anti-Slavery Bugle,* say that I will misrepresent you in England.[62] My theme in that land will be of better men, and better principles than you, or those which you possess. Will the *Bugle* please publish the letter, and send me the paper, and I will send him a year's subscription.

Some two months ago or more, Mr. Douglass challenged me, in connection with Ward and Bibb, to discuss the matter upon which we differed in New York in May last. I accepted, but you became frightened at the mere "shaking of my goose quill." *You could not be called out.* You affirmed that the project to give the slaves the Bible, is unworthy of the attention of philantropists. I dissent from you entirely.

Your servant,
Henry Highland Garnet

*Peterboro,* August 31. *The North Star,* September 7, 1849

## REV. HENRY HIGHLAND GARNET

A letter from this gentleman may be found in another column of this week's paper. The only answer to it we deem it necessary to make is to republish the article to which it purports to be a reply. Our readers can judge as well as we, how far Mr. Garnet has vindicated his position, and how much better is the spirit than ours. All that he says about his espousal of the Free Produce cause only confirms the truth of our statement on that point. He has *"humbly commenced practising it."* We said he was a *"practical man."* His espousal of the Free Produce cause will be quite news to all, we think, who know him. As to what he says about morals he has too often (in Zion Church, New York, and elsewhere) taught the doctrine that no people ever have nor ever can gain their freedom without fighting for it, even to make a reply, on this point, necessary for us. But, there is Mr. Garnet's letter, and the article to which it purports to reply. *Read and judge.* —F.D.

*The North Star,* September 7, 1849


# CONTROVERSIES AMONG COLORED MEN

We have received several letters recently, deprecating our course towards Henry Highland Garnet, and expressing profound regret that differences and controversies should occur among men of the same complection.[63] We admire the amicability more than we do the sagacity of our correspondents. Until they can prove that sameness of complexion produces harmony of opinion, they will fail to show that colored men have not as good right to differ from each other as have white men. These correspondents and advisors must find a more permanent and rational basis for their regrets than that of *"color."* The mind does not take its complexion from the skin; to be a colored man is not necessarily to be an abolitionist.

If we have, in any instance, accused a man unjustly, administered an untimely rebuke; or made any attack unwarrantably—let it be shown, and we shall not need to be asked to retract, or to make a needful apology. In the case of Mr. Garnet we merely spoke what we deemed at the time to be true—and what we since have had no evidence to disprove. We know nothing of that *charity* which is so forgiving that it can embrace an enemy that glories in his transgression. We neither forgive nor forget a man who insidiously seeks to destroy our character, and, thereby, to stab the cause with which we are identified; but we will hold him responsible for his conduct before God and man, until he shall repent. A peace founded on any other basis would be delusive and worthless. —F.D.

*The North Star,* October 19, 1849

## TO OLIVER JOHNSON

Rochester, 4th Sept. 1849

My Dear Mr. Johnson:

Your kind letter, honoring me with an invitation to be present at the contemplated Convention of the Young Men and Women of Ohio, is before me. I have no words to tell you how glad I should be to attend that convention, nor how much I regret my inability to do so. It is indeed soul-cheering to observe the activity of the Old Organized Anti-Slavery movement in your State. I say *Old Organized*—though in truth there is no *New* Organized Anti-Slavery in Ohio or elsewhere. That, if it ever did exist, is now dead and buried. The glorious cause now rests upon the shoulders of men and women who honor the principles more than men—and who are resolved to fight the battles of Freedom on the most disinterested grounds; turning neither to the right nor the left—attacking Church and State, Constitution and Government, principalities and power, and wickedness in high places, making war upon everything that opposes the high and Heaven-blest cause in which they are engaged—without compromise and without concealment. With this class I am proud to be connected. As our old Anti-Slavery Pioneer once said, in a speech of his in New York, I am willing at all times to be known as a *Garrison* Abolitionist. I must close, for I write in haste, by wishing the Convention all the harmony consistent with *Free Speech,* and every success in spreading Anti-Slavery truth in Ohio.

Yours, most sincerely,
Frederick Douglass

*The Anti-Slavery Bugle (Salem, Ohio), October 6, 1849*

## TO SIDNEY HOWARD GAY

Rochester, 11th, Oct. 1849

Dear Friend:

I am ready to second to the very best of my ability your proposition for holding a grand Anti-Slavery Convention at Syracuse this fall. The idea is an excellent one, and I have no doubt if carried out will do important service to our common cause. I agree with you that the thing should be well done or not done at all. Syracuse as you need not be informed is the center of all that remains of the Liberty Party, and hold the convention when we will, the men of that party will meet us. We should have our loins girt about, and be ready to defend our position. Let me know the course you intend to pursue as speedily as possible, and all your plans about the proposed convention, that I may shape my course accordingly.

Of course, Boston must be represented at the Convention or it would be a mistake I think, to hold it. It should be a grand rally of freedom's friends from all quarters. In haste

Yours faithfully,
Frederick Douglass

*Samuel Howard Gay Papers, Columbia University Library*


## PROSCRIPTION AND OPPRESSION TOWARDS COLORED CHILDREN IN ROCHESTER

In the *North Star* of 17th August 1849 we published an able and interesting Report to the Board of Education in this city, signed by four of its members, demonstrating the folly and wickedness of creating distinctions among equal citizens on account of complexion—and recommending the abolishment of the colored school on Washington Street, and the free admission of colored children into the District Schools in equal terms with white children.[64]

We are sorry to say that this excellent Report is rejected by the Board of Education, and that they have adopted a course towards our children as cruel as it is disgraceful. For some time past they have been at a loss to find a place whereon to build a achool-house for colored children; when almost wearied out in the pursuit, and almost-ready (from sheer necessity) to admit colored children into the District Schools, where they have a right to be, we record with shame and confusion the scandalous fact that *the trustees of the Zion Methodist Church, for the paltry consideration of two hundred dollars,* offered the use of the cellar of their meeting-house, and have thus become the servile tools of their own proscription and degradation. For such base and cringing servility we have no language sufficiently strong to express our indignation and contempt. These trustees have not only sanctioned by this conduct the spirit of *caste,* by which we are constantly haunted and tormented, but, for the sake of a paltry reward, they have been willing to endanger the health, and ruin the constitution of the whole generation of colored children in Rochester. The *cellar* of that church is about as fit for a school-house for tender children as an *ice-house* would be, and we have been credibly informed that *that* has been the use to which this *cellar* has been put. The house itself occupies a piece of very low ground, *and for three months in the year is surrounded by mud and water,* and into the low, damp and dark cellar of this house, these *recreant black* men have been willing to thrust the colored children of this community. Two hundred dollars have proved a sufficient inducement to these Trustees to sacrifice a vital principle and to peril the lives of their own children. Shame upon their narrow souls! and let every colored child in the city cry *shame!* It was to be expected that our white Negro haters would seek our degradation, it is their habit to do so, but for colored men to become their willing tools is a depth of infamy scarcely to be apprehended. We still hope, however, that this bribe will be withheld, and that these Methodist Trustees will be shamed and scorned out of their ignominious proposition by the justly indignant colored population of this city.—F.D.

*The North Star,* November 2, 1849

## LETTER FROM A SLAVEHOLDER

Biloxi, (Miss.) Mar. 26, 1850

F. Douglass:

I am in receipt of your letter of the 26th Feb. in which you remind me that I owe you two dollars. I herewith send that amount. Instead of adding another subscriber to your list, allow me to withdraw my name. I never was voluntary your subscriber as you know; and you published the circumstances under which I became so, in the first paper you sent me. The papers I have received have disappointed me. From what had been said of you by your friends, and what I had seen of you and heard from you while you were addressing a crowd of your own friends, in your adopted State, on one of the few occasions that I have ever been out of the slave States, I believed that you would do good, by exposing in strong language, the too common practice among many of the Creole population of Louisiana; such as requiring slaves[1] on a part of every Sunday, providing them scanty food and clothing and in some circumstances inflicting punishments which[2] degrade the slave, and destroy his health and usefulness. I thought that an exposure by you, on other States, of the unusual cruelties practised, which had fallen under your observation, would have the effect of removing those oppressions upon the black man, and of benefiting his physical condition. To effect this, I thought you would deal with the subject candidly; that

157

your object being to "benefit the perishing slave," your strong common sense would induce you to hold yourself strictly within the bounds of truth; that your pictures and descriptions would not be so highly colored, as not to be recognized by the slave-holders. I was prepared to make many allowances on account of your past condition—to excuse slight embellishments and pardon small exaggerations. In all this, I have been disappointed. Indeed your whole *policy* was misconceived. Your *indiscriminate abuse* of slaveholders—your inflammatory appeals to your colored and white brethren of the North,—your violence and wantonness in attacking the Constitution of our common country, and your willingness to see it violated in the most open and palpable manner, have convinced me that you are doing harm to the black race, and more firmly rivetting their chains. I am not therefore, your "dear friend," as you style me; I am not a co-worker with you in your crusade against the best interests of your race. I have heard you patiently for one year. I took your paper because it was offered as an argument by one of your friends, and I was willing to listen, not only to what your friends had to say on these exciting subjects. Deliberately and calmly I decide against you, your paper and your cause.

As far back as I can trace my ancestry, they were slaveholders— not "slave-dealers;" and without any desire to act on my own part, I have been always a slaveholder. I am working 122 slaves at my brickworks at this place. Some I own and some I have hired. I work Negroes, because their labor, from the very nature of the institution, under a Southern sun, can alone be *relied upon with certainty;* and not because slave labor is more profitable than white labor would be, if we had no slaves. If I could will the institution of slavery out of existence tomorrow, to-morrow there would be no other than voluntary slavery on this continent; and by the annihilation of the institution of slavery, I should feel that I had benefitted my own more than the black race.

In conclusion, I must add my firm belief, that it is not in the power of any human being to benefit the present condition of the slave, when owned and cared for by an honest man.

You will oblige me by a discontinuance of your paper.

Respectfully, &c.

W. G. Kendall

P.S. at New Orleans, 27th March. Since writing the above, I read it to a gentleman who is a native of the South—who has all his life been accustomed to slave labor, and has deliberately investigated the subject of slavery, and *therefore* has never owned a slave; and requests me to express to you his firm conviction, that slavery is a great blessing to the black race, and a great curse to the white race.

W.G.K.

REMARKS. When Mr. Bradburn[3] sent us the name of our slaveholding correspondent as a subscriber to the *North Star,* we could not but be glad, though we felt almost sure that the writer would soon become annoyed by our animadversions on slavery and slaveholders, and would abandon the paper. Two persons could not well be placed in any circumstances more unfavorable to harmony of feeling and unity of opinion, than the slave and the slaveholder. They are opposites and extremes, which can never meet. The lamb and the lion may lie down together, but the slave and the slaveholder never. Between these there is a great gulf fixed. With a full knowledge of these simple truths at this first, we cannot say with our slaveholding correspondent, that we are at all "disappointed" at the termination which he has put to our further intercourse with him. If we feel any surprise, it is more on account of his gentlemanly bearing towards us, than on account of the conclusion to which he has come. In this respect, his example might be copied to advantage, by many a white Northerner, whose estimate of his own great consequence is derived from the impunity with which he can insult a Negro. In this letter there are no wanton and meaningless flings or sneers at our complexion. He has written respectfully, if not cordially. If he does not esteem us as a friend, he does not despise us as a man. In our reply, we desire to be as respectful as he, without being unfaithful; though the need of praise we have extended to him, we have no idea will ever be meted out to us. Unfortunately for us, to be faithful to a slaveholder, is to be rude and vulgar in popular estimation. An enslaver of his fellow-man—a promoter of ignorance, vice and crime, must be branded before the world as a flagrant offender against the government of God and the happiness of man and in a Christian spirit exhorted to repent. Any other mode of treatment would be mere sham and of course utterly useless. And in pursuing an open and bold exposure of slavery and slaveholders, one of two results will always follow—the opponent will be converted or he will be repelled.

We regret that the latter alternative has fallen to our slaveholding correspondent. Would that his heart had been touched, softened and converted! Would that he could have risen superior to his condition, and broken the chain of selfishness which, like a huge serpent, has wound itself around him!

But, alas! Sir, you have decided to shut out anti-slavery light from your mind, and have already adopted the dark system of reasoning common to the most hardened slaveholders. We conjure you, by the high value of your own soul, to reconsider your determination. You cannot be satisfied with your present position. This is apparent in the very letter before us; for though you are now, and always have been a slaveholder you are careful to mention that you are so not by desire nor act of your own; and you are further careful to state, that your ancestors were slaveholders, *"but not slavedealers."* Now, in this evident desire to put the best face upon your position, may be easily read the workings of a disquieted conscience. Why not yield to its demands, and be at peace? Why attempt to appease its urgent and just requirements by mere wordwise distinctions? Why distinguish between the slaveholder and the *slavedealer?* Is not the latter comprehended in the former? If the one be right, can the other be wrong? You hold the slave as property. This comprehends all else. You can go no further than this. It is the highest crime you can commit. Then again, your becoming a slave-holder without any desire or act on your own part, may we ask: What does it avail, when you admit, as you must, that you do *now* hold slaves by your own desire, and by your own act? Why implicate your ances-tors, to exculpate yourself? Why use a reproach with which your post-erity may assail your own memory? If the plea thus made be a good one, how long will it remain so? does it strengthen or does it weaken under the weight of years? You say, that as far back as you are able to trace your ancestry; they have been slaveholders: tell us, have each generation of them thrown off their sins upon the preceding genera-tion, and is it not likely that succeeding ones will do the same? Oh! blinding and bewitching voice of selfishness! into what mazes of confu-sion, false logic and absurdity dost thou not lead?

It is more than implied in your letter, that you were induced to subscribe for the *North Star,* under a misapprehension of its character. We submit, that this is no fault of ours. You knew its editor to be an unconcealed denouncer of slavery, in all its forms, and identified with what are called, by way of reproach, the most radical class of abolitionists. We have deceived no man; and if you have been deceived, you have been self-deceived. The good you expected from the paper, was not that aimed at by its editor—nor that declared upon the face of every number of it which has yet been issued. It was not to correct the incidents of slavery, but to abolish it. It was not to expose the cruelty of *Creole* slaveholders, but all slaveholders, whether white or colored.

Nor are we at all conscious, that in the pursuit of this object, we have ever been reckless of truth, or unjust to any. We defy you to disprove a single charge ever made in its columns, against slavery in general, or slaveholders in particular. Our columns shall be held at your service for such a purpose, whenever you choose to occupy them.

You doubtless think that something is due to kind masters, and perhaps rank yourself among the number. To all such we say kind or cruel, you are bound to quit your grasp on your slaves. You have no right, but the right of a robber to your victims. Your fancied kindness, to what does it amount when set against the loss of liberty, the loss of progress, the loss of the means of education, and the overwhelming degradation to which the slave is subjected—the mere pack-horse of another—a man transformed into a beast of burden—a name which might be enrolled among the blest on the Lamb's Book of Life, sacrilegiously degraded to a place in the pages of your ledger, with horses, sheep and swine? Perish all shows of kindness, when they are thought to conceal or to palliate the damning character of slavery.—F.D.

*The North Star,* April 12, 1850

## LETTER OF M. R. DELANY

The letter of M. R. Delany, (which takes up a large share of our Editorial space) deserves perhaps a few words from us in reply. With all that he says as to the desirableness of cultivating amicable feelings among those whose end and aim is, the abolition of slavery, and the elevation of the free colored people, we most heartily agree. We shall probably go as far in promoting such feelings as he himself would desire, and as far as is compatible with the free expression of our honest convictions in respect to the conduct of our public men.

Identity of color, does not forbid a difference of opinion: and having a common object, does not prohibit a free expression of that difference; and in the light of these facts, we expressed our sentiments in respect to the conduct of Ward, in consenting to address a public meeting in Philadelphia in a colored church, where colored people themselves were, by the terms of the call that convened that meeting, expressly denied the right to a seat in the lower part of the building, which was expressly and exclusively appropriated to white persons.

We have re-examined what we said in the *North Star,* to which Mr. Delany takes exception and we find nothing in it so grossly personal as to justify the implied censure which our friend Delany has so freely lavished upon us.[4] One must be struck, on reading his letter, with the appropriateness of his advice, if applied to himself. In correcting our errors he has followed the example of many others who have presumed to give advice; by doing the very thing himself, which he disallows in us. He compares our comments upon Mr. Ward's hand-bill, to the *"uncivilized, vulgar,* attacks of the Mississippi *ruffian,"* and he goes on imputing, (by implication to be sure) such base motives for our conduct, as jealousy, envy, and mean ambition—all of which we think quite gratuitous, and uncalled for. We undertake to affirm that our whole course of conduct towards Mr. Ward, (and we think that the columns of the *North Star* will bear us out in our affirmation) up to his recent visit to Philadelphia, have displayed marked admiration of his very superior talents; and a high appreciation of his character, as a man. When we debated with him in New York, a year since, we bore this testimony to his deportment in that debate, "He showed himself a skillful debater, as well as a powerful declaimer, and certainly possessed a large power over the intelligent audience before him. With an opponent of such genius and magnanimity, it affords us pleasure to discuss any question of difference." These were our words one year since. On the 16th May 1850 we used the following language, with respect to Mr. Ward: "Frederick Douglass was followed by Samuel R. Ward, who, for about 20 minutes, poured forth a brilliant stream of wit, humor, and argument, fairly blistering the unfortunate Mr. Grant." Does this look like ambition, envy, or jealousy? When we found ourselves assailed on the platform, during the last Anniversaries, in New York, after encountering and silencing the clamor of the mob, on retiring from the platform, who, of all the talented colored men who were present, did we select to complete the triumph of human brotherhood, over vulgar prejudice, but Samuel R. Ward? If we differ with him now, it is not that we *love him less,* but freedom and equality more. And if M. R. Delany should ever venture to hold a public meeting in the City of Rochester, or elsewhere, on the pro-slavery conditions of driving the Negro into a separate pew, he shall find us equally ready to denounce such conduct on his part. Persons must be respected, but principles are above persons, and we must follow the latter, though they bring us into conflict with the whole world. —F.D.

*The North Star,* June 27, 1850

## TO O. DENNETT

Rochester, Aug. 9th, 1850

Dear Friend:

You will have already been furnished with the cause of my delay in writing to you, in reply to your kind letter of July 22d inviting me to lecture in Portland before your Anti-slavery Lyceum. I wish, I could say without hesitation or the shadow of a doubt *I'll come!* but that I am now unable to say. I am now nearly six hundred miles from you. Portland and the time appointed is some distance in the future. All that I can say is that should my circumstances call me to Boston during the winter, and there should be a vacancy in your list of speakers, it will give me pleasure to fill that vacancy.

I have been much from home of late and have labored very hard, and as a consequence I am greatly worn, but still my spirit is bright, and my courage invincible. With the truth and the right on our side victory is certain. Pleasure remember me kindly to Mrs. Dennett and all *the faithful.*

Sincerely yours,
Frederick Douglass

*Ms., Houghton Library, Harvard University*

## A LETTER TO THE AMERICAN SLAVES FROM THOSE WHO HAVE FLED FROM AMERICAN SLAVERY[5]

Afflicted and Beloved Brothers:

The meeting which sends you this letter, is a meeting of runaway slaves. We thought it well, that they, who had once suffered, as you still suffer, that they, who had once drunk of that bitterest of all bitter cups, which you are still compelled to drink of, should come together for the purpose of making a communication to you.

The chief object of this meeting is, to tell you what circumstances we find ourselves in—that, so you may be able to judge for yourselves, whether the prize we have obtained is worth the peril of the attempt to obtain it.

The heartless pirates, who compelled us to call them "master," sought to persuade us, as such pirates seek to persuade you, that the condition of those, who escape from their clutches, is thereby made worse, instead of better. We confess, that we had our fears, that this might be so. Indeed, so great was our ignorance, that we could not be sure that the abolitionists were not the friends, which our masters represented them to be. When they told us, that the abolitionists, could they lay hands upon us would buy and sell us, we could not certainly know, that they spoke falsely; and when they told us, that abolitionists are in the habit of skinning the black man for leather, and of regaling their cannibalism on his flesh, even such enormities seemed to us to be possible. But owing to the happy change in our circumstances, we are not as ignorant and credulous now, as we once were; and if we did not know it before, we know it now, that slaveholders are as great liars, as they are great tyrants.

The abolitionists act the part of friends and brothers to us; and our only complaint against them is, that there are so few of them. The abolitionists, on whom it is safe to rely, are, almost all of them, members of the American Anti-Slavery Society, or of the Liberty Party. There are other abolitionists: but most of them are grossly inconsistent; and, hence, not entirely trustworthy abolitionists. So inconsistent are they, as to vote for anti-abolitionists for civil rulers, and to acknowledge the obligation of laws, which they themselves interpret to be pro-slavery.

We get wages for our labor. We have schools for our children. We have opportunities to hear and to learn to read the Bible—that blessed book, which is all for freedom, notwithstanding the lying slaveholders who say it is all for slavery. Some of us take part in the election of civil rulers. Indeed, but for the priests and politicians, the influence of most of whom is against us, our condition would be every way eligible. The priests and churches of the North, are, with comparatively few exceptions, in league with the priests and churches of the South; and this, of itself, is sufficient to account for the fact, that a caste-religion and a Negro-pew are found at the North, as well as at the South. The politicians and political parties of the North are connected with the politicians and political parties of the South; and hence, the political arrangements and interests of the North, as well as the ecclesiastical arrangements and interests, are adverse to the colored population. But, we rejoice to know, that all this political and ecclesiastical power is on the wane. The callousness of American religion and American democracy has become glaring: and, every year, multitudes, once deluded by them, come to repudiate them. The credit of this repudiation is due, in a great measure, to the American Anti-Slavery Society, to the Liberty Party, and to anti-sectarian meetings, and conventions. The purest sect on earth is the rival of, instead of one with, Christianity. It deserves not to be trusted with a deep and honest and earnest reform. The temptations which beset the pathway of such a reform, are too mighty for it to resist. Instead of going forward for God, it will slant off for itself. Heaven grant, that, soon, not a shred of sectarianism, not a shred of the current religion, not a shred of the current politics of this land, may remain. Then will follow, aye, that will itself be, the triumph of Christianity: and, then, white men will love black men and gladly acknowledge that all men have equal rights. Come, blessed day—come quickly.

Including our children, we number in Canada, at least, twenty thousand. The total of our population in the free States far exceeds this. Nevertheless, we are poor, we can do little more to promote your deliverance than pray for it to the God of the oppressed. We will do what we can to supply you with pocket compasses. In dark nights, when his good guiding star is hidden from the flying slave, a pocket compass greatly facilitates his exodus. Candor requires the admission, that some of us would not furnish them, if we could; for some of us have become non-resistants, and have discarded the use of these weapons: and would say to you: "love your enemies; do good to them, which hate you; bless them that curse you; and pray for them, which despitefully use you." Such of us would be glad to be able to say, that all the colored men of the North are non-resistants. But, in point of fact, it is only a handful of them, who are. When the insurrection of the Southern slaves shall take place, as take place it will unless speedily prevented by voluntary emancipation, the great majority of the colored men of the North, however much to the grief of any of us, will be found by your side, with deep-stored and long-accumulated revenge in their hearts, and with death-dealing weapons in their hands. It is not to be disguised, that a colored man is as much disposed, as a white man, to resist, even unto death, those who oppress him. The colored American, for the sake of relieving his colored brethren, would no more hesitate to shoot an American slaveholder, than would a white American, for the sake of delivering his white brother, hesitate to shoot an Algerine slaveholder. The State motto of Virginia: "Death to Tyrants;" is as well the black man's, as the white man's motto. We tell you these things not to encourage, or justify, your resort to physical force; but, simply, that you may know, be it to your joy or sorrow to know it, what your Northern colored brethren are, in these important respects. This truth you are entitled to know, however the knowledge of it may affect you, and however you may act, in view of it.

We have said, that some of us are non-resistants. But, while such would dissuade you from all violence toward the slaveholder, let it not be supposed, that they regard it as guiltier than those strifes, which even good men are wont to justify. If the American revolutionists had excuse for shedding but one drop of blood, then have the American slaves excuse for making blood to flow "even unto the horse-bridles."

Numerous as are the escapes from slavery, thay would be far more so, were you not embarrassed by your misinterpretations of the rights of property. You hesitate to take even the dullest of your master's horses—whereas it is your duty to take the fleetest. Your consciences suggest doubts, whether in quitting your bondage, you are at liberty to put in your packs what you need of food and clothing. But were you better informed, you would not scruple to break your master's locks, and take all their money. You are taught to respect the rights of property. But, no such right belongs to the slaveholder. His right to property is but the robber-right. In every slaveholding community, the rights of property all center in them, whose coerced and unrequited toil has created the wealth in which their oppressors riot. Moreover, if your oppressors have rights of property, you, at least, are exempt from all obligations to respect them. For you are prisoners of war, in an enemy's country—of a war, too, that is unrivalled for its injustice, cruelty, meanness—and therefore, by all the rules of war, you have the fullest liberty to plunder, burn, and kill, as you may have occasion to do to promote your escape.

We regret to be obliged to say to you, that it is not everyone of the Free States, which offers you an asylum. Even within the last year, fugitive slaves have been arrested in some of the Free States, and replunged into slavery. But, make your way to New York or New England, and you will be safe. It is true, that even in New York and New England, there are individuals, who would rejoice to see the poor flying slave cast back into the horrors of slavery. But, even these are restrained by public sentiment. It is questionable whether even Daniel Webster, or Moses Stuart, would give chase to a fugitive slave; and if they would not, who would?—for the one is chief-politician and the other chief-priest.

We do not forget the industrious efforts, which are now in making to get new facilities at the hands of Congress for re-enslaving those, who have escaped from slavery. But we can assure you, that as to the State of New York and the New England States, such efforts must prove fruitless. Against all such devilism—against all kidnappers—the colored people of these States will "stand for their life," and, what is more, the white people of these States will not stand against them. A regenerated public sentiment has, forever, removed these States beyond the limits of the slaveholders' hunting ground. Defeat—disgrace— and, it may be, death—will be their only reward for pursuing their prey into this *abolitionized* portion of our country.

A special reason why you should not stop in that part of the Nation which comes within the bounds of John McLean's judicial district, is, that he is a great man in one of the religious sects, and an aspirant for the Presidency. Fugitive slaves and their friends fare hard in the hands of this Judge. He not only puts a pro-slavery construction on the Federal Constitution, and holds, that law can make property of man—a marketable commodity of the image of God, but, in various other ways, he shows that his sympathies are with the oppressor. Shun Judge McLean, then, even as you would the Reverend Moses Stuart.[6] The law of the one is as deadly an enemy to you, as is the religion of the other.

There are three points in your conduct, when you shall have become inhabitants of the North, on which we cannot refrain from admonishing you.

1st. If you will join a sectarian church, let it not be one which approves of the Negro-pew, and which refuses to treat slaveholding as a high crime against God and man. It were better, that you sacrifice your lives than that by going into the Negro-pew, you invade your self-respect—debase your souls—play the traitor to your race—and crucify afresh Him who died for the one brotherhood of man.

2d. Join no political party, which refuses to commit itself fully, openly, and heartfully, in its newspapers, meetings, and nominations, to the doctrine, that slavery is the grossest of all absurdities, as well as the guiltiest of all abominations, and that there can no more be a law for the enslavement of man, made in the image of God, than for the enslavement of God himself. Vote for no man for civil office, who makes your complexion a bar to political, ecclesiastic or social equality. Better die than insult yourself and insult our social equality. Better die than insult yourself and insult every person of African blood, and insult your Maker, by contributing to elevate to civil office he who refuses to eat with you, to sit by your side in the House of Worship, or to let his children sit in the school by the side of your children.

3d. Send not your children to the school which the malignant and murderous prejudice of white people has gotten up exclusively for colored people. Valuable as learning is, it is too costly, if it is acquired at the expense of such self-degradation.

The self-sacrificing, and heroic, and martyr-spirit, which would impel the colored men of the North to turn their backs on pro-slavery churches and pro-slavery politics, and pro-slavery schools, would exert a far mightier influence against slavery, than could all their learning, however great, if purchased by concessions of their manhood, and surrenders of their rights, and coupled, as it then would be, by characteristic meanness and servility.

And now, brethren, we close this letter with assuring you, that we do not, cannot, forget you. You are ever in our minds, our hearts, our prayers. Perhaps, you are fearing, that the free colored people of the United States will suffer themselves to be carried away from you by the American Colonization Society. Fear it not. In vain is it, that this greatest and most malignant enemy of the African race is now busy in devising new plans, and in seeking the aid of Government, to perpetuate your enslavement. It wants us away from your side, that you may be kept in ignorance. But we will remain by your side to enlighten you. It wants us away from your side, that you may be contented. But we will remain by your side, to keep you, and make you more, discontented. It wants us away from your side to the end, that your unsuccored and conscious helplessness may make you the easier and surer prey of your oppressors. But we will remain by your side to sympathize with you, and cheer you, and give you the help of our rapidly swelling members. The land of our enslaved brethren is our land, and death alone shall part us.

We cannot forget you, brethren, for we know your sufferings and we know your sufferings because we know from experience, what it is to be an American slave. So galling was our bondage, that, to escape from it, we suffered the loss of all things, and braved every peril, and endured every hardship. Some of us left parents, some wives, some children. Some of us were wounded with guns and dogs, as we fled. Some of us, to make good our escape, suffered ourselves to be nailed up in boxes, and to pass for merchandise. Some of us secreted ourselves in the suffocating holds of ships. Nothing was so dreadful to us, as slavery; and hence, it is almost literally true, that we dreaded nothing, which could befall us, in our attempt to get clear of it. Our condition could be made no worse, for we were already in the lowest depths of earthly woe. Even should we be overtaken, and resubjected to slavery, this would be but to return to our old sufferings and sorrows and should death itself prove to be the price of our endeavor after freedom, what would that be but a welcome release to men, who had, all their lifetime, been killed every day, and "killed all the day long."

We have referred to our perils and hardships in escaping from slavery. We are happy to be able to say, that every year is multiplying the facilities for leaving the Southern prison house. The Liberty Party, the Vigilance Committee of New York,[7] individuals, and companies of individuals in various parts of the country, are doing all they can, and it is much to afford you a safe and a cheap passage from slavery to liberty. They do this however, not only at great expense of property, but at great peril of liberty and life. Thousands of you have heard, ere this, that, within the last fortnight, the precious name of William L. Chaplin has been added to the list of those, who, in helping you gain your liberty, have lost their own.[8] Here is a man, whose wisdom, cultivation, moral worth, bring him into the highest and best class of men—and, yet, he becomes a willing martyr for the poor, despised, forgotten slave's sake. Your remembrance of one such fact is enough to shed light and hope upon your darkest and most disponding moments.

Brethren, our last word to you is to bid you be of good cheer, and not to despair of your deliverance. Do not abandon yourselves, as have many thousands of American slaves, to the crime of suicide. Live! live to escape from slavery, live to serve God! Live till He shall Himself call you into eternity! Be prayerful—be brave—be hopeful. "Lift up your heads, for your redemption draweth nigh."

*The North Star,* September 5th, 1850

## AMERICAN SLAVERY LECTURE NO. VII

DELIVERED in Corinthian Hall, on Sunday Evening, Jan. 12th, 1851.[9]

I rise to give my seventh lecture on American slavery under feelings of very deep seriousness. The return of Henry Long to all the horrors of a life of endless slavery, has shrouded my spirit in gloom.[10] But a few days ago, he walked abroad in the streets of New York in the full enjoyment of freedom, his mind occupied with thoughts, hopes and aspirations becoming the mind of a virtuous freeman. But, in a moment, he has been snatched away by a hand more dreadful than that of death. His hopes and aspirations, plans and purposes, have been cut off and destroyed. From a man, he has fallen to a chattel, and instead of breathing the free air of New York, in the pride of his liberty and in the society of freemen, he is now doomed to the appalling conditions of a slave, and must drag out his life in Virginia, under all the horrors of the whip and fetter.

Henry Long is the second victim surrendered by New York under the inhuman and barbarous provisions of the fugitive slave act,[11] and there are some circumstances affecting his surrender which make it even more alarming and distressing than the case of James Haskel. The latter was arrested and delivered up in a most secret and hasty manner, without the legal and friendly aid which might have been rendered, despite the furious haste required by the fugitive slave act. The case of Long is different. Between the time of his arrest and the time of his surrender, there was an ample opportunity for rendering him all the assistance of which the law and the case would allow. His arrest was known, and his trial open to the public gaze. There was time for the vigilance of his friends to be exercised; and that vigilance, to a certain extent, was exercised. Yet Henry Long was surrendered, and, in broad daylight, dragged out of the city of New York, without even an attempt being made to rescue him.

It is stated that there was not a sign of "disturbance" when the unfortunate man was taken to the ferry from which he departed to the South, and that the only thing unusual in that vicinity at the time, was the appearance of Captain Isaiah Rynders,[12] parading about with a rifle in hand, swearing vengeance against abolitionists. If this be so, it is a shame and a scandal which the colored people of New York should seize the first opportunity to wash out. It is humiliating in the extreme, that, in a city with a colored population of more than twenty thousand, such a high-handed and daring atrocity could be perpetrated without any intervention on the part of any among them. I know not what would have been the chances of success had any attempt been made to rescue Henry Long.—It is possible that no chance of success appeared in this case. For the credit of the colored people alone, I hope that the latter is true. It ought not to be said of a people like those of New York, that they stood mute spectators of a scene which might well have roused the courage even of *dastards* to deeds of blood. Some explanation, some apology for the apparent indifference and utter inactivity manifested by the colored people of New York City, is demanded. I say again, I do *not* know what the chance of success would have been in an effort at the rescue of Henry Long, but this *I do know* that the absence of any attempt to break the jaws of the oppressor, and to rend the victim from the horrid clutch, will form the strongest possible ground of encouragement to other slave-hunters who may be disposed to prosecute their infamous business in New York City. I am free to say that nothing short of physical resistance will render the colored people of the North safe from the horrible enormities which must result from the execution of the fugitive slave law; and I had rather have heard that colored men had been beaten down by the two hundred policemen employed on the occasion, than that there should have been no manifestation of physical resistance to the re-enslavement of poor Long. My very blood chilled, and I felt myself degraded, when I read that the demand of the slave catcher for a sufficient force to remove Henry Long from New York was answered by Judge Judson to the effect that "he *apprehended no disturbance!*" "*No disturbance!*" Doom the innocent to perpetual bondage, and no fear of "disturbance!" Why, when a guilty felon is to be hanged, a murderous assassin, who, for the love of gold, has plunged his dagger into the heart of an innocent brother, such are the sympathies of human nature, and such is the proneness of men to forget the crime of the criminal in reflecting on his horrible fate, that, even in such a case, there is always danger of "disturbance" for his rescue, and provision made against such an occurrence. But here, in the case of an innocent man—a man unstained by any crime, and against whom there is not even the shadow of an allegation, we see him hurried away to a fate more terrible than death itself, and "no disturbance" on account of it is apprehended. This reveals a popular acquiescence in the execution of this inhuman law, which is at once disgraceful and heart-sickening—an acquiescence which will not fail to inspire with hope other two-legged bloodhounds who are meditating Northern excursions in pursuit of their prey. The contemplation of these things makes me sad. But more saddening still is the present aspect of the public mind throughout the North.

It is impossible not to see a determination on the part of men in high places to put down, if possible, all efforts made to promote anti-slavery sentiment in this country. Politicians in and out of the country, are evidently conspiring against the agitation of the question of slavery, and are exerting themselves to the utmost to quiet the public mind on the subject. Distinguished individuals, both of the Whig and Democratic parties, whose voices rang through the land last winter, proclaiming manly hostility to the slave power, are now as hushed as though slavery had ceased to exist, and the slave powers were no more. Meanwhile, the pulpit is sending forth sermons, in pamphlet form, boldly and shamelessly advocating obedience to the fugitive slave law, and, in the sacred name of Jesus Christ, defending the slave system.—The Rev. Dr. Lord, of Buffalo, in a sermon enjoining obedience to the fugitive slave bill, says: "But there is higher authority for the determination of this question, than anything we have yet suggested. The existence of domestic slavery was expressly allowed, sanctioned and regulated by the Supreme Law-giver, in that divine economy which he gave to the Hebrew state. The fact is open and undisputed. The record and proof of it are in the hands of every man who has in his possession a copy of the Bible. All the ingenuity of all the abolitionists in the United States can never destroy the necessary conclusion of this admitted divine sanction of slavery, that it is an institution which may lawfully exist, and concerning which governments may pass laws and execute penalties for their evasion or resistance." Dr. Lord is the minister of a Presbyterian Church in Buffalo; and so gratifying was the sermon, of which the above extract is a fair sample, that nineteen of the respectable gentlemen and Christians of his church sent him a letter, requesting it for publication. With this request it seems he cheerfully complied, and the sermon now appears before the public in a pamphlet of 39 pages. Another Doctor of Divinity, the Rev. Dr. Lathrop, of Auburn, has signalized himself by devoting "Thanksgiving day" to rebuking disobedience to the fugitive slave law, and exhorting his brother Christians to a faithful discharge of their slave-catching duties. On the same day, the Rev. Dr. Sharpe preached a sermon in Boston, to the same end; and we are informed that sundry learned Doctors of Divinity have come out on this as on *"the Lord's side,"* in the struggle for human freedom. Dr. Lathrop says that the fugitive slave law is the law of the land, "enacted by the powers that be," and that they are "ordained of God." *"What*, then," he asks, "is the duty of the Christian and the citizen?" and he adds—"We answer, that both patriotism and religion require that the law should be obeyed." "Suppose," says he, "that we deny the right of property in a human being, and insist upon it that one man has no moral right to hold another as his property, still, we must admit that, for the time being, he has a legal right, according to the constitution and laws of the State in which he lives. Other States entering into a confederacy with this one, have agreed that it may hold slaves as property, and manage its own internal concerns in its own way. The confederacy is entered into for the security of other and commanding and common interests, which are of paramount importance. If by any act of legislation of this confederated government they are required to restore to them that property to which they have a legal right, however much we may doubt the morality of that claim, or the law upon which it is founded, the duty of good citizenship, and the claims of true patriotism, would demand obedience to the law.—The responsibility in regard to the morality or the wisdom of the law, rests not with us. That lies somewhere else. But with us is the responsibility of obeying the laws of the land, which have been established by the powers that be, and that are ordained of God."

In a lecture delivered in this hall a few evenings ago, I undertook to show why abolitionists are often called infidels. If I did not satisfy my hearers on that occasion, with the causes which first led to that popular cry, the foregoing extracts may succeed in doing so. Here we have all that is sacred in heaven and earth—God, Christ and the

Apostles, the Bible, Christianity and patriotism, all blasphemously in support of slavery, and in justification of obedience to that concentration of hellish cruelty, the fugitive slave law.

I believe this audience will agree with me, that the true enemy of the Christian religion and of the Bible, is *not* he who uniformly appeals to them in support of justice, mercy and goodness—*not* he who regards them as on the side of the abused and enslaved, but rather he who, though clothed in sacerdotal robes, and assuming to be the chosen minister of God, *dares* to quote the Bible in defense of robbery and wrong. *Such* men do more in one hour to undermine the reverence of mankind for the Bible, than the most skillful infidel could effect in ages!

I do not believe that the Bible sanctions American slavery. I do *not* believe that Christ and his Apostles approved of slaveholding, nor of slave-catching. From the depths of my soul I appeal with confidence to the pages of Holy Writ, in behalf of my imbruted and plundered fellow-countrymen. Despite the teachings of American divines (slave though I have been), I will continue to look to God and to Christ for support in my humble efforts for the emancipation of my race. But here I will say, that *should* doctors of divinity ever convince me that the Bible sanctions American slavery, that Christ and his apostles justify returning men to bondage, *then* will I give the Bible to the flames, and no more worship God in the name of Christ, for of what value to men would a religion be which not only permitted, but enjoined upon men the enslavement of each other, and which would leave them to the sway of physical force, and permit the strong to enslave the weak? What better would such a religion be than black atheism, which knows no God? To defend slavery in the name of God, is simply to reduce mankind absolutely to the law of brute force. It places men in relation to each other on a footing of the wild beasts of the forests which live and prey upon each other. If you may enslave the black man in America, of course the black man may enslave the American in Africa, and as the Bible is made for all mankind, of course if it sanctions slavery at all, it may be quoted by the African priest in favor of enslaving the whites, with as much propriety as it can be quoted by the whites as authority for enslaving the blacks, and the God of the Bible would be at once the God of slavery to all mankind. The law of force would in this case take the place of the law of love, and he who could succeed in man-stealing on the most extensive scale, would best represent the attributes of the Divine mind.

But away with this revolting and blasphemous theory! And away with those hypocritical Doctors of Divinity! They are wolves in sheep's clothing—thieves and liars, who wrest and torture the pages of the Holy Bible to sanctify popular crimes!

The fact that such sentiments as those which I have quoted from Dr. Lord and Dr. Lathrop can be taught with impunity from Northern pulpits, implies a depth of moral debasement and blindness in the community beyond the power of human language to describe.

The responsibility of politicians for slavery, is great; but *infinitely greater* is the guilt of the American clergy. They frame a tangled web of arguments in support of slavery, of which politicians would never dream, and urge them with a show of piety which, in any other men, would but provoke popular contempt and scorn. Common men would be utterly ashamed to shield villainy under such sophistry. In discussing the question of American slavery, I would far rather encounter *twenty lawyers*, than one *Doctor of Divinity*, for if I should convict the former of self-contradiction and falsehood, blind as the public are, they would decide according to the facts; it is only the doctor of divinity who, skulking in the shadow of his priestly office, is able to affright the common people from forming an intelligent estimate of his character and conduct.

The abolitionists of the United States have been objected to on the score of using harsh language; but what language is sufficiently stern and denunciatory to characterize the conduct of men who, while acting as the constituted guardians of the public morality, and claiming the reverence and respect due to those who hold their commission from the most high God, yet bring the whole scope of their influence to the side of the oppressor against the oppressed, to prop up a system in which is combined every sin and pollution that has a name. When I speak of *such* men, I can find no more appropriate language than the words of our Savior to the Scribes and Pharisees, and if any here deem the language I have already used harsh, or denunciatory, I commend to them the burning words of our Savior, applied eighteen hundred years ago to the same class of men as those who are now standing in the way of the slave's redemption: "*Woe* unto you, Scribes, Pharisees, hypocrites, for ye pay tithe of mint, and anise and cummin, and have omitted the weightier matters of the law, judgment, mercy and faith. Ye blind guides, which strain at a gnat and swallow a camel. Woe unto you, Scribes and Pharisees, for ye are like unto whited sepulchures, which, indeed, appear beautiful outward, but are within full of dead men's bones, and all uncleanness. Ye serpents, ye generation of vipers, *how* can you escape the *damnation of hell?*"

It would be easy to preach a sermon from these passages of scripture, and to show their literal application to the pro-slavery church and clergy of our day; but this is, I hope, unnecessary, as I have already had much to say on the subject in a previous lecture.

I turn, therefore, for the present, from the pro-slavery church, and its clerical defenders of slavery. The slave has nothing to hope from either. They are moved only as they are moved upon by popular sentiment, and when *that* becomes anti-slavery, they *will* become anti-slavery, and will be among the first to abrogate to themselves the glory of the achievement.

Not many weeks ago, a State election took place in this State; and important anti-slavery results were said to be depending upon that election. The Whigs and Democrats came before the people with their respective claims. Hunt and Seymour were the candidates for Governor of the State.[13] Seymour was openly in favor of measures adopted by Congress as a complete statement of the slavery question. Hunt was represented as a Seward Whig, and, of course, as opposed to the fugitive slave act; but how little there was to choose between the two, may be seen by perusing the recent message of Governor Hunt. Not *one* word could be found in it condemning the immorality, the unhumanity, and the unconstitutionality of the fugitive slave law; there is not one word in it recommending the repeal or the modification of the atrocious enactment. There is not *one* word of dissatisfaction with regard to the law; not one word of apprehension for the safety of the colored citizens of this State, but there is to be found in it, what in all the circumstances must be regarded as a cheerful acquiescence in all its horrid provisions. The Governor says:

Notwithstanding the violent discussions which have agitated the country, and the wide diversity of opinion which exists in respect to the questions involved in the recent action of Congress, a general disposition is evinced to acquiesce in the measures referred to, and to regard them as a final settlement of these territorial controversies. The people of the State continue to indulge a strong desire that harmony and mutual good will may prevail between all portions of our widely extended Republic. They are a law-abiding people; they cherish the most friendly sentiment toward their brethren of the South, and have always conceded to the slave States the entire right to maintain and regulate Slavery within their own limits, and to exercise all those rights without abridgement or hindrance which the Constitution confers. More than this ought not to be claimed or expected.

The fugitive slave law is not named especially here; but it is easy to see when the Governor assured the State that the people of this State are a law-abiding people, and that there is no disposition to abridge and to hinder the slave-holding rights, which the Constitution is alleged to confer, that the fugitive slave law is in his mind, for that is the only measure in which resistance is likely to be made, and about which there is any serious dispute between the politicians of the North and South. Rightly to appreciate the tame and submissive character of this part of the Governor's message, it should be contrasted with the message of southern Governors. They are loud and boisterous in their accusations of the faithlessness on the part of the North, high and proud in their demands; there are *no fawning and sickly* expressions of friendship for the North; their love of union is ever held *subject* to their love of slavery. They care for the North just as they care for their *slaves*—only so far as they are served by them. This open, and aboveboard; and, if *not* generous, it is, at least, frank; and if we cannot honor the men of the South in adopting this policy, we certainly cannot despise them. Their tone is bold and uncompromising—we know *where* to find them, but *not so* with Northern politicians. They are ever anxious to be understood as a *most harmless* set of beings, taking the world as they find it, and especially desirous of peace and concord. With them, the Union is above all earthly blessings, and to save it, they are willing to sacrifice *liberty, justice,* and all manly independence; and although they have ever been repaid for their undue devotion and deference to their self-imposed task-masters, with the bitterest contempt and scorn, yet they have not even the spirit of the *"fugitive* slave" to make their escape. This readiness to concede everything to the South is not only disgraceful, but is a great *political mistake* on the part of the North. If there be one political truth more evident, and more frequently illustrated than another, it is, that concessions to slavery only invite new demands and encroachments. The more they get, the more they want, and the more tamely the North may submit, the more imperious and arrogant will be their Southern masters. Nothing is more ridiculous and absurd than to suppose that the restless and ambitious spirit of southern slave holders will be content with their present advantages, when they know that they can have more at any time when they shall make the demand.

There is no history extant in which is furnished a more striking illustration of what a few men can do in getting possession of political power, than in the history of the American Government.

The actual slaveholders are a mere fraction of the American people, and a very small minority of the people in the Southern States. Three hundred thousand is the largest estimate ever made of them, and I have seen calculations with great show of accuracy, putting their number at one hundred and fifty thousand; yet these men rule, speak for, and represent the whole fifteen Southern States, as completely as though there was not a white man in the whole South besides themselves. They are the governors and officers of the State, and they enjoy a complete monopoly of all that pertains to the government of the State. They mold the politics, the morality, and the religion of that entire section of country, and the white workingmen are but a step removed from the slaves in their servility to this lordly and imperious class of men.

*You*, who reside in the free States, can but *poorly* understand how absolute is the authority of slaveholders, and *how* abject is the servility of their white dependents in the slave States. There is scarcely a shadow of difference between the cringing obsequiousness of the slave to the slaveholder, and that of the poor white man who is not so fortunate as to own a slave. But the power of the slaveholder is not confined to the Southern States.

Slavery is the only interest represented by Southern men at the Capitol of the nation; and he is a fortunate man that is elected from the South, who is not himself a slaveholder. The purchase of Louisiana, her immense south-western territory, the millions expended upon Florida, the annexation of Texas, the war with Mexico, were all measures commenced and carried forward to their consummation by that *mere fraction* of the American people, the Southern slaveholders.

Governor Hunt, in his recent message, thus confesses the readiness in which New York has ever bowed to the arrogant dictations and imperious policy of Southern slaveholders; and he assures them of the continued contentment of New York, in her servile condition. He says:

"Great injustice is done in assuming that we have intended or now meditate encroachments upon the just rights of any portion of the Confederacy. During the entire period of our national history, the people of New York have manifested a spirit of kindly deference to the feelings and prejudices of our sister States, and a readiness to sacrifice everything for principle and honor for the sake of Union and concord. Their course has been distinguished by a broad spirit of nationality, elevated far above the indulgence of local views or sectional prejudices. The limits of this communication will not permit me to recall all the evidences in which our history abounds of the generous spirit of concession which New York has uniformly manifested as a prominent member of the Federal Union.

"For more than three-fourths of the period which has elapsed since the adoption of the Constitution, Southern statesmen, elevated by the aid of her voice, have filled the Presidential office. Every peaceful extension of the Southern territorial limits was made with her concurrence, and by successive steps all the State territory on the North American Continent was brought within the boundaries of the United States. Although every new acquisition diminished the relative weight of New York in the National Councils, she waived all views of State power or aggrandizement, and yielded to the consideration urged by other sections in favor of annexing the contiguous countries."

A more true and humiliating statement never dropped from the lips of any Governor of any sovereign State in this Union; and I put it to you, citizens of New York, *how long* will you continue to manifest a spirit of kindly deference to the feelings and prejudices of Southern slaveholders? *How long* will you allow yourselves to compromise the dignity of this "the Empire State," by making base concessions to the ever-hungry slave power, whose cry, like that of the voracious horse-leech is, "give, give, give?"

It would be interesting on this occasion, if I had time, to enter into the causes, and the means by which this small knot of tyrants have acquired such indisputable power in the councils of the nation; *how* they have drawn the reins of government into their own hands; *how* completely they have brought both political parties to do their bidding; and how utterly impossible it has been for Northern statesmen to withstand their influence. I say, it would be interesting if we could go into a minute description of the causes of these things, for it is a marvel, until now, how readily every great man from the North, has been made to bow the knee to this mysterious power. There is one obvious explanation of all this. There is *but one* interest in the South, I mean there is *but one* that can get represented in the Congress of the United States, and that is *slavery*. All other interests are cast into the shade by the colossal greatness of this *one*, and around this *all-absorbing* and *all-commanding* interest, both the great political parties of the South rally, and make common cause. The South is united as one man, and nothing diverts them from the one common object, which is the maintenance, prosperity and propagation of slavery. They talk of their *"peculiar institutions,"* and about *"Southern rights,"* but the only thing meant by these euphonious terms, is *"slavery."* For this they are ready to sacrifice, "the Union," "the Constitution," the fraternal feelings between North and South, and the glory of this great Republic. They make no hesitation in declaring to the world that upon that question, there is but one party in the whole South; while the North is divided and subdivided, the South is united; and it is her unity of action which must account for the success which has attended her in every grand controversy which has occurred in the politics and legislation of this country.

Until the North shall be as true to liberty as the South has been to slavery; until she shall cease to worship the Union at the expense of everything good and great; until she shall be inspired with a true self-respect, and shall be represented in Congress by independent and high-minded men, men to whom Presidential honors are utterly worthless in comparison with an honest and faithful discharge of their duties as *men*, as *patriots* and as *Christians*, until then, the North must continue to be the mere cringing vassal of the South, and she must expect to receive the *wages of her servitude*, in an accumulation of kicks and disgrace.

*The North Star,* January 16, 1851

# THOMAS SIMS CONSIGNED TO SLAVERY[14]

Let the Heavens weep and let Hell be merry! Slavery has triumphed! Daniel Webster has at last obtained from Boston, the cradle of liberty, a living sacrifice, to appease the slave God of the American Union. A man guilty of no crime; and charged with none, has been seized at the point of the bayonet, and doomed to a lot more terrible than death. From the heights of freedom, he has been hurled into the depths of slavery; to gratify three of the most infernal propensities of man's malicious heart—*pride, avarice,* and *revenge.* Yes! we say *revenge—blood-thirsty, murderous* revenge. Had not this been the actuating motive, the victim might have been ransomed. *Money* could have sacrificed *avarice; success* might have soothed wounded pride; nothing can appease a slaveholder's revenge but the torn back, and warm blood of his helpless victim.

Thomas is to be made an example of; to deter slaves from escaping the hateful house of bondage. He is to be tortured for the amusement of his tormentors; and to strike terror to the hearts of his trembling companions in bondage. It is *Boston, civilized, refined, Christian,* and humane Boston, that has furnished this sacrifice! Great God! wilt thou not visit for these things? Wilt thou not be avenged on such a nation as this?

Amid the deep distress and anguish which this sad occurrence has brought us, there are points of consolation connected with it, which while they do not help the man now on the highway to slavery, serve to mitigate the disheartening effect of his surrender. He was carried off to slavery yet not with ease. He was overcome; yet not without a struggle, both on his own part and on the part of his friends. As soon as he found himself in the hands of a legalized kidnapper, he drew out his knife and stabbed the villain, although not fatally. Overcome by superior force, he was imprisoned in the Court-House to prevent a rescue on the part of his friends. The temple of justice was literally surrounded by chains and bayonets.

The horrid men-hunters only escaped a deserved death by the precaution of never allowing themselves to walk forth in broad daylight unprotected by an armed police, and the government, (strong and mighty as it is,) did not even venture to confront the burning indignation of the travelling public of New England, by taking the innocent man in fetters, by the usual travelling conveyances through the land; but under cover of night, (like a band of pirates on the coast of Africa,) they hurried their victim off to the lonely sea, surrounded by hired ruffians armed to the tooth, were towed away from the sight of humanity, by a steamer provided for the purpose.

These and many other circumstances, which we have not space to narrate, more than slightly relieve the dark transaction of its disheartening effect upon those who had fondly hoped that Boston, at least would escape the damning infamy of returning a man to slavery under the horrible provisions of the new Fugitive Slave Law.

For our part, shocked and sorrow stricken as we are at the recapture of Thomas Sims, we can confess to no surprise nor disappointment at this result. From the first, we believed, (and we declared that belief, even when the Fugitive Slave bill was first introduced into the Senate by Mr. Mason of Virginia,) that the law, once enacted, would never want villains to execute it. If we are surprised at all, it is that so strong a demonstration was made in Boston against its execution. It is gratifying to believe that nothing but this utter fruitlessness of any attempt to rescue Thomas Sims prevented his friends from rushing through the bristling bayonets of his captors, to liberate him.

The government, however, had their plans *too* well adjusted to make any such onset successful. The sole hope that we have of defeating the execution of the Fugitive Slave law, (while it remains of law,) is grounded in the belief that there are a few fugitives still remaining to be recaptured whose regard for their own lives and the lives of others, will not be so strong as to hinder their shooting dead any legalized robber who shall lay hand upon them.

The work, to be done successfully, must be done instantly; there must be no parleying. As soon as a man knows that there is a warrant out for him, he should place himself within his castle, and perish in his own defense, if need be. In these troublous times no colored man should be without arms in his house, if not upon his person. The having of weapons is of some consequence, and will inspire the disposition to use them when the time comes. A law that cannot be executed but by exposing the officers authorized to execute it to deadly peril, cannot long stand. — F.D.

*Frederick Douglass' Paper*, April 17, 1851


## TO GERRIT SMITH

Rochester, May 21st, 1851

My Dear Sir:

It needs no ghost to assure me, that I am to be made for a time, an object of special attack. I am not afraid of it, do not personally dread it, nor shrink from it, and yet I regret it and am pained in view of it. I know too well the temper of my old companions to hope to escape the penalty which all others have paid who have ventured to differ from them. The leaders in the American Anti-slavery Society are strong men, noble champions in the cause of human freedom, and yet they are not, after all, the most charitable in construing the motives of those who see matters in a different light from themselves. Insinuations have already been thrown out, and will be again.

There are two ways of treating assaults from that quarter and of that character. They can be replied to, or be allowed to spend their force unanswered. Judgment is needed here. A word of advice from you will at any time be most welcome. You will do me the kindness, and the cause of truth and freedom the service of giving a little attention to any controversy which may arise between my old friends and me, in regard to my present position on the *constitutional* question. That my ground is correct I am satisfied, and can easily, I think, defend it against the strongest. But I am persuaded that the war will be waged not against opinions, but *motives*, especially if the union of papers which we contemplate shall go into effect.[15] If in this, time shall prove me correct, I shall need a word from you which I am sure you will generously give. You can prove that even in the *North Star* more than two years ago I gave up the ground that the Constitution when strictly construed is a proslavery document and that the only point which prevented me, from declaring at that time, in favor of voting and against the disunion ground related to the intentions of the framers of the Constitution. I had not made up my mind then, as I have now, that I am only in reason and conscience bound to learn the intentions of those who framed the Constitution—*in the Constitution itself.*[16]

You yourself do know that before I could have had the slightest hope of affecting the union of papers which we now contemplate that I distinctly assured you, of the change in my opinion which I have now publicly avowed. For months I have made no secret of my present opinion. I talked the matter over with S. S. Foster. I told him soon after leaving your house this spring that I no longer held to the no voting theory. I assured S. J. May of the same thing. The only reason which I had for not publicly avowing before, the change in my mind was a desire to do so in open court. I espoused the doctrine among my old companions. I wished to reject it in their presence. I write from the office or I am sure that my wife would unite with Miss Griffiths[17] (who is industriously wielding her pen at another desk) in sending love to yourself and Dear Lady.

Your most truly,
Frederick Douglass

*Gerrit Smith Papers, George Arents Research Library, Syracuse University*

## TO GERRIT SMITH

Rochester, May 28th, 1851

My Dear Sir:

Pardon me for writing so often. I send this to say that, I have made the proposal to our friend, Mr. Thomas, which you suggest in the letter now before me; I have offered him the freedom of the office, assistant Editorship, and six dollars per week for his services. If he accepts this arrangement, the union of papers will be complete and we shall soon see the new paper afloat. I shall need, to begin with, four hundred dollars, to provide things suited to enlargement and beauty. This will be all sufficient. I do not wish to go in debt at the commencement of the enterprise, and I shall save ten percent by paying cash, for my new press and type. I tremble to ask it, and yet I know not what better to do. Will you be so good as to let me have *two hundred of that sum?* If so I will raise the other two, and you shall, if all be well, see the new sheet unfurled on the first of July, the day of cheap postage.

Most sincerely & gratefully your friend,
Frederick Douglass

I am sure that I can work with Thomas, and that together we can do true men's work in the cause of "*All rights for All*."[18] F.D.

*Gerrit Smith Papers, George Arents Research Library, Syracuse University*

# TO GERRIT SMITH

Rochester, May 29th, 1851

My Dear Sir:

I have no answer yet from our Friend Thomas. I wish it may be favorable when it comes. Should it be otherwise, I will not urge the union further, but press my "Star" onward with all the means I can command. I do not mean that the "Star" shall die at any rate, nor shall it take one step backwards as to the antislavery character of the U.S. Con. . . . nor of the duty of political action on the subject of slavery. I have got letters from Ward and have replied to it this morning. I think he will accept of the union. I offer him, first all the donations and collections he can obtain for the paper as a travelling agent. I offer him fifty cents for every cash yearly subscriber he shall obtain for the paper, and half that for half-yearly subscribers. I offer him, three dollars per week for his services as Corresponding Editor of the paper. Still further I offer him what you Gerrit Smith Esqr. shall designate as a fair price for his subscription list.

Mr. Thomas misapprehended me in one or two particulars. I was not surprised that he held his services so high, or so low, but was puzzled to know where the money was to come from to pay him. I told him that I preferred Rochester to Syracuse, as the place of publication.

A remark in Mr. Thomas's letter makes it necessary for me to say, that, in the event of the union of papers, you may hold me morally, intellectually, and mechanically responsible for the character of the paper. However important I may, in that event, deem the services of my friend, Mr. Thomas, and how much soever, I may avail myself of his friendly counsel, I shall not put the helm in other hands than my own. It is proper to be thus explicit to avoid future misunderstanding.

Julia Griffiths sends, with my own, her sincere regards to yourself and Mrs. Smith,

Most truly yours,
Frederick Douglass

*Gerrit Smith Papers, George Arents Research Library, Syracuse University*

## TO GERRIT SMITH

Rochester, June 4th 1851

My Dear Sir:

Mr. Thomas has *almost* signified his consent to the "union." He is only inflexible on one point, to wit place of publication. I have sent him a letter, giving reasons for establishing the new paper here, and expect soon to have an answer favorable to that proposition. The "union" I now consider a fixed fact. I have no word from Brother Ward since I wrote to you last. He will, I am sure, come out on the right side, and form a strong force in the new team.[19]

The paper must appear as early as the first of July. It should come forth with all the marks of strength, which can be given it. Your own highly valued name must not be wanting on the first sheet. Thomas and Ward and (I) myself, must come forth in our best clothes, and look as trim as any three officers in the French army. There must be nothing clumsy, hasty or awkward in our *debut.*

The paper must be clean, white and strong. The ink pure, black and glossy. The matter must be arranged with taste, skill and order, and our columns must be free from all typographical, grammatical, orthographical, and rhetorical errors and blunders.

The matter shall be such as shall secure the approval of your discriminating judgement.

To the necessary preliminary work. The new type should be bought at once. The new paper engaged at once. I ask for two hundred dollars from you to begin with, the rest I will raise myself.

Most truly and gratefully yours,

Frederick Douglass

*Gerrit Smith Papers, George Arents Research Library, Syracuse University*

## TO GERRIT SMITH

Rochester, June 10th, 1851

My Dear Sir:

I am most thankful for your ready compliance with my request for two hundred dollars, and, also, for the good letter you have sent me for my new paper. I have been absent from home, otherwise, I should have written immediately on the receipt of your letter, containing the money order.

It will be impossible to get the new paper out before the 26th June. The prospectus for it will be published today in the "Star" and will be at once forwarded to you. I do hope you will be pleased with it.

Julia Griffiths, my faithful friend, and co-worker, (to whom I am greatly indebted for many lessons of wisdom,) is all zeal in our new enterprise.

The call of L[iberty] Party convention shall appear next week. Thomas shall be written to come on here next Monday. In great haste

Yours most faithfully and affectionately,

Frederick Douglass

*Gerrit Smith Papers, George Arents Research Library, Syracuse University*

## TO MESSRS S. E. SEWALL, WENDELL PHILLIPS, THEODORE PARKER, COMMITEE

Rochester, June 11th, 1851

Gentlemen:

I am deeply sensible of the honor you have done me, by inviting me to join you, in the token of respect to George Thompson you propose to give in Boston, on the eve of his departure, from the United States to his native land. To participate how humbly soever in such a demonstration would afford me sincere pleasure. But I cannot be present, and I much regret that I cannot.

In common with all the Sable Sons of America, I owe George Thompson, a mighty debt of gratitude, respect and Love: His labors in behalf of my afflicted, enslaved and slandered people, have been productive of good, to an extent, which eternity alone can fully disclose. My heart grows warm at the mention of his name. That name is associated in my mind with the masses of the noblest benefactors of suffering man. There were two courses plainly set before George Thompson, when he landed on the shores of this Republic in the autumn of 1850.[20] He was a free man. He was not compelled to adopt any given course. There are men, many of them, who seem doomed by virtue of their very organization, to a limited and contracted sphere of action. In them the ability to wish is present, but the ability to do, is absent. George Thompson belongs not to this class. Long before he came to this country, his Philanthropy, zeal, industry and splendid genius, rendered him before the whole civilized world, a light of surpassing brightness, a gem greatly to be coveted, a prize worth securing.

Wealth, honor, and ease invited him to their sumptuous entertainments, only asking as a condition that he should array himself in the smartest garments of worldly prudence. Had he complied, instead of being assailed, maligned, calumniated, mobbed and threatened with assassination as he has been, he would have been welcomed, applauded, honored, caressed, and hailed everywhere, as a distinguished guest from one end of this Union to the other. His early antislavery sentiments, would have been charitably forgiven, as those of Theobold Matthew and Daniel Webster have been, and his course might have been one series of brilliant demonstrations. But George Thompson had a heart. He saw the poor, weak, emaciated bondmen in chains, his heart was touched by the mournful wail. Wealth, luxury, and ease lost their gilded charms. He turned his back upon the scorner, and his face to the despised, and generously gave himself to toil. With the disinterested spirit of the Israelite deliverer, he preferred to suffer affliction with the people of God, to enjoying the pleasures of sin for a season.

Honor him who is an honor to humanity. He is a man of many millions. We do not often meet his like, a miracle of true courage, daunted by no danger, disheartened by no opposition, a moral hero, not less than an intellectual giant, whom all the reproaches of a mighty nation have been unable to silence or subdue.

God bless George Thompson, and methinks I hear from every slave dungeon in the land a responsive amen.

I am, Gentlemen, with many regrets, that I cannot be with you

Very truly yours,

Frederick Douglass

A good old Farmer, an abolitionist of course, Gideon Ramsdell, to whom I have just read this letter, gave me for Mr. Thompson the enclosed two dollars. F.D.

*Frederick Douglass Ms., New York Historical Society*

## "STOP MY PAPER"

This is never a very agreeable order to an Editor. There are few more disagreeable, especially to those who can hardly keep their heads above water; but there are few editors who are not sometimes obliged to receive and obey such orders, and we have, therefore, all the consolation of company in our misery.

It was not be expected that all our readers would see "eye to eye" with us in regard to the United States Constitution, nor were we unprepared for a much greater curtailment of our subscription list than has yet taken place; still a considerable number of our old subscribers have dropped out, some of them, we are sorry to say, in a manner so *un*magnanimous and spiteful as to show that they, at least, would gladly see our paper die for want of support as a punishment for our anti-slavery *heresy*. We deny no man's right to discontinue our paper; certainly not, if his arrears are paid up, a condition which has not been scrupulously observed in every instance by their requiring us to *"stop their papers."* Meanness is no part of the character of an abolitionist— dishonesty *certainly* is not: yet to stop a paper without paying arrears, is both mean and dishonest. Mean, because the party to whom the money is due is almost destitute of the power to collect it; dishonest, because it is refusing to pay a just debt, and keeping back the wages of the laborer by fraud. We say again, we do not deny the right to discontinue a paper. If a subscriber becomes convinced that a paper for which he subscribes has ceased to be the useful paper for which he subscribed, and instead of being the means of propagating truth, justice and humanity, it has become the detestable instrument of error and falsehood, there is no question as to his right or his duty to abandon such a paper; nay, even to make war upon it, and seek its extinction by all honorable measures. That ours is not such a journal as that described, we plead the fact that our columns are open as well to those who differ from us, as to those who agree with us; and if we propagate error, it is accompanied with the condition that "truth is left free to combat it." No lover of truth, therefore, is obliged by his love of truth to abandon our paper, merely because the opinions of its editor are not in complete harmony with his own. A contrary doctrine would reduce the freedom of the press to a mere name, and make the very term liberty of opinion, a detestable mockery.

We do not make these remarks because we have not full confidence in the good sense and magnanimity of most of our readers. The majority, at least, see and feel that the claims of "Frederick Douglass' Paper" to their sympathy and support, do not rest merely upon the fact of the editor's agreement with their views of the United States Constitution. To them, there is an obvious desirableness that this paper should be sustained: the fact that it is edited by a fugitive slave, by one who has endured the hardships, the trials, and degradation of slavery; by one whose education has been gained without the aid of schools, snatched, as it were, by the way-side, as he was being hurried along by the driver's lash; the fact that he is identified with those who encounter a storm of prejudice and malignity, such as perhaps no nations, (the Jews excepted,) were ever called to endure.—These facts, with other considerations, command the sympathy of the generous in our efforts to bear aloft the banner in the grand contest for freedom. It is in these circumstances more than all others that we attribute the success of our enterprises thus far. If our readers were all of this generous description, our paper would be easily sustained and much of the reproach which has accumulated for ages on our unfortunate and inflicted people would be gradually removed. The existence of the paper itself would stand as an incontestable refutation of the oft-repeated slander of natural inferiority.

We need not say that we urgently desire the prosperity and perpetuity of our journal on other than selfish grounds. The paper has a great work to do for the slave, for the free colored people and for all men, for its sympathies are not limited to any particular color, creed, class, or crime. It aims to obtain "all rights for all," and to promote the happiness of all.

In conclusion, (pardon a little boasting,) if we have one subscriber who had conceived the idea, and has flattered himself with the fancy that he can dishearten us and control our opinion by withdrawing his patronage or by inducing others to do so, he has altogether mistaken the material upon which it is his purpose to operate. Our views do not depend upon the success of our paper. No dread of returning to manual labor is before our eyes. He who has followed the plow year after year in the corn-fields of Maryland, who has been taught the use of the spade, rake, and hoe under the whip of the man-driver; he who has caulked ships in the ship-yards of Baltimore, and has there been the drudge of a hundred masters, boring, driving, turning and carrying timber at the command of them all, and all this without the hope of a reward, (unless the exemption from cruel flogging be so considered;) he who has rolled oil casks, stowed ships, sawed wood, swept chimneys, and labored at the bellows in New Bedford for a living, until his hands became hard like horns, has, we say, no dread of returning to manual labor, bringing, as he well knows it does manly independence, sound sleep, and a good appetite.—If, therefore, the time should come which should make it necessary to abandon our paper, "the world is still before us where to choose," and we are ready for any alternative but the relinquishment of our opinions to gain the support of mean, narrow-minded and tyrannical subscribers. But our paper will not "down" at the bidding of any, and we appeal, in this connection, to the liberal and spirited readers and friends of our paper, to stand by us, and to give us the needful aid to place it beyond the apprehension of failure. Let each subscriber pay up what is due to us, and exert himself and herself to extend the circulation of our paper and the enterprise will speedily be "set in safety from him who pulleth at him."

*Frederick Douglass' Paper*, June 24, 1851

# IS THE UNITED STATES CONSTITUTION FOR OR AGAINST SLAVERY?

After the very considerable amount of skirmishing which has already taken place with Mr. Johnson, Mr. Treat, the *Pennsylvania Freeman*. &c., on the outer border of this field of inquiry, we may, perhaps, venture to solicit the attention of our indulgent readers while we attempt something more thorough, and we hope more decisive against the errors and assumptions which have been so imposingly marshaled against us.

Let no one imagine that this is either an unnecessary or an unprofitable controversy. So to regard it would be a great mistake.—The question of the constitutionality or the unconstitutionality of slavery involves the solution of other vital and important questions—questions which come home to the bosom of every abolitionist who desires to oppose slavery consistently and effectively. It involves the question as to whether abolitionists shall be restricted in their instrumentalities to pen and tongue, or whether they may wield against slavery the press, and the living speaker, and all the powers of the Constitution and Government. If we are correct in this, all will see the desirableness of having the question so decided as to leave abolitionists at liberty to use the most effective measures for the abolition of slavery.—The case is urgent; humanity is bleeding; ages of suffering and of wrong, cry, trumpet-tongued for redress; everything in morals, religion and politics, which can reasonably be made available to the grand consummation ought to be seized upon without hesitation.

It may be said that this is not a motive favorable to a candid consideration of the subject. We must not hope to find the Constitution right, the intention and motives of the framers and adopters of the Constitution right, lest, in wishing to find the character of the Constitution anti-slavery, we should accommodate our conclusions to our wishes. Now, it does seem to me that the error is quite on the other hand: there seems to be a resolute determination to see slavery in the Constitution, although it is nowhere to be found there, for nothing short of such resolute determination can account for the pertinacity with which our opponents insist upon it. It does seem to us highly commendable to take the most favorable possible view of the motives and intentions of men, and especially of those men who lived in the stormy and trying time in which the Constitution was orginated and adopted. Such a view is not incompatible with a just and intelligent judgment of the case in controversy, since it assumes no infallibility in men, but merely that there is in human nature a little more of honesty than knavery. It makes innocence the rule and criminality the exception, and God help the perishing world if this be not just and commendable charity.

If, instead, the Constitution be for slavery, if it has recognized and established the relation of master and slave; and if all who vote and take office under that instrument are the bound and sworn enemies of the imbruted slaves, are required by their obligations as citizens, to be the allies of slaveholders; to become the watch-dogs of the plantation; the blood-hounds to track and ferret out absconding humanity; the mere bodyguards of human fleshmongers, (revengeful, relentless and barbarous as they are) then we freely admit that reason, humanity, religion and morality alike demand that we do spurn and fling from us, with all possible haste and holy horror, that accursed Constitution, and that we labor, directly and earnestly, for revolution, at whatever cost and at whatever peril.

But who does not see that this position is fraught with imminent danger and disadvantage, and that it ought not to be assumed but from absolute moral necessity. It imposes upon the anti-slavery reformer the overwhelming work of abolishing the government, as a condition of abolishing slavery, and even when the first work is done, the theory of dissolution, as a remedy, leaves the slave still in his chains, to work out his deliverance through all the horror of blood and carnage. Still, we say, dark, gloomy and cheerless as is the work of "dashing this government in pieces," (bound as the parties to it are by geography, by language, by commerce, by interest, by railroads, by electric wires, by lakes and rivers, mountains and oceans, by postal arrangements, and by ten thousand religious and social ties,) yet, if the Constitution be the haggard and damning thing which it is alleged to be, duty to the enslaved shows no other path for the feet of the abolitionist but that leading to revolution, and *that* we are bound to follow, though the dungeon and the scaffold stare us in the face. But are the friends of emancipation in the country shut up to that dreadful alternative? Are they compelled by the nature of the case to assume the ungraceful and odious attitude of anarchists or to deny God, and to trample upon their heaven-ordained principles? To each of these questions our opponents say YES; and to each of them, we, on the other hand, say NO.

Let us to the inquiry. The *Pennsylvania Freeman* and those who agree with it, plant themselves upon what seems to them an impregnable basis—the *intention* of the framers and the adopters of the Constitution, and upon the uniform practice of our pro-slavery government under the Constitution. There they take their stand, and with amazing dogmatism and superciliousness pronounce all who differ from them as being *"pitiable and ridiculous."* But the *Freeman* shall speak for itself, and not in curtailed sentiments and chopped up paragraphs, but in sufficient length to afford the reader full means of understanding the argument as well as the position to which the *Freeman* assumes:

We can hardly conceive of a fact in law or history being proved more conclusively to an impartial mind, than is the fact that the Constitution was intended to protect slavery and does so protect it, in the points wherein we accuse it. A denial of it, and attempt to disprove, any other historical fact could scarcely seem more unreasonable.

The language of these debated clauses not only casts no doubt upon our construction but confirms it. The terms employed to describe slaves, ("persons held to service," from whom labor was "legally due," &c., and "persons imported,") had for fifty years before, and has ever since, been used in the slave laws of the South to describe slaves. It was used thus in the Ordinance of 1787, where it is directly applied to *slavery*, in the Fugitive law of '93, and in that of 1850, where Mr. Douglass and every man of common sense and intelligence *knows* that it applies to *slaves*. He and Mr. Spooner may spend ink and paper till they are grey, in trying to prove that the Fugitive slave law has no reference to slaves, and their success will be to make themselves pitiable and ridiculous. To us, it is melancholy to see men of their powers of intellect and capabilities for usefulness, wasting time and strength in such impracticable theories and frivolous absurdities.—And yet as a means of showing more clearly the absurdity of their whole argument, we are not sorry for their acknowledgment that consistency compels them to put the Fugitive Slave Law and the Constitution in the same category, and give an anti-slavery construction to both or neither.

But not only is the language of the pro-slavery clauses of the Constitution such as custom had then and has ever since made applicable to slaves, but, were it ambiguous, its meaning would be fixed beyond reasonable doubt, by the direct and public testimony of its authors, who surely ought to know their own meaning—the debates upon the adoption of the Constitution in the National and State conventions, the legislation, the judicial and executive action under it in the Federal and State governments, through the whole course of our National existence; and by the uniform acquiescence of the people in such an understanding.

Well, now, let us in a familiar way begin with the beginning of our text. "We can hardly conceive," says the *Freeman*," of a fact in law or history being proved more conclusively, than is the fact that the Constitution was intended to protect slavery." It is indirectly here affirmed with particular emphasis, that "history proves that the Constitution was intended to protect slavery."

This is decidedly a loose statement, and needs considerable pruning. We might ask our excellent friend, to tell us who the persons were who intended that the Constitution should protect slavery? We might ask him to give us the name of the author of that history who has so conclusively proved that the Constitution was intended to protect slavery; and being a little more severe, and to save time, we might ask the particular page upon which we shall find written in plain, *unmistakable* English, that the Constitution was intended to protect slavery. But we will not be unnecessarily exacting, nor must we, on the other hand, deal playfully with the *Freeman*. The oration of Mr. Noodle was, evidently, too much for him, and anything further in that line might prove that additional straw to the camel. The truth is (and the *Freeman* knows it,) that he has only dignified tradition with the honored name of history; the former being little suited to the use he proposed to make of it.

A grave constitutional question is not to be settled by apocryphal tradition. But let us call this tradition history, out of compliment to the *Freeman*, and we shall find many conflicting versions about the very point which is so conclusively proved. For instance, the late Mr. Calhoun held the radical doctrine, deduced of course, from history that slavery is co-extensive with the Constitution of the United States, and that slaveholders had a right to carry their slaves into any part of the United States, and that the right to property in slaves stood precisely upon the same constitutional basis as any other property. He held that the Constitution was intended to secure slaveholders an equality of political power with the Free States; and he clung to his opinion with a martyr's grip. This is version number one.

By another party, scattered over the entire United States, it is held that, by the Constitution of the U.S., the people of this country have no right to interfere with slavery in any way whatsoever, neither to uphold it nor to abolish it; that the framers and adopters of the Constitution intended to leave slavery just where they found it, strictly a State institution, which should neither be regarded with favor nor disfavor by the General Government, but that it should fall or flourish by the voice of the individual States in which it is located. This is version number two.

Opposed to both these versions, is that held by a very influential party North, East, and West. They tell us that the founders of this Government intended that the Constitution should promote the freedom and happiness of all the people of the U.S.; that contributing to the extension and perpetuity of slavery was never dreamed of by the men of the Revolution, and their immediate descendants; but that, on the contrary, the fathers of the Revolution sought to limit, to circumscribe, and to hasten the extinction of slavery. This is version number three.

"We can hardly conceive of a fact in law or history being proved more conclusively to an impartial mind, than is the fact that the Constitition was intended to protect slavery, and does so protect it in the points where we accuse it." This is the *Freeman's* version. All these versions are more or less based upon that sort of evidence which the *Freeman* indirectly calls history. The absurdity of relying on such evi-

dence is sufficiently manifest in the fact that no two versions agree.—
But as we are taken to history to decide the question, it might appear
shrinking if we did not furnish our version also. We give it readily
with confidence in its truth.

In reading the sentiments of the most influential men of the
period, and to which the Constitution was framed and adopted, it is
evident that slavery was looked upon as a great evil—not merely regarded with aversion by the North, but by many of the most distinguished men at the South. The writings of Washington, Franklin,
Jefferson, Adams, Madison, Monroe, Hamilton, Luther Martin, Patrick Henry, John Jay, and a host of other great men, fathers of the
Republic, all go to establish this conviction; and whoever else might
have intended that the Constitution should protect slavery, there were
those among the most illustrious in the country who entertained no
such intention.

Another thing, we take to be true—that the statesmen of that
early period held slavery to be an expiring instituion. We doubt if
there were more than a dozen men in the Convention that framed the
Constitution who did not expect that slavery in this country would
cease forever long before the year 1851. Nor is there anything in the
language of the Constitution which casts a shadow of a doubt upon this
version. There is, in our mind, every reason to believe that the framers
of the Constitution intended that it should permanently protect the
freedom of every human being in the U.S. The great principle which
they laid down as the fundamental objects of the Government and the
completeness with which they have excluded every word sanctioning
the right of property in man, is no slight testimony in proof of the
intention to make the Constitution a permanent liberty document. But
let us quit intentions and come to the language of the Constitution of
the U.S., for it is *here* (and we wish we could beat it into the heads of
our opponents) that the question is to be decided. It is not to this
tradition nor that intention that we are to look, for an authoritative
settlement of the point in dispute. We at once throw before our readers
all the alleged slaveholding clauses of the Constitution, and which
prove, according to the *Freeman*, that the Constitution was intended to
protect slavery:

Art. 1, Sect. 2. Representatives and direct taxes shall be apportioned
among the several States, which may be included within this Union, according to their respective numbers, which shall be determined by adding to the

whole number of free persons, including those bound to service for a term of years, and excluding Indians not taxed, *three fifths of all other persons.*

Art. 1, Sect. 8. Congress shall have power to suppress insurrections.

Art. 1, Sect. 9. The migration or importation of such persons, as any of the States now existing, shall think proper to admit, shall not be prohibited by the Congress, prior to the year one thousand eight hundred and eight; but a tax or duty may be imposed on such importation, not exceeding ten dollars for each person.

Art. 4, Sect. 2. No person, held to service or labor in one State, under the laws thereof, escaping into another, shall, in consequence of any law or regulation therein, be discharged from such service or labor, but shall be delivered up on claim of the party to whom such service or labor may be due.

Just run your eye over these clauses again, and ask yourself, if, by any just understanding of the English language, one word in the forgoing can be received as "intended to protect slavery."

Here are four articles. We give them all, because all have been referred to by our opponents, as fixing the proslavery character of the Constitution, although Art. 1st, Sec. 9, has long since expired by its own limitation, and no longer imposes any duty or obligation upon anybody. Art. 1st, Sec. 8th, Congress shall have power . . . to suppress insurrections, may also be read out of the lists; for it is only by the most extravagant and far-fetched reasoning that any man can be brought to believe that this clause was intended to "protect slavery." For one, we are very glad this clause is in the Constitution. To our thinking, there is no part of the Constitution from which slaveholders have more to apprehend, than from this.—John Quincy Adams, the most renowned statesman America has produced, gave it as his opinion, twelve years ago, that this clause of the Constitution confers upon Congress the right in certain contingencies to abolish slavery in the States. With a sound anti-slavery public sentiment, a pure anti-slavery party in power, the best thing which could happen would be a contingency in which Congress would be called upon to exercise this power conferred by this article. The slave's chains would be broken, and liberty would be proclaimed throughout the land.—The *Freeman* may say that this would be acting in bad faith with the slaveholder; that after promising to aid him in holding the slave, we use the power obtained by the promise to emancipate him. The answer to this is, that we have made no such promise. The Constitution requires none such. Many people read this article as if it read, Congress shall have power to subject slaves to the control and wishes of their masters, but how remote is this from the true reading of this article. The obligation imposed upon Congress is plainly this, and only this, to suppress insurrections, but incident to this is the power to remove the cause of insurrection. If, therefore, Congress shall come to regard as we have now come to regard the whole system of slavery to be a grand system of domestic violence, it will be the duty of Congress to abolish the evil in all its ramifications. If slaveholders intended otherwise, their intention was wicked, and contrary to the spirit and letter of the Constitution, and is by no means entitled to respect or regard. But, in reply to this position, the *Freeman* quotes Dr. Paley:

"Promises are to be performed in that spirit in which the promiser apprehended at the time the promised received it."

The rule here laid down may be well enough for the case to which it applies, but it is wholly without pertinence in the administration of the powers granted by the federal Constitution; first, because the Constitution is the record of its own intention; and second, because outside of that instrument we shall find conflicting and irreconcilable intentions. One state may have adopted the Constitution, intending that it should subserve one end; while another may have adopted it intending that it should serve another and quite a different end.

Then, again, how are we to know now, or a century hence, what were the motives and intentions of the various parties to the Constitution of the U.S.A. Nothing is more evident than that as slavery becomes strong, the pretensions of slaveholders range higher and broader, and their claims to be protected under the Constitution become more and more unreasonable and audacious. From every view of this subject, we are convinced that the only practical course is that which finds the intention of those who adopted the Constitution in the Constitution itself. The opposite argument is destructive of all written constitutions, covenants and agreements. If we are to be governed by supposed apprehensions, and not by the words of the bond, the bond is of no use whatever. The *Freeman* quotes many authorities, showing that great weight ought to be attached to the uniform practice of courts, contemporaneous usage, and history. This, too, is all well enough in the proper place, but cannot be of force when a foul, haggard, and damning crime like slavery is to have thrown over it the panoply of law.

When such an outrage is meant to be perpetrated, the intention must be expressed with irresistible clearness. There must be no ambiguity about it. The ugly monster must be there, with all his frightful peculiarities, open, clear, palpable and unmistakable.

On the side of nature, right, liberty and humanity, the judge, jury and advocate may make the circuit of the globe for evidence, but villainy is an exception, and the rules of legal interpretation hem it in on every side. We must now stop abruptly. We commenced this article when quite feeble, and our strength now fails us, so that we are unable to meet the expectation created by the first sentence of this article. We shall return to the subject again, Providence permitting.

*Frederick Douglass' Paper*, July 24, 1851

## COLORED AMERICANS, COME HOME!

We have felt in common, with every other well-wisher of the colored people of this country, highly gratified with accounts of the cordial reception and welcome everywhere extended to our distinguished co-workers who are now abroad. We have read these accounts with virtuous pride that our long despised people could boast such representatives as Pennington and Brown, Garnet and Crummell, Henson and Crafts.[21] Their example has done immense good both at home and abroad. But we begin to want them at home. The cause cannot well spare them longer. If ever there was a time when every intelligent colored American was needed at home, now is such a time. We need the MEN who can wield pen and tongue, whose character and intelligence will bring commendation even from the stony-hearted oppressor. We need them to inspire hope and to save our afflicted people from desperation. We beg them to heed the call to come home, for if they are seen hand to hand with the enemy, the most timid amongst us shall be brave. Come home and stand between our people and the hateful scheme of Colonization. Come home and help Samuel R. Ward, C.L. Remond and Amos C. Beman,[22] rouse the slumbering conscience of this nation to our wrongs. Of course you must judge for yourselves what is best for you to do. But we want you and know not how to do without you in these days of trial.

*Frederick Douglass' Paper*, July 31, 1851

## TO GERRIT SMITH

Rochester, Aug. 4th, 1851

My Dear Friend:

I thank you for your pamphlet on Civil Government. I hope to find room for the whole of it in next week's paper. I cannot profess to agree with you in all you say in that speech, especially in respect to the bounds you set to government.[22] Yet I am unable at present to refute your position. I have a notion that the State, not less than the church should cover the whole ground of morals, incorporating into itself all great moral truths. If government were the thing it ought to be, if it were what you are laboring for, *righteous* government, there could be little objection to committing the education of its subjects or citizens to its charge.

You did me a real kindness introducing Mr. Crocker. I spent an hour very agreeably with him. He is with and for Liberty, and I think he will prove a most valuable co-worker. He has promised to write for our paper, and to get subscribers for it. I had a call today from Professor Upham of "Bowdoin College." Full two hours did he labor with me in favor of colonization. The dear man thinks he is doing God's service, by advocating that manhating scheme. He is evidently a benevolent and pure minded man, but the thought of founding a number of "*States*" on the coast of Africa, blinds him to the malignant spirit which he is helping to spread. The pamphlets you have dispatched for me have not arrived. Be pleased to accept my thanks for them in advance. I purpose to take the field in the course of a fortnight. I shall then have a chance to see them. My friend Julia Griffiths sends her love to yourself & Mrs. Smith.

Your sincere and grateful Friend,
Frederick Douglass

*Gerrit Smith Papers, George Arents Research Library, Syracuse University*

## TO E. MONTFORD

Rochester, Aug. 8, 1951

Dear Madam:

Your letter informing me of a course of twelve lectures in Portland, designed to be secured by the Society which you represent, and that I am invited to give the ninth of said lectures came safely to hand more than three weeks ago, and should have had an earlier answer but for my continued absence from home.

I am quite sorry that I cannot give you a positive assurance of my presence with you at the time you appoint. I am at such a distance from Portland & am so variously and constantly engaged in the antislavery field west, that I feel it hazardous to make eastern engagements.

This however I will say. Should it be in my power to visit New England during the approaching autumn or winter, and your Society should desire my services they shall be forthcoming.

I rejoice to find that antislavery has again acquired a local habitation as well as a name in Portland and sincerely hope that the *Cause* may always lead to the abandonment of minor differences and secure the united co-operation of all your members to the end of the race.

Most truly yours,<br>Frederick Douglass

*Portland Anti-Slavery Society Papers, Box 14, Maine Historical Society, Portland, Maine*

## SPEECH DELIVERED AT NATIONAL CONVENTION OF LIBERTY PARTY, BUFFALO, NEW YORK, SEPTEMBER 17, 1851

. . . It is my purpose to occupy but a few moments of the meeting on this subject, as I know you are anxious to hear our other friend (Mr. Scoble) from England.[23] In listening to the remarks of our friend from Jamaica,[24] I was struck with the similarity of the reasons given by him for the emigration of colored persons from his country, to those which are given, but with very different motives, by the agents of the American Colonization Society—a society which ever has and, I hope, ever will receive the utter detestation of every colored man in the land. I know that our friend (Mr. A.) will find it difficult to appreciate the reasons which induce the free colored people of these states to insist upon remaining here. He sees us, a suffering people, hemmed in on every side by the malignant and bitter prejudice which excludes us from nearly every profitable employment in this country, and which, as he has well said, has had several of the states to legislate for our expulsion. In the extremity of our need, he comes to us in the spirit of benevolence, I believe, and holds out to us the prospect of a better country, the prospect of a home, where none shall molest or make us afraid. And he will think it strange that we do not accept of his benevolent proffer, and welcome him in his mission of mercy and good will towards us. And yet we must say that such a welcome cannot be given by the colored people of this country without stabbing their own cause to the vitals, without conceding a point which every black man should feel that he must die for rather than yield, and that is, that the prejudice and the mal-administration toward us in this country are invincible to truth, invincible to combined and virtuous effort for their overthrow. We must make no such concession. Sir, the slaveholders have long been anxious to get rid of the free colored persons of this country. They know that where we are left free, blacks though we are, thick skulled as they call us, we shall become intelligent, and, moreover, that as we become intelligent, in just that proportion shall we become an annoyance to them in their slaveholding. They are anxious therefore to get us out of the country.—They know that a hundred thousand intelligent, upright, industrious and persevering black men in the northern states must command respect and sympathy, must encircle themselves with the regard of a large class of the virtue-loving, industry-loving people of the North, and that whatever sympathy, whatever respect they are able to command must have a reflex influence upon slavery. And, therefore, they say "*out with them*," let us get rid of them! For my part, I am not disposed to leave, and, I think, our friend must have been struck with the singular kind of applause at certain sayings of his, during the address—an applause that seemed to come from the galleries, from the door, and from that part of the house that does not wish to be mixed up with the platform. Straws show which way the wind blows,. I fancied, too, that when our friend was portraying the blessings that would result from our removal from this land to Jamaica, that delightful visions were floating before the minds of those gentlemen in the distance. Now, sir, I want to say on behalf of any Negroes I have the honor to represent, that we *have been* with, and still *are* with you, and mean to be with you *to the end*. It may seem ungrateful, but there are some of us who are resolved that you shall not get rid of your colored relations. —Why should we not stay with you? Have we not a right here? I know the cry is raised that we are out of our native land, that this land is the land of the white man; that Africa is the home of the Negro, and not America.

But how stands the matter? I believe that simultaneously with the landing of the Pilgrims, there landed slaves on the shores of this continent, and that for two hundred and thirty years and more we have had a foothold on this continent. We have grown up with you; we have watered your soil with our tears; nourished it with our blood, tilled it with our hard hands. Why should we not stay here? We came when it was a wilderness, and were the pioneers of civilization on this continent. *We* levelled your forests; *our hands* removed the stumps from your fields, and raised the first crops and brought the first produce to your tables. We have been with you, are still with you, have been with you in adversity, and by the help of God will be with you in prosperity.

There was a time when certain learned men of this country undertook to argue us out of existence. Professor *Grant* of New York reckoned us of a race belonging to a by-gone age, which, in the progress of the human family, would become perfectly extinct. Yet we do not die. It does seem that there is a Providence in this matter.— Chain us, lash us, hunt us with bloodhounds, surround us with utter insecurity, render our lives never so hard to be borne, and yet we do live on—smile under it all and are able to smile. Amid all our afflictions there is an invincible determination to stay right here, because a large portion of the American people desire to get rid of us. In proportion to the strength of their desire to have us go, in just that proportion is the strength of our determination to stay, and in staying we ask nothing but justice. We have fought for this country, and we only ask to be treated as well as those who fought against it. We are American citizens, and we only ask to be treated as well as you treat aliens. And you will treat us so yet. Most men assume that we cannot make progress here. It is untrue, sir. That we can make progress in the future is proved by the progress we have already made. Our condition is rapidly improving. Sir, but a few years ago, if I attempted to ride on the railroad cars in New England, and presumed to take my seat in the cars with white persons, I was dragged out like a beast. I have often been beaten until my hands were blue with the blows in order to make me disengage those hands from the bench on which I was seated.—On every railroad in New England this was the case. How is it now? Why, a Negro may ride just where he pleases and there is not the slightest objection raised, and I have very frequently rode over those same roads since, and never received the slightest indignity on account of my complexion. Indeed the white people are becoming more and more disposed to associate with the blacks. I am constantly annoyed by these pressing attentions. I used to enjoy the privilege of an entire seat, and riding a great deal at night, it was quite an advantage to me, but sometime ago, riding up from Geneva, I had curled myself up, and by the time I had got into a good snooze, along came a man and lifted up my blanket. I looked up and said, "pray do not disturb me, I am a black man." "I don't care who the devil you are, only give me a seat," was the reply. I told you the white people about here are beginning "to don't care who the devil you are." If you can put a dollar in their way, or a seat under them, they don't care "who the devil you are." But I will not detain you longer. I know you are anxious to hear our friend from England.

*Frederick Douglass' Paper*, October 2, 1851

## FREEDOM'S BATTLE AT CHRISTIANA

The fight at Christiana between the slavecatchers and the alleged fugitive slaves,[25] continues to excite general discussion. The sensation produced by the death of the kidnappers is not surpassed by that which occurred throughout the country on hearing of the fate of the Cuban invaders.[26] The failure of these two patriotic expeditions, undertaken so nobly by our *law-abiding* citizens, must long be regarded as among the most memorable events of this eventful year.

Everybody seems astonished, that in this land of gospel light and liberty, after all the sermons of the *Lords, Lathrops, Spencers, Coxes, Springs, Deweys, Sharpes, Tyngs,*[27] and a host of other Doctors of Divinity, there should be found men so firmly attached to liberty and so bitterly averse to slavery, as to be willing to peril even life itself to gain the one and to avoid the other. Pro-slavery men especially are in a state of amazement at the strange affair. That the hunted men should fight with the biped bloodhounds that had tracked them, even when the animals had a *"paper"* authorizing them to hunt, is to them inexplicable audacity. "This not that the Negroes fought the kidnappers (no, let no one misrepresent) that we are astonished, but that they should fight them and kill them when they knew they had *'papers'*." That they should kill the men-hunters is, perhaps, natural, and may be explained in the light of the generally admitted principle "that self-preservation is the first law of nature," but, the rascals! they killed their pursuers, when they knew they had "*papers!*" Just here is the point of difficulty. What could have got into these men of sable coating? Didn't they know that slavery, not freedom, is their natural condition? Didn't they know that their legs, arms, eyes, hands and heads, were the rightful property of the white men who claimed them?

Can we in charity suppose these Negroes to have been ignorant of the fact that our "*own dear Fillmore*" (than whom there is none higher—not according to northern Whiggery, not even in the heavens above nor in the earth beneath) did, on the eighteenth day of September, in the year one thousand eight hundred and fifty of the Christian era and in the seventy-fifth year of the freedom and independence of the American people *from the bondage of a foreign yoke*, approve and send forth a decree, (with all the solemn authority of his great name.) ordaining that thereafter *Men Should Cease to be Men!*[28]—Oh! ye most naughty and rebellious fellows! Why stand ye up like men, after this mighty decree? Why have not your hands become paws, and your arms, legs? Why are you not down among four-footed beasts with the fox, the wolf and the bear, sharing with them the chances of the chase, but constituting the most choice game—the peculiar game of this free and Christian country? We say again that here is the point of difficulty which demands explanation. For you see, friends and brethren, if the story gets afloat that these Negroes of Christiana did really hear the words of the mighty *Fillmore* commanding them to be brutes instead of, men, and they did not change as ordered, why, the dangerous doctrine will also get afloat presently that there is a law higher than the law of *Fillmore.* If his voice cannot change the nature of things, it is certain that there is a power above him, and that that frightful heresy, (which has been so justly condemned by the most learned clergy,) called the "Higher Law,"[29] will be received, the evil consequences of which, even the great Daniel cannot portray.

We have said that the pro-slavery people of this country don't know what to make of this demonstration on the part of the alleged fugitive slaves of Christiana. This, however, is possibly a mistake. There is in that translation a lesson which the most obtuse may understand, namely, that all Negroes are not such fools and dastards as to cling to *life* when it is coupled with chains and slavery.

This lesson, though most dearly bought is quite worth the price paid. It was needed. The lamb-like submission with which men of color have allowed themselves to be dragged away from liberty, from family and all that is dear to the hearts of man, had well nigh established the impression.that they were conscious of their own fitness for slavery. The frequency of arrests and the ease with which they were made quickened the rapacity, and invited these aggressions of slave-catchers. The Christiana conflict was therefore needed to check these aggressions and to bring the hunters of men to the sober second thought. But was it right for the colored men to resist their enslavers? We answer, Yes, or the whole structure of the world's theory of right and wrong is a lie.—If it be right for any man to resist those who would enslave them, it was right for the men of color at Christiana to resist. If an appeal to arms may ever be innocently made, the appeal in this instance was innocently made; and if it were wrong in them to fight, it can never be right in any case to fight.—For never were there, never can there be more sacred rights to defend than were menaced on this occasion. Life and liberty are the most sacred of all man's rights. If these may be invaded with impunity, all others may be for they comprehend all others. But we take still higher ground. It was right in the light of absolute justice, which says to the aggressor, he that leadeth into captivity shall go into captivity, and he that taketh the sword shall perish by the sword. The man who rushes out of the orbit of his own rights, to strike down the rights of another, does, by that act, divest himself of the right to live; if he be shot down, his punishment is just.

Now what are the facts in the case, for these have been most scandalously misrepresented by the newspapers? The slaveholder's side of the story has been told, but the other side has been dumb, for colored men cannot write. Could they speak for themselves, we dare be sworn that they would testify substantially as follows: Early in the evening of September tenth, a colored man, a fugitive slave, went to the house of Wm. Parker, a sober, well-behaved, and religious man of color,[30] and said to him, William, there is a warrant out for the arrest of some of us, and it is said the kidnappers will be up to-night from Philadelphia. What had we better do? The answer to this was worthy of the man. Come to my house said Parker. Accordingly, five men of color, all told, spent the night at William's house. They sat up late in the apprehension of an attack, but finally went to bed, but sleep—they could not. About two hours before day-light, one of the colored men went into the yard, and on raising his eyes, saw, at that unseasonable hour, fifteen men, coming stealthily along the lane. He ran into the house, and told the inmates that the slave-catchers had come, and the truth of his story was soon confirmed, for a minute elapsed before the whole fifteen were in Parker's yard. The man who went into the yard, did not fasten the door securely, and it was therefore easily forced. The slaveholders rushed into the lower part of the house, and called upon the occupants to give themselves up. Here commenced the conflict. The kidnappers undertook to force their way upstairs, but were met, and compelled to retreat. A parley ensued. Gorsuch was spokesman for himself and his kidnapping comrades, and Parker for himself and guests. Gorsuch said, you have got my property in your house. I have not, said Parker; there is no property here but what belongs to me. I own every trunk, and chair and article of furniture about this house, and none but robbers and murderers would make any attack upon me at this hour of the night. You have got my men in your house, said Gorsuch, and I will have them, or go to hell in the attempt to get them. Parker said I have got none of your men, I never owned a man in my life. I believe it to be a sin to own men; I am no slave-owner. Gorsuch here interrupted Parker, saying, I don't want to hear your abolition lecture. After a long parley, during which Parker repeatedly advised the slave-catchers to go away, stating that he did not wish to hurt them, although they had fired into his house fifteen times, shooting once through his hat crown, the five colored men came downstairs, and walked in front of the slave-catchers, and both parties were now arrayed face to face. Parker then took the old man, Gorsuch, by the arm, and said to him, old man, we don't want to harm you. You profess to be a Christian; you are a Methodist class-leader, and you ought to be ashamed to be in such business. At this point, young Gorsuch, "father, do you allow a 'n----r' to talk so to you? why don't you shoot him, father?" Parker than answered: "Young man, I would say to you, just what I have said to your father, you had better go about *your* business." Young Gorsuch then fired at Parker, but missed him, and he, Gorsuch, was instantly shot down. —There was now general shooting, and striking with clubs, during which the elder Gorsuch was killed, his son shot through the lungs, and his nephew dangerously wounded. We must not omit to state that the first man to take the advice of the colored preacher, (as Parker is called,) was the Marshal from Philadelphia. *He topped his boom* before the heat of the battle came on, undoubtedly feeling that he had barked up the wrong tree, and that it was best for him to make tracks! The time occupied in parleying between the two parties, was full two hours.

The colored men who are alleged to have taken part in the conflict at Christiana, are to be tried, we are informed, for high treason.[31] This is to cap the climax of American absurdity, to say nothing of American infamy. Our government has virtually made every colored man in the land an outlaw, one who may be hunted by any villain who may think proper to do so, and if the hunted man, finding himself stript of all legal protection, shall lift his arm in his own defense, why, forsooth, he is arrested, arraigned, and tried for high treason, and if found guilty, he must suffer death!

The basis of allegiance is protection. We owe allegiance to the government that protects us, but to the government that destroys us, we owe no allegiance. The only law which the alleged slave has a right to know anything about, is the law of nature. This is his only law. The enactments of this government do not recognize him as a citizen, but as a thing. In the light of the law, a slave can no more commit treason than a horse or an ox can commit treason. A horse kicks out the brains of his master. Do you try the horse for treason? Then why the slave who does the same thing? You answer, because the slave is a man, and he is therefore responsible for his acts. The answer is sound. The slave is a man and ought not to be treated like a horse, but like a man, and his manhood is his justification for shooting down any creature who shall attempt to reduce him to the condition of a brute.

But there is one consolation after all about this arraignment for treason. It admits our manhood. Sir Walter Scott says that treason is the crime of a gentleman. We shall watch this trial in Philadelphia, and shall report the result when it transpires. Meanwhile, we think that fugitives may sleep more soundly than formerly.

*Frederick Douglass' Paper*, September 25, 1851

## IS CIVIL GOVERNMENT RIGHT?

This question is raised and summarily disposed of in a letter which appears in another column, addressed by Mr. Wright to Gerrit Smith, Esq. The writer thinks a just civil government *"an impossibil-*

*ity.*"[32] He does not, in this, object to the abuses of power, but to the power itself, and he classes the assumed right of government with robbery, piracy and slavery. *"To speak of a righteous human ruler is the same as to speak of a righteous thief, a righteous robber, a righteous murderer, a righteous pirate or a righteous slaveholder."*

To those unacquainted with Mr. Wright's style, this letter will seem an outburst of unusual extravagance on his part; but we must pronounce it *tame* as compared with many of his productions, on this and on kindred subjects. There is in it an absence of startling assertion, and an attempt at reasoning such as Mr. Wright does not always condescend to in dealing with opponents. We, therefore, take pleasure in laying his letter before our readers, that they may have both sides of a subject which is to them, and to us, one of unspeakable interest.

Were we to presume to criticize Mr. Wright's letter, we should object to his limited statement of the assumed right upon which civil government is based. He says, *"the assumption is, that man is invested by God with power to dictate law to man and to punish him if he do not obey."*

To this statement we object, that the vital principle of Government is left out. It contains the skeleton, but the life is not there. — The bones and sinews are retained, but the vital spark which should animate them is gone. Were we to make an inquiry into the rightfulness of civil government, we should (perhaps owing to the diffuseness of our intellect) begin by assuming, first, that man is a social as well as an individual being; that he is endowed by his Creator with faculties and powers suited to his individuality and to society. Second, that individual isolation is unnatural, unprogressive and against the highest interests of man; and that society is required, by the natural wants and necessities inherent in human existence. —Third, that man is endowed with reason and understanding capable of discriminating between good and evil, right and wrong, justice and injustice. Fourth, that while man is constantly liable to do evil, he is still capable of apprehending and pursuing that which is good; and that, upon the whole, his evil tendencies are quite outweighed by the powers within him, impelling him to good. —Fifth, that rewards and punishments are natural agents for restraining evil and for promoting good, man being endowed with faculties keenly alive to both. Finally, that whatever serves to increase the happiness, to preserve the well-being, to give permanence, order and attractiveness to society, and leads to the very highest development of human perfection, is, unless positively prohibited by Divine command, to be esteemed innocent and right. The question then comes, Is human government right? Mark, the question is not: Is arbitrary, despotic, tyrannical, corrupt, unjust, capricious government right? but is society (that is a company of human beings) authorized by their Creator to institute a government for themselves, and to pass and enforce laws which are in accordance with justice, liberty and humanity? Mr. Wright says that they *have not*. His reasons are, that "*to admit the rightfulness of such government is to admit that human will or discretion is the only tenure by which we hold life, liberty, or happiness. That the existence of each one is at the discretion of each and every other. That we must all live or die, be slaves or freemen, be happy or miserable, by act of Congress or Parliament*," *and much more in the same strain*. (See letter.)

From a conclusion so revolting and terrible, he, naturally enough recoils with a shudder. The fallacy and fatal error which form the basis of this reasoning, are the assumptions that human government is necessarily arbitrary and absolute; and that there is no difference between a righteous and a wicked government. Human government, from its very nature, is an organization, like every other human institution, limited in its powers, and subject to the very wants of human nature which call it into existence. A community of men who will organize a government, granting it the power to make them slaves or freemen, to kill them or to let them live, to make them happy or miserable at discretion, is in a pitiable condition, and far behind the Liberty Party in right apprehension of the nature and office of civil government.

"But," says Mr. Wright, "if a man may rightfully tell his fellow-beings how to act, he may tell them how to speak, how to feel, and how to think." Well, what of it? Mr. Wright is constantly telling men how to act, how to think, how to feel, and how to speak; and it would be well for the world if it followed some of his telling at least. But we apprehend that objection to government does not consist in its telling men how to think, speak, feel or act, but in the punishment which government may see fit to inflict, and that involves the question of the rightfulness of physical force, of which we shall speak anon. Mr. Wright does not object to societies expressing by their votes their dissent or approval of the thoughts, sayings, feelings and actions of men. He, doubtless, deems this proper and praiseworthy; nor does he, as we understand him, object to the principle that majorities ought to rule; at any rate, he certainly cannot think that the minority of the members of the American Anti-Slavery Society ought to adopt measures which are condemned by the majority. Why is this respect to be shown to the majority? Simply because a majority of human hearts and intellects may be presumed, as a general rule, to take a wiser and more comprehensive view of the matters upon which they act than the minority. It is in accordance with the doctrine that good is the rule, and evil the exception in the character and constitution of man. If the fact were otherwise, (that is, if men were more disposed to evil than to good,) it would, indeed, be dangerous for men to enter into a compact, by which power should be wielded by the mass, for then evil being predominant in man, would predominate in the mass, and innumerable hardships would be inflicted upon the good. The old assertion of the wickedness of the masses, and their consequent unfitness to govern themselves, is the falsehood and corruption out of which have spring the despotic and tyrannical conspiracies, calling themselves governments, in the old world. They are founded not in the aggregate morality and intelligence of the people, but in a fancied divine authority, resulting from the inherent incompetency of the people to direct their own temporal concerns. Kings and despots flourish in such a soil, poisoning the moral atmosphere with oppression and paralyzing the spirit of progress by choking the utterance of free speech from the platform and the press. It is confounding such government with a righteous democratic government, and charging the crimes of the former upon the latter, that has led such men as Mr. Wright to array themselves against the Liberty Party.

But how different is the ground assumed by Gerrit Smith and his associates, from that upon which despotic governments are based. The one assumes that the people may be trusted, and the other, that the people should have nothing to do with the laws but to obey them; or (to use a favorite sentiment of Mr. Wright) one regards institutions for men, and the other regards men for institutions. But it is alleged that the power claimed for government by the Liberty Party, is, in essence, the same as that which is claimed by despots, and is, therefore, to be rejected. This allegation is unfounded, since there is all the difference between the cases, that exists between limited and restricted power, and power unlimited and unrestricted. In the one case, the governing power is in the hands of the people, who are supposed to know their rights and to understand their interests; and in the other, the governing power is in the hands of an individual, who, from his very circumstances and environments, can be supposed to have very little sympathy with the people, or very little desire to promote their intelligence as to their best interests.

Mr. Wright will, however, insist that the exercise of government power is practically the same, whether, it be wielded by King Individual or King Majority; that the will, caprice, or what not, of the majority is as imperious in its tone, and must be as implicitly obeyed as that of the king.

The answer is, that the Liberty Party concedes no governmental authority to pass laws, nor to compel obedience to any laws, against the natural rights and happiness of man. It affirms that the office of government is protection; and when it ceases to protect the rights of man, they repudiate it as a tyrannical usurpation. But our friend asks, *"Who is to decide?"* We answer, the Constitution and the common sense of the people, manifested in the choice of their lawmakers. It may still be further asked, will they always decide rightly? They may not, for the individual does not always decide for himself what is for his best interest. What then? Shall we abolish the individual, and deny him the right to govern himself because he may sometimes govern wrongly? The reasoning which would deny the right of society to frame laws for its own protection, preservation and happiness, would, if rigidly adhered to, deny to man the right to govern himself; for is he not a frail mortal, and has he any more right to ruin himself than he has to ruin others? But again, the very fact that a government is instituted by all, and rests upon all for support and direction, is the strongest guarantee that can be given that it will be wielded justly and impartially. With all the drawbacks upon government which fancy can depict, or imagination conjure up, society possessing it, is a paradise to pandemonium, compared with society without it.

Mr. Wright objects to civil government because "there is no crime which man may not and will not perpetrate against man." A strange reason against government.—We use the fact in favor of government, not against it. Because there are hardened villains, enemies to themselves and to the well-being of society, who will cheat, steal, rob, burn and murder their fellow-creatures, and because these are the exceptions to the mass of humanity, society has the right to protect itself against their depredations and aggressions upon the common weal. Society without law, is society with a curse, driving men into isolation and depriving them of one of the greatest blessings of which man is susceptible. It is no answer to this to say that if all men would obey the laws of God, lead virtuous lives, do by others as they would be done unto, human government would be unnecessary; for it is enough to know, as Mr. Wright declares, that "there are no crimes which man may not and will not perpetrate against his fellowman," to justify society in resorting to force, as a means of protecting itself from crime and its consequences.

If it be alleged that to repel aggression by force is to promote aggression; and that to submit to be robbed, plundered and enslaved is the true way to establish justice and liberty among men, the answer is, that the theory is contradicted by the facts of human nature, and by the experience of men in all ages. The present condition of the slave population of this country is a striking illustration of the fallacy that submission is the best remedy for the wrongs and injustice to which they are subjected. Here we have two hundred years of non-resisting submission, and equally two hundred years of cruel injustice: and so far, from this submission to the imposition of still greater hardships, and this is the lesson taught by the facts of human nature, and by the history of the world. Men need to be taught, not only the happy consequences arising from dealing justly, but the dreadful consequences which result from injustice; their fears, therefore, may be as legitimately appealed to as their hopes, and he who repudiates such appeals, throws away an important instrumentality for establishing justice among men, and promoting the peace and happiness of society. All tyrants, all oppressors should be taught, by precept and by example, that, in trampling wantonly and ruthlessly upon the lives and liberties of their unoffending brother-men, they forfeit their own right to liberty, and richly deserve the slavery and death that they inflict upon others. Mr. Wright may say that the slave should appeal to the humanity and to the sense of justice of his master, and thus overcome evil with good; but, once enslaved, the master may forbid such an appeal; for, to use the language of Mr. Wright, the power claimed is such as may enable the slaveholder to tell his slave not only "how to act," but how to speak, think and feel; and he may deprive his victim of every means of reaching his sense of justice, except through his bodily fears. This, then, is our reasoning: that when every avenue to the understanding and heart of the oppressor is closed, when he is deaf to every moral appeal, and rushes upon his fellow-man to gratify his own selfish propensities at the expense of the rights and liberties of his brother-man, the exercise of physical force, sufficient to repel the aggression, is alike the right and the duty of society.

Truth may withstand falsehood, love may overcome hatred, opinion may be opposed to opinion, the theory of liberty may be opposed to slavery, and common sense alike teaches that physical resistance is the antidote for physical violence.

It is asked, in view of these conclusions: when will wars cease? We answer, when man shall learn to respect the rights of man: *"first pure, then peaceable."* There can be no peace while there is oppression. The true way to give peace to the world is, to establish justice in the world; and regarding righteous civil government as an important means to this great end, we unhesitatingly and heartily consecrate ourselves, within our humble sphere, to its advocacy.

*Frederick Douglass' Paper*, October 23, 1851

# NOTICE TO SPORTSMEN AND HUNTERS

There are in Rochester, for private sale, a large pack of Negro Dogs, strong of limb and keen of scent, completely obedient to the *Lower Law*, capable of enduring hunger and thirst for a long period, and of undergoing any amount of fatigue when animated by the chase. All sound in wind and limb, except one, which the subscriber is happy to state, is rapidly recovering from wounds experienced in a recent Slave Hunt, in which he distinguished himself by sundry dexterous evolutions including lofty jumping and rapid running.

Persons wishing to purchase Negro Dogs will do well to call at the Intelligence Office of George Bloodhound, Inhuman Street, Rochester.

*Frederick Douglass' Paper*, October 23, 1851

# ON BEING CONSIDERED FOR THE LEGISLATURE

To F. Gorton, B. E. Hecock, N. H. Gardner, James Abrams, of American office, Joseph Putnam, S. F. Witherspoon, William Breck, United States Deputy Collector, G. S. Jennings, James H. Delly, John C. Stevens, L. R. Jerome, United States Deputy and of American office, Sulivan Gray, Edward French, William Thorn, Justin Day, Jr., E. R. Warren, John Cornwall, Rev. Charles G. Lee, formerly preacher in Syracuse, M. H. Jennings, Jared Coleman, United States Deputy Collector.

Gentlemen: I have learned with with some surprise, that in the Whig Convention held in this city on Saturday last, you signified, by your votes, a desire to make me your representative in the Legislature of this State. Never having, at any time that I can recollect, thought, spoken, or acted, in any way, to commit myself to either the principles or the policy of the Whig party, but on the contrary, having always held, and publicly expressed opinions diametrically opposed to those held by that part of the Whig party which you are supposed to represent, your voting for me, I am bound in courtesy to suppose, is founded in a misapprehension of my political sentiments.

Lest you should, at any other time, commit a similar blunder, I beg to state, once for all, that I do not believe that the slavery question is settled, and settled forever. I do not believe that slave-catching is either a Christian duty, or an innocent amusement. I do not believe that he who breaks the arm of the kidnapper, or wrests the trembling captive from his grasp is a "traitor." I do not believe that human enactments are to be obeyed when they are point blank against the laws of the living God. And believing most fully, (as I do,) the reverse of all this, you will easily believe me to be a person wholly unfit to receive the suffrages of gentlemen holding the opinion and favoring the policy of that wing of the Whig party, denominated "the *Silver Grays*."

With all the respect which your derision permits me to entertain for you,

I am gentlemen,
Your faithful fellow-citizen,
Frederick Douglass

*Frederick Douglass' Paper*, October 30, 1851; reprinted in the *New York Times*, November 6, 1851

## THE COLORED PEOPLE AND OUR PAPER

We have often, during the last four years, felt an earnest desire, and that, too, far apart from any personal considerations, to appeal to the free colored people of the United States to sustain us in keeping our free banner unfurled to the breeze. We have resisted that desire out of a delicate sense of propriety, considering that other papers, conducted by colored men were in the field, and that, in the judgment of their proprietors and projectors, were deemed as well worthy of patronage from the colored people as our own. These papers have now faded from the view. The *Mystery*, the *Disfranchised American*, the *National Watchman*, the *Ram's Horn*, the *Hyperion* and the *Impartial Citizen* have all disappeared; and the only paper regularly published now in the United States by colored man is *Frederick Douglass' Paper*, standing alone now in the field as it does, and in danger, as it is, of being swept down by the malignant assaults of foes, or of languishing inactivity of its friends, we deem it highly proper to appeal to you to aid. It is for you to say whether this journal shall be numbered with the disheartening catalogue of colored newspapers, the history of which failures has gone far to strengthen that prejudice and presumption on the part of our oppressors which continues to brand us before all the world as an inferior race. It is for you to say whether you can dispense with the services of the only Journal in this country which is, in every sense, identified with the interests and happiness of yourselves.

We put it to you, whether this is the time to relax your efforts for that improvement and elevation for which your reform Conventions, held during these last twenty years, in various parts of the country, have contended. *Ought* we, *shall* we, while we are hunted like wild beasts, expelled from the States by Legislative enactments, and while the American Colonization Society is putting forth most strenous endeavors for our removal, calling for appropriations from the National Government, in aid of its people from the face of this land, can we consent to give up our efforts, and allow our only banner to be trampled in the dust? This cannot be your decision.—The night is a dark and stormy one—and the sea which we traverse is fearfully agitated. We have lost some of our strong men.—Ward has been driven into exile; Loguen has been hunted from our shores; Brown, Garnet and Crummell, men who were our pride and hope, have we heard signified their unwillingness to return again to their National field of labors in this country. Bibb has *chosen* Canada as his field of labor—and the eloquent Remond is, comparatively, silent.

We protest, from the depths of our soul, against all this—and especially against the despair into which it has plunged our people.

The times demand heroes of our race.—men of stuff as stern as that which formed the character of John Knox. But enough of this. The question is—will you sustain your own Journal? your own advocate?—or will you allow both to be driven from the field, and prove by your indifference, the injurious allegations of your enemies?

A proposition was made, more than a month ago, by one of our number[33] whose influence and position are second to those of no other colored man in the United States, to raise a fund, with which to publish our paper semi-weekly, and to this hour, not one colored man in the United States has responded to the earnest appeal of the proposer. Now we ask, in view of these facts, and of certain others which we will not name: could any colored man in this country blame us if we also should lay aside our banners, and abandon our common cause, and the country? Such an act on our part would, at least, have the excuse which is always deemed satisfactory—that of being abandoned by the very men in whose cause we are battling. But we will not despair.— We shall stand so long as we have a leg to stand upon, and we shall not strike down our flag until the last hope of sustaining it shall be dispelled. We will not multiply words. We have said enough to reveal our state of mind to our people in the present almost *desperate circumstances* in which we are mutually placed. We call upon them to act promptly in the premises. Let each individual subscriber lay the subject of sustaining this paper before his neighbor, and point out the special reasons which should induce him to subscribe, and *pay for it*; and thus to increase the circulation to a living point. Every colored man should feel himself an agent, and take pleasure in forwarding the interests of the Journal devoted to his cause; for identified, as the paper is with the colored man in this country, its failure could not fail to affect our whole people disastrously. Let this paper go down; let the colored people show to the world that they are destitute of public spirit; let them, while the Irish and German population are contributing with their hard earned mites, to establish journals to defend them from the narrow spirit of *"Nativeism"*—we say, let them at such a time, and in such circumstances, desert the only Press in the country wielded by a colored man, and allow it to languish and die; and they will inflict upon their own cause a blow (it may be our vanity to say it) by far more destructive than any which either Slavery or Colonization can inflict. Men of color awake, and do your duty, and deprive your malignant enemies of the demoniacal joy with which the downfall of *Frederick Douglass' Paper* would be hailed throughout this Negro-hating land.—We say nothing to our white friends here; for their kind co-operation we are grateful. They have already, done much more for the paper than those in whose cause its energies are enlisted. We will only solicit them to hold up our hands awhile longer, and if then it shall be found that those who ought to rally around it still stand away from it, it will be evidence to the writer of this article that his services are no longer wanted, and that he may retire from the public advocacy of this cause, to a pursuit which, although more humble, may better enable him to provide for his household, and thereby escape the malediction of being "worse than an Infidel."—After years of arduous labor in lecturing, in four of which we have combined the duties of both Editor and Lecturer, have led us to a sense of our limited powers, and taught us the painful lesson that however zealous, devoted and industrious one may be, he may yet lack those qualities which inspire the confidence, and secure the support of the very people for whom he may be even willing to lay down his life.

Let no man think, however, that we have not our true and faithful *friends* among the colored people. *We have them*, but unfortunately, they are the few, not the many; and we still hope that their numbers will be augmented, and their spirits cheered by the "smiling face" of that Providence which now seems veiled in darkness and terror.

*Frederick Douglass' Paper*, November 27, 1851

## EXTRACT

FROM A SPEECH at Providence, Nov. 6. Phonographic Report by J. L. Crosby.

God, the foundation and source of all goodness, must be loved in order that we may love our fellow-man. In order to produce and cultivate this love, abolitionists should pray, abolitionists should meditate, abolitionists should make it a matter of thought, of deep thought; they should make it so when they come before the people, and that God who seeth in secret will reward them openly. This may seem rather ministerial, than after the fashion of an anti-slavery speech; but I am not sure that we have not, in our utter detestation of the subserviency of the ministry and of the church, cast aside something which we might justly highly prize. I know I have. I know that a few years ago, when engaged more especially in exposing the pro-slavery character of the American Church and clergy (and, as I now believe, justly) still, in coupling together all manner of churches and ministers, I have no doubt that I destroyed in myself that very reverence for God and for religion which is necessary to give vital power to my anti-slavery efforts; and hence I am led to make confession of having erred—greatly erred. I believe that others will make the same confession before long—that they have to some extent undermined that principle in the human mind which is essential for carrying forward a great and holy cause, namely reverence.

Now I believe, it is good for us to meditate on this question, and to take the slave with us in our meditations, to take the slave with us everywhere, to take the slave into our thoughts when we go before God; and if we do this, we shall not be wanting in words to say on this subject.

We believe that there never was a time when we had more strong and powerful reasons for being active in the cause than now. The time was when abolitionists could gather themselves together, when they spoke and prayed, and sang and had a good meeting, and returned to their homes with none to molest them or make them afraid; but at this time we are all prostrate under the arm of the Slave Power to an extent which we never were before and this consideration if no other, should induce greater activity on our part, greater earnestness, greater determination to wage war upon this inhuman *slave* system, of which the Fugitive Slave Law is but a branch, a shoot, a leaf. This, I say, should prompt us to more energetic exertion in behalf of the slave.

I have been, for the past year under a cloud. I have never been so hopeful of the American people on this subject as many of my friends. I never believed, for instance, that slavery would be limited by any action of the last Congress. I never believed that the Fugitive Slave Law would not be enacted and if enacted that it would not be enforced. I believed that the Slave Power would be extended. I believed that the

Fugitive Slave Law would be enacted, and, if enacted the nation would be ready to execute it. It has been enacted and it has been executed.

Scarcely a week passes, but some poor fugitive is hunted down in the streets of some of our large cities. In Philadelphia, week after week, instances of this kind are occurring; men and women hunted down in the streets of brotherly love! Men and women hunted down, chained and fettered under the very steeples, and in the shadow of the very churches of our land or dragged through the streets with none to pity, none to succor them, none to help them, Man after man is dragged and chained and fettered into hopeless bondage—hopeless, unending bondage, so far as bondage in this life can be unending. Facts like these are occurring over our land and if there are souls within us, we cannot be indifferent at such a time as this.

*Frederick Douglass' Paper*, December 11, 1851


# SELECTIONS

FROM the Writings and Speeches of William Lloyd Garrison. By R. F. Wallent, 21 Cornhill, Boston.

We have been prevented, by a protracted and distressing illness, from sooner noticing this Book, and we are even now too feeble to write out the thoughts and feelings which the perusal of it has excited. Among the first things that we did after breaking the chains of our thralldom, and reaching the free State of Massachusetts, (now more than thirteen years ago,) was to subscribe for the *Liberator*, and through that medium we became acquainted with the writings of William Lloyd Garrison.[34] It was from his pen that we first obtained definite information respecting the Anti-Slavery movement.

To him we were first indebted for a full exposure of the wickedness of slavery for a powerful assertion of the manhood, and equal rights of the slave; for a bold rebuke of the stupendous criminality of slaveholders; and for a high proclamation of the duty of immediate, unconditional and universal emancipation. It is natural, therefore, that we should feel an especial interest in the book before us; and we should be pardoned if we regarded it with a respect almost amounting to veneration.

In this collection of the writings of Mr. Garrison, though the book is much smaller than it might have been, the reader will find a pretty ample presentation of the leading views, opinions and doctrines which have made him peculiar and conspicuous, and have caused him to be loved, hated, persecuted and honored perhaps above any other living man in the United States. To all who wish to know Mr. Garrison better, this book offers a ready mode of accomplishing it. There may be found his "wildest fanaticism," his *most dangerous heresies; his most shocking blasphemies,* and his darkest "infidelity,"—These four hundred pages are four hundred witnesses. Blessed with a mind singular for its clearness, as well as its power, Mr. Garrison conveys his thoughts in a manner distinct, direct, well defined, eloquent and forcible. There is seldom a possibility for misunderstanding him. An honest man, understanding himself, he aims to be understood by others and he succeeds.

On the subject of American Slavery, the subject which has most deeply engrossed his thoughts, and enlisted his feelings, he has written that which will live long after the Republic itself shall have faded from the great circle of nations. There he has earnestly enforced eternal principles, which must remain unaltered and unalterable through all terrestrial mutation. For this, his name will be handed down from generation to generation, and will be held in loving remembrance by all the friends of Liberty and Equality who may yet come after him. While we bear this testimony to the writings of our friend Garrison, there are yet parts of the book before us from which we dissent. But as these points have been often argued in our columns, there is little need for discussing them here.

All know that we have repudiated the views of Mr. Garrison respecting the Constitution of the United States.

In regard to the doctrine of *non-physical* resistance to evil, so eloquently maintained by Mr. Garrison, we reject it, with deference, to be sure, but with a full conviction of its unsoundness. The only "Peace" principle which we are able to comprehend, is justice. We contend that he who does most to establish this principle, does most to establish *"Peace on earth and good will towards men,"* and further, without at all dispensing with or losing faith in moral force, we hold that physical resistance to evil has often been, and is now a solemn duty in the sight of God and man. In short, it is evident that when oppressors and tyrants silence all appeals in behalf of justice and mercy, blot out all right rules for the guidance of man toward man, and consult only their own selfish pride, and pleasure, he is a benefactor of all mankind, and the servant of the God of Peace, who traces the straight line of immutable justice with the blood of such oppressors and tyrants, as a warning to all who would trample in the *dust* the precious lights of human nature. The time for "non-resistance" has not yet come. There are lessons needful to mankind, which will be learned only when written in blood; and however it may be deplored, it is which can secure *"peace,"* to the sons of man. Where there are Oppression and Slavery, there can be no *"Peace,"* and the removal of these, it seems to us, will never be effected until tyrants are taught that it is perilous to stand upon the quivering heartstrings of outraged humanity.

We purposely refrain from offering a single remark in regard to the strictly theological speculations contained in this book, for the reason that our paper is an anti-slavery paper, and devoted only to such reforms, the need of which can be demonstrated from the necessities of Society.

*Frederick Douglass' Paper*, January 29, 1852

## TO GERRIT SMITH

Rochester, Feb. 5th, 1852

My dear Sir:

I am much in your debt for kind notes and messages during my late illness. My health is improving and I am on my legs again. My joints have not yet attained their wonted elasticity, but they work pretty well and I am thankful for the good service they do me. My hands are somewhat stiff and swollen. Yet you see I can use my pen, which to me is a source of much happiness. I look forward to warm weather for complete restoration, but until then, I shall have to play the *old* man. Mrs. Smith smiled upon us yesterday, having ascended the long dark stairs of the office for the purpose. I fear the exertion cost her dearly. How I wish that her health were better. My happiness on seeing her was much shaded by the thought that she had exerted herself too much in making her call. Poor Julia to whom the sunlight of a sympathising face is as cordial, was delighted. They rode up from the office to our new home together.

God will bless you, my dear Friend: for the interest you have taken in the cause of Jerry's rescuers.[35] The time and money devoted, though great, has been I think wisely and beneficially expended. My heart leaped up, when I read your name among the counsel for the rescuers. I assigned you a place in that trial which would send your name down to posterity beside that, of Granville Sharpe. You were to be made (under God) the honored instrument of making the soil of New York like that of England, too sacred to bear the footprints of a slave or a slavehunter. I need not tell you that I feel disappointed that the trial did not go on. I hope you will follow up the case. It was a happy thought, leaving Mr. Thomas at Albany. I will write you again soon. Most truly and affectionately yours,

Frederick Douglass

*Gerrit Smith, George Arents Research Library, Syracuse University*

# IMPORTANT TRUTHS

SPEECH Delivered to Church Congregation at Harveysburg, Warren County, Ohio, May, 1852[36]

We have assembled here for the true worship of God—to sympathize with the oppressed, and act our part in breaking their bonds. This is true religion. That is not true religion which is not Godward, and also manward. Christianity teaches the doctrine that if any man has ought against his brother he should leave his gift at the altar, and go and first be reconciled to his brother and then make the offering. There is a sable brother—yea three millions of brethren in this land, to whom the American church, and clergy have yet to be reconciled.

In addressing you at this time we do not expect to present any new truth. It will be time to present new truth, when old truths are reduced to practice. There *is* no new truth—truth is eternal. The abolitionists have endeavored to present by lectures and through the press, this truth, *that every man is himself, belongs to himself, that singly he comes into the world, singly he breathes, singly he lives, singly he dies, and singly his spirit goes to God who gave it.* That every man has a right to be free, needs no proof. It is self-evident. The assertion of freedom touches a sympathetic cord which sends a thrill around the world—a denial of it, a shriek.

Nine years have elapsed since it was my privilege to stand here. I hardly know what were the aspects of this subject then, and it is no difference, things are substantially the same. The nation is guilty as ever, and the church is more guilty, for she has more light. When I first commenced disussing this subject I thought five or six years would accomplish the work. I had not comprehended the deep root this Upas had taken in American soil. I did not know the power slavery had to beget sentiments like itself. But my disappointment in some respects has served to increase my confidence, and faith, in the goodness and forbearance of God. I have a bright faith, and strong hope that slavery will come to an end. It is opposed by the principles of the great Jehovah, by the Constitution of our government and the genius of American Institutions. I see its destruction in every railroad bar, in the electric wire, in the improvements of the age.[37] Something more must be done for the abolition of slavery. There must be a struggle to unmask the hypocrisy of those who profess to love God, and yet hate man. The war must be carried into the church. The church is the light of the world. There are individuals out of the church frequently who seize the torch of God's truth and outstrip the multitude, even the church remains behind. But the church is still the light of the world. The slave can never be redeemed until the organized religion of this land pronounces its *fiat* against slavery. I need not go to the Presbyterian synods, the Methodist conferences, the Baptist associations to show you their numerous resolutions declaring that they have no sympathy with the abolitionists. The two hundred years this curse has sat in the sanctuary proves that there is no warfare between slavery, and the church. The church has remained on the side of slavery, and is linked, and interwoven with slavery, she has bolted her doors, barred her gates against anti-slavery truth. The true representatives of a nation are but the full length and character of the nation itself. No people are better than their lawmakers. The lawmakers are the representative characters of the nation or people. The two old parties aim at availability, not righteousness.

When the Whigs were about to nominate a candidate for the presidency in the last campaign, they took a survey of the morals of the American people; and of the American church, they tried their thurmonitor, [sic] and it stood precisely at *Zachary height*.[38] They said he is a war man—and in the circumstances we would have been so too; he will swear—he did say in the midst of the groans and shrieks of the dying at Buena Vista, "*Give them hell*"—we would have done so too under the circumstances. He owns slaves, traffics in human beings, but he once honored by his presence a Methodist Episcopal Conference, which is evidence he is a *little* disposed to religion, and that is as much as we are. What did our people care for that? Show me the man at whose presence the drum beats, and the houses and streets are illuminated on account of his deeds of blood, and I will show you a man much more popular than a man imbued with the principles of Jesus Christ. The church must be opposed, in this enterprise. Necessity compels us to do it, we attack it because we feel it to be our duty.

The noble Garrison thought that he would only have to announce to the church her duty relative to this subject and it would rush to the rescue. Therefore he asked the clergy to come with their learning, their logic, their influence, their eloquence, to the slave's rescue, but they thundered their anthems upon him, and any other that would plead the cause of the dumb. Slavery had coiled itself in the pulpit, vaulted itself over the sanctuary. It had traced the sacred pages of the New Testament finding no comfort. It came to the church praying for protection, the church threw its mantle over it, stood by it, and declared it a Bible Institution. The most learned doctors of divinity came forth and advocated the doctrine that man may hold property in man. God is favorable to it, nature not opposed to it. Drs. Sharp, Spring, Spencer, Lord, Dewey, and others declared that Bible Christianity is in favor of slavery. This causes us to make war upon the church. Such organizations as these are opposed to Christianity. We must have a better religion—a religion which is love to God and man. Love to man only is not sufficient, this might render us selfish, it is not sufficient to hold us up. To use a homely expression, I might as well expect to raise myself up by my boot straps as to raise man up looking only to man. I look to God, and in proportion as I get a glimpse of God I embrace Christianity, love God, and love his purity.

The mass of the religionists of the day would call me an infidel. But I think I now drink at the true fount of Christianity.

In the middle of the nineteenth century, you may see the church and the slave-prison next door to each other, while the groans of the slave are drowned by the deafening shouts of the church. Revivals of religion and revivals of slave selling at the same time. Devils clothed in

Angel's robes stand in the church and pray, Our Father who art in Heaven, hallowed be thy name, thy kingdom come, thy will be done, on earth as it is done in Heaven, &c., and we thank thee, O God, that we live in a land of liberty where every man can worship thee under his own vine and fig tree, when none dare to make him afraid &c. We pray for righteous rulers that they may rule this people in fear, &c. And the next day go to the ballot-box, and vote for the oppressor, the warrior! for Whigs. But what is a Whig—a compromise man. Goes for Negro hunting, Negro catching. Perhaps there are Whigs here who this morning prayed that God would bless their families, that God would enable them to love him, while they are the very men of all others who are upholding the system of man-stealing, women-catching, and cradle-plundering. That minister who does not preach against the sin of slavery is not a minister of God. Men may be converted under their preaching to Methodism, &c., but not to Christianity. We want a better ministry, men who will preach in the name of God and not man. There are powerful temptations presented to the minister and the editor to let these sins alone. If the minister feels like preaching a little on land reform, as he is convinced land monopoly is oppressive and wrong, wherein there sits a large landholder of the church, and it won't do, it may drive him away and he then might lose his precious soul!!

(Mr. Douglass then made a few remarks in regard to the national party. He said until we have a party established independent of all support of slaveholders—a party that will render itself distasteful to the South, we can never effect much.) The two old parties are like two large serpents throwing their bodies across this whole land, their tails twisting about in the North while their heads are in the South together, and they looking most placidly in each other's eyes. The South rules the North. You may talk here in the North about nominating a candidate for the presidency, but you have no voice, you are proscribed by the South and have to vote for the man the South tells you to. You may talk about your choice of candidates, but you are like little boys playing upon the pond. You would acknowledge this to me if we were in the woods together.

Do you mean to continue to be the vassals of the Slave power? There are interests at the North dearer to us than any which can be attained by a co-operation with the parties. We are met by the assertion that we must have a disruption of this confederacy before Slavery can be overthrown. (Mr. Douglass avowed that this formerly was his opinion, and he had withdrawn from all action under or support of the Constitution, denouncing it as the deadly foe of humanity. He had once said in view of the evils of Slavery that he would welcome the bolt whether it came from the North or the South, from Heaven or Hell, which should shiver the Union into fragments. But he has since examined the question here carefully and now believes the Constitution to be an Anti-Slavery instrument and that it should be so construed and enforced. His reasons for the change in opinion in part are that though he always knew that taken in its plain reading, it did not uphold Slavery, yet he had got the impression we were to look beneath the surface and to find an occult meaning. There are several passages which look like sustaining Slavery. He had not then read law, and knew little of the debates on the adoption of the Constitution or the history of the times. When he came to examine the rules and principles by which such instruments should be construed, his opinions changed.) We are taught by tradition that what is said in the Constitution was the intent of the so called pro-slavery portions. When we look at it through the pro-slavery action of the Government, it bears a still worse appearance.

The proper rules in construing the Constitution are:

1st. In all cases an instrument which is ambiguous in its terms should be construed favorably to freedom and natural right. Any lawyer will tell you that. It has been adjudged by the Supreme Court that an evil intent in any written document must be expressed with irresistible clearness.

2nd. Another rule is where two interpretations, an innocent and a guilty can be given, the innocent should always be taken, and,

3rd. Where it is sought to sustain anything against the rights of man we are to be confined to the strict letter of the instrument authorizing it. (Thus construed he maintains there is no pro-slavery in the Constitution. Under the opposite belief persons supposing we must have Slavery or anarchy, choose to continue to support the former. But there is no such alternative presented by the case. The speaker holds that one of the great purposes of the adoption of the Constitution was to secure the overthrow of slavery.) In proof of this look at the intent expressed in the preamble. 'We the people of the United States, in order to form a more perfect union, establish justice &c. and to secure the blessings of liberty to ourselves and our posterity do ordain and establish this Constitution.' Hear it, old men and young, and especially the young who are coming up to construe and sustain it. Humanity may range throughout the universe for proof in her favor, but crime must have the letter on its side and that above to abide by. This was once shown rather ludicrously in the Legislature of Connecticut. A law was passed there that Negroes should not be allowed to travel after nine at night unless they carried a lantern. It was resolved to cast a light upon their dark countenances. Accordingly the colored people bought lanterns and carried them but without candles in them. When hauled up for trial it was proved they were taken up with lanterns in their hands but no candles. The proof was satisfactory they had complied with the letter of the law and they were acquitted as such a law must necessarily be construed strictly. Another law was passed that Negroes should carry lanterns with candles in them. This they complied with but without lighting them and were again hauled up and acquitted.

The law was amended so as to require them to carry lanterns with lighted candles in them and anon the Negroes were found parading with lighted candles in dark lanterns and being again acquitted the Legislature gave in and let the matter drop.

It is evidently our interest to make Legislators find it difficult to enact villainy into law. If then, the Constitution may be used to sustain natural right and against slavery, what we need is a party which will deal out equal and exact justice to all men. Here is a work for those to do who pray for just rulers, and it is necessary to place vital questions before the people.—Whilst we cling to the old parties we can do nothing against Slavery.

We feel for Hungary and for Ireland,[39] but how can we as a nation exert an influence favorable to freedom in the old world, while we are oppressors at home. Since I last addressed you I have seen the effects of American Slavery in other countries. The Irish cannot complain of the oppression of the British Crown, or speak of the land where they would gladly go without having it hurled at them, it is the land of oppression. They enslave the Blacks and he that would enslave one man would another. He may look at it but he sees no protection for him, he may be seized under it, and in the midst of the light of the religion of this day and hurled into the hell of slavery. The old world knows this, it delights the despots of Europe.

(The speaker then made some remarks in regard to the light in which the great O'Connell looked upon this land of blood and slaves, said that O'Connell was true to liberty everywhere, hated oppression in all lands, and dealt his bolts wherever the oppressor was seen to rear his head, and then proceeded to remark that he would to God that the great Hungarian had been as true, and faithful to human liberty as O'Connell; but that Kossuth had injured his cause.)[40]

We want our land to be something more than a by-word, and a hissing. Let us up to the work. The truth must accomplish it. Let us proclaim this truth to the state and to the Court, which have established Oppression for Liberty. Don't think you can do nothing; you are armed with the power to move the millions.

*Wilmington (Ohio) Herald of Freedom,* May 7, 1852, *reprinted in Larry Gara, editor, "Brilliant Thoughts and Important Truths: A Speech of Frederick Douglass," Ohio History,* Winter, 1966, pp. 3-9.


# I CONTEND

I contend that I have a right to co-operate with anybody, with everybody, for the overthrow of slavery in this country, *whether auxiliary or not auxiliary to the American Society*, when I am permitted to do so without sanctioning that which I disapprove, or sacrificing that which I do approve, and without withholding any part of my anti-slavery testimony. If I happen to be found in company with anybody who entertains a spirit more narrow than my own, I will not withdraw from him, but do what I can to enlarge his spirit, remove his prejudices, and impart to him more universal ideas than he had previously entertained; and this, (do not mistake me,) I hold to be *sound*, when tried by the standard of the American Anti-Slavery Society, whatever the agents may say to the contrary.

*Frederick Douglass' Paper,* May 20, 1852


# THE RECENT ANTI-SLAVERY FESTIVAL AND CONVENTION IN ROCHESTER

. . . Humanly speaking, all power in this country is in the hands of the people. Public opinion, is in this sense omnipotent; and this public opinion is the matter with which we have to do. In order to achieve the abolition of slavery, the great and and primary work still remains to be done; and still remaining to be done, and still demanding all our moral energies, is that of abolitionizing public sentiment. It is quite obvious, that until this fundamental and primary work is considerably advanced beyond what it now is, it will be as rational to expect good fruit from a bad tree, or sweet water from a bitter fountain as to expect extensive anti-slavery political action, or righteous legislation, in this country. It is, then to regenerate the public mind that we are called; and to do this we rely, under God, upon the power of truth, faithfully preached, and honestly reduced to practice. Slavery, with all its horrors must be exposed. The great principles of justice and liberty must be enforced, and the conscience of the nation must be quickened. This can be done by means of the *press*, and the living voice. But how shall these agencies be sustained? Mainly, we answer, by associated effort. Individual effort cannot do it, nor should it be left to any political party; for while political action against slavery is a duty, we deem the conditions under which it must be performed, if performed consistently, unfavorable to uniting all the elements necessary to be directed against slavery. The philosophy of reform, and our own anti-slavery experience clearly teach one, and the same lesson on this point. It is this, that the great moral and primary work to which we are invited, can be much more easily, economically, and successfully prosecuted by a Society exclusively devoted to this one great mission, and with which all the friends of the slave can cordially co-operate, be they voters or non-voters, than by any political party, how excellent soever its character. The reason is plain. A political party must from its very nature, declare itself upon many points of public policy; and how wise soever its declarations may be, there will be some about wisdom of which there is ever likely to be widely different and conflicting opinions, even of those, who are of one mind and one heart, in respect to slavery itself. There is also another reason for forming a New York Anti-slavery Society.—While woman is deprived of the right to vote it is impossible that she shall feel the same interest in political anti-slavery meetings as she would do in the meetings of an anti-slavery Society.

We, therefore, want just such an organization as that now found, to unite the sympathies and call forth the activities of anti-slavery women. We call upon the woman to take notice of this organization.

Their equal rights are *here* recognized; and *here* they may work for the deliverance of the slave and the salvation of their country. We call upon abolitionists throughout the State to welcome the appearance of this new engine for agitating and educating the public minds.—Let *towns, villages* and *counties* assemble and form auxiliary societies throughout the State; let the means be put into the common treasury and be used by the executive committee for securing able and eloquent agents, who shall carry the cause to every county, town, and village in the State. This is precisely what is wanted to agitate the public mind, to quicken the conscience, to elevate the moral sense, and to direct the public opinions against slaveholding. Let this be done at once, and the slaveholder will feel his grasp grow less firm on the throats of his victim; and the crushed and sorrow-stricken bondman will be made to rejoice in the hope of coming deliverance. But let it not be forgotten that it were *far* better that the Society had never been formed, if it should be allowed to languish in its infancy, for that support and sympathy which are needful to bring it into vigorous life and activity.

*Frederick Douglass' Paper*, May 25, 1852

## COLOROPHOBIA

If we may believe the clerk of the Forest City House, in Cleveland, the whole traveling community are now suffering under the most violent paroxysms of this disease, and it is the especial business of hotel keepers to accommodate themselves to the insane vagaries it may prompt.

When Frederick Douglass was on his way to Cincinnati, he stopped in Cleveland at the Forest City House. The following is Mr. Douglass's narrative of the transactions there:

But to the accident, in which I design the foregoing as the preface. On arriving at Cleveland, and finding that the train had departed for Cincinnati, I went to the *"Forest City Hotel"* to pass the night. I was readily received and handed a book by the clerk, in which he desired me to write my name, my place of residence, and my destination; with all of which, I complied with alacrity; feeling greatly pleased that my entrance had not at once subjected me to insult; for such is the hard fate of the colored traveler, that instead of being grateful for kindness, he has to thank his fellow-men for allowing him the commonest amenities of life, and permitting him to pass among them without insult. The civility extended to me at the commencement, induced the hope that nothing would occur during the twenty-four hours which I was to pass there, to ripple the current of good feeling which appeared to exist. The following circumstances will show the deceitfulness of outward appearances, and the groundlessness of my hope.

At the ringing of the morning bell for breakfast, I made my way to the table, supposing myself included in the call; but I was scarcely seated, when there stepped up to me a young man, apparently much agitated, saying: "Sir, you must leave this table." "And why," said I, "must I leave this table?" "I want no controversy with you. You must leave this table." I replied "that I had regularly enrolled myself as a boarder in that house; I expected to pay the same charges imposed upon others; and I came to the table in obedience to the call of the bell; and if I left the table, I must know the reason." "We will serve you in your room. It is against our rules." "You should have informed of *your rules* earlier. Where are your rules? Let me see them." "I don't want any altercation with you. You must leave this table." "But have I not deported myself as a gentleman? What have I done. Is there any gentleman who objects to my being seated here?" (There was silence around the table.) "Come, sir, come, sir, you must leave this table at once." "Well, sir, I cannot leave it unless you will give me a better reason than you have done for my removal." "Well, I'll give you a reason, if you'll leave the table and go to another room." "That, sir, I will not do. You have invidiously selected me out of all this company to be dragged from this table, and have thereby reflected upon me as a man and a gentleman; and the reason for this shall be as public as the insult you have offered." At these remarks, my carrot-headed assailant left me, *as he said*, to get help to remove me from the table. Meanwhile I called upon one of the servants (who appeared to wait upon me with alacrity) to help me to a cup of coffee, and assisting myself to some of the good things before me, I quietly and thankfully partook of my morning meal without further annoyance. To relieve the picture a little, I must mention that the proprietor of the house was absent; and I was informed that the conduct of his clerk was unauthorized. I am persuaded that such treatment will meet with no favor with a large and increasing class on the Western Reserve; and that such proscription, like that on the railroads of New England, will pass away under the enlightening influence of anti-slavery discussion and the practical assertion of their rights by colored men.

The True Democrat, in alluding to it, expressed the conviction that such treatment of gentlemanly guests, as Mr. Douglass received from the clerk was by no means a fair representation of the character of the house. In reply, the clerk issues a card, assuring the "traveling public" that this treatment or worse, is just what the travelling public demand, and that it shall be his especial business to gratify their whim in this particular.

We publish this statement, that that portion of the travelling public which may visit Cleveland, and who have sufficient self-respect to feel the insult offered them by the Forest City House, may hanceforth avoid it.

On Mr. Douglass's return, a similar incident occurred on board the steamer Queen City. We give an account in Mr. Douglass's own words:

On the steamer Queen City from Cleveland to Buffalo, I met with another illustration of American servility and toadyism. The facts are similar as those that transpired at the Forest City Hotel, with the exception that, on this occasion, the scamp who was about to drag me from the table was rebuked from an unexpected quarter, and never was there a more striking instance of Northern servility, than followed the rebuke. I was taking my seat, unwittingly opposite a Kentuckian, and a slave holder, and knew not of it until in a firm and commanding tone, he bade the fellow to depart, and to allow the gentleman to take his seat, adding that *"he was a Southerner."* This was enough. The contemptible creature of brief authority, skulked away like a spaniel at the stamp of his master. I had no further trouble, but received, thereafter, marked attention from all quarters. In subsequent conversation with the chivalrous Southerner, I found that he was no less a person than the Hon. Mr. Marshall, Representative to Congress, from California. Thus, going and coming from Cincinnati, I was afforded an opportunity to bear effective testimony against the unhallowed spirit of caste and proscription.

*The Liberator,* June 11, 1852

## TO PROFESSOR H.W. LONGFELLOW

Rochester, June 16th 1852

Dear Sir:

Do not deem me over importunate. My kind friend, Mrs. Porter, has just handed to me, your kind note: in which you decline (not peremptorily) to write anything on Slavery for the "Autograph."[41] That excellent Lady, with a perseverance characteristic of zeal in a good cause, says, "Do write at once to Mr. Longfellow *yourself*." My friend seems to think that my "*fugitive Slaveship*" will go a great way towards obtaining the desired treasure. *I* have no such vanity, and yet I am acting as though I had.

If, my dear Sir, you can but favor us with twenty lines, the favor will be highly prized.

For your kind disposition toward me, please, accept my grateful acknowledgements.

Very Respectfully yours etc.,
Frederick Douglass

*Ms., Houghton Library, Harvard University Library*

## HENRY CLAY IS DEAD

He died in Washington on Tuesday,[42] at half-past 11 o'clock, A.M. The court-House bell is tolling out the mournful tidings as we write; and we make no doubt that thousands are now doing what[43] his decease. —Wherever the lightning has flashed the news, a common shock will be felt, and common emotions will be manifested. —For whatever may be said (and much ought to be said) in derogation of the character of Henry Clay, his place in the affections of the American people, was higher than that of any other statesman, living or dead. It is no contradiction to this, that he never was honored with the chief magistracy of this republic; for affection happens not to be the controlling element in President-makings; that business rests upon quite other foundations, as many facts might be adduced to show. Friendship and affection are impotent before the power of selfishness and intrigue. The fact that a man has been chosen President, is far from being conclusive proof that he shares the affection of the American people.

*Henry Clay* was, personally, the most popular man of this nation; and he doubtless goes to his grave sincerely mourned by a larger number of people than any other statesman since George Washington. He was the man of his nation; and fully stained with their vices and crimes. He was an American; nothing more, nothing less; and he will be missed, mourned over, and remembered by Americans, as the great statesman of America. The press will unfold his career, the orator will kindle as he magnifies his eloquence and statesmanship, the American Church will own him as an American Christian, and American ministers will preach the great American statesman into "the rest that remains for the people of God." They see him from their point of view, and love his character, prize his deeds, mourn his death, honor his memory, and exalt his fame. In nothing of this can we join. So far as his statesmanship has affected us, we have vastly more reason to condemn, than to applaud his character; to rejoice, than to mourn his death; to hate, than to prize his deeds; and to execrate than to honor his memory.

In the blaze of his nineteenth century, with all the lights of Christian truth burning around him, with the *Declaration of Independence* sounding in his ears, from childhood to old age, with the profession of religion on his lips, Henry Clay has gone up to his Maker a holder of slaves, a man-stealer, having done more than any other man in this country to make slavery perpetual.

In his early years of public life, he gave his best energies to the cause of emancipation in Virginia. Some of his higher strains of eloquence were poured out over the wrongs of the African race. But, when he found that the pathway to power and position in this country led through palliating, excusing, and defending slavery, he seems deliberately to have decided to stifle his generous feelings, to blunt his moral sense, and fit himself for the debasing work which has, for many years, engaged his time and talents. In conversation with the noble Gerrit Smith, of Peterboro, 20 years ago, when asked by him if he held slaves he answered in words which contain a history of his character and his course, "Yes," said he, regretfully, *"I have floated down with the current."* A melancholy reply; certainly. What he might have done, had he braved that current and been true to his early convictions of truth and duty, who can tell? His country, now staggering under a heavy curse, intoxicated with human blood, tossed by the winds and waves of agitation, inventing new schemes of oppression, to make former tyranny secure, might have been delivered from its guilt and shame; and robed in that *"righteousness"* which *"exalteth a nation;"* but alas for him and his country, he *"floated down the current;"* and by his example dragged thousands of the brightest luminaries of the land with him; and at last, dies himself—*a slaveholder*. The dragon he denounces in the shell, and which he might have easily crushed, has grown to frightful dimensions, causing the land to tremble under its dreadful tread. It was said by Lamartine,[44] that *"Wilberforce went up to the throne of God with a million of broken fetters* in his hands as evidence of a life well spent." But what must be said of Henry Clay? Where are the monuments of his good deeds? Where are the widows, whose tears he has dried? the orphans he has left protected? the poor he has succored? the fetters he has broken? and echo answers, *Where?*

His career may be traced by the blasted soil of Virginia; by the whipping posts of Kentucky; by the slave-hunts of New England; and by the domineering pride of men, whose property is human flesh; whose motive to industry is the lash; whose protection is in the ignorance of their victims; and who are driven, by their iniquitous position, to plot, war, and repine upon their neighbors. From a life and death like his, we may all reverently say, "Good Lord! deliver us."—He *"floated down the current;"* and the object for which he flung himself in like a false light, drifted ever beyond his grasp, and he died without obtaining the aim of his ambition.

The occasion is full of profitable suggestions, but we forbear.

*Frederick Douglass' Paper*, July 1, 1852

## TO GERRIT SMITH

Rochester, July 20th, 1852

My dear Sir:

Many thanks for your present. I shall not be able to go to Pittsburgh by way of Philadelphia. The journey would cost too much, and besides I should encounter the "American demon" that way, more than by way of Cleveland.[45]

I shall however meet you at the convention. I share the doubt you express, as to our being received as members of the convention. If *they* don't receive us, the people will. Our western friends must know something of the Liberty Party and thou art the man to tell them.

I am off for Tomkins county tomorrow morning, and shall probably go to McGrawville before I return home. A letter from Wm. R. Smith this morning expresses his belief that Wm. Goodell will go to England, to collect the Chaplin bail.

In haste yours most truly,<br>
Frederick Douglass

*Gerrit Smith Papers, George Arents Research Library, Syracuse University*

## LETTER FROM THE EDITOR

I found Mr. Schuyler deeply interested in the improvements of the colored people in Ithaca. He often addresses them on subjects connected with their elevation at their meetinghouse, and he is evidently doing a good work there. I am to speak to my colored friends to-night in Zion Church, and, as much interest is felt, a large meeting is expected.

July 22d.—It was exceedingly warm last night, but this morning the air is cool and reviving. The meeting at Zion Church was contrary to my expectation, and partly to my wishes, largely composed of white persons. There are some things which ought to be said to colored people in the peculiar circumstances in which they are placed, that can be said more effectively among themselves, without the presence of white persons. We are the oppressed, the whites are the oppressors, and the language I would address to the one is not always suited to the other.

I found the meeting-house just the cleanest and neatest colored meeting-house into which I ever stepped. I remark on this fact purposely; for I have been in many colored churches which were a disgrace to the colored people, and this was just for the want of a little *taste* and industry. Men cannot well have clean hearts who worship in dirty meeting-houses. I have been in some not far from Rochester, that confer no credit on the people worshipping in them. All along the side wall you may see, in *grease spots*, just where the uncles Tobeys and Johnsons rest their heads to sleep during public worship! The meeting-house at Ithaca is kept in creditable order, and is a place into which the colored people of that village need not be ashamed to invite anybody. I aimed to impress upon my friends, in my speech, the importance of helping themselves, and relying upon their own efforts for attaining an honorable position among the people of this country. I was sorry to find in Ithaca that the colored people had, like those in other places, adopted the miserable habit of coming into meeting much later than other people. I call this a *miserable* habit, and so it is. It is a slavish habit, for which only slaves could offer an excuse. When men are held as slaves, they are usually compelled to get their masters ready for meeting before themselves, and in this there is an excuse for such persons; but there is none for free men and free women. It is often the case that those who live nearest to the church get into meeting last; thus showing that it is not distance nor employment, but a *miserable slavish*, lazy habit that leads them to put everything off to the last. This habit must be broken off before we can boast of being equal to white people! I dwell on this because I think that we are about as much behind the whites in other things as we are in this; and have hopes that if colored people will try to imitate the whites in this, they will try to imitate them in other things, and finally make honorable progress. The lazy, sleepy heads will be full of wrath at these remarks, and denounce me without measure; but the prompt and industrious will justify all I have said. WAKE UP! and go to meeting in time.

July 23d.—The County Anti-Slavery Convention held here yesterday, in the Town Hall, was in numbers, spirit, zeal and determination highly gratifying, and fitted to cheer the hearts of all who would see this guilty nation repent, and the poor slave redeemed from his chains. The whole affair showed a pleasing change in the public opinion of the place, since it was my privilege to visit Ithaca ten years ago. At that time the community seemed sunk to the most hopeless depths of pro-slavery. Anti-slavery was bitterly and intensely hated. The advocates of liberty were subject to brutal persecution, and colored people were held in contempt and scorn. The public halls and the meeting houses in the place were shut against the anti-slavery lecturer. At that time I was compelled, if I spoke at all, to speak in the open air, but not even there was I protected, for I spoke amid insults and jeers from a menacing mob. The hotels would hardly shelter an abolitionist; and then there were no kind friends to invite the lecturer home. Dr.

Wisner's Divinity had done an evil work for Ithaca, and such as at that time, it seemed difficult to counteract.

A change, however, has taken place, and it is very plainly seen. The exactions of the slave power and the Fugitive Slave Law, have had something to do with changing the public mind on this subject, as well as anti-slavery lectures and papers. But it must be conceded that the most efficient agent in changing the sentiment of Ithaca, as well as elsewhere, must be set down to the circulation of "Uncle Tom's Cabin." That book is but at the beginning of its career,[46] and it goes like fire through a "dry stubble," sweeping all before it.

The Convention met at ten o'clock, A.M., and notwithstanding the press of work on the hands of the farmers at this season of the year, they were present in goodly numbers, with hard hands and warm hearts, showing that the Whig and the Democratic parties have yet a large share of work to do, before they will have suppressed all agitation against slavery. Those noble farmers, as they flocked in, seemed to take the parties by surprise. The demonstration was altogether more imposing than was expected and its effect was powerful. Ithaca was quite roused from her slumbers, and I was told that no anti-slavery meeting had ever awakened such a sensation in the place before.

The forenoon meeting was addressed by P.C. Schuyler and Frederick Douglass. The former made a calm statement of the objects of the Constitution, briefly noticed the present position of the great national pro-slavery parties, and insisted upon the strictest adhesion to anti-slavery principles in the coming election.

A series of resolutions were presented by a business committee, especially directed against the Fugitive Slave Bill. This done, and the meeting adjourned till two o'clock P.M.

I learned from Mr. and Mrs. Love, that an excellent impression was made in Ithaca last winter, by *Miss Sallie Holley*. Miss Holley seems to have been very successful in winning friends, not less for herself, than for the holy cause to which she is devoting her time and talents. It is pleasant to find good impressions left behind those who plead the cause of the slave. Where the hearts of the people are not reached, no matter how much light and truth have been poured around them, they are not yet in their sins, and it may be only the more hardened in their sins by what they have heard. Miss Holley seems to have won the hearts, as well as the heads of her hearers. And this may safely be set down as proof of her fitness for the arduous work to which she is earnestly devoting herself.

### Afternoon Session

Prof. Allen of Central College,[47] and J.W. Loguen,[48] of Syracuse, have joined us, the first by appointment, and the latter by accident; both were warmly received by the audience, who recognized them as old friends and acquaintances. Messrs. Allen and Loguen were called upon to speak, and speak they did, and with eloquence and power. Loguen never did better than at this meeting. His exile in Canada has not weakened his spirit, nor abated his natural force. He is the very picture of health, and is the embodiment of manly energy. a kind-hearted, gentle, good man, naturally a lamb, and evidently capable of playing the part of a lion. The skull of a kidnapper would stand no chance beneath the strong arm and heavy hand! I was glad to hear him say that he should not again consent to be exiled; but that he should stand his ground, and sell his life or liberty at the highest price, should there be an attempt to drag him back to bondage. A few such men as Loguen could easily expose the folly of the Fugitive Slave Law, and make it of no effect.

The evening meeting was thronged. Prof. Allen and Frederick Douglass were the speakers. Mr. Allen made one of the best anti-colonization speeches I ever heard. It was not a passionate outburst of indignation at the impudence and wickedness of the Colonization scheme, but a calm, philosophical, and historical argument; well fitted to convince the audience that the presence of the colored people in this country is important to the progress of civilization, and to the highest elevation of the whole American population. I venture to say that this speech of Mr. Allen removed more prejudice against color than anything which has been done in Ithaca for a long time. He brought learning and logic, as well as feeling to the work so that he reached the judgments, as well as the hearts of men. The colored people present looked delighted, as they saw their champions, scattering one after another, the barricades of their enemies. It was a proud night for them, and it was cheering to observe that they so regarded it. Let them warmly espouse their own cause, and bear a part of the burden of keeping up the movement, and the victory gained may be a glory, as well as a benefit to them.

Frederick Douglass followed Prof. Allen, commencing at half past nine, and ending at eleven o'clock, when the meeting adjourned.

The Convention appointed delegates both to the Pittsburgh and the Buffalo Conventions. A strong desire to bring the whole anti-slavery strength of the country to bear upon the approaching election was apparent; nor did there seem to be a disposition to lay much stress on minor points, as conditions for uniting their energies with the Pittsburgh Convention. Anti-slavery fitness seemed to be the main thing they required in the candidate who should receive their votes.

I have spent a part of to-day in visiting among the colored people here, with brother Loguen; and was happy to find them "very well-to-do" in the world. I found them as neat in their homes, as at the nice little church of which I have spoken. Colored and white children go to the same school here; prejudice cannot do much where that is the case.

Loguen, Allen and I go from here to Dryden, about ten miles distance. We are to hold another meeting there to-night.

Frederick Douglass

*Frederick Douglass' Paper*, July 30, 1852

## WHY FRED. DOUGLASS GETS INTO DIFFICULTY

Fred. Douglass seems to get into difficulty wherever he goes. The Cleveland *Forest City* states that when he was there, in the early part of the season, he made a great ado because the Forest City House did not desire to drive the rest of the guests from the dining rooms, and leave him the sole occupant. Now he comes out in the *Wellington Journal* severely consuring the officers of the 'Northern Indiana' for not giving him a cabin passage; and we believe he had some difficulty with a keeper of an eating-house on the Pittsburgh road, for driving him from the table, which was adjusted by taking a vote of the guests. Douglass came out ahead, the vote being two in his favor to one against him. We never had an attack of the colorphobia, and can respect genius, whether its possessor be a man of sable hue or a ruddy Anglo-Saxon; but it strikes us that Douglass could arrange it so, in his travels, as not to have cause for as much trouble as he does.—He seems to court a collision when altogether unnecessary. His talents none will deny, but a deep-rooted prejudice must be worked out gradually, without compulsion or precipitancy. He may be a 'perfect gentleman,' but he is a very unfortunate man.

The above, is taken from the *Buffalo Courier* of Monday morning; and the writer must have thought himself a clever fellow.—"*Frederick Douglass* gets into difficulty wherever he goes;" not because he is either intrusive, insolent, or querulous, but simply, because, presuming to be a man, he recognizes himself as entitled to the rights and privileges of a man. These rights and privileges are shamefully trampled upon by the community at large. Hence, he is constantly "*in difficulty*," not of his own seeking, but "*difficulty*" forced upon him by the manhood of himself, and the meanness of the community. It seems to us superlatively selfish and mean for one human being to sit down to a table and appease his own hunger, while he drives his hungry brother from the table for no fault save the color of his skin. It is not true that a single passenger of the hundreds present objected to sitting at dinner with Fred. Douglass, in the Hotel at Alliance. The vote in favor of his admission to the dinner table was unanimous and enthusiastic, and much indignation was felt at the landlord for his insulting conduct. The delegates to the Convention on returning from Pittsburgh through Alliance remembered Mr. "*Sourbeck*," and six hundred of them passed by his house to another, and left his *dinner* to those who can bear colored men at the table only as servants. This number was exceedingly small, six only dined with "*Sourbeck*" and *six hundred* at the house which accommodated all passengers on equal terms. We ought, perhaps, to say that "*Sourbeck*" apologized in a very submissive manner when he found himself arrayed against public opinion. The friends of freedom should acquaint the proprietors of steamboats and hotels, that there is public opinion on both sides of this question.

It was pretended by the clerk on board the "Northern Indiana" that Frederick Douglass was deprived of a cabin passage because white passengers would object to his presence in the cabin. The absurdity of this pretense will be quite obvious when it is remembered that the passengers on board of the "Northern Indiana" were the same that had rode side by side with him by railway, without the slightest objection, or manifestation of dissatisfaction. There was no objection in the cars; why should there be in the cabin? The fact is, that the officious clerk, proud of his brief authority, anxious to appear superior to somebody on earth, took especial pleasure in asserting his superiority over a Negro. "*I am not for mixing up*," said he.—But he had no objection to mixing up Frederick Douglass with the white deck passengers, showing that he thought Negroes and poor white people were about on a level, and that he did not object so much to the mixing of *white* and *black* as to the mixing of *rich* and *poor*.

The railroad, when completed from Buffalo to Cleveland, will put an end to this contemptible conduct on the lake. Frederick Douglass was ill prepared (having no overcoat) for a night in the open air, on Lake Erie; and although he pleaded this circumstance, and offered to give an extra sum for his passage to obtain a place, in which to lay his head, his offers were rejected in the most brutal and insulting manner; yet, on this very boat, strange to tell, and in the same cabin, as a servant, a colored man will find his color no barrier whatever. Our countrymen do not understand us, if they for a moment imagine that we are animated by a love of contention or collision, simply because we do not recognize the wisdom or the justice of the distinctions that they set up; and meanly slink away from the *practical* assertion of our rights, under their bitter and contemptuous scowl. Nor, do they comprehend our spirit, if they fancy that, by *such* repulses, they can crush the hope or the aspiration within, us, that,

> "Man to man the world all o'er,
> Shall brothers be for a' that."

*Frederick Douglass' Paper*, August 20, 1852

# IT IS NOT TO THE RICH BUT TO THE POOR THAT WE MUST LOOK

SPEECH at the Tenth Annual Convention of the Western Anti-Slavery Society, Salem, Ohio, August 23, 1852

I want my good will for the W.A.S. Society understood and I desire to show it especially in this matter of sustaining its operations. I know, notwithstanding I am a politician and have become a Liberty party man, that the pioneers of this A.S. movement, the men upon whom this cause rests most fully, those who will have to bear the burden and heat of the day, are those who are connected with this Society. I know that political action is necessary only in the rear of public sentiment, and whenever public sentiment is strongly anti-slavery enough, then will be generated a party who will "crystalize" as Wendell Phillips said, "this sentiment into law." I think I understand the philosophy of Reform well enough to know that the man or society which utters the truth most pointedly, and applies it most closely and stringently to the public mind, no matter if a small minority, that man or body is doing most to promote the A.S. cause. They may not be doing all the work. They who scorn all abuse on account of principle, and believe only in flinging that principle before the public mind, are the men who are bringing about the abolition of the wrong against which they are so contending and their hands ought to be held up. Now I can vote one day in the year against slavery, and think it my duty to do so, but every other day I want the burning coals of truth to be thrown upon the nation's naked breast, and because you are working thus it is our duty as Free Soilers to aid you in your work.

Besides, we know that political parties are a very uncertain sort of machinery, we do not know to what base uses these organizations may be put, and we want a force outside of them, something to fall back upon in the day of trial when these parties fail us. We need a body who *will* be faithful and who will apply the principles of truth continually. I have engaged for life in this work, but I am going to be a man. A free man. Free to adopt any views, any instrumentalities, which I think will advance the good cause, and although I vote, I believe that the great instrumentality after all, is the "foolishness of preaching." The work is to be done by exposing the damning deeds of Slavery, the abominations of the church, in short, by agitation. Agitate, *agitate.* This is the grand instrumentality, and without this you Free Soilers will come to nothing. I go as a Liberty party man for sustaining all the moral movements of the country. I have no idea that you abolitionists of the W.A.S. Society, will ever be able to bring all the people up to your platform; and it is not necessary, for long before you have converted the whole people to your doctrine of "No union with Slaveholders," slavery will be blotted out. Go on then with your preaching, you can all do something, both men and women.

It is the poor man's work. The rich and noble will not do it. I know what it is to get a living by rolling casks on the wharves, and sweeping chimneys, and such like, and this makes me able to sympathize with the poor, and the bound everywhere. It is not to the rich that we are to look but to the poor, to the hardhanded working men of the country, these are the men who are to come to the rescue of the slave. I tell you my friends and fellow citizens, there is room enough for us all, there is a niche in the temple of Reform for everybody. Abolitionism has made me a great man, (beg pardon for the egotism,) but it delivered me from the bondage of sectarianism and priestcraft, from the bondage of my color even, and false notions of human brotherhood, and has opened the wide world of humanity, and taught me that though my heart is small, yet there every man under the wide canopy of heaven can find room. Why what has it not done for me, for us all? It has taught us that we have a heart and conscience, that we are a part of the great whole of humanity. Let us up then and be doing, and learn to labor and to wait. What matters it if you are few in numbers, let me tell you friends, that even if a man be alone and be right, he is a majority in the universe. If he does not represent the present state of things, he represents the future. If not what men are, what they ought to be. Be true then to your convictions, and I will try and be true to mine, and so far as we can, let us unite for the common cause. I did not come here to subserve the interests or ends of any party, but to subserve the interests of the cause, and I shall go back cheered and strengthened by what I have seen and heard. Let us devote ourselves heart and hand to the work, and go on rejoicing in the proclamation of truth.

*Anti-Slavery Bugle,* January 1, 1853

## SPEECH DELIVERED AT THE MASS FREE DEMOCRATIC CONVENTION AT ITHACA, NEW YORK, OCT. 14TH, 1852

Mr. Chairman:

I esteem it a very great privilege to address this Convention.

I take you to represent the spirit of freedom and progress in Tompkins.

Sir, I am not sensible of possessing any special aptitude or qualification to instruct you in minute political questions, which may affect your material interests. I know little of banks or tariffs, of commerce or currency. Yet, I have one great political idea, and so far as that can bear upon your political relations and duties, I am willing to present it this evening.

That idea is an old one. It is widely and generally assented to;

nevertheless, it is very generally trampled upon and disregarded. The best expression of it, I have found in the Bible. It is in substance, Righteousness Exalteth a Nation—Sin is a Reproach to any People.

Sir, this constitutes my politics, the negative and positive of my politics, and the whole of my politics.

I hold that nations, no more than individuals, may hope for peace and prosperity while they trample upon the sacred principles of *justice, liberty,* and *humanity;* and as a member of our society, under the laws and institutions of this country, I feel it my duty to do all in my power to infuse the idea into the public mind, that it may speedily be recognized and practiced upon by our people.

Fellow-citizens, I am not an old man, nor have I had great opportunities for studying the history of this country. My sphere of observation and experience was, for more than twenty years, limited to the slave plantation.

I have been a slave, and could learn but little, when a slave, of what was going on in this country and world about me. A slave prison is worse than a States prison. In the States prison a man may know something and think something of the past; but the inmates of the slave prison know nothing of the past, present or future. Clouds and darkness overshadow them, and facts familiar to others are unknown to them.

Humble, however, as I am, and limited as is my knowledge, I must be allowed to say that, never has there been a time when the great principles of *justice, liberty* and *humanity* were put in more imminent peril than at the present moment. Never was there a time when the friends of these great principles were more loudly and imperatively called upon to stand by these principles than now.

The ruling parties of the country have now flung off all disguises, and have openly and shamelessly declared war upon the only saving principles known to nations. Their platforms, adopted at Baltimore, embrace the whole slave system, as worthy of their regard and support. To expose those platforms and to rebuke those parties, becomes the duty of every intelligent and patriotic voter in the republic,

These parties, fellow citizens, are now soliciting you for your votes. They want the reins of government to enable them to accomplish certain objects.

What these objects are, you are to learn from their platforms.

They want power, and want you to give it to them, and in their platforms they tell you what they mean to do with power when they get it.

There is quite a gain here, for in whatever else these parties are to be condemned, they are certainly to be commended for their frankness. I repeat, they want power, and ask you to give it to them; and they have boldly told you just what use they mean to make of it when they get it. No man who votes for General Scott or for General Pierce can so vote without knowing precisely the use to which his vote is to be put.[49]

You all know, gentlemen, that there was an attempt, both in the Whig and in the Democratic Convention at Baltimore, to nominate candidates before adopting their platform.—The motive for this was to leave candidates room for double dealing and to make them independent of the platforms. But the South scouted this as a cowardly policy, and it failed. They cried out principles, not men; and that cry prevailed.

The candidates are, therefore, subject, not superior to the platforms. The candidates are *after,* not before the platforms. The whole matter is here in a nut shell. The candidates who have stepped upon these platforms, pledge themselves, before God and the world, to carry out the policy set forth in the platforms. There is no escape from this common sense view of the case. There is no back door here. There is no other way which men can climb. The way of entrance and the way of exit are the same.

The efforts of certain Whigs and Democrats to escape from this dilemma are very miserable. They tell us they mean to vote for the candidates of their parties, but that they repudiate the platforms. They hold the platforms to be simply the opinions of the men who voted for them in the Convention[50] matter, it strikes a death blow at all political integrity and destroys confidence in all political creeds, and in all the men who adopt them. Honesty is the best policy even in dealing with slaveholders. Carry out this dodging doctrine, and no man voting would know to what use his vote is to be put—what measures his vote will support, and what measures his vote will defeat. Upon this theory, the Whig slaveholders may vote for Scott, because he is on the platform, and the Whig abolitionists may vote for him because he is too good to be on the platform, and because he will cheat the South if he shall be elected. Now I hold this to be a desperate piece of political dishonesty; eating the devil, while piously repudiating his broth is nothing to this.

There is something really amusing in the evolutions of the anti-slavery Whigs who have brought themselves to vote for the Whig candidates. When we tell them that by voting for General Scott they vote for the Baltimore platform, they say not at all. We vote for the candidate, not the platform.

Now it would be quite as sensible to say we vote for the men, not their principles.—These candidates were selected to carry out the platforms upon which they secured their nominations, and this everybody knows.

The authorship of this pro-candidates, anti-platform theory, must go to the credit of Mr. Greeley of the *N. Y. Tribune*[51]—a man whose moral convictions are always kept beyond hearing distance behind his political action. He tells us that he defies, repudiates and spits upon the Baltimore platform; that he is not bound by it, and doesn't mean to be. Yet he claims to be a Whig, and gives his support to the Whig candidates.

Gentlemen, I fight no shadow. Mr. Greeley is keeping back from our cause in this country thousands whose hearts are with us. Almost every man with whom I have met in your country who avows his intention to vote for Scott and Graham, does so, with a kick at the Baltimore platforms.—They shield their inconsistency under this Greeley sophistry.

It is true, sir—this is a very shallow sophistry—a very miserable covering; but you know a drowning man will catch at a straw. Like almost all sophistry, its effect is produced by a skilful substitution of a false for the real issue. It calls attention from the vote to the state of mind of the voter, from his pro-slavery vote to his anti-slavery character, from his actions to his professions.

Now, we who call ourselves of the Free Democracy do not deny that the Whig platform ought to be defied and spit upon. That is our doctrine exactly. We not only think so, believe so, and feel so, but we are prepared to *act* so.

We do not deny that Mr. Greeley and other anti-slavery Whigs, think, believe and feel as we do. They spit, repudiate and defy; but that does not meet the case. The question is not whether they thus spit and defy; but does this spit and defiance go along with their vote, or does it, like spit to the windward, come straight back in their faces?

We know you hate your platform in your hearts; but we complain that you do not in your votes. You love liberty and vote against it. You hate slavery and the fugitive slave act, and then vote for the twin abominations. When we condemn your votes, you vindicate your opinions; when we assail your deeds, you defend your motives. Is this honest? Is it manly?

What matter is it to the man in chains, whether his chains are voted on by an anti-slavery or by a pro-slavery man, by a Christian or by an infidel? It is not the motives nor the opinions of the voter, but it is the vote that either rivets or breaks his fetters.

It does seem strange that men can be found who can act so inconsistently.

The candidates of the two great parties have accepted their nominations, understandingly and distinctly. And these nominations have not been more distinctly and understandingly accepted than have the platforms; both came from the same bodies, and were presented at the same time, and accepted at the same time. There can be no mistake about it.

Now, for these candidates to allow themselves to be voted for while on these platforms, and then turn round after getting into power and violate the principles and measures set forth in them, would be nothing less than political treachery of the basest kind.

General Scott might well say of that class, save me from my friends; for just in proportion to the success of Mr. Greeley at the North, must be General Scott's unpopularity at the South.

Sir, I leave this miserable paper castle to be disposed of by that hailstorm which is beginning to show itself in the political firmament. With the remark, that considering how much the Whig party North has had to complain of in the way of treachery, bad luck and the like; how much Mr. Greeley belabored the unfortunate accidental President eleven years ago, for treachery to Whig principles and Whig measures; it does seem that this spit and repudiation theory should have emanated from another quarter than the Whig party, and from another pen than that of Horace Greeley. Whig principles and obligations were quite loose enough before this shock. Whiggery cannot stand much more. I apprehend that this one will kill it, at least in the South, where it has heretofore had little better than a name to live.

But we were asked by the Whig Democratic parties to give them power. What they want with power they have frankly told us.

The question is, Can we innocently and wisely give them our votes, and secure to them the reins of government which they crave? Ought we to vote for them, or ought we to vote against them, is the question?—Let us see. There is, in this country, a system of injustice and cruelty, shocking to every sentiment of humanity—a crime and scandal, making this country a hissing and a bye-word to the world and liable to the judgements of a righteous God.

This stupendous iniquity, this giant crime, this murderous system is Slavery.

There is nothing to which we can liken it. It is barbarous, monstrous, and bloody.—Crushed beneath this most horrible institution, are three millions of our countrymen. These are subject to the terrible inflictions of the fetter, the lash, and the chain. These suffering men and women have been held, and are now held to gratify the pride, to indulge the indolence, to minister to the lasting pleasure of three hundred thousand slaveholders.

For a long time, these slaveholders have, with greater or less completeness, ruled this nation. They have had the lion's share in all the honors and emoluments of office.—They govern the state in which they live. They monopolize all state offices, unless it be the office of Negro-whipper. This they are willing to have Northern ruffians to do for them. It is next to impossible for any man in the Southern States, not a slaveholder, to get into any respectable office above that of a constable or a Negro-driver.

In South Carolina, a man who is not able to own ten slaves cannot be a member of the Legislature. He may be, in every respect, qualified as a legislator, a sober, honest, intelligent and patriotic man; but if the blood of his brother man be not in his skirts, he is, by law, disqualified in South Carolina.

What is *law* in South Carolina, is *custom* in nearly all the slave states of this Union.

The slaveholders gather up the reins of the government, and pocket the rewards of office to the exclusion and degradation of the honest and industrious free white man of the South. The thirst of the slaveholder for power is insatiable. The more they get, the more they want. Every concession is followed by a new and still more unreasonable demand. To comply with one demand, is only to pave the way to a new exaction. The history of this country shows that between freedom and slavery there has been a constant systematic effort on the part of the latter to extinguish and destroy the former. The struggle has been long and fierce, and the combatants are still in the field.

It may be well, in this connection, to call to mind a few facts in the history of this struggle, and to take a general view of the different phases of the slave power.

Daniel Webster said at Springfield, Mass., that nations, no less than individuals, do well to pause at certain periods, and survey the past, examine the present, and in the light of these, contemplate the future. This is but one of many sage suggestions from the same quarter. What of the night?—Whither are we tending? Is the ship of State sound, tight and free? Or is she leaky and liable to sink? Are we out of danger? or are we in the midst of sharp and flinty rocks? Are we advancing? or are we retrograding? These questions concern every American citizen.

The Slavery power has aimed at two objects from the beginning. First, to acquire a wide and fertile territory; second to control the government. It needs endless, limitless fields over which to pour its poisoning and blasting influence. Its province is not to replenish, but to wear out the earth. Its course is like that of the locusts of Egypt; ruin and desolation are in its track.

The virgin soil of Virginia, once the most fertile, inviting and beautiful, is now spread out like a withered branch on the Republic, cursed and blighted by slavery. Whole villages, once thronged with people are now deserted, and crumbling in ruins.

North Carolina is rapidly going to decay; and all the older slave states are witnesses to the ruinous influence of slavery. The contrast between Kentucky and Ohio is familiar to you all; and the causes of that contrast are known to every intelligent American.—Cassius M. Clay,[52] himself a Kentuckian, has unfolded their causes, and demonstrated, beyond all questions that emancipation tomorrow, so far from making his native state poorer, would on the very instant make that State richer. Yet, there she lies, in the ruinous embrace of Slavery, venting her curses and repining over the prosperity, progress and intelligence of her neighboring sister. Her children, instead of remaining with her, making all her hills valleys, and plains cheerful, are straying away into the limitless Southwest, to plant, only to poison the virgin soil, with slavery. As with the slaveholders of Kentucky, so with the slaveholders of all the older slave states.

When I was a boy, the most dreaded doom to which a slave could be subjected, was being sold to Georgia. That was our Southern slave market thirty years ago. Since then, the surplus increase of human stock has demanded new outlets and new markets. Virginia has asked for fresh markets for her human produce; and the North has consented and conceded the request.—We are starving, said Virginia. Our Negroes are swarming around us, and are literally eating us out of house and home. We must have relief. We must have a market for human flesh, or we are ruined. We have sometimes been told that Virginia was moving for the abolition of slavery; but that the injudicious course of Northern abolitionists has put back the cause in that State, and defeated the benevolent designs of Virginia in this matter.

I am persuaded that this statement is far from the truth. The real cause for the defeat of the anti-slavery movement in Virginia is found in the fact that Northern pro-slavery men have, whenever slave property has decreased in value, opened new markets for human flesh, and raised its price. Thus, when slavery was dying from its utter unprofitableness, new life and vigor have been imparted to its expiring frame by Northern men and by Northern votes.

The purchase of Louisiana,[53] the annexation of Texas, the war with the Seminoles,[54] and the war with Mexico, were all measures commenced and carried on for the purpose of giving prosperity and perpetuity to slavery and for maintaining the sway of the slave power over the republic. Any man who doubts this, has only to read *"Jay's view of the action of the federal government,"* and his *"Review of the Mexican war,"* to have his doubts entirely removed.

Gentlemen, let us inquire, What was the state of the anti-slavery question four years ago? I mean in its political aspects. Fourteen legislatures had solemnly instructed their representatives in Congress to vote for the Wilmot Proviso.

Innumerable political conventions throughout the North had declared in favor of excluding slavery from the newly acquired territories from Mexico. This policy had the support of leading men of the North. Daniel Webster had declared his unalterable determination to oppose the farther extensions of slavery. Whigs and Democrats vied with each other in professions of hostility to the slavery propagandism of the ultraslave-holding politicians of the South. This sentiment became so strong that a powerful party was organized, solemnly pledging itself to *"fight on and fight ever"* against slavery, and the ascendency of the slave power in the councils of the nation. The agitation in this direction was general and wide spread. The North was in flame. The eloquence of the Stantons, the Van Burens, the Butlers, the Kings, roused the Northern feeling and excited intense and burning enthusiasm among the people. No more Slave States, No more Slave Territory, Free States, Free Men, and Free Territory, leaped joyously from Northern lips of all parties and creeds. The movement appeared formidable. The South became alarmed and it was evident that leading men at the South felt that their crafty wisdom was about to be confounded, and their counsels brought to nought. They changed their aggressive tactics for a defensive attitude. They declared that Congress had no right to decide what should be the character of the institutions established in the territories, and that that question should be left to the territories themselves.

Such, gentlemen, was the state of this question four years ago. The cause of freedom looked auspicious. For the first time in the political history of this nation there did appear a strong likelihood that the people and the politicians in the North would remain firm and unyielding; that they would withstand the shock of Southern aggression with manly courage; and that freedom would come off victorious.

But, alas! Northern integrity and spirit were no match for the dogged persistence, seductive blandishments, and bribery of the South. The slaveholders entirely outgeneralled the men of the North at the very outset of the winter of '49, with a boldness creditable to their sagacity. The slaveholding members of Congress, under the lead of Mr. Calhoun, organized themselves into a sort of Congress of their own, and marked out the kind of legislation which the legitimate Congress should adopt, and threatened that direful consequences would ensue if Congress should, in its wisdom, desregard the views and opinions held by them, the slaveholders. We all remember how this movement operated. The cry of Danger to the Union was raised. Foote, the fire-eater and hangman, led the American Senate in this cry. He was followed by the late, Mr. Clay, who boldly assailed the policy of Gen. Taylor, and drew vivid pictures of *"dismal terror and dire confusion,"* of *"disunion,"* and civil war. Cass followed in the same course. Douglas, with characteristic wariness, encouraged the idea that something really terrible was at hand. He, of course, was for concession; everything was to be done to save the Union.

Gentlemen, the trick worked admirably.—Man after man gave in his adhesion, to the cry of danger to the Union. Papers of all parties flamed with it; and the land was filled with dread and apprehenson.

Still, gentlemen, there was hope. The great "Expounder" had not spoken. He stood before the country openly and strongly committed to the principles of the Free Soil party; and he was known in private to have encouraged the young Whigs of New England to stand by the principle of the ordinance of '87. But to the disappointment and mortification of all who had confidence in him, Daniel Webster fell; and "what a fall was there, my countrymen!"

> "Then I, and you, and all of us fell down,
> And bloody treason flourished o'er us."

The North stood appalled and paralyzed, deserted, abandoned, and betrayed—cowed and bowed down under the proud domination and impudence of the lords of the lash. Such was the state of this question after the seventh of March, '50.[55] The slaveholders waxed bolder every hour; and the men of the North humbler. There was now no doubt that the South could get its most extravagant demands complied with.

Texas, that most powerful and warlike State, wanted ten millions of money. She only had to threaten that she would whip the United States, to get every dollar of it. I am only surprised that she did not ask for twenty millions, instead of *ten*. She might have got it easily. I drop this glance at the past. It is a sickening theme. I have alluded to it with a view to refresh your memories and to awaken that indignation which it is fitted to inspire.

I come now to the more immediate question before us. I presume I speak to some men who have not made up their minds as to who they shall vote for in the coming election; and that they are candidly considering that question. To them I would speak.

There are now three parties in the field—the Whig, the Democratic, and the Free Democratic party.

The two large parties are now, if they were not before, united on the only great question which really and seriously divided the country.

Old differences have subsided; old issues have been laid aside.

The only question about which there seems a division of opinion, respects the matter of river and harbor improvements; and here the difference is seeming, rather than real.

The Whigs are in favor of making constitutional appropriations for this purpose; and the Democrats are opposed to unconstitutional appropriations. So that there is after all, on direct issue—no great principle in the matter of public policy which divides them.

The struggle seems purely one of men, *which* men shall have the dispensing of power and place the next four years. Here, there is a strong division, and the contrast is warm. But what are the measures, sentiments, and principles which both parties ask you to support?

This question is important. I will answer it in my homely way. They ask you to give them power to make the compromise measures of 1850 a final settlement of the slavery question. The resolutions on this point stand at the head of many of their papers, as the corner-stone of those parties.

The first objection, and a very important one to these platforms, is the idea that human enactments may be *"final"* in this country; that one generation may tie the hands of another; that the darkness of the past shall be preferred to the light of the present; that like the laws of the Medes and Persians, the laws of the Republic shall remain unchanged. I say that this is an idea that every American citizen is bound to oppose. It strikes a deadly blow at the spirit and the hope of progress; and reduces the growing limbs of the Republic to cramping cast-iron moulds. The thing is unnatural, and no more to be countenanced in this country, than iron shoes for the feet of American women.

Besides, if one law can be put beyond the reach of future generations, all laws may; and one generation may not only enjoy the right of making laws for themselves, but do up the legislation for all generations to come.

Now I think that one legislature ought to be satisfied with making such laws as it in its wisdom or its folly may determine, without reaching its death fingers into the living, futile, and controlling future legislatures.

The next thing they ask you to do, is to authorize them to admit unnumbered States into the Union, with Slavery. You are to bind yourselves, that when one of these States ask admission into this Union, you will not raise the questions of the wisdom or the wickedness of admitting another slave-cursed member into this Republic. There is *no* fiction. Those States are to be admitted with or without slavery. But everybody knows that the *"without"* means nothing and meant nothing at the time.

Hon. Horace Mann,[56] in a speech of surpassing power and eloquence, has shown that slavery already exists in New Mexico. It has been long known that slaveholders design to force the slave system upon Utah.—In this they may not succeed; but the question of success or failure depends upon you.

The votes of the North are to decide the case. Should there be a strong vote for Hale and Julian,[57] slavery will be checked.—Northern men will be made to feel there is a North. Otherwise, slavery may run rampant.

Again; the Whig Party and the Democratic Party ask you for power; the one to discountenance, and the other to resist agitation; or in other words, to discountenance and resist the exercise of the right of speech. These parties express themselves with great emphasis on this point, leaving no doubt of the importance which they attach to this particular item of their creed.

The Whigs mean to discountenance, and the Democrats mean to resist agitation.—They are going to do so whenever and wherever the evil may appear, whether in Congress or out of Congress, they will discountenance and resist.

Here, then, is a deliberate, open, and decided attempt to discourage and fetter the constitutional and natural right of speech.—Whigs and Democrats, in their party and organized capacity, have resolved to discourage and resist agitation at all times, in all places in Congress or out of Congress.

We are bound to regard this declaration on their part, not merely as a vague sentiment, but one which may be incorporated into the legislation of this country. It appears in their political platforms, and is presented with other objects to be accomplished by the parties adopting them. If these parties mean anything more than mere bravado, they mean to make their discountenance and resistance a reality, even to the extent of suppressing agitation by law, making it penal to discuss the question of slavery.

This right of speech is very dear to the hearts of intelligent lovers of liberty. It is the delight of the lovers of liberty, as it is the dread and terror of tyrants.

Why then, have these two great parties arrayed themselves against its exercise?—*Why* have they imitated the crowned heads of the old world in warring upon it?

The answer is, we have got in this country a system of wickedness which cannot bear the light of free discussion. We have here 3,000,000 of God's children bound in chains, and who are murderously robbed of all their dearest rights; and to save their atrocious system from the execration of the American people, these parties have openly declared it to be their purpose to abridge the right of speech. The purpose, and the means to accomplish it, are alike worthy of each other. To chain the slave, these parties have said we must fetter the free! To make tyranny safe, we must endanger the liberties of the nation, by destroying the palladium of all liberty and progress—the freedom of speech.

It is idle and short-sighted to regard this question as merely relating to the liberties of the colored people of this country. The wrong proposed to be done touches every man.

If, to-day these parties can put down the right of speech on one subject, to-morrow they may do so on another. If they can prohibit the discussion of the rights of black men, they may also, bye and bye, prohibit the discussion of the rights of white men.—*"Liberty for all, or chains for all."*

Daniel Webster said, in his earlier and better days:

"Important as I deem it, to discuss on all proper occasions the policy of the measures at present pursued it is still more important to maintain the right of such discussion in its full and just extent. Sentiments lately sprung up and now growing fashionable make it necessary to be explicit on this point. The more I perceive a disposition to check the freedom of inquiry, by extravagant and unconstitutional pretenses the firmer shall be the tone, and the freer the manner in which I shall exercise.—It is the ancient and the undoubted prerogative of the people to canvass public measures, and the merits of public men. It is 'a home-bred right,' a fire-side privilege. It hath ever been enjoyed in every house, cottage, and hamlet in the nation. It is not to be drawn into the controversy. It is as undoubted as the right of breathing the air, or walking on the earth. Belonging to private life as a right it belongs to public life as a duty; and it is the last duty which those whose representative I am shall find me to abandon. Aiming at all times to be courteous and temperate in its use, except when the right itself shall be questioned. I shall then carry it to its extent. I shall place myself on the extreme boundary of my rights, and bid defiance to any arm that would move me from my ground.—This high constitutional privilege I shall defend and exercise within this house, and without this house, in all places, in time of peace, in time of war, and at all times. Living, I shall assert it; dying I shall assert it, and should I leave no other inheritance to my children by the blessing of God I will still leave them the inheritance of free principles, and the example of a manly, independent, and conscientious discharge of them."

Now it is just this "high constitutional right" which you are called upon by the Whig and Democratic parties to crush. Slavery is so false, unnatural, brutal, and shocking, that it won't bear the light of discussion, and, therefore, discussion must be put down. The system is like Lord Grandy's character; it can only "pass without censure, as it passeth without observation;" and, therefore, the nation must be blindfolded.—Its lips must be padlocked; and you, fellow-citizens, are called upon to aid by your votes this blindfolding and padlocking system.

And this is to be done, fellow-citizens, to give peace to slave-holders. These parties have attempted to do what God has declared impossible to be done. *"There can be no peace, saith my God, to the wicked."*

Suppose it were possible to put down the free speech, what would it avail the guilty slaveholder? Pillowed as he is upon the bosoms of ruined souls, he would still be troubled. If the tongue of every abolitionist were cut out, and every pamphlet and periodical treating of slavery were carried to Washington and burnt in the presence of the assembled nation, and the whole history of the abolition movement were blotted out, still the guilty slaveholder could have "no peace;" bubbling up from the depths of his sin-darkened soul, would come the terrible accusation, *"Thou art verily guilty concerning thy brother."*

It would be easy to enlarge on this point, but I must pass on. They ask you to give them power to violate the Constitution and to make that violation *"final."* The Constitution of the United States declares that, in suits where the amount in controversy exceeds twenty dollars in value, the right of trial by jury shall be preserved; and that no person shall be deprived of life, liberty, or property, without due process of law.

Now, the Fugitive Slave Act notoriously violates both these provisions at once. It scouts the idea of a trial by jury. Instead of "due process," it gives a summary process, and that most scandalously destitute of all show of justice. The judge is bound to hear only one side of the case. The oath of any two villains may consign an American citizen to the hell of slavery for life under this Fugitive Slave Act.

A man may not throw the noose of a rope over the horns of an ox without having his right to do so submitted to a jury; but he may seize, bind and chain a man—a being whose value is beyond all computation, and doom him to life-long bondage by a summary process. Thus, the beast of burden is more sacred in the eye of the law, than in the image of God! Thus, the right of man to himself is deemed of less consequence than the right of man to a brute. Man's dearest interests may be passed upon by a single judge; but the ownership to an ASS must be determinded by a jury of twelve impartial men!

Just this monstrous anomaly the Whig and the Democratic parties ask the aid of your votes to make final.

Once more. It has ever been deemed a thing of immense importance among the governments, that the judicial power be placed above every temptation to make corrupt and unjust decisions. The founders of this government had this point distinctly and constantly in view.

To place the judicial officers of this government beyond the possibility of corruption, they inserted these plain and wisely arranged words in the federal Constitution: "The judges, both of the supreme and inferior courts, shall receive for their service a compensation which shall not be diminished during their continuance in office." The Fugitive Slave Act violates both in spirit and letter. The judges created under it are supported by their fees. Their support depends upon the number of cases which they can get before them. They are not only to try cases; but to get cases to try. They are made to feel a direct and personal interest in getting cases before them. They are tempted to engage in setting nets for the feet of their fellow-men; and when they have caught one, they try him, and get the coveted fee.

Let it not be said that honorable men would not do this mean thing. An honorable man would not hold such an office. The work to be done is a work for scoundrels, and scoundrels will be found to do it.

But a still darker shade. This "slave act," and slave-acting judges, are paid ten dollars for every man they decide to be a slave; and only five dollars when they fail to do so. An honorable man would have his right hand cut off before he would sit as a judge under such a disgusting bribe. Yet the horrid law is *"final."* Fellow-citizens, there was a time when it was quite common to hear it asked, *"what* have we to do with slavery?" It was affirmed that slavery is a local institution, with which *we of the North* have nothing to do.

The Fugitive Slave Law has taken away this excuse. Slavery is no longer *"sectional,"* (if it ever were), but *"national"*—no longer a mere State institution, but a United States institution. If it never was before, it is now an American institution, to be maintained by all the powers of the American government.

Within the limits of the American government, slavery knows no limits. Wherever the star-spangled banner waves, there may men hold men as slaves.

There is not one spot in the Republic sacred to freedom; but every inch of soil is given up to slavery, slave-hunting, slave-catching, and slaveholding.

Our citizens are compelled to fly from a Republic to a Monarchy for liberty. They fly to the paw of the British Lion for protection from the devouring talons and bloody beak of the American Eagle.

*"Hail Columbia! Happy land!"*

The Israelites had their cities of refuge, to which even the guilty might escape; but our model Republic, under the corrupt and debasing policy of our two parties, has not even a refuge for innocent men. The murderer is better protected than the man without crime. The robber is better protected than the robbed. And this is to be *"final."*

Gentlemen, I call attention to a matter of still deeper concern. You, yourselves; you—fathers, sons, and brothers, freemen of the North—are compelled, by this "final" act, to throw off the dignity of manhood, and become bloodhounds; to scent out, and hunt down your fellow-men!

This is the Whig and Democratic entertainment, to which you are invited. You are to leave off your honest and honorable employment when you are called upon by the blood-thirsty man-hunters to join in the chase. You are commanded, as good citizens, to do this; and subjected to pains and penalties if you do it not. You are commanded to bound forth at the sound of the hunter's horn.

Are you prepared for this dignified avocation? I will not believe it; yet this constitutes a part of the *"finality"* which the Whig and Democratic party stand pledged to maintain, and to ma ntain which they ask your votes in November.

In conclusion, I will present what I deem to be the greatest objection to voting for the candidates of the old parties. It is this:— The system of measures which they have pledged themselves to regard as a *"final settlement"* of the slavery question, aims a death-blow to Christian, religious liberty. A more deliberate or skillfully aimed blow was never given against Christianity, than is found in this fugitive slave act. I have shown that the law is opposed to the Constitution. It would be quite as easy to show that it is contrary to the gospel, and to the spirit and aim of Christianity. It is true that this law does not interfere with the forms and ceremonies of the Christian religion. It is , however, much worse; in that it is directed against the fundamental principles of Rhristianity. It strikes at the weightier matters of the law, judgement, mercy, and faith.

Christianity commands us, as we would inherit eternal lif, to "feed the hungry"' clothe the naked, and take in the stranger. This law makes it penal to obey Christ. In the language of Wm. Lloyd Garrison, "we are asfed by these political parties to damn our own souls."

Again; it would be impossible to point out a more glaring contempt of the religious sentiment of the religious people of this country, than is furnished in these two platforms. They virtually say to the Christian people of this country, we regard your conscience as mere convenience; your religion as a sham; your faith in God, and love of Christ as things having no connection with your daily practice; and, therefore, not to be considered in connection with your political duties.

Now, I think, Mr. Chairman, and gentlemen, that it becomes the Christian duty of the people of this country to rebuke the contemptuous disregard of Christianity by our political organizations. Whether they will do so or not, remains to be seen. But, in any event, sir, Itrust this Convention has thoroughly made up its mind to go in and come out of the contest with clean hands.

*Frederick Douglass' Paper,* October 22, 1852

## TO GERRIT SMITH                    Ithaca, Oct. 28th, 1852
My dear Sir:

You may rely upon my presence at Peterboro on the twentieth, then and there, to commence my labors in your District. May I hope that you will map out my work for me? I am speaking twice a day in this county and am having fine meetings, large and spirited.[58] I find in Phillip C. Schyler, an active and faithful friend, one too, who loves Gerrit Smith and the great principles with which Gerrit Smith is associated.

That was a magnificent and glorious celebration at Syracuse. Boston abolition, that allowed Sims to be dragged into slavery did seem to me less efficient than Syracuse abolition, that rescued Jerry, though it might be considered egotistical to say so!

I doubt not that my friend Miss Griffiths had a good visit at Peterboro, and left you with her strength renewed.

Yours always for freedom and humanity,

Frederick Douglass

*Gerrit Smith Papers, George Arents Research Library, Syracuse University*

## TO SAMUEL J. MAY[59]

Nov. 10, 1852

My dear Sir:

Your letter came yesterday, and I immediately ordered the numbers of my paper to your addresses for which you sent. I hope you will get them safely.

I hope your plan for agitating this State will succeed. I will pledge whatever of influence I possess in aid of such agitation. A Series of such meetings as you propose could not fail to act beneficially on our cause throughout the country.

The election of *Gerrit Smith*[60]—what an era! But this grand event will be comparatively lost unless the agitation is kept up. With men and money, we could carry the State for freedom in *1856*.

I was sorry not to have seen more of you at the celebration, but in a crowd so large even a tall man might pass unobserved.

Very truly yours,

Frederick Douglass

*Frederick Douglass Ms., New York Historical Society*

# ABOLITION IN RUSSIA

In his second lecture, speaking of Russia, Dr. Baird expressed his conviction that serfdom in that country will soon come to an end.[61] He represented the Emperor as being not only favorable to its abolition but determined upon it. To the reply of one of his nobles that the serfs were too ignorant, and altogether unfit for freedom, the Emperor is said to have answered that his brother before him had not the energy to free the serfs, that he was afraid that his own son who might succeed him would not have the needed resolution and courage, but he believed that God had given him the requisite energy to do this thing, and do it he would, cost what it might.

If this be true (and Dr. Baird is pretty good authority in foreign matters,) there is trouble ahead for that class of American Statesmen whose policy it is to prevent, by all means in their power, the occurrence of "dangerous examples." The abolition of slavery in Russia would be a blow at slavery in South Carolina. This is a matter to which we would call the special attention of our *republican* Legislators. Our diplomatic agent at St. Petersburg should be instructed to remonstrate against the adoption of a measure fraught with so much danger to the stability of *our institutions,* and to the peace of the Republic.

It would be a spectacle worth beholding, to see the mightiest despot in the world, covering himself with the glory of emancipating slaves to the number of forty millions, against the remonstrances of his own nobles, and those of the model republic. It will be seen from the above that the old objection to the emancipation of the black slaves of America is considered equally applicable to the white slaves of Russia. So it seems that ignorance is not peculiar to black slaves—the important concession.

As to Dr. Baird, it is a little inconsistent with his position in regard to American abolitionists to be extolling the merits of this Imperial abolitionist of Russia. The Doctor is one of those divines who have never felt it his duty to utter aught that approached anti-slavery sentiments—looking to the abolition of slavery in this country.

*Frederick Douglass' Paper,* January 7, 1853

## EDITORIAL CORRESPONDENCE—THE RESCUE TRIALS

Albany, Jan. 29, 1853

Well, the union, the American Union, that which was to fall asunder unless the Fugitive Slave Act should be successfully enforced, is now saved! The awful moment, that which precedes a dreadful, impending calamity, is now past. After many, and as we may say, extraordinary efforts, the glorious, but greatly imperiled, Republic of Liberty-loving men and women, has succeeded in vindicating the *sacred* majesty of a slave-catching enactment. The first Northern victim of our blood-stained Moloch is *Enoch Reed,* a colored man, a carman, an industrious and quiet man. It will be seen, by reference to the proceedings in our other columns,[62] upon what sort of evidence and ruling *Enoch Reed* was convicted. It may not be improper for us to say a word as to the evidence and the rulings of Judge Hall in the case. Thank God, there are two tribunals to which the injured have a right to appeal, in this country—From Courts of *law,* we can appeal to courts of men. Public opinion is ever open, and will be, unless slavery shall padlock our lips, and pens, as well as chain our hands.—Supposing *Enoch Reed* to have committed the act, alleged against him, namely, "aided and abetted" in the rescue of Jerry, we would even now, while he is under the heels of this government, most gladly exchange situations with him. To be convicted of such acts is an honor to him, only equalled by the shame which belongs to the government, for making such deeds a crime.—While, however, we glory in the acts alleged to have been committed by *Enoch Reed,* and would gladly have done as he is alleged to have done, it must be apparent to all who carefully read the proceedings in the case that the Government failed to prove these acts against him beyond a reasonable doubt. Both the evidence and the rulings may well draw out unfavorable comments. From the first moment we went into Court, we felt that it would go hard with the defendant.—Judges are men, and being men there is a certain transparency about them, no matter what may be the drapery about them, that enables a looker-on to see even the subtle workings of their mind. One interposition of his honor, when the witness *Geer* was under examination—showed most conclusively that though justice may be *blindfolded,* Judges are not always so. In order to test the knowledge of the witness, Mr. Sedgwick asked, did you *ever go* on a pleasure excursion with *Enoch Reed?* when, in a most insolent and insulting tone, *Geer* answered, "I don't associate with "n----s." The question was certainly a very proper one and the Court, if it interposed at all, should have rebuked the insolence and evasion of the witness; but no—the opportunity must not be lost to show the contempt of the Judge for "n----s." Leaning back into his chair with an air of sympathy with the wounded pride and malignant prejudice of witness, the Judge said, that *counsel must not "insult the witness!"* Contemptible in a man, disgraceful in a judge. The witness had protested to know Reed, knew his voice, knew him as well as to know him even in the *dark,* and even in a crowd of more than two thousand persons when the wildest excitement and confusion prevailed, he could distinguish his voice. In these circumstances, it was clearly consistent for the defense to make the above enquiry. That the question was deemed an insult by the Judge, as well as by the witness, showed, that neither witness nor Judge were in a state of mind to respect the rights of the prisoner. We do not say that either would, knowingly, injure or deal unjustly with Reed—but, unhappily for our afflicted people—they are often made victims by men who are unconscious of their own state of mind.

We have spoken of the vindication of the Fugitive Slave Law, as it is called. But in truth the victory, after all, is not a victory of the Fugitive Slave Law. Enoch Reed has not been committed under that law. He has not been tried under it. So far as his trial is concerned, that inhuman enactment is still under the mud of Syracuse, where it was trampled down by the feet of three thousand freemen on the first of October, 1851. The Government refused in Enoch's case so much as to touch it with one of its fingers. It lies there, soiled, torn, insulted, despised and spit upon, with "none so poor as to do it reverence." We know little of the forms of law, and willingly confess that our ignorance may expose us to ridicule, and even to contempt, but it does seem to me that there was something discreditable, mean and cowardly in the government, in thus trying the case of Enoch Reed. His crime (if crime it was), was that of obstructing a process under the Fugitive Slave Act of 1850. He was indicted under that act. The penalty attached to a violation of that act, is plainly set forth in the *act itself.* The act is more stringent than that of 1793. The penalty in the former is much heavier than in the latter.

Now the question is, (and it will be asked by the slaveholders, as well as by the people of the North), "Why did the government refuse to make an issue on the law of 1850, the law, and the only law intended to be defied and trampled upon by those who rescued Jerry from the officers who had him in charge on the 1st October, 1851?" Why did they make an issue with the defendant on the law of '93, instead of the law of '50? They made an issue on a law of which the defendant had, probably, never heard until he was brought into court for trial. Why did they try him under a law in no way odious, when the law alleged to have been violated, provided the measure and manner of the punishment for its own infraction? Does the vindication of a general and popular law vindicate and establish a peculiar, umpopular, and hateful one? Is not the fact that the law of *ninety three*, instead of the law of *fifty*, was selected, a virtual confession of the doubtful constitutionality of the latter, by the Court? So it looks to us. So it will look at the South. If the Court had regarded the Fugitive Slave Law adapted to accomplish the desired end, namely, the conviction and punishment of offenders against it, why did he not allow the case to be tried under that law, that it (not the law of '93) might be vindicated. Again, we ask, why was Enoch tried under the law of '93? Was it to lessen his punishment, if convicted? or was it to make his conviction difficult, and give him a better chance to escape the punishment which must be meted out under the Fugitive Slave Law? It would be pleasant to assign this last reason for the action of the government, if any one sane man in ten thousand would give it the slightest credence. Most plainly, the government took this course, to make the conviction of Enoch easy and certain. The law of *fifty* lay bleeding at their feet—its wounds all open, and calling for help; and instead of coming to its relief, they hunt up a law nearly as old as the federal government itself, and harrangue the jury about the "sacredness" and majesty, when no one questioned either its majesty or sacredness. The whole thing, upon the face of it, bears the marks of being a most cowardly manouver. Had Reed been tried under the law of 1850, the whole question of the constitutionality of that law would have been open. The counsel for the defense would have laid bare its gross unconstitutionality. They were ready and ripe for that question. General Nye, Messrs. Sedgwick, Hillis, and Gerrit Smith, would have shaken the horrid structure to the ground. But not a word would his Honor, Judge Hall, hear on the subject. Mr. Smith, the body and soul of whose speech, was to have been marshalled against the Fugitive Slave Law, to show its gross inhumanity, and its entire unconstitutionality, was completely cut off by the adroit ruling of the

Court. To the marked astonishment of not a few bystanders, Judge Hall declared that the constitutionality of the Fugitive Slave Law had already been decided. To prove this, he cited several cases, where it had been decided, in which cases, in reality, that question was not before the Court. He would not hear a word of argumentation on that point. This, of course, compelled Mr. Smith to desist, and, to some extent, it crippled the defense. It gave the government marked advantage in summing up their side. The advantage was not rejected by the government; it was used most skillfully. H. G. Wheaton is not a man to refuse to use an advantage, of which he finds himself *honorably* possessed.—At least one hour of the lengthy address to the jury was directed against those who resist as unconstitutional, the Fugitive Slave Law, and in a weak attempt, to ridicule them as *"big-hearted men,"* *"soft-hearted men,"* giving the best proof thereby, that his own heart (if he has any) is neither "big" nor "soft." A "big heart" or a "soft heart" would scarcely be in place in a cause like his—a cause with neither justice nor mercy in it.

Then, the evidence; it is really hard to see how a jury, in such a case, could convict. The circumstances of the rescue, the darkness of the night, the general excitement which prevailed, where friends and foes were united in one inextricable mass, so dense, so confused and so wild as to prevent one from knowing even the members of his own family. We say these circumstances weaken the most positive testimony. The jury convicted really against good ground for reasonable doubt, of which the prisoner was entitled. The witnesses themselves were not the men whose words were to be greatly relied upon. They had been in the *melee* and were foiled. They had been *hired* by the slavecatchers to help hunt Jerry; and their prey had been wrested out of their cruel paws.—They lied when they arrested Jerry; told him he was arrested for what he was not. If men will lie when *not* under oath, will they always be careful to tell the truty when they *are* under oath? Then, too, men base enough to hunt down an innocent fellow-man, lie to him, put fetters on him for a few paltry dollars, are entitled to very little respect for their veracity. Again, every act which was alleged to have been committed by Enoch Reed, was shown to have been done by Peter Hornbeck—a man just about the size and complexion of Reed.—There is another consideration which should have been considered by the jury—it is this: the great mass of white poeple of this country really cannot detect any difference between the looks of colored people. To them, *we all look alike.* They take so little interest in us, think so little of us, and care so little about us that they do not even distinguish our names, to say nothing of our features. To them we are *Negroes*—that's all. But those witnesses could not only detect differences where resemblance was almost perfect, but they could do so in the dark!

We have little complaint to make against the *charge* to the jury. It was, upon the whole, much less one-sided than we had reason to expect; and what he said against prejudice against the color of a man's skin was worthy of the high place from which it was said, and in strong contrast with the sympathy for the wounded feelings of Geer, who said he did not associate with "n-----s," yet better judges than we are, hold that the "charge" was one-sided and jesuitical. We did not say so much, but *this we do say*, that when a judge, here in New York, endeavors to impress a jury, that the Courts of the slave States are freely open to colored persons who may be given up under the fugitive slave laws, he exposes his honesty and fairness to suspicion. It is next to impossible for a man, torn away from friends and acquaintances at the North, thrown on a slave plantation amongst the slaves, and placed under an overseer, worked and whipt with them, to get before the Courts of the South. Then, too, there is not a slave State in the Union where a colored man is allowed his oath against that of a white man, thus it is rendered next to impossible for a black man to get before the Courts, or to get justice when he succeeds in getting before the courts. Yet, Judge Hall took pains to impress that idea upon the jury, in the case of Reed. We hope his honor will see the unfairness of that course, and abandon it in the other cases which are to come before him.

The counsel for the defense, we need not say, did their duty. General Nye's speech to the jury was almost a matchless effort of eloquence, wit and power.

No remarks are necessary from us to show up the weakness, looseness, uncertainty and unlikelihood of the evidence upon which Enoch Reed has been convicted. That is done most successfully in the synopsis which we give of General Nye's address to the jury. Nor is it necessary to remark upon the most important witnesses. It is enough to say that they were the very men who had been gathered up for the hunt when Jerry was first scented out by the slave dogs in Syracuse—men who would engage in a slave hunt for the love of the thing, are not the men whose testimony should be believed.

Frederick Douglass

*Frederick Douglass' Paper*, February 4, 1853

# H. O. WAGONER

The letter, in another column of the present edition,[63] is the first indication of a sense of the greatest outrage recently committed against the colored people of Illinois, which we have received from any colored man in that State. In view of the cruel enactment in question, our good brother asks with a feeling bordering on desperation, "Oh whither shall we fly? The Almighty, it would seem, has brought into the world human beings, for whom He has made no provision to live anywhere!" So, indeed, it would seem, in view of the harassing legislation of *Illinois*, and of the national government.

We agree with friend Wagoner, that the time has arrived when the Free Colored people of the Northern States should assemble together, for the purpose of seriously and solemnly considering our present state and condition, and of deliberating as to the best course to be pursued in relation thereto; but a Convention of our people, to be in any way effective, must come together in no "flourishing" mood. It must be sober, thoughtful, wise, cool, and determined in its character, or it will fail to comprehend, in any degree, the gravity of the crisis which is rapidly approaching and for which we are admonished to prepare, or be overwhelmed. A Convention of the description thus given could not be held without producing a strong, moral effect, not only in the United States, but abroad; and the time has come when we must not only appeal to the sense of justice in the American people, but to the sympathies and influence of THE WHOLE CIVILIZED WORLD. There is a power, even in a statement of wrongs endured by an oppressed people, when there is no physical force to redress those wrongs. Let us meet, then, in Convention, and the name of our deeply outraged people, and let us appeal to *our country* and to *the world*, in behalf of those principles of justice and humanity which have been struck down in our persons.

*Frederick Douglass' Paper*, March 18, 1853

## THE BLACK LAW OF ILLINOIS

What kind of people are the people of Illinois? Were they born and nursed of women as other people are? Or are they the offspring of wolves and tigers, and only taught to prey upon all flesh pleasing to their bloody taste? If they are members of the human family, by what spirit are they animated? is it from heaven or is it from hell? Have they any churches among them? have they the Bible? have they Sabbath schools? Do they look up to God in prayer for mercy? or do they invoke the foul fiends in the regions of darkness, aid to distress and afflict the helpless who may venture within their reach? The enactments which may be found on our first page, in their appropriate place, make these questions pertinent. The wickedness framed by law in that State, is of a peculiarly shocking description, and may well prompt the questions thus presented.

A nation of savages, to whom the names of God and of Christ, of the Bible, and of religion are unknown, could not be guilty of more inhuman and barbarous legislation than that perpetrated by the "Democratic Legislature" of Illinois.

The 1st Section of the law in question prohibits the bringing any Negro or mulatto slave (whether said slave is set free or not) into the State; so that if a slaveholder, in any of the Southern states, wishes to emancipate his slave, and to remove him beyond the Slave Code, and the power of slavery, Illinois says it shall not be done on her soil; and he who attempts to do it shall be liable to a fine of from *one* to *five* hundred dollars, and imprisonment in the County Jail.

The 2d Section provides for the extradition of any person indicted under the law, who may have escaped into another State or Teritory; so that Illinois means not only to get rid of Negro residents in a State of freedom, but in imitation of other slave States, and *"the Fugitive Slave Law,"* the means to hunt them and fetch them back for punishment.

But the bill is before our readers, and it is a terrible one. There is a stringency and a bitterness in its purpose, and in the manner of accomplishing it, equal to the edicts of the most heartless tyrants that ever afflicted mankind.

*Frederick Douglass' Paper*, March 18, 1853

# MAKE YOUR SONS MECHANICS AND FARMERS—NOT WAITERS, PORTERS, AND BARBERS.[64]

Do we hear you say, "this is more easily said than done?" So be it. But do not say the thing required is impossible. If it can be done and ought to be done, the more industry, self-sacrifice, fortitude and perseverance involved in doing it, the more full and complete will be the measure of reward. We have done easy things long enough already. Such things have been done by us until we have become contracted and enfeebled, instead of being enlarged and strengthened. Our energies have waned because we have not given them appropriate exercise and scope. The writer of this has found out, what almost every other worker has found out, that within certain limits, the more a man does, the more he is able to do—and on the other hand, the less he does, the less he is able to do. Our faculties and powers were given to be used, and using them is the main condition of keeping them fit for use. To lift plates from the table, or to place them on the table; to carry a man's trunk in the hateful idleness for another; to shave a half dozen faces in the morning, and sleep or play the guitar in the afternoon—all this may be easy; but is it noble, is it manly, and does it improve and elevate us? We speak not to offend or wound the feelings of any who are now engaged in these occupations. Indeed, the intelligent ones among them are with us on this question, and rejoice that we are moved to speak on this subject.

Observation has completely convinced us that a great proportion of the vice and crime, found amongst us at the North, may be traced directly to the fact of our having no steady and continuous employment. The porter waiting at the station, or at the wharf—the barber waiting for a customer, and the waiter (done his work and out in the afternoon) waiting for the tea hour, are all peculiarly exposed and liable to be led into temptation. For idleness is the parent of vice.

It is said that they can make more money in these menial employments than as mechanics. This is not true; but if it were true, the argument would be worthless—for it is the direct effect of these employments to beget, in those engaged in them, improvidence, wastefulness, a fondness for dress and display. Catering to the pride and vanity of others, they become themselves proud, vain and foppish. Called out to wait upon the balls and tea-parties of the rich, they, too, must must have balls and tea-parties, and the money got by waiting on others is expended in dress, tea, dancing and in paying others for waiting on us. Thus, in our poverty, we expend our all in trying to imitate the customs and to follow the fashions and follies of the rich, with whom our vocations bring us in contact. The difference between us and our rich employer, is the difference between two ships setting out to sea—the one with ballast, and the other without. So, while the one sails on, defying winds and waves, we are capsized and lost.

Now, we desire most sincerely to see our people made happier and better than we believe it possible for them to be in the employments to which we have thus referred; and therefore we say to the parents and guardians of colored boys, make them mechanics and farmers—not waiters, porters and barbers.

In asking you to follow this advice, we would not seem to be unreasonable, demanding that which cannot be performed. Nor would we seem blind to the mighty difficulties that beset the path which you are advised to pursue. We only ask you to do all in your power to get your sons and daughters out of menial employments into profitable and respectable trades, and to do so on principle. It is no answer to this advice, to say that, as a general rule the circumstances should avail themselves of exceptions to general rules. If most men will not teach our sable children trades in this country, some men will; and of the aid of the latter, we should quickly avail ourselves. There are mechanics and farmers, scattered over the country, who could be prevailed upon to take our sons into their workshops and upon their farms, and no colored man is excusable who does not seek out for his children such advantages. He who omits to give his son a trade when he can do so is guilty of degrading his own blood, and of perpetuating the degradation of his race. It is a sin and a shame to us to leave our children to stagger under a load through life, when we could easily throw it off for them.

Let us inquire, how many colored parents really desire to have their sons become farmers and mechanics? How many have taken the pains to inquire for such master mechanics as would receive a colored boy? How many have used argument and persuasion, and even money, to open the door of the workshop to their sons? We fear that the number of these would, on a counting, be found to be very small.

It is unjust, oppressive, mean and tyrannical in the whites to refuse to teach our children the methods of gaining a living; but it is cruel, unnatural, brutal and scandalous for parents to cast their off-spring upon a selfish world without using every means in their power to give them useful trades. In our sojournings up and down the land, we have often been chilled to the heart in witnessing the cold indifference of colored parents to the real welfare of their children. Such remarks as these are by no means uncommon: *"Bless the Lord! my children are now big enough to help me saw wood, and I aint a going to put them out to no white man." "Let my son do as I has done afore him." "I mean to get some good out of him now; he'll be getting married bine bye."*

We might multiply sayings of this kind to any extent—sayings which are so general among the colored people, that no body will venture to question our truthfulness in attributing them to this source. Now, the policy which keeps a boy at home to help his father saw wood, wash windows, beat carpets, run errands and the like, when that son could be learning a trade, is most selfish, short-sighted and mean in the parent, and it is cruelly unjust to the son. What right has a father to serve himself temporarily, at the expense of tying his son's hands for life?—We say serve himself temporarily—for the service is but slight and transient; it is more seeming than real, and in many cases, even in a pecuniary point of view, the parents would be immediate gainers by having their sons put out to learn trades, while the future and remote gain cannot be calculated. To hire your son out at the age of sixteen, and at $10 per month, and out of that amount to board him when out of employment; to take care of him and pay doctor's bills for him when he is sick; keeping him in clothing, such as is deemed fit for a table waiter, and at the end of five years, in nine cases out of ten, the parents will have really lost money by the operation. So that even in a pecuniary point of view, to say nothing of the morality of the case, the parents entail on themselves the very evil they seek to avoid. Ah! but then we have the society of our children. Yes, that is something, to be sure; nevertheless, you purchase the society of your children at a rate altogether too dear; for it is at the cost of their manhood and respectability. We love our children, Heaven knows— they are dear to us; but by all the love we bear them, we would much rather think of them doing well at a distance, than to see them doing ill at home, as they certainly would be doing ill, if they were growing up without a knowledge of some useful and honorable calling by which to provide for their wants as men and as citizens.

Let the black man become an industrious and skilful mechanic, or a steady and industrious farmer, and there will be an end to all schemes for colonizing him, and all that wicked legislation designed to drive him out of the State. Let colonizationists bestow one tenth of the sum they expend in sending us out of country in efforts to make us useful where we are, and they will soon find no motive for removal elsewhere.

*Frederick Douglass' Paper*, March 18, 1853

## LETTER FROM M. R. DELANY

Pittsburgh, March 23, 1853
Frederick Douglass, Esq., Dear Sir:

I notice in your paper of March 4th an article in which you speak of having paid a visit to Mrs. H. E. B. Stowe, for the purpose as you say, of consulting her, "as to some method which should contribute successfully, and permanently, to the improvement and elevation of the free people of color in the United States." Also, in the number of March 18th, in an article by a writer over the initials of "P. C. S." in reference to the same project, he concludes by saying, "I await with much interest the suggestions of Mrs. Stowe in this matter."

Now I simply wish to say, that we have always fallen into great errors in efforts of this kind, going to others than the *intelligent* and *experienced* among *ourselves*; and in all due respect and deference to Mrs. Stowe, I beg leave to say, that she *knows nothing about us*, "the Free Colored people of the United States," neither does any other white person—and consequently can contrive no successful scheme for our elevation; it must be done by ourselves. I am aware, that I differ with many in thus expressing myself, but I cannot help it; though I stand alone and offend my best friends, so help me God! in a matter of such moment and importance, I will express my opinion. Why, in God's name, don't the leaders among our people make suggestions and *consult* the most competent among *their own* brethren concerning our elevation? This they do not do; and I have not known one, whose province it was to do so to go ten miles for such a purpose. We shall never effect anything until this is done.

I accord with the suggestions of H. O. Wagoner for a National Council of Consultation of our people, provided *intelligence, maturity,* and *experience*, in matters among them, could be so gathered together; other than this, it would be a mere mockery—like the Convention of 1848 a coming together of rivals to test their success for the "biggest offices." As God lives, I will never knowingly, lend my aid to any such work while our brethren groan in vassalage and bondage, and I and mine in oppression and degradation such as we now suffer.

I would not give the counsel of one dozen *intelligent colored* freemen of the *right stamp*, for that of all the white and unsuitable colored persons in the land. But something must be done, and that speedily.

The so called free states, by their acts, are now virtually saying to the South, "you *shall not* emancipate; your blacks *must be slaves*; and should they come North, there is no refuge for them." I shall not be surprised to see, at no distant day, a solemn Convention called by the whites in the North, to deliberate on the propriety of changing the whole policy to that of slave states. This will be the remedy to prevent dissolution; *and it will come, mark that!* anything on the part of the American people to *save* their *Union.* Mark me—then non-slaveholding states *will become slave states.*

Yours for God and Humanity,

M. R. Delany

REMARKS: That colored men would agree among themselves to do something for the efficient and permanent aid of themselves and their race, "is a consummation devoutly to be wished," but until they do, it is neither wise nor graceful for them, or for any of them to throw cold water upon plans and efforts made for that purpose by others. To scornfully reject all aid from our white friends, and to denounce them as unworthy of our confidence, looks high and mighty enough on paper; but unless the background filled up with facts demonstrating our independence and self-sustaining power, of what use is such display of self consequence? Brother Delany has worked long and hard—he has written vigorously, and spoken eloquently to colored people—beseeching them, in the name of liberty, and all the dearest interests of humanity to unite their energies, and to increase their activities in the work of their own elevation; yet where has his voice been heeded? and where is the practical result? Echo answers, where? Is not the field open? Why, then, should any man object to the efforts of Mrs. Stowe, or anyone else, who is moved to do anything on our behalf? The assertion that Mrs. Stowe "knows nothing about us," shows that Bro. Delany knows nothing about Mrs. Stowe; for he certainly would not so violate his moral, or common sense if he did. When Brother Delany will submit any plan for benefitting the colored people, or will candidly criticize any plan already submitted, he will be heard with pleasure. But we expect no plan from him. He has written a book—and we may say that it is in many respects, an excellent book—on the condition, character, and destiny of the colored people; but it leaves us just where it finds us, without chart or compass, and in more doubt and perplexity than before we read it.

Brother Delany is one of our strong men; and we are therefore all the more grieved, that at a moment when all our energies should be united in giving effect to the benevolent designs of our friends, his voice should be uplifted to strike a jarring note, or to awaken a feeling of distrust.

In respect to a national convention, we are for it—and will not only go "ten miles," but a thousand, if need be, to attend it. Away, therefore, with all unworthy flings on that score.—Ed.

*Frederick Douglass' Paper*, April 1, 1853

## TO HON WM. H. SEWARD[65]

Rochester, April 16th (1853)

My Dear Sir,

I thank you sincerely for your prompt and *promising* response to my begging note. I wish Sir, to make myself thoroughly acquainted with the public Labors of your life, and although I have already made some progress in this line, I feel that there is much yet to be learned. I am even now but a boy of fifteen, less than that space of time has past since I escaped from Slavery. He who helps fit me for the voyage of life, shall not lack my gratitude. Pardon me for trespassing upon your time.

I am most truly yours,<br>
With high esteem,<br>
Frederick Douglass

*William Henry Seward Collection, Rush Rhees Library, University of Rochester*

## TO HON. WM. H. SEWARD

Rochester, April 28th, 1853

My very dear Sir:

Give me leave to thank you for your encouraging words, and for the valuable donation of your "Works," which have just come to hand. I shall read every Syllable in these volumes, and, shall try to master (so far as my Negro intellect is capable) the various subjects, which have there engaged your attention, thought, and Study. I promise this as the best return I can now make for your great kindness in Sending me the Books.

In looking on these compendious volumes, it seems almost incredible that their author is so young. The labors of three score years seem piled up in these volumes. I thank God, My dear Sir, that you are still young, vigorous and strong, inspiring hope in the hearts of the poor and the oppressed, and striking terror in those of oppressors and tyrants. The great truths uttered by you in the hearing of the nation still ring in the ears of all who would shut out the spirit of God from the councils of men. My Dear Sir, as a friend to the Slave with whom I am identified, I put my trust in you as far as I dare put trust in an arm of flesh. Slave holders fear you. I will trust you. Your philosophy is not my philosophy, but you have said and done that which removes from me all timidity in addressing you and the timidity of my people is great.

Allow me to say one word further. The political parties are much out of joint. The peace of the Democratic party is, evidently, but a patched up affair. It is, simply, a putting of new wine into old bottles. The Whig party has failed, and fallen to pieces. *You,* my dear Sir, have the organizing power, and have the voice to command, and give shape to the cause of your country, and to the cause of human liberty. For my part, I long to see the day when it shall be proclaimed, from one end of this Union, to the other, that *Wm. H. Seward* is no longer a member of the old Whig party, but is at the head of a great party of freedom, of justice, and truth, whose business it will be to find out and to re-enact the Laws of the Living God.[66] Can a State rest upon selfishness, upon injustice, cruelty, oppression, & Slavery? No! And the salvation of this republic can only be secured by the utter repudiation of these abominations. Disentangle the Republic from Slavery, and the Republic may live, link its destiny with the frightful monster, and the bolts of offended Heaven will rain down on both.

May God give you strength for the great work which is before you, and shield you from every hurtful influence.

I am, dear Sir, most truly your grateful friend,

Fred Douglass

*William Henry Seward Collection, Rush Rhees Library, University of Rochester*

## THE LETTER OF M. R. DELANY[67]

This letter is premature, unfair and uncalled-for, and, withal, needlessly long, but happily, it needs not a long reply.

Can brother Delany be the writer of it? It lacks his generous spirit. The letter is premature, because it attacks a plan, the details of which are yet undefined. It is unfair, because it imputes designs (and replies to them) which have never been declared. It is uncalled for, because there is nothing in the position of Mrs. Stowe which should awaken against her a single suspicion of unfriendliness towards the free colored people of the United States, but, on the contrary, there is much in it to inspire confidence in her friendship.

The information for which brother Delany asks concerning Mrs. Stowe, he has given himself. He says *she* is a colonizationist,[68] and we ask, what if she is?—names do not frighten us. A little while ago, brother Delany was a colonizationist. If we do not misremember, in his book he declared in favor of colonizing the eastern coast of Africa. Yet, we never suspected his friendliness to the colored people; nor should we feel called upon to oppose any plan he might submit, for the benefit of the colored people, on that account. We recognize friends wherever we find them.

Whoever will bring a straw's weight of influence to break the chains of our brother bondmen, or whisper one word of encouragement and sympathy to our proscribed race in the North, shall be welcomed by us to that philanthropic field of labor. We shall not, therefore, allow the sentiments put in the brief letter of George Harris, at the close of *Uncle Tom's Cabin*, to vitiate forever Mrs. Stowe's power to do us good. Who doubts that Mrs. Stowe is more of an abolitionist now than when she wrote that chapter?—We believe that lady to be but at the beginning of her labors for the colored people of this country.

Brother Delany says, nothing should be done for us, or commenced for us, without "consulting us." Where will he find "*us*" to consult with? Through what organization, or what channel could such consulting be carried on? Does he mean by consulting "*us*" that nothing is to be done for the improvement of the colored people in general, without consulting each colored man in the country whether it shall be done? *How many*, in this case, constitute "us?" Evidently, brother Delany is a little unreasonable here.

Four years ago, a proposition was made, through the columns of *The North Star*, for the formation of a "*National League*,"[69] and a constitution for said League was drawn up fully setting forth a plan for united, intelligent, and effective co-operation on the part of the colored people of the United States—a body capable of being "*consulted*." The colored people, in their wisdom, or in their indifference, gave the scheme little or no encouragement—and it failed. Now, we happen to know that such an organization as was then proposed, was enquired for, and sought for by Mrs. Harriet Beecher Stowe, who wished, most of all, to hear from such a body *what could* be done for the *free colored people* of the United States? But there was no such body to answer.

The fact is, brother Delany, we are a disunited and scattered people, and very much of the responsibility of this disunion must fall upon such colored men as yourself and the writer of this. We want more confidence in each other, as a race—more self-forgetfulness, and less disposition to find fault with well-meant efforts for our benefit. Mr. Delany knows that, at this moment, he could call a respectable

Convention of the free colored people of the Northern States. Why doesn't he issue his call? And he knows, too, that, were we to issue such a call, it would instantly be regarded as an effort to promote the interests of our *paper*. The consideration, and a willingness on our part to occupy an obscure position in such a movement, has led us to refrain from issuing a call. *The Voice of the Fugitive,*[70] we observe, has suggested the holding in New York, of a "World's Convention," during the "World's Fair." A better proposition, we think, would be to hold, in that city, a "National Convention" of the colored people. Will not friend Delany draw up a call for such a Convention, and send it to us for publication?

But to return, Brother Delany asks, if we should allow *"anybody"* to understand measures for our elevation? Yes, we answer:—anybody, even a slaveholder. Why not? Then says brother Delany, why not accept the measures of "Gurley and Pinney." We answer, simply because *their measures* do not commend themselves to our judgment. That is all. If "Gurley and Pinney" would establish an industrial college, where colored young men could learn useful trades, with a view to their becoming useful men and respectable citizens of the United States, we should applaud them and co-operate with them.[71]

We don't object to colonizationists because they express a lively interest in the civilization and Christianization of Africa; nor because they desire the prosperity of Liberia, but it is because, like Brother Delany, they have not sufficient faith in the people of the United States to believe that the black man can ever get justice at their hands on American soil. It is because they have systematically and almost universally sought to spread their hopelessness among the free colored people themselves; and thereby rendered them, if not contented with, at least resigned to the degradation which they have been taught to believe must be perpetual and immutable, while they remain where they are. It is because, having denied the possibility of our elevation here, they have sought to make good that denial by encouraging the enactment of laws subjecting us to the most flagrant outrages, and stripping us of all the safeguards necessary to the security of our liberty, persons and property.—We say all this of the American Colonization Society; but we are *far* from saying this of many who speak and wish well to Liberia. As to the imputation that all the pecuniary profit arising out of the industrial scheme will probably pass into the pockets of the whites, it will be quite time enough to denounce such a purpose when such a purpose is avowed. But we have already dwelt too long on a letter which perhaps carries its own answer with it.

*Frederick Douglass' Paper*, May 6, 1853

# REMARKS AT ANNIVERSARY MEETING OF THE AMERICAN ANTI-SLAVERY SOCIETY, NEW YORK CITY, MAY, 1853

*Frederick Douglass was then called upon, and, on coming forward, was loudly cheered. He said:* "I will not detain you more than a very few minutes at this stage of the proceedings. I experience great pleasure in appearing before an audience in the City of New York, at the Anniversary of the American Anti-Slavery Society. I rejoice that it has again taken place among the Anniversaries of this month. I regard it as an earnest of our future triumph. I rejoice that this is so. There has been much said this morning as to the hopeful and the fearful sides of this great contest with Slavery. I feel both hopeful and fearful. It seems to me that the Slave power has determined upon fixed and definite policy with regard to the colored people of the country. They appear determined to suppress the freedom of speech, to expatriate every free colored man and woman from the United States, and they seem determined also on the perpetration of Slavery forever in the Southern States. —They are determined to make Slavery respected in every State of the union. The history of the past few years, is not unfavorable to some of these designs. It seems to me Mr. Phillips is right, when he tells you that the Fugitive Slave Law has succeeded; he is right when he pictures to you the ruin that has followed in its truck. Hundreds and thousands of men and women have virtually had their property confiscated, and have been driven forth wanderers on the highways of the earth by this law. But to make the law respected in the North cannot be done by law. The relation of master and slave is so shocking—so monstrous—that men cannot look upon it with respect; they cannot look upon the slave as on any other piece of property; no law, no enactment can ever blot out the manhood and the consciousness of manhood in the slave and he can never feel, when he sees him escape, as he does when he sees a loose horse. —They endeavor to bring all others to look on him as a horse or an ox; but that can't be done. They endeavor to secure peace to the slaveholder; the slaveholder cannot have peace; "No peace to the wicked, saith my God." They might silence the voice of Wendell Phillips, or the pen of Lloyd Garrison; they might cut out my tongue, and gather together all the anti-slavery literature in the United States, set a match to it, and scatter its ashes to the four winds, but then the slaveholder will be ill at ease. "Thou art verily guilty concerning thy brother." I cannot resist the hopeful, the fearful; yet I have faith. I believe it will be crushed. I take this assembly as a guarantee that ere long no chains will clank in our ears.

*Frederick Douglass' Paper*, May 27, 1853

## TO GERRIT SMITH

Rochester, June 1st, 1853
My Dear Friend:
    Yours with the letter from Mr. Green came this morning. I am sorry to learn of your illness. Do not venture to Syracuse unless fully restored to health. My own health is good. Never better. My family are well, and my good friend, Julia, is well also. I appreciate your kind wish to see and talk with me, for I desire always to have your counsel. The meetings at New York are well got along with. Just as you wished, opportunity offered and I embrace the same, to speak at both meetings.[72] So the Garrisonians could not say that I deserted them, nor the new organization that I failed to recognize them as workers in the slave's cause. My paper which goes to press this afternoon, contains your call for a "Christian Union Convention" at Syracuse.[73] The good women are now holding their State temperance meeting here, and I want to be there.[74] Excuse haste.

Always truly yours,
Fred Douglass

*Gerrit Smith Papers, George Arents Research Libraty, Syracuse University*

# ANOTHER WAR WITH MEXICO

The war demon is abroad amongst us.—Having tasted of Mexican blood, and revelled in the rewards of human slaughter, his ferocious appetite is unappeasable except by a repetition of the late bloody *course.* The entertainment may not be forthcoming; but if it does not come, it is evident that the fault will not be in our Democratic administration, nor in the leading Democratic journal at the North, (Bennett's *Herald.*) Fire and brimstone, gunpowder and bullets roll down their columns wordwise in attractive profusion; and there is reason to believe that the war of words may end in blows. The accursed love of gain—the ambition of the Americans to make themselves masters of the continent—to own and possess it—to prevent any alliance between any nation upon it, and any other in Europe—are at the bottom of our movements in this otherwise contemptible controversy about the Mesilla Valley.[75] There is a continent, and a valley at stake. This little valley, and the debate upon it, explains the speeches of Cass and others, made a few months ago, in favor of the Monroe Doctrine, and against the Clayton and Bulwer *treaty.* We mean to have the continent, and to have it if possible for slavery.

If the disputed boundary were on the North, instead of the South, very little danger could be apprehended. Aside from the question of slavery, in that case, there would be restraining and peaceful influences at work, which could not fail of bringing about an amicable adjustment of all difficulties—for our glorious Republic, gallant and brave as she is, need never be expected to go to war unless she has a reasonable probability of whipping somebody. There must be something more than justice and honor on her side to induce her to go to battle. It is not here insinuated that Americans are not courageous—but that they are calculating, and like to fight most where there may be the least fighting to be done. Poor Mexico, disjointed, scattered, torn to pieces by contending factions, is scarcely allowed to "peep or mutter," without being threatened with the beak and talons of our rapacious eagle.— Not so with our neighbor on the North.—There is little disposition in America to disturb the pacific relations so "happily subsisting" between these two Governments.—Indeed, England, not less than America, is desirous of maintaining peace on the North, and probably with motives not wholly unlike those cherished by Americans.

But in respect to Mexico, our course is different. We talk war to her, without ifs, or buts, or whys, or wherefores. The secret of this is—Mexico is weak, and our ideas of magnanimity are so largely mixed with meanness as not to be shocked by such bravado. It is but just to observe, however, in this instance, a slight hesitation is seen on the part of the press, growing not out of where the right is, but out of a wise solicitude as to what part France and Spain may take in the matter. War is a hateful thing; and every man, having the happiness and well-being of mankind at heart, must exert himself to check the war; but we cannot but console ourselves, in the prospect of a war in which France and Spain would be parties, with the belief that slavery could not survive such a war. America, however, is too wise, as we said before, to go to war when the odds are at all doubtful.

*Frederick Douglass' Paper*, June 17, 1853

# THE U.S. CONSTITUTION ANTI-SLAVERY

A highly important and instructive letter from the pen of Hon. Horace Mann,[76] is published on our first page, in which that gentleman gives the opinion in respect to voting, under the Constitution, supposing it in some sense, to support slavery. Like everything else from Mr. Mann, this letter is brilliant, eloquent and able. Its reasoning is powerful, and we see not how it can be answered. We shall, next week, lay before our readers another document from the same pen, which carries us gloriously to an Anti-Slavery Constitution, by three distinct *routes*.

The first route is by the well-established and well-understood rules of legal interpretation, as old as the science of law itself; this route conducts us unfailingly to an Anti-Slavery Constitution. The next is by a route a little less direct than the first, yet equally certain; it is contemporaneous history; this brings us, like the other, to an Anti-Slavery Constitution. The third is the plain literal reading of the Constitution, which defies ingenuity itself, to fasten slavery upon it. We shall publish this important letter next week.

We look upon the Mann and Phillips' controversy as the last serious one which we shall have on the question of the propriety and rightfulness of voting under the Constitution. Efforts to persuade abolitionists that it is a sin to vote for the abolition of slavery; and that their true work is to dissolve the political Union between the confederated States, will, we trust, give place to efforts, more wisely directed, urging to the exercise, by the people, of all the moral, religious and political power of the nation for the abolition of slavery. If this shall result from this controversy, it will not have been held in vain, and Mr. Mann will have performed a most excellent work.

The question whether an honest man can vote and hold office under the American Constitution, has been pressed by Mr. Garrison and his friends during the last ten years.—They have held the Constitution to be a "covenant with death, and an agreement with hell," and have, therefore, refused to vote under it. The unsoundness of their conclusions, and the fallacies by which they have reached them, have been repeatedly exposed by such men as Lysander Spooner, Wm. Goodell, Alvan Stewart, and Gerrit Smith. Still, they have held on to their conclusions, and fancied themselves to occupy, what in their humility, they are pleased to term "higher ground," than is occupied by any other abolitionists beside. It is true that slaveholders could ask no higher service from them, than that which they are promptly rendering; for what more do the slaveholders want than to have the character of the Constitution, the character of the great men who framed and adopted it, and the facts of history so perverted as to stand between them and the terrible crime and scandal of slaveholding. They do not desire to be found more upright and just than the fundamental law of the land, or more virtuous than their revolutionary fathers. The fact is, non-voting abolitionists have been conscientiously weaving garments to shield the consciences of slaveholders during the last ten years, claiming all this while that they occupy higher ground than all other opponents of slavery. May we not now hope to hear no more of it, in view of Horace Mann's extinguisher.

*Frederick Douglass' Paper*, June 24, 1853

# THE ANTI-SLAVERY ADVOCATE
## AND THE TESTIMONIAL TO MRS. STOWE.

It will be remembered that we copied from the *Advocate*, in our paper of 7th May, a letter purporting to have been written by *"an*

*American Abolitionist," opposing the appropriation of Mrs. Stowe's funds, to the "instruction and amelioration" of the condition of the free and fugitive slaves portion of the colored people of the United States; denouncing all schemes of "instruction and amelioration," as delusive and cruel, while slavery lasts; ridiculing them as childish philanthropy; regarding such efforts as harmful to the anti-slavery cause, and humiliating to the colored people.*[77]

We felt called upon as soon as we saw this letter in the discharge of a duty incumbent upon us, as an advocate of the cause of the *nominally free*, as well as of the slave population of the United States, to expose with some severity, the mischievous suggestions of this "American Abolitionist;" and it affords us much satisfaction to know that our "club" did good execution in the promises.

The *Advocate* of this month gives us the benefit of nearly three columns, which we do not produce here, because we like, sometimes to follow the example of our elders. —The *Advocate* having been careful to omit, from its columns, every connected sentence . . . professes to reply.[78]

Of course, the man of the *Advocate* has everything his own way. He can attribute to us every absurdity, cruelty, injustice, and egotism he likes; and his readers have to swallow all on his authority; having nothing withal to excuse their incredulity.

We, however, will not follow the *Advocate*, literally; but, to whatever point we reply, that point shall be stated in his own words:

"The anti-slavery enterprise was not undertaken for the purpose of feeding, clothing, or educating the Free Colored People; nor for the purchase and liberation of individual slaves, or the relief of isolated cases, of suffering or to promote the escape of fugitives, or to found industrial institutions in Canada, or to forward emigration to the West Indies or anywhere else."

Stripped of all disguise, this *Anti-Slavery Advocate* affirms that it is no part of the duty of abolitionists to assist the struggling Free Colored man in efforts to educate and improve the conditions of "the Free Colored people" of the United States. The enumeration which he makes is, evidently, intended, simply to strengthen the general argument in favor of his main position. It is much to be regretted that this sort of abolitionism is not confined to Ireland. The editor of the *Advocate* has sympathizing friends on this side the Atlantic in this view of the case; but we usually regard such abolitionists as sham abolitionists.

The *Advocate* is altogether mistaken in supposing the Free Colored people not to have been contemplated in the objects of the Anti-slavery enterprise—the original declaration of sentiments pledged the American Anti-Slavery Society not merely to emancipate the slave; but to elevate the free people of color;[79] and that has been considered quite orthodox work, among abolitionists generally, until very lately. Some few who have no notion of associating with colored people on terms of equality, would like "this elevation" part of abolitionism thrown tastefully into the background.

Such persons will exclude a colored man from their offices and stores, and will not have him seen there, except in the capacity of a porter or a waiter.

The *Advocate* assumes, throughout its article, that improving the condition of the Free Colored people is not appropriate anti-slavery work; that the Free Colored people may not receive the benefit of any funds intended for anti-slavery purposes; and that to help them is not necessarily to advance the anti-slavery cause. He says:

"We rejoice in everything that is done to help them, provided the funds for the promotion of the anti-slavery cause be not diverted to the benefit of those who have gained the priceless treasure of liberty. This would be like appropriating the funds of an hospital for the sick, to establish and support a gymnasium for the benefit of the healthy."

It is evident, from the foregoing that the *Advocate* has undertaken to plead a cause about which, with all the assistance of "*An American Abolitionist*," he is but slightly informed. *He* is grossly ignorant of the real identity of the slave and the Free Colored people of the United States, who affirms the one to be sick and other "healthy." There is, indeed, a difference between the slave and the free; but it is a difference to be described by no such extravagant simile as the *Advocate* makes. To talk of the Free Colored people as "healthy," while State after State passes laws for their expulsion; while the Fugitive Slave Law renders the liberty of every one of them insecure; while their children are excluded from schools in most of the States; and it is impossible for them to learn trades, and they are compelled to be the hewers of wood and drawers of water, proscribed, insulted and spit upon because of their identity with the slave—we say that to talk of the Free Colored people as "healthy," in these circumstances, is to add insult to injury. The Editor of the *Advocate* will have to change his philosophy on this point, before he can *fitly* speak for the American slave.

We, in this country do not measure any man's abolitionism by his

professed love of the slave at the South. We have a better way than this.
It is, "How does he treat his black neighbor at the North?" If he care
nothing about the education, improvement, and elevation of the blacks
where he is, we have no difficulty in disposing of his claims as an
abolitionist. Stupid as pro-slavery men are over here, they have been
sagacious enough to apply this test, and a capital one it is. It is the old
scriptural method, "For he that loveth not his brother whom he hath
seen, how can he love God, whom he hath not seen?"

However strange it may seem to the impersonal *Advocate*, the Free
Colored Man in the United States is but *half* free; for although not a
slave to an *individual*, he is a slave to society; and the genuine
abolitionists so regard him. The *Advocate* takes refuge behind *"The
American Abolitionist."* He cracks him up very high; he says "the obnox-
ious remark to which we replied, was communicated by one who has
been much longer connected with the anti-slavery cause than himself;
whose services to it have been far greater than his own; and who has
sacrificed more to its promotion than he has ever done or is likely to
do."

We do not object to any of this. It seems perfectly proper for the
*Advocate* to compliment his friend, *"the American Abolitionist,"* who,
evidently, (for wise purposes,) prefers to be *incog.*

The anti-slavery enterprise, however, doesn't belong to anybody
in particular, on the ground of priority; it is not an *invention* about
which there need be any quarreling. We have never *"served"* the cause
too faithfully, though we've done what we could, and can boast of
having emancipated others before emancipating ourselves. We should
like, however, (for the mere fun of the thing,) to know *who* this very
self-sacrificing abolitionist is, and then we should be better able,
perhaps, to appreciate his deep concern, that lost money, designed to
promote the cause of the slave, should be squandered in *"delusive and
cruel"* efforts to educate the *"Free Colored people."*

The *Advocate* finds, however, another standard, before he gets
through by which to determine the merits of men; for, with the
consistency of a true Hibernian, he says, when referring to *Gerrit Smith*:

"Still, there are many laborers, in the anti-slavery cause, who, in
their measures and according to their gifts, have done as well [as Gerrit
Smith.] It does not follow, because everybody has not vast possessions
and a heart to distribute them, that they cannot do as much for the
slave in some other way."

*Very good*; and perhaps, if you, Mr. *Advocate*, had thought of this in disposing of our *poor* merits, you might have raised us a peg higher than the estimate just given of us above; but neither our want of services, not the services of that "American Abolitionist" in question, has anything to do with the point in controversy. Good men have erred, and will, probably, err again; and no good man, according to Mr. Phillips, should wish to be exempt from criticism.

Whatever the editor of the *Advocate* may think, we believe that no better appropriation could be made (even with a view to the emancipation of the slave) of the funds of Mrs. Stowe, than that of establishing in this country, an *institution*, in which colored youth can be instructed in certain lucrative mechanical branches; and we are very happy to know that in this opinion, the excellent authoress of *"Uncle Tom's Cabin,"* fully unites.[80]

*Frederick Douglass' Paper*, July 22, 1853

## ARGUMENTS ON THE CALL FOR A NATIONAL EMIGRATION CONVENTION

TO BE held in Cleveland, Ohio, August, 1854

We have no sympathy with the call for this convention, which we publish in another column.[81] Whatever may be the motives for sending forth such a call, (and we can say nothing as to these) we deem it uncalled for, unwise, unfortunate and premature; and we venture to predict that this will be the judgment pronounced upon it by a majority of intelligent thinking colored men. Our enemies will see in this movement, a cause of rejoicing, such as they could hardly have anticipated so soon, after the manly position assumed by the colored National Convention held in this city. They will discover in this movement a division of opinion amongst us upon a vital point, and will look upon this Cleveland Convention as opposed in spirit and purpose to the Rochester Convention. Looked at from any point, the movement is to be deprecated.

Then the call itself is far too narrow and illiberal, to meet with acceptance among the intelligent. A Convention to consider the subject of emigration, where every delegate must declare himself in favor of it beforehand, as a condition of taking his seat, is like the handle of a jug, all on one side! This provision of the call looks cowardly. It looks as if the Conventionists are afraid to meet the colored people of the United States on the question of emigration.

We hope no colored man will omit, during the coming twelve months, any opportunity which may offer to buy a piece of property, a house, lot, a farm, or anything else in the United States, which looks to permanent residence here. On account of any prospective Canaan which may be spread out in the lofty imaginations of the projectors of this Cleveland Convention.

*Frederick Douglass Paper,* July 25, 1853

## J.M. WHITFIELD IN REPLY TO F. DOUGLASS

Buffalo, Sept. 25th, 1853

Frederick Douglass, Esq.—Dear Sir:

I have noticed, in your comments upon the call for the Convention of the friends of Emigration to be held at Cleveland, many severe, and, in my opinion, unjust strictures upon the movement, and as I have seen objections of a similar import raised by others, I desire, with your permission, briefly to answer some of them.

One of the prominent objections raised against us by yourself and others, is that while we have issued a call for a National Convention of the friends of Emigration, for the purpose of devising the best means of carrying into operation what we believe to be just and wise policy, that is, the concentration, as far as possible, of the black race in the central and southern portions of America, so that it may exercise its proper influence in molding the destiny, and shaping the policy of the American Continent, and in securing a proper field for the full development of its own power and resources, and while that call is emphatically for the friends of the measure, and none others—we are assailed on all sides as though we had no right to issue such a call—a course which can be accounted for only on the ground that the assailants suppose that we are incapable of acting for ourselves, or of knowing our own wants.

You say that "whatever may be the motives for sending forth such a call," you "deem it uncalled for, unwise, unfortunate, and premature;" and you "venture to predict that the same judgment will be pronounced upon it by a majority of intelligent thinking colored men." It may, perhaps, be a sufficient answer to this, to say that the signers of the call (many of whom are men of cultivated minds, not accustomed to rash and hasty action upon important subjects) after mature deliberation and interchange of views are fully convinced that it is imperatively called for, eminently wise and timely, and if conducted with energy, cannot fail of being salutary in its influences. You also say "our enemies will see in this movement a cause of rejoicing, such as they could hardly have anticipated so soon, after the manly position assumed by the colored National Convention held in Rochester. They will discover in this movement, a division of opinion amongst us upon a vital point, and will look upon this Cleveland Convention as opposed in spirit and purpose to the Rochester Convention."

So far from rejoicing, I believe that our enemies will see as much greater cause for dreading the holding of the Cleveland than of the Rochester Convention, as a master would have greater reason for fearing the loss of the slave, who arms himself and leaves his premises with the determination to be free or die, than he would the one who, after a few vain supplications, submits to the lash, and devotes the energies which should be employed in improving himself and his children, to building up the fortune of a tyrant, whose constant endeavor is to crush him lower in degradation, and entail the same hopeless condition upon his posterity. I suppose the purpose of the Cleveland Convention to be as much superior to that of the Rochester Convention, as deeds are superior to words—as strenuous efforts to obtain freedom, even if unsuccessful, are superior to whining or supplicating submission to slavery. The purpose of the Rochester Convention (for which it deserves great credit as a step, and that, too, an important one, in the right direction) was to endeavor to create a union of sentiment and action among the colored people, and, to give it efficiency, by forming a kind of national organization here, under the overshadowing influence of our oppressors. I believe that movement to be a good one, because it must ultimately lead *"intelligent thinking* colored men" to the conclusion which many of us ignorant and thoughtless ones have arrived at intuitively—that is, that colored men can never be fully and fairly respected as the equals of the whites, in this country, or any other, until they are able to show in some part of the world, men of their own race occupying a primary and independent position, instead of a secondary and inferior one, as is now the case everywhere. In short, that they must show a powerful nation in which the black is the *ruling* element capable of maintaining a respectable position among the *great* nations of the earth; and I believe that the reflex influence of such a power with the increased activity that its re-action will excite in the colored people of the country, will be the only thing sufficiently powerful to remove the prejudices which ages of unequal oppression have engendered, unless the bleaching theory of Henry Clay should prevail, and be carried into practice, by which the Negro race in this country is to be absorbed and its identity lost in that of the Caucasian—a consummation in my opinion not to be wished for. I believe it to be the destiny of the Negro, to develop a higher order of civilization and Christianity than the world has yet seen. I also consider it a part of his "manifest destiny," to possess all the tropical regions of this continent, with the adjacent islands. That the Negro is to be the predominant race in all that region in regard to numbers, is beyond doubt. The only question is, shall they exercise the power and influence their numbers entitle them to, and become the ruling political element of the land in which they live? or shall they, as too many of our brethren in this country seem to be willing to do, tamely submit to the usurpation of a white aristocracy, naturally inferior to themselves in physical, moral, and mental power, and devote their lives to building up a power whose every energy will be wielded to crush them? If the Cleveland Convention gives, as we hope it will, a proper response to these great practical questions, its position will be as much more manly than that assumed by the Rochester Convention, as freedom is superior to slavery, or self-reliance to childish dependence on others.

To the charge that "our enemies will discover a division of opinion amongst us upon a vital point," I would answer, what if they do? All but bigots and fanatics know that there ever have been, and probably ever will be, divisions of opinion among men upon questions vitally connected with their temporal and spiritual welfare; and the more vital the question, the greater the differences of opinion, and the harder to reconcile conflicting views— consequently all reasonable men are willing to make allowances for honest differences of opinion, because they know that entire unanimity is to be expected only where tyranny on the one hand dictates, and servility on the other submits. The only opposition that I am able to discover, either in spirit or in purpose, to the Rochester Convention, is, that it goes a step further in the same direction, and purposes to walk in the path which the Rochester Convention has pointed out. The child who has ventured to stand alone, must, of necessity, either step on, or fall down again and crawl in the dust; and if we prefer walking forward, although it may be with feeble and tottering steps, in the path where freedom and a glorious destiny beckon us on, to crawling again in dust at the feet of our oppressors, we think that we deserve praise rather than censure for the choice.

The last objection that you make to the call, that it "is illiberal and cowardly," because it excluded all but the friends of the measure, is too ridiculous to deserve serious comment. What would be thought of the Whig or Democrat who should bring serious charge against the opposite party, because they would not admit him as a delegate to their Conventions, with the right to vote on shaping the policy, and nominating the candidates of his opponents! It strikes me that such a claim would be regarded as transcendently impudent, were not its impudence surpassed by its absurdity, and I doubt very much whether his opponents could be brought to recognize the justice of such a claim, however willing or anxious they might be to discuss the question at issue between them. The friends of Emigration are *not* afraid to meet the colored people on the subject, but they choose to rest under the imputation of cowardice, sooner than *prove* themselves fools by admitting the avowed enemies of a measure, as the ones to devise ways and means for promoting its success. However, if the opponents of Emigration desire, we are ready and willing to discuss it, either in a Convention, if they choose to appoint one for the purpose, or through the press; and all that we ask is that equally fair hearing shall be allowed to each party. We apprehend, however, that anything like a fair discussion of the subject is not desired by the opponents of the measure; but that an attempt will be made to excite the prejudices of the people beforehand, by raising the cry of Colonization, Expatriation, &c. If any of our brethren have arguments addressed to our reason as men, by which they think they can convince us of the folly of our measures, of the wisdom of their own, we will endeavor to receive and reply to them in the same spirit; but if wholesale denunciations and misrepresentations are to take the place of facts and arguments, we must respectfully but firmly decline entering into any such controversy. Life is too short, and our foes too numerous and powerful for us to waste our time wrangling with brethren because we differ in relation to the means necessary to promote the same great end which we have equally at heart—the elevation of our race.

We hope that our brethren that differ from us in opinion will do us the justice to believe that our position in favor of emigration is the result of no rash and hasty speculation, but of full and well-matured deliberation; and that, therefore, the stereotyped and commonplace objections raised by them have been thoroughly examined by us in all their bearings, without at all shaking our confidence in the wisdom and policy of Emigration. We wish it also to be understood that we consider the line of argument usually pursued by the colonizationists and abolitionists, pro and con, in relation to Colonization or Emigration *en masse* to be a tissue of nonsense on both sides—because contending for the practicability, or impracticability, of a measure which is absolutely impossible. We do not wish it to be supposed that we are so utterly ignorant of the laws which govern population, as to think that a nation or class of people scattered through all the ramifications of society, in a great and civilized nation like the colored people in the United States, ever did, ever will, or ever can emigrate *en masse*. No fact is better fixed in the world's history than this, that a people who have passed the pastoral state, never can by any possibility be brought to emigrate *en masse*. If our brethren will bear these things in mind, it may lead them to form a more correct opinion of our position than they seem to have done hitherto.

Respectfully yours,<br>
J.M. Whitfield.[82]

*Arguments, Pro and Con, On the Call for a National Emigration Convention, to be held in Cleveland, Ohio, August, 1854, by Frederick Douglass, W.J. Watkins, & J.M. Whitfield. . . . Detroit, 1854, pp. 7-11. Copy in Howard University Library.*

## THE LETTER OF J.M. WHITFIELD

Just before our paper was put to press, we accidentally caught a glimpse of the letter of this gentleman, being in the lecturing field at the time of its reception, and from which we have just returned.

The letter is written in a good spirit, and despite its exorbitant length, we cordially welcome it to our columns; at the same time we would remark that communications from whatsoever source they may emanate and however ably they may be written, will prove more acceptable to our readers generally, if the ideas attempted to be conveyed, be not clothed in such interminable prolixity. Again, we would remark to our friend that we notice the fact that *his* letters are caught up with avidity, and published in the *Alienated American* and *Voice of the Fugitive*, and our *short responses* do not, somehow, find way into their columns.

Our friend finds fault with the "inference" which we consider the irresistible deduction of his own logic. He believes, then, that the two races can live, and move, and have their being together, in this country. But we would ask the plain question, does he not, in company with those whom he parades before the public as the heroes of the "Emigration" movement, maintain the position, that "colored men can never fully and fairly be respected as the *equals* of the whites in this country," and *therefore* they must leave the United States? Now, if they do not make this affirmation in so many words; their actions, which speak more loudly than words, certainly warrant such an interpretation of their position. If they believe with us, that by remaining *here*, and battling for the right we shall evidently stand out in the sunlight on the broad platform of equality, why turn their backs upon the contest, and flee from the country under the protext of "shaping the policy of the American continent?" We make the broad, unqualified assertion, that we regard any movement which contemplates the removal or emigration of the Free Colored People of these U.S. to *any* land, near or remote, as a virtual endorsement of the fundamental principles which underlie the whole fabric of African Colonization. Colonizationists affirm that we can never in the United States rise superior to the adverse circumstances by which we are surrounded; that the color of our skin, the textures of our hair, and diversity of our physical conformation, preclude the possibility of our elevation here.

Mr. Whitfield declares that "the mass of the colored people in this country must ever remain here, and can never, by any possibility be brought to emigrate *en masse*."

Then what an egregious absurdity is the contemplated "Cleveland Convention?"—For what purpose is the Convention called? Why, of course, to "consider and decide upon the great and important subject of emigration from the United States." Individual emigration? No! Not if words are the representatives of ideas. The call is for a *National* Emigration. National Emigration means emigration of the *nation*. This Convention is to be held, then, for the purpose of carrying out a measure which our friend himself declares to be "unworthy of a moment's consideration."

Again; Mr. W. informs us that "the tendency of political events is towards the formation of a great nation, or family of nations, occupying the tropical regions of this continent and its islands," &c. This may be so; but it by no means follows that it is *our* "manifest destiny" to become a member of this illustrious family. "Tropical regions, forsooth!" Now, we would seriously inquire of our Emigration friends, whether they are in earnest when they urge, among other considerations, an objection to their abode in Africa, the "uncongeniality" of tropical climate. We know some men whose names are appended to the "Call," who have prated very loudly about the *fatal* folly which our people would exhibit, by leaving a climate *so congenial with our constitution*, for one of sickness, devastation, and death; or, in other words, the exchanging of a temperate for a torrid zone. When they are urged to emigrate to Africa, they cry out "No, we can't live in a *tropical* clime." Now, so far as this family of nations is concerned—this family that is destined to occupy the "tropical regions," we fancy that the *very few* who will leave the States—would hardly come up to the idea of a *nation*. We believe with Mr. W., that it is our manifest destiny to remain *here*, and this opinion is based upon a limited knowledge of the laws which govern population.

Then let the nations occupy, if they please, the tropical regions of this continent, or any other; and if the reflex influence of such a power will remove existing prejudice on us in this country, then, with all our vigor will we exclaim Amen!

The remainder of this gentleman's letter will be considered at a future period. We consider this Cleveland Convention movement as one affording aid and comfort to the enemy. We do not believe that those whose names are appended to this Call seriously contemplate emigration. They will meet in public Convention, and adopt a long series of resolutions, then return to their homes, and stay there. They will not leave the country and neither will we. We here inform them, and all others concerned that unless they show to our people more convincing evidence of *their* intention to leave the country, we shall henceforth regard them as insincere in the theory they promulgate. When these men leave the country, may we be there to see. This Emigration question is an important one, and we have no disposition to pass it lightly by, but consider the work of our elevation here, as one of transcendant importance, shall act accordingly; and we cannot understand gentlemen so well-informed as Messrs Whitfield and Delany, can consent, for a moment to occupy a position which obviously confounds them with that despondency which has ever embarrassed and clogged them of our efforts at elevation in the United States. And we call upon them in the name of our already too deeply bowed down people to drop their Emigration Scheme, and put their shoulders to the wheel of the first in motion in these United States.

*Frederick Douglass' Paper*, November 25, 1853

## THE LETTER OF J.M. WHITFIELD

We have, since our last issue, re-perused the letter of Mr. Whitfield, and carefully weighed the contents. Before entering upon the merits or demerits, we have a word to say to our readers. We wish it distinctly understood, that the proclivity of some men to enter the arena of conflict, is something wholly foreign to our nature. We have seen people who were like the troubled sea, unless an opportunity favorable to the development of their warlike propensities, continually presented itself. This was one of the leading characteristics of the *bellique* Caesar. "Never mind, brother Toby," he would say, "by God's blessing, *we shall have another war break out again*, some of these days, and when it does, the belligerent powers, if they would hang themselves, cannot keep us out of play."

We lay not the flattering unction to our souls, that we possess a particle of Caesar's *courage*. We do not voluntarily and cheerfully leap into the gladiatorial arena; but, if forced thither, we will fight to the best of our ability, unless we can effect an honorable retreat.

These remarks are induced from a consciousness of the fact that too many of our leading men, or would-be leaders, apparently delight in being submerged in the turbid waters of strife; but, amphibious-like, they can live also when ranging the pleasant fields of love and harmony. With these land and water men we have no sympathy. So far

as Mr. W. is concerned, we make no personal allusion. We suppose
him to be a gentlemen of noble and generous impulses. We believe,
also, that the policy he so ably advocates, is one which involves an
admission detrimental to the interests of those with whom we are
identified. We regard the ground-work of this theory radically defec-
tive. The Emigration movement receives its vitality, if it has any, from
assumptions which are untenable and gratuitous, and we shall contribute our humble quota toward the development of their fallacy.

First, then, those who advocate the policy of the Emigration of
the Free Colored People of these United States to *any* country, we care
not whether the locality be a desirable one on account of its proximity
to the slave population, or otherwise, virtually admit the truthfulness
of the position which Colonizationists assume, viz: *that our elevation in
this country* is an absolute impossibility; that it is an incongruity wholly
irreconcilable with the law of our destiny.

This is a most suicidal assumption, the correctness of which we
are not yet willing to concede. We do not assert that our friend W. and
others, admit the *righteousness* of that barbarous policy which mer-
cilessly compels us to occupy a secondary position in the country.
Certainly not. But, simply, that the very fact of our friends having
called a Convention "to consider and decide upon the great and important subject of Emigration from the United States," proves, if it proves
anything, that they have lost that faith which has hitherto nerved us
onward, unparalleled by the terrific thunders of the wrath of man.
Their prospects of the ultimate triumph of our heaven-born cause, have
been quenched by the pitiless peltings of the storm.

Their action demonstrates their belief in the ultimate discomfi-
ture of those, who cling with unyielding tenacity to those signs of the
times, which we regard as auguring its final triumph. Here, then,
really, is the point at issue. Not, exactly, as some of our friends would
declare, whether or not our condition "can be made worse by Emigration," but whether or not we have implicit confidence in the ultimate
success of the anti-slavery movement; *whether Might or Right shall
triumph in the present conflict.* —What, then, is the position which Emigrationists and Colonizationists assume? Whoever will take the pains to
read the first paragraph of the Call for the Cleveland Convention, will
readily discern that those who sympathize with it regard their condition in this country as one from which they can, by no contingency,

hope to emerge. "The time has now *fully* come when we, as an oppressed people, should do something effectively, and use those means adequate to the attainment of the great and long-desired end, to do something to meet the actual demands of the present and prospective necessities of the rising generation of our people in this country." Now, in order to effect this desirable consummation, what policy must be pursued? Must we remain here battling in defense of our rights as men, implicitly relying upon the willingness, and ability, and intention, so to speak, of Jehovah, to crown our efforts with signal success? Not at all. What then? The idea of Emigration is held out to our oppressed people as a "sovereign balm for every wound." To meet these "present demands, and prospective necessities, we must occupy a position of entire *equality*, of *unrestricted* rights," &c. For the purpose of attaining this equality and preparing for these "prospective necessities," all those in favor of "emigrating out of the United States," are invited to assemble in Cleveland, in Convention. Here is the position assumed: We can never be the equals of the whites in this country, and we must, therefore, prepare for our exodus.

This, we consider a most fatal admission, and one which, at *this crisis*, operates as mollifying ointment upon the gangrene heart of American Despotism.

Here, then, do we make the issue with Emigrationists. *They are confounded with that despondency and despair which preclude the possibility of their working for their elevation here, with that hopeful ardor which is the life-blood of the anti-slavery enterprise.*

We, who are opposed to Emigration, occupy a different position. In waging war with the enemy, and believing in the final triumph of the right, we do not believe that we are the victims of a miserable delusion. A contemplation of the past, and its contrast with the present, inspire us with confidence and hope for the future. We, therefore, intend to work faithfully and fearlessly, and hopefully, for our elevation HERE, till victory perch upon our banner.

Believing with Mr. W., that it is *"our manifest destiny to remain here,"* it is our respective duty, to march onward, in the path of progress, and look upward, and if it be the destiny of that *"family of nations* to occupy the tropical regions of this continent, and its islands," we, who are an integrant part of THIS nation, (though crushed and bleeding,) should, instead of preparing for our exodus to other lands, calmly and stoically suffer our hardships here, cordially awaiting the arrival of that auspicious era, when "the reflex influence" of that potent family, will "remove the existing prejudice against us" here.

We do not believe in herding ourselves together, in this country, or in any other. We will not *willingly* segregate ourselves from the rest of mankind. We are part and parcel of the *American Nation*. At any rate we will join this tropical family, only as a *last resort*. If Slaveholders, and their apologists succeed in driving us from the country; if our star of *Hope* go out in darkness, then we'll join this family, and not till then. This was the position assumed by Frederick Douglass, in his Broadway Tabernacle Speech, May 11th, '53.[83] Said he:

Sir, I am not for going anywhere. I'm for staying precisely where I am, in the land of my birth. But, Sir, if I must go from this country; if it is impossible to stay here, I am then for doing the next best, and that will be to go wherever I can hope to be of most service to the colored people of the United States. Americans, there is a meaning in those figures I have read. God does not permit twelve millions of his creatures to live without the notice of his eye. That this vast people are tending to one point on this continent is now without significance. All things are with God. Let not the colored man despair then. Let him remember that a home, a country, a nationality, are all attainable this side of Liberia. But for the present the colored people should stay just where they are, unless where they are compelled to leave. I have faith left yet; the wisdom and justice of the country and it may be that there are enough left of these to save the nation.

Again; neither Colonization, nor Emigration, is a remedy for the ills of the Colored American. He cannot emigrate from himself. He cannot destroy his own identity. If he leaves the country, he must carry his predilections with him. *If these are as they should be, he will here rise, superior to all adverse circumstances by which he is surrounded. If they are not, he will rise nowhere but must ever occupy a degraded position.*

Our friend W. virtually accuses us of dishonesty, in uttering sentiments, which do not emanate from the heart. We stated in a former article on this subject, that Colonizationists are resolved to drive us from the country and care but very little where we go. What they dread is, our proximity to our brethren in bonds. To prove we did not mean what we wrote, he triumphantly inquires why we did not remain in Maryland, instead of going to Massachusetts and New York.

Now, we reiterate our declaration. We would ask Mr. W. if he does not know it to be true? We might, had we time, point to the speeches of the great leaders of the Colonization movement, in which this fact stands out in bold relief. They declare without reservation, that our presence in this country exerts an unfavorable influence upon the Slave population. We render the slave discontented, and, consequently, we must be separated from them. But friend W., suppose we did leave Maryland? What if we are not in contact with the Slave; does this fact prove the fallacy of our assertion? We are still in the country. When we wrote the word "proximity," we did not mean immediate. We merely wished to convey the Idea that we should remain in the country, where our brethren are in bonds, and plead for them, (which we could not do in Maryland), rather than leap over the wall, under the pretext of "shaping the policy of the American Continent."

But *we too*, have a question to ask. Our friend W., remarks that he has entertained the same opinions of the policy of emigration, from boyhood; aye, fifteen years ago he was an emigrationist. "Did *you* mean what you wrote then?" If you did, how happens it that you are here, in 1853 still talking *loudly* about *leaving?* Why have you not been borne to the "tropical regions" by the current of "political events." We think we are at liberty to take your past history as a precedent for the future. Time will continue to "strengthen your conviction," but after all, you will settle down and resolve to *receive*, rather than impart that "reflected influence" which your imagination beholds so plainly, "removing the existing prejudice."

We believe with you, that Colonizationists would prefer that we would go to our "fatherland." We know they deprecate the "existence of an independent community on their southern frontier." But they more deprecate our existence in their midst. We are not disposed to compromise the matter with them' *by removing but not removing FAR.*

But our friend concludes his letter by suddenly assuming a very hopeful mood. Well, better late, than never. But his hope is *sui generis*. If he really hopes for our elevation here, why flee *from* the country? He declares that "those who would be for themselves, must strike the blow." But do you mean what you wrote then? If so Mr. W., *you* must help *strike*, and not just *receive* the blows and kicks of our enemies and then depart in peace, for the tropical regions. But we must conclude by a call upon our Emigration friends, to cast the evil spirit of despondency from their thoughts, and remember that "God is just and His justice shall not sleep forever."

Ye fearful saints, fresh courage take
The clouds ye so much dread
Are big with mercy, and shall break
In blessings on your head.

*Frederick Douglass' Paper*, December 2, 1853

## A TERROR TO KIDNAPPERS

Such is the title of a huge and highly finished cane, recently presented to Frederick Douglass by John Jones and J.D. Bonner, members of the National Council for Illinois. This was a happy thought, this *stick*— present not altogether inappropriate, for it is believed in these parts that a good stick is sometimes as much needed as a good speech and often more effective. Where you have a dog deal with, stick will perform wonders where speech would be powerless!—There are among the children of men, and I have gained the fact from personal observation, to be found representatives of all the animal world, from the most savage and ferocious, to the most gentle and docile. Everything must be dealt with according to its kind. What will do for the Lamb will not do for the Tiger. A man would look foolish if he attempted to bail out a leaking boat with the Bible, or to extinguish a raging fire by throwing in a Prayer Book. Equally foolish would he look if he attempted to soften a slave-catcher's heart without first softening his head. This is a capital stick, and I thank my friends for it. I hope never to meet with a creature requiring its use; but should I meet with such an one, I shall use it with stout arm and humane motive.

*Frederick Douglass' Paper*, November 25, 1853

# REMARKS

AT THE ODD FELLOWS FESTIVAL in Minerva Hall, Rochester, New York, on Thursday evening, January, 1854

Ladies and Gentlemen:

I really do not know what is expected of me on an occasion like this. I am not initiated into the mysteries of this association, and, what is more, have for a long time had a very strong prejudice against associations of this kind. I have however, learned some important lessons on respect to nearly all human institutions. Among these lessons, I have learned this one, namely, commend what you know to be good wherever you find it—condemn whatever you know to be evil wherever you find it—and be silent about whatever you do not know enough of either to condemn or approve.

When called upon to be present on this occasion, I asked the gentlemen, who kindly invited me, the object of this festival; they told me it was to benefit our own poor and helpless ones. This is a good object.

Anything which looks to assisting the helpless, has my heart and has my hand.—This, ladies and gentlemen, is my feeling generally; but where it relates to my own afflicted fellow-countrymen, those who suffer a common oppression with me, I feel an especial interest. We are one people in point of position and destiny, and cannot, if we would, and ought not, if we could, separate from each other, in efforts of this kind to improve our condition. I esteem the invitation to address you this evening as a high honor. You are my fellow citizens, you know me, and if you who know me best, think me worthy to address you on this high festival occasion, I shall be excused, if I do not heed the selfish clamor raised against me abroad.

Another thing I understand to be comprehended in this invitation—and that is, I am to deal honestly with you—the members of this association—both as members of this Society—and as citizens, and also, and more particularly as related to our enslaved and oppressed people throughout the country.—You style yourselves *United Friends*, and, of course, set some value upon friendship.—This is right and beautiful. The term friend is a delightful one, filled with a thousand sweet harmonies. In journeying through this vale of tears, life is desolate indeed, if unblest by friendship. A friend is a very precious gift. A brother is not always a friend—a sister is not always a friend, and even a wife may not always be a friend, nor a husband always a friend. The central idea of friendship, and the main pillar of it is "trust." Where there is no *trust*, there is no friendship. We cannot love those we cannot trust. The basis of all *trust* is truth. There cannot be trust—lasting trust—where the truth is not. Men must be true to each other, or they cannot trust each other.

If I have been called upon to lend my neighbor five dollars, and have received the positive assurance that he will pay me at a given time, and that time comes and the pay does not, the grounds of my *trust* are shaken. But if that friend and neighbor comes soon after, and explains that causes which he could not control, made it impossible for him to meet that engagement, I hold him excused and restore him to my confidence and regard even though I may disapprove of his rashness in making promises. But again, if this neighbor of mine, not only fails to meet his engagement, but also fails to explain the cause of his failure, and instead of seeking me, seeks to avoid me, I cannot—you cannot—living man, knowing the facts, cannot trust him. He is not only not a man of truth—but he is in good earnest a liar—and the truth is not in him. Such a man must repent and bring gospel fruit meet for repentance—or it will be impossible to love or to trust him. You may pity him, you may despise him—but you cannot regard him as a man of honor.

If, therefore, you ask me what is the basis of friendship, I answer, *"Truth and trust." Love* does not form the basis of friendship, it simply crowns and glorifies a friendship already established on the basis of *"Truth and trust."* If, further, you ask me, how shall friendship already in existence be perpetuated—I answer simply, that this can be done only by being true to each other. Do all you promise to do, and as much more as you can. Pardon me for hinting at this matter. I deem it of vital importance. No society, no family, can hang together without it.

Now, a word about our relations to each other as a people. These are peculiar. As a people, we are poor, and are limited in point of mental attainments. We must improve our condition, and here the work is ours. It cannot be done by our friends. They can pity as they can sympathize with us. But we need more than sympathy— something more than pity. *We must be respected.* And we cannot be respected unless we are either independent or aiming to be. We must be as independent of society as society is of us, and lay society under as many obligations to us as we are under to society. We cannot be paupers and be respected, though we may be paupers and be pitied. The fact is, my friends, we must not only work, but, we must make money—not only make money, but save it; and when we use it, we must use it wisely. Knowledge, too, we must get. We must get it by exertion, by patient study and perseverance. It is fortunate for our down-trodden race, that knowledge is power, and that this power is accessible to us, as well as the rest of mankind. Armed with truth and with the high approval of the God of truth, may you go on in the *work* before *you* to certain triumph.

*Frederick Douglass' Paper*, January 6, 1851

# TO CALVIN ELLIS STOWE

Roch., Jan. 17th, 1854

Dear Dr Stowe:

Please accept my sincere thanks for the volumes five in number just come to hand, intended to assist me in the study of the claims of the Bible as a Divine revelation. The thought that I am an object of your care has comfort in it. I will read and study these books, and some day give you some idea of the progress I have made on the subject. At present I shall be too much in the lecturing field to study, but if all be well, shall have more time in Summer. Tomorrow evening I begin a series of appointments made for me in New Hampshire. Please remember me kindly to Mrs. Stowe and believe me very gratefully your friend,

Frederick Douglass

*Ms., Chicago Historical Society*

## AMERICAN SLAVERY

LECTURE No. 11, Delivered before the New Lyceum, Rochester, January 24, 1854.[1]

Ten years since, I came to this city, and found it impossible to secure a place in which to speak on the subject of American slavery. I rejoice at the evident change that has taken place in the state of feeling in this part of New Hampshire. and I take this meeting as an evidence of the onward progress of the principles of freedom. I cannot hope, in view of the vast amount that has been said by abler and more eloquent men, to being before you any new truths connected with this question. Indeed, it is scarcely necessary to search for new truths, till the old truths, which have been uttered from the Declaration of Independence until now, shall have become recognized and reduced to practice. Properly speaking, there is no such thing as new or old truth. Error may be either new or old; it has its beginnings and must have its endings. But truth is from everlasting to everlasting. Such is the great truth of man's right to liberty. It entered into the very idea of man's creation. It was born with us, and no laws, constitutions, compacts, agreements or combinations can ever abrogate or destroy it. It is so simple a truth that we have no occasion to look into the moldy records of the past, in order to demonstrate it; it is written on all the powers and faculties of the human soul, the record of it is in the heart of God, and, until tyrants can force the portals of heaven, and wrest from the bosom of the Almighty the precious record of human rights, slavery cannot be sanctioned by law or truth.

The great truth, which the anti-slavery men have been laboring to establish, is, that every man is *himself*, and belongs to no one else. Some eminent Doctors of Divinity have made the discovery that slavery is divine; that the Almighty sanctions it. These men are doing more to undermine the religious faith of the American people, and more to destroy reverence for God, to encourage atheism and infidelity, than all the writings of Paine, Kneeland, Voltaire, or all the infidels combined. Those who defend slavery as an instituion of the Almighty among men, prove more than they would like to prove, for if they succeed in proving this, then out of the great heart of God, there is constantly springing all manner of torture and wrong and crime. To maintain their assumption that slavery is divine, they must also assume that the necessary conditions upon which it exists are also divine.—But what are the conditions necessary for the maintenance of this system?

First, *force* is necessary. Men do not yield to the mandates of their fellow men without cause. They do not bow down their necks to the yoke of bondage because they love it. When you find a man in slavery, you may know that force has been brought to bear upon him. He has been given to understand that he must sustain that relation or die. And that is the language of slavery to every slave in the United States. It is said he is kindly treated, but what kindness can compensate for the loss of liberty! If the slaveholder wanted the slave in the place of a bronze statue, merely to beautify and adorn his household, he might possibly keep him, for we are a vain people, and not without a pretty firm belief in our own beauty as a race. But they don't want us for any such purpose; they want us *to work*.—They have a slight prejudice against work themselves. They think it is all well enough for cadaverous, dank and hungry-looking Yankees, as they call them; but, for their part, they wish to be excused. There is gold in the earth, and it must be dug out, but this digging is the rub which is to be *rubbed* by. They want Negroes to do this rubbing.

Secondly, they do not wish to *pay* for their work; they think this paying to be a Yankee notion. In the absence of pay there must be force. The slave must be made to feel, that unless he shall work a worse thing will come unto him. I admit there are slaveholders who do not treat their slaves as I have indicated in my foregoing remarks but they are the exceptions, and besides, they are able to hold their slaves by terror inspired by cruelty inflicted by other slaveholders.

*Ignorance* is necessary to the maintenance of slavery. Education is incompatible with it. Give a slave a knowledge of geography, and he

# 308    LIFE AND WRITINGS OF FREDERICK DOUGLASS

will give you a lesson in locomotion. Give him a knowledge of the free states, and he is off, not on his master's legs, but on his own. The mental eye must be bored out.—His mind must not be enlightened. Do this and his chains snap. There is not power enough in the southern or northern states, to bind down intelligence among three millions of people. It is only by darkening the soul, by crushing the spirit, by over-awing the man, that the slave is kept in bondage.

I am not here, this evening, to dwell at length upon the nature and character of slavery, or the arguments in its defense. Indeed, I have very little to do with southern slavery or slaveholders now; but I have much to do with the men and women of these northern states over which slavery has spread its death-like pall. Slavery is here. The men who hold three millions in bondage yonder, are *here*. The men, who make slavery possible in this republic, are north of Mason and Dixon's line. There is a purely slavery party in the United States, that exists for slavery alone. Its members will be Whigs or Democrats or neither, in order to maintain slavery. The purpose of this party are briefly these: First, the silencing of all agitation on the subject of slavery.—Second, to extend slavery over this whole continent. Third, to make slavery respected in every State of this Union. And its fourth purpose is the expatriation of every free colored man in the U.S.

The first purpose avowed by this party is pretty distinctly avowed. also, by the Whig and Democratic parties. They declare they are both in favor of putting down agitation. These parties are united at this point, and I believe they are at all other points, except in name. The Democrats go for—*democracy*. Their platform says they will resist agitation. The Whigs say they will discountenance, that is make-mouths at agitation. The Democrats hold that the compromise of 1850 was a final settlement. The Whigs think it was a settlement final. The Whigs resolve they are in favor of constitutional apropriations for internal improvement. The Democrats say they are in favor of prohibiting unconstitutional appropriations. The difference between them and their platforms, is the difference between "Jenny come in," and "come in Jenny." They both are for putting down agitation, that our southern brethren may have peace. They have undertaken to do what God Almighty has declared cannot be done. "There can be no peace for the wicked, saith my God," and the slaveholder can have no peace. Daniel

Webster lived long enough after the passage of the compromise measure to say:

> Now is the winter of our discontent
> Made glorious summer.

And Henry Clay lived to say—"Peace and tranquility reign throughout all our borders," but it was a very deceitful and unreal peace. If the mouths of Northern men could be closed, the tongues of all anti-slavery men be cut out, and all the literature, all the Uncle Tom's Cabins and Bibles burned, still the slaveholders could have no peace. Deep, down in his own soul God has planted an abolition lecturer; and while he has that monitor he sleeps on quivering heart-strings. Slaveholders and the abettors of slavery cannot, if they would, stop talking on this subject. They tell us to be silent, still they cannot be silent themselves. Like the wandering Jew they cannot stop. God Almighty is at the bottom of this agitation, and Whigs and Democrats will find it hard to stop what he commands to go forward.

I said the north was the great supporter of slavery. I feel I walk now not on a free soil. The star spangled banner affords no protection. The fugitive slave bill covers the whole country. The slave may be started from the far west and chased to the far east; there is no valley so deep, no mountain so high, no plain so boundless, no glen so secluded, no cave so secure, no spot so sacred, as to give him shelter from the bloodhound and hunter. He may pass into the New England States, to Concord and Bunker Hill, and ascend that shaft, and ask in the name of the first blood that was shed at its base for protection, and even there, the hungry, biting bloodhound, and the master with his accursed chains can go and snatch the bondman away. They can do it right under the eave droppings of old Fanueil Hall, and under the stately spires of your magnificent churches.

We are told the Fugitive Slave Law is constitutional; that there is a clause in the Constitution that authorizes the recapture of slaves. But the clause is not there. When it says "no person shall be deprived of life, liberty or property without due process of law," it looks right. Men have tried to see a recognition of this law there, but it is not. I used to think it was there, but like the Irishman's flea, "when I put my finger on it, it wasn't *thar*." But there is an article in the Constitution, that declares "no person, held to service or labor in one State under the laws thereof, shall in consequence of any law be released from such service or labor, and shall be delivered up," which article was intended to secure to every man what is due to him. Mr. Webster, in his seventh of March speech, said this clause of the Constitution was introduced in consequence of a wide spread system of apprenticeship and on account of a large class of redemptioners, that existed at that time. There is nothing there to leave the impression that it was intended for the recapture of slaves.—And it is a strange fact, that, not until the lapse of twenty-five years, was a slave returned from the north to the south. This fugitive law is a *modern* invention; we have constitutions outside of the Constitution. I believe in denying everything to *slavery*, and claiming everything for *Liberty*.

Some men have supposed every law pro-slavery until it has been proved otherwise; they proceed on the presumption that the Constitution is in favor of slavery. The great mistake of the anti-slavery men of modern times, is that they have too easily given up the Constitution to slavery. If our fathers introduced a clause into it for the purpose to return the bondman, then they transcended their authority, they leaped out of the orbit of their rights. Had your fathers any right to make slaves? Look over your rights, and have you one which gives you liberty to make a slave of your brother man? If you have not, your fathers had not, and they had no right to command others to make them. Suppose in some fit of generosity I should write each of you a title deed, giving you three hundred acres of clear blue sky, all full of stars. What then?—Why, the stars would stay up there, and shine as bright as ever, the sky would not fall down. You could not appropriate it to yourself. So if I should give you a title deed to own somebody else as property, would your right to that person hold good? You may pile statutes to the heavens affirming the right of one class of men to hold another in servitude, yet they will be null and void.

Now we have the fugitive slave law, how shall we get rid of it? I do not think it will ever be repealed, it is too low and bad for that. It is not only to be trampled upon and disregarded, but scorned and scouted at by every man and woman. It was enacted for the basest of purposes; it was to humble you; to make you feel that the south could command you, and make you run on the track of the bondman and hunt him down.

A law of this kind is to be met with derision, and if the poor slave, escaping from his pursuer, shall find himself unable to get beyond the reach of the tyrant, and he should turn around and strike him down to the earth, there is something in the heart of universal manhood that will say, "you served the villain right."

This law goes directly against religious liberty. We hear much about religious liberty in Tuscany, Rome and Russia, but you can point to no law in Russia, Turkey, Austria or any of the Papal States, that can equal this law in its warfare against religious liberty, if this liberty means the liberty to practice Christianity. The law tells you good ministers and elders "We shall expect you to forget the law of God, at the ballot box, and enforce the law of the Devil." To be sure it does not strike down any of the ordinances of religion, but it strikes down *man*. There is no other system of religion so benevolent and merciful as Christianity! It reaches down its long, benevolent arm through every grade of suffering and seizes the last link in the chain and says, "stand up, thou art a man and brother." But this law makes Christianity a crime; it has made the law of God an *out*law. It tells ministers they shall no longer learn their duty to their fellow men from the Bible, but from the statute book. There comes the slave from Alabama. He comes in the dark night—he dare not trust himself if by moonlight—he travels toward the north star—

> Star of the North, I ask to thee.
> While on I press—for well I know
> Thy light and truth shall make me free.
> Thy light, which no poor slave deceiveth,
> Thy light, which all my soul believeth.

On he comes, he reaches us, he comes to the door of a Christian, and says, "give me bread and shelter or I die;" but the law of the country says, if you do that you shall have a home in a cold, damp cell, and shall see the light of day through granite windows for six months, besides paying a fine of $1000.

I wish Americans did not love office so well, It is strange how fascinating it is, however mean it may be. How many men at the north have made shipwreck of their principles, honor and everything else, while listening to the promise of office! It makes me think of a dog I once saw. A fellow held up a biscuit before him and said "speak," and the dog spoke. "Stand up," and he stood up. "Roll over," and he did so, and the fellow, very complacently, put the biscuit in his pocket, and said, "Now go and lay down." This is the way southerners have treated northern statesmen. They have told him to "speak," and they have stood up and spoken for slavery. Then they said "roll over," and they have rolled over, and cast off their old principles of freedom. Then they say, "go and lay down forever—you are of no further service." It is time northern men should wake up. There is no need of allowing the slave power to control you any longer. It is degradation intensified for you to suffer yourselves to be the vassals of women whippers, and the dupes of northern aspirants for office and power.

*Manchester (New Hampshire) Democrat reprinted in Frederick Douglass' Paper*, February 10, 1854

# LETTER FROM THE EDITOR

Providence, R.I., Feb. 8, 1854

Oh! when will the accursed system of human bondage, with all its infernal accompaniments of cruelty and blood-guiltiness, cease out of the land, and Liberty—blest Liberty! man's inalienable birth-right— be enjoyed by our poor outcast and heart-broken race. In going the rounds—travelling over ground which I trod twelve years ago, and pouring out the same sad tales of wrong and outrage to the same people, making the same appeals, urging the same arguments, asserting the same rights, pressing the same claims, till voice and strength sink down under the arduous labor—I pause and survey the apparently gloomy prospect, and cry, in the anguish of my spirit, for the day of my people's redemption from chains. The response is,

Learn to labor and to wait.

Well, labor and wait I will, assured that the arm of the Lord is not shortened, and that the day of freedom will come at last. Here is comfort, encouragement and support.

Since my last, I have lectured twice in Pawtucket, once in New Bedford, once in Newport, and three times in Providence, besides attending a meeting of the State Council of colored men for Rhode

Island, and a Liberty Festival got up under the supervision of said Council. These meetings have all been largely attended, and, to me, deeply interesting. The interest taken in the cause of emancipation and improvement by the colored people of Providence, New Bedford and Newport, is evidently greatly on the increase.

There is also an evident improvement going on among them in the matter of their physical and mental condition. Poverty is disappearing—intelligence is spreading—and they are comprehending more fully the obligations and duties of their relations to the enslaved of the land. The good effects of the National Convention, held in Rochester last July,[3] are quite visible here.—It cleared away the fogs and mists that overhang the present, and spread out, if not a future, at least the hope of a future to their view. I was happy to observe that both in Providence and in New Bedford the colored people came forward, and did not hang on the outskirts of the congregation like mere idle spectators. On the platform, as well as in the congregation, they looked and acted as if they had a work to do, and felt willing to engage in it to the best of their ability. In these remarks I ought not to except Newport—for there, as well as in New Bedford and Providence, the same commendable spirit was manifest. It was quite a new thing to see halls crowded with white people, presided over by a colored man, and colored men occupying conspicuous places on the platform. So far as I could judge, the audiences assented to the propriety of the innovation, and seemed pleased with the dignity and manliness which it evinced. What is there more natural or more desirable than that colored people should stand forth with such prominence as to convince all that the efforts being made for their freedom and elevation are not gratuitously made on the part of their white friends? Who could long and cheerfully work for the freedom, elevation, and advancement of a people who evinced no interest in such objects.—It may be a higher virtue in the white man, himself being free, to labor for the freedom of the colored man; but it seems to me quite certain that the chariot wheels of freedom will never roll on till the colored people both North and South, shall give startling evidence of discontent with their condition.—The inspiration of liberty must be breathed into them, till it shall become manifestly unsafe to rob and enslave men. The battle of freedom in America was half won, when the patriotic Henry exclaimed, *Give me Liberty or Give me Death.* Talking of insurrection, yes, my friends, a moral and bloodless one. An insurrection has been raging in this country for more than two hundred years. The whip has been cracking and the chains clanking amid the shouts of liberty, which have gone up in mockery before God. The Negro has been shot down like a dog, and the Indian hunted like the wolf, by our prayer-making and hymn-singing nation.—Yes, let us have a moral insurrection. Let the oppressed and down-trodden awake, arise, and vindicate their manhood by the presentation of their just claims to liberty and brotherhood. Let them think and speak of liberty till their chains shall snap asunder; and their oppressors shall feel it no longer safe to ensnare and plunder them.—But briefly to my tour. In my visits to New Bedford and Newport, I had the happiness to be accompanied by my esteemed friend, George T. Downing[4] a man known well and favorably to all my readers, white and colored. His kind attention and generous co-operation with me in Providence, Newport and New Beford, shall not soon be forgotten.

On Sunday, at noon, we addressed the Sabbath school connected with Rev. Mr. Ward's Church, in New Bedford. In the evening we both spoke to the people in Liberty Hall. Monday, in the face of one of the most wintry and pitiless storms we went to Newport, and on Tuesday, proceeded to Providence to attend our Liberty Festival. On this occasion, I should like to say much, partly to express my sense of the kindness of my friends in Providence, and partly to cheer them on in the good work to which they have nobly laid their hands. The time may come when I shall have occasion to allude to the good words and works of the friends of freedom in Providence, when I can do the subject something like justice.—I even now may get home before this shall appear in print.     F.D.

*Frederick Douglass' Papers*, February 17, 1854

## THE JUDGMENT PRONOUNCED BY HON. RICHARD H. BAKER UPON MRS. DOUGLASS FOR LEARNING CHILDREN TO READ IN VIRGINIA—HER FINE AND FINAL IMPRISONMENT.[5]

Judge Baker, in his address to the prisoner, Mrs. Douglass, appears conscious that posterity will hold him responsible for every word which fell from his lips, on this most extraordinary occasion.

A lady, admitted by the Court to be of "fair and respectable standing in the community," excepting only the crime of teaching children to read the Bible, punished, in February 1854, in Virginia by fine and imprisonment!! No language, no power of illustration, no fancy of imagination, can enlighten or impress more than a simple statement of the fact itself. Therefore, we hand the case over to the whole civilized world for dissection.

To the honor of the age in which we live, we record the significant fact, that Judge Baker's whole sentence, reads, as though he was ashamed of his position, and would thank the earth, over which he stood, to open and swallow him up, where he could hide himself from the gaze of an insulted world. The Judge performed his part about as well as almost any man could have done, with such a *delicate* matter to manage. If the Judge had stolen a sheep, and been caught with it on his back, he could not have had more special pleading than is here exhibited. It is evident the Judge had no taste for the unenviable notoriety that the pronouncing this decision upon Mrs. Douglass was about to impose upon him, which, of course, reflects credit upon him as a man and as a Judge. This poor man could not *resign* or run, as that would have reflected severely upon his friends and neighbors around him, who are slaveholders. And the only way to sustain the slaveholders was, to bring public opinion to bear upn the Judge, and thus compel him to hold himself up, while he performed the degrading and dirty duty the slaveholders' laws had imposed upon him.

In confirmation of this, Taywell Taylor, M. Cooke, H. Woods, Wm. G. Dunbar, Simon S. Stubbs, Wm. T. Henren, John S. Lovett, and P. P. Mayo, members of the Norfolk Bar, all united, in a published written request to Judge Baker, for a copy of his judgment. All this was probably arranged previously, and is so unusual, as to prove that the public mind was not entirely encrusted in the moral influence of the infernal institution. It proves that the moral conscience of the public mind was not *dead*, but had merely been *asleep*. This is certainly a favorable symptom! Suppose this transaction had been performed, *without all this parade of the Norfolk Bar*, and as quietly as a similar punishment would have been inflicted by the Court in a case tolerated by the civilized world, then surely there would be less hope for the "Virginians" than there now is—the conviction of the public mind, is generally followed by reformation. At the South, as well as at the North, and in the East, and in the West, and among the languages this transaction is to be examined and discussed. "What a great matter a little fire often kindleth!"

In our own Revolution, a few chests of tea were the instrument to place the ball in motion. The burning Lattimer at the stake, and Luther's conversion—none of these, and similar events which have revolutionized the world, promised in their introduction to do as much as the imprisonment of Mrs. Douglass now promises. At every slaveholding fire-side it will be discussed. The "rights and wrongs" of slavery will be analyzed.—And who can foresee what will be the end of this? The slaves, by overhearing these conversations, will get more light than twenty schoolmasters could have given them.

The world never saw a people with so bad a cause as the poor slaveholders have. It cannot be touched, without impairing it.—If friends talk in its favor, or enemies talk against it, the same fatality follows—every word "for or against" weakens it. In short, it is such a vile, stinking institution, that nothing but the most "masterly inactivity" can hold it together. Only have Judge Baker's judgment published in all languages, and the world will speak to the slaveholders upon the subject.

*Frederick Douglass' Paper*, February 24, 1854

## SHOOTING A NEGRO

On Monday last Mr. _____ Patmon, overseer for Mr. L.D. Crenshaw, at his farm about three miles from Richmond, was compelled to shoot and dangerously wound a Negro man in Mr. C's employ to save himself from bodily harm, if not death. Mr. P., if we are not misinformed, entered the employment of Mr. Crenshaw the first of the year, and found, as now overseers often do, great difficulty in enforcing obedience to his authority. In order that all his hands might have an equal opportunity to enjoy the Sabbath, he determined to apportion the feeding of stock and other necessary duties equally between them, directing them to take it by turns, two staying at the farm on Sunday, and two another, throughout the year. On Saturday last he ordered the wounded Negro to be in place the next day, as that was his turn, and was given to understand that he would not be there. Mr. P. remarked to him that he had better be, and said no more. The next day the fellow absented himself as he had threatened to do, and Mr. P. informed Mr. Crenshaw of it, telling him of all that had passed. Seeing the importance of discipline, Mr. Crenshaw directed Patmon to show his authority at once, and, when the disobedient fellow returned, to give him a proper flagellation, and he would probably then get along without further trouble. On Monday morning, the Negro, returned to his labors, and soon thereafter Patmon went to him, demanded to know why he had absented himself contrary to order, and told him he intended giving him a flogging. The Negro promptly replied, "You will do no such thing." With this Patmon seized him, and the Negro having a currying-comb in his hand, gave P. a severe blow with it, and then collared him, when a scuffle ensued. Finding that he could not manage the fellow, Patmon called to a Negro man by to give him a stick, and the fellow, seeing a heavy one not far off, picked it up and handed it to his overseer, but this was promptly seized by the refractory slave, who wrenched it from Patmon's hands and gave him a violent blow over the head with it. Believing his life to be in danger, Patmon stepped back, drew his revolver, and told the fellow to surrender, or he would shoot him. "Shoot and be d---d," replied the Negro, "I am not afraid of your shooting," and, raising the club, was about renewing the assault, when Patmon fired, lodging a ball in the left side of the Negro, from which he fell, severely wounded.

Patmon then had the ruffian properly cared for, and when we heard from him yesterday he was alive, and hopes were entertained of his recovery.

From all that transpired before and after the shooting, it is generally believed that it was the intention of the Negro to kill the overseer, and that other servants on the farm were in the conspiracy with him. This being the case, it is really a pity that Patmon ceased pulling his trigger until he had planted his six balls in the assassin's body. —*Richmond (Va.) Dispatch.*

*Comment.* —What white man would not have struck down Patmon, the overseer, and Crenshaw, the owner also? The case is simply this: The owner is a robber, and the overseer is his assistant, in villainy. Together they were robbing the slave, not only of his liberty, and of his wife and children, but of all their earnings, and that of all their posterity. The slave, it is true, was a rebellious man; and it is also true that Patrick Henry was rebellious. He would have knocked over, not only owner and overseer, but King George III into the bargain. He excited other white slaves to rebellion, by yelling at the top of his voice, *"Give me liberty or give me death."* George Washington, Benjamin Franklin and John Adams, all joined in the rebellion, and not only knocked over their overseers, but killed thousands upon thousands of those who undertook to enslave them, and in a much milder form than this poor Negro was enslaved. They had not a thousandth part of the provocation to rebel, to kill and destroy their oppressors, that this poor Negro had. All honor was awarded to them for their rebellion. Now let us have a monument erected in front of some pro-slavery church, to commemorate this struggle for freedom on the part of this poor slave.

What a mean craven villain this Crenshaw must be, to stand, day by day, and rob such a noble specimen of a man as this slave was. Look at his very coat on his back, and the very shoes on his feet—all the fruits of his robbery from this poor slave—and then the poor miserable wretch of an overseer, who agreed to be hired to thrust his hands in this poor Negro's pocket, and rob him of every cent he had, while the miserable culprit of a master held him. Two such monsters as this owner and overseer ought to be daguerreotyped and placed where the scorn of the whole world should be pointed at them.

A common thief who robs the hen roost of a white man, is a prince of a fellow compared with those two wretches whose whole business is to rob poor defenseless Negroes. Can anyone deny this view of the case?—Halls may be torn down, rotten eggs may be thrown at anti-slavery men, but *that* doesn't exonerate the slaveholder. His villainy remains unimpaired; and soon the whole civilized world will arrive at the conclusion to brand *all* as the meanest kind of robbers who rob a n----r!

*Frederick Douglass' Paper*, February 24, 1854

# TO GERRIT SMITH

Rochester, March 6, (1854)

My dear Sir:

I am slowly recovering from my illness, and hope soon to be at work again. I am, with you, quite sorry that W. H. Seward's abolitionism is not of a more decided type, and that he annexes so many hard conditions to the freedom of the slave, in the D.C.[6] Yet so anxious am I to see emancipation there, I would see it at almost any price, and since we cannot have you, and such as you, to propose plans in Congress for Emancipation I am glad of even so much as Wm. H. Seward's plan. As to "indemnifying" slaveholders, that is by no means so repulsive to me since your great speech on the Nebraska Bill,[7] which speech by the way, I was reading but yesterday. I hope it will not be long before I shall see and hear you again, for I always feel the better for having seen and heard you. I am Dear Sir,

Yours as ever truly and affectionately,

Frederick Douglass

*Gerrit Smith Papers, George Arents Research Library, Syracuse University*

# THE WORD "WHITE."

The *Homestead Bill*,[8] which has just passed the House of Representatives, and is now likely to pass the Senate, contains a provision limiting the advantages which it is designed to secure, solely to that part of God's children, who happen to live in a skin which passes for white. Blacks, browns, mulattoes, and quadroons, &c., are to have no part or lot in the rights it secures, to the settlers on the wild lands of the Republic. In the political eyes of our legislators, these latter have no right to live. The great Legislator above, according to our magnanimous republicans, legislated unwisely, and in a manner which independent Americans can never sanction, in giving life to blacks, browns, mulattoes, and quadroons, equally with his dear white children! and this, Congress is determined to make evident before Heaven and Earth and Hell! Alas! poor, robbed and murdered people! for what were we born? Why was life given us? We may not live in the old states; we may not emigrate to the new, and are told not to settle with any security on the wild lands! Were we made to sport?—given life to have it starved out of us?—provided with blood simply that it may gush forth at the call of the scourge? and thus to gratify the white man's love of torture. Some deeds there are, so wantonly cruel, so entirely infernal, as to stun the feeling, and confound all the powers of reason.—And such an one is this. What kind of men are those who voted for the Homestead Bill with such an amendment! Do they eat bread afforded by our common mother earth? and do they ever pray that God, the common father of mankind, will preserve them from famine? Men that act as they have now acted, do not appear to believe either in the existence of, or in the justice of God. It is impossible for us to argue against such mean, cowardly and wanton cruelty. Americans by birth—attached to the country by every association that can give a right to share in the benefits of its institutions, the first successful tillers of the soil—and yet foreigners, aliens, Irish, Dutch, English and French, are to be made welcome to a quarter section of American land, while we are to be kept off from it by the flaming sword of the Republic. Shame on the outrage!

*Frederick Douglass' Paper*, March 17, 1854

## THE PLAN FOR THE INDUSTRIAL SCHOOL[9]

The Plan for the Industrial School, which we publish elsewhere in our present number, should not pass without a word from us, in our character as editor of a paper devoted to the interests of the colored people of the United States.

The first question which benevolent and enquiring men will put in respect to this school will be: is there a necessity for it?—The second will be, (after admitting the necessity,) is such a school the best means of meeting that necessity?

Our answers to these questions are briefly: There is a necessity for facilities for giving colored youth a Practical Knowledge of Useful Trades. At present such facilities are very few, and not at all equal to the wants of the colored people. Trades, at the North, are completely monopolized by the whites, and there is an evident determination to keep them so monopolized. This is shown by the fact that not one in a thousand master mechanics of the country, will take into his shop, and into his house, as an apprentice any youth in whose veins there is one drop of African blood. The truth of this statement is beyond all controversy among intelligent colored men who have made efforts to procure places for their sons. Admitting this statement as true, every man will see at once that there is a necessity for placing some means within reach of our proscribed people for learning useful trades. No one who has studied the social relations of mankind, will say it is good for any one class to be known only in the community as domestics and menial laborers. Such laborers are necessary; but no one class or variety of people can furnish them exclusively without degradation. It is evident that any such class must, from the very nature of the case, be regarded as a degraded caste; and such is precisely the case with the colored people of the Republic. It therefore appears impossible that this people can be elevated and improved without an extension of their employments. They must become *mechanics* and *farmers*, and be connected with society through the cardinal wants, or be forever looked upon as a degraded and comparatively useless class of the community.

To the second question, is the proposed school (a school in which several of the most important and permanent branches of mechanical trades can be learned), the best that can be devised to meet the necessity in consideration? No better plan seems available. Shut out from the ordinary methods of learning trades, and being for the most part poor and scattered, we can, as a people, offer no inducement to master mechanics to receive our youth in our different localities, sufficient to secure their admission as apprentices. Could we obtain the admission of colored youth to the work-shops and factories in our neighborhood, it would be far better to do so, than to build up an institution of this kind. But the fact that we cannot, is the point of the case. Herein is the necessity for the proposed industrial school. It has been objected to this school, that it will serve to keep up the spirit of caste, since it will merely be looked upon as an affair of the colored people. The objection is not well founded. The school will be open to white as well as colored youth.

If it shall be looked upon merely as a colored school, the blame will not rest with us, whom inexorable necessity has forced to the measure but upon them whose pride and prejudice had imposed the necessity upon us. It is also objected that the enterprise cannot succeed, that the funds which are required to build the Institution, can be more wisely expended in keeping up general anti-slavery agitation. To the first part of this objection it may be stated that *"where there is a will, there is a way,"* and to the latter part of the objection, we say it comes with an ill grace from the parties who urge it. They are men who earn their living by agitation, and get thousands of dollars, where the poor colored men are compelled to pick up a penny here and there, carrying trunks, or putting away a load of coal, in order to eke out an existence. But we intend that our columns shall have much on this subject hereafter. Meanwhile, we call upon the friends of this practical measure for the elevation of our people to come up to the work, and send their subscriptions and donations for the same.

The successful establishment of this industrial school, by the colored people themselves, for themselves, and with the aid of such of their white friends as deem it consistent with their regard for the freedom of the slave at the South to assist the nominally free colored man in his laudable efforts at self-elevation at the North, will afford, in itself one of the most striking proofs of the colored man's capacity for improvement and will oppose a killing refutation of the slander, so often pronounced against us, of being naturally inferior to what is proudly denominated the superior race.

*Frederick Douglass' Paper*, March 24, 1854

# THE COLORED PEOPLE OF CINCINNATI

It is not to cover our brethren in Cincinnati with extravagant praise, that we are about to notice them. There are others who can do that far more gracefully and skillfully than we. Indeed, it is becoming about as fashionable to praise as to blame our people, and we are likely to suffer as much from the latter as from the former.

During our recent visit to Cincinnati, we are happy to state that we saw many evidences of progress and prosperity, which were exceedingly grateful to our feelings; and as it is a cherished object of our journal to encourage and cheer on the oppressed, in the pathway of improvement, we deem it quite proper to notice these evidences of an upward tendency, in our columns. Among the first signs of progress in Cincinnati, worthy of mention, is the organization, recently, of a Young Men's Library Association. This body is composed of a number of the most intelligent young men of the city; and it bids fair to become highly serviceable to the colored people thereof. It has, already established, in a central postition, and in one of the finest buildings, a Library and Reading Room, and has obtained a choice selection of books, together with many valuable periodicals. The rooms are beautifully furnished, and are, every way, attractive. We believe this is the first institution of the kind established by colored people in any city in the Union, and we certainly wish it every success. The Association is young, and far from rich; and we submit to our white friends, whose libraries are overstocked with works of history, philosophy, poetry and science, that they cannot more worthily dispose of their surplus volumes, than by donating a few of them to this worthy institution. We make this request or suggestion (call it what you please), on our own responsibility, but have reason to know that any such donations would be thankfully received.

We were quite struck with the variety of employments, engaged in by colored men in Cincinnati; that city resembles more, in this respect, Baltimore and other Southern cities, where colored men are ship-carpenters, joiners, cabinet-makers, wheel-wrights, bricklayers, draymen, cartmen, coachmen, &c. &c. There are also, in Cincinnati, mechanics, traders and merchants of color, who are doing a good business, getting an honest living, and giving the *lie* to the slander that the colored people are deteriorating in a state of freedom. We walked through the market at Cincinnati, and saw that some of the best stalls were occupied and owned by colored men. Some of these traders of sable hue supply, with produce, ten and twelve different steamers plying between Cincinnati and New Orleans. *Money* "is *power*," as well as "*knowledge*;" and we are happy to know that this secret is beginning to be known and pretty thoroughly believed in by the colored citizens of Cincinnati.

We were glad to find that our esteemed friend, W. W. Watson, (the first to welcome us to his hearth and home in Cincinnati,) has recovered his health, and is flourishing in his business. We were indebted to Mr. John L. Gaines for many kind attentions during our stay; and to him and family we tender our acknowledgements, assuring his colored friends who heard him at the National Convention at

Rochester, that we found him still in his *"native land, Sixth Street, Cincinnati,"* and with no more probability of emigrating with our Cleveland brethren than of our undertaking a mission to the moon. We look upon John L. Gaines as a *"fixed fact,"* and rejoice to know that prosperity attends his endeavors, as a worthy citizen. One of the most creditable indications of enterprise, furnished in behalf of our people, is the flourishing business, and magnificent Daguerrean Gallery of Mr. Ball in Cincinnati. We shall treat our readers and friends to a picture of this gallery, with a particular account of it on the first page of our next week's edition. It is one of the best answers to the charge of natural inferiority we have lately met with.

For the purpose of being more accessible to our friends, we lodged at the "Dumas House," kept by Mr. Whett, a colored gentleman, and though in point of style and gentlemanly deportment on the part of its conductors there is much to commend, yet we regret to say there are some things about the establishment, which go far to make it a dangerous place for the colored youth of Cincinnati. It has a Billiard Room, frequented by idle and thoughtless persons, who, imitating the follies of the whites, will be likely to end where they end. Highly respectable gentlemen and ladies board at this house but the billiard fraternity is no credit to the "Dumas Hotel," and ought to be shunned and detested by all who desire to see the colored people of Cincinnati advance in virtue, knowledge and temperance. It is not to injure this otherwise respectable house, that we write thus. We wish it every success—not based on the moral deterioration of the colored people. The magnificent store formerly owned by our enterprising (and in our belief honorable) friend, Sam'l Wilcox, and which was for a long time the pride of the colored citizens of Cncinnati, is now owned by Mr. Roxborough, Mr. W. having met with reverses, which compelled him to relinquish the establishment. Regretting this, it is yet consoling that a colored gentleman is still the proprietor. We hope again to see our friend Wilcox flourishing in a lucrative and honorable business.

After the close of the Convention in Cincinnati, we had a meeting in the Zion Baptist Church, owned by a colored congregation in the city, and although it was designed to be a *select* audience, many of our white friends came in, and remained with us till a late hour. We shall give in another paper, unless otherwise determined, a sketch of this meeting.

*Frederick Douglass' Paper*, April, 28, 1854

# ANTHONY BURNS RETURNED TO SLAVERY[10]

> Now are our brows bound with victorious wreaths;
> Our bruised arms hung up for monuments;
> Our stern alarums chang'd to merry meetings,
> Our dreadful marches to delightful measures.

Now let all true patriotic Christian Republicans rejoice and be glad! Let a grand Festal day be at once proclaimed from the august seat of government. Let the joyous thunders of ten thousand cannon jar the earth and shake the sky with notes of gratitude, in fitting acknowledgement of this mighty victory! Let the churches be flung open and the pulpit resound with thanksgiving, that our beloved country has been saved, and that Republican Liberty is still secure, and the example of the model republic still shines refulgently, to the confusion of tyrants and oppressors in Europe. After a mighty struggle continued through a great many bitter, dreadful, stormy and anxious days and nights the arms of the Republic have gloriously succeeded in capturing Anthony Burns—the clothes cleaner—in Brattle Street, Boston! Under the Star Spangled Banner, on the deck of our gallant warship Morris, the said Burns, whose liberation would have perhaps rent asunder our Model Republic, has been safely conveyed to slavery and chains, in sight of our nation's proud Capitol!

How sweet to the ear and heart of every true American, are the shrieks of Anthony Burns, as the American eagle sends his remorseless beak and bloody talons into him!! How grateful to the taste and pleasant to the eye, is the warm blood of the sable fugitive. He is now getting his desert. How dare he walk on the legs given him by the Almighty? He thought to take possession of his own body! to go at large among men, but he forgot that this is a civilized and Christian nation, and that no such unnatural and monstrous conduct could be allowed.—Had our churches been dens, and Christians been but tigers, he might have escaped. But he knows by this time that Christian bayonets are more terrible than the claws of the tiger or the fangs of the wolf! He perpetrated the folly of calling upon our churches and ministers to pray for him. He might as well have prayed to the devil to keep him out of hell! Did he not know that our churches are built up, and our religion is supported by the blood and tears of such as he? Was not the Fugitive Slave Bill defended by the very lights of Christianity? Had he forgotten that Rev. Doctor Stewart, of Andover, Doctor Spring, of New York, Doctor Cox, of Brooklyn, and Doctor Lord, of Buffalo, all mighty in doctrine, read in all the languages of the sacred books, enforced his capture as a Christian duty? How foolish was it, then, of him to look to the church for sympathy and to the pulpit for prayers. Was he not the property of brother Suttle, bought with his money, and would it not have been a piece of naked robbery to have deprived dear Brother Suttle of his rightful property?—A few madcaps—dangerous ones—whose infatuation would almost surpass belief, but for their reckless deeds, sought to rescue him; they said he was a man; that he was a brother; that God and nature proclaimed him free; and that it was a sin to enslave him; that it was monstrous and inhuman to enslave him; but we sent these mischievous and infidel persons to prison, and told them to read the Bible. Oh! how our brave troops did trample them down; and how our cannon would have swept them into eternity, had they lifted a finger for the release of our prey!

Hail Columbia! happy land.

*Frederick Douglass' Paper*, June 9, 1854

# THE TRUE REMEDY FOR THE FUGITIVE SLAVE BILL

*A good revolver, a steady hand, and a determination to shoot down any man attempting to kidnap.* Let every colored man make up his mind to this, and live by it, and if needs be, die by it. This will put an end to kidnapping and to slaveholding, too. We blush to our very soul when we are told that a Negro is so mean and cowardly that he prefers to live under the slavedriver's whip—to the loss of life for liberty. Oh! that we had a little more of the manly indifference to death, which characterized the Heroes of the American Revolution.

*Frederick Douglass' Paper*, June 9, 1854

# IS IT RIGHT AND WISE TO KILL A KIDNAPPER?

The answer, to all this is that the entire argument assumes a case of *revolution*, where everything desirable is to be gained and preserved by violence. And, as if to leave no doubt on this point, the illustrations are the famous saying of PATRICK HENRY and the destruction of tea in the Boston harbor. If the people of this country were in arms for the purpose of prostrating the present Government and establishing a different one on its ruins, as when Henry spoke, and the tea was destroyed then the positions of Mr. Douglass would be intelligible and consistent. Such too might be the case, if like his former associates Garrison, Phillips and Parker, he avowed himself an enemy to the Constitution and the Union. But the ground he now occupies— that of a professed upholder of the Constitution, while at the same time he argues in favor of revolutionary violence, which if successful on a large scale, would be nothing short of an overthrow of the Government itself—involves a self contradiction and lands him in absurdity. It may be a man's duty to become a revolutionist—to seek the subversion of one Government, for the purpose of setting up a better. That we do not deny. But if while carrying on open resistance to the recognized authority of the existing Government, he still pretends to uphold it, our belief in his honesty, or our respect for his understanding—one or the other—must give way. We need not go at large into the legal argument respecting the Fugitive Slave Law. Mr. D. is aware that there is a provision in the Constitution requiring Fugitive Slaves to be given up; that the law of 1793 and that of 1850 were regularly enacted in pursuance of such provision; and that the validity of that legislation is maintained by the judicial tribunal having the right to decide. He cannot, therefore, fail to see, as a necessary conclusion, that opposition by force to the execution of that law, can only be general and successful by triumph over the power of the Government—in other words by revolution.

We need not waste words to show how utterly inconsistent such a doctrine as Mr. D. advocates is, with the allegiance to and support of the Constitution and Government of the country.—*Roch. American.*

The instinctive and spontaneous convictions of mankind, without the aid of theories, respond to the doctrine that laws against fundamental morality are not binding upon anybody; and the theory which holds to the binding character of that most infernal of all modern enactments, the Fugitive Slave Law, must not hestitate to accept, as Law, Decrees for the commission of Rape, Robbery, Piracy and Murder. Why not?—A law, commanding every husband to cut the throat of his wife—to burn the house of his neighbor—to poison the fountains of water—to slaughter the infirm, would possess as much claim to respect and obedience as this atrocious Law to hunt down defenseless men and women, with a view to reducing them to slavery. If any one truth is more firmly established in the American mind than another, it is this—"RESISTANCE TO TYRANTS IS OBEDIENCE TO GOD." But the *American* tells us that this is "Revolution." So, however, we do not regard it. Revolution implies a subversion of the Government; this is a simple resistance to the enforcement of one enactment, standing alone. If there is any revolution about it, that revolution is to be found in the Fugitive Slave Bill itself, which offers a bribe to the Judges under it—which makes the writ of *Habeas Corpus* of no effect—which suspends the right of trial by jury—thus violating and overthrowing the Constitution. Here was the Revolution; and it was for those who deprecate Revolution, like the *American*, to direct their batteries against the revolutionary measure. Mr. Douglass is not, by any means, aware that there is a provision in the Constitution, requiring Fugitive Slaves to be given up.—Hence the point of inconsistency made by the *American* does not stand. We hold that the clause of the Constitution to which we suppose the *American* refers, but which it does not quote, to affirm anything else, than to require the giving up of Fugitive Slaves. The plain reading of that clause, together with the history of its adoption, prove that the framers of the Constitution purposely omitted to recognize the hellish claim now set up by the slave hunters and their Northern tools.

*Frederick Douglass' Paper*, June 9, 1854

## TO SYDNEY HOWARD GAY ESQR

Rochester, June 12, 1854

My dear Sir:

I drop this to ask a favor of you—it is this: In the month of August 1847 an address of mine, delivered at Canandaigua, was published in the *National Anti Slavery Standard* (I cannot tell you the number,)[11] but you will find it in the "*Standard*" of that month—The address in question I wish to obtain—and I hope there is nothing existing between us, to prevent you from putting me in possession of it—or to prevent me from being quite thankful to you for the favor.

Truly yours with respect,

Frederick Douglass

*Sidney B. Gay Collection, Columbia University Library, Rare Book Division, Special Collections*

## THE SPIRIT OF THE PRESS

On the first page of this week's number, we have taken what some may regard a course which violates proper modesty, in laying before our readers a few of the many notices called forth by the suggestion made some time ago, by we know not who, and we know not why, that the editor of this paper is to be sent to Congress.[12] In publishing these comments, we are more desirous to mark and record the state of public sentiment in regard to a great public question, than to make ourselves conspicuous before the public.—The matter is one which concerns the colored people, rather than any one individual identified with them. These comments of the press illustrate the present relations of the white and colored races in America, and may be read with instruction on both sides of the Atlantic. The possibility of electing a Negro to the American Congress, is a modern suggestion. The idea is a new one, as little hoped for by the despised colored people, as dreamed of by their white friends.—We accept it simply as an indication of a slightly altered state of mind in the country; but without the slightest belief that the idea will ever be realized in our own person, tho' we do hope and expect to see it realized in some competent colored man before we shall have done with the journey of life. The thing is in itself reasonable, and therefore, probable. It is consistent with all the elementary principles of the American government, though it is in conflict with all our national prejudices and practices. It is evidence of some progress that the subject has called forth an expression so general and so decided at this time—and this is the only importance we feel at liberty to allow it.—We certainly do not believe in the existence of any serious intention to offer us, or to accept us, as a candidate for Congress, or for any other office in this government, State or National.

*Frederick Douglass' Paper,* August 4, 1854

## SPEECH DELIVERED IN THE COURT HOUSE, AT CHATHAM, CANADA, C. W. AUGUST 3RD, 1854[13]

This gentlemen addressed a very numerous and respectable assemblage of our citizens in the Court House, on the evening of Thursday last, and rarely, indeed, has it been our good fortune to listen to an address so replete with sound sense, forcible illustration, and fervid eloquence. From Mr. Douglass' fame, both as a speaker and writer, we were led to expect much; yet we must confess, the reality even exceeded our anticipation. We do not call him a first-rate orator—that is, as far as gracefulness of manner, and a studied elegance and ready flow of language are concerned—but he has that instead, which far exceeds those ornate arts of oratory—a persuasive earnestness and sincerity, a power of thought and feeling, which cannot fail to arrest the attention, and seize upon this judgement. You are convinced, while you listen, that the man *feels* what he says—that, the thoughts and sentiments he utters are in reality his own; and while he is pleading the wrongs of his injured brethren—the evils, the horrors, and the cruelties of slavery— you are spell-bound, not with the assumed pathetic appeals of the paid advocate, but with the heartful sentiments of one who has himself experienced what he so touchingly illustrates.

We regret not being able to give Mr. D.'s address in the exact words in which it was delivered. This is impossible, and therefore we have endeavored to convey, as accurately as possible, merely the ideas of the speaker.

When we entered the room, he was saying that slavery destroys the power of the human mind, and deadens every feeling of the human heart. To illustrate this he need not appeal to the merciless slave-dealer, whose interests are bound up in the demoralizing traffic in which he is engaged; but he would appeal to the candid judgement of those whom interest has not biased, nor whose hearts are not callous to the groans and agonies of their enslaved fellow beings. He would go beyond the boundaries of slavery, where a Christian Ministry is appointed, where Christianity is preached and practiced, where its humanizing influence is exerted over the evil passions and propensities of the corrupt heart, and where slavery has not extinguished its kindling emotions, and here the truth of his assertion would be fully acknowledged, and ample testimony borne to the depth of moral degradation, into which slavery plunges its unfortunate subjects.

He might be asked, what right had he to come here to speak on the subject of slavery—to unfold its horrors, its sad tales of suffering and of woe; but he boldly proclaimed his fullest right to speak in Canada, England, Ireland, Spain, France, Germany, any and everywhere he could get men to hear him, on a subject fraught with so mighty, interests to so many millions of his own race. The slave ought to break loose from his chains, burst the bonds of a base and ignominious servitude, go abroad and tell of the cruelty he has witnessed, the ignorance from which he has escaped, to excite the sympathies of the world in behalf of those he has left behind.

The slaveholders represent their slaves to be happy, comfortable, and well off—supplied with all the necessaries and many of the comforts of life. For this they have written and spoken. They will tell you they are better off than either the poor of England or Ireland; but this he denied. It is impossible in the very nature of the institution, that the condition of the slave can be any other than the most miserable and deplorable.—The poor slave is seldom permitted to go abroad. He is denied the privileges of altering his condition, or earning a living by honest industry. Ask the slave how he is treated, and he is as silent as the grave. No answer escapes those lips, that are sealed with the lash of a brutal master. Ask those three and a half millions of slaves that people the Southern States, to meet on the banks of the Mississippi, and to pass resolutions, that the world may know whether they are free or not, and you receive no answer. They dare not speak. The Irishman, no matter what his condition—hungry, and in rags, a wandering outcast—still breathes the air of liberty, and possesses the right of speech.—In all that beautiful land, from the lofty hill of Howth, to the Giant's Causeway; on the Liffy, and on the green banks of the Shannon; in its fertile valleys and deep retired glens, can Irishmen assemble and utter grievances and miseries, while an active press takes them up to disseminate abroad, and a sympathizing humanity eloquently pleads in their behalf. But no such privilege belongs to the poor and oppressed sons of Africa.—They toil and labor beneath a burning clime, with backs furrowed by the relentless driver's lash, and yet there is none to whom they dare whisper their sufferings and their wrongs.

Was there not, therefore, an excuse for him to bring this momentous question before them tonight—a question on which there is yet a great deal to be learned.

No term is more abused, or missapplied, that that of *Slavery*. It is frequently connected with drunkenness, hard-working, legal dis-abilities, and many other things. Men are said to be slaves of their propensities, passions, or of circumstances; but none of these are applicable to slavery in the strict sense in which he would wish to bring it before them. It is one man claiming and exercising an uncontrolled right over the body and soul of another—losing his manhood and being converted into a merchantable commodity—men stamped with the image of the living God, endowed with rationality, whose souls are immortal, with minds capable of grasping the great interest of eternity—whose names may be inscribed in the book of life—it is such beings degraded on a level with sheep, and with swine, that constitute alone the idea of slavery. In the language of South Carolina, "a slave can own nothing, earn nothing, but all that are his belong to his master."—no mind, no will, his individuality lost, and personality destroyed, humanity gone, and ranked with the beasts of the field! Such does slavery accomplish.

From this condition spring up innumerable evils. There is no impulse so strong as that of liberty, because it is the normal condition of man; hence to hold a man in bondage, *cruelty* must necessarily be resorted to, and this is one of the saddest evils of slavery. In all slaveholding States, the justice and right are founded.—But, would it not be more reasonable to establish its *humanity*, before undertaking to prove its *Divinity*? The Lights of the church have endeavored to estab-lish the position that God sanctions slavery. To what conclusions must such an absurd argument lead, and who is there that will follow out these conclusions? God never established a relation, but He also sanc-tions its conditions: thus the relations existing betwween husband and wife—between parent and child—between the pastor and his flock—are all beautiful in themselves, and sanctioned by Jehovah; but what are the conditions of slavery? Cruelty is one—does God sanction that? Without this, men will not voluntarily resign their liberty into the hands of another. A slave is made to feel that he must either continue such or die.—For, were it otherwise, he would immediately assert his freedom, and cease to be a slave. Hence, where there is slavery, there must be the whip, the cat-o'-nine tails, the thumbscrew, the gag, with all the paraphernalia necessary to its very existence, and which, of course, must necessarily be sanctioned by God!

Slaveholders want slaves to do their work. They know there is gold in the earth, but it must be dug. They cannot do it. To beg they are ashamed. They must have the comforts of life—be arrayed in fine linen—travel to Saratoga and the Falls—to France and London—their fingers covered with costly rings—breasts ornamented with sparkling diamonds, and yet they are indisposed to work to acquire these luxuries and ornaments. They have hands, but they are not made for earning an honest living, which is merely an antiquated Northern notion, British or Canadian in its origin, but scowled at in the Southern States. Slavery breaks the mainspring of honest industry; it holds out no hope or reward, for which free men toil and labor; instead of which it uses the lash, in order to obtain work, and, therefore, if God sanctions the existence of slavery. He must also sanction the infliction of punishment and cruelties, by which it can be maintained.

But it may be asked, do all slaveholders use the whip, are there not many humane and kind to their slaves, attend to their comforts and wants, and never have recourse to such severe punishment or unnecessary cruelty? Yes. Then what becomes of your argument, for Slavery is only a sin in the abuse, not in the use? By no means; for the great evil of Slavery consists in a man's liability to be sold. His master claims the right to do so, and this ever hangs like a night-mare over the poor slave. He may tell him he had never used him badly always clothed and fed him well; but if he is disobedient or lazy, he will sell him to another, from whom he will receive different treatment; and here the very terror which such threats inspire in the mind is employed to ensure subjection and acquiescence from the slave. Take away the bloody lash and thumb screw; let the dagger and bowie-knife be absent, and soon would the slave burst the bonds that encircle him, and walk forth to breathe the pure atmosphere of Freedom.—No sentiment of justice attaches him to his master; no acts of kindness inspire in him a feeling of affection to him. We can see no Divine right which [binds] him over, body and soul to another. He knows his hands and feet are his own, and in using them to assert his freedom, he uses what belongs to himself and to nobody else.

Ignorance is another evil of, and indispensable to slavery. Knowledge enlightens and expands the mind, elevates the thoughts and makes the slave dissatisfied with his condition and to pant after liberty. Hence, in all the slaveholding States, the most stringent laws are enacted, the violation of which entails the severest punishment, to forbid the slave either to read or to write, aye, to forbid even to learn the nature and existence of that God who breathed into him the breath of life. Hear it, Christians—for it is safer for the missionary to transport the bible into the very heart of Africa, than to carry it to the benighted slaves of Christian America.

He does not wish to arouse in the minds of Canadians any feeling of exasperation toward, the people of the United States; but he believes the moral influence of Canada ought to be brought to bear against a system which destroys every principle of humanity, saps the foundation of religion and morality, and prostrates the individual into the lowest depths of degradation.

The less character a nation has, the more sensitive do we find it. America is vain, arrogant and jealous, always inquiring of the world what do you think of me? Behold us extending our territory far and wide; soon will we lay our hands on Cuba, then Mexico, by and by Brazil; and in a little time Canada will be added to our glorious Republic! We would like to know how the people of Canada would like the embrace.

America stands prominently forth as a land of inconsistencies and contradiction—aspiring to be honest, and yet a nation of liars; for in her Declaration of Independence, and the gateway of her Constitution, she proclaims "all men equal," while she holds in bondage three millions and a half of her subjects—robbed of every right, deprived of every privilege, and sold and bought like beasts that perish. Her hills are studded with poles crowned with the cap of *liberty*. Her coins bear the impress of the same deity. The stranger, on landing, is congratulated for having set his foot on free soil, while the vainglorious boast of "free country," "glorious country," everywhere meets his ears; and yet land more steeped in slavery and all its concomitant evils nowhere exists on the face of the earth. The political feeling of the country has ever been enlisted on the side of slavery. In every successive Government it has been the controlling power.—When England was sympathizing with the Hungarian Patriot, he lands on the shores of America and there he finds the national sympathies directed towards Russia, rather than to the cause of liberty. And it cannot be otherwise; for how can America take side with oppressed freedom, so long as the chains of slavery bind the feet of many million of her subjects? It is a lasting disgrace on that boasted land of liberty, to stand aloof from the struggle in which England and France are patriotically engaged, to crush the Despot of Russia, who aims to destroy the last vestige of European liberty. Why is it so? Because infidel France is more consistent than Protestant America. The one has snapped the fetters of slavery in all her dominion, while the other refuses to listen to the voice of humanity, which loudly pleads for the emancipation of her own sable subjects, whereby her sympathies could be consistently enlisted in behalf of the threatened oppression of others. There is not a spot in all the vast territory of the United States sacred to the cause of freedom. The Israelites had their cities of refuge, where the poor and oppressed could fly, and while standing within their precincts, could bid defiance to the oppressor.—But in America, there is no hill so high, no valley so deep, no glen so sequestered as to afford a safe retreat for the poor unfortunate man of his colony. He may be started at Detroit and chased over the lake to Buffalo, from thence to the Hudson, to Canada, even to the foot of Bunker Hill Monument, and there under the shadow of the Monument, and while imploring mercy in the name of that blood, which was first shed by a black soldier, in the cause of American Independence—he may be chained and handcuffed and dragged back to the presence of his brutal owner. But beneath the pale light of the North Star, where the Lion reposes with his foot on the Virgin's lap—fit emblem of England's Queen—and nestling in his name, can the sable sons of Africa find a refuge, free from the bloody beak of the American Eagle.

But he is aware that he is treading on dangerous ground. He may be told, we don't want all the colored people in Canada. Neither does he. He wants some to remain behind. It will not be detrimental to the interests of this country, to have a large infusion of colored people in her borders. Let only justice and kindness be meted out to them, and soon will they become the most loyal, sober, and industrious of her population.

There never has been a fair opportunity afforded to the black man, to show what he would become, under the influence of good treatment, and the proper direction of his mind. What has been accomplished in the United States by coercion, can be effected here by the hope of reward. The prejudice against a colored man is principally owing to too much being expected from him. He comes here ignorant, degraded, despised, and suddenly thrown on his own responsibilities; and hence, it is natural that excesses may be frequently traced to his door. But what does Christianity say? Let us elevate the race, let us ennoble their minds, and soon will they be divested of their peculiarities, acquired in the house of bondage. Prejudice can best be removed by kindness. Let the object be rendered less offensive, and prejudice soon ceases to exist. If ignorant, enlighten; if immoral, infuse into the mind the principles of practical religion. There is no nobler work than this, nor one that is more certain to yield its own reward.

He would not now stop to discuss the natural capabilities of the Negro. It is well known he is a descendant of those, from whom the world first derived the germs of civilization—the ancient Egyptians and Abyssinians. All the knowledge imported to Rome and to Europe originated among those people; and if the flat nose, the high cheek-bone, the thick lips—the sure characteristics of the Negro—were no barriers to civilization among the Egyptians and Abyssinians, why should they separate from the civilized world, their descendants now? Once it was a curiosity to see the Negro read; and a book was formerly written to prove that it *was not a sin* to baptize a Negro—but now we behold the sable brow redolent with intellect, and uplifted under the inspiring influence of the highest and noblest thoughts. Need he mention the Garnetts, the Cromwells, the Smiths, the Wards, and a host of others, who are not considered unworthy to pace the platform with the most learned and eloquent Divines of the day.

We (said he) have among us, Doctors of Law and Medicine, Editors, Ministers and Lawyers, and in every way are we progressing, though comparatively slow, owing to the great prejudices existing in the public mind against our color.

It is in vain, however, to resist the influx of Negro population. There are twelve millions on this continent, all of whom are under the eye of God, and cannot be legislated out of existence. They will not all make their way to Canada, but he hopes enough will come to exert a moral influence over slavery in the United States. If Canadians want to get rid of us, they must banish slavery from the neighboring Union, for if they do not render themselves more unchristian, more inhuman than they, we will cling to this and to liberty; for where else can we go?

He was happy to meet his colored brethren on this occasion, and to them he would now speak plainly and affectionately. In escaping from slavery, and to the full enjoyments of freedom, they had assumed rights, and taken responsibilities and duties, which did not belong to them in a state of bondage; and it was necessary that they should be instructed how to act in accordance with those newly acquired relations. If there be here prejudice against the race, the colored man alone is responsible. He can, by his conduct either increase or disarm all antipathy in the public mind towards him. If he has no character capable of acquiring respect, he must undoubtedly be disposed. A black man may so far elevate himself by sobriety, industry, integrity and honesty, as to demolish opposition, while on the other hand, he may sink so low as to be an object of dislike and distrust to all who know him. The colored people in every community must do what the whites wish them. They must be orderly, temperate, cleanly, possess good manners, taste and modesty, besides integrity and honesty in all their social intercourse with others. They must neither be vain nor arrogant, impudent nor vulgar, but manifest both courtesy and respect to those among whom they have come. He saw a few colored people a day or two ago in this town, occupying the whole width of the side walk and refusing to allow a respectable white couple to pass, without going on the street. Such conduct ought to be strongly censured, because it has a tendency to increase the very prejudice against the Negro, which already is so prevalent among the whites. Manners are never incompatible with self-respect, while low-bred vulgar, insolent airs are sure to engender prejudice in those towards whom they are practised.

*The colored man must also read.* They are not a reading people. As for himself he was born a slave; never was at a school in his life; has acquired some knowledge of men and things, since he escaped from servitude; and has found that the higher he ascends in the scale of intelligence, the more does he grow in respectability. Formerly his daughter was prohibited to enter the public school in Rochester; now she is admitted like others, and all prejudice towards her has ceased to exist. He has been made a member of the various literary societies of that city, because he has ever exhibited a thirst for the acquisition of knowledge.—Therefore, it is that prejudice towards any man or people—no matter what their color—is not innate but arises entirely from their ignorance. It is not imported from England or Wales; for he has travelled through all parts of that land; has sat in the House of Lords and Commons; has been admitted to the places of the nobles; visited the Museums and Universities, and never did he see the first look of scorn, nor hear the first word of insult directed towards him on account of his color. The custom is not British, but American, pro- duced either by the slaveholder, or by the conduct of the black man himself. Natural equality is nothing for the Negro to possess, if he cannot at the same time show his pale-faced brother that he has exerted his natural abilities as much as he.

It is of no use, said Mr. D., concealing the fact, that as a people, the blacks are inferior to the whites. While the whites makes the boots, the poor Negro blacks them—While the whites are giving to the world the noblest achievements in the arts and sciences, the indolent and idle black is doing nothing but kicking up his heel, or strumming on the banjo. (Here Mr. D. humorously imitated the movement.) They must go to work. They cannot be expected to gain admission to the house of lords and dukes, as long as they remain in profound ignorance. Even the ignorant white man is spurned from the doors of the rich; and what right have the former to ask for privileges not conceded to the latter. Besides, colored people ought to be as careful of their associates as the whites, and those who have no self-respect, nor wish to be decent and industrious, ought to be made to feel their inferiority. The black man, therefore, can never command respect from the world, so long as he allows himself to be unfit for any, except the most menial occupation—the boot-black, the cook, or the wood-sawyer.

The respectability of a man will always be in accordance with his capabilities of supplying the wants of society, but if it be merely the artificial wants, he has got but a flimsy hold on society. He leaves no monuments behind him, to which posterity can look and admire. It is the employment of the intellect, and making it subservient to the practical uses of life, as well as to the cultivation of the higher duties of the social state, that acquires for the individual an enduring name. While the white mechanic points with pride and pleasure to the house he has planned and constructed; or to the ships he has modeled, he asks Sam what he has been doing, and the answer is, *white washing*. Let the colored man therefore, put forth the energies of his mind, lay aside his menial occupations, endeavor to assume the same elevated position occupied by his white neighbor, as soon will he obtain that respect whichever belongs to the employment of intellect in its legitimate and proper sphere. Let him leave the grog shops and taverns, and no longer stand idling at the corners of the streets, but go out into the world, and devote his hands and his mind to some useful and honorable occupation. He was proud of his race today, when on visiting the Elgin association, at Buxton,[14] he saw men, women, and children, who, but a short time ago, were under the rod of the slave driver, engaged in the

peaceful and noble pursuit of agriculture, settled down on their own
estates, administering to their own comforts, and growing in intelligence and wealth. The efficiency of their common school, where the
higher branches of education are taught, and eagerly acquired, did his
heart good, and filled him with hopes for the future. He would again
impress upon his race to quit the rumshops; to quit, quit them at once,
or they never can hope to acquire the good will or esteem of those,
amongst whom they dwell. They must feel that they have in this free
country duties and responsibilities devolving upon them,—that if they
are shielded alike with Britons by the protecting arm of British laws,
they must live and act in a manner to make themselves worthy of the
exalted privileges to which Britain, in her overflowing sympathy, has
generously admitted them.

The world says the black man is unfit to live in a mixed society—
to enjoy, and rightly appreciate the blessings of independence—that he
must have a master to govern him, and the lash to stimulate him to
labor. Let us be prepared to afford, in our lives and conversation, an
example of how grievously we are wronged by such a prevailing opinion of our race. Let us prove, by facts, not by theory, that independence
belongs to our nature, in common with all mankind—that we have
intelligence to use it rightly, when acquired, and capabilities to ascend
to the loftiest elevations of the human mind. Let such examples be
given in the mental cultivation, and moral regeneration of our children, as they increase in knowledge, in virtue and in every ennobling
principle of man's nature.

He was sorry to see that many of the colored people forget in this
land of freedom, that they ever were slaves. They neither take any
interest in the cause of anti-slavery, nor would they contribute a six
pence to spread intelligence among those they have left behind in the
house of bondage. Well might they hang their heads for shame, when
they behold the whites more deeply interested in their emancipation
than they themselves are—when they witness the generous sympathies
of a British people actively aroused in behalf of that liberty, which the
black man too often abuses when obtained.

He is fully aware that he may incur the censure of many of his
brethren, for having spoken thus plainly, perhaps saucily. But they
must ever bear in mind that he is closely linked with them; and in
proportion as they ascend in the scale of intellectual and moral improvement, so will he; whereas if they allow themselves to sink into

degradation, he also is dragged down along with them. Truth can never be too plainly told. Error loves concealment, and shrinks from the light of day. He has said nothing but the truth and those who wish to assume a position of respectability—to be esteemed by all with whom they come into social intercourse—will tender to him their sincere thanks for his plainness of speech; while the rowdy, the idler, and the loafer, only will censure him. Let them do it. He cares not. No blame, no censure from any man will ever deter him from pursuing that course, by which alone, he believes, the moral, the social and the intellectual elevation of his race can be secured—by which they will be enabled proudly to take their stand among the various orders and distinctions of men in the world, their equals in everything, except in vice, in crime and immorality.

(*The Western Planet* has, for the most part given here a report of the remarks made by us at Chatham with admirable accuracy; and we cannot withhold a grateful acknowledgement to the Editor of the *Planet* for allowing us to be so fully heard through his columns. There are, however, several inaccuracies in the speech, as published above, which it is proper to correct at once. We never said *"the colored people in every community must do what the whites wish them;"* but we did say, that the colored people, in every community, must do for their elevation, precisely what the whites do for theirs; and that they must make the white community as largely dependent on them, as they are upon the whites. Again, we never said, that as a people, *"the blacks are inferior to the whites,"* but we did say, that they are inferior in attainments to the whites. There are other lights and shades, perhaps quite unavoidable in a report like the above, which might be rendered more accurate, but the most important corrections are those already noticed.)—*Editor.*

*Frederick Douglass' Paper*, August 18, 1854

## TO GERRIT SMITH

Rochester, August 23d, 1854.

My Dear Sir:

Now that you have laid down the burden of Congressional duties, and are among your native Peterborough hills, allow me to solicit (what, if given, I am sure, will be of service to the Anti-Slavery cause) your views,[15]

1st. Of the present posture of the Anti-Slavery question generally.

2dly. What hope, if any, may be predicated of the present Congress.

3dly. The nature, character, and extent of influence exerted in Congress, by the Anti-Slavery members of the House.

4thly. Who are the most effective supporters of Slavery there, and the means of their efficiency.

5thly. Your impressions concerning the character, learning, ability, of members generally, and anything touching the House of Representatives, which may serve to give the public an insight into the proceedings of that body.

A compliance with the above, will be gratefully appreciated, by

Your faithful friend,

Frederick Douglass

*Frederick Douglass' Paper*, August 25, 1854

## TO GERRIT SMITH

Rochester, Sept. 7th, 1854

My dear friend:

I have this moment got your letter. The great wrong done to our mutual friend, (for he is my friend as well as yours), Hon. Thomas Davis, has been as well repaired as it could be in this week's edition of my paper.[16] The whole thing is bad, and I have suffered much about it. Yet I cannot say as you do, that the loss of a thousand dollars from my pocket book, could not have hurt me so much as that mistake. Money is too useful, too scarce with me, too hard to get hold of and too easily got rid of in a thousand ways, and I am too often called upon by printers and paper makers to pay what I owe, to make the thought of such a comparison, possible with me. Your letter was addressed to me. I was proud to have, what I must call the most beautiful letter I remember ever to have read, addressed to me. I was anxious from the moment I received it, and knowing my inaptitude as to little niceties in composition, I did not trust myself to read the proof but gave it into the hands of my friend Miss Griffiths and the printer with every injunction that the letter should appear absolutely free from errors. That great pains were taken with that letter I know. I am pained and mortified at the result. Had I read the proof myself, while other errors might have crept into your letter, I think this would not, for I know Thomas Davis, have known him long. I have heard him speak often. To me, he is even more than a plain and forcible speaker, he is really eloquent. I have heard him, when his words have had that in them, which goes straight to the soul, and shakes the spirits of men. The best place in the world to try a man's eloquence is among his friends and neighbors, at a moment when some great interest is excited, and there is division. The man that can arrest his neighbors and compel them to stand still, when they were just about to rush on, or who can rouse them to action, when they have been riveted to the spot by doubt is what I call an eloquent man, and such a man is Thomas Davis. I have seen the proof of what I say in him. At the time when the Suffrage Party of Rhode Island committed the sad mistake of restricting the right of suffrage to white persons in the new Constitution,[17] a mistake the effects of which that party is suffering from at this day, though it was committed under strong temptation and twelve years ago, Mr. Davis, was deeply moved against the injustice, and poured out repeated denunciations against it, which would have commanded attention for the speaker, in the most dignified body on earth. His speeches were usually short but I observe that the effect they produced was lasting. Knowing Mr. Davis as I do know him, I should have detected the injustice my typos have done him.

But Thomas Davis is not only an eloquent man, he is also a reasonable man, and I am sure you can make all right with him.

I would write to him myself, but I much dislike to intrude myself upon the attention of men so much engaged as he is.

Always yours Truly,

Frederick Douglass

*Gerrit Smith Papers, George Arents Research Library, Syracuse University*

# WILLIAM WELLS BROWN[18]

While our distinguished brother, Brown, was abroad, laboring, with admirable industry in the cause of human freedom, and adding to his stock of knowledge of men and things, we esteemed it not less a pleasure than a duty to commend him and his work. We rejoiced that so much of talent and industry could be pointed to, (in vindication of our common people), as were exemplified in Mr. Brown. We do *not* regret any kind word we then said of him; but we do regret that he should feel called upon, to show his faithfulness to the American Anti-Slavery Society, by covering us with reproach and dishonor. If Mr. Brown has aught against us, he need not retail his complaints to cliques, parties, and anti-slavery circles, or allow them to be so retailed for him. Put your charges against us, Mr. Brown, in a suitable shape, and they shall appear, not only in the anti-slavery office at Boston, in the private ear of prejudice, but we promise you to publish them to our readers. As an honest man, we hold it to be your duty to do this, or to cease circulating as facts what we know can be shown to be the merest fictions. Come, Mr. Brown, let us have the facts.

*Frederick Douglass' Paper*, March 2, 1855

# REPLY TO WILLIAM WELLS BROWN[19]

To Frederick Douglass:

Sir: Had not your many changes and re-changes, prepared me to be astonished at nothing that you might say, or do, I would have been somewhat surprised at the attack made upon me by you, in your paper of the 2d of March. You commence by saying "we do regret that he should feel called upon to show his faithfulness to the American Anti-Slavery Society by covering us with dishonor." Let me say to you, Frederick Douglass, that my difference with you has nothing whatever to do with the American Anti-Slavery Society, and no one knows that better than yourself. And I regard such an insinuation as fit only to come from one whose feelings are entirely lost to all sense of shame. My charge against you is, that, just before I left the United States for England, you wrote a *private* letter to a distinguished Abolitionist in Great Britain, injurious to me, and intended to forestall my movements there. In a note which I forwarded to you, to your address at Rochester on the 20th of January last, I gave you to understand that I have been made aware of your having acted in that underhand manner. The following is a part of the note I sent you more than a month ago. During my sojourn in England, and several months after my arrival there, and while spending a few days with a friend of yours, the post brought me a letter, which had been remailed in London, and it proved to be from you, dated at New Bedford. After I had finishing reading the letter, your friend seemed anxious to learn its contents. I handed it to her, with the request that she would read it; your friend appeared much astonished at the kindness expressed by you to me, and exclaimed, 'Douglass has done you a great injustice,' and immediately revealed to me the contents of a letter which she had received from you, some months before, and which was written a short time previous to my departure from America. I need not say that the very unfavorable position in which your letter placed me before your friend, secured for me a cold reception at her hands. I need not name the lady; you know to whom I refer, unless you wrote to more than one. Your attack upon me in your paper of the 2d inst., in which you ask for "facts," when my note containing the above had been in your possession more than a month, shows too well your wish to make a sneaking fling at me, instead of seeking for "facts," and acting the part of an honorable man. Why did you not give my note a place in your paper, and make such comments as you thought best? No, that would not have suited you. But, anxious to heap insult upon injury, you resort to the mode most congenial in your feelings and sense of justice. Had I not thought it due to the public to state the above "facts," I would have treated your scurrilous paragraph with that silence and contempt that all such articles so justly deserve. However, no future insinuation of yours, no matter how false or unjust, shall provoke from me a reply.

William Wells Brown


*Reply to Mr. Brown*

A statement more adroit, with a view to fix a stigma upon the honor of a man, I do not remember lately to have seen than is this statement of Mr. Brown. The charge is palpable enough; the manner of sustaining it is plainly indirect, unfair, and one-sided.—There is no man in the world, who knows better than Mr. Brown, how entirely different the face of his letter would appear, were he but to tell the whole truth connected with the transaction to which he refers; not the truth as we know it, but as he, himself knows it. This truth, I shall make another effort to force or *"provoke"* out of him. He shall not fire his gun, and retire in this manner, under the plea of offended dignity, as he proposed to do at the close of his letter. It was cowardly of him, in view of the nature of his charge, thus to retire. —I deem myself fortunate in having drawn forth to public view, a slander which, evidently, he designed simply for private circulation, where I could have no means of defense or explanation. And now, Mr. Brown, I say, give us the *facts*. Your indignation and "contempt" may be well enough in their place, but they are beneath consideration here. However annoying the demand may be—I repeat it—give us the "facts." I don't mean your *charges*; these I understand very well; but I mean some tangible evidence of their truth. You shall not be prosecutor and judge, and the only witness in your own case. The facts wanted are, in brief, these:

1st. Who is the *"distinguished abolitionist to whom* you allege I wrote a private letter *injurious"* to you? Give the name and the local habitation. Certainly one so prompt to have *"justice"* done, can have no objection to come before the world in defense of justice.

2d. State precisely—and if not precisely—state the *substance* of what I said in that letter, that the public may judge, not only whether it was *injurious* to you, but, secondly whether it was intentionally *"injurious."* I admit that the charge is a serious one; and if it be established beyond contradiction or reasonable explanation, I am willing to fall not only beneath the contempt of my brother Brown, but that of all honorable men. I call for the *"facts,"* and should do so in the face of a dozen such letters as the above.

Reserving my defense till the whole case is presented, I may ask brother Brown how it happens that he has corresponded with me repeatedly, during the last five years—that he has written for my paper repeatedly, and sent me his books "with his kind regards," and yet, during that entire time, he has never once intimated that I had dealt with him in the manner he now alleges? The whole thing is most extraordinary, and I demand the facts. Brother Brown may refuse to state the facts; he may refuse to have the truth *"provoked"* out of him; but if he does so refuse, the public will know why.

*Frederick Douglass' Paper*, March 16, 1855

## TO GERRIT SMITH

Rochester, March 27, 1855

My dear Sir:

I am glad my speech pleased you.[20] I had a pretty high opinion of it before, and your kind approval has not detracted from that opinion. I did, in my spoken speech, accord all due honor to the clearlighted, and righthearted Elizabeth Herrick. The omission is only in my printed speech. The correction shall be made in the pamphlet edition, which I am about to publish.

Oh! yes, do let us have a *National Liberty Party Convention.* Let us have a strong call.[21] We must leave the Free Soilers and Garrisonians to uphold their own standards, and stand on our own grounds. You have but to speak the word, to have a grand convention here, and here is the place to have it. Do *you*, my dear Sir, write the call. No other man must write the call for the Liberty party, while *Gerrit Smith* lives, and is able to wield a pen.

Most truly yours, always,

Fred Douglass

*Gerrit Smith Papers, George Arents Research Library, Syracuse University*

## COLORED PEOPLE OF PENNSYLVANIA

In a very neatly printed pamphlet, prepared by a Committee of the "Colored Citizens of Philadelphia," asking for the same right of suffrage they enjoyed for forty-seven years prior to the adopting of the present Constitution, in '38, it is stated that they number 30,000 persons in Philadelphia; that they possess $2,680,693 of real and personal estate; and have paid $9,766,782 for house, water, and ground rent.

Should not such a people have the right of suffrage, and all the rights and immunities enjoyed by other citizens?[22] If so, why not? This is the question to be answered. The only answer that *the enemy* gives, is "because their Creator has made some of them black!" Yes! because their eyes, *some of them*, are not blue, and their hair, *some of it*, is not straight. This physical diversity is regarded as the index of a degraded condition. But this is *not* the reason. The colored people of Pennsylvania, it is well known, are a thrifty, enterprising and industrious class of the population. The whites are jealous of their growing strength.

They buy and sell property, own lumber yards, (two of the most extensive, if not the largest lumber merchants in the State are colored men) and till the soil; there are mechanics, professional men, and artists among them; they are developing not only their *identity*, but their equality with the whites; and the latter do not wish to recognize or acknowledge this equality. They wish the political disabilities, and others under which colored citizens labor, to remain, to harass them into the belief that they are, after all, an inferior race. They are told they never can rise in this country; and their disabilities are pointed at, as evidence of the truthfulness of the assertion. O no, we can never rise with the millstone around our neck. They fear, that if they assist us in taking off the millstone, and dashing it into the sea, we will become hopeful of the final success of our holy cause and will plant more stakes, instead of digging up those already planted, and what is worse than all, we will doggedly persist in remaining here; we will buy houses and lands, and we WILL not leave for Africa.

But let our brethren in Pennsylvania, and throughout the country, take courage. Our enemies are strong, but our Great Deliverer is stronger. Darkness may now gather around us, but the morning cometh. We shall yet chase from our firmament the gangrenous clouds that lower o'er us. Press on! *Nil desperandum!*

*Frederick Douglass' Paper*, April 20, 1855

# EQUAL SCHOOL RIGHTS

We are glad of an opportunity to "report progress" in any matter which involves the well-being of our oppressed people. The subject of exclusive organizations among our people is one, in which we have long been interested. As a general thing, we consider them detrimental to our interests, having a tendency to foment the spirit of proscription where it already exists, and to engender it, where it does not. But we can easily understand of certain exigencies, in which they may be absolutely necessary to our well-being. We would not have our people support a colored school, or colored church, in those places, where they can procure admission into schools and churches, in which there are no complexional distinctions, where they will be in the possession of the same rights and privileges, that others enjoy. This is our private opinion, publicly expressed. For a long time the majority of the colored citizens of Boston have been battling against the existence of a separate school for their children. Boston is the only place in Massachusetts where such a distinction is made. The time was, when other cities and towns refused equal privileges to their colored inhabitants. But they have conquered their prejudices. White children, and black, and all the intermediate grades go to the same school, sit upon the same seats, are arranged in the same classes, and nothing very alarming has transpired in consequence, *that we ever heard of.*

But old aristocratic Boston has refused to abolish her proscriptive school. Had the colored people themselves refused to permit their children to attend it, and adhere to their determination, that simple act would have abolished the school. But the "authorities" declared that just so long as any considerable number of colored children attended the school, they should have the privilege. But this was only an ostensible reason for its continuance—for it was well known that the majority of the colored citizens of Boston, were arrayed in bitter and open hostility to the Smith School. And, for a long time, no considerable number has attended it. Several of the best tax paying citizens have removed from Boston to adjacent towns, and elsewhere, where their children would receive treatment, necessary to a full expansion and development of their mental being, and treatment, too, calculated to inspire them with the idea, not of inferiority, but of *Equality.*[23]

But even Boston, the residence of the Rev. Nebemiah Adams, and the scene of the rendition of his Baptist brother, is becoming ashamed of her iniquity. The friends of Equal School Rights, are with commendable zeal, still striving for the mastery they are bound to obtain; the victory of Right over Wrong, Humanity over Despotism.

Six years ago, the case of Sarah C. Roberts vs. the city of Boston, for equal school privileges was brought before the Supreme Judicial Court. Hon. Charles Sumner made a most eloquent argument in behalf of the plaintiff in the case.[24] He asserted that "according to the Constitution of Massachusetts, all men without distinction of color or race, are equal before the law; that the legislature of Massachusetts, in entire harmony with the Constitution, had made no discrimination of color or race in the establishment of public schools; that the courts of Massachusetts had never recognized any discrimination, founded on color or race, in the administration of the public schools, but had recognized the equal rights of all the inhabitants; that the exclusion of colored children of practical inconvenience to them and their parents, to which white persons were not exposed, and was, therefore, a violation of equality; that the separation of children in the public schools of Boston, on account of color or race, was in the nature of *caste*; that the Committee of Boston, charged with the superintendence of the public schools, had no power under the Constitution and laws of Massachusetts to make any discrimination on account of color or race among the children in the public schools; and he asked the court to declare the by-law of the School Committees of Boston, making a discrimination of color among children of the public schools, unconstitutional and illegal, although there were no express words of prohibition in the Constitution and laws."

Judge Shaw, in behalf of the court, rendered a decision adverse to the plaintiff.—But this decision did not place a quietus upon the anti-exclusive movement. It only animated its ardent friends to redoubled diligence, and a renewed determination to conquer. They have had public meetings over the subject, they have presented petitions again, and again, to the proper authorities; they have appeared in *propria personae* before them, but seemingly to little or no avail.

During the session of the present Legislature, some dozen petitions or more, numerously signed by taxpaying citizens, of all complexions, were presented to that body.—They were referred to the Committee on Education who have made a report favorable to the wishes of the Petitioners. The Report is an able document creditable to the head and heart of the writer, and the good sense and humanity of the whole Committee.[25]

*Frederick Douglass' Paper*, April 20, 1855

# THE PROPERTY QUALIFICATION

The Assembly resolution, proposing to amend the Constitution of our State, so as to extend the right of suffrage to colored citizens, without the property qualification,[26] was defeated in the Senate, by being "tabled" under the rule. So we must try again. We shall conquer by and by. While the slaveholders in North Carolina and Alabama are endeavoring to relieve the Slave Code of some of its most repugnant features, we, in the State of New York, must attend to the barbarous enactment on the Statute Book, by which we are proscribed and trodden under foot. Our petitions may be laid upon the table again, and again; but we shall never be hushed into silence. We have, we trust, as a people, come to the determination to worry and weary our adversary, until our prayers are granted. Let us, then, prepare for the next Legislature. Let our lecturers on Slavery at the South, see to it, that they do not forget Slavery at the North. Let them agitate this question of our enfranchisement, as they ought, and petitions shall flow into the next Legislature, which, from the character of the Petitioners, must receive attention.

*Frederick Douglass' Paper*, April 20, 1855

# COMMUNIPAW AND THE AMERICAN A. S. SOCIETY

In last week's paper, our esteemed New York correspondent treated our readers to a well-written paper, explaining the grounds of the coldness of the colored people towards the American Anti-Slavery Society.[27] His right, as a colored man, to enter upon such an explanation is unquestionable. Our columns are free and fully open to the consideration of all subjects properly connected with the great questions of slavery and anti-slavery. They are as free to those who dissent from, as those who agree with, the views of our respected friend, *"Communipaw."*

In regard to the article now in question, we are free to say, that had we been at home, it should not have gone before our readers without the expression of our dissent from one point which it contained.

We cannot think with *"Communipaw"* that it is the *"Unitarianism"* of the "American A. S. Society," which has interposed a gulf between the colored people and that organization. The cause, we take it, lies deeper. "Unitarians" have shown as much *heart* in the cause of liberty, as the members of any other religious faith in the country. The true reason, we believe, to be a conviction entertained by that Society, but of which that Society is itself unconscious—that we are inferior, and not to be treated in all respects as other men. It is the Anglo-Saxon pride of race, which not even anti-slavery has been able to obliterate, which makes the black man stand off a respectful distance.—There is, as Mr. Phillips would say, a kind of mesmerism encircling that Society, telling the colored man that he cannot be at home in it. Individual men in the Society have divested themselves of the quality in question, but the old leaven is still in the lump, and occasionally shows itself quite unmistakably.

Our relation, as a people, towards the American Anti-Slavery Society will be changed when we have changed it toward the mass of the American People, and very little sooner. We are *pitied* by the American A. S. Society, and are *despised* by the American people—both must be supplanted by the feeling of *respect.*

*Pity* may be invited, *contempt* may be attracted, but *respect* must be commanded.—The colored people must show themselves not one whit behind their white friends, either in the abundance or the excellence of their work in the great cause of our liberty and enfranchisement. While the abolitionists can say that they are more concerned in labors to promote our welfare than we are in such labors, they may pity us, but they cannot respect us. We would, therefore, in dealing with this subject, take blame to ourselves, as well as charge much upon the American Anti-Slavery Society.

*Frederick Douglass' Paper*, May 18, 1855

# THE CASE OF REV. DR. PENNINGTON[28]

Our members are aware the Rev. Dr. Pennington, of New York City, a gentleman of high intellectual, moral worth, was recently ejected from a public car, in Sixth Avenue, by the conductor, in a worse than brutal manner.—It seems that the Dr., shortly after taking his seat, was notified by the Conductor that he must leave the car, as the regulations of the Company strictly prohibited colored people from riding in any of their cars, save those provided for their especial *accommodation.* The Rev. gentleman very properly refused to accede to the Conductor's wishes, whereupon the Conductor and driver pounced upon him, and forcibly ejected him. He, however, knowing his rights, and resolving, like a man, to maintain them still held on to the car, behind which he ran as far as the lower depot, where, finding a policeman, he demanded the arrest of the cowardly assailants. The policeman endeavored to dissuade the Dr. from taking any legal course to punish the offenders; but he very wisely resolved to have the question settled at once, whether or not, a man can be thus assaulted by his fellowman in the public conveyances of the city of New York with impunity? In the meantime, the driver was suffered to return upon his upward trip without molestation. It appears that a misunderstanding occurred between the Dr. and the policeman; the former was taken to the Tombs, and the case dismissed by Justice Connelly. These are the circumstances as we have narrated them from memory, the *Tribune* containing an excellent article on the subject, having been mislaid, and the *Anti-Slavery Standard* of last week, which we have on file, containing not even the slightest allusion to the transaction.

What a commentary is this shameful outrage upon the institutions of free, humane, enlightened and Christian America! Boasting and ranting about Freedom and Equality, the American people, as a whole, are the most inconsistent, and the most tyrannical people, the sunlight ever revealed to the gaze of men or of devils. Caste is the god the nation delights to honor. Caste is in their preaching, their singing and their praying. They talk about the caste of the Hindoo, while they out-Hindoo, in the development of this insatiate and malignant spirit, every nation under heaven. This spirit follows us by day and by night. It follows us at every step. *"Wherever thou goest, I will go;"* this is the language addressed to us in every avenue of life. It goes with us to the market, to the workshop, to the polls, to the church, to the cars, to the graveyard, and when our dust returns to our mother dust, feeds upon the effluvia arising from our dead bodies. Yes! it pounces upon us at birth, goes with us through life, and, like a starved jackal, is seen flashing its lustful eyes at our new-made graves. Thank God! It cannot go beyond the tomb.—It can enter neither Heaven nor Hell.

The spirit which dragged Dr. Pennington from the *public* car in New York City, and which drives the colored man from the lower floor of her Christian (?) churches, the majority of them, would not (could it do otherwise?) suffer him to enter the regions of the blessed upon terms of equality with the white man. It would only allow him, and all our oppressed people, on condition of suffering in this world, with the resignation and meekness of Uncle Tom, the ills we have, as our reward, the exalted privilege of being somewhere in the neighborhood of the *white man's* heaven and having a peep now and then into the transcendent glories. We might swing back and forth upon the

"golden gates, on golden hinges turning;"

but not be allowed to trespass *within the gates!* If we had on earth, as the French have it, *une goutte de sang noir*, one drop of African blood, this fact being known, we could not enter *there*. This is no exaggeration. There is no rhetoric about it, but a living, breathing, burning reality.

The spirit of caste reflects anything but credit upon the character of the American People.—It makes those who possess it, a hissing and a by-word among all civilized nations. Gustave de Beaumont, a French author, who visited this country eighteen or twenty years ago, was much disgusted with the exhibitions he witnessed of the silly prejudice of the Americans, and upon his return to his native country, wrote a work, entitled, *"Maria, or Slavery in the United States, A Picture of American Manners,"* in which he alludes, in very sarcastic language to the prevalence of this abominable spirit:

"That which long astonished me," says de Beaumont, "was to find this separation of whites and blacks in the religious edifices. Who would believe it?—ranks and privileges in Christian churches! Sometimes the blacks are confined in an obscure corner of the temple, sometimes wholly excluded. Imagine what would be the displeasure of a genteel assembly, if it were obliged to be mingled with coarse and ill-clad people. The meeting in the holy temple is the only amusement which the Sabbath authorized. For American society, the Church is promenade, concert, ball, and theatre;—the ladies there display themselves elegantly dressed. The Protestant temple is the salon where one prays. Americans would be distressed to meet there people of low condition. Would it not be grievous, too, if the hideous sight of a black face should come in to tarnish the lustre of a brilliant assembly? In a congregation of fashionable people, the majority will necessarily have a mind to shut the door against the people of color; the majority willing so, nothing can hinder it.

"The Catholic Churches are the only ones which admit neither of privilege nor exclusion; the black population finds access to them as well as the white. This tolerance of Catholicism and this rigorous policy of the Protestant temple, is not accidental, but pertains to the very nature of the two systems."

This high-minded and courteous foreigner, it may be well to add, was associated with Mr. de Tocqueville, in a deputation from the French Government, to examine our penitentiary system. After accomplishing the object of their mission, the former published the work to which we have alluded, and the latter, gave the world a masterly treatise upon our *democratic* institutions.[29]

In conclusion, we remark, with reference to the case of Doctor Pennington that we hope that the matter will not be suffered to rest here. We do not believe that the people will sanction any such regulation of the company to which we have alluded. We do not believe they would prefer sitting by the side of a white man, a dirty white man, with a cod-fish, or a bunch of onions in his hands, to sitting by the side of a respectable colored man. And in this case, the conductor has ejected the *right man*, a respectable Doctor of Divinity! What will his brother Doctors say? Suppose Dr. Bethune had been ejected from the same car, for his *physical rotundity,* what a time there would have been in New York! And yet the conductor had no more right to eject Dr. Pennington than Dr. Bethune.

We anxiously await the issue of the present struggle of the colored people in New York, to ride in the public conveyances. They will ultimately triumph; let them persevere, let them develop their manhood, and it will, at length, be recognized.

*Frederick Douglass' Paper*, June 8, 1855

# THE DISSOLUTION OF THE UNION

We regard the conclusion to which our correspondent, U.B. has arrived on this subject, unsafe, unsound, and unwarrantable.[30] Let us take up his *"results"* in the order in which he has narrated them.

*First*, by the withdrawal of the Northern free States, from the Southern States, the Slave power would be weakened, leaving it with a population of four or five millions to sustain slavery. He does not call in question the ability of these 5 millions with their bayonets, etc., at their command, to keep the slaves in subjection, but simply declares that the disgrace would be shifted from the North, wholly upon the South. What good would accrue *to the slave*, from this shifting scene? A pretty thing, indeed, that after the Northern States have received their share of the profits, after having been *particeps criminis*, in the outrage upon the rights of the slave, they should walk out of the Union, and coolly request the South to pocket all the disgrace. No, friend Boston, this will never do. You fall into a lamentable error, indeed, by designating the Slaveholding States, *"the guilty parties only."* There is a fearful responsibility resting upon the Northern States, which no mere withdrawal from the Southern States will be sufficient to discharge.

Your *second* result might be a final release of the Northern States from expenses now incurred in supporting Slavery, but then, *you* know this would not be equivalent to a "release," "final" or otherwise, of the slave population.—Certainly not.

*Thirdly,* you assume that were the Union dissolved, there would be no necessity for any further agitation of the Slavery question. We have no sympathy with any movement, which, in the event of its successful issue, proposes to leave the slave fettered as before, and even desires, during his enslavement, *to ignore "his deplorable situation,"* and to take no part in the *"unpleasant and disagreeable agitation of the slavery question."* Would *you* be satisfied, Friend B., in the event of a dissolution of the Union, conscious of the perilous condition of the slave, to say nothing, by way of *continuing* the *"disagreeable agitation?"* Such is the irresistible deduction of your logic.

And now a word in relation to the unpleasant results which would be felt by the South.

First, the slaves would flee without let or hindrance in every direction. We don't believe a word of it, friend U.B. Without let or hindrance? Not a word of it. They would be watched by their masters with unslumbering vigilance. Doubtless, some would get away.— They run away without waiting for a dissolution of the Union. But as for any southern gate being thrown open wide for their egress, or as you have it, their fleeing without let or hindrance, it is all moonshine.

Your second unpleasant result to the South would be slave insurrections. But you have forgotten to enlighten us in respect to the chance of success, in these insurrectionary movements. Your "final and grand result" would be the Abolition of Slavery. A *grand* result truly!

But, friend B., how did you jump to this conclusion? You have made a grand leap from premise to conclusion.—You see farther than most people. We confess, that we fail to be convinced by your logic.—But you are not the only one who has failed to convince us on this point. Try again.

*Frederick Douglass' Paper*, August 31, 1855

## PROSCRIPTIVE SCHOOLS ABOLISHED

We are indebted to the Boston *Evening Telegraph*, for an account of a meeting of our colored fellow citizens, in Rev. Mr. Grimes' Church, with reference to the abolition of Caste Schools in that city, and the anticipated admission of *all* children, without regard to color, into the various public schools. There was a large gathering of those especially interested, and the meeting was of a most interesting character. Addresses were made by Messrs. Garrison, Logan, Slack, and Nell, and well received by the audience.

We have always felt an interest in this Equal School Rights' question. It was upon this question that we made our advent into the arena of public life. We would not willingly subject courselves to the imputation of an egotist, but our friends in Boston, will bear us witness that while a resident of that city, we labored faithfully in conjunction with others, for the abolition of the Smith School, believing it a curse to the colored, and a disgrace to the colored, and a disgrace to the white community. And now we rejoice with our Boston friends in the victory they have achieved. The Right, at last, lifts up its head in triumph. We most sincerely hope that our friends will show unto all, *by sending their children punctually to the public schools* in their respective wards, that they know, in this degenerate age, how to appreciate every recognition of their manhood. Let the Smith School be *forever* abolished; there is no excuse for its existence one hour. The Legislature had virtually abolished it; let no one be foolish enough to incur the disgrace of posterity by still clinging to its shattered remains.

We think our friends should have a grand celebration, in honor of the successful issue of this hard fought battle. Let them shake old Fanueil Hall with their jubilant thunders.—The enemy is vanquished;

blow the trumpet loudly. An intelligent demonstration evincing to all around them, a hearty appreciation of the merited triumph, will tell effectively upon the Bastille of Prejudice.

We now behold another illustration of the motto: *"Truth is Mighty and Will Prevail."* In this triumph of Justice over Injustice, we see clearly how much can be accomplished, in time, by an inflexible adhesion to the Right and an unwavering confidence in the God truth. Let us not, then grow weary in well doing. Press on, through every opposing influence. We shall yet *stretch forth our withered arm, and it shall be made whole.*

The following Resolutions reported by W. C. Nell, Esq. were unanimously adopted:

Resolved, that we tender our heartful thanks to the Massachusetts Legislature and to all who have contributed to the result, for the act whereby colored and all caste schools are abolished in this Commonwealth.

Resolved, That in this act we recognize, through the providence of God, the sure and rapid progress of the anti-slavery enterprise, which, based upon the recognition of the truth of the fatherhood of God and the brotherhood of the race, deserves the advocacy of every lover of humanity.

Resolved, that to attest our appreciation of the passage of this anti-colored school act, we the colored parents of Boston, do hereby pledge ourselves to have our children punctually at school, and neat in their dress, and in all other ways will aid their instructors in the task which has been assigned them.

Resolved, That a copy of these resolutions be sent to the Superintendent of Public Schools, and that the public press be respectfully requested to give them an insertion.

*Frederick Douglass' Paper*, September 7, 1855

# SPEECH DELIVERED AT CONVENTION OF COLORED CITIZENS OF THE STATE OF NEW YORK, TROY, NEW YORK, SEPTEMBER 4, 1855.

Gentlemen and Ladies:

It is with no little embarrassment that I rise on this occasion, and under the circumstances in which I am placed, to address you. This has been a long, laborious, fatiguing day with me, and I have had no repose, no retirement, no opportunity, to fling together such thoughts as the intelligence of the audience which I now see before me leads me to believe necessary, and proper to enforce on this occasion. I never, perhaps, felt a profounder desire to say something worthy of the great cause in which we are engaged, than I do now, and at the same time, I never felt more incapable of doing so. But, since I have been called upon to speak, I will try, if you will be patient and forbearing towards me, to say a few words.

It is very evident that the great question now before the American people—the question upon which the nation will soon be called to decide—is Slavery.

In the Southern States there is no institution, no party, save the slaveholding institution and party. By this institution, 3,700,000 of the human family are stripped of every right, robbed of all justice, whipped, outraged, and compelled to be marketable chattels. Fifteen hundred millions of dollars are said to be invested in this species of property at the South.—Fifteen hundred millions of dollars is said to be the money representation of this enslaved portion of the human race. This vast accumulation of wealth—this immense conglomeration of interest—has made the South a unit on the Slavery question—bound them together in every action. So overshadowing has it become as to eclipse, and swallow up every other consideration. In the Southern States of our Union, the non-slaveholder is almost a cypher—literally a nonentity. This is the case with him, even more than with the colored population of this State. One fact alone will illustrate this fact. At the recent State Convention in Kentucky, notwithstanding the non-slaveholding power, that State embraces a population of over 700,000, and the slaveholding interest a population of only 30,000, the slaveholding interest was so powerful, so all-pervading, that not a single delegate appeared in the Convention as a representative of the 700,000 people embraced in that non-slaveholding population. This fact will show you the tremendous power of this institution in the Southern States. In South Carolina, no man, no free, white American citizen, is eligible to a seat in the Legislature of the State, unless he is the holder of ten slaves—unless he can call ten human beings his property. Thus, this institution rules everything at the South. It has given to the South its laws, its morals, its social code, its interpretation of the Bible, its definition of the Declaration of Independence, its understanding of the Constitution of the United States. The nonslaveholding citizens have thus become a mere cypher, and we scarcely ever speak of the South, without speaking of the slaveholders as the South. This Southern institution has also given it a peculiar style of religion. It has so materially changed the religion of that section from what it was in the primitive days of the Quakers and others, who opposed the principle of human oppression, as to give it what may be termed a slaveholding religion—a religion which can be practised in perfect conformity with the whip, the gag, the fetters, the thumbscrew, and all the horrid, hellish paraphernalia of the slave system. The South has also given us its own peculiar interpretation of the laws. The system and practise formerly was this: that every man was presumed to be free until he was proved to be otherwise. But this principle is found to be incompatible with the great Southern institution; so they have established one diametrically opposite, and they call upon the North to endorse and sustain it in the fugitive slave bill. This new principle is, that every man is presumed to be a slave until he proves himself to be otherwise. This is what the South is demanding and will continue to demand of the North. There are two principles in this country—Slavery and Liberty. One of these kings is bound to reign in this country. The question for the North to answer is— "Under which king?" There is in this Northern country what may be styled a Slavery party. Its members are distributed through every other political organization, save perhaps the Liberty Party and the Free Soil Party of the North. This Slavery party will sink every other policy and lose sight of every other constitution in order to advance the interests of the South. For this purpose, its members will become Whigs and Democrats, or *neither* Whigs nor Democrats. It entered the political caucuses of 1852 in the city of Baltimore, and demanded the incorporation principle into the platforms of the Whig and Democratic organizations. And both parties bowed themselves before this gigantic interest, and consented to take upon themselves the "mask of the beast." They then and there abandoned all other issues to give way to the Slave policy of the South. There was no living issue between the Whig and Democratic party in the election of 1852. It has been inserted that the Whig party was in favor of the improvement of Rivers and Harbors, and so forth, while the Democratic party was not—and that this constituted the issue. What are the facts? The Platform of the Whig Party said—"We are opposed to the *unconstitutional* improvement of Rivers and Harbors." And that was no issue. Both parties endorsed, with all their hell-black etceteras, the Compromises of 1850. Both parties endorse the Southern interpretation of all these questions which divided the North and South on the subject of Slavery. What were those questions?—What was the standard taken by the South?—Let us see. It has been said that the North is opposed to Slavery. But the South has discovered that the chain on the Negro slave will not cut, and fasten, and fester securely in the flesh, unless the other end of that chain is held by a padlock in the lips of the North.

It is one of the compensating laws of Providence that a wrong done by one section of the nation against the other cannot go unpunished. A man cannot build his mansion on a hill-top, be it so fair and lovely, if its base be reeking with nuisance and corruption, without suffering the baneful influences of that deadly corruption. So you of the North, freemen and non-slaveholding citizens, cannot sit idly by, and see 3,700,000 of your fellow-beings wronged, robbed of their rights, whipped, outraged, and driven to toil by day and by night, without the shadow of right or justice, without the consolation and revivifying influences of intelligence and of the gospel, and not suffer from the baneful effects of this hideous wrong. You at the North cannot suffer this dark enormity to be perpetrated, without suffering the consequences. And one of the consequences will be that your limbs will be stricken down at your side, your thoughts fettered, yourselves deprived of the freedom of action.—No man is really free south of Mason & Dixon's Line, but the slaveholder. And soon no man north of Mason & Dixon's Line will be free but he who will succumb to the demands of the slaveholders.

I speak rather by sight then by hearing.—The objects of the slaveholding party are becoming open to the sight. They are five in number. The first is the suppression of all anti-slavery discussion. The second, the extension of Slavery over all the Territories of the United States. Every one of my hearers who is a political reader knows that I have facts to bear me out in asserting this to be the policy of the South. The third is, the nationalization of Slavery in every State of the Union, so as to do away with all Conventions, Associations, and discussions of an anti-slavery character, and abolish everything tending to disturb the relations between the master and the slave. The fourth is, the expatriation of every free citizen of color in the United States. Ten millions of dollars is the amount of money which is to be devoted to bringing about this result. The fifth and grand object is, the absorption by the

United States, of Mexico, Southern California, Cuba, the Sandwich Islands, all the islands of the Caribbean Sea, and Nicaragua, bringing them into the Confederacy of our Union, and placing their black population, fourteen millions in number, under the ban of the slave power.—Let us look this in the face. What is necessary to secure all their aims and objects? Why, first, this anti-slavery agitation must be put down. And unfortunately, most unfortunately for the ends of right, liberty and justice, both the Whig party and the Democratic Party have lent themselves to the Slave Power, to engage in putting it down. This was the determination of these parties on that point, as expressed in the Platforms put forth by them at Baltimore. They would resist agitation—noblest patriot in the American Republic.—They would read out Horace Greeley, that champion of the rights of free men, to accomplish this end. The Democratic Party proposes to go as far or a little farther than the Whig party on this point. It is strong and nervous in its declarations, and strong as thunder in its action. It says it will not only resist agitation, but it will assist in putting down agitation.—That is the decision of the Democratic National Party. Now, what does putting down agitation mean? It means putting down the right of speech on a particular subject in this Republic. It means closing the mouth of all those who utter principles designed to operate to the injury of the slave power. Remember, this was a political, not an individual declaration, A political declaration differs from an individual declaration in this—that it is supposed to be capable at some time of being crystalized, of being molded into a law of the land. *They mean to put down agitation.* How will they put it down? How have they put it down already in the Southern States? By making every statement uttered in opposition to the slave power an incendiary sentiment. These parties, then, acted in obedience to that law of the South when they said they intended to put down agitation. The question now is, fellow-citizens, are you quite ready to give up to the South your right of speech? Are you quite ready to relinquish to a section the right of the discussion of any particular political subject? For if you give up the right in regard to slavery to-day, you may have to give it up for something else to-morrow. Experience has taught us that the Southern slaveholders are capable of any action, and you know not what they may next demand of you.

This right of speech was once regarded as a very precious institution in our country. It was looked upon as the sentinel on the outer bulwarks of Liberty. Daniel Webster so regarded it in a speech made by him in Congress in 1814, when he declared that it was a principle he should assert to the last—that he should relinquish it only when he relinquished his life.—That living he should assert the right or dying, he should transmit to posterity the honor of a brave defense. He had not then forgotten that this right is sacredly guaranteed in the Constitution of the United States, in the Constitution of every State in our Union.

Well, the two great political parties have found that the free exercise of the right of speech is incompatible with Southern feelings and interests—that it disturbs our Southern brethren. So they have, therefore, in their kindness attempted to give peace to the slaveholders. They have endeavored to do what God in his infinite wisdom has decreed that it shall be impossible to do. "There shall be no peace to the wicked, saith my God."

This is a confession that the exercise of free speech is incompatible with the relations of master and slave. It is a tacit admission of guilt. Innocence has nothing to fear from discussion. It folds its arms and throws itself open to the severest scrutiny. It is only the dark wing of iniquity that seeks to burrow out of sight—to hide itself from the observation of man. It was said by Junius of Lord Granville that his character would only pass without censure so long as it passed without observation. Such is the case with Slavery. With it, observation and censure are synonymous. Therefore, they aim to put down all discussion. If it were possible for the South to do so, it would disband every anti-Slavery organization in the land. Still, the slaveholders would have no peace. For down in the heart of every one of them, God has planted an abolition lecturer, which is continually saying to him, "Thou art verily guilty in regard to thy brother." Cowper was quite right, after all, in regard to slavery, when he said:

> I would not have a slave to till my ground,
> To fan me when I sleep,
> My heart would throb at every sound.

I have experienced slavery in my own person. Before I formed a part of this living, breathing world, the scourge was plaited for my back. and the fetter forged for my limb. But though my blood still burns, and my heart bounds as I look back to those dark days of slavery, I would rather at this moment exchange places with the veriest whipped slave of the South, than the wealthiest slaveholder of that region. He can have no peace. His mind must be constantly casting up mire and dirt. You can see him gather up his bowie-knife and revolver and place them under his pillow at night. That bowie-knife is intended to pierce the heart of the slave, and that revolver to scatter his brains to the four winds of Heaven. But they first pierce the heart of the slave owner's happiness, and scatter his peace to the winds, ere they reach the poor slave. The slaveholder can know no peace. There is no safeguard for the South save in the preservation of the relations of master and slave. Just let it be rumored that ten slaves have been overheard to say that they are tired of being flogged, and they mean to fight, and the whole South is in a tremor. —This is why the South wish you to give up the right of free speech.

Let us view the encroachments of the slave power in another light. The Constitution of the United States provides that in all cases at law where the value of the property concerned is more than twenty dollars, trials by jury shall be provided. The South has found that this will not do. It has found that there is a species of property in the South which must not come under this jury definition. Congress passed such a law in 1850, in the shape of the fugitive slave bill. The writ of *habeas corpus* was formerly regarded as a most valuable provision. It provided for the delivery from imprisonment of any person, unless good cause was shown for his detention. The Constitution provides that this writ of *habeas corpus* shall not be suspended, unless when, in cases of rebellion or riot, the public good requires it. —But it has been found to be in opposition to the designs of the slave power, and the two grand parties have united together, and declared that it shall be nullified. The presumption of the law formerly was, that every man is free until he is proved to be otherwise. But now, the slave power, bold and arrogant, has asserted the contrary principle. Every colored man, under the Fugitive Slave Bill, is presumed to be a slave unless he proves himself to be otherwise.

A pure and unbribed judiciary used to be thought something of here in the North. But slavery demands something else. And in the Fugitive Slave enactment it has secured its demands. It demands and provides that when a judge shall convict any prisoner of being a slave, or in other words, of being worthy of imprisonment for life, he shall receive the sum of $10. But if, on the contrary, he acquits the prisoner, he is to receive only $5. Isn't that a "Hail, Columbia, happy land," provision?

Mr. Douglass then proceeded to establish the position that the Slave States demand that the North shall execute their laws, and cited the case of Passmore Williamson in proof.[31] He contended that Mr. W. had committed no crime. He had broken no law of Pennsylvania, but was incarcerated for breaking the laws of Virginia. He dwelt upon the provisions of the Fugitive enactment, which decrees that there shall be "no refuge for the stricken slave thro' the length and breadth of this fair land—no spot upon which he can plant his foot and say, 'Here, by the blessings of God's Providence, and my own right, I am a free man.' " He contended that the nation is at present in a state of anarchy—that the government of the United States has resigned its functions to three thousand lawless border ruffians of Missouri.[32]—A struggle has gone on in that territory [Kansas] and it has resigned its ballot-boxes and its liberties with an ease which puts to shame the fighting before Sebastopol. The reason is obvious. The walls at Sebastopol are of granite. The walls of Kansas are of *dough!*[33] . . . facetiousness upon the attempts being made to drive the free colored men out of the country. He says they do not mean to go to Liberia, if they can avoid it. On this point we are somewhat in the position of the boy John when he was going to visit his Uncle Robert. Said he, "I am going to Uncle Robert's. I am going to stay six weeks. And I am going to do just as I please—that is, if Uncle Robert will let me." We intend to remain in this country—*if you will let us.* And although there is physical force enough here to drive us out, I do not think there is *moral force* enough to do it. So we may embody our sentiments in the old song which they used to sing at camp meetings:

> Bredren, we hab been wif you,
> And still is wif you,
> And mean to be wif you to the end!

He argued at some length upon the ground that prejudice against color was not natural, but conventional, and quoted many happy anecdotes to strengthen his position. On retiring he said: "I am thankful for your kindness in listening to me, and beg you not to forget in the playfulness of my last remarks, the sober earnestness of the first."

*Frederick Douglass' Paper,* September 14, 1855

# COLORED AMERICANS, AND ALIENS—T. F. MEAGHER

If native born colored Americans experienced the same treatment at the hands of the National and State governments, as aliens do, we should not have so much about which to murmur and complain. We are, some of us, descendants of those, who, fought for our country, who bled for it, and died for it. Let us be treated as well as the sons of those who fought against it. We are victims, even here in the "free North," of a relentless hate. Everything is done to crush out our vitality. In the Southern States we are placed in the same category with horses, sheep, and other cattle, to be sold to the highest purchaser. Here in New York, we are looked upon as half-sheep, and half-horses, and of course, denied the rights of *men*. These Rights we demand; these Rights we intend to have.

We say unto our white fellow-citizens; treat us as well as you treat the foreigners swarming in your midst, those who *fill* your jails, and alm-houses *as well as build them.*

We see that Mr. Thomas F. Meagher, one of the Irish repealers who emigrated to this country from Van Diemen's Island, has been admitted to practise as an attorney and counsellor in all the Courts of this State, by a special order of the Supreme Court. Mr. Meagher is not a citizen of the United States, and was not eligible to a regular examination. But the Judge, taking into consideration the fact of his being an Irishman, and one, too, who had not meddled with the "peculiar Institution," admits him by *courtesy.*

Now, we have not one word to utter about the admission of Mr. Meagher, on the account of his being an Irishman. We call attention to the fact; and ask those who voted against us on the equal suffrage question, to consider it, and contrast it with the fact of our treatment. The colored man, the native born American receives nothing by "courtesy." He lives and breathes in one continual storm, and walks through a wilderness of sorrow and of toil. —We receive nothing by "courtesy," gentlemen. Now, why should we be treated *so much worse* than aliens, and the sons of aliens? We ask the question. Who, among our ostracizers, will answer it? Are we not as virtuous, as honest, as useful, and as intelligent as they?—Let the jails and the poor houses answer the question.

We hope that when the question of Equal Suffrage shall again be presented to the consideration of the citizens of this State, they will ponder well upon the impracticability (to use no stronger term) of extending to aliens, rights and privileges, denied to their own fellow-citizens. At the polls, we were defeated on this very question, by the Irish, who rushed, as it were, *en masse* to the ballot-box, and impudently declared that *we should not have equal rights* with them. Look to it, fellow-citizens, that they triumph not again. Probably, they will have something else to attend to *now*, as *they*, too, are to come in for a share of proscription, if Know Nothingism[34] succeeds in its cruel exactions. A fellow feeling should make us wondrous kind. We throw this remark to those *"foreigners"* who proscribed *us* at the polls.

But we are told that we are not citizens!—Well; all we have to say in reply to this absurd declaration, is, if we are not, we ought to be. *We have been in the country long enough to entitle* us to all the rights and immunities of citizenship, having been born on the soil. The colored man cannot be an alien for aliens, we believe, are not born in the country. He cannot be naturalized as foreigners only are naturalized. Not a citizen, not an alien! In the name of the Constitution, what is he?

We hope our Irish fellow-citizens who despise this proscriptive spirit, will take no exception to these remarks, but let them exert their influence in bringing their brethren to a proper apprehension of the reciprocal duties and obligations, existing between man and his fellow.

*Frederick Douglass' Paper,* September 14, 1855

# THE VARIOUS PHASES OF ANTI-SLAVERY

All men desire Liberty. They desire to possess this inalienable birthright themselves, if they are not concerned about others being the recipients of its countless blessings. They instinctively shrink from the idea of having their Intellectual, their Moral, and their Physical organism, subjugated to the entire control of Tyranny, clothed in the vesture of assumed superiority. This love of their own identity is inseparably connected with their desire and hope of immortality. And even those who attack the citadel of man's personality, and seek to reduce him to a thing, are jealous of any invasion of their own Rights, and will resist to the death any encroachment upon the sacred domain of their own personal liberty. They are Abolitionists, as they seek to abolish any system of Oppression *which has them* for its victims, even though they trample their own principles in the dust, when the Rights of others are invaded. This is neither just nor generous. No man should crave the possession of that which he assiduously endeavors to withhold from another.

Again, we maintain that no man has a Right to make any concession to Tyranny, which he would refuse to make if *he* were the victim.—He has no Right to make any compromise of contract in reference to the "Institution" of slavery, as it is falsely called, which he would be unwilling to make, were he, himself the slave. He should place himself, as it were, in the position of the slave, and advocate those principles and measures, which, judging from his stand-point, he would deem just and advisable.

Now, we hold that there is but one class of men and women in the land, who stand upon the slave's platform, and advocate the principles and measures which he would advocate, had he the opportunity. Abolitionism in this country is a sort of heterogeneous compound. It is composed, too, of certain elements, some of which are totally dissimilar. They have no affinity, in some respects, the one for the other; and the lack of homogeneousness must, in some way, be supplied, before a perfect fusion, or commingling of the elements can be effected.

We have the Free Soil, or Republican Party,[35] as the representative of Principles and Measures which are themselves totally distinct, and diverse from those which are advocated with so much zeal and ability by those who rejoice in the cognomen of Garrison Abolitionists. Then we have the Radical Abolitionists, who profess to believe the Principles and Measures adverted to, unsound, unjust, impracticable, and, of course, wholly intenable.

What, then are the distinctive features of these respective organizations? Wherein do they differ? What do they propose to accomplish? Let us briefly examine them. This is the Age of Inquiry, of deep, sober, rational Investigation. All systems, and opinions, and creeds, and Institutions, which cannot withstand the ordeal of the most rigid Investigation, cannot, at this crisis, find a lodgment in the popular heart; they cannot receive the approving smiles of the popular conscience.

First, then we have the Free Soil, or Republican Party. This is a powerful Party, so far as numbers and influence is concerned, and is sweeping over the country with restless efficacy. What are *its* characteristics? The Principle which imparts vitality to the Republican organization, is, simply, the *Non-Extension of Slavery*. Its motto is, "No Slavery Outside the Slave States." It proposes to restrict Slavery, and keep it within what is called its *constitutional limits*. It does not propose to interfere with Slavery where it already exists, but seeks to prevent the spread of the infectious malady. It virtually concedes to slaveholders, the constitutional right of plundering their helpless victims and plundering them as long as they are able, *provided they do so in a certain locality*. In a word, it proceeds upon the gratuitous assumption of the legality and constitutionality of Slavery, and, at the same time, seeks to relieve the Federal Government from all responsibility for its existence or continuance. It thunders in the ear of the Government, the declaration that "Slavery is Sectional; Liberty, National." Not one of its leading advocates, so far as we have any knowledge, has ever intimated a desire in public, to abolish Slavery, by Legislation; thus to strike off the fetters of the three millions and a half of men, women, and children, *who are the present victims of the insatiate rapacity of American Despotism*. To intimate such an intention would place them in advance of the party with which they are identified. They, indeed, hate Slavery, and affirm, that by surrounding the slave States with a girdle of Freedom, Slavery will eventually die, for lack of room and air in which to breathe. This, we believe, is a fair and impartial statement of the position of the Free Soil, or Republican Party. If we have erred in stating its true position, we have done so unintentionally, and stand ready to be corrected.

Secondly, we have another body of Anti-Slavery men in the country, who style themselves Garrison Abolitionists. These, too, are powerful, if not in numbers, in the array of talent, wealth, and energy, at their command.—The motto of the Garrison party, is "no union with slaveholders." They affirm the Constitution of the United States to be pro-Slavery in its character, and therefore denounce it, as "an agreement with Death and a covenant with Hell." They are opposed to *political action, for the Abolition of Slavery,* and refuse to vote for the officers of the Government, because of the alleged pro-Slavery character of the Constitution, by which it professes to be guided in its administration. Its dis-union sentiments were thus distinctly stated at an annual meeting of the Pennsylvania Anti-Slavery Society, convened in the city of Philadelphia, Oct. 25th, '52:

*Resolved.* That, independent of all questions as to the meaning of particular clauses of the Constitution, and whether it be admitted or denied that it contains certain guarantees for the benefit of slavery, the effort to establish a union between States that are slaveholding and States that are free must in the nature of things be abortive, since the legislation demanded by the former is diametrically opposed to that required by the latter; and therefore we reiterate the doctrine of the American Anti-Slavery Society, 'No Union with Slaveholders.'

At the same meeting W. Lloyd Garrison thus stated the position of those who occupy the Platform of the American Anti-Slavery Society. Said he:

The position of this Society upon the Constitution is well known. We hold that it contains certain wicked compromises of the rights of the Slave. It gives the Slaveholders a political representation for their slaves, thus bribing them to hold and multiply their human chattels. I cannot swear to give such power to Slaveholders. Does our Declaration of Sentiment require me to do it? On the contrary, the principles and spirit forbid such an oath.—So of the obligation to put down a slave insurrection and return fugitive slaves. To be faithful to the principles of that Declaration, I must stand outside of the government organized upon pledges to do such acts. So if I find that the church of which I am a member, is pro-slavery, as I recognize its Christian character by that membership, I must stand outside the church.

So much then, for the position of the Garrison Abolitionists. They are *in* the country, but at the same time, they profess to stand outside of the Government. But this is not all. The Free Soil or Republican Party says, "Let *Slavery* take care of its own interests." The Garrison Party, through one of the most eloquent exponents of its theory, virtually tells the Slave to take care of *himself.* This may seem to be an unjust and ungenerous assertion. But what says one of the most able advocates of the disunion movement. Hear him:

All the slave asks of us, is to stand out of the way, withdraw our pledge to keep the peace on the plantation; withdraw our pledge to return him, withdraw that representation which the Constitution gives in proportion to the number of slaves, and without any agitation here, without any individual virtue, which the times have eaten out of us, God will vindicate the oppressed, by the laws of justice which he has founded, Trample under foot your own unjust pledges, break in pieces your compact with hell by which you become the abettors of oppression. Stand alone, and let no cement of the Union bind the slave, and he will right himself.

The idea of the slave righting himself, presupposes his ability to do so, unaided by Northern interference. O no! the slave *cannot* "right himself" any more than an infant can grapple with a giant. He must receive the effective aid of those who, at the North, are, despite their denial, the members of the confederacy, and, as such, "verily guilty concerning their brother."

But we have another Anti-Slavery or Abolition Party, the Liberty Party, or Radical Abolitionists. Who are they? What do they propose to effect?

They deny that Slavery can be legalized, and, therefore, affirm that all slaveholding enactments are illegal. They also deny that the Constitution of the United States is a pro-slavery instrument, and affirm that it is, legitimately, susceptible only, of an Anti-Slavery interpretation. They regard it as having been established for the express purpose of establishing justice, &c., and of securing the blessings of Liberty to all the people of the Confederacy, not merely one class of People, but the whole, *we,* the people, as well as *you,* or *they,* the People. Radical Abolitionism asserts, that if the various provisions of the Constitution, (right of trial by Jury, *habeas corpus,* and others,) were faithfully executed, it would instantly free every Slave in the land. All they ask, is, that the present Constitution, imperfect as it is, shall receive a righteous, a correct interpretation, that its manifold provisions be executed, and Slavery will find no refuge under it.

Radical Abolitionism lays the axe at the root of the tree. It proposes not only to hew down the Upas Tree, but to tear it up root and branch. It believes that the Federal Government has the power to abolish Slavery everywhere in the United States, and that such is the duty of the Government. They are opposed to a dissolution of the Union, *unless a Southern Confederacy could be organized in which there would be no abolitionists, white or black, and a Northern Confederacy, in which there would be no apologists for Slavery.* By withdrawing from the Slave States, we withdraw from nearly four millions of Abolitionists, black and white. And on the other hand, we retain in our midst some of the most influential supporters of the traffic in human flesh. These are some of the leading views entertained by Radical Abolitionists. We believe them to be just, tenable, and practicable; and thus believing, can conscientiously give our adhesion and our support to no other.—Of their ultimate triumph, we have not the shadow of a doubt. We know they are regarded as impracticable. But those who assume their impracticability, pronounced, a few years ago, the same judgment upon the views they now cherish so ardently, and promulgated with so much zeal and ability. They even deprecated the idea of any agitation, whatever, upon the subject. And we do not despair of yet congratulating them upon their admission into the ranks of Radical Abolitionists. We shall, therefore, contribute our mite toward effecting this desirable consummation.

*Frederick Douglass' Paper,* November 16, 1855

# TO GERRIT SMITH

Rochester, Jan. 1st, 1856

My Dear Friend:

Your letter has made quite a flutter among the long skirts, and I fear the consequences. Mrs. Gage seems to think that Mrs. Stanton[36] is not a match for you, and summons all the sisterhood to stand forth against the common foe. If but one in a thousand shall respond to her call, my poor paper will have little room for ought else than their contributions. I shall publish Mrs. Stanton's this week, and draw the curtain. In truth, I think you were a little hard upon us all in that letter. Yet I cannot say more against it, than that it was the truth overstrongly stated. I have just returned from a short tour in Ohio. I have had good meetings.

Accept from me the heartiest compliments of the Season, for yourself and Dear family.

Yours most truly,
Frederick Douglass

I leave home to spend a month lecturing in Maine, Saturday.

*Gerrit Smith Papers, George Arents Research Library, Syracuse University*

## TO WILLIAM LLOYD GARRISON ESQR.

Springfield, Mass., Jan. 13th, 1856

Mr. Garrison:

Sir. I find the following from your pen in the last number of the "Standard," copied into that paper from the "Empire," published in London, England, and Edited by George Thompson, Esqr.

My object in calling your attention to this last effort to injure, is respectfully to ask you, (if not incompatible with your chosen mode of dealing with me), to point out in the pages of My Bondage and My Freedom, the offensive portions of the Book to which you refer, that the readers of the *"Standard"* and the *"Empire"* may read and judge for themselves, of the justice of your denunciations.[37]

Respectfully yours,
Frederick Douglass

*Anti-Slavery Collection, Boston Public Library*


## TO MRS. WALLINGFORD

New Market, Jan. 28th, 1856

Dear Mrs. Wallingford:

I am sorry that the snowdrifts of Maine, which entirely blocked the wheels of travel last week, made it impossible for me to spend yesterday in Dover, and further, prevented me from expressing to you in person, my sincere thanks for the valuable addition, Mrs. Adams, Kate, & yourself and perhaps, others—including Dear Mr. Wallingford, have been pleased to make to my wardrobe. It would have given me some pleasure to have appeared in my New Suit at Dover, but failing of this, I take the Liberty of reminding of my grateful appreciation of your kindness and continued interest in my welfare, prosperity and happiness. I esteem you among my earliest anti-slavery friends and whatever differences may arise in respect to men or measures I hope our friendship will ever survive.

Please remember me kindly to Mr. Wallingford, to Miss Kate, and especially to your kind sister, Mrs. Adams.

I shall not be able to lecture in Dover before I return to my home in the West, and probably not again before next fall.

I am, Dear Madam,

With Best wishes for your Health and happiness,

Your faithful friend,

Frederick Douglass

*Ms., New Hampshire Historical Society*

## SLAVERY UNCONSTITUTIONAL

Whether or not the Constitution of the United States is a pro-slavery document, is a question, the decision of which is of vast importance, as deeply affecting the interests of the great cause in which we are engaged. The majority of the people of the United States affirm that Slavery has *unconstitutional* existence. Some affirm that the Constitution *does* sanction Slavery, others, that it *intended* to sanction it.—On the other hand there are some who distinctly deny these assertions, and affirm that the Constitution "contains no designation, description or necessary admission of the existence of such a thing as slavery, servitude, or the right of property in man." It will be admitted by all, that the Constitution itself does not contain the words slave or slavery, that it contains no *distinct* recognition of the right of property in man. The pro-slavery interpretation of the instrument is wholly dependent upon inferences, implications, assumptions, and imputations, all of which are peremptorily forbidden by the well established rules of legal interpretation. These imperatively require, that in our interpretation of this document, we must confine ourselve strictly to the words of the instrument and not wander amid the fertile region of intentions and inferences.—We have to do with these intentions, only so far as they are collected from the words of the Constitution. The Supreme Court of the United States, has laid down the following rule: "Where rights are infringed, where fundamental principles are overthrown, where the general system of the laws is departed from, the legislative intention must be expressed with *irresistible clearness,* to induce a design to effect such objects."

No one has the hardihood to affirm that the sanction of American Slavery is "expressed" in the Constitution "with irresistible clearness."—Mark the phraseology. "Expressed with irresistible clearness." The casual reader is not apt to attach that importance to the word "expressed," in this rule, which legally belongs to it. In law, we are told, that a thing is said to be expressed, "when it is *uttered, or written out, embodied in distinct words,* in contradistinction to its being inferred, *implied,* or gathered from evidence exterior to the words of the law."

If this be true, this rule disallows the imputation of an unjust intention to the law, unless it be denominated in the bond; it must be expressed or written out so plainly, that he who runs, may read it. If the "fathers" intended that the Constitution should sanction the atrocious wickedness of dealing in new-born babes, very unfortunately for them, they failed to make their intention sufficiently clear. This intention to chattelize the image of God, is one thing: the *expressed* record of that intention, is another. No such record appears in the Constitution, and we have neither the time nor the desire to go outside of the instrument, and hunt up evidence to prove that they were both liars and traitors.

But again; another very important rule of legal interpretation is, "that where the prevailing principles and provisions of a law are favorable to justice, and general in their nature and terms, no *unnecessary exception* to them, or to their operation, is to be allowed." The law requires that an exception to a rule, be stated, with as much distinctness as the rule itself, or it cannot be established. The question natural[38] . . . exception in favor of slavery, in compliance with this principle? There is none whatever.—Where is the exceptional word? Where, the "provided," or "nevertheless," or "except," or "however," or any word of this character?—Yet, despite the stubborn fact, that the Constitution contains no proviso, no word of exception, &c., Slaveholders, their apologists, and, strange to say, the mass of professed Anti-Slavery men, make two exceptions of the most flagrant character. "One of these exceptions," says Lysander Spooner,[39] is an exception of principle, substituting injustice and slavery, for "justice and liberty." The other is an exception of *persons;* excepting a part of *"the people of the United States"* from the rights and benefits which the instrument professes to secure to the whole; and exposing them to wrongs, from which the people generally are exempt.

Now we solemnly inquire, what right has any man or any class of men in the country, or out of it, to adduce any argument for slavery, *making* these exceptions to the Constitution? In other words what right have Slave-holders, or any other class of men, to substitute injustice and slavery, for justice and liberty? The results to be attained by the adoption of the Constitution, are plainly set forth in its preamble. Are injustice and slavery placed in the category?—If not, why attempt to force them therein.—*Cui bono?* And with regard to the other exception, that of excluding a portion of the people of the United States, from an equal participation in the rights and immunities guaranteed to the whole people by the organic law of the Nation, is there anything in the phrase, "the people of the United States," of an exceptional or exclusive character? Then why substitute "a *part* of the people" for "*the people?*"

But we must not dwell longer on this point. Let us glance at another rule of legal interpretation, viz., that we are to be guided, in doubtful cases, by the Preamble.

The Preamble is regarded as indicative of the import of what is to follow, when there is any doubt or ambiguity as to its precise or definite meaning. Even admitting, for the sake of argument, that the real meaning of the Constitution in respect to Liberty were involved in doubt, the doubt is at once dissipated by the Preamble, which reads as follows:

"We. the people of the United States, in order to form a more perfect union, establish justice, insure domestic tranquility, provide for the common defense, promote the general welfare, and secure the blessings of liberty to ourselves and our posterity, do ordain and establish this Constitution for the United States of America!"

Noble objects to be accomplished! Glorious results to be attained! but it is well known, that certain clauses in the Constitution have been claimed as sanctioning Slavery. We are bound by the rule of interpretation now under consideration, to determine the meaning of these clauses by the Preamble. This being the test, it is plainly seen, that there is in them no sanction of the inhuman traffic in human flesh, no recognition, whatever, of the right of property in man. "Justice" and "liberty" are among the declared objects of the Constitution. If the Preamble has no meaning, neither has any portion of the Constitution; for, (as Story remarks,) "we find it laid down in some of our earliest authorities in the common law, and civilians are accustomed to a similar expression, *cessante legis pramio, cessat et ipsa lex.* (The preamble of the law ceasing, the law itself ceases.)"

To suppose that one portion of this instrument sanctions Slavery, and another sanctions liberty, is to array the Constitution in conflict with itself. And this brings us to the consideration of another rule of interpretation, which is, that one part of an instrument must not be allowed to contradict another unless the language be so explicit as to make the contradiction inevitable." No one will fail to discover, that if the Constitution sanctions Slavery, it would be full of contradictions; for it cannot be shown that this instrument has made any exception to its general provisions restricting the sphere of their operations to a part of "we, the people."

Again; if we had no other foundation to stand upon, so far as the rules of legal interpretation are concerned we might stand upon the following, and feel secure. In the interpretation of the Constitution, we must not forget that "all reasonable doubts must be decided in favor of liberty." Where rights are infringed, where fundamental principles are overthrown, where the general system of the laws is departed from, the legislative intention must be expressed with *irresistible clearness* to induce a court of justice to suppose a design to effect such objects. — Now, admitting that the Constitution is susceptible of two constructions, one in favor of Liberty, another, in favor of Slavery; and suppose it *was* the intention of "our fathers," to give constitutional sanction to Slavery. What follows? This "sum of all villainies," certainly constitutes an infringement of man's natural rights; and as the despotic "intention" of these "liberty-loving fathers" is *not* expressed with "*irresistible clearness*," their meaning, therefore, is involved in reasonable doubt, and the rule requires that "*All reasonable doubts must be decided in favor of Liberty.*" This, then is sufficient, for our purpose. Contrary to this rule of interpretation—rule not arbitrary, but inflexible—these "reasonable doubts," are decided not only by pro-Slaverymen, in favor of Slavery.

But we must not devote too much of our space this week, to the consideration of this all important subject. We propose to continue its discussion, until we think we have clearly proved what we affirmed in the outset, that the Constitution can only, by a forced construction, be made to "sanction" the hell-black business of breeding men and women, like the beasts that perish.

*Frederick Douglass' Paper,* February 1, 1856

# MORE AGITATION: ANOTHER MESSAGE FROM THE PRESIDENT

A considerable portion of our present issue is occupied with what purports to be a message from the President of the United States. A baser document never emanated from the Presidential chair. It is, from beginning to end an atrocious falsification of the history of Kansas affairs,[40] which no honest man in the country will fail to regard with unutterable loathing, and burning indignation. Quite warlike in its tone, it was evidently written for the purpose of terrifying the Free State men in Kansas, and bringing them in subjugation to the tyrant will of Atchison, Stringfellow, and their ignoble coadjutors.

The President is, doubtless, "very wroth," but there is method in his madness. He has not thrust another bombshell into the camp without consideration. He is somewhat solicitous to *remain* in a position, in which he can have a golden opportunity of ministering to the necessities of those whose interests he seems to have so much at heart. He doubtless, hopes to secure the nomination at Cincinnati, but the hope of the wicked, we are told, shall perish.

But how will the non-agitators regard this ridiculous ebullition of Presidential wrath?—Will *they* be satisfied with this renewed attempt to fan the flames of discord, and intensify the hostility already developing itself in "sectional agitations?" If they are content that he shall thus forfeit his claim to the title of "National President" which has been thrust upon him, surely a most marvellous change has come over the spirit of their dreams.

But to this remarkable Message: Mr. Pierce professes to find an apology for insulting the country so soon after his recent *pronunciamento,* in "the circumstances which have occurred to disturb the course of governmental organization in the territory of Kansas," and then proceeds to give what he is pleased to describe a "brief expostion" of these circumstances, and also to recommend an appropriation of the public money to be expended in "crushing out" the spirit of Freedom in the newly settled territory. A considerable portion of this "intensely border ruffian" Message, is occupied with a gross assault upon Governor Reeder and abuse of the people of the Free States who encouraged emigration to Kansas, for the avowed purpose of making it a Free State; and the President assigns as a reason for the removal of the former from the office of Executive Magistrate of the Territory, his delay in organizing the Territorial Government. It would, we dare say, have been quite congenial with the wishes of the present successor of Washington, if the territory had been organized, (as the projectors and official supporters of the bill intended), when a handful of Presidential lackeys, called Government officers and a few border ruffians could have arranged everything to suit their own convenience.

He regards such emigration as an "unjustifiable interference" on the part of Free State emigrants and stongly insinuates that hanging would be too good for them. He is, however, forced to admit that even this unjustifiable interference was not sufficient to justify the action of the Missouri Ruffians, whose cause he advocates with more zeal than ability. but it is quite inconsistent on the part of the President, after designating the counter movements of the Border Ruffians as "illegal and reprehensible," to give them his sanction and support and threaten to enforce, by the aid of the militia under his control, the enactments which are but the offspring of these illegal demonstrations. Mr. Pierce assumes and endeavors to establish the legality of the Ruffians' Legislature, and after recognizing the election of Whitfield, pounces upon the Free State Convention, like one fresh from the battlefield, denouncing the movement of the Free State men as rebellion and treason and promising to have the rebels shot whenever the exigency of the case shall require it, or whenever his Southern brethren shall deem advisable. After a few rhetorical flourishes concerning the "inflammatory agitation which for twenty years, has produced nothing save unmitigated evil, North and South," (is he an agitator?) he proposes that "when the inhabitants of Kansas may desire it, and shall be of sufficient numbers to constitute a State, a convention of delegates, duly elected by the qualified voters shall assemble to frame a Constitution, and thus to prepare, through regular and lawful means, for its admission into the Union as a State," and recommends a law to that effect. We have no doubt that a speedy admission of Kansas into the Union as a slave State would meet his decided approbation, but we are told, that some things can be done as well as others, and believe that the threats of the President to shoot down the Free State men will not intimidate those who are laboring to prevent what would be to him a "consummation devoutly to be wished." We shall see what we shall see.

*Frederick Douglass' Paper*, February 1, 1856

# PROSPECTUS
## of the
## NINTH VOLUME OF
## FREDERICK DOUGLASS' PAPER,
### Published at Rochester, N.Y.
### Frederick Douglass, Editor and Proprietor.
### Wm. J. Watkins, Assistant Editor.

The increased activity of the Pro-Slavery Propaganda demands on the part of the advocates of Human Liberty renewed exertions. The Slave Power never, never slumbers; nor should the friends of Freedom. No one can now plead ignorance of the startling events which stamp our country's history with deathless infamy. Slavery is indeed developing itself. Its character is emblazoned upon the blackened brow, in letters of blood.

No time could be more propitious than the present, for Anti-Slavery action. The great masses of the People are thinking for themselves. The wolfish cry of "fanaticism," which once deterred many from identifying themselves with the cause of Liberty, has lost its wonted potency. Men are thinking more of individual responsibility, and less of party predilections.—This almost miraculous change in public sentiment, has been effected through the continued agitation of *the great question of the age.*

It is to help on this thrilling, this Heaven-directed agitation, to help swell the tide of regenerated public sentiment, that *Frederick Douglass' Paper* has been established. Agitation is the life blood of all moral Reforms.—No one at all acquainted with the history and progress of any Reform, will deny this simple assertion.

We call, then, upon all who sympathize with us in our efforts to break the chains of our fellow-men, to help us pour out, in common with others, a flood of Light and Truth upon the great quesion, which shall, in its onward course, bear down all opposition, causing not only the oppressor to tremble, but the oppresssed to stand up in all the dignity of manhood, redeemed, regenerated, and disenthralled.

We think our paper has *a special claim* upon the advocates of Equal Rights. Owing to the inflexible exigency of our position, it is apparent to every reflecting mind, that circumstances over which we can have no control must come in conflict with the circulation.

Everything is done in the United States to crush the colored man. He has not an open field, and a fair fight. The Press and the Pulpit stand up in battle array, to oppose his progress, and precipitate his disastrous doom. The incentive held out before our white fellow-countrymen, to virtue, and wealth, and honor, are purposely withheld from the colored American. Yes, everything is done by *soi disant* Republicans, to drive back the development of his mental, moral being, and then in his face is contemptuously hurled the absurd allegation of inherent inferiority. He is excommunicated not only from the pale of American citizenship, but, virtually, from the pale of Humanity itself, and then, held up before the world as a connecting link between man and the brute creation; to make the best of him, a well-developed monkey. Strange as it may appear, while the dog, and the sheep, and the horse, regardless of their complexion, or conformation, find no difficulty in obtaining a recognition of their identity with their respective races, the colored man, in this enlightened country, (but no other,) is called upon by his fellow-man, to prove, by elaborate argument, his affinity with the *genus homo*.

We, then, reiterate the assertion that *Frederick Douglass' Paper* has a special demand upon all the friends of the Anti-Slavery movement, to rally around our standard, *and, by enrolling their names upon our subscription list*, to help us to do battle for the Right.

It is needless for us to enumerate, in a special manner, the Principles which it sustains, and the measures which it proposes and advocates.—It is sufficient to state, that it is a Journal devoted to the cause of Human Rights, generally, at home and abroad. It claims to be the especial advocate of the Liberties of the downtrodden People, with whom its editor, by complexion and position, is identified. It urges upon the American People the duty of immediately undoing the heavy burdens, leaving God to take care of the consequences. And while it rebukes the foul spirit of Caste which lives and breathes, and burns in this land of Equal Rights, it urges upon the nominally Free Colored man, the necessity and the duty of self-elevation. It holds that the colored man is a citizen of these U. States, and, as such, entitled to all the rights and immunities of other citizens, and is opposed to all wholesale movements for removing him from the land which invites to its shores the oppressed of the world.

It holds that the Constitution of the United States is an Anti-Slavery document, and should be so interpreted; that there is not constitutional slavery in the land, and therefore, the Slaveholder, *as such, has no Rights.* Its motto is Freedom National and Universal—Slavery, an Outlaw. Knowing no Law for Slavery, it regards all its enactments null and void, and of no binding authority whatever.

It is opposed to all secret political Parties, whether Protestant, or Catholic. It acts with the Liberty Party, or Radical Abolitionists, and will contribute its mite to the support of its Principles and Measures. We are now near the close of the Eighth Volume, and we are desirous of commencing our NINTH under as favorable auspices as possible.

In addition to our Assistant Editor, Wm. J. Watkins, we are favored with contributions from Dr. James McCune Smith, Prof. Geo. B. Vashon, W. J. Wilson, Rev. Wm. Watkins, John Mercer Langston, Esq., John U. Gaines, Esq.,[41] and others among the most cultivated colored citizens of the United States. We are, also, favored with communications from philanthropic white persons, engaged in our common cause. Mrs. Julia Griffiths, now on a visit to her native land, will, upon her return, continue to write the Literary Notices for this Paper.

## TERMS OF SUBCRIPTION

| | |
|---|---:|
| Single copy, one year | $2.00 |
| Three copies, one year | 5.00 |
| Five copies, one year | 8.00 |
| Ten copies, one year | 15.00 |
| Single copy, six months | 1.00 |
| Ten copies, six months | 8.00 |

Voluntary Agents are entitled to retain 50 cents commission on each new yearly subscriber, *except in the case of Clubs.*

*Frederick Douglass' Paper*, February 1, 1856

## TO MRS. WALLINGFORD

Rochester, March 14, 1856.

My dear friend:

You could not have regretted more than myself, my inability to reach Dover for a second lecture in February. For my own sake and for the *Cause's* sake, I would have been glad if the case had been otherwise. I had a warm, fresh word to utter there, in behalf of the slave and in behalf of universal freedom, which might have been of service. I wanted too to meet again yourself and other Dear friends, who have manifested an interest in my welfare and happiness, but the elements were against this and I was compelled to submit to their decision. This winter has found me abundant in Labor, and left me much work. I travelled during the winter about four thousand miles, and have delivered nearly Seventy Speeches to large meetings of the people. I have lectured in Maine, N. Hampshire, Massachusetts, R. Island— Conn.—New York, and Ohio. My extreme point in the east was Bangor, and in the west, Cincinnati. During my visit to Ohio, while at Painesville, I had the good fortune to spend an afternoon and evening with Mrs. N. P. Rogers and several of the children of our gifted friend now resting from his labors, where the treachery of professed friends, and the malice of open foes, are alike harmless. I had a very pleasant interview, and was much reminded both of sunny and shady moments spent with the same children and mother when the Father was living, and mantled us all in the bright sunshine or the pensive shades of his powerful mind and heart. I am to lecture this evening in Brockport, N. York about 20 miles from home. Pardon the brevity of this note—Love to Mr. Wallingford, to your sister, Mrs. Adams, and to all that love this cause of human progress in your Dear family and out of it in Dover. Yours most truly and with great respect,

Frederick Douglass

*Ms., New Hampshire Historical Society*

# TO MRS. TAPPAN

Rochester, March 21st, 1856

Dear Madam:

The notice of the death of Miss Weems, was already in my paper when your letter came. You will receive the dozen papers as you direct. You will be glad to know that Mr. Garnet is now in the United States, and that you may learn more from him of one in whom you have taken so lively an interest. I have now been at home about one week, and am resting a little from my winter's labors. I have travelled this winter between four and five thousand miles, visited communities as far east as Bangor, and as far West as Cincinnati, delivered about Seventy lectures, been in snow drifts oft, but have reached this season, always very trying to my health with nothing more serious than a sore throat which is now on the mend.

Please say to My good friend, your Husband, that I am very glad that his mind is for the present, especially directed to the Subject of enquiry; how can the condition of the free colored people be best improved? I am yet of the opinion that nothing can be done for the free colored people remaining in their present employment. These employments, such as waiting at Hotels, on Steamboats, Barbering in large cities, and the like, contribute to no Solid character. They require Servility, beget dependence, destroy Self reliance, and furnish pleasure and temptation to every possible vice, from smoking cigars to drinking whisky. What we want is Steady employment at respectable trades, or on the land. To this end if I had money, I would establish an industrial school to begin with, where the education of the hands and heart should be the main feature. I have now five colored Boys in My family, three my own children, and two adopted ones taken from the street. They have been with me nearly a year. They are good boys both, and may make good men, but if my paper should fail, they would be flung out of employment and I know not where they would find any other than those which would be sure to degrade them, and perhaps ruin them. A small amount of money expended in this direction, I mean, in securing places for colored boys to learn trades would bring good results. But I write in haste. I have not heard Mr. Finny for I have scarcely spent a Sabbath in the city this winter. Two Sundays ago, I had the high pleasure of hearing able discourse from Mr. Tappan's friend, Mr. Boynton, at Cincinnati. He made mention of the late tragedy in that city in his prayer in a manner wonderfully solemn and impressive. I hope to hear Mr. Finny on Sunday.

Yours with great respect,
Frederick Douglass

*Henry P. Slaughter Collection: Frederick Douglass, Sr., Papers, Trevor Arnett Library, Atlanta University*


## TO GERRIT SMITH

Rochester, April 12, 1856

My Dear Sir:

My throat is better, and for ten days I have been out on a lecturing tour. I am now quite hoarse, and am withal to lecture in Watertown, Jefferson Co. Tuesday and Wednesday of next week. My meetings are fully attended, and I believe make a good impression for the cause. I, however, find it hard work to get new subscribers, or to keep old ones, and my list has fallen off considerably from what it was last year. The coming presidential campaign will severely try and perhaps break down my paper. Radical abolitionism is too far ahead of these degenerate times to be well supported. I shall, however, nail my colors to the mast, and if I go down, it will be with all colors flying. I shall not be able to be present at our nominating convention in Syracuse. I have appointments in Ohio at that time. My presence there would be more important to myself than to anybody else. Upon this rely I shall stand by the action of the convention, unless it shall be less radical than I expect it will be. Please accept my thanks for your kind mention of me, to the assembled wisdom of the state in your speech on the Negro suffrage question.

With love to your Dear family,
Yours truly,
Frederick Douglass

*Gerrit Smith Papers, George Arents Research Library, Syracuse University*

# TO GERRIT SMITH

Rochester, May 1st, 1856.

My dear Friend:

Mrs. Douglass wishes me to tender her thanks for the Garden seed kindly sent from Peterboro. These are little things, but little things rather than large things, reveal the real qualities of the heart. I had to laugh right out when I saw that neat little bag so carefully enclosing a few seeds, intended to speak to senses already refined. We both thank Mrs. Smith and yourself, for remembering us in these nice little tokens. Did you notice Mr. Garrison's reply to Mr. Granger's speech?[42] It is full of sophistry. I have reviewed it in part in the paper just going to press. In doing so I have been more concerned for the argument than for the style. I have made free use of your ideas in my review. Yours most Truly,

Fred Douglass

*Gerrit Smith Papers, George Arents Research Library, Syracuse University*

# THE DANGER OF THE REPUBLICAN MOVEMENT

SPEECH Before the First National Nominating Convention of the Radical Abolition Party, Market Hall, Syracuse, New York, May 28, 1856

Mr. Chairman:

There are a great many people in this country, who have special reasons—special causes—for liking the sentiments of that Address.[43] I think that we have seldom had a document submitted to this country, or to any country from a political party, to be compared with the one to which we have listened this afternoon. Political parties have concerned themselves less, hitherto, with the principles of our common humanity, essential to the preservation of our own humanity, than with popular prejudices and cunning methods of securing power.

We have before us to-day, a document which begins with the truth so beautifully expressed by Elihu Burritt[44]—"The Fatherhood of God, and the Brotherhood of Man." Upon this truth we have a platform basis, as comprehensive as our humanity, as high as the throne of God, and as eternal as his immutable laws.

The Irishman listening to this address, might feel that it sprung from an Irish heart. The German listening to this Address, might feel that it spring from a German heart. The genuine American, born upon the soil, might feel that it sprung from an American heart; and surely the Negro with his woolly head and black skin, might feel that it might be the offspring of a Negro heart. I love that address, because it takes in the Negro.

I have had some temptation, as many have, to mingle in the immediate strife of the Republican issue, and presume I should have acted with them, could I have seen with them anything like a full recognition even of the humanity of the Negro. I have almost come to the conclusion that "no more slave territory," in the mouth of most of our Republican leaders, means no more Negroes, anyhow.[45] It certainly means no more Negroes in Kansas. Well, I don't want you to abolish Negroes just now! I, for one, am not disposed to be abolished just now. I want a place to stand in this world, and want to be doing something, and to meet with men and brethren looking towards the same end—the realization of the great idea of human truth and perfection, and the perfection of society. I think it would be quite easy to lose sight of the Negro, if it were not that some of us here have insisted upon holding up the Negro before the country.

The Anti-slavery movement—a movement undertaken for the abolition of slavery, for giving to four millions of human beings their freedom—is every hour liable to be entirely superseded by a movement to uphold the political strength of the North—to promote the freedom of *white* men, without in any way promoting the freedom of *black* men. And this is the danger of the Republican movement. Its design is— what? To put down the slave oligarchy in Kansas; to limit slavery to the states in which it is, and confine it there. When this is said, all is said. It does not even propose to emancipate the slaves in the District of Columbia, or to abolish the commerce in slaves between the different States. It does not aim at the abolition of slavery in the arsenals and forts that are under the control of the Federal Government. It aims simply to limit slavery, and drive it from one point; and that is Kansas and Nebraska.

Now, I say, that in looking at that movement, it seems to be a movement in open forgetfulness of the first great idea that inspired the anti-slavery movement. Our movement might have contemplated the freedom of white men collaterally; but the great end and aim of anti-slavery in this country, is and must be the abolition of American slavery. To leave slavery unfettered where is now exists, is to leave it with all the power which it has ever had, to protect and reproduce itself.

This Republican party cuts off, as I think, all hope of the abolition of slavery, by denying us the right to any of the powers of the General Government for the abolition of slavery. I wish to be particularly understood, here. That movement, by declaring that we are prohibited from interfering with slavery in the States, surrounds slavery by a wall, as it were of iron, and protects it from the shafts we hurl against it.

The slaves of this country can never be emancipated unless emancipated by forces extraneous to the southern States. Nothing short of the judgments of God, or interference from the outside of the southern States can ever put slavery down. Where are the forces to remove it from the slave States? Is there a literature in those States to effect this? No; it is expunged of everything tending to elevate and enlighten humanity.

Shall we look to their schools? No! These institutions are under the control of the slave power, and are ready to do its bidding.

Shall we look to the church? No! The church, alas! is also bound hand and foot, and cannot help us. Shall we look to the pulpit? The auction block and the pulpit are in the same neighborhood, and the gold gained by the sale of human flesh, goes to sustain the pulpit! The shaky head of slavery may be seen in every pulpit in the land, telling the minister what he shall preach, and what he shall not preach. If he comes to the passage:—"Woe unto him that keepeth back his neighbor's wages," he is commended to pass that by, and he does pass it by. If he comes to the passage—"Remember those that are in bonds as bound with them," he must keep that back, and he does keep it back. Or, if he comes to that most glorious rule—"All things whatsoever ye would that men should do unto you, do you even so unto them," he must pass that by. If he dares to quote it, and to say that because you would be free yourselves, you must make others free, he will soon find himself with a halter around his neck.

We cannot have freedom of speech in Congress, until slavery is abolished in the District of Columbia. So long as it exists there, waiters will continue to be shot down for insolence. And, by the way, men at the North don't generally know what insolence is, among slaveholders. But I happen to know; and have been punished for it more frequently than for any other crime. I was born insolent, and have always been insolent. Insolence, at the South, means presence of anything like manhood and consciousness of one's humanity. To look as though one thought himself a man—to lift his arm or his leg as if one thought himself a man, is insolence. I have been punished for insolence for answering, when asked why I had done a thing thus or so, that I thought it the best way. "Who gave you the right to think, you scoundrel!" was the reply. And when that Irish waiter dared to tell Herbert that the breakfast hour had passed, he was guilty of insolence, and punished with death for the act. And to this hour—I want the Irish to remember it—Herbert sits in his seat at Washington, lauded by Southerners for punishing that insolence. We are apt to think that the black servant is the only one that is looked down upon with contempt. But this is not so. The poor laboring white man of the South is looked down upon with as withering a contempt as a slave. And if you will not fight them you are despised as much as a slave. If there is one who, when smitten upon one cheek, will turn the other also to be smitten, these men are "the boys that will do it."

But as I was saying, the moral power that shall overthrow slavery, must come from quarters uncontaminated by that dark and withering curse. The idea which slavery generates is favorable to its continuance. It makes the slaveholder a helpless wretch, by placing him in possession of power and luxury, without his efforts, and depriving him of the incentives to industry. The condition upon which I have strong arms is that I use them. I can only have strength in that right arm, by bringing it into exercise. And slaveholders have no necessity for doing that. Night after night, the poor creatures toss about, unable to sleep. The sleep of the meanest slave in the South is more sweet than that of the slaveholder. His arms are weak—his fingers are depressed—his strength is gone; and he, of all creatures beneath the sky, appeals to us as being *incapable of taking care of himself*. He is rendered so lazy that he cannot consider the question of emancipation. "If," says he, "the slaves were to be emancipated, how could I get along without them?" The poor neighbor of the slaveholder, who is unable to own slaves himself, is kept in love of the system, by being allowed at times, the luxury of whipping a slave. He is sometimes called in, to administer a flogging to a slave; and as everyone wants to be above somebody else, they like the idea of slavery, and are opposed to emancipation, as it would place the slaves upon an equality with themselves. In this state of affairs it is impossible to hope that a regenerating power can be found in the slaveholding States themselves. The deliverer from American slavery, like the deliverer from spiritual slavery, must come from Heaven. Within the dark prison-house of bondage, we cannot look for a moral power sufficient to overthrow the system.

Now I believe it is our duty to hold up the great truth, that it is our right and intention to abolish slavery in the States—to abolish it everywhere—that it, is our purpose to abolish (it) in the States, because it exists in the States; and to abolish it, if we can, through the judiciary—through Congress, if we can—through moral means if we can; but to abolish it, any way. Slavery must come down; we have a right to abolish it. This, is no longer a mere Confederation of States. We are under a Constitution—a Constitution which I am glad to see so ably vindicated in the Address. This Constitution sets forth several propositions, which, if carried out, would abolish slavery. What are they? The Constitution declares its object to be "to form a more perfect Union." How can you form a more perfect Union with Slavery? Only by abolishing the Free States, entirely. There is no such thing as a perfect Union while we have both Liberty and Slavery! They are as opposite as light and darkness—as Heaven and Hell; and there can never be a real Union formed between the two. The only union that can be formed between them, is a union struggle between them, for the death of one or the other. Liberty must either cut the throat of Slavery, or have its own cut by Slavery.

And then, too, the Constitution proposes "to provide for the general welfare"—the welfare of the people. If the general welfare was cared for, would four millions be doomed to Slavery? Would two million women be left to the unbridled lust of three hundred and fifty thousand slaveholders? Would the marriage institution be annulled in fifteen States of the Union? Would the measureless wrongs of the Southern States be perpetrated, if the general welfare was provided for?

Then, too, one of the avowed objects of our Federal Constitution, is, "to establish Justice"—to render to every man his due; for such is Justice. There could be no slavery, if Justice were established; for slavery is a nameless injustice.

"To secure the blessings of liberty, to ourselves and our posterity." Some say this has a limited meaning, and does not apply to slaves. Some of our Garrisonian friends take the position that Negroes were not contemplated in that or any liberty clause of the Constitution; and since they were not, it is fraudulent and jesuitical for us to insist that the liberty clauses of the Constitution apply to colored people!

How strangely do our friends act towards us! Where is the necessity of making any such admission as this, in behalf of slavery? There is no necessity for it. The Constitution is declared to be established for the people. And who are the people? The men and women of the country. We are a part of the people; and it is the most unkind—I was going to say it was the most wicked—concession ever made to the slave power from any quarter, to admit that the Constitution does not apply at all to colored people.

The Constitution partakes of the spirit of that Address. It does not know anything of Irishmen, of Englishmen, of Germans, of white men or black men; but of *men*. It knows nothing of a north, south, east or west; but the *people*.

At the time of the adoption, of the Constitution of the United States, as every man who has made himself familiar with those times, knows, there was a strong anti-slavery feeling, which looked forward to an ingathering of all people of this country, into the enjoyment of their liberty.

Mr. Chairman, the friends of of the slave are under a pressure just now; and that pressure is, to meet those fellows in Kansas, where they wish to be successful, and put them down there, even at the sacrifice of holding great principles in abeyance for a time. But let us not take this position; but a position by which every slave will be redeemed, and every slave set free. We have a right to interfere with slavery everywhere in this country, because it interferes with us everywhere in this country. While the pure air of America is disturbed by the crack of a driver's lash, we are involved in a common disgrace and a common crime; and it becomes us to wipe out that disgrace by repenting of that crme—wash our hands in innocency, and compass the altar of our God.

*Radical Abolitionist,* July, 1856

# TO S. J. LESLIE

Rochester, Sept. 6th, 1856

Dear Madam:

It will give me pleasure to serve you and your friend in bringing Mother and Son together so far as I am able. At present I am totally ignorant of the young man's whereabouts—but I have Several acquaintances on different parts of the Country from North Carolina of whom I will gladly make enquiries—and should any trace of him reach me, I will gladly inform you of the facts. It is however, exceedingly difficult to find colored people from the South. They change their names—and conceal their origin for obvious reasons. I have been looking for a friend of mine from Slavery this 10 years—and in a measure, know how to Sympathize with your poor friend in Search of her Son—

Very Respectfully,

Frederick Douglass

*Leslie Papers, American Philosophical Society Library*

# TO MRS. LYDIA DENNETT

Rochester, April 17, 1857

My Dear Mrs. Dennet:

You said to me when I was leaving your house, after a good breakfast, and a pleasant interview with the frank and spirited Miss Charlotte Thomas, *"do write to me."* Well, I am writing to you. The request so kindly made, was none the less grateful to my ear because it is one which it is often my privilege to be the recipient of. I have many such requests made of me in my journeyings among the children of men, but poor mortal that I am, with hands full and head full of public pressing matters, I have fallen far short of responding to this very amiable and most friendly request. I sometimes satisfy my conscience for failing of this duty by assuming, that I am merely asked to write by way of harmless compliment; and it is therefore, of little or no consequence whether I respond or no. In ninety-nine cases out of every hundred this assumption is doubtless well founded. You, my dear friend, must consider yourself the *"one"* not the *"ninety and nine"*! Ask Charlotte if she hears that. But in asking me to write, you very sagely selected the subject of the wished for letter. You want to know something of my family, my wife and children. I confess that you have given me a *"large"* subject to discourse upon. You could not have given me a theme more fruitful, and yet for the soul of me (if black men of African descent have Souls) I do not know where to begin. Suppose I begin with the wife. I am sad to say that she is by no means well—and if I should write down all her complaints there would be no room even to put my name at the bottom, although the world will have it that I am actually at the bottom of it all.[46] She has the face, I was going to use terms scarcely up to the standard of modern elegance, neraligia.[49] She has a great deal to do, but little time to do it in, and withal much to try her patience and all her other very many virtues. You have doubtless in your experience, met with many excellent wives and mothers, who have been in much the same condition in which my wife is. She has suffered in every member except one. She still seems able to use with great ease and fluency her powers of speech, and by the time I am at home a week or two longer, I shall have pretty fully learned in how many points there are need of improvement in my temper and disposition as a husband and father, the head of a family! Amid all the vicissitudes however, I am happy to say that my wife gives me an excellent loaf of bread, and keeps a neat house, and has moments of marked amiability, of all which good things, I do not fail to take due advantage. I cannot say much for my children.[48] I cannot be expected (with my known good taste) to praise them, and with my natural partiality, any criticisms of mine would be of little value. I can only say they are human, with a certain degree of human nature about them, enough to make them as bad as other children, and capable, I trust, of being as good. I am doing my best to give them a plain, practical English education, a thing I value all the more, perhaps because I never had any of any sort. I am trying to teach them to work, and eat bread that comes by earnest Labor, and I have some hope of success in this, & not in much more than this. My Dear friend Lydia, I do not write letters in these days of speech, I cannot take the time, and you must accept this note for the present. I was more than glad to see you when in Portland and shall be most happy to meet you again. Please make my regards to Miss Thomas, and also to the kind young Ladies in your family.

> I am, Dear friend, very truly yours,
> Frederick Douglass

*Ms., Houghton Library, Harvard University*

## TO GERRIT SMITH

Rochester, December 14, 1857

My dear Sir:

I am most sincerely glad to see again a letter in your well known handwriting. In your own behalf and that of your Dear family, and in behalf of my woe-smitten people and the thousands to whom your life is precious, I thank my God that you have been raised up from your recent illness, and that you begin to feel again the strength of returning health. Yes, My dear Sir, I saw you, as yourself, Mrs. Smith, Green and Mr. Morton glided by the cars in the station at Albany. The night air was cold and piercing and your step though quick was feeble. I quickly determined that it was more kind to let you pass in silence than to stop you for a moment's recognition. I deemed myself quite fortunate that I got this early glimpse of you. I had just been on a lecturing tour in Massachusetts and was returning home, and thought I should be telling news to my family when I should say that you had started for home, but the highway had already made them acquainted with the fact. I am just home now from a short tour in Canada where I found much desire to hear me. The great increase of colored people, most of them quite ignorant and some of them vicious, has raised up prejudice against colored people in Canada as well as here. The masses do not look into causes. If they find a people degraded, they pity them for a while and at length despise them.

Please remember me kindly to your Dear Household, all my family join me in Love to you,

> Yours Most Truly,
> Frederick Douglass

*Gerrit Smith Papers, George Arents Research Library, Syracuse University*

# THE REPROACH AND SHAME OF THE AMERICAN GOVERNMENT

SPEECH delivered at the First of August celebration,
Poughkeepsie, New York, August 2, 1858

Ladies and Gentlemen:

We have met to-day in your hospitable and beautiful city to celebrate no common event. No deed of partial and selfish patriotism claims our homage on this occasion. No towering monument is to rise here in honor of any naval or military heroism. We come among you to rejoice, but not over the warlike conqueror, nor his fallen foe. We meet to proclaim neither the glory of the one, nor the shame and disgrace of the other. Our intents are charitable, not wicked. Physical courage has its uses, and I would not disparage it or those who have distinguished themselves in the exercise of it. It has played an important part in the cause of Liberty as well as Slavery; but I am not here on this sacred day to explain its office, trace its history, or to applaud its merits, either in the abstract nor in the concrete. Without rejecting or calling in question the right of an enslaved people to gain their freedom by a resort to physical force, we present to you, in the great fact which brings us here, a happier result of a nobler warfare, a holier strife, than any which have distinguished the most successful conqueror. To see a giant wrong like Slavery literally falling before the arms of truth and love, made mighty, through God, to the pulling down of strongholds, must ever be more grateful to human contemplation then to behold the hard-hearted, persistent and inflexible tyrant perishing amid the flames of his own kindling, and falling amid the clash and glitter of carnal weapons. Thank God, there is nothing in the associations of this day to revive national antipathies, ancient or modern. For aught that properly belongs to this occasion, the hot embers of human hate may slumber forever in the depths of oblivion. No hand is here to stir them—no breath is here to blow them into life and flame. The event we celebrate naturally addresses itself to the highest and most ennobling attributes of human nature.

The annals of the world show no brighter page than that on which West India Emancipation is recorded. It is an exhibition of conscience—a manifestation of Christian virtue—an acknowledgement of duty—a confession and a renunciation of profitable sin at great expense, on a grand and commanding scale, by a great nation. It is this which surrounds the event we celebrate with a halo of dimless glory, brighter and more enduring than the stars that fret the hollow sky. After long years of patient labor on the part of Thomas Clarkson, William Wilberforce and their noble associates; after repeated defeats in Parliament and out of Parliament; after coldness, indifference, sneers and persecution had become abashed and silenced by the power and majesty of sincere and earnest devotion to a great principle; after the abolition sentiment had spread from individuals to multitudes all over the United Kingdom of Great Britain and Ireland, and the voice of the nation was united in one earnest and determined demand for the realization of a merciful, just and beneficent measure, we behold the statesmen of the British monarchy at last moved to action; and against all devices for delay which ingenuity and subtlety could invent; against all the Satanic and selfish appeals addressed to human prejudice and pride; against all excuses and protests which insolent oppressors know how to wield when their power is about to be wrenched from their cruel grasp—I say, against all these, and after all these, we behold the British Parliament calmly proceeding to dissolve the relation of master and slave in the British West Indies, and to make freedom the law of Britain for all time.

In reward of time well spent, of means well employed, of measures well directed and energetically prosecuted, and in answer to the ascending prayers of all the God-fearing and man-loving Christians of England, Ireland, Scotland, and Wales, on the morning of the 1st of August, 1834, eight hundred thousand colored members of the human family were instantly declared free, emancipated; and this vast multitude, as if at the voice of God, the trump of the Archangel, rose from Slavery as from the grave, lifting their scarred and mutilated bodies up as from the jaws of death and hell. The account given of the scene in the West Indies on the 1st of August, is the most affecting and thrilling I ever read. The very thought of it now sends the blood in quicker pace around the circuit of my system. They had been ranked, as our slaves are, with the beasts of the field, rated with bales of goods and barrels of rum, driven before the taskmaster's lash, marked and branded, bruised and wounded, robbed and plundered, but all at once they learn that their bondage is ended, the taskmaster is dismissed, the whip and chains are buried; they are no longer slaves, but free men and women. The effect upon them must have been electrical. I can well believe that they staggered and fell down, rose up, ran about, shouted, laughed, cried, sung, prayed as they are described as having done, by Thome and Kimball.[49]

We are here again to congratulate our brethren of the British West Indies upon their peaceful disenthrallment, and to tender them the assurance that we, the oppressed, and our friends in the United States, watch with the deepest interest their career in the new life upon which they have entered. We are here to acknowledge and manifest our gratitude to God, the giver of every good and perfect gift, for the merciful deliverance of that people. We are here, too, to bless the memory of the noble men, through whose wise, unwearied, and disinterested labors this grand result was wrought out, and to hold up their pure and generous example for admiration and imitation throughout the world. But above all, our profoundest wish, our intensest desire, our chiefest aim, is to make this ever memorable day, in some small measure the means of awakening a deeper interest in the cause of the fettered millions in our own land. We think it nothing unreasonable to ask the citizens of this Republic to be as true to liberty, to be as just, as generous, and as Christian-like as the subjects of the British monarchy have shown themselves to be.

How long, may we ask, shall it be the standing reproach and shame of the American Government, that while England is exerting her mighty power, and her all-pervading influence, to emancipate mankind from Slavery, and to humanize the world, the American Government is taxing its ingenuity, and putting forth its power, to thwart and circumvent this policy of a great and kindred nation? Only a few weeks ago the American people were placed in a most disgraceful and revolting position. We were made the patrons of pirates, the protectors of the vilest band of robbers and murderers which the sea ever floated—I mean the slave-traders of the year of our Lord one thousand eight hundred and fifty-eight. Our government virtually gave notice not merely to slave-traders, but to all manner of sea-pirates, that the American flag is broad enought to protect them all, and that the American arm is strong enough to defend them all. Mr. Buchanan virtually gave notice to all the Spanish, American, and Portuguese stealers of men, that they have only to run up the stars and stripes, when pursued by an honest man-of-war, to be safe. The American flag would shield them, if loaded to the gunwales with human flesh for Cuba and Texas. Talk about the law of nations—talk about the freedom of the seas—the rights of independent nations! Who does not know that this is all a refuge of lies? Who believes that our opposition to the exercise of the right of visit by England arises innately out of our respect for the law of nations, or our regard for the freedom of the seas? Who is there so inept in the discernment of motives of State, not to know that the real explanation of our belligerent assertion of the freedom of the seas—our opposition to the right of visit, is that England is an Anti-Slavery nation—while we are a slaveholding and slave-trading nation. But for this, the men-of-war of both nations would move as fraternally to the Gulf of Mexico to put down the Slave-trade, as the *Niagara* and the *Agamemnon* proceed to the middle of the Atlantic to lay down the electric wire. A slaveholding Government cannot consistently oppose the Slave-trade, is the logical and legitimate deduction of Slavery—and the one is as hateful as the other. They are twin monsters both hatched in the same nest. Slavery and the Slave-trade together constitute what the pure-minded and pious-hearted John Wesley denominated the sum of all villainies.

But to return. I rejoice to see before me white people as well as colored people to-day; for though this is our day peculiarly, it is not our day exclusively. The great truths we here recognize, the great facts we here exhibit, and the great principles which truth and fact alike establish, are worldwide in their application, and belong to no color, class or clime. They are the common property of the whole human family.

It is natural that I should attempt on this occasion something like a defence of Emancipation in the West Indies, and perhaps you expect this at my hands. You know it has been charged that the West India *"experiment," "experiment"*—that is the word—is a failure, and you would doubtless wish to know what answer can be made to this charge. I shall make short work with it, for I believe that my esteemed and eloquent friend, Henry Highland Garnet, made this charge the subject for your consideration on a similar occasion in this city last year.

One word as to the propriety of calling West India Emancipation an experiment. I take it that this is one of the tricks of Slavery and is of a piece with the character of their fraudulent business. There is obviously no more reason for calling West India Emancipation an experiment than for calling the law of gravitation an experiment. Liberty is not a device, an experiment, but a law of nature dating back to man's creation, and if this fundamental law is a failure the responsibility is not with the British people, but with the great author of this law. Slavery is the experiment in this case. God made man upright, but man has sought out many inventions, and Slavery is one of them. It is an experiment by which men seek to live without labor, to eat bread by the sweat of another man's brow, to get gold without digging it, and to become rich without using one's own faculties and powers to obtain riches. This is the real experiment.

But in answer to the charge that West Indian Emancipation is a failure, I frankly admit that in some respects it has failed. It has failed to keep Slavery under the name of Liberty. It has failed to change the name without changing the character of the thing. The Negroes have really been emancipated, and are no longer slaves. Emancipation has failed to keep Negroes out of civil office, it has failed to keep them out of the jury box, off the judge's bench, and out of the Colonial Legislature, for colored men have risen to all these stations since Emancipation. It has failed to keep the lands of Jamaica in the hands of the few and out of the hands of the many. It has failed to make men work for a planter at small wages, when they can work for themselves for larger wages. In a word, West Indian Emancipation has failed just as putting new wine in old bottles, or sewing new cloth upon an old garment, will fail. The failure is not with the new, but with the old—not with the present, but with the past. Plain enough it is, to common sense and common reflection, that liberty cannot prosper upon the old conditions and with the old methods and machinery which are adapted to a state of Slavery. The old plantation system of the Southern States of the American Union, grow out of, and are adapted to, Slavery. They belong to feudal ages and to feudal circumstances, where the land and the people are alike owned by a few lordly proprietors. In such circumstances, where the toiling masses are all sacrificed to a limited and privileged class of slaveholders, it is easy to keep up great establishments, flourishing estates. The explanation of the failure of West India emancipation will become very clear if these facts are kept in mind.

The complaint is, you are aware, that certain great States which were once prosperous and flourishing, have greatly declined since the abolition of Slavery. I do not dispute the fact. All, or nearly all that is alleged at this point, may be admitted, but I deny that the failure of these States proves emancipation to be a failure. On the contrary, they prove that a new order of things adapted to a state of freedom is indispensable to the growth and prosperity of these Islands. It is no proof that the people of Egypt are not as well off now as they were in the days of the Pharoahs, because no more pyramids are seen rising to meet the Eastern sky. It is no proof that the people of England are not as well off now as they were in the feudal ages, because huge castles with towers and turrets, walls and battlements, are not seen rising in different parts of the British islands. It is no proof either that Britain is declining because most of those old piles, belonging to a semi-barbarous age, are fast crumbling to ruin. So neither is it any proof that the West Indies are declining because the old plantation system of other days is giving place to small farms—as is the case in Jamaica and elsewhere.

But it is said that the emancipated Negroes will not work—that it is absolutely necessary to import coolies to the West Indies to supply the places of the slaves on the plantations, and estates, which were once flourishing. I do not dispute a word of it. It may be all just as the slaveholders would have it, and I answer in a similar manner to that already adopted. You cannot get men to work on plantations for a lordly proprietor when they can do as well, and better, for themselves in other ways. I will not assume that Yankees are a lazy, good-for-nothing set because we are compelled to import Irishmen to dig our canals and grade our railroads. They find employment more congenial—better suited to their taste; and so will the Irish when they are here awhile. Grading railroads and digging canals are well enough in the absence of anything better. The same is true of plantation labor. I have no doubt that the Negroes are lazy—it is not an uncommon fault of some men who are not Negroes. Thackeray remarks, very truly, that, as a general rule, men are about as lazy as they can afford to be. This rule is perhaps as true under a tropical sun as in a temperate climate.

It is said that the morals of the people of Jamaica are deplorably low. This too I frankly admit. So are the morals of our Slave-trade. So were the morals of Jamaica before the act of emancipation; so are they in all slave countries. Slavery and low morals go together. It is a low morality that permits one man to enslave another. I would not apologize for the shocking state of morals in Jamaica, but this I may do, show that Slavery, more than all other causes, must account for it. Liberty shall not bear the blame, when slavery is the real offender. You cannot expect that a people, cradled in Slavery, and sunk to the condition of brutes, in the eye of the law, will have a very high opinion of

the marriage institution. Immediately succeeding physical emancipation, the British Parliament could remove the fetters off the bodies of
the bondmen—but not from their souls. That is a work for time, for
religion, and for education. The moral habits of a people cannot be
changed in a day, perhaps not for generations. Jamaica is now good
ground for missionary reforms, not for malicious reproaches. Let those
who paint her moral and religious destitution, and content themselves
by assuming that West India Emancipation was a failure, exert themselves to send good men there with the Bible, with knowledge, with
purity, and with order, and no doubt the good seed thus sent would
bring forth good fruit. This work is now being done by England and
Scotland, and by the American Missionary Society, of which Louis
Tappan, Esq., is Secretary. Mr. Loren Thompson, who has been a
Missionary in that island for many years; is now in this country, asking
for means to help forward the good work of the moral and mental
elevation of the people. Let him be sustained in his endeavors. Far more
creditable and becoming will this be, than standing aside and giving
aid and comfort to American dealers in the bodies and souls of men by
denouncing Emancipation as a failure. But I promised to make short
work of those objections, and will keep my promise.

It is well to bear in mind an important truth here. Whether men
should be slave or free, does not depend upon the success or failure of
freedom in any given instance. Some things have been settled independently of human calculation and human adjudication. One of these
things is, that every man has by nature a right to his own body, and
that to deprive him of that right is a flagrant violation of the will of
God. This is settled. And if desolation and ruin, famine and pestilence
should threaten, Emancipation would still be the same urgent and
solemn duty that it ever was. When the God of all the earth ordained
the law of freedom He forsaw all its consequences. Do right though the
Heavens fall. We have no right to do evil that good may come, nor to
refrain from doing right because evil may come.

This celebration comes opportunely just after your National Anniversary. It taps on, and supplies a deficiency, in the exercises of that
day. It takes up the principles of the American Revolution, where you
drop them, and bears them onward to higher and more beneficent
applications. American Slavery, with its millions of caves[50]nd mountains of gold, is a most captivating power, a great corruptor of men, as
well as institutions. Few of our great public men have been able to

withstand its fascinations. Strangers and citizens alike fall before it. Our Doctors of Divinity seem especially susceptible and alive to its charms. For it they readily find a warrant in the Bible. It has seduced and bribed American orators into the most shameless contraction, mutilation and falsification of the Revolutionary principles of American Freedom and Independence. What our brave fathers intended for the whole world, some of the most distinguished orators in America would confine to a section, a latitude, a climate, a soil—or would abandon altogether at the bidding of the great abomination. Principles which your fathers intended to apply to all mankind, their sons, meanly and wickedly, in the cowardliness of their souls, limit to one race, to one complexion, to one type of features, to one variety of men. Before they can tell you whether a man ought to be free, they want to know the color of his cuticle and the texture of his hair. They read the Declaration of American Independence with exceptions. They read the Bible with the exceptions—and while they are careful to include themselves, they are careful to exclude all others.

The American Republic is not very old. Only eighty-two years and thirty-one days have transpired since, in an hour of darkness and trial, it was launched on the broad sea of national existence. The great act which gave it being was the Declaration of Independence. You all know what are the principles laid down in that great instrument. The central and most comprehensive principle there asserted is that 'all men are entitled to life, liberty, and to an equal chance for happiness.' The Fathers of this Republic told us, and told a then listening world, that, according to their sense, civil Government, fit for the name and fit to exist at all, should secure these fundamental rights. They pledged themselves, by implication at least, that they would establish a Government which should secure these cardinal rights to the weakest and humblest of the American people. They not only appealed to earth, but solemnly appealed to Heaven, not only to man, but to God. They flung open their hearts for the scrutiny of the world.

I do not doubt that it was the purpose of your fathers to form just such a government as the Declaration of Independence shadows forth as the true one, and the only one which men are authorized to establish and perpetuate. They really believed in liberty, they believed in humanity, they believed in human progress and in human elevation. They steadily ignored all distinctions between men in respect to rights, and stated their principles in the broadest and most comprehensive terms they could command. Regarding Slavery as a transient, not a permanent, feature of American society, they made no provision for the hateful thing in the Constitution. They looked upon it as an alien, and treated it as such. They nowhere tell us that black men shall be Slaves and white men shall be free. They nowhere make any distinction among men in respect to rights on account of color. They say, "we, the people," never we, the white people. Neither in the Constitution nor in the Declaration of Independence, is there a single reference to the subject of color. The sentiment of the leading statesmen of that day—the sentiment of leading divines, as well as the position of the church—show that Slavery was regarded as a perishing system, only requiring the silent operation of free principles and the certain advances of time to blot it out forever.

Great is the apparent ignorance of the present generation respecting this point. *Slavery has bewitched us*. It has taught us to read history backwards. It has given us evil for good—darkness for light, and bitter for sweet. We have been sitting at the feet of its Calhouns and its Taneys so long that we have ceased to comprehend the elements out of which the nation sprung into existence. A Government which was expressly ordained to establish justice and to secure the blessings of liberty, we have pathetized into thinking was especially intended and solemnly ordained to preserve the right of one man to hold property in the body and soul of another man. The fact is, there is scarcely a single great man of Revolutionary memory who was so ignorant, and so base, and so lost to the sentiments of shame as to defend the principle of Slavery—while, on the other hand, the chief and recognized builders of the Republic almost without exception, openly condemned that principle. Washington, Franklin, Jefferson, Adams, Madison, Monroe, Patrick Henry, Roger Sherman, George Mason, Luther Martin, and other distinguished men of the earlier and better days of the Republic, condemned the system of slavery as a great moral and political evil, alien to the laws of nature.

But how different from this is the sentiment of the present among our public men! What was regarded as a curse at the beginning, is now cherished as a blessing. What your fathers thought it the highest patriotism to limit, circumscribe and discourage, it is now called patriotic to nationalize, spread and protect. It has now come to pass that Freedom is the evil to be shunned, and Slavery the blessing to be sought. Those who denounced the accursed thing at the beginning, were deemed wise, humane and patriotic. Those who denounce it now, are called disorganizers, enemies of the Union, 'freedom-shriekers,' 'negro-worshippers,' infidels and traitors. The contrast is striking and instructive. The great men who pledged their lives, their fortunes, and their sacred honor to the principles of the Declaration of Independence, would to-day be banished from the councils of the nation. They would stand no chance with the Buchanans, Casses, Touceys and Cobbs[51] of the present day.

Pardon me, I am only stating what must be evident to all. Let me glance at another topic, or rather at another phase of the same topic. Only a few weeks ago the American people celebrated the eighty-second year of their freedom and independence. The celebration was this year quite remarkable and noteworthy, in several of its features. You know that our national birthday, like the word "Liberty" on the old-fashioned copper cent, has been regarded with increasing suspicion of late. The new-fashioned coin, now passing for a good cent, has banished the old copper and "Liberty," and some doubts have been expressed if the Fourth of July will be much longer retained among our institutions, since the principles which make that day glorious have been buried out of sight, and Slavery, with the Negro's bleeding bones in his mouth, is now *stamping* on Freedom's grave. It was supposed that so frightful a reminder of the people of slaughtered Liberty might be gotten rid of in much the same way. But no, the Fourth of July is still celebrated, but not as a festival of Liberty. With many it is the great day selected for the assassination of Liberty.

But to the late celebration. Of course, though remarkable as I have said, in some of its features, it was, in its general character, about the same as for some years past. There were not more than the custom-ary number of accidents. The killed and wounded did not, perhaps, exceed the number of previously reached by similar celebrations. There was evidently a good deal of villainous saltpeter burnt; a few arms blown off—a good deal of bad whisky imbibed, perhaps in imitation of our worthy President, who, the public are informed, takes nothing in the way of liquor but old rye whisky. There was also a little fighting done. There was, as a Western man would phrase it, tall drinking, tall fighting and tall swearing that day. I judge of it by the papers, and from these I infer that it was altogether a lively day, especially in certain northern localities.

Among those of our public men who figure conspicuously that

day, we may name (for public men are for public mention) Honorable Edward Everett, Honorable Rufus Choate[52] and Honorable Caleb Cushing[53], the latter [the] late Attorney-General under the Administration of General Franklin Pierce, whose Pro-Slavery glory is now eclipsed by Mr. James Buchanan. Mr. Cushing was the honored orator of Old Tammany, that favored resort of all that is decent, patriotic, and Democratic, in the City of New York. Mr. Everett was favored with a select audience of Democrats (Democrats again, you see) at the Revere House, over or under a dinner table—only costing $10 a plate. Quite a democratic dinner that. While Mr. Cushing was addressing the Democracy of Old Tammany, and Mr. Everett saying his speech at the Revere House, Mr. Choate was discharging a perfect whirlwind, (not of periods, for he doesn't use any) but of words, no doubt to the wonder and astonishment of the Boston Democratic Club. He talked gloriously, vaingloriously, and furiously, for it is no trouble for Mr. Choate to talk.

But what, think you, these three distinguished sons of old Massachusetts had to say on that day which was to remind us of the days when men dared to rebuke tyranny, and to look danger full in the face? What had they to say in favor of the principle of Liberty, which your fathers nobly asserted, and bravely defended with their lives, their fortunes and their sacred honor? I say, what idea was made prominent? Turn to Mr. Choate, and if you can understand him, you get this idea. The Union of these States is a great blessing, and that the Northern people, in their wild devotion to liberty, are putting the Union in peril. You gather from his "glittering generalities" that there are certain forces operating in the country prejudicial to unity and nationality, and it is plain that that opposition to Slavery is, in his judgment, the disturbing and dangerous force to be met, resisted and put down. Not a word against Slavery—not a word in denunciation of tyranny—not a word in sympathy with the advancement of freedom throughout the world—but nationality was beginning, middle and end with Mr. Choate. Thus the strength of the eloquent orator was spent for naught. He insists upon what is not denied—he rebukes where there is no transgression—he warns where there is no danger, and leaves unsaid the only word which is in keeping with the great principles and purposes of the Declaration of Independence. It is just such a speech as any old Tory might have made against the Whigs in 1776. As they would have had your fathers seal their lips on the subject of British oppression for the safety of the union with England, so Mr. Choate would have us seal our lips on the subject of American Slavery for the sake of the Union with the South. It was a plea for silent acquiescence in all the domineering pretentions of the slave power of the country.

A word of Mr. Everett[54]—and only a word. Notwithstanding this man's early Bible defense of Slavery; notwithstanding his shameless declaration of a preference to fight against slaves to any other warfare, knowing no other military service in which he would rather buckle on his knap-sack and gird on his sword than to put down a slave insurrection; notwithstanding his cowardly suppression of the most significant feature of the moral portrait of Washington lest the exhibition of it should give offense to slaveholders; notwithstanding his singular desertion of the Hon. Charles Sumner and the cause of freedom in the American Senate, and his general reprehensible truckling to the dark spirit of Slavery, I, for one, had followed him with a certain degree of hope. He is a man of great and splendid abilities, and knows what is right on the subject of Slavery as well as any man in America. He knows that Slavery is the mistake, is the curse, the crime, the disgrace, and the shame of America. Yet in all his travels, amid all the scenes through which he has passed in delivering his popular lecture on Washington, he has found nothing in the country to condemn, except a little something he calls Buncombe. That's all—a little spot called Buncombe. The enslavement of four millions of men and women is nothing to condemn; the efforts making to spread the withering curse of human bondage is nothing to condemn; but only a little spot called Buncombe, a spot to which his own speech belongs—for a more palpable piece of Buncombe than this speech of his—made over the golden plates of the Revere House, and by the side of slaveholding Commissioner Ben Hallett—never found place in an American newspaper. It is national flattery on a large scale, such as few would attempt when sober, and which could not have been expected of Mr. Everett when drunk.

Now, for the sake of symmetry and completeness, let me say a word of the other performance at Tammany Hall. Among the first Anti-Slavery speeches I ever heard, was one from the lips of Hon. Caleb Cushing, at Liberty Hall, in New Bedford, Mass. It is now nearly twenty years ago. It was a passing eulogy on the lamented Young Alvard, lately deceased, one of the most promising Anti-Slavery men of that day. Mr. Cushing then stood upon the old Whig platform. He was fishing for Abolition votes then, as he is fishing for Pro-Slavery votes now. But there was something in the sudden burst of grief and lamentation over the early death of Alvard, that cheated me for the moment into the belief that Caleb was really in sympathy with the great and beneficent aims of that rising young statesman. But it was not so. Mr. Cushing was then, as now, the same gifted, learned, crafty, unscrupulous corruptor of the public heart that he now is. His speech at old Tammany Hall would convert the great celebration of Liberty into a means of making friends for Slavery and for stirring up the bitterest and most brutal passions of the country, of every prominent and consistent friend of the principles of the Declaration of American Independence.

Such is the use made of the birthday of Freedom by these three eminent public men. Under all the gauze and face of their bewitching rhetoric, under all the high sounding phrases of their devotion to the Union, there is veiled the hideous and hell-black imp of Slavery. Sitting there on his throne of bleeding hearts, he drives, by proxy, his sable serfs to unrequited toil, keeping back the wages of the laborer by fraud, and giving him nought for his work. For him, these searchers after fame and funds have no rebuke on the Fourth of July. Their bolts are forged for the head of Liberty—not for the head of slavery. They love the Union, but not the objects for which the Union was formed. They quote the great words of the father, but only to excuse the sins of their children. They would preserve the form, but murder the spirit of Liberty

> Paltering in a double sense,
> They keep the word of promise to the ear,
> And break it to the heart.

Yet, even in this quarter, there is much to cheer and gladden the hearts of the friends of impartial freedom. Old Massachusetts does not allow such treachery to liberty to go unpunished. Under the teachings of the Sumners and Wilsons, the Parkers and Higginsons, she has put the broad brand of her condemnation upon the whole brood of poetic, brilliant panderers to slaveholding lust and love of power. She has taught them, by precept and by example, that they cannot serve two masters. If they bask in the smiles of Slavery, they must confront the frowns of old Massachusetts. She admires their eloquence, she is proud of their learning, but, having no faith in the integrity of the men, she consigns them to political oblivion. Before these three, no men in Massachusetts could have risen higher, yet no three men in that State have sunken lower. But, let us leave the old Bay State. She has done well, and promises to do better. She has sent Everett, and Choate, and Cushing, to political oblivion, and driven from the bench a minion of the law for slave-catching. And, above all, she is now moving for the enactment of a law which will make her soil too holy for the footprints of a slave or a slave-catcher.

How stands the case in other directions? for wherever we look and wherever we listen, our eyes are greeted by the same sights, and our ears are saluted by the same sounds. Slavery and Freedom are everywhere in the field face-to-face, in open conflict, and the war is one of extermination. Vanquish, or be vanquished, is the desperate alternative. This lesson—long taught by the Abolitionists at the North, and by the extreme men at the South—is beginning to be learned by the rank and file of both parties. The contest going on just now in the State of Illinois is worthy of attention. Stephen A. Douglas, the author of the Kansas-Nebraska bill, is energetically endeavoring to hold his seat in the American Senate, and Mr. Abraham Lincoln is endeavoring as energetically to get that seat for himself. This, however, is only a partial view of the matter. The truth is, that Slavery and Anti-Slavery is at the bottom of the contest. As matters now stand, Douglas has a desperate case on his hands. He is fighting at immense disadvantage. The planks of his platform are as opposite as the Kilkenny cats. He has to defend the Dred Scott decision in one breath, and popular sovereignty in the next. He has to conciliate the Democratic Party and oppose the Democratic Administration upon the only important question about which the public mind is divided and agitated. He hopes for the support of individual Republicans, while he denounces the Republican Party. The doctrine of popular sovereignty holds that the Territory, while it is a Territory, and in the interim of its Territorial existence, may admit, or may exclude Slavery. This doctrine is diametrically opposed to the Dred Scott decision. That decision denies the right of a Territory to exclude Slavery at all. Nevertheless, Mr. Douglas accepts the Dred Scott decision, and goes on talking about popular sovereignty all the same. During the last congress you remember that he managed to produce the impression on the country that he was about to abandon his old slaveholding policy. He gave out that he had gone as far South as he ever meant to go, and that he was quite prepared to take the consequence of this resolution. We of the North, you know, shouted aloud over this demonstration of Mr. Douglas. He boasted thereafter that while, in 1854, he could have traveled all the way from Washington to Chicago by the light of his own effigy, that now he should receive nothing but plaudits all along such a journey.

He was promptly denounced by the South as a renegade—a traitor. The President denounced him, and he defied the President. His friends were removed from office, and his enemies were put in. In a word, he was marked out for political destruction. At this juncture Mr. Douglas held conversations and conferences with his old enemies, the Republicans; and the lightning from Washington told us that these conferences were mutually satisfactory. The nature of the satisfaction was not published, but for a time it was a matter of doubt as to which party had sold out, the Little Giant or the Republicans. But the tone of the Republican speeches made thereafter induced painful doubts as to the stability of the Republican Party. It was feared, and not without reason, that Cincinnati was to be the platform, and Douglas the leader of the Republican forces thenceforth. But just before the close of the session the spell was broken. Some rumbling sounds of danger and discontent reached all parties from the State of Illinois. Mr. Douglas was assured that however cordial Republicanism might be at Washington, Republicanism in Illinois had no terms to offer him—no proposals of peace to make with him—and that as for his seat in the Senate he could expect no help from them in retaining that; in fact, that they should get him out of it if they could. So matters were shaped just before the close of the session. What did the brave Douglas do? The circumstances were perplexing in the extreme. I will tell you. He made the very natural—but very desperate, if not fatal—move to get back into the good graces of the old Democratic Administration. He went about it in the old-fashioned way of doing such things. He made a speech—it was a queer speech—in which he wanted the past forgotten. Let by-gones by by-gones. The English swindle had carried—question was settled, and the only point of difference between him and the Administration was now out of the way. Hereafter, as heretofore, he was ready to fight the battle of Democracy.

I do not profess to give his words, but his ideas. Mr. Douglas was heard, as a culprit, under the gallows, is heard, with patience, and even with pity—and yet no one who heard him had their opinions altered by anything he said. Here, I take it, was the great mistake of that man's political life. He admitted his crimes, he owned his rebellious conduct—but wished all forgotten, because the reasons which moved him thereto had ceased to exist, After his speech there was no expression of regret on the Republican side—none of joy and congratulation on the Democratic side. He left without a single good-bye—and entered without a single expression of welcome. I say, here was the great mistake. His Kansas-Nebraska bill, with all its train of atrocities, might have been forgiven him; his repeated, virulent assaults upon the leading Republicans might have been excused upon the ground of general hostility; his standing by in perfect silence and permitting an armed assassin to strike down a brother Senator might have been forgiven if not forgotten. But this double treason—this attempt to cheat two great parties in a single session, right before the eyes of all, was an extravagance in political profligacy which can neither be forgiven nor forgotten while Stephen A. Douglas lives. The Democrats pitied and despised him; the Republicans felt relieved by his departure, and he went home to Illinois with a mill-stone of condemnation round his political neck.

Nevertheless, Mr. Douglas has money, he has talent, and he has a party, and may even yet get back into the Senate of the United States. He is no trifling opponent. His zeal is quite equal to his ability, and his success would, for many reasons, be a deplorable calamity. He is one of the most restless, ambitious, boldest, and most unscrupulous enemies with whom the cause of the colored man has to contend. It is for this reason that I have given him so lengthy a paragraph in my present address. It seems to me that the white Douglas should occasionally meet his deserts at the hands of a black one. Once I thought he was about to make the name respectable, but now I despair of him, and must do the best I can for it myself. 1 I now leave him in the hands of Mr. Lincoln, and in the hands of the Republican Party in Illinois, which seemed about to be compromised and sacrificed at the very heart of the Government.

The key-note of Republicanism in that State, at present, is given in the following extract from the great speech of Mr. Lincoln:

We are now far into the fifth year since a policy was initiated with the avowed object and confident promise of putting an end to Slavery agitation. Under the operation of that policy, that agitation has not only not ceased, but has constantly augmented. In my opinion it will not cease until a crisis shall have been reached and passed. 'A house divided against itself cannot stand.' I believe this Government *cannot endure permanently half Slave and half Free*. I do not expect the Union to be dissolved—I do not expect the house to fall—*but I do expect it will cease to be divided*. It will become all one thing, or all the other. Either the opponents of Slavery *will arrest the further spread of it*, and place it where the public mind shall rest in the belief *that it is in the course of ultimate extinction*; or his advocates *will push it forward till it shall become alike lawful in all the States*—old as well as new, North as well as South.[56]

Well and wisely said. One system or the other must prevail. Liberty or Slavery must become the law of the land. And men, communities, parties, churches and public measures are ranged on one or the other side, favoring the ascendancy of one or the other.

But I call your attention to another speech on the political firmament. Atchison,[57] while attempting to curse Kansas with Slavery, seems about to lose Missouri itself to the slave interest. A phenomenon is presented in the tone of sentiment reaching us from that Slave State. Emancipation is openly discussed in the streets of St. Louis. Emancipation leaders are written and published in the daily journals published in different parts of the State. Emancipation speeches are made on the stump in open daylight. Emancipation candidates are run for Congress, and the same for other offices.

I know that the chief motive of this movement is to benefit white men. I know that the moral character of the slave system is not brought into discussion; but I am willing that men should do right from any motives. Two kinds of arguments can be urged in favor of any right measure. If men will not do right from a love of principle, I am glad to have them do right from a love of the results of right doing. I look therefore with hope to the emancipation movement in Missouri. I know that many of the present slaves of that State would be speedily put beyond the beneficent reach of any act of emancipation which might be passed in the State. No doubt thousands would be hurried off down the river, in fetters and chains. It would be like most slave masters to do this. The same was done in this State and elsewhere, and the same would be done there. Nevertheless, Emancipation in Missouri will be great gain. Some at least, of our enslaved brethren would reap its benefits, and the accession of another free State, without the trouble of admitting her into the Union, would help on the Anti-Slavery movement immensely. It would inaugurate a new and dangerous model of thinking and talking on the whole subject of Slavery, and lead to combinations against the Slave system in other States. Maryland, Delaware and Kentucky would follow.

I make little account of the talk made of driving the colored people out of the State. This is an effort not likely to succeed. It has been threatened in Virginia and elsewhere, but the cruelty and meanness of the proposition are too gross and monstrous for the assent of even the slaveholders of Virginia. I, therefore, see nothing to discourage us in that quarter, but everything to cheer us on in the work of enlightening the public mind and winning the public heart to the side of liberty and justice.

The speaker was unable to finish his address at the afternoon session, having already spoken two hours. He therefore claimed the indulgence of the audience to break off at the point now reached, and promised to speak again at the meeting in the evening.[58]

*New York Times*, August 3, 1858

# THE LETTER OF BENJAMIN COATES,[59] ESQ.

Our views and opinions in respect to all schemes yet broached for the removal of the free colored people from the United States to Africa, or to other parts of the globe, have been so frequently and fully stated recently, and our readers are so completely in possession of them, as to render any formal and lengthy reply to the eloquent and elaborate letter of Mr. Coates, wholly unnecessary. We publish that letter, as a friend of free discussion, and as an act of courtesy to the author, whose philanthropic spirit we love, and whose many labors for the freedom and elevation of our people we gratefully approve and admire yet all the more, because Mr. Coates is so good a man are we to point out, denounce and shun his errors, for all the more are we adopting them. His arguments and appeals for Colonization sound so much like genuine Abolitionism, that one is at a loss, upon first blush, to know why he is tolerated in the Colonization camp. This very quality, as we have said, makes him the more effective. We say this, not to awaken prejudice, but as a needful warning to those who read this letter.

The tendency of all such arguments and appeals, as those of Mr.

Coates', is to draw off the attention, and allure the colored people from what they *can and ought to do for themselves, here in their native land*, and to set them thinking and speculating what they may *possibly do and be* in a far distant country, among a strange people, and in a climate for which they have been unfitted by two hundred years residence in this temperate zone Assuming that we are a very excitable people, very imaginative, delighting in fancies, these arguments and appeals of Mr. Coates are admirably adapted to draw us away from immediate, and practical advantages and duties here, to magnificent, but we more than fear, Utopian and impossible enterprises abroad. This we take to be a present and obvious evil, very mischievous and hurtful, both in paralyzing our own energies, and keeping alive the miserable idea in the minds of our oppressors, that the colored man can never be at home in this country. Eternity alone will tell how we have been injured, and retarded in our progress by this Colonization scheme. With soft and gentle persuasions in one hand, and gloomy threats and forebodings in the other, changing its arguments to suit the times, whether they were tranquil and peaceful, or boisterous and violent, smiling, it, with matchless perseverance, has pursued us with its crippling influence, during the last forty years. In vain have the colored people protested against it; in vain have they besought the specter to depart and refrain from following after and tormenting them; it has pursued them still.

At the North, the idea of the ultimate removal of the colored people from the country, has been urged and supported by the known haters and maligners of the Negro race; at the South it has been supported by the more sagacious and crafty of the slaveholders, as an apology for slavery, and as a means of getting rid of that part of the free colored people of the slave States, supposed to endanger the peace of the slave system.—Between these two main classes, who support the Colonization scheme, stands our correspondent, "solitary and alone," neither a slaveholder, nor a Negro-hater, yet, unconsciously, doing the work of both—for he can reach those who cannot be reached by either of the others. Mr. Coates, we believe, is about the last of a large class who entered the Colonization ranks, as did the Tappans, and Gerrit Smith, because they thought they saw in it a means for freedom of the American slave, the abolition of the slave trade on the African coast, the civilization and evangelization of Africa, by commerce and the gospel. What others of this better class early believed, and have now abandoned, Mr. Coates still believes and adheres to. These noble objects fire his soul, and move his pen; hence the sheets of flame, the eloquence and power with which he writes.

While we do not, for reasons already mentioned, intend to go fully into the controversy with Mr. Coates, we must enter our most emphatic protest against the injustice of the charge, direct in some cases, and only implied in others, that they who labor for the emancipation and elevation of the colored people in America, and have not seen the necessity or the desirableness of Colonization, are in any measure wanting in a proper interest in the welfare, happiness, improvement and progress of Africa. For our part, no sign of progress in that quarter of the globe, no new light is shed upon the better character of its people, fails to awaken grateful emotions in us. We watch Liberia, with nothing but friendly eyes, and learn with pleasure that the natives, in Yoruba are extensively engaging in the culture of cotton, and that English manufacturers are getting large supplies for their mills from the African coast. The trade, though now in its infancy, is nevertheless, in a very vigorous infancy, and we know not but these intelligent Yorubans are quite equal to its prosecution without our interference. The difference between ourselves and Colonizationists generally, is quite remarkable, and is characteristic of the springs of action in each party. They show their care and good will towards the Negro at *home*, by their advocacy of the claims of the Negro *abroad*. They advocate our improvement and elevation in Africa, and denounce the same as impossible in America. The prime difference here is about as broad, as loving God, whom we have not seen, and hating our brother, who we have seen.

With all deference to our friend Mr. Coates, (whom we except from the generality of Colonizationists,) we must continue to hold that this home work is also good foreign work and that, after all, the suffering man nearest us, and most within the reach of our influence is, in the strictest sense, our neighbor, and has the first claim on our powers for his relief.

Africa is, indeed, in some parts of it, in a deplorable condition. Among the heaviest curses which keep her floundering in the depths of barbarism, are slavery and the slave trade. These give rise to the terrible wars, the neglect of agriculture, and of legitimate commerce, and general improvement. All this we admit, and lament. But because this is so, it does not follow that the Colonization of a few shiploads of colored people from the United States, is to solve the problem of the redemption of Africa. Experience has shown that the slave trade now flourishes in the neighborhood of Liberia itself; and the charge has not yet been entirely disproved, that men, high in authority, in that Republic are deeply interested in trade with the murderous pirates, Portuguese, Spanish, French, and American, who prowl along the African coast, like tigers in pursuit of their prey. But whether Liberia is , or is not a check upon the slave trade, does not materially affect the argument. The difference of opinion respects the best modes of helping our fellow-men in given circumstances. It is said that the colored man must go to Africa to free the slave, and elevate his race in America. This is the upshot of it. The good you free colored people can do, depends upon where you are located; and the *further* you are from America, the greater and better will be your influence upon the condition of the slaves of America. This is the sentiment in the rough, to which we object. And why must we go to Africa to do this great good? Cannot Africa as readily receive the good effects of our moral and mental elevation in America, (seeing that we are already here,) as America can receive back those good effects from us, when elevated in Africa? The slave trade and slavery, and their gross, and scandalous crimes, and cruelties, are deplorable evils in Africa; but no less deplorable are the same barbarous and shocking evils, in sight of the dome of our National Capitol, and within hearing of the sermons, prayers, and hymns of American Christian Churches. The putting down those evils here seems quite as desirable as putting down the same in Africa. But the grand reason why we are to get Africa is that while here, in contact with a race which outstrips us in civilization and progress, we cannot but be disheartened and hindered, and drag along through life an abject class, unable to contend against the heavy competition.—When we have listened carefully to the argument of Colonizationists at this point, we have been led to inquire why it is, that contact with a superior class should be urged as a disadvantage in America, and extolled as a great blessing in Africa. If the superiority of the whites should so dishearten and overshadow us in America, why will not our superiority have a like effect upon the natives in Africa? Is superiority, when colonized, [better] than it is to a people living for centuries in the midst of the said superiority? The history of Colonization shows that colonists generally take up an anti-native position. It has been so in this country. It has been so in Africa, Western and Southern, and the doctrine of the Dred Scott decision[60] is, perhaps, nowhere acted upon with less scruple, than by colonists towards natives, in Africa, California, and Oregon. But it may be said that, being of the same color and race with the natives, we should easily harmonize and unite with them. So, indeed, it would seem, and yet the facts are all against it. Human nature, in its good and bad qualities, is, in white and black, the same. We do not have to change the skin of a Negro to make a slaveholder, as exacting and haughty, as any who can be furnished by the white race, either in Brazil, or Louisana. Black men hold slaves in both these countries and in Africa. Altogether too much is made of similarity of color in estimating the good effects of Colonization in Africa. In our judgment, similarity of color is about the least qualification for propagating civilization and Christianity in Africa. There is one objection to the persistent agitation of the Colonization scheme which we sincerely wish we possessed adequate ability to enforce. Even our friend Mr. Coates does not fully comprehend this objection. We have several times had occasion to bring it forward of late, and we press it now with increased earnestness. This it is: the agitation of the removal of the colored people from the United States keeps them constantly in a perturbed, unsettled, neither-go-nor-stay, state of mind. That a people thus disturbed, thus apprehensive, restless, and anxious, cannot improve the opportunities immediately surrounding them, must be plain to every one. We are made to sleep with our luggage on our backs, and keep looking for our command to depart. This constanr agitation makes us feei that we have no continuing city, but that we are like a "stranger that turneth aside to tarry for a night"—denied a home in the land of our birth, and told that we must look elsewhere for an abiding place. What right have Colonizationists, what right have you, Mr. Coates, what right have any, to take advantage of a popular prejudice, which else might soon die out, and keep this struggling people perpetually in a state of uncertainty and even alarm? How can a people, thus situated, improve their condition?—If they think of buying land, building houses, planting trees, and making provision for respectable and permanent residence here, Colonization whispers this is not your home. You must sooner or later look out for another country; you can't stay here; you must give place to the European nations who are coming in. If you plant, you cannot reap; if you build you can't occupy; if you educate, you can't get employment; if you prepare for usefulness this is not the place for your usefulness, listening to these evil prophets, who make use of every new oppression imposed by State or Nation, Church or Government, as an additional proof of their own foresight, and urge it as evidence of the certain fulfillment of their worst predictions concerning us—is it to be wondered at, we say, that so few are found among us who are endeavoring to build up their fortunes here, and that we do not present to the world the aspect of a people vigorously at work in their natural calling. Menaced with threats on the one hand, and coaxed by persuasions on the other, allured at one time, and driven at another, we have hardly time for anything but to provide for the pressing wants of the moment. We Negroes are kept under a constant strain, either in contemplating magnificent enterprises, for which we have but little qualification, or looking for the shadow of the cruel arm which we are told must sooner or later smite us, if we do not get out of this land.

If free colored men, self-moved, wish to go to Africa or elsewhere, as individuals or as masses, and choose to form themselves into emigration societies or committees, preparatory to final removal from the United States, however much we might regret their determination on other grounds, we should be saved from the mortification of their having acted upon the suggestions, urgency, and representations of those whose pride and prejudice were the cause of their removal.

Let colored men go to Africa, and go to St. Domingo, to Jamaica, Mexico, or elsewhere, just as they list, but let them be selfmoved in the matter. The free colored people have not shown themselves wanting in migratory qualities. The American people are an exceedingly restless and enterprising people; colored people are not entirely unlike them. The black man's voice was heard amid the first shouts raised by emigrants on the banks of the Pacific, after the glitter of its gold dazzled the world's eye. They follow the white man's lead in the most daring enterprises. One of the best means of getting us in the notion of going to Africa will be for our white fellow countrymen to make a rush for that country themselves. We should have gone as freely to Kansas with our enterprising fellow citizens, as to California, but for the intervention of a Slave state, and the powerful effort to degrade us there in advance and even to forbid our going there at all. This natural tendency to emigration may be safely left to direct and control us, just as the same is left to direct and control the Englishman, Frenchman, German, Irishman, or the white American, in fixing his habitation of the earth.

How long shall we be called upon to establish a *"nation in Africa,"* as a condition to respectability? We have an African nation on our bodies. A million of sable people have been governing themselves, in freedom and independence, more than half a century, right under our *national* nose; but America has never acknowledged her independence, and Colonizationists seldom point to Haiti as an example of what the black race are capable of. Liberia, whose national existence is recognized by almost a dozen crowned heads in Europe, is unknown to our Democratic Government at Washington. Why is this? The *"Nationality"* is not wanting. The answer is—Slavery, Slavery, not in Timbuctoo, not in Ashantee, not in Dahomey, not in Africa, but in the enlightened and civilized "nationality" of the United States.[61]

What is the natural inference of this state of facts? Plainly this: it is not the abolition of Slavery in Africa, not the abolition of the slave trade on the gold coast, not the establishment of African nationalities, that can change the estimate now set upon the colored people of the United States, but rather the emancipation and gradual improvement of these people upon the soil of the United States.

Our correspondent, referring to our reference to the Jews, illustrating the vincibleness of prejudice, in our article on Mr. Harper's letter, thinks us unfortunate in that reference, and puts to us the following question: "Are you willing and desirous that the *whole mass* of the colored population of the United States should remain here contending against oppression even for *one* century, if at the expiration of that time some one of their number could be admitted into the British Parliament?" This question causes us neither difficulty nor hesitation. Our answer is, that for all that Colonization in Africa is likely to do for us, a century spent here in battling against oppression will be as wisely and as worthily spent as the same number of years spent on the western coast of Africa. Our respected correspondent does not frighten us by the picture of color destitution he draws in his supposed case. We are contending not for the rights of color, but for the rights of men. But we need not be contending against oppression a century nor a half century in this country, if gentlemen like Mr. Coates will abandon the Colonization scheme, cease to give the aid and comfort which it affords to Slavery and prejudice. The battle would be more than half won.

But we meant to make no formal reply to the various points presented in friend Coates' letter; and while we admit that he has made the best reply that could be made from the Colonization side to our former article, he has not shaken a single position taken in that article, and the most visible impression his letter makes, is, that Mr. Coates, the writer of it, is sincerely desirous of improving the condition and character of the African race, whether in the United States or in Africa, *but especially in Africa.* In would be far easier to deal almost with any other Colonizationist than he to whom we are referring; for we know his works in Philadelphia, the city where he resides; how that, even more than the so-called Abolitionists of that city, he is vigilant, active, and earnest, going about doing good to our oppressed people, visiting their schools, encouraging their efforts at obtaining an education, cheering on their teachers, inspiring them with hope, circulating valuable books among them to increase their stock of knowledge, and otherwise employing his time and means to promote the improvement and elevation of the colored people. For these things we love and honor the man. He is not far from being a genuine Abolitionist, and has but to drop his *special* preferences for Africa as the final home of the colored people of the United States and other countries, through which they are scattered, to put himself in harmony with the laws of human brotherhood—the tendency of which is, to blot our all *"selfish nationalities,"* and to establish one law, one religion, one language, one government, and one human family, in which all members shall have Equal Rights and Equal Protection.

*Frederick Douglass' Paper*, September 17, 1858

# RESOLUTIONS PROPOSED FOR ANTI-CAPITAL PUNISHMENT MEETING, ROCHESTER, NEW YORK, OCTOBER 7, 1858[62]

Resolved, That life is the great primary and most precious and comprehensive of all human rights—that whether it be coupled with virtue, honor, or happiness, or with sin, disgrace and misery, the continued possession of it is rightfully not a matter of volition; that it is neither deliberately nor voluntarily assumed, nor to be deliberately or voluntarily destroyed, either by individuals separately, or combined in what is called Government; that it is a right derived solely and directly from God—the source of all goodness and the center of all authority—and is most manifestly designed by Him to be held, esteemed, and reverenced among men as the most sacred, solemn and inviolable of all his gifts to man.

Resolved, That the love of man as manifested in his actions to his fellows, whether in his public or private relations, has ever been the surest test of the presence of God in the soul; that the degree in which the sacredness of human life has been exemplified in all ages of the world, has been the truest index of the measure of human progress; that in proportion as the tide of barbarism has receded, a higher regard has been manifested for the God-given right to life, its inviolability has been strengthened in proportion to the development of the intellect and moral sentiments, and that conscience, reason and revelation unite their testimony against the continuance of a custom, barbarous in its origin, antichristian in its continuance, vindictive in its character, and demoralizing in its tendencies.

Resolved, That any settled custom, precept, example or law, the observance of which necessarily tends to cheapen human life, or in any measure serves to diminish and weaken man's respect for it, is a custom, precept, example and law utterly inconsistent with the law of eternal goodness written on the constitution of man by his Maker, and is diametrically opposed to the safety, welfare and happiness of mankind; and that however ancient and honorable such laws and customs may be in the eyes of prejudice, superstition and bigotry, they ought to be discountenanced, abolished, and supplanted by a higher civilization and a holier and more merciful Christianity.

Resolved, That in the opinion of this meeting, when a criminal is firmly secured in the iron grasp of the government, and on that account can no longer endanger the peace and safety of society; that when he is wasted and emaciated by heavy chains and horrid thoughts, and long confinement in a gloomy cell—when, as is often the case, he is completely transformed, both in temper and spirit—the execution of the death penalty on such an one is an act of cold blooded and barbarous enormity, and is as cowardly as it is cruel, and that instead of repressing and preventing the horrid crime of murder, it really serves by shocking and blunting the finer and better feelings of human nature, to undermine respect for human life, and leads directly to the perpetration of the crime which it would extinguish.

Resolved, That the time to advance opinions and principles is when those opinions and principles are upon trial, and threatened with outrage; and that while we have respectfully remained silent till the ends of justice have been served in fixing the guilt of the criminal, we now come in the sacred office of humanity and benevolence, to appeal for mercy at the hands of his Excellency, Governor King, on behalf of young Ira Stout, and to ask that his punishment shall be commuted from being capitally executed to imprisonment for life.

Resolved, That punishment as such, is a form of revenge, wreaking upon the criminal the pain he has inflicted on another, wrong in principle and pernicious in practice; arises out of the lowest propensities of human nature, and is opposed to the highest civilization; that it has no sanction in the spirit and teachings of Christ, which everywhere abound in loving kindness and forgiveness.

Resolved, That rather than visit the crime upon the head of the criminal, thus descending to his level, we ought to place him in a position to develop his higher nature; and instead of descending to a spirit of revenge, and degrading ourselves on the one hand, and the criminal on the other, we should urge a thorough reform in our criminal laws—basing them on the truly Christian principle of love and good will towards man, and to reject forever the cold blooded and barbarous principle of retaliation.

Resolved, That a copy of the foregoing resolutions, and the proceedings of this meeting, be transmitted to his Excellency, Governor King, as an expression of the sense of this meeting, and that the same be subscribed by the Chairman and Secretary thereof.

Frederick Douglass, Chairman.

J. Bower, Secretary.

*The Liberator,* October 22, 1858

# OUR RECENT WESTERN TOUR

It has not been many years since the West was contemplated by us as new and hard soil for anti-slavery labor, and when going thither, we set out, prepared for rough duty, resolutely determined to meet with calm front whatever in the shape of opposition might be flung in our pathway. In those days, it was common to meet with church doors bolted and barred against the cause of the slave, the minister warning his flock against the pestilent disturbers who were going about to turn the world upside down, to disorganize society, and break up the churches, destroy the revivals, turn the minds of the people from the claims of religion, to look after the mere temporal interests of men. It was common then, too, to meet with a cold and sullen indifference on the part of many, and a fierce and bitter spirit of persecution on the part of others.—The press was full of appeals to the basest passions against our cause, and poured out its scorn and contempt upon its advocates as either traitors or madmen. Brutal indignities met the anti-slavery lecturer, on stage coach, and at the hotels, and everywhere.—He was often compelled to get up his own meetings, hire a house, buy his candles, light up the house and ring the bell to call the people together, and sometimes after going to this trouble to get a meeting, he drew together only a few of the baser sort, who, stupefied with tobacco, or maddened by rum, would answer his arguments with bad eggs and brick bats, This state of things was not confined to the West alone. Within a dozen years, Mr. Garrison and the writer of this were mobbed, and their lives endangered in the civilized capital of Pennsylvania, for the utterance of simple abolition sentiments.—In those days, friends were few, and enemies abundant. An Abolitionist was a proscribed man, and the proscription reached him in all the relations of life; his business was made to languish, and his social standing lowered, and his children pointed at in the streets as n-----s and "amalgamationists." The men who stood up in their isolation in those degenerate times, firm for God and Humanity, carried hearts in their bosoms and benignance in their faces, which shed hope even then upon the reigning moral desolation. It is good even now to get one of these tried men by the hand and talk with him about other days, when friends were few, and our cause covered with odium and everywhere spoken against. Then Abolitionists loved each other with an ardor inspired by a common cause and a common persecution.

But times have changed very much of late. The Abolition lecturer speaks to a different audience, moves in a different atmosphere, and treads a less rugged pathway. The public sentiment has been gradually rising, the distance between the people and the reformer has been steadily decreasing. The repellency has become less and less strong, so that Abolitionism has become comparatively respectable, even in the West, where less anti-slavery labor has been performed than in the East. We, therefore, bring no discouraging news from the West—none from Michigan, none from Wisconsin, none from Illinois—the cause of freedom is onward and upward in them all. The work is not done; there is much more to be done, and will remain to be done, till the last yoke is broken and the last captive set free; but it is soul cheering to observe how much has been accomplished in spreading right views, sowing good seed, and the abundant fruit which has followed the labors already performed.

We think a Negro lecturer an excellent thermometer of the state of public opinion on the subject of slavery, much better than a white man. And for this reason, a hated opinion is not always in sight—a hated color is—and whatever of prejudice and pride, or other malign feeling may exist, are promptly called forth on the first appearance of a Negro. The Negro is the test of American civilization, American statesmanship, American refinement, and American Christianity. Put him in a rail car, in a hotel, in a church, and you can easily tell how far those around him have got from barbarism towards a true Christian civilization. We go about taking the measure of the times, scanning the field to ascertain the state of the contending moral forces, and the probabilities in favor of the final triumph of freedom over slavery.

We have, during the last seven weeks, visited Battle Creek, a fine flourishing young city in Michigan, where we met with a most hearty and cordial reception, by Abolitionists of all schools, Garrisonians, as well as others—Chicago, the home of Artemas Carter, L. C. Paine Freer, John Jones, H. O. Wagoner, and other long tried men—men who may always be relied upon to stand by the cause of God's poor in every emergency—men who stood by James H. Collins, now gone to his rest, in those days when he stood against the whole combined forces of slavery; but we must not stop here to name the men.—Waukegan, Elgin, Belvidere, Rockford, James, Freeport, Beloit, Princeton, (the home of Owen Lovejoy, brother to the noble martyr, Dixon, Mendota, Galesburg, Peoria, Bloomington, Ottawa, and Morris—towns in Illinois and Wisconsin—Jackson, Marshall, Albion, Ann Arbor and Detroit in Michigan, were all visited; and during our tour we made nearly fifty speeches, a part of the time speaking twice a day, besides talking much of the time in rail cars and elsewhere.

We came home somewhat fatigued, but much gratified by what we have met with, seen and heard during our journey. Those who came to hear us, were confessedly the most valuable and intelligent of the people in each community visited, just the class before whom it is of importance to get the claims of our people. And no matter what might be the subject of our discourses, whether before lyceums or elsewhere, slavery was really the thought uppermost in the minds of our hearers. Our own connection with slavery and identity with the oppressed, makes any good thing we are, under God, able to do, or say, tell in favor of the cause of our whole race.—Every town we visit, every audience we address, seem to regard us as the medium of an acquaintance with our enslaved people; and we have cause to rejoice when we see, as we have often seen during this and other tours through the country, a better feeling toward the colored man, a higher estimate of his qualities, and a deeper respect for his rights, as the results of our labors.

Our readers have already learned that we met with one incident of a slightly unpleasant character while at the American House at Janesville. The landlord, a rampant Democrat, wishing to signalize his devotion to the Dred Scott decision and to slavery generally, by making an example of us, and for that purpose caused a table to be set at the extreme end of the dining room, with two hall doors and a street door opened directly upon it, where all the loafers of the bar room could come and feast their ill natured curiosity upon us and indulge a morbid feeling of pleasure at our isolation. The table was covered with a dirty and ragged table cloth, and the whole appearance of the breakfast preparations made to resemble *"Negro fare"* on a slave plantation as nearly as it conveniently could. We, with our friends H. Ford Douglass[63] and John Jones, who accompanied us, seeing that the whole thing was a premeditated attempt to degrade and insult us, paid our bill and went to another hotel, where we were treated with the same consideration extended to other travelers. We made no noise, put on no airs, nor showed any marked sense of dissatisfaction, but simply told the landlord that we would pay our bill and leave, as we did not choose to gratify the feeling of prejudice and contempt which he has essayed to make us serve. We regret that this miserable affair has got into the papers at all, for it is every way exceptional, it being the only case of the kind we met with during our whole journey, the rule being all the other way; but since it has been made the subject of comment, we are thus particular to state the facts, as they really are. We have been represented as imposing ourselves upon those who did not want us, forcing ourselves among white people, simply because when traveling we do not wish to be stowed away in a separate car from all other travelers, and when at hotels opened to the public, do not like to be sat aside as a moral leper, unfit to be in the presence of other men. This is our offense, and our only offense. No one can say, either in or out of Rochester, that we ever took special pains to get into the society of white people or of any other people. We have no prejudices nor preferences based upon color.

Our Democratic contemporary over the way thinks us too sensitive; that we should feel it no disgrace to sit apart from others at hotels. He is another instance of the philosophy and cool equanimity with which men can bear insults when offered to others. We hold that when at home, in one's own house, a man is at liberty to say who shall and who shall not come to his table, and to choose his own associates; but when he goes into a public hotel, his right of choice is qualified by the rights of other travelers, whose rights are equal to his. He has a right then to what he pays for, no more, no less. He may not say that the man with red hair shall not sit at the same table with him, nor that a man with a colored skin shall not sit at the same table with him; the right of the men with the red hair, and him of the black skin is as good as the right of any. Men who travel should leave their prejudices at home, and determine their conduct in the light of their just rights— rights which are equal, and which can only be forfeited by a violation of them in the persons of others. If guests have no right to set up their prejudices as the rule for the government of public houses, landlords have not.—They keep a public table, advertise to accommodate the public, and have no arbitrary right over the table. The table really belongs to those who pay for it, and equally to all who pay for it. Each person has a right to the knife, fork, and plate, and the good things before him, but he has no right to say who shall sit at the other end or the other side of the table, nor who shall sit next to him. Both landlord and guests ought to take *"pot luck"* in this respect. Strange as these common sense suggestions may appear now to some who may read them, they are certain to prevail in this country, and our visit to the West has done much to establish this conclusion. *"It's coming yet for a' that."*

*Frederick Douglass' Paper*, March 25, 1859

# PIERCE M. BUTLER'S SLAVE AUCTION

There are, undoubtedly, many points connected with slave life, which strike and sting the heart with a sharper and more terrible sensation than a mere slave auction. In some of its manifold features, the slave system strikes home at once, instantly overwhelming the soul with frantic horror. In others, its grim and ghastly enormity is revealed only by degrees; the sense of its great wickedness deepens and widens the longer the mind dwells upon it. Such is the effect of a slave auction. The mind becomes stupefied and the heart sick over it. At the first, the wickedness is too great for words, too great for comprehension, and oppresses the senses, loading them down with unutterable disgust and loathing. Those who would witness to the truth of this statement, have only to read the article which occupies the entire first page of our present number. The man who can read and think of the scene there described, and do so without a deep and heart-rending sense of the infernal character of American slavery, has lost the quality that separates men from demons. We fling this ghastly picture, not of human but of diabolical depravity, before our readers in its whole length. Let it be read all over the country, and by everybody. Let it be scattered broadcast over the Northern States; let it be published especially in England, that the Christian people of that land may see with distinctness one feature, at least, of our sacred institution. It is a source of much encouragement and hope, that we perceive special efforts are being made to give this document a very wide circulation at home and abroad. The Rochester Ladies' Anti-Slavery Society will, we trust, take hold of this work in earnest, and do its share in exposing the true character of the great evil. Slavery must be abolished by the peaceful weapons of *light* and *truth,* or by force and bloodshed; therefore let the light shine, and let the truth be told, that slavery may meet a peaceful, not a bloody end.

A notable circumstance about this grand vendue of "slaves and souls of men," is that the owner of the slaves is a citizen of a free State, a resident of the city of Philadelphia, a gentleman—aye, a gentleman, if one can be such, who can breed men for the market, and drag a woman from a bed of confinement with a baby six days old in her arms to the auction block, and there sell her and her baby to pay debts which this prodigal gentleman had contracted by riotous living. No wonder that the noble-hearted Fanny Kemble[64] refused to remain under the roof of such a gentleman! and prefers now to earn the "staff of life," by her own energies, to living upon the gold and silver of Pierce M. Butler, stained as it is with the blood of five hundred slaves. We remember at the time this noble woman was endeavoring to free herself from this gentlemanly manstealer, one of the reasons was alleged to be his slaveholding; but we feared that such a report was quite too creditable to human nature to be true. We now learn that what we thought too creditable to human nature, was entirely true of Fanny Kemble.—There are, doubtless, many other Pierce M. Butlers in the city of Philadelphia, and other Northern cities. They are the moral pests of Northern society, and the explanation of the slow growth of anti-slavery opinion in all our large cities. They are wise in coming North to defend slavery, for here its fate is to be decided. All the munitions of war which endanger the slave system are North, and nothing furnishes such a barricade against assaults from our pulpit and press, as money and social position. Who knows but that Pierce M. Butler is now suffering patriotically? Who knows but that he has spent the earnings of his Negroes too lavishly, it may be, but still at the call of his country, or rather at the call of slavery, the reputed mother of a thousand blessings, especially to the slaves themselves? If this be the case, his brother slaveholders have dealt ungratefully with him in allowing him thus to fall beneath the weight of his debts. They should have made common cause with him in this bitter hour of his need.

But hand around the account of the grand slave auction. It is an admirable anti-slavery document, and the *N.Y. Tribune* is entitled to much credit for furnishing the public with it. Of all things dreadful, slaveholders and slave-traders dread most open exposure of the slave system. Slavery loves darkness and cannot endure the light. Hence, Speech is gagged; the Press is fettered; patrols, spys, eaves-droppers and informers everywhere accompany the hateful thing. All moral life demands its death, hence all moral life must be extinguished, in order that slavery may live and flourish. But read the heart-sickening details of Pierce M. Butler's slave auction, and circulate it largely among your neighbors.

*Frederick Douglass' Paper*, March 25, 1859

# H. FORD DOUGLASS

The nature of this young colored orator, who has quite distinguished himself at the West as an eloquent advocate of the emancipation and elevation of our enslaved people, has often, of late, been seen in our columns. We owe it to him, and to the cause of our people, which he is so well able to serve, to say a word of him to our readers, and to commend him to their regard. We do this the more freely since we have made his acquaintance and learned something of his spirit as a Reformer, his character as a man, his principles of action, the history of his self-education, and his ability as a speaker. During our recent visit to Illinois and Michigan, we had many opportunities of listening to H. Ford Douglass; and we only speak the general conviction of other men, competent judges of true eloquence, when we pronounce him a man of rare and noble powers, one who may rise to any height of usefulness and fame in the cause of his people. He has that quality without which all speech is vain—*earnestness.* He throws his whole soul into what he says, and all he says. His person is fine, his voice musical, and his gestures natural and graceful. The question was frequently put to us, when leaving halls where H. Ford Douglass had spoken, "Where was he educated?" and we remarked the look of astonishment when we told them that our young friend was a self-made, a self-educated man, and owes nothing to schools or colleges. He entirely surprised us, and not more by the power of his speech, than by the extent and accuracy of his information. He has read and heard. This would not avail him much, but that he is a man of a fine sense of the beautiful and the true, and knows well what to appropriate and use, and what to reject as improper and useless.

We write this not as a puff to H. Ford Douglass, not as incense ofered to vanity, but from a desire to enlarge the field of his usefulness, to awaken an interest in the man, that the man may the better serve the cause. When we heard him, we wanted others to hear him; we wish every slaveholder and Negro-whipper in the land could hear the scorching denunciations poured out upon them from his lips. We call upon H. Ford Douglass to put himself unreservedly into the lecturing field, not upon the platform of an "African Civilization Society,"[65] (which makes no issue with the guilty conscience of this nation, and aims to remove us from our depressing circumstances, instead of counselling us to make war upon them and overcome them.) Let him stand upon the platform of Radical Abolitionism, and go to the people of the country with a tangible issue. He will then have something to fire his soul, engage his energies, unfold his powers, and make him a strong man, a hero, in the service of his people. No better issue can be made to the State of Illinois, with slavery, than the repeal of her Black Laws. All that is malignant and slaveholding in that State, clings around and supports these atrocious laws. The immediate repeal of these cruel enactments, (which the white Douglas is endeavoring to sustain,) should be the demand of the black Douglass of Chicago.—He is just the man for the place, and the friends of freedom in that city should urge him forward and hold up his hands in doing it. At any rate, we give him our good word, with a hearty good will, and pledge him whatever co-operation we are able to give to the good work to which we invite him.

*Frederick Douglass' Paper*, March 25, 1859

## OLD BROWN IN ROCHESTER

We have had a hero among us, and we wish to make a note of the fact for *future* reference. "Old Brown," of Kansas memory,[66] has been here. He was received at the City Hall on Saturday evening by an audience exceedingly and discreditably small, considering the Republican professions of our citizens, and the character and history of the brave old man , to whose courage and skill, more than to those of any other man in Kansas, the freedom of that Territory is now indebted. It is hard to account for the indifference of Republicans to the claims of John Brown, on any grounds which do not imply an impeachment of their sincerity and honesty. Have they been sincere in what they have said of their love of freedom? Have they really desired to head off, hem in, and dam up the desolating tide of slavery? If so, does it not seem that one who has suffered, and perilled everything in accomplishing these very ends, has some claims upon their grateful respect and esteem? Where were they on Saturday night? Why were they not present to grasp the hand that disarmed the Border Ruffian, Henry Clay Pate, and captured his company of Missouri invaders? the hand that cut up General Read's army of four hundred ruffians, who were running roughshod over the trembling Free State settlements in Kansas in 1856? the hand that made it possible for Free State men to remain in that Territory at all; we say, why were they not present to grasp the hand by which the tide was turned in favor of freedom in Kansas?

Had John Brown been a man of words, rather than deeds, had he been noted for opposing slavery with his breath, rather than with blows, some apology might be made for the indifference with which he has been received in this city. It might be said that we have enough of that sort of courage among us for all the homage and admiration we have to lavish upon courage of that quality. Had he come to us from Washington, where he had spoken eloquently for free Kansas, instead of from the dangers and hardships of border life, where he had acted his part bravely, his reception here would have been cordial, and perhaps enthusiastic. Only give us a sham instead of a real man and Rochester is not behind the chief cities of the Republic. Even our newly appointed Republican Janitor of the City Hall ran off with the key of the bell of the City Hall, and refused to ring it on the occasion! Shame upon his little soul, and upon all the little souls who sustained him in his conduct!

John Brown does not really need the sympathy such souls can give. though he comes here from a three years' campaign in the cause of justice and liberty, and stripped of all earthly possessions, he has with him that which is more precious than silver or gold, or the hollow-hearted approbation of the crowd. The consciousness of having honestly and fearlessly performed his duty, in a crisis which demanded the courage and skill of a hero, is his. A man who will forsake home, family, ease, and security, and in the cause of liberty go forth to spill his blood, if need be, is a man who can look down upon a large part of this world of ours. The time is coming when we shall be quite ashamed of the reception given to John Brown, for the country has not reached such an absolute security from the aggressions of slavery as to make it safe and wise to discharge a man so noble, and a soldier so brave.

It is poosible that Mr. Brown is a trifle too thorough in his devotion to the cause of freedom to suit the professed friends of that cause. His recent demonstration against slavery in Missouri, in which he released a dozen slaves from bondage by force, may have produced the conviction that he is not altogether so politic and discreet as a leader should be. Indeed, that act of his has raised a question both of his honesty and his sanity in some quarters, and made him an object of suspicion in some others. For the benefit of all such, we would say that Mr. Brown is neither insane nor inconsistent.[67] He says that slavery is only one form of robbery, and he acts just as he talks. He does not think himself a sinner, because he plucks the spoiled out of the jaws of the spoiler, but simply in the way of his duty, as a man, and a Christian. The basis of his idea of duty is comprehensive and philosphical.—The enslavement of the humblest human being he declares to be an act of injustice and wrong, for which Almighty God will hold all mankind responsible; that a case of the kind is one in which every human being is solemnly bound to interfere; and that he who has the power to do so, and fails to improve it, is involved in the guilt of the original crime. He takes this to be sound morality, and sound Christianity, and we think him not far from the right.

*Frederick Douglass' Paper*, April 15, 1859


# EULOGY ON THE LATE HON. WM. JAY

DELIVERED on the invitation of the Colored Citizens of New York City in Shiloh Presbyterian Church, New York, May 12, 1859

Friends and Fellow-Citizens:

. . . Honorable William Jay is dead! Since our last Anniversaries in this city—in the objects of which he took so lively an interest—he has been summoned the way of all the earth! The broad, mysterious curtains, which separate the busy scenes of Time and Sense from the solemn and measureless plains of Eternity, have silently fallen between us and him. We shall no more see the fragile form of William Jay upon the earth. His pale and benignant face, so well and gratefully remembered by most of us, has been veiled in death! We have often seen his countenance glow with fervor and spirituality as he sat in our meetings, cheering on the utterance of the great truths of Liberty and Humanity, which were ever dear to his warm and generous heart. But his place on the Abolition platform is now vacant. His beneficent mission among men is now completed. His good work on the earth is done, and he is gathered home to his exceeding great reward. His sleeping dust lies among the ancestral tombs of his great family, and ancient patrimonial trees now fling their plaintive shadows upon his new-made grave. His body, amid solemn ceremonies, has been committed to the dust from whence it was taken, and his immortal spirit has gone up to the God who gave it. In the death of William Jay, the cause of Emancipation in the United States has lost one of its ablest and most effective advocates. Our peeled and woe-stricken people, both of the North and of the South, have lost an invaluable friend. We have, as a people, too few real friends, even among our professed friends; and we have now lost one of the truest and best of that few. Some of the heaviest and bitterest reproaches under which we have been compelled to stagger, as a people, in this country, have come, unfortunately, from persons who affect to regard us as objects of compassion—men who actually trade in our sorrows, and live by our afflictions. All the more, on this account, we feel, and shall feel, the loss of our friend Wm. Jay. His friendship for us had its basis in principle. It was unaffected by the ebbs and flows of the national feelings, for or against us, and stood inflexibly and unalterably the same in every hour of trial.

In view of the mighty struggle for freedom in which we are now engaged, and the tremendous odds arrayed against us, every colored man, and every friend of the colored man, in this country, must deeply feel the great loss we have sustained in this death, and look around with anxious solicitude for the man who shall rise to fill the place now made vacant. With emphasis it may be said of him, he was our wise counsellor, our firm friend, and our liberal benefactor. Against the fierce onsets of popular abuse, he was our shield; against governmental intrigue and oppression, he was our learned, able, and faithful defender; against the crafty counsels of wickedness in high places, where mischief is framed by law, and sin is sanctioned and supported by religion, he was a perpetual and burning rebuke.

Poetry and eloquence will search in vain for nobler themes, with which to enlighten and inspire the minds of men, than those which form the basis of the character and history of William Jay. All that is commanding in virtue—all that is exalted and sublime in piety—all that is disinterested in patriotism—all that is noble in philanthropy— all that will bear, like the unblenching marble, the searching judgments of after-coming ages, in which all our works shall be tried as by fire, stand out gloriously in the life of William Jay.

One qualification, which may serve me as an apology for venturing to speak in the name and memory of one so eminent as our honored friend—a friend whose name must confer honor upon all who seek to honor it—this it is: In common with you, my friends, I wear the hated complexion which Wm. Jay never hated. I have worn the galling chain which Wm. Jay earnestly endeavored to break. I have felt the heavy lash, and experienced in my own person the cruel wrongs which caused his manly heart to melt in pity for the slave.

Who but the slave should lament, when the champion of the slave has fallen! Who but the black man should weep, when the black man's friend is no more! Who should rise to vindicate, honor, and bless the memory of William Jay, if the colored people of this State and country may not properly do so?

While other rights may be denied us—while other privileges may be withheld from us—while we may not share in the honor of building the tombs of other great men of the country, whose actions, so far as they touched us, tore open our wounds instead of healing them—surely, no man will shut against us the offices of love and gratitude in this special instance. All will admit that those who have witnessed the scenes, and have endured the hardships of Slavery, may be permitted to make some sign, however rude and awkward, in generous token of the love and gratitude with which the memory of William Jay is cherished. It is meet that some broken accents, not less acceptable because broken, should rise from the sable ranks of untutored millions, as a testimonial to one who stood by us and befriended us, in all the vicissitudes of our anomalous and forlorn condition. Of one thing we may feel assured: Whatever may be thought of our assembling here this evening, and whatever aversion it may excite here on the earth, that pure spirit which did not disdain us when in this world of pride and show, will from his celestial abode look down approvingly upon the humble offering we venture to bring to his memory. He who had respect for us among those who despised us; he who bound up our wounds, when the priest and the Levite had left us to die; he who lifted us up when the church and State had wantonly and maliciously trodden upon us—will not reject the only offering a fettered and enslaved people have to bring. The principles of Mr. Jay knew no selfish and partial limitations. They reached to the very outer-most boundaries of the outcast, embracing in their broad beneficence, the poorest, the rudest, and most neglected of men; and he may therefore fitly be the object of marked and decided expression of living remembrance on our part.

The liberal press of the country, to which he was an able, learned, and voluminous contributor, often anonymously, and as often over his own signature, has taken respectful, lengthy and gratifying notice of the death of William Jay. The legal profession, represented by the bar of Westchester county, where he lived and presided—where he was most intimately known as a man and as a minister of justice—has recorded its unhesitating testimony to his eminent worth, as a man, and as an upright judge. Religion, to which he was an unblemished honor through all the years of his life, has dropped its tear upon his sacred grave. Learning, not less than Law, has recognized with fitting tokens of bereavement the loss of one of its brightest ornaments. The cause of international Peace, to which Mr. Jay was deeply devoted, and for the promotion of which he labored with that skill, fidelity, and efficiency, which distinguished him in every department of reform that engaged his energies, has summoned the ancient prophet-like eloquence of George B. Cheever, to Boston, before the American Peace Society, of which Mr. Jay was long an honored President, to speak in memory of his good works in that department of Christian Philanthropy. Old personal friends, companions in the Christian reforms, to which he was earnestly attached, and for which he wrought with the pious zeal of a true Christian, have recorded in affectionate and most touching language, their sense of the beauty and excellence of his life and the great value of his friendship. The New York Historical Society, of which he was a member, describes him "accomplished as a scholar, eminent as a citizen, just as a Judge, candid and benevolent as a man, and sincere as a Christian," and esteems his name among the most illustrious on its roll.

In this grateful procession, who can have a better right to join than we? In the great cause of universal freedom his name was a tower of strength, and his pen a two-edged sword. His mightiest works were wrought for us. Our freedom, our elevation were special objects of his regard. We have a right to cherish his memory as a precious legacy. We may bind it upon the altars of our heart's best affections, and offer it the ever-increasing tribute of our respect and gratitude.

The name of William Jay should hereafter be associated in our minds and hearts with the venerated names of William Wilberforce, Thomas Clarkson, and Granville Sharpe, the most illustrious friends of our people, who now rest from their labors. It was given unto Clarkson and Wilberforce to remain long enough on the earth, to see the ripening fruits of their devoted labors. They were permitted to see the triumph of the great principles and measures which they with almost matchless perseverance pressed home upon the hearts of the British nation. They lived long enough to behold their beloved Britain a free country, the safe asylum of the enslaved of all lands, and of all colors. They saw the dark stain of human bondage washed out, and the moral sentiment of their country so purified that a slave cannot breathe in England; and the whole policy of the British Government was changed in their very presence, and in direct and immediate response to their indefatigable exertions to bring about that very result. They saw the slaves emancipated. Their living ears caught the glad shouts and songs of eight hundred thousand souls redeemed from slavery in the West Indies. Joyous anthems of Freedom, sweeping across the wild waves, and rising above the thunders of the mighty deep, brought joy to the hearts of the noble and aged emanicpators, ere they quitted the shores of Time. They beheld, while yet in the flesh, the finger of God, writing their heavenly welcome upon discarded whips, severed chains and broken fetters—"Well done, good and faithful servants."

So, however, hath it not been with our great friend in America, whose character and labors, so beautifully resemble theirs. The toils of the seed time, but not the joys of the harvest, were his. He sowed in tears, but the golden sheaves of rejoicing have yet to be gathered into the garner of righteousness. Nevertheless, it was his great privilege to see after a long course of severe labor, patiently and cheerfully performed, the great cause of emancipation rapidly rising to power and importance in this country fully justifying his best hopes for its ultimate success. The important truths which he brought forward and illustrated, and enforced, by utterance and by action, and with marked fidelity, although yet falling on unwilling ears, have certainly rallied in their defense, a mighty host, whose advancing footsteps already rock the continent and fill the halls of American tyrants with alarm and terror, *and the huts of the slave with joy and hope.*

Though Mr. Jay saw with grief, as his pure spirit passed away from us, the slave still toiling in hateful chains, and the slave power madly intent upon the endless perpetuation of slavery, he evidently took with him to his blissful abode, the happy assurance that he had not labored for the honor of his country and the freedom of the slave in vain. Like another great Liberator, who was not permitted to see the full realization of his hopes, he endured as seeing him who is invisible! He died just as he had dared to live, a true man, and an honest Abolitionist. To the very last he remembered the American bondman as bound with him.

Happy and glorious is the lot of that man, who, when standing on the verge of the grave, winding up his affairs in this life, surveying the whole course of his career of the earth, can truthfully say, in full view of the past, and the great incoming future, I have no regrets for the uses to which I have put my time and talents.

I well remember, and shall never forget, the impression made upon my mind, by the declaration made to me on this point, by the good and great Thomas Clarkson. Standing face to face with me, in his study at Playford Hall, erect, calm, and collected in the eighty-seventh year of his age, his long flowing silvery locks falling gracefully upon his shoulders, assured by his advanced age, and his gathering infirmities, that he was fast verging toward the tomb; he said, while holding my right hand firmly in his, "Go on, go on, in the good work, Mr. Douglass; I have given sixty-seven years of my life to the Abolition cause, and if I had sixty-seven more, they should all be sacredly given to the same cause!" Mr. Jay has given proof of the same satisfaction with his anti-slavery life. He was as certain of the ultimate triumph of emancipation as he was of its righteousness, and he committed himself to its whole course without reserve and without qualification.

His last *will and testament* contains a lesson to our country and the world on this subject. That sacred document exposes anew the futility and the blasphemy of attempting to control and overawe a good man's conscience by the force and authority of inhuman and wicked laws.

Mr. Jay's example at this point stands alone, I think, in the history of American philanthropy. No American Christian or Abolitionist has left a better testimony for the truth, or a nobler defiance of wrong. You have heard of bequests to popular institutions, to churches, colleges, tract societies, missionary societies, and even to piles of stone in honor of the successful man-slayer, but never, I think, such a bequest as the following: "I bequeath to my son *one thousand dollars* to be applied by him at his discretion in promoting the safety and comfort of fugitive slaves." Here is not only a thoughtful concern for the most needy of all the poor of this land, but a burning protest and a sublime prophecy. It is a cutting rebuke to the present, and an appeal to the future by a righteous man looking steadfastly into the immeasurable continents of eternity, and winding up his affairs for his long journey, and unending home with God.

However, those who maintain the divine right of Christian white men to hunt down and to hold the black man in slavery, may affect to regard this defiance of the fugitive slave statute, in the glorious coming future—when Doctors of Divinity shall find a better use for the Bible than in using it to prop up slavery, and better employment for their time and talents than in finding analogies between Paul's Epistle to Philemon and the slave-catching bill of Millard Fillmore, this act of Christian charity on the part of Mr. Jay, will be regarded as the crowning act, the most glorious climax to a great and benevolent life.

My friends, I can attempt here no general and detailed account of the life and the services of William Jay. Only a few of the leading facts of his ample history can be properly noticed and compressed within the narrow limits suited to the present discourse, and to this occasion. The relation of Mr. Jay to any one of the good causes, to which he gave his sympathy and his earnest co-operation, if minutely and faithfully examined, would fill a volume. We can scarcely hope to bring him before you in more than one of these relations. His connection with the great cause of human freedom, is the most prominent, as it is the most significant and important feature of his life. It is the feature of the life and history of Mr. Jay which will longest keep his memory fresh and green, at home and abroad.

Mr. Jay was born in New York, on the 16th of June, 1789, and died at his home in Westchester county, on the 14th of October, 1858, having nearly filled up the scriptural measure of human life. He was the second son of John Jay—a man whose name and fame stand worthily connected with those of George Washington.

The father of our deceased friend was one of the most eminent men of his day, and ranked with such as Hancock, Adams, Hamilton, Jefferson, and Franklin—the most renowned of all the American patriots. The history of John Jay is in fact the history of the American Revolution, and the American Independence; as, indeed, it is also the history of Emancipation in this State. For the father, not less than the son, was an Abolitionist. Abolitionism seems hereditary in the family—from father to son and from son to grand-son. In the darkest hours, and the deepest perils, which surrounded the American cause, and they were far more numerous and direful than many at this day suppose, John Jay never wavered, John Jay never doubted. It is, indeed, hard to say, in view of the slender margin between success and failure in that great undertaking, how the Revolution would have ended, whether independence itself would have been achieved had it lacked the support of John Jay. Certain it is, that to his devotion, vigor, sagacity, address, unflagging industry and determination, the American people are to-day largely indebted for their freedom and independence. He served his country as few had the ability to serve it. His singular purity of character shed light and gave strength to the revolutionary cause.

At home and abroad, by his talents, by his learning, by his voice, and by his pen, in council, in the field; as a member of Congress, as a foreign minister, as Chief Justice of the United States, both before and after the Revolution, John Jay won for himself a high place among the Patriots of the Revolution.

William Jay was fortunate in being the son of such a father. A man so faithful to the impulses of true liberty, animated by the loftiest patriotism, was just the man to be scrupulously concerned for the proper education of his children; for love of family and love of country go hand in hand together. Ambition may, indeed, sometimes mask itself in the attractive forms of patriotism—but the genuine sentiment springs up in its fullness and purity only at the fire-side.

When but eleven years old, William Jay was placed at Albany under the charge of Rev. Mr. Ellison, an Oxford scholar noted for his strict discipline, and devotion to the classics. Here he, no doubt, acquired that habit of order and regularity of proceeding, for which he was ever afterwards remarkable, and to which, in part, may be ascribed the facility with which he accomplished any and every work undertaken by him.

Yale College, an institution already loaded down with honors, has the great honor of completing the education of Mr. Jay. He entered Yale in 1804, and took his degree in 1807, having ranked throughout the course among the severest students.

Turning his attention to the law—of which in after-life, he became an able exponent of its highest attributes in its application to human rights—he was again placed at Albany, in the office of John B. Henry, an eminent lawyer, in that city of eminent lawyers.

Here Mr. Jay took the degree of Counsellor, but owing to failing health he abandoned the practice of the profession, and rejoined his father's family and assisted in the management of his estate at Bedford, which estate he inherited upon the death of his father, in 1829.

From this sacred old homestead, hallowed by glorious revolutionary memories—the scene of many an anxious consultation, in the troubled times that tnen's souls—the steady light of William Jay's clear intellect has streamed out over the country and the world, blessing all it has touched.

While in Mr. Henry's office, earnestly pursuing the study of the law, Mr. Jay wrote to his friend and class-mate, Mr. Henry P. Strong, who was then studying for the ministry, a letter which gives us a key to his own character and history:

"The pursuit," writes Mr. Jay, "in which you are engaged, is the most important, and the most interesting that can occupy the attention of man. I have devoted myself to the law, to protect the weak from the power of the strong. To shield the poor from the oppression of the rich, is the part for which I am preparing myself. God grant that I may not labor in vain."

Here is a noble and generous purpose declared, and I undertake to say that it has been as nobly and generously performed.

Fortunate in his parentage, fortunate in his education, fortunate in the choice of his profession, fortunate in all his early surroundings, Mr. Jay was not less fortunate in his marriage. In any condition of life, marriage is a matter of great moment. Even in private life, it may be the tide taken at the flood that leads on to fortune, or it may lead on to wreck and ruin. But its power for good or for evil is increased in a ratio with the magnitude of a man's public sphere and duties.

Here it may be an exalted blessing, or a withering curse—it may bear us upward towards success, or cast us down to failure. In all his noble plans and purpose our departed friend had the good fortune to be seconded by his excellent wife—in whose character were harmoniously blended, like his own, all the Christian virtues.

Subsequent to his marriage, which took place in 1812, Mr. Jay was appointed first Judge of the County of Westchester, and was continued upon the bench by successive Governors, of opposite and conflicting politics, through all the varied contests and changes of parties, until the year 1843. Speaking of Mr. Jay, as a judge, the *Historical Magazine* remarks, that his charges to grand juries, commanded attention from his clear exposition of the law, without the slightest concession to the popular current of the day, and with careful regard to constitutional rights, morality and justice. All who know anything of Judge Jay will assent to the justice of this encomium.

Mr. Jay never sought office. He belonged to other and better days of the Republic—when other and better tastes prevailed in respect to holding civil office. General Jackson, while President, appointed him to an important Commissionership, but the office which had been unsought, was declined. Important Commissionerships are seldom declined in our day. With talents, learning, and ability, a man of his position and connections, with a different ambition might have risen to almost any station in the country, but he contented himself in his office of County Judge. In this office, which enabled him to be of immediate service to those of his fellow-citizens, who know his character and uprightness best, he would have remained probably to the day of his death but for his anti-slavery sentiments and principles.

Having been successively commissioned by Governors Tompkins, Clinton, Marcy and Van Buren, Mr. Jay was superseded by Governor Bouck, who had been elected in the pro-slavery reaction which followed the retirement of Governor Seward from office. The removal of Judge Jay was notoriously in compliance with the demands of the pro-slavery press, urged on by the slave power of the nation. The circumstance at the time of its occurrence excited strong and decided disapproval in the county of Westchester. A letter addressed to Judge Jay by Minot Mitchell of White Plains, a gentleman who then stood at the head of the bar, expressed the unqualified regret and indignation of the people.

On some accounts, Mr. Jay's removal from the judgeship is to be regarded as fortunate. He was left all the more leisure to devote to the different objects of Christian benevolence which had already largely occupied his thoughts and feelings. The world is all the better for his removal from the bench. It was meant for evil, but it worked for good, for he could have scarcely found time to write so much and so efficiently had he continued to perform the duties of his judicial office.

In religion Mr. Jay was a low church Episcopalian, and though a devoted and conscientious churchman, he was singularly free from that self-righteous bigotry which can see and appreciate nothing as good, that does not bear the image and superscription of a particular religious denomination. His estimate of the tenets of other Christian denominations was like the man, broad, catholic, philosophical and liberal.

In politics he was like his honored father, a Federalist of the old school. Subsequently he acted with the Whig party, and finally with the Free Soil and Republican parties. Independent and honest, having no favors to ask of any party, his utterance of truth was never trammelled by his party connections. He was never prominent as a politician, and he was equally never of those who esteem themselves too righteous to take part in the government of their country.

The labors of Mr. Jay were very quietly performed. He was often found serving upon committees of religious, benevolent and scientific associations, giving them the great benefit of his presence, knowledge, experience and his wisdom; but he seldom appeared as a speaker before the public. While, however, he had no taste for the noise and ostentation of public assemblies, he did not despise those popular instrumentalities for flinging the great truths of liberty, virtue, and humanity among the people.

The very last time it was my privilege to see Judge Jay, was on one of those great public occasions four years ago. It was at that memorable meeting when Charles Sumner, now suffering from assassin blows,[68] (which may God heal,) was thrilling with his surpassing eloquence an audience of your most refined and cultivated citizens at Metropolitan Theatre. Judge Jay was there. He was there and on the platform. Among all the radiant faces, making up that grand and brilliant scene, there was not one which seemed more in sympathy with the great theme of the orator than his. It was a benediction to look upon that good man's face that night. I remember it as one of the most pleasing and imposing features of that great occasion.

But the crowded hall, the clash and glitter of public speech and debate were not the favorite surroundings of Judge Jay. He is not to be contemplated to the best advantage in that direction and amid such scenes. The slender frame and delicate health which led him to abandon the profession of the law, made him unsuited to the physical hardships and excitements incident to frequent attendanse upon, and participation in the proceedings of public meetings.

The pen was the weapon of his choice, and the weapon of his power. His quiet study was the scene of his most efficient warfare with wrong. It was here that he met the dark legions of error, selfishness, sin, and moral death, as they sallied forth from the gloomy gates of hell and vanquished them. Slavery, intemperance, war, duelling, treachery, hypocrisy, wickedness in high places, in church and state, found in him a steady and uncompromising enemy, while nearly every

good cause of his time received the aid of his countenance and cooperation. Mr. Jay's zeal and industry with his pen are proved by the great
number and quality of his works. These are his perpetual eulogy.
Letters, essays, pamphlets, books, newspaper articles on a variety of
subjects, mostly of immediate and of practical importance, and all
looking to the establishment of just principles for the well government
of society, flowed from his pen in rapid succession, and prove him to
have been a man of immense industry and abundant mental resources.
In this respect, Mr. Jay appears to very great advantage. The world
may have many pleasing and gratifying spectacles to present us. We
meet in life many noble examples, worthy of our study and of our
imitation; but a man born to the inheritance of large wealth, able to
draw around him all that the cultivated taste and the peculiar pride of
riches can suggest as the luxuries and indulgences proper to opulence;
relieved of the necessity of making any exertion to supply real or
artificial wants; left wholly at leisure, having the option to work or
play, to seek his own pleasue, or to do otherwise; such a man, thus
favored, thus surrounded, and, *I may say, thus temped,* all forgetful of
himself, deaf to every selfish entreaty to ease and to idleness, deliberately choosing to devote himself to earnest, persevering, indefatigable
labor, not to increase his own worldly gains, either in purse or in
position, but with only the motive to add his mite to the welfare and
happipness of his suffering fellowmen, is one of the most hopeful,
gratifying and noble examples which in this selfish and ease-loving age
and world, it is permitted mankind to behold. Precisely such an example has been given to the world in the life and in th works of William
Jay. Compared with such a life, how vastly inferior, in all the elements
of true greatness, are the lives of most men to whom the world has
accorded fame and greatness. Such a man has conqured himself, and is
greater than him who has taken a city. Starting at the point where
other men have usually ended their labors, he has gone forward and
reached a point of excellence immeasurably beyond them. The man
who makes great exertions to be rich, the man who will endure untold
hardships and privations for the world's applause and honor, who seeks
the bubble, reutation, in the cannon's mouth, may, indeed, be a great
man; but how small is such a man, when measured by the example of
one who, though born to the inheritance of wealth, of ease, of leisure,
and of a name already illustrius, instead of reposing on what is alredy
attained, devotes all that he has an is to a cause of mercy and benevo-

lence, which he well knows must direct against him the bitter hostility of power, the scorn of pride, and the vindictive frown of public opinon. The men are few who can stand this test of greatness. How few of the rich and mighty men of the land have even yet earnetly identified themselves with the Abolition cause, and given it the benefit of their manful exertions.

Abolitionists have been called men of one idea, but if Judge Jay shall be embraced in this charge, it mut be confessed, upon a survey of his life and his labors, that his one idea was immensely comprehensive, and capable of manifold applications. Few men have taken a broader view of human life. Few men have better understood and better performed its various duties.

To Mr. Jay belongs the merit of not only studying many subjects, but also the merit of considering well whatever he considered at all. In 1826 he received a prize for an essay on the Sabbath, viewed as a civil institution; the year after he received another for an essay on the Sabbath viewed as a divine institution. In 1830 he was honored with a medal from the Savannah (Georgia) Anti-Duelling Society, for another essay upon the nefarious custom of duelling. In 1833 he published two octavo volumes, of the life and writings of his father, Chief Justice Jay. These volumes are among the most readable and reliable of any that treat of the early political history of this country.

He was a friend to the Bible, Tract, Peace, Temperance, Sunday School, Sabbath, Missionary and Educational causes. He was President of the Westchester Bible Society, and a Vice-President of the American Bible Society. His time, his money, and his talents were freely given in all these and other departments of benevolent effort. He was, however, by no means a worshipper of any particular organization or combination of men. He looked at such organizations in the broad, intense light of truth, and esteemed them simply as means to important ends. When any of them were guilty of substituting their dead forms for the living objects which brought them into being, as most of them were, he never hesitated to withdraw his countenance from them, and to expose and rebuke them with all faithfulness. The American Bible Society, Tract Society, Sunday School Union, and the American Board of Commissioners for Foreign Missions have all been subject to his public censure. His chief controversy with all these popular bodies was either their culpable indifference to the wrongs of the slave, or their directly aiding and abetting those who hold the slave in bondage.

These bodies were, and are lamentably open to rebuke, both for sins of omission and for sins of commission. They are yet on the side of the oppressor, and deaf to the cries of the slave. He loved the great objects for which these various associations were combined, but was unwilling to build up with one hand and tear down with the other; and to him nothing beneath the sky was more sacred than the rights of the American slave. He was unwilling to subordinate this cause to any other, and much more unwilling to sustain those who were using their influence and position to put down that hated cause.

Judge Jay wrote voluminously on the whole subject of slavery. I will name only a few of his publications: 'Letter to the Hon. Theodore Frelinghuysen, respecting his declaration that he was not an Abolitionist, but an ardent friend of the Colonization Society'—'Esamination of the Mosaic Laws of Servitude'—'Letter to the Committee chosen by the American Tract Society'—'Inquiry into the American Colonization and American Anti-Slavery Societies'—'A View of the Action of the Federal Government in behalf of Slavery'—'On the Condition of the Free People of Color in the United States'—'Address to the Friends of Constitutional Liberty on the Violation by the United States House of Representatives of the Right of Petition"— "Introductory Remarks to the Reproof of the American Church, contained in the recent History of the Protestant Episcopal Church in America, by the Bishop of Oxford"—"A letter to the Right Rev. L. Silliman Ives, Bishop of the Protestant Episcopal Church in the State of North Carolina"—"Address to the Inhabitants of New Mexico and California on the omission by Congress to provide them with Territorial Governments, and on the social and political evils of Slavery"—"A letter to Hon. William Nelson, Member of Congress, on Mr. Clay's Compromise"—"A letter to Hon. Samuel A. Elliott, Representative in Congress, in reply to his apology for voting for the Fugitive Slave Bill"—"An Address to the Anti-Slavery Christians of the United States, signed by a number of Clergymen and others" —"Letter to the Rev. R. S. Cook, Corresponding Secretary of the American Tract Society"—"Letter to Lewis Tappan, Esq., Treasurer of the American Missionary Association."

Mr. Jay was remarkable for his great readiness. He wrote precisely at the right time. No great occasion escaped him. He was ready for every emergency. Besides his public works, Mr. Jay wrote a great many private letters. He had a long list of correspondents. His anti-slavery relations alone gave him a great deal of this sort of occupation. His advice was constantly solicited by the leaders of the anti-slavery movement, and it was never withheld when it could be of service to the anti-slavery cause. Some idea can be formed of the extent of Judge Jay's anti-slavery correspondence, by the list of those with whom he was in most frequent communication.[69]

To form any just estimate of the character of a reformer, and to comprehend the value of his services, it is important to notice whether he embraced the cause early or late in the morning, or at the eleventh hour, whether he bore the burthen in the scorching heat of the noon-day sun, or came only in the refreshing cool of the evening, when the heaviest work was already done, and the space between labor and reward reduced to the smallest possible point. To this inquiry the history of Mr. Jay answers very satisfactorily. He was not behind the chiefest apostle of *immediate* emancipation. He, himself was too noble to set up any claims as to priority in the assertion of the doctrine of modern Abolitionism. He never asked to be considered the originator of the anti-slavery movement; and yet impartial history will accord to William Jay the credit of having affirmed all the leading principles of modern Abolitionism long before modern Abolitionism was recognized as a reformatory movement. There has been much said about "immediatism," as the peculiarity of the present movement, and when that principle was first applied to the abolition of slavery in this country. Some have attributed the doctrine to Mr. Garrison, and insist upon denouncing, as traitors, all who deny this claim. The absurdity of this pretension on the one hand, and the folly and injustice of the denunciation on the other, have become equally apparent in looking at the letters and papers of William Jay. Without, for a moment, wishing to call in question the eminent services which Wm. Lloyd Garrison rendered to the cause of aboliton when organized a quarter of a century ago, it can be shown that the doctrine of immediate Abolitionism was affirmed by W. Jay befor Mr. Garrison was so much as heard of in the anti-slavery cause. In 1819, Mr. Jay wrote to Hon. Elias Boudinot, as follows:

I have no doubt that the laws of God, and as a necessary and inevitable consequence, the true interests of our country, forbid the extension of slavery. If our country is ever to be redeemed from the curse of slavery, the present Congress must stand between the living and the dead, and stay the plague. Now is the accepted time, now is the day of salvation. If slavery once takes root on the other side of the Mississippi, it can never afterwards be exterminated, but will extend with the future western empire, poisoning the feelings of humanity, checking the growth of those principles of virtue and religion which constitute alike the security and happiness of civil society.

On the 22d of September, 1826, he wrote to Hon. Mr. Miner of the House of Representatives:

Since I read the resolution introduced by you in relation to slavery in the District of Columbia, the subject has been scarcely absent from my mind, and the late imprisonment in Washington of a citizen of this county, (Westchester County, N.Y.,) afforded an opportunity which I gladly embraced of obtaining an expression of public opinion. I do not entertain the slightest hope that our petition will be favorably received, nor the slightest apprehensions that the cause we espouse will not finally triumph. The history of the abolition of the slave trade teaches us the necessity of patient perseverance, and affords a pledge that perseverance will be ultimately crowned with success. We have nothing to fear, but much to hope from the violence and threats of our opponents. Apathy is the only obstacle we have reason to dread, and to remove this obstacle it is necessary that the attention of the public should be constantly directed to the subject. Every discussion in Congress in relation to slavery, no matter how great may be the majority against us, advances our cause. We shall rise more powerful from every defeat.

On the 4th of November, 1826, he writes to Mr. Thomas Hall:

In consequence of a resolution passed at a public meeting in this county, (a meeting called through Mr. Jay's effort in relation to the arrest and imprisonment, at Washington, of Gilbert Horton, a free black man of Westchester,) a petition will be forwarded to Congress for the immediate abolition of slavery in the District of Columbia. It is not easy to calculate the vast importance of the object of this petition. The District, it is true, is small, and the number of slaves to be emancipated comparatively few; but the moral influence of the measure will be felt on every plantation, and in every Legislature in the several States. It is an act which is required by our national character, as well as by humanity and religion. Congree possesses an undoubted constitutional right to abolish slavery in the District of Columbia, and it is in the power of the free States to carry the measure.

Thus we see the criminal character of slavery declared, the non-extension of slavery insisted upon, the Negro recognized and called a citizen, and the immediate abolition of slavery demanded as early as 1819 and 1826, by William Jay.

This was no sudden and temporary outburst of feeling against slavery, by Mr. Jay. Writing to Mr. Chas. Miner, member of Congress, from Pennsylvania, who had introduced a bill for the abolition of slavery in the District of Columbia, he says:

In our exertions to promote the welfare of our fellow men, we must, for our encouragement, recollect that we are not answerable for success. It is our duty to plant and water, while the conviction that it is God who giveth the increase, ought to teach us both confidence and resignation.

Writing to Mr. Miner at another stage of the effort for the abolition of slavery in the District of Columbia, Mr. Jay thus joyfully announces to his friend and co-worker, a position gained in the State of New York:

Mr. Dear Sir:—The mail this evening brings the news that resolutions instructing our Representatives in Congress to vote for the abolition of slavery in the District of Columbia, have past our Assembly by a vote of 57 to 39. In the fullness of my heart, I thank God, and congratulate you on the result.

It is worthy of remark that Mr. Jay takes no credit to himself for the passage of these resolutions in the Legislature of the State of New York. The truth is, however, that his exertions in procuring petitions, and by correspondence with influential men, such as Hon. Walker Todd of the N. Y. Senate, and Wm. L. Stone of the New York *Commercial,* had greatly aided to bring about the result, upon which, with a full heart, he thanks God, and congratulates his friend and co-worker for the abolition of slavery.

Like many other good men, (Gerrit Smith among the number,) Mr. Jay at one time was disposed to co-operate with the Americn Colonization Society, that old enemy of the colored people of the U.S. It has always worn two faces—one a face of humanity, and the other a face of hatred—one was for the South, and the other was for the North, so as to deceive, if possible, the very elect. Mr. Jay was among the first of the North to get his own eyes open, and to open the eyes of others, to the real character of this malign and mischievous scheme. He had regarded it, as many others had done, as a means of doing away with slavery—the removal of them to Africa as fast as they should be emancipated, supplying a motive for emancipation. When he found that in this he was mistaken, and that, instead of furnishing a motive for emancipation, it only increased the motive for slaveholding; that, instead of supplying an asylum for the oppressed free colored people of this country, it promoted and encouraged their oppression, to get them to *consent* to leave the country—when, in a word, he found it to be an engine of wickedness, and not an instrument of mercy, he promptly exposed it as a hypocrite, a deceiver, and renounced it. As early as 1829, in answer to an invitation to assist a meeting of the Colonization Society, Mr. Jay wrote to Mr. Stone, saying:

I confess, I entertain no hope that the efforts of the American Colonization Society will produce any direct and sensible diminution of the number of slaves in our country.

This early expression of a want of confidence in the American Colonization Society, shows that Mr. Jay had not taken his views second hand, but had, for himself, thoroughly examined the claims of the Colonization scheme, and for himself had found it the stupendous sham which it was afterwards proved to be by overwhelming facts and arguments brought out three years afterwards in *"Garrison's Thoughts"* on African Colonization.

At this point of time, the American Colonization Society ranked among the most popular institutions of the country. It combined the support of all classes, anti-slavery men and pro-slavery men, and enjoyed a monopoly of the pulpits North and South. Monthly sermons were preached in its favor by the pastors, and collections were taken up to aid in sending the Negroes out of the country. The most distinguished divines, and the most influential statesmen, everywhere stood forth as its champions, regarding it as the ample and all-sufficient answer to all inquiries concerning slavery, and concerning the free colored people of the United States. Hence, to dissent from it, and worse still, to oppose and attack it, was to unstop all the vials of concentrated wrath, and to bring down their malignant contents upon the naked heads of such offenders.

That all this had no terror for such a man as William Jay, stands boldly out to his credit, He did not hesitate either to dissent from, to oppose or attack this popular Goliath. His "Inquiry into the character and tendency of the American Colonization and American Anti-Slavery Societies," is one of the most clear, searching and masterly publications now to be found upon the subject.

The next great work of Mr. Jay, was his views of the Federal Government. The facts and arguments brought forward in this work exerted an incalculable influence upon the public mind. It showed how completely the slaveholders had for years wielded the Federal Government to extend and strengthen slavery. It is a book of facts, and was a manual in the hands of anti-slavery agents all over the country, and is such still.

The subject of slavery is an exciting one. Oppression is apt to make even a wise man mad. The bare relation of master and slave, unaccompanied with its grosser manifestations of ignorance, depravity, cruelty and blood, shocks and stuns the mind by its enormity. O'Connell used to say, that when he first heard the idea of property in man, it sounded to him as if some one were stamping upon the grave of his mother. The very thought chills the blood in the veins of the strong man, and stirs a fever in the blood of age. The heart becomes sick, and the spirit frantic with horror over its brutal atrocities and crimes. In writing upon a system of such boundless and startling enormity, where the wildest fancy is over-matched by the terrible reality, it is not easy to steer clear of exaggeration in individual cases. Some extravagance may indeed be looked for and excused in treating of such a subject, but such extravagance will be looked for in vain in the writings of Judge Jay on slavery.

As a writer, that can be said of him which can be said of but few reformatory writers in any age, he not only relied implicitly upon, and believed in the simple undistorted truth as the safest and best means of accomplishing his benevolent purposes, but was never, to the knowledge of any, tempted or driven by eager anxiety for immediate results into distortion or exaggeration. He had an earnest heart. It was always alive with the fires of justice and liberty; but with all, he possessed that accurate and well-balanced judgment which controlled and directed wisely and discreetly all his writings on the subject of slavery. No fact, no statement, of Judge Jay, how fiercely soever his opinions may have been combated, has ever been called in question.

His burning indignation which came down upon the pro-slavery wickedness of the nation like a mantle of unquenchable fire, was recognized as the natural product of his well-known love of justice. Those who contended with him, contended not against him but against the truth, within which Mr. Jay was always fortified.

Some men rebuke sin with such manifest levity as only to amuse the sinner. Others denounce wrong as if exulting over the wrongdoer, while others show their zeal for the truth by stretching it into falsehood and absurdity. All these will offend, disgust and drive the wrongdoer from the teacher or reformer. He will say, your cause may be good, but you are not the man to advocate it. Mr. Jay's exemption from this sort of criticism did not arise out of any timidity either of character or manner; but it is to be traced to his scrupulous regard for truth, his entire and transparent honesty. When truth failed to produce conviction, he could bide his time without resorting to artifice. He ever scouted the doctrine of doing evil that good might come, and in the midst of all discouragements, he held that it is ours to plant and to water, but it is God who giveth the increase.

I am not of that sentimental school of moralists, who think it right to speak only of the virtues of the dead. The power exerted by some men, after death, is far greater than in life, and it frequently happens that to expose the faults of departed great men, is a much higher and more commanding duty than to extol their virtues. Wrong and injustice to the living are remarkably disposed to conceal themselves from the light of truth, under the overshadowing examples of the great among the dead.

Examples of this sort are abundant in all the ages, and our own among the number. Thus, while Jefferson wrote that all men are created equal, and are entitled to life, liberty and the pursuit of happiness, and while Washington fought for the principle which Jefferson wrote down, both Jefferson and Washington are today quoted in proof that colored people have no rights that white people are bound to respect. The fact that these great men were slaveholders, is triumphantly cited as sanctioning the idea of property in man.

Their anti-slavery declarations are less potent for good than their pro-slavery examples have been made for evil. From a careful survey of the life and works of Mr. Jay, no fear need be entertained that evil will get the advantage over good by means of his memory. If he had faults, they were to his whole character like the spots on the resplendent orb of day, not to be seen by the ordinary means of vision.

As we walk under the light of this glorious orb, never thinking of any possible speck upon its surface, but thanking God for the brilliant illumination, so let us accept gratefully the shining example of the late Honorable William Jay. He has taught us the great purposes of life. He has taught us how to live; he has taught us how to die.

*Pamphlet, Rochester, New York,* 1859

# THE KANSAS CONSTITUTIONAL CONVENTION

Few states, young or old were ever blessed with a larger supply of constitutions, or of constitution makers, than the embryo State of Kansas. Since the moment she was handed over to the tender mercies of squatter sovereignty, she has been an inviting field to that class of statesmen who fancy they possess a special genius for organizing and shaping the destiny of new States. Constitutional lawyers and constitution makers have flocked to her borders from every section of our extended country, as to a field upon which to win glory for their skill, and perhaps something a little more substantial. New constitutions, new Governors, new political leaders and new turns to political affairs there generally have followed each other in rapid succession; and still that country has yet to be astonished by the discovery of s single Solon among all her statesmen. The whole machinery of Government, and all the wisdom of statesmanship stand paralyzed in the presence of the 'Negro.' He balks every exertion, defeats every plan, and baffles all their wisdom. He is the rock of offense, the stone of stumbling, and the severest test of all their political skill. There have been in Kansas from the first, as in most other States, *apparently* two parties, essentially hostile one to the other in their estimate of the rights of men of color, and the true policy of the State toward this particular variety of the human family. While, however, parties are nominally divided in Kansas, the cause of division does not thus far rise to the importance of a principle. *The Democrats have declared themselves our enemies, and the Republicans have not declared themselves our friends.* —The first would admit the black man into Kansas as a *slave*, and the other would seem to wish to exclude him as a *freeman*; one party would enslave him, and the other party would drive him from the face of all the earth over which they have power. Thus, while nominally and apparently at sword's point on the subject of Negroes, these parties, at heart, show but little difference. Neither party aims to be entirely just and humane to the black man. The Republican party has consented to the exclusion of the colored man from Oregon.[70] A more flagrant injustice and wrong could not well have been crowded into any constitution than in that of Oregon; yet Republican votes were given for that constitution. The far-famed Topeka constitution put the black man's rights in contempt, by putting them in question; and yet the party that framed and adopted that constitution claims to be the party of freedom and humanity, of honesty and decency. While they affirmed their own right to live in Kansas, and to live there in freedom, they submitted to the people the question as to whether colored men should have that right. Almost forty years ago, the State of Missouri was kept out of the Union on the ground that she had no right to exclude colored citizens from her borders, and a slaveholding President refused to proclaim her admission until she should blot out her wicked prohibitory law. This fact, stated in contrast with the statements of our statesmen and the character of our legislation of to-day, gives some idea of the distance we have drifted from the landmarks of liberty laid down by the fathers.

We have alluded thus to the animus of parties in Kansas at this time, because a new Constitutional Convention is about to undertake to supply that State with another constitution. In this Convention the Republican party has a clear majority of twelve members, and, of course, has the power to determine the character of whatever constitution shall be adopted by the Convention. We have observed, with some degree of alarm, that while there is no doubt that slavery will be prohibited, it is intimated that free Negroes are likely to be excluded. We have no doubt that an effort will be made to fasten this new wrong upon a people already muted, peeled and crushed beneath the terrible force of wrongs too numerous for specification, and we regret to say that there are indications that the effort will succeed. —The true policy of the Republican party is as plain as the sun in mid-heaven. That policy is to make a free State of Kansas, free to all the people of the country without distinction of any kind, for though such a course may excite the hatred of the slave power it cannot excite contempt. The cruelty of dooming a whole race to exclusion from a State or Territory, needlessly branding them with inferiority, is a policy very little superior in humanity to slavery itself. The Republican party upon perpetrating such a wrong, would appear quite as devilish in spirit as the Democratic party itself. For the credit of humanity, let it be hoped that the Republican party in Kansas will step to the line of justice, and prove itself worthy of its name and professions in its present efforts of constitution making for that inchoate State.

*Frederick Douglass' Paper*, July 8, 1859

# EQUAL POLITICAL RIGHTS FOR WOMEN

Some of the women in Kansas are signing petitions to the new Constitutional Convention, asking for equal political rights with men, on the popular sovereignty principle. The men will find it easier to vote against the petitions than to answer its arguments.

*Frederick Douglass' Paper*, July 8, 1859

# THE AFRICAN CIVILIZATION SOCIETY

If this Society does not make a favorable impression for itself upon our readers, the fault must rest with its friends, for they seem to have the field of discussion all to themselves, and this, too, notwithstanding the impatience of friend Garnet at the apparent exclusion of his friends from our columns. In our number before the last, we had a long letter from Dr. Pennington, disclaiming all connections with the the Society, but earnestly advocating its claims; and in our present number we have another long letter on the same side from Mr. Herries, also disclaiming all connection with the Society, but advocating its claims. Mr. H. must have the credit of being a little more discriminating in the bestowment of praises than our confiding friend Dr. Pennington, who easily sees anti-slavery in men who were never before suspected of it, and perhaps never suspected themselves of it. But giving Mr. Herries all credit for this better discrimination, we yet think him unfortunate in quoting the *New York Herald* in favor of this new African movement. That paper would no doubt make merry over any plan to get Negroes out of this country. Its instincts are keen. It goes to its own side with certain step and without hesitation. The fact that the *Herald* sided with the African Civilization Society should be rather a cause of regret than encouragement to its friends.

Mr. Herries is severe upon our esteemed friend George T. Downing, a man abundantly able to take care of himself, and we will not therefore undertake to defend him, except to say that the charge, whether implied or expressed, that Mr. Downing makes a *color* distinction between his guests is to our own experience false. If such a distinction was made by his father in early times, before the present day of light on this subject, it certainly does not become those who now go and dine at his establishment, to rise in a public meeting to reproach either father or son for that past transgression. Mr. Garnet was told at that very meeting at which he adroitly insinuated the charge, that he himself had been repeatedly served in the establishment of the Downings; and we were quite glad that he did not deny it, though we were sorry that it could be shown that H.H. Garnet did accept hospitality in an establishment, without one word of protest or complaint at the time, and yet turned upon its proprietor in a public meeting with an accusation which, if true, ought to have excluded and kept the accuser from Downing's premises. If Mr. Garnet goes to Mr. Downing's and gets his dinner and pays his bills, knowing he is there subject to degrading conditions as a colored man, when he might go elsewhere and be treated in a respectful manner, he becomes a needless party to the insult offered to his own manhood.

*Frederick Douglass' Paper*, July 8, 1859

# A PLAN OF ANTI-SLAVERY ACTION

Our respected correspondent, J.H.J., wishes our opinion of his plan of anti-slavery action, published in our paper two weeks ago. We shall comply with his request briefly, and without hesitation or reserve. The plan, in our opinion, is the least fault about it—in other words, the plan is good enough if there were men and heart enough to set the plan in motion. Anti-slavery has never suffered in this State or languished elsewhere for want of a plan. Plans have been our least want.—We have had anti-slavery societies for towns and counties—anti-slavery societies for State and nation. In addition to societies, we have had parties, with plans and platforms, We have had Liberty Party, Liberty League, town committees, county and State committees; so that whatever of virtue there may be in plans, the cause of the slave has certainly shared the full benefit of such virtue. To us it is manifest that the cause now needs far less of plan than a cohesive principle and a co-operating spirit among Abolitionists. The letter killeth, but the spirit giveth life. We need less of the letter of anti-slavery, and more of the zealous and laborious self-sacrificing spirit.— It is a sad fact, that in the hands of all these societies and committees, nearly all our anti-slavery instrumentalities have disappeared.—We have neither press nor speech. This is not for the want of plan, but for the want of men. The Radical Abolition Society, organized at Syracuse, was built on a faultless plan, but where is that Society to-day? Where is its committee? where its paper, its lecturers and patrons? All gone! In view of the history of plans, Bro. Johnson, we prefer to work for the present on the plan of individualism, uttering our word for freedom and justice, whereever we may find ears to hear, and writing our thoughts for whoever will read them. There will come a time for organized effort for the aboliton of slavery; but for the present we see nothing better than to fight slavery in an individual way.

*Frederick Douglass' Paper*, July 8, 1859

# TO ROBERT KINSICUT ESQ., WARREN (R.I.)

Rochester, Oct. 9, 1859.

My dear sir:

I am about leaving for Europe,[71] but am to lecture at one or two places in New England before I go—among others, in the Fraternity course at Boston.

My lecture in Boston will take place in the first of November— and I can lecture for you on the 4th of November.

My lecture for this season will be on "Selfmade Men." I shall deliver the same in Boston.

My terms are twenty five dollars. If this will suit please drop me a line to that effect by return mail. I ask this because I am to leave home on Friday next for Phila.

I am, Dear Sir,
Respectfully yours,
Frederick Douglas

*Ms., New York Public Library, Schomburg Branch*

# AMERICAN CIVILIZATION

The pride of the American people, the thing which they most frequently cite as a proof of their superiority over other nations, is the high degree of civilization which they have attained—a civilization as rapid in its progress as it is peculiar in its features, and strikingly different from that of other countries. It may be truly called *American civilization*. If a stranger should look at some of our largest cities, the centers of commerce, business life, and industry of all description, and should be told, as he might be by persons very far from claiming the honor of being counted among 'the oldest inhabitants,' that they distinctly remember the time when the place so full of life and bustle was covered with the primeval forests, he could hardly credit the story, and would be inclined to think that they had been called into existence by the command of some magician; but upon looking deeper into the machinery and the network of this truly astonishing spectacle, he would perceive that America had availed herself of the unparalleled inventive development of the nineteenth century, doing the work in a day by two men which forty years ago would have required a week or a month to be performed by twenty men.

By availing herself of the capital of other nations, she has surpassed all other nations in the rapid increase of her railroads.—With foreign capital, foreign skill, and the Irish laborer, she has been able to reduce to cultivation enormous tracts of land, to level the forest, to remove the rocks, to tunnel mountains, to span the broadest and deepest chasms, and overcome ten thousand other difficulties in rendering her borders accessible, each to all, and all to each. The contact into which men are brought by those means of communication, is one of the most powerful promoters of general and uniform culture; and in vain would one look here for the isolated, secluded places which a traveler will frequently meet with even in the middle of the most cultivated countries of Europe, where a small population is found entirely isolated, cut off from the rest of the world, speaking their own peculiar dialect, preserving their own manners, and perpetuating a style of dress of unknown origin, forming a little world by themselves, whose frontiers they hardly ever cross, and whose mental horizon does not reach farther than the extent of the acres they cultivate. Here, on the contrary, everywhere, in the middle of deserts, on nearly inaccessible mountains we hear our own language almost uncorruptedly spoken, and meet with people hardly different from outselves in manners, notions and knowledge. Even foreigners soon show the influence of that general leveling civilization. The clumsy appearance, the awkward and queer behavior of the German and Irish peasant, are soon modified and made to give way to the force of American manners, and to take upon them an American appearance. The miserable clay huts, sometimes without chimney or windows, in which they may be found in their native countries, are supplanted by snug frame houses and shanties like those of the American farmer. But it is not only in respect to the material acquisitions that the Americans claim the front rank in civilization, for while they generously admit that in the fine arts they cannot yet compete with the old world, they do not forget to claim superior excellence over the nations of Europe in respect to social and political institutions, as well as in almost all branches of knowledge and science. It is their pride that owing to the system of public schools, there are hardly any Americans found within the free States who do not know how to read and to write.

Now, it must be submitted that if civilization naturally tends to improve the material and intellectual as well as the moral state of a nation, it would seem as if the Americans really had excellent reasons for claiming, as they do, to be the first nation on the face of the earth. Unfortunately, however, for this claim, American civilization abounds in strange and puzzling contradictions. It is true we have unequalled means of communication, and may fly with almost the speed of an eagle from the shores of the Atlantic to those of the Pacific, but it is also true that we do it at the peril of our lives. One of the first features which mark the distinction between a civilized, and a rude nation, is the value attached to human life, and the protection given it by the former, while the bold risking of it, the cold braving of death, is considered one of the chief virtues among savage tribes. Respect for human life, and vigilant protection of it, is a feature of civilization sadly absent in this country. In slow, conservative Europe, by railroad or by steamer, a journey is not thought much more of as being dangerous than a walk on a promenade. When in the course of several years an accident happens by which there is a loss of life, the whole country is seized with horror and consternation; while here their frequency is so great as to project one over another, and it is with difficulty in speaking of the last accident not to confound it with some other that just occurred. The same insecurity is found concerning the protection of health. All sorts of quackery run with a loose rein here. In Europe, the government provides for the people in this respect by not allowing any physician to practice unless he has undergone the strictest examination;

but such restraint would not agree with the principle of liberty peculiar to this Republic. Any quack, any runaway barber or apothecary's clerk may cure, kill or poison as he pleases. No apothecary here, as in Romeo and Juliet, hesitates to sell poison. What was penal in this respect even before Shakespeare wrote, is now free and unrestricted.

This peculiarly American carelessness in the protection of life appears still more strikingly in the almost undisturbed freedom allowed to Rowdyism. In fact, Rowdyism is itself a plant of genuine American growth; for however wild, coarse and rude the mob may be in other countries, they do stand in fear of the law. Outbreaks of such brutality and ferocity as that witnessed lately in Baltimore, when a gang of those outcasts of humanity wantonly, and without the slightest provocation, attacked a whole party of unoffending and peaceful passengers of a steamer, would be nearly impossible anywhere in Europe. Even in poor, uncultivated Turkey, such a thing could not happen; and it may be doubted if such an outrage finds its equals in the darkest times of the Middle Ages. Here, however, such outrages are by no means exceptions.—It is but a few months since a similar occurrence took place within sight of New York City, on Staten Island ferry, where an unoffending man was suddenly attacked and beaten by a group of rowdies, without any attempt being made by the bystanders or the officers of the boat to interfere or arrest the ruffians. It is not a year yet since a citizen of Baltimore was shot on the threshold of his house, and not two years since a colored man was shot for mere sport in New York. And now the papers are discussing an outrage perpetrated at Hartford on the reception of Gov. Seymour, which is an exhibition of the superlative contempt for human life in America, even in the best parts of it. Here the perpetrator of the murder was not a rowdy by profession, but a genuine citizen, a member of the armed force for the maintenance of law and order; yet he deliberately kills a citizen to make way for the carriage of another fellow-citizen! Has the reign of King Bomba an outrage more savage to boast of? But even this fades into nothingness compared with the numberless instances of lynch law, tarring and feathering, so characteristic of American civilization, and which are pointed to by the conservative classes in monarchical Europe as the natural and inevitable accompaniments of popular sovereignty.

The fact that such outrages and crimes are almost always committed by the outcasts of humanity, and are generally condemned and denounced by the higher and better classes of society, does not make them less chargeable to American civilization; for when we compare them with other enormities, the chief distinction is, that the one class is perpetrated in the name and under the sanction of law, and the other is not. And shocking and brutal as are the first, the latter are more pernicious in their consequences, since they corrupt by example the whole body of society. It was the wealth and respectability of our country which formerly mobbed the Abolitionists, which burned Pennsylvania Hall,[72] which passed the Fugitive Slave Law, which gave us the Nebraska Bill, and which gave us the Dred Scott decision, dooming a whole race to insult, outrage and outlawry. Where else under the whole heavens can be found States solemnly passing laws compelling a part of their people to choose between enslavement or banishment? Where but in America can be found in the nineteenth century a church built up out of the proceeds of the sale of human flesh? Where but in America are men excluded from public halls, degraded in churches, insulted on the side-walk, proscribed in theatres, kicked out of omnibuses, dragged from the cars, hooted at in the street, denied admission to schools and colleges, for no better reason than that such persons differ in complexion from the majority?

All these facts certainly ought not to shake our faith in civilization, whose wholesome and ennobling effects are known by the examples of other countries; but certainly they do demonstrate that the American people have yet attained only the outside, the mere surface of civilization and refinement; that while boasting to be first, they are little more than last in the true elements of high civilization; that in fact every phase of it, aside from mere material improvement, is still in its infancy. Part of this defect may be properly ascribed to the astonishing rapidity of its growth. Everywhere else, civilization was the result of an internal process, slow in its progress, taking deep roots, modifying, shaping and governing life in all its ramifications. Here it came like a whirlwind, sweeping over the land unequally, leveling mountains, cutting down forests, covering all that it touches with an outside polish, without the power to penetrate under the surface. A sort of sham civilization, which resembled the savages of whom Humboldt tells, who painted themselves coats, pants and vests on their bare skins, that they might appear in European style.

*Douglass' Monthly*, October, 1859

## TO HELEN BOUCASTER, SECR., SHEFFIELD A.S.A.

North Parade, Halifax, Dec. 7, 1859

My dear Friend:

Having, for the moment, very much upon my hands, I cannot go fully into the question of the right of an enslaved people to gain their freedom by a resort to force. Nor indeed is it necessary that I should. I can, however, at once, give you the assurance that my advocacy of the cause of the slave in England has no reference whatever to any plan or purpose involving a resort to arms, for the liberation of my Brothers & Sisters in slavery. My mission is wholly peaceful. On that point you may feel wholly at rest. On the subject of Harper's Ferry, I can be equally explicit. I neither took part in that transaction nor counselled the taking it, but opposed the measure as fraught only with disaster and ruin to the main object of the enterprise, which was to run off slaves into the mountains, and into Canada where they could protect and defend themselves.[73] I do hope that a difference of opinion on any one point will not defeat our co-operating against slavery at other points where we agree; but of that you must judge. The liberties of England are bulwarked about by ten thousand cannon. The slave is a victim of a constant *insurrection*, by which his blood is drawn out drop by drop! It may not be altogether impartial to lay down the rule of submission to him, too sternly, especially since he has submitted already two hundred years. First pure, then peaceable.

Very truly & gratefully your friend,

Frederick Douglass

*Ms., The John Rylands University Library of Manchester, Deansgate, Manchester, England*

## TO MRS. CASH

Huddersfield, December 1859

My dear Friend Mrs. Cash:

My good friend Julia assures me that you would be pleased to have a line from me in company with hers. I have not at all forgotten that I was once the guest of your dear home in Coventry, nor that you and your dear household have kindly stood by me in my antislavery labors during the last dozen years. I do hope much to see you all at Shereborne House during my present tour in England. The Halifax Antislavery friends met me last night at the house of Dr. Crofts,[74] where I make my home, and all seemed to take an earnest interest in the Anti-Slavery question. I shall have much to tell you about the Anti-Slavery Movements and its prospects when it shall be my good privilege to see you. Please, if you are seeing or writing to your daughter Ellenor, remember me kindly to her, tell her I am as much like the picture she took of me as the wear and tear of thirteen years will permit me to be. Do not forget to remember me also to dear Mary Ann and your dear husband—indeed all your dear household. I love to remember you all, and shall be most happy to see you all. I have hardly yet determined anything as to when I shall leave this vicinity but probably not before January, than I expect to go North.

Very truly yours,
Fredk Douglass

*Alfred William Anthony Collection, New York Public Library*

# REPORT OF SPEECH AT ANTI-SLAVERY MEETING

Wakefield, England, January 15, 1860[75]

Mr. Frederick Douglass then stood forth, and was greeted with deafening bursts of applause, which broke out again and again over all parts of the immense audience. He said that he was very glad to be present there that evening. He had very pleasant recollections of the hall he had been there before thirteen years ago and he now found very little alteration in it or in the people of Wakefield, though, if there were any, it appeared to be for the better. There seemed to be no declension in the anti-slavery spirit of Wakefield, and that was a gratifying circumstance to him he assured them. He hardly knew where to begin to speak on the question that had been so ably and so eloquently brought before them; and, indeed, he had been in doubt whether he should have a chance at them that night. He found that they were to have a very important subject brought before them for consideration; and that was the propriety of forming an Anti-Slavery Society, which should assist in the work of the abolition of slavery in the United States. He did not think it was necessary among Englishmen, who had paid so much for emancipation in their own West Indies, to go into the question of slavery; nor did he think that he who came from a slave plantation to Maryland could enlighten Englishmen with regard to the principles of civil and religious liberty.—He did not come there either to unfold new truths, for the advocates of a holy and righteous cause need not look round for new truths, until the old truths had been reduced to practice. Truth never changed, and such a truth was a man's right to liberty. That right did not depend upon moldy records, or old parchments, but every man—not excluding the slaveholder—knew it for himself. They would have heard that the slavery question was called a difficult one, and ought to be discussed only in a calm, temperate, common sense kind of way, which was all very pretty and very cool though for himself he did not see that it was anything but a plain case in which there could be no intelligent difference of opinion. Why the very dogs of England seemed to understand the question better than they did in America, for the dogs of Wakefield seemed to know that he was a man and thus it appeared that they were as well informed as the doctors of divinity in America, who told them that they must not look at slavery in connection with any system of ethics which applied to the white man.—But to look at it from a different stand-point, Slavery was declared by some to be too bad to be human, and just good enough to be divine; but in his opinion it was an insult to God to charge upon him, as the American churches and divines had charged upon him, the authorship of that hell-black system. So untenable, however, was this view that he did not care to argue it, and therefore he should pass it by. He might tell them that there was a moral power in the voice of a meeting like theirs, and that was the reason that he was among them; for though the slaveholders of America did not care for his voice alone, they found themselves compelled to listen to black sentiments when they were backed up by white authority. One reason, therefore, why he was there that night was that the slaveholders would rather that he were not there, for they preferred to keep such as himself and the lady who had been addressing them, at home. He said that the slaveholders did not want them to visit England; but they could come themselves and tell the people of this country what a beautiful system they had over there; though they never

brought a slave with them to tell their side of the question. Another
singular fact was that they never heard of the slaves in the plantation
getting up meetings and passing resolutions, declaring how contented
and happy they were, and that they wouldn't be free if they could. No,
they did not do that, but their masters did it for them; though in the
absence of testimony from their own side they might easily conclude
that their condition was miserable, wretched, and destitute beyond
expression.

Something had been said about Englishmen going over to
America and coming back with the story that they had not witnessed
the horrors in connection with slavery that had been described. Was it
likely that they should? If he were a slaveholder, and had an English
guest on whom he should like to make a favorable impression, was it
likely that if his slave offended him, he would drag him up for
punishment in the very presence of his guest? He should think not,
when he knew that he could punish as he would when that guest had
gone away. No, if they wanted to see slavery they must not go as these
went; but just put on a black skin, if they could borrow one and he
would lend them a part of his wool; and they would see the system as it
really existed, the slaveholder not being afraid to let the "darkies" see
how black it is. He would not, however, talk to them about the
cruelties of slavery, thinking, as they were considering the propriety of
forming an Anti-Slavery Society, it more desirable to give them some
accurate information with regard to the present state of the question in
America. There were in the States not only different sections of pro-
slavery men; but different sections of those who were opposed to it.
The anti-slavery friends of the States were by no means united; but
advocated different means, as they might say, of attaining the same
end. One class were known as "free laborers,"—they were the friends of
"free labor," and "free produce."—They wanted to starve slavery out;
and they accounted those who held commercial relations with the
slaveholders as *particeps criminis* with them. They were doing a good
work but he did not himself agree with them, for the reason that the
principles they laid down could not be practically carried out.—Were
they to attempt to carry them out, they could not even print their
anti-slavery journal without going out of the country, nay more, for on
that principle of action they must need go out of the world. Then there
was another class of men, who were known as "compensationists," at
the head of whom stood the honored name of Elihu Burritt.—Well,

they knew Elihu Burritt (yes;) so did he they loved him; so did he; but, at the same time, he did not agree with him, and for the reason that he was not prepared to transfer this question from the bar of conscience to the counter. It might be when the moral sense of the people demanded the abolition of slavery at any cost, that the question about their sharing the loss with the slaveholders would arise, but not until then.

Then there was another class of abolitionists who were known as the Garrisonians—a name which they had received before with applause that night. These held the necessity of dissolving the Union, and breaking up the Government as it now exists. Their argument is, that the Constitution of the United States is a slaveholding document, and their principle of action is to have no union with slaveholders, no union with the slave states, and to decline to have anything to do with the Government which does not unite with them. He (Mr. Douglass) did not, however, agree with this section of abolitionists, believing that if the union were to be dissolved, it would be a great loss to the cause, inasmuch as the free states could no longer influence the slave states any more than they could Cuba. —Again, however, there was another class of abolitionists, who differed from Mr. Garrison's friends respecting their method of abolishing slavery. They said that the Constitution of the United States, so far from being a pro-slavery document, was distinctly an anti-slavery document. They held there was not a single sentence in the Constitution which, rightly interpreted, gave the slightest sanction to the slave system; and therefore they held that they could not only vote under that Constitution but seek office under it, and administer it so that it would become a mighty instrument for the destruction of slavery, root and branch; and he must say that he agreed with those who held these views. He had read the Constitution of the United States carefully, had studied it long, had looked at it on both sides, and he declared that he had been unable to find one line or sentence, or one word, that sanctioned the system of slavery. Therefore, he agreed with those who declared that on account of the Constitution sanctioning slavery, there was no necessity to abolish the Union. It was a universal legal maxim that when an instrument was capable of bearing two interpretations, one innocent and the other villainous, they were to take that which was innocent; and if they did that, remembering that the men who drew up the Constitution were in favor of the gradual abolition of slavery, they would come to the same decision as himself. No, it was not the Constitution which looked forward to its abolition that supported slavery. That which had given the Constitution the pro-slavery interpretation it would not else have had, was the invention of the cotton gin, which had raised the value of the slave from 200 dols. to 800 dols., and 1,000 dols. and which had, consequently, made the planter a wealthy man, and humbled the church and the people at his feet. But, as slavery was the creature of law, it could be abolished by law, and this was the ground of action on which the abolitionists, with which he was the more especially connected, proceeded. They respected the power of moral suasion, of which the lady who had before addressed them was a representative, but they required something more than that. They acted on the people in every possible manner, diffusing information and working through the elections, and they had been successful, for they would now see that they were at a standstill in Columbia. They had been so for a month, and he hoped they would be so for a month longer. There was a time, however, when there was no trouble with regard to the matter; but there had been some fighting since then.

In 1844, when the anti-slavery party took part in the election of President for the first time, bringing out Mr. Birney as a candidate,[76] he received 60,000 votes, while Mr. Van Buren, in 1848, received a much larger number. In 1856 two million votes were cast for J. C. Fremont[77]. . and in 1860, he expected that they would cast three millions for their candidate, and carry Mr. Seward, the anti-slavery man, triumphantly up to the White House. It was true that Seward was not altogether an abolitionist; but he believed that slavery should not be extended one inch beyond the present limits; held that there should be no slavery in the District of Columbia; and that, in all parts of the Union there should be the right of freedom of opinion and free speech with regard to the question. If he were elected President, too, Mrs. Remond would not have had to ask a second time for her passport to be *vised* to Paris.[78] Though Seward was not an abolitionist, those with whom he acted looked at the matter in the common sense way in which they treated these questions in England. His party, when they wanted to reach Boston from Rochester, would be content to be conveyed as far on their journey as Albany, if they could not find anyone to take them the whole way to Boston. Thus it was with Mr. Seward; they were content to be taken as far as he could convey them, waiting their opportunity to proceed further on their journey.

Speaking generally of the policy of his party, he said that they thought it right to use the ballot box in their contests with the pro-slavery party; and, as we understood him, he thought it was not wrong to have the bullet-box at the back of that. He did not hold that Christianity required the slave tamely to submit to his fate; but that it was in accordance with its spirit he should compass his liberty if he were able, and for this reason he more admired the Christianity of Harris than that of Uncle Tom, inasmuch as the former had a little more of the 'man' left within him.

In referring to the case of John Brown, Mr. Douglass said he did not mean to dwell upon it, but he knew that some people regarded the attempt forcibly to emancipate slaves as a very injudicious and unwise thing. He was willing that the same rule of judgment should be applied to the undertaking that was applied to all such undertakings. The success or failure of such enterprises made them wise or foolish in the world's judgment. Let them bear in mind, that if John Brown had succeeded he would have been a hero—John Brown failed, and he failed like a brave and true man—and they should see to it that no words of theirs should drop upon his memory to tarnish it. He was a true and a good man, as he (Mr. Douglass) knew full well. For seven weeks Captain Brown was an inmate of his house,[79] and it was there he heard him say that he had no other use for his life than to give it for the ransom and freedom of the four millions in chains.—He would tell them that this man, who was branded as a blood-thirsty destroyer of the peace, was no such thing. He was a man of prayer, a man of Divine and startling piety; of a warm and generous heart—no one more so. Even his enemies had to confess that John Brown did not go into the slave state for the purpose of shedding blood; that was not his object. He did not go to lift the standard of insurrection, in which lives and property should be sacrificed; but he went with motives as pure as those which took Moses into Egypt to lead out the Israelites. He went to conduct a grand movement of slaves out of bondage, and he merely took his arms with a view to protect himself and his friends if assaulted or stopped in his proceedings. He (Mr. Douglass) was not advocating forcible emancipation, neither did he advocate any theory of peace which left the slave helpless in the hands of their masters. Slavery was itself an insurrection, and the slaveholders were a band of insurgents armed against the rights and liberties of their fellow men—for there was no time when the blood of the Negro was not being shed. Brown was a good and true man, and he went to the scaffold with the consciousness of having only discharged his duty to God and his fellow man.

Mr. Douglass, again speaking of the cause and prospects of anti-slavery, called upon his hearers to give them as much assistance as they could. Their money contributions would be useful, for they had many expenses to meet in connection with the cause. There was the diffusion of information through the press, for instance, and by means of agents, and there was also the necessity of assisting fugitive slaves on their way to Canada, he himself being the keeper of one of the "underground" railway-stations at Rochester.

*Douglass' Monthly,* March, 1860


## TO GEORGE THOMPSON

21 Albion Street, N. Castle-on-Tyne, Feby. 18, 1860.

My kind friend, Ellen Richardson, assured me that you would not object to getting a line from me, and although I had about made up my mind that writing would be of no value or interest to you without my first seeing you, I yet take pleasure in complying with the wish of one who is a friend to me and "how much more to thee."

I have many things to say to you, Dear George Thompson, many things to ask and many things to explain, but laying aside all these till we meet, as I do most confidently hope we shall meet, allow me to express my great pleasure in learning that your natural force has so far returned to you, and your friends are so true to you that you are again able to be seen and heard on the Subject of Slavery and to plead the cause now and always dear to your heart.

From my heart I thank you for your noble words in speaking of me to the people of New Castle upon Tyne. I was very glad to know from your friend, Ellen Richardson, that you believed that all would be right should we meet and speak together.

Until then don't hold me as an enemy.

Fredk Douglass

*Frederick Douglass Papers, Rush Rhees Library, University of Rochester*

# TO JAMES REDPATH

Rochester, June 20, 1860

My Dear Sir:

Your kind note, inviting me to meet with yourself and other friends on the 4th of July, at North Elba, came into my hands only yesterday. Had it reached me only a day or two earlier, I certainly should have complied with it. Very gladly would I assemble with you and others on that revolutionary day, to do honor to the memory of one whom I regard as THE man of this nineteenth century. Little, indeed, can you and I do to add lustre to his deathless fame.—The principles of John Brown, attested by a life of spotless integrity and sealed by his blood, are self-vindicated. His name is covered with a glory so bright and enduring, as to require nothing at our hands to increase or perpetuate it. Only for our own sake, and that of enslaved and imbruted humanity, need we assemble. To have been acquainted with John Brown, shared his counsels, enjoyed his confidence, and sympathized with the great objects of his life and death, I esteem as among the highest privileges of my life. We do but honor ourselves in doing honor to him for it implies the possession of qualities akin to his.

I have little hope of the freedom of the slave by peaceful means. A long course of peaceful slaveholding has placed the slaveholders beyond the reach of moral and humane consideration. They have neither ears nor hearts for the appeals of justice and humanity. While the slave will tamely submit his neck to the yoke, his back to the lash, and his ankle to the fetter and chain, the Bible will be quoted, and learning invoked to justify slavery. The only penetrable point of a tyrant is the *Fear of Death*. The outcry that they make as to the danger of having their *Throats Cut*, is because they know they deserve to have them *Cut*. The efforts of John Brown and his brave associates, though apparently unavailing, have done more to upset the logic and shake the security of slavery, than all other efforts in that direction for twenty years.

The sleeping dust, over which yourself and friends propose to meet on the 4th, cannot be revived; but the noble principles and disinterested devotion which led John Brown to step serenely to the gallows and lay down his life, will never die. They are all the more potent for his death.

Not unwisely are the eyes and hearts of the American slaves and their friends turned to the lofty peaks of the Alleghanies. The innumerable glens, caves, ravines and rocks of those mountains, will yet be the hiding places of hunted liberty. The eight-and-forty hours of John Brown's school in the mountains of Virginia, taught the slaves more than they could have otherwise learned in a half century. Even the mistake of remaining in the arsenal after the first blow was struck, may prove the key to future success. The tender regard which the dear old man evinced for the lives of the tyrants—and which should have secured him his life—will not be imitated by future insurgents.— Slaveholders are as insensible to magnanimity as to justice and the measure they mete out must be meted to them again. My heart is with you.

Very truly,<br>
Fred'k Douglass

*Douglass' Monthly*, September, 1860


## TO GERRIT SMITH

Rochester, Sept. 7th, 1860

My dear Sir:

The more I think of that Worcester convention[80] the more I feel the importance of your attending it. I do hope that no surmountable difficulty will prevent your being there. Your health is as precious to me as to anyone outside your Dear family circle and I would urge nothing that might endanger it. I really think that your health of body and mind would be improved by taking that Eastern trip. The friends of freedom and humanity know their obligations to you. You have served your day and generation as a workman who need not be ashamed of his work; but you have not done yet. When I see Lord Brougham over *eighty* years old, standing up and delivering an address of two hours, I cannot think of your ceasing to attend public meetings. I am not a physician and my opinion may not be worth much, but I think I never saw or heard you at any time within the last ten years when you seemed better able to withstand the wear and tear of public meetings. I did not urge you very strongly when in your presence, to go. Dear Mrs. Smith did that much better than either Mr. Foster, or I, could do. I do hope she succeeded.

The special subject on which you would be most expected to speak, relates to the powers of the Federal Government. You could show as no other man can how the Federal government can reach and overthrow American Slavery. Will you my friend take this matter into account and do attend the convention if possible.

Yours Very truly,

Fredk Douglass

*Gerrit Smith Papers, George Arents Research Library, Syracuse University*

# TO WILLIAM LLOYD GARRISON

*Rochester,* Oct. 15th, 1860

Mr. Garrison:

You will oblige me by allowing me to say in your columns, that the letter of J.A.H., which appeared in the *Liberator* of September 28th,[81] does me an injustice in the part it represents me as having taken in the proceedings of the recent Political Abolition Convention held in Worcester. Neither Mr. Foster, nor I, undertook the formidable work which your correspondent, in his letter, ascribed to us. I beg to assure you, that the "annihilation of the American Anti-Slavery Society" was no part of the business of the Convention. The language of your correspondent is much too strong. It conveys an exaggerated idea of what took place on the occasion which it purports to describe. Everybody knows that to criticise the position of an association in respect to a single point in its plan of operation, is a very different thing from discrediting an association altogether, and working for its destruction. I plead guilty to the first, but not the last impeachment. There is no good reason for misrepresenting even an enemy, if I must be deemed such. I did freely dissent from one of your leading doctrines, and did my best to prove it unsound, but in no such spirit as would be inferred from the language of your Worcester correspondent. My objection to the American A.S. Society respected its *plan*—not its life. So far from working for the annihilation of that Society, I have never failed, in the worst times of my controversy with it, to recognize that organization as the most efficient generator of anti-slavery sentiment in the country; and this I did, repeatedly, at Worcester.—The compliment which J.A.H. pays Mr. Howland for the part he took in the Convention, is natural, perhaps—but it is scarcely modest—since the complimenter and the complimented is one and the same person. If "manliness" consists in calling a man a *liar* to his face, or what is about the same thing, telling him he knows he tells a falsehood, I must prefer manners to "manliness." To me, Mr. Howland's manner and language on that occasion, and of which he now boasts in the *Liberator*, was better becoming a slave plantation among slaves, than an anti-slavery Convention among equals.

What had I said to call forth this ill-mannered charge from Mr. Howland? Why, in substance this: that the plan of operation adopted by the American Anti-Slavery Society did not embrace the abolition of slavery by means of the Government, and that the Radical Abolition party was the only organization which proposed such abolition. This is what I said, and what I meant to say. Mr. Howland, by suppressing a part of what I did say, and adding a little that I did not say, makes out to his own satisfaction a case of falsehood against me. His zeal has, in this instance, outrun his discretion, and I leave him to retrace his steps, as I am happy to see he has had to do in the case of Mr. Higginson.

Respectfully yours,<br>Frederick Douglass

*Douglass' Monthly*, November, 1860

## TO GERRIT SMITH

Rochester, December 18th, 1860

My dear Sir:

I am just home from the east. I found all your kind notes and thank you for them, I have been roughly handled, but not much hurt. The jar of dragging down the steps of Tremont Temple was considerable,[82] and left me a little sore, but this is hardly worth mentioning. I was well heard on the following Sunday morning in Music Hall. My fighting on the day of the mob was after a very small pattern, not large enough to shock even your peace views. My aim was less to injure than to keep from being injured, and in this my success was truly marvelous, for the crowd was at one time truly ferocious. The *Tribune's* account of the mob was the best. That in Mr. Garrison's paper the worst. It was taken from the Boston Pilot,[83] while there were far more accurate and truthful accounts of the affair in the *Boston Traveller* and other papers of the city. Mr. G. felt a little nettled that he had not been counselled with about holding the meeting. As much as this comes out in his Editorial notice of the affair. He should have indulged no such feeling in view of his non-resistant principles. Mr. Whipple was less affected. Phillips never appeared more truly grand than when facing the mob. I am soon to leave home again. I was in Potsdam all last week, and had the misfortune of being told by an indignant proslavery man that you and I should both be hanged! He said that the present deplorable condition of the country was due to just such men as yourself. Will the Republicans surrender?[84] Better the dissolution of the Union many times over. I can get only a small print of your sermon into the present monthly.

Your faithful friend,
Fredk Douglass

*Gerrit Smith Papers, George Arents Research Library, Syracuse University*


# HAYTIAN EMIGRATION

Pottsville, Pa., Feb. 5, 1861.

Mr. Editor:
    Will you be kind enough to answer the following questions for my information and others?
    1. As our old and well-tried friend, are you positively in favor of the emigration of our people to Hayti?
    2. Are you fully satisfied with the truthfulness of the representations of the Haytian Government, etc., as set forth by Mr. James Redpath's 'Guide to Hayti?'
    3. Do you expect to emigrate there at any time, providing the elevation of our people in the United States progresses at the same ratio that it has for the last, say, seven years?
    Will you be kind enough to give me a decisive answer upon these points, and I would be happy to have it publicly noticed in your next issue?

Yours, Geo C. Anderson


Emigration to Hayti is wise or foolish, commendable or otherwise, according to the circumstances of the emigrant himself. There are individuals and classes of our people who would undoubtedly succeed well in Hayti. —Those accustomed to the culture of cotton, rice, sugar and tobacco, and who have been driven North by the oppressive laws of the slave States, would do well to turn their course towards Hayti. But we are not in favor of wholesale and indiscriminate emigration to Hayti, or elsewhere. Such of our number as have acquired property, are making a good living, and have the means of educating their children, would be quite unwise to part with their property and leave a useful position for the uncertainties of emigration to Hayti, or elsewhere. We are in favor of emigration as a colored man, just as we should be if we were an Englishman, or an Irishman living in England or Ireland. To you who have no foothold *here,* we should say, *go there.* But as we should not be in favor of saying to all the people of these countries, be off, so we are not in favor of saying to all the colored people here, *move off.* We are far from calling upon any part of our people to emigrate, for public reasons, such as inability to live among white people or for the charms of a "Colored Nationality." The things for which men should emigrate are food, clothing, property, education, manhood, and material prosperity, and he who has these where he is, had better stay where he is, and exert the power which they give him to overcome whatever of social or political oppression which may surround him. So much for the first question.

2d. Yes; we are fully satisfied with the truthfulness of Mr. Redpath's representations of the Haytian Government. We believe him to be an honest man, and a sincere friend of the colored race.

3d. No; we do not expect to emigrate to Hayti under any circumstances now existing or apprehended.[85] We have personal and peculiar reasons for staying just where we are.—The same work to which we have given the first years of our manhood, requires our last, and shall have them. Nevertheless, we shall rejoice in the success attending our people who shall seek homes in Hayti, and if ever able to do so, we are resolved to visit them and see how they get along in their new homes.

We think the above a sufficiently explicit answer to the questions of our friend, Mr. Anderson, and to many others who have made similar inquiries of us about going to Hayti.

*Douglass' Monthly*, March, 1861

# Appendix

## THE HEROIC SLAVE

### PART I.

Oh! child of grief, why weepest thou?
Why droops thy sad and mournful brow?
Why is thy look so like despair?
What deep, sad sorrow lingers there?

The State of Virginia is famous in American annals for the multitudinous array of her statesmen and heroes. She has been dignified by some the mother of statesmen. History has not been sparing in recording their names, or in blazoning their dead. Her high position in this respect, has given her an enviable distinction among her sister States. With Virginia for his birthplace, even a man of ordinary parts, on account of the general partiality for her sons, easily rises to eminent stations. Men, not great enough to attract special attention in their native States, have, like a certain distinguished citizen in the State of New York, sighed and repined that they were not born in Virginia. Yet not all the great ones of the Old Dominion have, by the fact of their birth-place, escaped undeserved obscurity. By some strange neglect, one of the truest, manliest, and bravest of her children,—one who, in after years, will, I think, command the pen of genius to set his merits forth, holds now no higher place in the records of that grand old Commonwealth than is held by a horse or an ox. Let those account for it who can, but there stands the fact, that a man who loved liberty as well as did Patrick Henry—who deserved it as much as Thomas Jefferson,—and who fought for it with a valor as high, and arms as strong, and against odds as great, as he who led all the armies of the American colonies through the great war for freedom and independence, lives now only in the chattel records of his native State.

Glimpses of this great character are all that can now be presented. He is brought to view only by a few transient incidents, and these afford but partial satisfaction. Like a guiding star on a stormy night, he is seen through the parted clouds and the howling tempests; or, like the gray peak of a menacing rock on a perilous coast, he is seen by the quivering flash of angry lightning, and he again disappears covered with mystery.

Curiously, earnestly, anxiously we peer into the dark, and wish even for the blinding flash, or the light of northern skies to reveal him. But alas! he is still enveloped in darkness, and we return from the pursuit like a wearied and disheartened mother, (after a tedious and unsuccessful search for a lost child,) who returns weighed down with disappointment and sorrow. Speaking of marks, traces, possibles, and probabilities, we come before our readers.

In the spring of 1835, on a Sabbath morning, within hearing of the solemn peals of the church bells at a distant village, a Northern traveller through the State of Virginia drew up his horse to drink at a sparkling brook, near the edge of a dark pine forest. While his weary and thirsty steed drew in the grateful water, the rider caught the sound of a human voice, apparently engaged in earnest conversation.

Following the direction of the sound, he descried, among the tall pines, the man whose voice had arrested his attention. "To whom can he be speaking?" thought the traveller. "He seems to be alone." The circumstance interested him much, and he became intensely curious to know what thoughts and feelings, or, it might be, high aspirations, guided those rich and mellow accents. Tieing his horse at a short distance from the brook, he stealthily drew near the solitary speaker; and, concealing himself by the side of a huge fallen tree, he distinctly heard the following soliloquy:—

"What, then, is life to me? It is aimless and worthless, and worse than worthless. Those birds, perched on you swinging boughs, in friendly conclave, sounding forth their merry notes in seeming worship of the rising sun, though liable to the sportsman's fowling-piece, are still my superiors. They *live free,* though they may die slaves. They fly where they list by day, and retire in freedom at night. But what is freedom to me, or I to it? I am a slave,—born a slave, an abject slave,—even before I made part of this breathing world, the scourge was plaited for my back; the fetters were forged for my limbs. How mean a thing am I. That accursed and crawling snake, that miserable reptile, that has just glided into its slimy home, is freer and better off than I. He escaped my blow, and is safe. But here am I, a man,—yes, a man!—with thoughts and wishes, with powers and faculties as far as angel's flight above that hated reptile,—yet he is my superior, and scorns to own me as his master, or to stop to take my blows. When he saw my uplifted arm, he darted beyond my reach, and turned to give me battle. I dare not do as much as that. I neither run nor fight, but do meanly stand, answering each heavy blow of a cruel master with doleful wails and piteous cries. I am galled with irons; but even these are more tolerable than the consciousness, the galling consciousness of cowardice and indecision. Can it be that I dare not run away? Perish the thought, I dare do anything which may be done by another. When that young man struggled with the waves, for life, and others stood back appalled in helpless horror, did I not plunge in, forgetful of life, to save his? The raging bull from whom all others fled, pale with fright, did I not keep at bay with a single pitch-fork? Could a coward do that? No,—no,—I wrong myself,—I am no coward. Liberty I will have, or die in the attempt to gain it. This working that others may live in idleness! This cringing submission to insolence and curses! This living under the constant dread and apprehensions of being sold and transferred, like a mere brute, is too much for me. I will stand it no longer. What others have done, I will do. These trusty legs, or these sinewy arms shall place me among the free. Tom escaped; so can I. The North Star will not be less kind to me than to him. I will follow it. I will at least make the trial. I have nothing to lose. If I am caught, I shall only be a slave. If I am shot, I shall only lose a life which is a burden and a curse. If I get clear, (as something tells me I shall,) liberty, the inalienable birth-right of every man, precious and priceless, will be mine. My resolution is fixed. *I shall be free.*"

At these words the traveller raised his head cautiously and noiselessly, and caught, from his hiding-place, a full view of the unsuspecting speaker. Madison (for that was the name of our hero) was standing erect, a smile of satisfaction rippled upon his expressive countenance, like that which plays upon the face of one who has but just solved a difficult problem, or vanquished a malignant foe; for at that moment he was free, at least in spirit. The future gleamed brightly before him, and his fetters lay broken at his feet. His air was triumphant.

Madison was of manly form. Tall, symmetrical, round, and strong. In his movements he seemed to combine, with the strength of the lion, a lion's elasticity. His torn sleeves disclosed arms like polished iron. His face was "black, but comely." His eye, lit with emotion, kept guard under a brow as dark and as glossy as the raven's wing. His whole appearance betokened Herculean strength; yet there was nothing savage or forbidding in his aspect.

A child might play in his arms, or dance on his shoulders. A giant's strength, but not a giant's heart was in him. His broad mouth and nose spoke only of good nature and kindness. But his voice, that unfailing index of the soul, though full and melodious, had that in it which could terrify as well as charm. He was just the man you would choose when hardships were to be endured, or danger to be encountered,—intelligent and brave. He had the head to conceive, and the hand to execute. In a word, he was one to be sought as a friend, but to be dreaded as an enemy.

As our traveller gazed upon him, he almost trembled at the thought of his dangerous intrusion. Still he could not quit the place. He had long desired to sound the mysterious depths of the thoughts and feelings of a slave. He was not, therefore, disposed to allow so providential an opportunity to pass unimproved. He resolved to hear more; so he listened again for those mellow and mournful assents which, he says, made such an impression upon him as can never be erased. He did not have to wait long. There came another gush from the same full fountain; now bitter, and now sweet. Scathing denunciations of the cruelty and unjustice of slavery; heart-touching narrations of his own personal suffering, intermingled with prayers to the God of the oppressed for help and deliverance, were followed by presentations of the dangers and difficulties of escape, and formed the burden of his eloquent utterances; but his high resolution clung to him,—for he ended each speech by an emphatic declaration of his purpose to be free. It seemed that the very repetition of this imparted a glow to his countenance. The hope of feedom seemed to sweeten, for a season, the bitter cup of slavery, and to make it, for a time, tolerable; for when in the very whirlwind of anguish,—when the heart's cord seemed screwed up to snapping tension, hope sprung up and soothed his troubled spirit. Fitfully he would exclaim, "How can I leave her? Poor thing! what can she do when I am gone? Oh! oh! 'tis impossible that I can leave poor Susan!"

A brief pause intervened. Our traveller raised his head, and saw again the sorrow-smitten slave. His eye was fixed upon the ground. The strong man staggered under a heavy load. Recovering himself, he argued, thus aloud: "All is uncertain here. To-morrow's sun may not rise before I am sold, and separated from her I love. What, then, could I do for her? I should be in more hopeless slavery, and she no nearer to liberty,—whereas if I were free,—my arms my own,—I might devise the means to rescue her."

This said, Madison cast around a searching glance, as if the thought of being overheard had flashed across his mind. He said no more, but, with measured steps, walked away, and was lost to the eye of our traveller amidst the wildering woods.

Long after Madison had left the ground, Mr. Listwell (our traveller) remained in motionless silence, meditating on the extraordinary revelations to which he had listened. He seemed fastened to the spot, and stood half hoping, half fearing the return of the sable preacher to his solitary temple. The speech of Madison rung through the chambers of his soul, and vibrated through his entire frame. "Here is indeed a man," thought he, "of rare endowments,—a child of God,—guilty of no crime but the color of his skin,—hiding away from the face of humanity, and pouring out his thoughts and feelings, his hopes and resolutions to the lonely woods; to him those distant church bells have no grateful music. He shuns the church, the altar, and the great congregation of Christian worshippers, and wanders away to the gloomy forest, to utter in the vacant air complaints and griefs, which the religion of his times and his country can neither console nor relieve. Goaded almost to madness by the sense of the injustice done him, he resorts hither to give vent to his pent up feelings, and to debate with himself the feasibility of plans of his own invention, for his own deliverance. From this hour I am an abolitionist. I have seen enough and heard enough, and I shall go to my home in Ohio resolved to atone for my past indifference to this ill-starred race, by making such exertions as I shall be able to do, for the speedy emancipation of every slave in the land.

## PART II.

> The gaudy, babbling and remorseful day
> Is crept into the bosom of the sea;
> And now loud-howling wolves arouse the jades
> That drag the tragic melancholy night;
> Who with their drowsy, slow, and flagging wings
> Clip dead men's graves, and from their misty jaws
> Breathe foul contagions, darkness in the air.
>
> Shakespeare

Five years after the foregoing singular occurrence, in the winter of 1840, Mr. and Mrs. Listwell sat together by the fireside of their own happy home, in the State of Ohio. The children were all gone to bed. A single lamp burnt brightly on the center table. All was still and comfortable within; but the night was cold and dark; a heavy wind sighed and moaned sorrowfully around the house and barn, occasionally bringing against the chattering windows a stray leaf from the large oak trees that embowered their dwelling. It was a night for strange noises and for strange fancies. A whole wilderness of thought might pass through one's mind during such an evening. The smouldering embers, partaking of the sprit of the restless night, became fruitful of varied and fantastic pictures, and revived many bygone scenes and old impressions. The happy pair seemed to sit in silent fascination, gazing on the fire. Suddenly this reverie was interrupted by a heavy growl. Ordinarily such an occurrence would have scarcely provoked a single word, or excited the least apprehension. But there are certain seasons when the slightest sound sends a jar through all the subtle chambers of the mind; and such a season was this. The happy pair started up, as if some sudden danger had come upon them. The growl was from their trusty watch-dog.

"What can it mean? Certainly no one can be out on such a night as this," said Mrs. Listwell.

"The wind has deceived the dog, my dear; he has mistaken the noise of falling branches, brought down by the wind, for that of the footsteps of persons coming to the house. I have several times to-night thought that I heard the sound of footsteps. I am sure, however, that it was but the wind. Friends would not be likely to come out at such an hour, or such a night; and thieves are too lazy and self-indulgent to expose themselves to this biting frost; but should there be any one about, our brave old Monte, who is on the look-out, will not be slow in sounding the alarm."

Saying this they quietly left the window, whither they had gone to learn the cause of the menacing growl, and re-seated themselves by the fire, as if reluctant to leave the slowly expiring embers, although the hour was late. A few minutes only intervened after resuming their seats, when again their sober meditations were disturbed. Their faithful dog now growled and barked furiously, as if assailed by an advancing foe. Simultaneously the good couple arose, and stood in mute expectation. The contest without seemed fierce and violent. It was, however, soon over,—the barking ceased, for, with true canine instinct, Monte quickly discovered that a friend, not an enemy of the family, was coming to the house, and instead of rushing to repel the supposed intruder, he was now at the door, whimpering and dancing for the admission of himself and his newly made friend.

Mr. Listwell knew by this movement that all was well; he advanced and opened the door, and saw by the light that streamed out into the darkness, a tall man advancing slowly towards the house, with a stick in one hand, and a small bundle in the other. "It is a traveller," thought he, "who has missed his way, and is coming to inquire the road. I am glad we did not go to bed earlier,—I have felt all the evening as if somebody would be here to-night."

The man had now halted a short distance from the door, and looked prepared alike for flight or battle. "Come in, sir, don't be alarmed, you have probably lost your way."

Slightly hesitating, the traveller walked in; not, however, without regarding his host with a scrutinizing glance. "No, sir," said he "I have come to ask you a greater favor."

Instantly Mr. Listwell exclaimed, (as the recollection of the Virginia forest scene flashed upon him,) "Oh, sir, I know not your name, but I have seen your face, and heard your voice before. I am glad to see you. I know all. You are flying for your liberty,—be seated,—be seated,—banish all fear. You are safe under my roof."

This recognition, so unexpected, rather disconcerted and disquieted the noble fugitive. The timidity and suspicion of persons escaping from slavery are easily awakened, and often what is intended to dispel the one, and to allay the other, has precisely the opposite effect. It was so in this case. Quickly observing the unhappy impression made by his words and action, Mr. Listwell assumed a more quiet and inquiring aspect, and finally succeeded in removing the apprehensions which his very natural and generous salutation had aroused.

Thus assured, the stranger said, "Sir, you have rightly guessed, I am, indeed, a fugitive from slavery. My name is Madison,—Madison Washington my mother used to call me. I am on my way to Canada, where I learn that persons of my color are protected in all the rights of men; and my object in calling upon you was, to beg the privilege of resting my weary limbs for the night in your barn. It was my purpose to have continued my journey till morning; but the piercing cold, and the frowning darkness compelled me to seek shelter; and, seeing a light through the lattice of your window, I was encouraged to come here to beg the privilege named. You will do me a great favor by affording me shelter for the night."

"A resting-place, indeed, sir, you shall have; not, however, in my barn, but in the best room of my house. Consider yourself, if you please, under the roof of a friend; for such I am to you, and to all your deeply injured race."

While this introductory conversation was going on, the kind lady had revived the fire, and was diligently preparing supper; for she, not less than her husband, felt for the sorrows of the oppressed and hunted ones of earth, and was always glad of an opportunity to do them a service. A bountiful repast was quickly prepared, and the hungry and toil-worn bondman was cordially invited to partake thereof. Gratefully he acknowledged the favor of his benevolent benefactress; but appeared scarcely to understand what such hospitality could mean. It was the first time in his life that he had met so humane and friendly a greeting at the hands of persons whose color was unlike his own; yet it was impossible for him to doubt the charitableness of his new friends, or the genuiness of the welcome so freely given; and he therefore, with many thanks, took his seat at the table with Mr. and Mrs. Listwell, who, desirous to make him feel at home, took a cup of tea themselves, while urging upon Madison the best that the house could afford.

Supper over, all doubts and apprehensions banished, the three drew around the blazing fire, and a conversation commenced which lasted till long after midnight.

"Now," said Madison to Mr. Listwell, "I was a little surprised and alarmed when I came in, by what you said; do tell me, sir, why you thought you had seen my face before, and by what you knew me to be a fugitive from slavery; for I am sure that I never was before in this neighborhood, and I certainly sought to conceal what I supposed to be the manner of a fugitive slave."

Mr. Listwell at once frankly disclosed the secret; describing the place where he first saw him; rehearsing the language which he (Madison) had used; referring to the effect which his manner and speech had made upon him; declaring the resolution he there formed to be an abolitionist; telling how often he had spoken of the circumstance, and the deep concern he had ever since felt to know what had become of him; and whether he had carried out the purpose to make his escape, as in the woods he declared he would do.

"Ever since that morning," said Mr. Listwell, "you have seldom been absent from my mind, and though now I did not dare to hope that I should ever see you again, I have often wished that such might be my fortune; for, from that hour, your face seemed to be daguerreotyped on my memory." Madison looked quite astonished, and felt amazed at the narration to which he had listened. After recovering himself he said, "I well remember that morning, and the bitter anguish that wrung my heart; I will state the occasion of it. I had, on the previous Saturday, suffered a cruel lashing; had been tied up to the limb of a tree, with my feet chained together, and a heavy iron bar placed between my ankles. Thus suspended, I received on my naked back, forty stripes, and was kept in this distressing position three or four hours, and was then let down, only to have my torture increased; for my bleeding back, gashed by the cow-skin, was washed by the overseer with old brine, partly to augment my suffering, and partly, as he said, to prevent inflammation. My crime was that I had stayed longer at the mill, the day previous, than it was thought I ought to have done, which, I assured my master and the overseer, was no fault of mine; but no excuses were allowed. 'Hold your tongue, you impudent rascal,' met my every explanation. Slave-holders are so imperious when their passions are excited, as to construe every word of the slave into insolence. I could do nothing but submit to the agonizing infliction. Smarting still from the wounds, as well as from the consciousness of being whipt for no cause, I took advantage of the absence of my master, who had gone to church, to spend the time in the woods, and brood over my wretched lot. Oh, sir, I remember it well,—and can never forget it."

"But this was five years ago; where have you been since?"

"I will try to tell you," said Madison. "Just four weeks after that Sabbath morning, I gathered up the few rags of clothing I had and started, as I, supposed, for the North and for freedom. I must not stop to describe my felings on taking this step. It seemed like taking a leap into the dark. The thought of leaving my poor wife and two little children caused me indescribable anguish; but consoling myself with the reflection that once free, I could, possibly, devise ways and means to gain their freedom also, I nerved myself up to make the attempt. I started, but ill-luck attended me; for after being out a whole week, strange to say, I still found myself on my master's grounds; the third night after being out, a season of clouds and rain set in, wholly preventing me from seeing the North Star, which I had trusted as my guide, not dreaming that clouds might intervene between us.

"This circumstance was fatal to my project, for in losing my star, I lost my way; so when I supposed I was far towards the North, and had almost gained my freedom, I discovered myself at the very point from which I had started. It was a severe trial, for I arrived at home in great destitution; my feet were sore, and in travelling in the dark, I had dashed my foot against a stump, and started a nail, and lamed myself. I was wet and cold; one week had exhausted all my stores; and when I landed on my master's plantation, with all my work to do over again,—hungry, tired, lame, and bewildered,—I almost cursed the day that I was born. In this extremity I approached the quarters. I did so stealthily, although in my desperation I hardly cared whether I was discovered or not. Peeping through the rents of the quarters, I saw my fellow slaves seated by a warm fire, merrily passing away the time, as though their hearts knew no sorrow. Although I envied their seeming contentment, all wretched as I was, I despised the cowardly acquiescence in their own degradation which it implied, and felt a kind of pride and glory in my own desperate lot. I dared not enter the quarters,—for where there is seeming contentment with slavery, there is certain treachery to freedom. I proceeded towards the great house, in the hope of catching a glimpse of my poor wife, whom I knew might be trusted with my secrets even on the scaffold. Just as I reached the fence which divided the field from the garden, I saw a woman in the yard, who in the darkness I took to be my wife; but a nearer approach told me it was not she. I was about to speak; had I done so, I would not have been here this night; for an alarm would have been sounded, and the hunters been put on my track. Here were hunger, cold, thirst, disappointment, and chagrin, confronted only by the dim hope of liberty. I tremble to think of that dreadful hour. To face the deadly cannon's mouth in warm blood unterrified, is, I think, a small achievement, compared with a conflict like this with gaunt starvation. The gnawings of hunger conquers by degrees, till all that a man has he would give in exchange for a single crust of bread. Thank God, I was not quite reduced to this extremity.

"Happily for me, before the fatal moment of utter despair, my good wife made her appearance in the yard. It was she; I knew her step. All was well now. I was, however, afraid to speak, lest I should frighten her. Yet speak I did; and, to my great joy, my voice was known. Our meeting can be more easily imagined than described. For a time hunger, thirst, weariness, and lameness were forgotten. But it was soon necessary for her to return to the house. She being a house-servant, her absence from the kitchen, if discovered, might have excited suspicion. Our parting was like tearing the flesh from my bones; yet it was the part of wisdom for her to go. She left me with the purpose of meeting me at midnight in the very forest where you last saw me. She knew the place well, as one of my melancholy resorts, and could easily find it, though the night was dark.

"I hastened away, therefore, and concealed myself, to await the arrival of my good angel. As I lay there among the leaves, I was strongly tempted to return again to the house of my master and give myself up; but remembering my solemn pledge on that memorable Sunday morning, I was able to linger out the two long hours between ten and midnight. I may well call them long hours. I have endured much hardship; I have encountered many perils, but the anxiety of those two hours, was the bitterest, I ever experienced. True to her word, my wife came laden with provisions, and we sat down on the side of a log, at that dark and lonesome hour of the night. I cannot say we talked; our feelings were too great for that; yet we came to an understanding that I should make the woods my home, for if I gave myself up, I should be whipped and sold away; and if I started for the North, I should leave a wife doubly dear to me. We mutually determined, therefore, that I should remain in the vicinity. In the dismal swamps I lived, sir, five long years,—a cave for my home during the day. I wandered about at night with the wolf and the bear,—sustained by the promise that my good Susan would meet me in the pine woods at least once a week. This promise was redeemed I assure you, to the letter, greatly to my relief. I had partly become contented with my mode of life, and had made up my mind to spend my days there; but the wilderness that sheltered me thus long took fire, and refused longer to be my hiding-place.

"I will not harrow up your feelings by portraying the terrific scene of this awful conflagration. There is nothing to which I can liken it. It was horribly and indescribably grand. The whole world seemed on fire, and it appeared to me that the day of judgment had come; that the burning bowels of the earth had burst forth, and that the end of all things was at hand. Bears and wolves scorched from their mysterious hiding-places in the earth, and all the wild inhabitants of the untrodden forest, filled with a common dismay, ran forth, yelling, howling, bewildered amidst the smoke and flame. The very heavens seemed to rain down fire through the towering trees; it was by the merest chance that I escaped the devouring element. Running before it, and stopping occasionally to take breath, I looked back to behold its frightful ravages, and to drink in its savage magnificence. It was awful, thrilling, solemn, beyond compare. When aided by the fitful wind, the merciless tempest of fire swept on, sparkling, creaking, cracking, curling, roaring, out-doing in its dreadful splendor a thousand thunderstorms at once. From tree to tree it leaped, swallowing them up in its lurid, baleful glare; and leaving them leafless, limbless, charred, and lifeless behind. The scene was overwhelming, stunning,—nothing was spared,—cattle, tame and wild, herds of swine and of deer, wild beasts of every name and kind,—huge night-birds, bats, and owls, that had retired to their homes in lofty tree-tops to rest, perished in that fiery storm. The long-winged buzzard and croaking raven mingled their dismal cries with those of the countless myriads of small birds that rose up to the skies, and were lost to the sight in clouds of smoke and flame. Oh, I shudder when I think of it! Many a poor wandering fugitive, who, like myself, had sought among wild beasts the mercy denied by our fellow men, saw, in helpless consternation, his dwelling-place and city of refuge reduced to ashes forever. It was this grand conflagration that drove me hither; I ran alike from fire and from slavery."

After a slight pause, (for both speaker and hearers were deeply moved by the above recital,) Mr. Listwell, addressing Madison, said, "If it does not weary you too much, do tell us something of your journeyings since this disastrous burning,—we are deeply interested in everyting which can throw light on the hardships of persons escaping from slavery; we could hear you talk all night; are there no incidents that you could relate of your travels hither? Or are they such that you do not like to mention them?"

"For the most part, sir, my course has been uninterrupted; and, considering the circumstances, at times even pleasant. I have suffered little for want of food; but I need not tell you how I got it. Your moral code may differ from mine, as your customs and usages are different. The fact is sir, during my flight, I felt myself robbed by society of all my just rights; that I was in an enemy's land, who sought both my life and my liberty. They had transformed me into a brute; made merchandise of my body, and, for all the purposes of my flight, turned day into night,—and guided by my own necessities, and in contempt of their conventionality, I did not scruple to take bread where I could get it."

"And just there you were right," said Mr. Listwell; "I once had doubts on this point myself, but a conversation with Gerrit Smith, (a man, by the way, that I wish you could see, for he is a devoted friend of your race, and I know he would receive you gladly,) put an end to all my doubts on this point. But do not let me interrupt you."

"I had but one narrow escape during my whole journey," said Madison.

"Do let us hear of it," said Mr. Listwell.

"Two weeks ago," continued Madison, "after travelling all night, I was overtaken by daybreak, in what seemed to me an almost interminable wood. I deemed it unsafe to go farther, and, as usual, I looked around for a suitable tree in which to spend the day. I liked one with a bushy top, and found one just to my mind. Up I climbed, and hiding myself as well as I could, I, with this strap, (pulling one out of his old coat-pocket,) lashed myself to a bough, and flattered myself that I should get a good night's sleep that day; but in this I was soon disappointed. I had scarcely got fastened to my natural hammock, when I heard the voices of a number of persons, apparently approaching the part of the woods where I was. Upon my word, sir, I dreaded more these human voices than I should have done those of wild beasts. I was at a loss to know what to do. If I descended, I should probably be discovered by the men; and if they had dogs I should, doubtless, be 'treed.' It was an anxious moment, but hardships and dangers have been the accompaniments of my life; and have, perhaps, imparted to me a certain hardness of character, which, to some extent, adapts me to them. In my present predicament, I decided to hold my place in the tree-top, and abide the consequences. But here I must disappoint you; for the men, who were all colored, halted at least a hundred yards from me, and began with their axes, in right good earnest, to attack the trees. The sound of their laughing axes was like the report of as many well-charged pistols. By and by there came down at least a dozen trees with a terrible crash. They leaped upon the fallen trees with an air of victory. I could see no dog with them, and felt myself comparatively safe, though I could not forget the possiblity that some freak or fancy might bring the axe a little nearer my dwelling than comported with my safety.

"There was no sleep for me that day, and I wished for night. You may imagine that the thought of having the tree attacked under me was far from agreeable, and that it very easily kept me on the look-out. The day was not without diversion. The men at work seemed to be a gay set; and they would often make the woods resound with that uncontrolled laughter for which we, as a race, are remarkable. I held my place in the tree till sunset,—saw the men put on their jackets to be off. I observed that all left the ground except one, whom I saw sitting on the side of a stump, with his head bowed, and his eyes apparently fixed on the ground. I became interested in him. After sitting in the position to which I have alluded ten or fifteen minutes, he left the stump, walked directly towards the tree in which I was secreted, and halted almost under the same. He stood for a moment and looked around, deliberately and reverently took off his hat, by which I saw that he was a man in the evening of life, slightly bald and quite gray. After laying down his hat carefully, he knelt and prayed aloud, and such a prayer, the most fervent, earnest, and solemn, to which I thank I ever listened. After reverently addressing the Almighty, as the all-wise, all-good, and the common Father of all mankind, he besought God for grace, for strength, to bear up and under, and to endure, as a good soldier, all the hardships and trials which beset the journey of life, and to enable him to live in a manner which accorded with the gospel of Christ. His soul now broke out in humble supplication for deliverance from bondage. 'O thou,' said he, 'that hearest the raven's cry, take pity on poor me! O deliver me! O deliver me! in mercy, O God, deliver me from the chains and manifold hardships of slavery! With thee, O Father, all things are possible. Thou canst stand and measure the earth. Thou hast beheld and drove asunder the nations,—all power is in thy hand,—thous didst say of old, 'I seen the affliction of my people, and am come to deliver them',—Oh look down upon our afflictions, and have mercy upon us.' But I cannot repeat his prayer, nor can I give you an idea of its deep pathos. I had given but little attention to religion, and had but little faith in it; yet, as the old man prayed, I felt almost like coming down and kneeling by his side, and mingling my broken complaint with his.

"He had already gained my confidence; as how could it be otherwise? I knew enough of religion to know that the man who prays in secret is far more likely to be sincere than he who loves to pray standing in the street, or in the great congregation. When he arose from his knees, like another Zacheus, I came down from the tree. He seemed a little alarmed at first, but I told him my story, and the good man embraced me in his arms, and assured me of his sympathy.

"I was now about out of provisions, and thought I might safely ask him to help me replenish my store. He said he had no money; but if he had, he would freely give it me. I told him I had one dollar; it was all the money I had in the world. I gave it to him, and asked him to purchase some crackers and cheese, and to kindly bring me the balance; that I would remain in or near that place, and would come to him on his return, if he would whistle. He was gone only about an hour. Meanwhile, from some cause or other, I know not what, (but as you shall see very wisely,) I changed my place. On his return I started to meet him; but it seemed as if the shadow of approaching danger fell upon my spirit, and checked my progress. In a very few minutes, closely on the heels of the old man, I distinctly saw fourteen men, with something like guns in their hands."

"Oh! the old wretch!" exclaimed Mrs. Listwell "he had betrayed you, had he?"

"I think not," said Madison, "I cannot believe that the old man was to blame. He probably went into a store, asked for the articles for which I sent, and presented the bill I gave him; and it is so unusual for slaves in the country to have money, that fact, doubtless, excited suspicion, and gave rise to inquiry. I can easily believe that the truthfulness of the old man's character compelled him to disclose the facts; and thus were these blood-thirsty men put on my track. Of course I did not present myself; but hugged my hiding-place securely. If discovered and attacked, I resolved to sell my life as dearly as possible.

"After searching about the woods silently for a time, the whole company gathered around the old man; one charged him with lying, and called him an old villain; said he was a thief; charged him with stealing money; said if he did not instantly tell where he got it, they would take the shirt from his old back, and give him thirty-nine lashes.

" 'I did not steal the money,' said the old man, it was given me, as I told you at the store; and if the man who gave it to me is not here, it is not my fault.'

" 'Hush! you lying old rascal; we'll make you smart for it. You shall not leave this spot until you have told where you got the money.'

"They now took hold of him, and began to strip him; while others went to get sticks with which to beat him. I felt, at the moment, like rushing out in the midst of them; but considering that the old man would be whipped the more for having aided a fugitive slave, and that, perhaps, in the melée he might be killed outright, I disobeyed this impulse. They tied him to a tree, and began to whip him. My own flesh crept at every blow, and I seem to hear the old man's piteous cries even now. They laid thirty-nine lashes on his bare back, and were going to repeat that number, when one of the company besought his comrades to desist. 'You'll kill the d——d old scoundrel! You've already whipt a dollar's worth out of him, even if he stole it!' 'O yes,' said another, 'let him down. He'll never tell us another lie, I'll warrant ye!' With this, one of the company untied the old man, and bid him go about his business.

The old man left, but the company remained as much as an hour, scouring the woods. Round and round they went, turning up the underbrush, and peering about like so many bloodhounds. Two or three times they came within six feet of where I lay. I tell you I held my stick with a firmer grasp than I did in coming up to your house to-night. I expected to level one of them at least. Fortunately, however, I eluded their pursuit, and they left me alone in the woods.

"My last dollar was now gone, and you may well suppose I felt the loss of it; but the thought of being again free to pursue my journey, prevented that depression which a sense of destitution causes; so swinging my little bundle on my back, I caught a glimpse of the Great Bear (which ever points the way to my beloved star,) and I started again on my journey. What I lost in money I made up at a hen-roost that same night, upon which I fortunately came."

"But you didn't eat your food raw? How did you cook it?" said Mrs. Listwell.

"O no, Madam," said Madison, turning to his little bundle;—"I had the means of cooking." Here he took out of his bundle an old-fashioned tinder-box, and taking up a piece of a file, which he brought with him, he struck it with a heavy flint, and brought out at least a dozen sparks at once. "I have had this old box," said he, "more than five years. It is the only property saved from the fire in the dismal swamp. It had done me good service. It has given me the means of broiling many a chicken!"

It seemed quite a relief to Mrs. Listwell to know that Madison had, at

least, lived upon cooked food. Women have a perfect horror of eating un-
cooked food.

By this time thoughts of what was best to be done about getting Madison
to Canada, began to trouble Mr. Listwell; for the laws of Ohio were very
stringent against any one who should aid, or who were found aiding a slave to
escape through that State. A citizen, for the simple act of taking a fugitive
slave in his carriage, had just been stripped of all his property, and thrown
penniless upon the world. Notwithstanding this, Mr. Listwell was determined
to see Madison safely on his way to Canada. "Give yourself no uneasiness,"
said he to Madison, "for if it cost my farm, I shall see you safely out of the
States, and on your way to the land of liberty. Thank God that there is such a
land so near us! You will spend to-morrow with us, and to-morrow night I
will take you in my carriage to the Lake. Once upon that, and you are safe."

"Thank you! thank you," said the fugitive; "I will commit myself to your
care."

For the first time during five years, Madison enjoyed the luxury of
resting his limbs on a comfortable bed, and inside a human habitation.
Looking at the white sheets he said to Mr. Listwell, "What, sir! you don't
mean that I shall sleep in that bed?"

"Oh yes, oh yes."

After Mr. Listwell left the room, Madison said he really hesitated
whether or not he should lie on the floor; for that was far more comfortable and
inviting than any bed to which he had been used.

We pass over the thoughts and feelings, the hopes and fears, the plans
and purposes, that revolved in the mind of Madison during the day that he was
secreted at the house of Mr. Listwell. The readers will be content to know that
nothing occurred to endanger his liberty, or to excite alarm. Many were the
little attentions bestowed upon him in his quiet retreat and hiding-place. In
the evening, Mr. Listwell, after treating Madison to a new suit of winter
clothes, and replenishing his exhausted purse with five dollars, all in silver,
brought out his two-horse wagon, well provided with buffaloes, and silently
started off with him to Cleveland. They arrived there without interruption, a
few minutes before sunrise the next morning. Fortunately the steamer Admi-
ral lay at the wharf, and was to start for Canada at nine o'clock. Here the last
anticipated danger was surmounted. It was feared that just at this point the
hunters of men might be on the look-out, and, possibly pounce upon their
victim. Mr. Listwell saw the captain of the boat; cautiously sounded him on
the matter of carrying liberty-loving passengers, before he introduced his
precious charge. This done, Madison was conducted on board. With usual
generosity this true subject of the emancipating queen welcomed Madison,
and assured him that he should be safely landed in Canada, free of charge.

Madison now felt himself no more a piece of merchandise, but a passenger, and, like any other passenger, going about his business, carrying with him what belonged to him, and nothing which rightfully belonged to anybody else.

Wrapped in his new winter suit, snug and comfortable, a pocket full of silver, safe from his pursuers, embarked for a free country, Madison gave every sign of sincere gratitude, and bade his kind benefactor farewell, with such a grip of the hand as bespoke a heart full of honest manliness, and a soul that knew how to appreciate kindness. It need scarcely be said that Mr. Listwell was deeply moved by the gratitude and friendship he had excited in a nature so noble as that of the fugitive. He went to his home that day with a joy and gratification which knew no bounds. He had done something "to deliver the spoiled out of the hands of the spoiler," he had given bread to the hungry, and clothes to the naked; he had befriended a man to whom the laws of his country forbade all friendship,—and in proportion to the odds against his righteous deed, was the delightful satisfaction that gladdened his heart. On reaching home, he exclaimed, "He is safe,—he is safe,—he is safe,"—and the cup of his joy was shared by his excellent lady. The following letter was received from Madison a few days after.

Windsor, Canada West, Dec. 16, 1840.
My dear Friend,—for such you truly are:—

Madison is out to the woods at last; I nestle in the mane of the British lion, protected by the mighty paw from the talons and the beak of the American eagle. I AM FREE, and breathe an atmosphere too pure for slaves, slave-hunters, or slave-holders. My heart is full. As many thanks to you, sir, and to your kind lady, as there are pebbles on the shores of Lake Erie; and may the blessing of God rest upon you both. You will never be forgotten by your profoundly grateful friend.

Madison Washington.

PART III.

————His head was with his heart,
And that was far away!
Childe Harold.

Just upon the edge of the great road from Petersburg, Virginia, to

Richmond, and only about fifteen miles from the latter place, there stands a somewhat ancient and famous public tavern, quite notorious in its better days, as being the grand resort for most of the leading gamblers, horse-racers, cock-fighters, and slave-traders from all the country round about. This old rookery, the nucleus of all sorts of birds, mostly those of ill omen, has, like everything else peculiar to Virginia, lost much of its ancient consequence and splendor; yet it keeps up some appearance of gaiety and high life, and is still frequented, even by respectable travellers, who are unacquainted with its past history and present condition. Its fine old portico looks well at a distance, and gives the building an air of grandeur. A nearer view, however, does little to sustain this pretension. The house is large, and its style imposing, but time and dissipation, unfailing in their results, have made ineffaceable marks upon it, and it must, in the common course of events, soon be numbered with the things that were. The gloomy mantle of ruin is, already, outspread to envelop it, and its remains, even but now remind one of a human skull, after the flesh has mingled with the earth. Old hats and rags fill the places in the upper windows once occupied by large panes of glass, and the molding boards along the roofing have dropped off from their places, leaving holes and crevices in the rented wall for hats and swallows to build their nests in. The platform of the portico, which fronts the highway is a rickety affair, its planks are loose, and in some places entirely gone, leaving effective mantraps in their stead for nocturnal ramblers. The wooden pillars, which once supported it, but which now hang as encumbrances, are all rotten, and tremble with the touch. A part of the stable, a fine old structure in its day, which has given comfortable shelter to hundreds of the noblest steeds of "the Old Dominion" at once, was blown down many years ago, and never has been, and probably never will be, rebuilt. The doors of the barn are in wretched condition; they will shut with a little human strength to help their worn out hinges, but not otherwise. The side of the great building seen from the road is much discolored in sundry places by slops poured from the upper windows, rendering it unsightly and offensive in other respects. Three or four great dogs, looking as dull and gloomy as the mansion itself, lie stretched out along the door-sills under the portico; and double the number of loafers, some of them completely rum-ripe, and others ripening, dispose themselves like so many sentinels about the front of the house. These latter understand the science of scraping acquaintance to perfection. They know every-body, and almost every-body knows them. Of course, as their title implies, they have no regular employment. They are (to use an expressive phrase) hangers-on, or still better, they are what sailors would denominate holder-on to the slack, in every-body's mess, and in no-body's watch. They are, however, as good as the newspaper for the events of the day, and they sell their knowledge almost as cheap. Money they seldom have; yet they always have capital the most reliable. They make their way with a succeeding traveller by intelligence gained from a preceding one. All the great names of Virginia they know by heart, and have seen their owners often. The history of the house is folded in their lips, and they rattle off stories in connection with it, equal to the guides at Dryburgh Abbey. He must be a shrewd man, and well skilled in the art of evasion, who gets out of the hands of these fellows without being at the expense of a treat.

It was at this old tavern, while on a second visit to the State of Virginia in 1841, that Mr. Listwell, unacquainted with the fame of the place, turned aside, about sunset, to pass the night. Riding up to the house, he had scarcely dismounted, when one of the half dozen bar-room fraternity met and addressed him in a manner exceedingly bland and accommodating.

"Fine evening, sir."

"Very fine," said Mr. Listwell. "This is a tavern, I believe?"

"O yes, sir, yes; although you may think it looks a little the worse for wear, it was once as good a house as any in Virginy. I make no doubt if ye spend the night here, you'll think it a good house yet; for there aint a more accommodating man in the country than you'll find the landlord."

Listwell. "The most I want is a good bed for myself, and a full manger for my horse. If I get these, I shall be quite satisfied."

Loafer. "Well, I alloys like to hear a gentleman talk for his horse; and just because the horse can't talk for itself. A man that don't care about his beast, and don't look after it when he's travelling, aint much in my eye nay how. Now, sir, I likes a horse, and I'll guarantee your horse will be taken good care on here. That old stable, for all you see it looks so shabby now, once sheltered the great Eclipse, when he run here again Batchelor and Jumping Jenny. Them was fast horses, but he beat 'em both."

Listwell. "Indeed."

Loafer. "Well I rather reckon you've travelled a right smart distance to-day, from the look of your horse?"

Listwell. "Forty miles only."

Loafer. "Well! I'll be darned if that aint a pretty good only. Mister, that beast of yours is a singed cat, I warrant you. I never see'd a creature like that that wasn't good on the road. You've come about forty miles, then?"

Listwell. "Yes, yes, and a pretty good pace at that."

Loafer. "You're somewhat in a hurry, then, I make no doubt? I reckon I could guess if I would, what you're going to Richmond for? It wouldn't be much of a guess either; for it's rumored hereabouts, that there's to be the greatest sale of N-----s at Richmond to-morrow that has taken place there in a long time; and I'll be bound you're a going there to have a hand in it."

Listwell. "Why, you must think, then, that there's money to be made at that business?"

Loafer. "Well, 'pon my honor, sir, I never made any that way myself; but it stands to reason that it's a money making business; for almost all other business in Virginia is dropped to engage in this. One thing is sartain, I never see'd a n-----buyer yet that hadn't a plenty of money, and he wasn't as free with it as water. I has known one on'em to treat as high as twenty times in a night; and, ginerally speaking, they's men of edication, and knows all about the government. The fact is, sir, I alloys like to hear 'em talk, becase I alloys can learn something from them."

Listwell. "What may I call your name, sir?"

Loafer. "Well, now, they calls me Wilkes. I'm known all around all the gentlemen that comes here. They all knows old Wilkes."

Listwell. "Well, Wilkes, you seem to be accquainted here, and I see you have a strong liking for a horse. Be so good as to speak a kind word for mine to the hostler to-night, and you'll not lose anything by it."

Loafer. "Well, sir, I see you don't say much, but you've got an insight into things. It's alloys wise to get the good will of them that's acquainted about a tavern; for a man don't know when he goes into a house what may happen, or how much he may need a friend." Here the loafer gave Mr. Listwell a significant grin, which expressed a sort of triumphant pleasure at having, as he supposed, by his tact succeeded in placing so fine appearing a gentleman under obligations to him.

The pleasure, however, was mutual; for there was something so insinuating in the glance of this loquacious customer, that Mr. Listwell was very glad to get quit of him, and to do so more successfully, he ordered his supper to be brought to him in his private room, private to the eye, but not to the ear. This room was directly over the bar, and the plastering being off, nothing but pine boards and naked laths separated him from the disagreeable company below,—he could easily hear what was said in the bar-room, and was rather glad of the advantage it afforded, for, as you shall see, it furnished him important hints as to the manner and deportment he should assume during his stay at that tavern.

Mr. Listwell says he had got into his room but a few moments, when he heard the officious Wilkes below, in a tone of disappointment, exclaim, "Whar's that gentleman?" Wilkes was evidently expecting to meet with his friend at the bar-room, on his return, and had no doubt of his doing the handsome thing. "He has gone to his room," answered the landlord, "and has ordered his supper to be brought to him."

Here some one shouted out, "Who is he, Wilkes? Where's he going?"

"Well, now, I'll be hanged if I know; but I'm willing to make any man a bet of this old hat against a five dollar bill, that that gent is as full of money as a dog is of fleas. He's going down to Richmond to buy n-----s, I make no doubt. He's no fool, I warrant ye."

"Well, he acts d---d strange," said another, "anyhow. I likes to see a man, when he comes up to a tavern, to come straight into the bar-room, and show that he's a man among men. Nobody was going to bite him."

"Now, I don't blame him a bit for not coming in here. That man knows his business, and means to take care on his money," answered Wilkes.

"Wilkes, you're a fool. You only say that, because you hope to get a few coppers out of him."

"You only measure my corn by your half-bushel, I won't say that you're only mad because I got the chance of speaking to him first."

"O Wilkes! you're known here. You'll praise up anybody that will give you a copper; besides, 'tis my opinion that that fellow who took his long slab-sides up stairs, for all the world just like a half-scared woman, afraid to look honest men in the face, is a Northerner, and as mean as dish-water."

"Now what will you bet of that," said Wilkes. The speaker said, "I make no bets with you, 'case you can get that fellow upstairs there to say anything."

"Well," said Wilkes, "I am willing to bet any man in the company that that gentleman is a n-----r-buyer. He didn't tell me so right down, but I reckon I knows enough about men to give a pretty clean guess as to what they are arter."

The dispute as to who Mr. Listwell was, what his business, where he was going, etc., was kept up with much animation for some time, and more than once threatened a serious disturbance of the peace. Wilkes had his friends as well as his opponents. After this sharp debate, the company amused themselves by drinking whiskey, and telling stories. The latter consisting of quarrels, fights, rencontres, and duels, in which distinguished persons of that neighborhood, and frequenters of that house, had been actors. Some of these stories were frightful enough, and were told, too, with a relish which bespoke the pleasure of the parties with the horrid scenes they portrayed. It would not be proper here to give the reader any idea of the vulgarity and dark profanity which rolled, as "a sweet morsel," under these corrupt tongues. A more brutal set of creatures, perhaps, never congregated.

Disgusted, and a little alarmed withal, Mr. Listwell, who was not accustomed to such entertainment, at length retired, but not to sleep. He was too much wrought upon by what he had heard to rest quietly, and what snatches of sleep he got, were interrupted by dreams which were anything than pleasant. At eleven o'clock, there seemed to be several hundreds of persons crowding into the house. A loud and confused clamor, cursing and cracking of whips, and the noise of chains startled him from his bed; for a moment he would have given the half of his farm in Ohio to have been at home. This uproar was kept up with undulating course, till near morning. There was loud laughing—loud singing—loud cursing—and yet there seemed to be weeping and mourning in the midst of all. Mr. Listwell said had heard enough during the forepart of the night to convince him that a buyer of men and women stood the best chance of being respected. And he, therefore, thought it best to say nothing which might undo the favorable opinion that had been formed of him in the bar-room by at least one of the fraternity that swarmed about it. While he would not avow himself a purchaser of slaves, he deemed it not prudent to disavow it. He felt that he might, properly, refuse to cast such a pearl before parties which, to him, were worse than swine. To reveal himself, and to impart a knowledge of his real character and sentiments would, to say the least, be imparting intelligence with the certainty of seeing it and himself both abused. Mr. Listwell confesses, that this reasoning did not altogether satisfy his conscience, for, hating slavery as he did, and regarding it to be the immediate duty of every man to cry out against it, "without compromise and without concealment," it was hard for him to admit to himself the possibility of circumstances wherein a man might, properly, hold his tongue on the subject. Having as little of the spirit of a martyr as Erasmus, he concluded, like the latter, that it was wiser to trust to the mercy of God for his soul, than the humanity of the slave-trader for his body. Bodily fear, not conscientious scruples, prevailed.

In this spirit he rose early in the morning, manifesting no surprise at what he had heard during the night. His quondam friend was soon at his elbow, boring him with all sorts of questions. All, however, directed to find out his character, business, residence, purposes, and destination. With the most perfect appearance of good nature and carelessness, Mr. Listwell evaded these meddlesome inquiries, and turned conversation to general topics, leaving himself and all that specially pertained to him, out of discussion. Disengaging himself from their troublesome companionship, he made his way towards an old bowling-alley, which was connected with the house, and which, like all the rest, was in very bad repair.

On reaching the alley Mr. Listwell saw for the first time in his life, a slave-gang on their way to market. A sad sight truly. Here were one hundred and thirty human beings,—children of a common Creator—guilty of no crime—men and women, with hearts, minds, and deathless spirits, chained and fettered, and bound for the market, in a Christian country,—in a country boasting of its liberty, independence, and high civilization! Humanity converted into merchandise, and linked in iron bands, with no regard to decency or humanity! All sizes, ages, and sexes, mothers, fathers, daughters, brothers, sisters,—all huddled together, on their way to market to be sold and separated from home, and from each other forever. And all to fill the pockets of men too lazy to work for an honest living, and who gain their fortune by plundering the helpless, and trafficking in the souls and sinews of men. As he gazed upon this revolting and heart-rending scene, our informant said he almost doubted the existence of a God of justice! And he stood wondering that the earth did not open and swallow up such wickedness.

In the midst of these reflections, and while running his eye up and down the fettered ranks, he met the glance of one whose face he thought he had seen before. To be resolved, he moved towards the spot. It was MADISON WASHINGTON! Here was a scene for the pencil! Had Mr. Listwell been confronted by one risen from the dead, he could not have been more appalled. He was completely stunned. A thunderbolt could not have struck him more dumb. He stood, for a few moments as motionless as one petrified; collecting himself, he at length exclaimed, "Madison! is that you?"

The noble fugitive, but little less astonished than himself, answered cheerily, "O yes, sir, they've got me again."

Thoughtless of consequences for the moment, Mr. Listwell ran up to his old friend, placing his hands upon his shoulders, and looked him in the face! Speechless they stood gazing at each other as if to be doubly resolved that there was no mistake about the matter, till Madison motioned his friend away, intimating a fear lest the keepers should find him there, and suspect him of tampering with the slaves.

"They will soon be out to look after us. You can come when they go to breakfast, and I will tell you all."

Pleased with this arrangement, Mr. Listwell passed out of the alley; but only just in time to save himself, for, while near the door, he observed three men making their way to the alley. The thought occurred to him to await their arrival, as the best means of diverting the ever ready suspicions of the guilty.

While the scene between Mr. Listwell and his friend Madison was going on, the other slaves stood as mute spectators,—at a loss to know what all this could mean. As he left, he heard the man chained to Madison ask, "Who is that gentleman?"

"He is a friend of mine. I cannot tell you now. Suffice it to say he is a friend. You shall hear more of him before long, but mark me! whatever shall pass between that gentleman and me, in your hearing, I pray you will say nothing about it. We are chained here together,—ours is a common lot; and that gentleman is not less your friend than mine." At these words, all mysterious as they were, the unhappy company gave signs of satisfaction and hope. It seems that variable accompaniment of genius, had already won the confidence of the gang and was sort of general-in-chief among them.

By this time the keepers arrived. A horrid trio, well fitted for their demoniacal work. Their uncombed hair came down over foreheads "villainously low," and with eyes, mouths, and noses to match. "Hello! hallo!" they growled out as they entered, "Are you all there!"

"All there," said Madison.

"Well, well, that's right! your journey will soon be over. You'll be in Richmond by eleven to-day, and then you'll have an easy time on it."

"I say, gal, what in the devil are you crying about?" said one of them. "I'll give you something to cry about, if you don't mind." This was said to a girl, apparently not more than twelve years old, who had been weeping bitterly. She had, probably, left behind her loving mother, affectionate sisters, brothers, and friends, and her tears were but the natural expression of her sorrow, and the only solace. But the dealers in human flesh have no respect for such sorrow. They look upon it as a protest against their cruel injustice, and they are prompt to punish it.

This is a puzzle not easily solved. How came he here? what can I do for him? may I not even now be in some way compromised in this affair? were thoughts that troubled Mr. Listwell, and made him eager for the promised opportunity of speaking to Madison.

The bell now sounded for breakfast, and keepers and drivers, with pistols and bowie-knives gleaming from their belts, hurried in, as if to get the best places. Taking the chance now afforded, Mr. Listwell hastened back to the bowling-alley. Reaching Madison, he said, "Now do tell me all about the matter. Do you know me?"

"Oh, yes," said Madison, "I know you well, and shall never forget you nor that cold and dreary night you gave me shelter. I must be short," he continued, "for they'll soon be out again. This, then, is the story in brief. On reaching Canada, and getting over the excitement of making my escape; sir, my thoughts turned to my poor wife, who had well deserved my love by her virtuous fidelity and undying affection for me. I could not bear the thought of leaving her in the cruel jaws of slavery, without making an effort to rescue her. First, I tried to get money to her; but oh! the process was too slow. I despaired of accomplishing it. She was in all my thoughts by day, and my dreams by night. At times I could almost hear her voice, saying, 'O Madison! Madison! will you then leave me here? can you leave me here to die? No! no! you will come! you will come!' I was wretched. I lost my appetite. I could neither work, eat, nor sleep, till I resolved to hazard my own liberty, to gain that of my wife! But I must be short. Six weeks ago I reached my old master's place. I laid about the neighborhood nearly a week, watching my chance, and, finally, I ventured upon the desperate attempt to reach the window, but the noise in raising it frightened my wife, and she screamed and fainted. I took her in my arms, and was descending the ladder, when the dog began to bark furiously, and before I could get to the woods the white folks were roused. The cool night air soon restored my wife, and she readily recognized me. We made the best of our way to the woods, but it was now too late,—the dogs were after us as though they would have torn us to pieces. It was all over with me now! My old master and his two sons ran out with loaded rifles, and before we were out of gunshot, our ears were assailed with 'Stop! stop! or be shot down.' Nevertheless we ran on. Seeing that we gave no heed to their call, they fired, and my poor wife fell by my side dead, while I received but a slight flesh wound. I now became desperate, and stood my ground, and awaited their attack over her dead body. They rushed upon me, with their rifles in hand. I parried their blows, and fought them till I was knocked down and over-powered."

"Oh! it was madness to have returned," said Mr. Listwell.

"Sir, I could not be free with the galling thought that my poor wife was still a slave. With her in slavery, my body, not my spirit, was free. I was taken to the house,—chained to a ring-bolt,—my wounds dressed. I was kept there three days. All slaves, for miles around, were brought to see me. Many slave-holders came with their slaves, using me as proof of the completeness of their power, and of the impossibility of slaves getting away. I was taunted, jeered at, and berated by them, in a manner that pierced me to the soul. Thank God, I was able to smother my rage, and to bear it all with seeming composure. After my wounds were nearly healed, I was taken to a tree and stripped, and I received sixty lashes on my naked back. A few days after, I was sold to a slave-trader, and placed in this gang for the New Orleans market."

"Do you think your master would sell you to me?"

"O no, sir! I was sold on condition of my being taken South. Their motive is revenge."

"Then, then," said Mr. Listwell, "I fear I can do nothing for you. Put your trust in God, and bear your sad lot with the manly fortitude which becomes a man. I shall see you at Richmond, but don't recognize me." Saying this, Mr. Listwell handed Madison ten dollars; said a few words to the other slaves; received their hearty "God bless you," and made his way to the house.

Fearful of exciting suspicion by too long delay, our friend went to the breakfast table, with the aid of one who half reproved the greediness of those who rushed in at the sound of the bell. A cup of coffee was all that he could manage. His feelings were too bitter and excited, and his heart was too full with the fate of poor Madison (whom he loved as well as admired) to relish his breakfast; and although he sat long after the company had left the table, he really did little more than change the position of his knife and fork. The strangeness of meeting again one whom he had met on two several occasions before, under extraordinary circumstances, was well calculated to suggest the idea that a supernatural power, a wakeful providence, or an inexorable fate, had linked their destiny together; and that no efforts of his could disentangle him from the mysterious web of circumstances which enfolded him.

On leaving the table, Mr. Listwell nerved himself up and walked firmly into the bar-room. He was at once greeted again by that talkative chatter-box, Mr. Wilkes.

"Them's a likely set of n------ in the alley there," said Wilkes.

"Yes, they're fine looking fellows, one of them I should like to purchase, and for him I would be willing to give a handsome sum."

Turning to one of his comrades, and with a grin of victory, Wilkes said, "Aha, Bill, did you hear that? I told you I know'd that gentleman wanted to buy n------, and would bid as high as any purchaser in the market."

"Come, come," said Listwell, "don't be too loud in your praise, you are old enough to know that prices rise when purchasers are plenty."

"That's a fact," said Wilkes, "I see you knows the ropes—and there's not a man in old Virginy whom I'd rather help to make a good bargain than you, sir."

"Mr. Listwell here threw a dollar at Wilkes, (which the latter caught with a dexterous hand,) saying, "Take that for your kind good will." Wilkes held up the dollar to his right eye, with a grin of victory, and turned to the morose grumbler in the corner who had questioned the liberality of a man of whom he knew nothing.

Mr. Listwell now stood as well with the company as any other occupant of the bar-room.

We pass over the hurry and bustle, the brutal vociferations of the slave-drivers in getting their unhappy gang in motion for Richmond; and we need not narrate every application of the lash to those who faltered in the journey. Mr. Listwell followed the train at a long distance, with a sad heart; and on reaching Richmond, left his horse at a hotel, and made his way to the wharf in the direction of which he saw the slave-coffle driven. He was just in time to see the whole company embark for New Orleans. The thought struck him that, while mixing with the multitude, he might do his friend Madison one last service, and he stept into a hardware store and purchased three strong files. These he took with him, standing near the small boat, which lay in waiting to bear the company by parcels to the side of the brig that lay in the stream, he managed, as Madison passed him, to slip the files into his pocket, and at once darted back among the crowd.

All the company now on board, the imperious voice of the captain sounded, and instantly a dozen hardy seamen were in the rigging, hurrying aloft to unfurl the broad canvas of our Baltimore-built American Slaver. The sailors hung about the ropes, like so many black cats, now in the round-tops, now in the cross-trees, now on the yard-arms; all was bluster and activity. Soon the broad fore topsail, the royal and top gallant sail were spread to the breeze. Round went the heavy windlass, clank, clank went the fall-bit,—the anchors weighed,—jibs, mainsails, and topsails hauled it to the wind, and the long, low, black slaver, with her cargo of human flesh, careened and moved forward to the sea.

Mr. Listwell stood on the shore, and watched the slaver till the last speck of her upper sails faded from sight, and announced the limit of human vision. "Farewell! farewell! brave and true man! God grant that brighter skies may smile upon your future than have yet looked down upon your thorny pathway."

Saying this to himself, our friend lost no time in completing his business, and in making his way homewards, gladly shaking off from his feet the dust of Old Virginia.


# PART IV.


Oh, where's the slave so lowly
Condemn'd to chains unholy,
    Who could he burst
    His bonds at first
Would pine beneath them slowly?
    —Moore


—————Know ye not
Who would be free, themselves must strike the blow.
    —Childe Harold


What a world of inconsistency, as well as of wickedness, is suggested by the smooth and gliding phrase, *American Slave Trade*; and how strange and perverse is that moral sentiment which loathes, execrates, and brands as piracy and as deserving of death the carrying away into captivity men, women, and children from the African coast; but which is neither shocked nor disturbed by a similar traffic, carried on with the same motives and purposes, and characterized by even more odious peculiarities on the coast of our MODEL RE-PUBLIC. We execrate and hang the wretch guilty of this crime on the coast of Guinea, while we respect and applaud the guilty participators in this murderous business on the enlightened shores of the Chesapeake. The inconsistency is so flagrant and glaring, that it would seem to cast a doubt on the doctrine of the innate moral sense of mankind.

Just two months after the sailing of the Virginia slave brig, which the reader has seen move off to sea so proudly with her human cargo for the New Orleans market, there chanced to meet, in the Marine Coffee-house at Richmond, a company of ocean birds, when the following conversation, which throws some light on the subsequent history, not only of Madison

Washington, but of the hundred and thirty human beings with whom we last saw him chained.

"I say, shipmate, you had rather rough weather on your late passage to Orleans?" said Jack Williams, a regular old salt, tauntingly, to a trim, compact, manly looking person, who proved to be the first mate of the slave brig in question.

"Foul play, as well as foul weather," replied the firmly knit personage, evidently but little inclined to enter upon a subject which terminated so ingloriously to the captain and officers of the American slaver.

"Well, betwixt you and me," said Williams, "that whole affair on board of the *Creole* was miserably and disgracefully managed. Those black rascals got the upper hand of ye altogether; and, in my opinion, the whole disaster was the result of ignorance of the real character of darkies in general. With half a dozen resolute white men, (I say it not boastingly,) I could have had the rascals in irons in ten minutes, not because I'm so strong, but I know how to manage 'em. With my back against the caboose, I could, myself, have flogged a dozen of them; and had I been on board, by every monster of the deep, every black devil of 'em all would have had his neck stretched from the yard-arm. Ye made a mistake in yer manner of fiting 'em. All that is needed in dealing with a set of rebellious darkies, is to show that ye're not afraid of 'em. For my own part, I would not honor a dozen n-----s, by pointing a gun at one on 'em,—a good stout whip, or a stiff rope's end, is better than all the guns at Old Point to quell a n----r insurrection. Why, sir, to take a gun to a n----r is the best way you can select to tell him you are afraid of him, and the best way of inviting his attack."

This speech made made quite a sensation among the company, and a part of them indicated solicitude for the answer which might be made to it. Our first mate replied, "Mr. Williams, all that you've now said sounds very well here on shore, where, perhaps, you have studied Negro character. I do not profess to understand the subject as well as yourself; but it strikes me, you apply the same rule in dissimilar cases. It is quite easy to talk of flogging n-----s here on land, where you have the sympathy of the community, and the whole physical force of the government, State and national, at your command, and where, if a Negro shall lift his hand against a white man, the whole community, with one accord, are ready to unite in shooting him down. I say, in such circumstances, it's easy to talk of flogging Negroes and of Negro cowardice; but, sir, I deny that the Negro is, naturally, a coward, or that your theory of managing slaves will stand the test of salt water. It may do very well for an overseer, a contemptible hireling, to take advantage of fears already in existence, and which his presence has no power to inspire; to swagger about whip in hand, and discourse on the timidity and cowardice of Negroes; for they have a smooth sea and fair wind. It is one thing to manage a company of slaves on a Virginia plantation, and quite another thing to quell an insurrection on the lonely billows of the Atlantic, where every breeze speaks of courage and liberty. For the Negro to act cowardly on shore, may be to act wisely; and I've some doubts whether you, Mr. Williams, would find it very convenient were you a slave in Algiers, to raise your hand against the bayonets of a whole government."

"By George, shipmates," said Williams, "you're coming rather too near. Either I've fallen very low in your estimation, or your notions of Negro courage have got up a button-hole too high. Now I more than ever wish I'd been on board of that luckless craft. I'd have given ye practical evidence of the truth of my theory. I don't doubt there's some difference in being at sea. But a n---r's a n----r, on sea or land, and is a coward, find him where you will; a drop of blood from one on 'em will skeer a hundred. A knock on the nose, or a kick on the shin, will tame the wildest 'darkey' you can fetch me. I say again, and will stand by it, I could, with half a dozen men, put the whole nineteen on 'em in irons, and have carried them safe to New Orleans too. Mind, I don't blame you, but I do say, and every gentleman here will bear me out in it, that the fault was somewhere, or them n-----s would never have got off as they have done. For my part I feel ashamed to have the idea go abroad, that a ship load of slaves can't be safely taken from Richmond to New Orleans. I should like, merely to redeem the character of Virginia sailors, to take charge of a ship load on 'em to-morrow."

Williams went on in this strain, occasionally casting an imploring glance at the company for applause for his wit, and sympathy for his contempt of Negro courage. He had, evidently, however, waked up the wrong passenger; for besides being in the right, his opponent carried that in his eye which marked him a man not to be trifled with.

"Well, sir," said the sturdy mate, "You can select your own method for distinguishing yourself;—the path of ambition in this direction is quite open to you in Virginia, and I've no doubt that you will be highly appreciated and compensated for all your valiant achievements in that line; but for myself, while I do not profess to be a giant, I have resolved never to set my foot on the deck of a slave ship, either as officer, or common sailor again; I have got enough of it."

"Indeed! indeed!" exclaimed Williams, derisively.

"Yes, indeed," echoed the mate, "but don't misunderstand me. It is not the high value that I set upon my life that makes me say what I have said; yet I'm resolved never to endanger my life again in a cause which my conscience does not approve. I dare say here what many men feel, but dare not speak, that this whole slave-trading business is a disgrace and scandal to Old Virginia."

"Hold! hold on! shipmate," said Williams, "I hardly thought you'd have shown your colors so soon,—I'll be hanged if you're not as good an abolitionist as Garrison himself."

The mate now rose from his chair, manifesting some excitement. "What do you mean, sir," said he, in a commanding tone. "That man does not live who shall offer me an insult with impunity."

The effect of these words was marked; and the company clustered around. Williams, in an apologetic tone, said, "Shipmate! keep you temper. I meant no insult. We all know that Tom Grant is no coward, and what I said about you being an abolitionist was simply this: you might have put down them black mutineers and murderers, but your conscience held you back."

"In that, too," said Grant, "you were mistaken. I did all that any man with equal strength and presence of mind could have done. The fact is, Mr. Williams, you underrate the courage as well as the skill of these Negroes, and further, you do not seem to have been correctly informed about the case in hand at all."

"All I know about it is," said Williams, "that on the ninth day after you left Richmond, a dozen or two of the n-----s ye had on board, came on deck and took the ship from you;—had her steered into a British port, where, by the by, every woolly head of them went ashore and was free. Now I take this to be a discreditable piece of business, and one demanding explanation."

"There are a great many discreditable things in the world," said Grant. "For a ship to go down under a calm sky is, upon the first flush of it, disgraceful either to sailors or caulkers. But when we learn, that by some mysterious disturbance in nature, the waters parted beneath, and swallowed the ship up, we lose our indignation and disgust in lamentation of the disaster, and in awe of the Power which controls the elements."

"Very true, very true," said Williams, "I should be very glad to have an explanation which would relieve the affair of its present discreditable features. I have desired to see you ever since you got home, and to learn from you a full statement of the facts in the case. To me the whole thing seems unaccountable. I cannot see how a dozen or two of ignorant Negroes, not one of whom had ever been to sea before, and all of them were closely ironed between decks, should be able to get their fetters off, rush out of the hatchway in open daylight, kill two white men, the one the captain and the other their master, and then carry the ship into a British port, where every 'darkey' of them was set free. There must have been great carelessness, or cowardice somewhere!"

The company which had listened in silence during most of this discussion, now became much excited. One said, I agree with Williams; and several said the thing looks black enough. After the temporary tumultuous exclamations had subsided,—

"I see," said Grant, "how you regard this case, and how difficult it will be for me to render our ship's company blameless in your eyes. Nevertheless, I will state the facts precisely as they came under my own observation. Mr. Williams speaks of 'ignorant Negroes,' and, as a general rule, they are ignorant; but had he been on board the *Creole* as I was, he would have seen cause to admit that there are exceptions to this general rule. The leader of the mutiny in question was just as shrewd a fellow as ever I met in my life, and was as well fitted to lead in a dangerous enterprise as any one white man in ten thousand. The name of this man, strange to say, (ominous of greatness,) was MADISON WASHINGTON. In the short time he had been on board, he had secured the confidence of every officer. The Negroes fairly worshipped him. His manner and bearing were such, that no one could suspect him of a murderous purpose. The only feeling with which we regarded him was, that he was a powerful, good-disposed Negro. He seldom spoke to anyone, and when he did speak, it was with the utmost propriety. His words were well chosen, and his pronunciation equal to that of any schoolmaster. It was a mystery to us where he got his knowledge of language; but as little was said to him, none of us knew the extent of his intelligence and ability till it was too late. It seems he brought three files with him on board, and must have gone to work upon his fetters the first night out; and he must have worked well at that; for on the day of the rising, he got the irons off eighteen besides himself.

"The attack began just about twilight in the evening. Apprehending a squall, I had commanded the second mate to order all hands on deck. to take in sail. A few minutes before this I had seen Madison's head above the hatchway, looking out upon the white-capped waves at the leeward. I think I never saw him look more good-natured. I stood just about midship, on the larboard side. The captain was pacing the quarterdeck on the starboard side, in company with Mr. Jameson, the owner of most of the slaves on board. Both were armed. I had just told the men to lay aloft, and was looking to see my orders obeyed, when I heard the discharge of a pistol on the starboard side; and turning suddenly around, the very deck seemed covered with fiends from the pit. The nineteen Negroes were all on deck,[2] with their broken fetters in their hands, rushing in all directions. I put my hand quickly in my pocket to draw out my jack-knife; but before I could draw it, I was knocked senseless to the deck. When I came to myself, (which I did in a few minutes, I suppose, for it was yet quite light), there was not a white man on deck. The sailors were all aloft in the rigging, and dared not come down. Captain Clarke and Mr. Jameson lay stretched on the quarter-deck,—both dying,[3]—while Madison himself stood at the helm unhurt.

"I was completely weakened by the loss of blood, and had not recovered from the stunning blow which felled me to the deck; but it was a little too much for me, even in my prostrate condition, to see our good brig commanded by a black murderer. So I called out to the men to come down and take the ship, or die in the attempt. Suiting the action to the word, I started aft. 'You murderous villain,' said I, to the imp at the helm, and rushed upon him to deal him a blow, when he pushed me back with his strong, black arm, as though I had been a boy of twelve. I looked around for the men. They were still in the rigging. Not one had come down. I started towards Madison again. The rascal now told me to stand back. 'Sir,' said he, 'your life is in my hands. I could have killed you a dozen times over during this last half hour, and could kill you now. You call me a black murderer. I am not a murderer. God is my witness that LIBERTY, not malice, is the motive for this night's work. I have done no more to those dead men yonder, than they would have done to me in like circumstances. We have struck for our freedom, and if a true man's heart be in you, you will honor us for the deed. We have done that which you applaud your fathers for doing, and if we are murderers, so were they.'

"I felt little disposition to reply to this impudent speech. By heaven, it disarmed me. The fellow loomed up before me. I forgot his blackness in the dignity of his manner, and the eloquence of his speech. It seemed as if the souls of both the great dead (whose names he bore) had entered him. To the sailors in the rigging he said: 'Men! the battle is over,—your captain is dead. I have complete command of this vessel. All resistance to my authority will be in vain. My men have won their liberty, with no other weapons but their own *Broken Fetters*. We are nineteen in number. We do not thirst for your blood, we demand only our rightful freedom. Do not flatter yourselves that I am ignorant of chart or compass. I know both. We are now only about sixty miles from Nassau. Come down, and do your duty. Land us in Nassau, and not a hair of your heads shall be hurt.'

"I shouted, 'Stay where you are, men,—when a sturdy black fellow ran at me with a handspike, and would have split my head open, but for the interference of Madison, who darted between me and the blow. 'I know what you are up to,' said the latter to me. 'You want to navigate this brig into a slave port, where you would have us all hanged; but you'll miss it; before this brig shall touch a slave-cursed shore while I am on board, I will myself put a match to the magazine, and blow her, and be blown with her, into a thousand fragments. Now I have saved your life twice within these last twenty minutes,—for, when you lay helpless on deck, my men were about to kill you. I held them in check. And if you now (seeing I am your friend and not your enemy) persist in your resistance to my authority, I give you fair warning, you *Shall Die*.'

"Saying this to me, he cast a glance into the rigging where the terror-stricken sailors were slinging, like so many frightened monkeys, and commanded them to come down, in a tone from which there was no appeal; for four men stood by with muskets in hand, ready at the word of command to shoot them down.

"I now became satisfied that resistance was out of the question; that my best policy was to put the brig into Nassau, and secure the assistance of the American consul at the port. I felt sure that the authorities would enable us to secure the murderers, and bring them to trial.

"By this time the apprehended squall had burst upon us. The wind howled furiously,—the ocean was white with foam, which, on account of the darkness, we could see only by the quick flashes of lightning that darted occasionally from the angry sky. All was alarm and confusion. Hideous cries came up from the slave women. Above the roaring billows a succession of heavy thunder rolled along, swelling the terrific din. Owing to the great darkness, and a sudden shift of the wind, we found ourselves in the trough of the sea. When shipping a heavy sea over the starboard bow, the bodies of the captain and Mr. Jameson were washed overboard. For awhile we had dearer interests to look after than slave property. A more savage thunder-gust never swept the ocean. Our brig rolled and creaked as if every bolt would be started, and every thread of oakum would be pressed out of the seams. 'To the pumps! to the pumps!' I cried, but not a sailor would quit his grasp. Fortunately this squall soon passed over, or we must have been food for sharks.

"During all the storm, Madison stood firmly at the helm,—his keen eye fixed upon the binnacle. He was not indifferent to the dreadful hurricane; yet he met it with the equanimity of an old sailor. He was silent but not agitated. The first words he uttered after the storm had slightly subsided were characteristic of the man. 'Mr. mate, you cannot write the bloody laws of slavery on those restless billows. The ocean, if not the land, is free.' I confess, gentlemen, I felt myself in the presence of a superior man; one who, had he been a white man, I would have followed willingly and gladly in any honorable enterprise. Our difference of color was the only ground for difference of action. It was not that his principles were wrong in the abstract; for they are the principles of 1776. But I could not bring myself to recognize their application to one whom I deemed my inferior.

"But to my story. What happened now is soon told. Two hours after the frightful tempest had spent itself, we were plump at the wharf in Nassau. I sent two of our men immediately to our consul with a statement of facts, requesting his interference in our behalf. What he did, or whether he did anything, I don't know; but, by order of the authorities, a company of *black* soldiers came on board, for the purpose, as they said, of protecting the property. These impudent rascals, when I called on them to assist me in keeping the slaves on board, sheltered themselves adroitly under the instructions only to protect property,—and said they did not recognize persons as *property*. I told them that by the law of Virginia and the laws of the United States, the slaves on board were as much property as the barrels of flour in the hold. At this the stupid blockheads showed their *ivory*, rolled up their white eyes in horror, as if the idea of putting men on footing with merchandise was revolting to their humanity. When these instructions were understood among the Negroes, it was impossible for us to keep them on board. They deliberately gathered up their baggage before our eyes, and against our remonstrances, poured through the gangway,—formed themselves into a procession on the wharf,—bid farewell to all on board, and, uttering the wildest shouts of exultation, they marched, amidst the deafening cheers of a multitude of sympathizing spectators, under the triumphant leadership of their heroic chief and deliverer, *Madison Washington.*"[4]

Frederick Douglass

*Autographs for Freedom,* edited by Julia W. Griffiths, 1853, pp. 174-238[5]

# Reference Notes

## Introduction

1. New York, 1973, p. vii.
2. In 1964 the biographical sections were combined and published separately under the title, *Frederick Douglass*, by the Citadel Press.
3. The papers of Booker T. Washington are edited by Louis R. Harlan and those of W.E.B. Du Bois by Herbert Aptheker.
4. The entire Douglass library including twelve volumes (1848 to 1860) of *The North Star* and *Frederick Douglass' Paper* were destroyed. Douglass was fairly certain that the fire was "the work of an incendiary." Referring to his having been denied shelter at the Congress Hall in Rochester when he returned home upon being notified of the fire, he informed his readers: "I may be wrong, but I fear that the sentiment which repelled me at Congress Hall burnt my house." (Philip S. Foner, *Frederick Douglass*, New York, 1964, p. 302.)
5. Originally the papers were in the care of the Douglass family, but they passed into the care of the Frederick Douglass Memorial and Historical Association. Limited funds made "Cedar Hall" difficult for use by scholars.
6. Philip S. Foner, *The Life and Writings of Frederick Douglass*, New York, 1950, vol. I, p. 11.
7. *The Crisis*, November, 1915, p. 81.
8. *See*, for example, Howard Brotz, editor, *Negro Social and Political Thought 1850-1920. Representative Texts*, New York, 1966; Philip S. Foner, editor, *The Voice of Black Americans: Major Speeches of Negroes in the United States, 1797-1971*, New York, 1972; Herbert Aptheker, editor, *A Documentary History of the Negro People in the United States*, New York, 1951; Benjamin Quarles, "Abolition's Different Drummer: Frederick Douglass" in *The Anti-Slavery Vanguard: New Essays on the Abolitionists*, edited by Martin Duberman, Princeton, N.J., 1965, pp. 123-34; August Meier, "Frederick Douglass' Vision for America: A Case Study in Nineteenth Century Negro Protest," in *Freedom and Reform*, edited by Harold M. Hyman and Leonard W. Levy, New York, 1967, pp. 127-48; William H. Pease and Jane H. Pease, "Boston Garrisonians and the Problem of Frederick Douglass," *Canadian Journal of History*, vol. II, September, 1967, pp. 29-48; George Shepperson, "Frederick Douglass and Scotland," *Journal of Negro History*, vol. XXXVIII, July, 1953, pp. 307-21; Robert Factor, *The Black Response to America*, Reading, Mass, 1969, pp. 3-106.
9. Carleton Mabee, *Black Freedom: The Nonviolent Abolitionists from 1830 through the Civil War*, New York, 1970, p. 294.
10. Benjamin Quarles, *Black Abolitionists*, New York, 1969, p. 64.
11. Mabee, *op. cit.*, p. 203.

12. Eric Foner, *Free Soil, Free Labor, Free Men: The Ideology of the Republican Party before the Civil War*, New York, 1970, p. 275.

13. Victor Ullman, *Martin R. Delany, The Beginnings of Black Nationalism*, New York, 1971, p. 76.

14. However, it should be noted that in the latest *Encyclopaedia Britannica* Douglass' biography, a very brief sketch at that, appears in the "Ready Reference Section" only, and not also in the "Knowledge in Depth" section of the "Micropaedia."

15. Foner, *Life and Writings of Frederick Douglass*, vol. I, p. 12.

16. Benjamin Quarles, "Frederick Douglass: Black Imperishable," *Quarterly Journal of the Library of Congress*, vol. XXIX, July, 1972, p. 161.

# PART ONE

1. James Miller McKim (1810-1874), anti-slavery leader, publishing agent of the Pennsylvania Anti-Slavery Society in Philadelphia, who succeeded John Greenleaf Whittier as editor of the *Pennsylvania Freeman* in 1840.

2. Charles Lenox Remond (1810-1873), son of a prosperous businessman in Salem, Massachusetts, he served for many years as an agent of the American Anti-Slavery Society. Remond was the first black Abolitionist speaker to address large audiences, and the best known before the emergence of Frederick Douglass. A delegate to the World Anti-Slavery Convention in London in 1840, he refused to take his seat because women delegates were excluded. Returning home after two years on the anti-slavery circuit in Great Britain and Ireland, he addressed Massachusetts legislators, convincing them to end segregation on the railroads of the state.

3. This is both a reference to the type of soil in this part of Pennsylvania and to the fact that Henry Clay was the Whig candidate for president in the election of 1844.

4. Ten years later Oxford, Pennsylvania, became the seat of the first black college in American history—Ashmun Institute, the forerunner of Lincoln University.

5. In 1845 Douglass left the United States for an antislavery tour of Ireland, Scotland, and England. His departure was hastened by the publication of his *Narrative of the Life of Frederick Douglass*, the first of his three autobiographies, which by divulging his identity and that of his master, made it no longer safe for him to remain as a fugitive slave in the United States. Another reason for the trip was to lay before the people of England "the claim of the Slave."

6. Slavery was abolished in the British West Indies on August 1, 1833. August 1, Emancipation Day, was annually celebrated in antislavery circles in the United States until the Civil War, especially by Black Abolitionists.

7. James N. Buffum (1807-1887), abolitionist from Lynn, Massachusetts, and vice-president of the Friends of Social Reform, a Fourier organization. In 1845-1846, he accompanied Douglass on his tour of Britain.

8. In a letter to William Lloyd Garrison from Dublin, September 16, 1845, Douglass wrote: "I have attended several temperance meetings, and given several temperance addresses." (Philip S. Foner, *The Life and Writings of Frederick Douglass*. Volume I, New York, 1950, p. 120. Hereinafter cited as *Life and Writings of Douglass*.)

9. In the same letter, Douglass also wrote: "I went out last Sunday to Bootertown,

and saw Father Mathew administer the pledge to about one thousand." (*Ibid.*)

10. The Corn Laws, passed in 1815, raised the price of bread and led to the anti-Corn Law agitation of the 1840's. The abolition of the Corn Laws in 1846 was a great triumph for radical England.

11. In reporting the meeting, the *Cork Examiner* noted that the "Independent Chapel was crowded by a most respectable audience. The platform was occupied by men of influence of our city." The Mayor, who chaired the meeting, read the "Address to Frederick Douglass from the Anti-Slavery Society of Cork," which stated that by Douglass' labors "here, we have been stirred up to renewed and active life for the deliverance of the captive."

12. Annexation of Texas was accomplished by joint resolution of Congress in 1845, after failure to achieve senatorial ratification of a treaty in 1844. Texas entered as the 28th state after nine years of independence as a republic.

13. Between 1820 and 1830, about 20,000 Americans with approximately 2,000 slaves had crossed into Texas, largely from the lower Mississippi frontier. In 1830 the Mexican government both called a halt to further American immigration and passed a measure abolishing slavery.

14. The night before the *Cambria*, the Cunard steamer on which he sailed from the United States, docked at Liverpool, Douglass, at the invitation of the captain, lectured on American slavery. He was constantly interrupted by catcalls from the Southerners, and as soon as he finished a sentence, several slaveholders would yell out, "That's a lie!" When he offered to present documentary proof, they rushed at him with clenched fists. The captain knocked down one man and quieted the others by threatening to put them in irons.

15. Richard Davis Webb (1905-1872), Dublin printer and reformer (advocate of abolition and temperance) and his wife Hannah (1809-1862), also an active abolitionist, were close friends of Douglass during his tour of Europe. Webb handled many of the details connected with Douglass' speaking engagements, and many of the latter's letters while on tour in Ireland, Scotland and England were to Webb. Most of them are in the Anti-Slavery Letters to William Lloyd Garrison in the Boston Public Library.

16. Webb was in charge of furnishing Douglass with copies of his *Narrative* which he sold during his speaking engagements. The proceeds from the sale of the *Narrative* went to support Douglass and his family while he was in Europe. "It is a great loss to me to be without my Narrative as I am dependent on it for all my support in this country," Douglass wrote to Webb from Perth on January 30, 1846. Writing to John B. Estlin from London, September 8, 1846, Garrison noted of Douglass: "As to his means of support, he is chiefly dependant upon the sale of his Narrative, but I believe he is at this time receiving a small stipend from the Edinburgh friends, though they do not defray his travelling expenses." (Walter M. Merrill, editor, *The Letters of William Lloyd Garrison*, vol. III, "No Union With Slaveholders, 1841-1849, Cambridge, Massachusetts, 1973, p. 400.) This work contains many letters from Garrison relating to Douglass during the period covered, but none to Douglass himself.

17. "I shall . . . briefly notice some of the most glaring falsehoods contained in the afforesaid Narrative," Thompson introduced his testimony, "and give a true rep-

resentation of the character of those gentlemen who have been censured in such an uncharitable manner, as murderers, hypocrites, and everything else that is vile." Thompson characterized Douglass' *Narrative* as "a budget of falsehood, from beginning to end."

18. From the very outset of his career as an anti-slavery speaker, Douglass made such an enormous impression for his qualities as an orator that immediately reports began to appear in the press that he could not possibly be a fugitive slave. "Many persons in the audience," wrote a Philadelphia correspondent in the *Liberator* of August 30, 1844, "seemed unable to credit the statements which he gave of himself, and could not believe that he was actually a slave. How a man, only six years out of bondage, and who had never gone to school a day in his life, could speak with such eloquence—with such precision of language and power of thought—they were utterly at a loss to devise." To dispel such doubts, Douglass wrote his *Narrative*.

19. Edward Covey was a "breaker" of slaves, and at Covey's farm, Douglass was "made to drink the bitterest dregs of slavery." In his *Narrative*, Douglass described that not only was he pushed beyond the limits of human endurance by the physical requirements imposed upon him by Covey, but he was virtually destroyed also in soul and spirit: "My natural elasticity was crushed, my intellect languished, the disposition to read departed . . . the dark night of slavery closed in upon me; and behold a man transformed into a brute."

20. "My former name"—footnote in original.

21. The "black Douglass" was a character in Sir Walter Scott's *Lady of the Lake*, and it was suggested as the name Frederick Bailey should assume in freedom by Nathan Johnson, a free Negro of New Bedford, Massachusetts.

22. Douglass may have been referring to the assertion by Polk in his inaugural address in March, 1845, that "the right of the United States to that portion of our territory which lies beyond the Rocky Mountains . . . to the country of the Oregon, is 'clear and unqestionable'. . . ."

23. The Free Church of Scotland (an organization based on the right of congregations to control the appointment of their own ministers) had sent a deputation to the United States in 1844 to solicit support for its cause. When the deputation went into the slave-holding South and collected about $3,000 from slaveholders, an immediate furor arose on both sides of the Atlantic. Douglass made the demand that the Free Church send back the money a key feature of his speeches in Scotland. By the time he lectured in Arbroath, his fiery oratory against the Free Church had begun to have such an effect that the words, "The Slave's Blood," adorned the walls of the Free Church in the city, and the slogan "Send Back the Money!" appeared in both poster form and letters of blood red paint on the walls where Douglass spoke. (Edward Dixon, "The American Negro in Nineteenth Century Scotland," unpublished dissertation for the Degree of M. Litt. in North American Studies, Edinburgh University, May, 1969, p. 64.)

24. On January 30, 1864, Douglass wrote to Webb that he had given "directions to the engraver to make the prints of the portrait shorter." He was referring to the portrait of himself in the frontispiece to the *Narrative*.

25. The Arbroath press emphasized that "the Abbey Church was densely crowded, and the utmost excitement prevailed."

26. Thomas Chalmers was the illustrious leader of the Free Church, and Douglass was regarded as his chief opponent. (*See* George Shepperson, "The Free Church and American Slavery," *Scottish Historical Review*, vol. XXX, 1951, pp. 130-33.)

27. Douglass was challenging the view that the conditions of the white workers in the industries of England were either the same or even worse than those of the black slaves in the United States. On his return to the United States, he declared: "Say what you will of England— of the degradation—of the poverty—and there is much of it there—say what you will of the oppression and suffering going on in England at this time, there is Liberty there, not only for the white man, but for the black man also."(*Life and Writings of Douglass*, vol. I, p. 235.)

28. Douglass may also have been referring to the fact that English courts asserted that the air of England was too pure for slaves to breathe. Lord Holt, the Chief Justice, declared early in the 18th century in the case of *Smith v. Brown and Cooper* that "as soon as a Negro comes into England he becomes free; one may be a villein in England but not a slave."

29. Douglass also addressed meetings in Paisley on the Free Church of Scotland. Copies of his speeches at these meetings are in the Anti-Slavery Cuttings, Central Library, Paisley, Scotland.

30. Granville Sharpe was one of the trio of great British Abolitionists, which also included Thomas Clarkson and William Wilberforce.

31. Thomas Clarkson (1760-1846), pioneer British Abolitionist, was active for over sixty years with Sharpe and Wilberforce in the battle against slavery and the slave trade.

    William Wilberforce (1759-1833), aroused to the anti-slavery cause by Thomas Clarkson, began to work in Parliament in 1787 to end the slave trade. The slave trade was abolished in 1807.

32. Although George Thompson, the British Abolitionist, contributed considerably to arousing sentiment in Scotland against slavery in the British West Indies, Edward Dixon maintains that James McCune Smith, the black American who was in Scotland studying medicine, also played an important role in this connection, "since his mere presence in the ranks of the [Glasgow Emancipation] Society was considered to be enough to bring the cause of freedom home to the Scottish people." (*op. cit.,* p. 30)

33. For a detailed answer by Douglass to this charge, *see* his speech "The Right to Criticize American Institutions," *Life and Writings of Douglass*, vol. I, pp. 234-43.

34. Hugh Auld, Douglass' former master, did not have the opportunity to catch his slave and return him to slavery. Late in 1846, Douglass' England friends, led by Ellen and Anna Richardson of Newcastle, raised $700.96 and purchased Douglass' emancipation from Auld. (For the text of the manumission document, see *ibid.*, pp. 432-33.)

35. In the summer of 1846 at a speech at the World Temperance Convention in London, Douglass used the incident in Philadelphia to denounce the official

American temperance movement for failing to speak up boldly for the rights of slaves and free Blacks. (*See ibid.*, pp. 67-69, 189-99.)

36. Douglass is referring to the fact that Maria Weston Chapman, leader of the Boston Female Anti-Slavery Society and editor of its gift-book, the *Liberty Bell*, had written to Webb warning the Irish Abolitionist to keep an eye on Douglass and Buffum lest they be won over by the anti-Garrisonian wing of the English anti-slavery movement. Mrs. Chapman, it seemed, was not too concerned about Buffum who was wealthy, but was worried lest Douglass "might be bought up by the London committee." Douglass was shown the letter.

37. William Smeal (1793-1877), Quaker admirer of William Lloyd Garrison, was the co-secretary of the Glasgow Emancipation Society, founded in 1833.

38. In his biography, *Frederick Douglass* (New York, 1899, p. 110), Booker T. Washington quotes an extract from this speech as proving "to what an extent he [Douglass] at this time shared the illusions of the Abolitionists, who, while preaching the doctrine of nonresistance, were steadily feeding the passions that made war eventually inevitable." Clearly Washington is blaming the Civil War upon the Abolitionists and not on the system of slavery which they denounced.

39. Robert Dale Owen (1801-1877), son of Robert Owen, the British Utopian Socialist, was a member of the U.S. House of Representatives from Indiana (1843-47).

40. The "true antislavery society" was, of course, the American Anti-Slavery Society under the leadership of William Lloyd Garrison, as distinguished from the American and Foreign Anti-Slavery Society founded in 1841 by a small group, led by Lewis Tappan, after they had separated from Garrison and his group. Tappan maintained correspondence with British Abolitionist sympathizers.

41. Anna Murray Douglass, a free Negro whom Douglass came to know while a slave in Baltimore, and who afterward became his wife.

42. For the storm aroused by this incident, which produced an apology from S. Cunard and a promise that "nothing of the kind will *again take place in the steamships with which I am connected,*" see *Life and Writings of Douglass,* vol. I, pp. 73-74.

43. An account of the meeting of the black people of New York City "to extend a welcome to Frederick Douglass on his return from his late tour in Great Britain," was published in the *National Anti-Slavery Standard* of May 27, 1847. The meeting was chaired by Reverend Samuel Ringgold Ward, and all of the speakers except one were blacks. The one white speaker was William Lloyd Garrison, who entered the meeting during Douglass' speech, "and was greeeted by the crowded assembly by vehement and protracted applause. When it had subsided, Mr. Garrison addressed them in a few words. . . ."

44. For Douglass' writings denouncing the Mexican War, *see Life and Writings of Douglass*, vol. I, pp. 291-300.

45. Sidney Howard Gay was one of the editors of the *National Anti-Slavery Standard.* There is a small collection of his papers in the manuscript division of the New York Public Library, but it contains no letters from Douglass.

46. *The Ram's Horn* was a Negro newspaper published in New York City, which lasted from January 1, 1847 to June, 1848. Thomas Van Rensselaer and Willis Hodge

were its editors, and Douglass assisted in editing the paper for a time. For Douglass' letter to Van Rensselaer, *see Life and Writings of Douglass*, vol. I, pp. 243-46.

47. On August 12, 1847 the *National Anti-Slavery Standard* carried the following under the heading "Frederick Douglass": "We take great pleasure in announcing to our readers that Mr. Douglass is engaged as a regular contributor to the columns of the Standard. His first communication we shall give next week, in the form of a written address, delivered by him at the First of August meeting at Canandaigua; and thereafter we shall receive a letter from him for the paper as often as his other duties will permit. . . . We are sure that this announcement will be received with universal satisfaction. The great esteem in which Mr. Douglass is held as a man, and the great and peculiar interest which is everywhere felt for him, would alone cause these letters to be sought for with avidity. But in addition to all this, he is a writer of no common power, and on that account alone, if no other, would give increased value to any paper."

48. The Negroes of Philadelphia had paraded to celebrate the progress of the temperance cause and the emancipation of the slaves in the British West Indies. The cause of the anti-Negro riot, which lasted several days, was said to be a banner in the parade which carried the motto "Liberty or Death" over the figure of a Negro and showed Santo Domingo in flames, with white people massacred by the slaves. A reporter for the *Philadelphia Public Ledger* investigated this charge and found it to be completely false. "The banner," he wrote, "contains nothing more than the figure of an *emancipated slave*, pointing with one hand to the broken chains at his feet, and with the other to the word 'Liberty' in gold letters over his head. The burning town turns out to be a representation of the *rising sun*, and a *sinking ship*, emblematic of the dawn of freedom and the wreck of tyranny." (*Public Ledger*, August 4, 1842.)

49. Actually, Portugal had been the country mainly engaged in the African slave trade. Italy had little to do with that trade, and Spain, by a Papal decree in 1493, was fairly well eliminated from Africa.

50. *Clarkson's History of the Slave Trade*, p. 54.—footnote in original. Douglass, however, does not mention that Queen Elizabeth, learning of the profit Hawkins had gained from his slave trade expedition, invested in his second voyage to Africa.

51. Douglass is quoting from Hannah More's celebrated poem *The Slave Trade* which urged England to abolish the slave trade:
     Restores the lustre of the Christian name,
     And clears the foulest blot thad dimm'd its fame.

52. Richard Baxter (1615-1691), English clergyman who preached against slavery and the slave trade.

53. Joseph Addison (1672-1719), English essayist who wrote against slavery and the slave trade.

54. Charles Louis de Secondat, Baron de Montesquieu (1689-1755), social analyst and philosopher of the French Enlightenment. His attack on slavery was in his masterpiece, *L'Espirit des Lois (Spirit of the Laws)*, published in 1748.

55. William Godwin (1756-1836), British social philosopher, whose works influenced reformers in a number of countries. His attack on slavery and the slave trade

was especially strong in *Enquiry Concerning Political Justice and Its Influence on Morals and Happiness*, published in 1793.

56. Sir Richard Steele (1672-1729), English essayist who wrote against slavery and the slave trade.

57. William Shenstone (1714-1763), English poet who dedicated several of his poems to the antislavery momement.

58. Lawrence Sterne (1713-1768), English clergyman and author who wrote against slavery and the slave trade.

59. William Warburton (1698-1779), English prelate and writer who voiced opposition to slavery.

60. John Wesley (1703-1791), founder of Methodist societies who spoke out against slavery and the slave trade.

61. George Whitfield (1714-1770), English evangelist and antislavery spokesman.

62. David Hartley (1705-1757), English philosopher and antislavery spokesman.

63. Gillaume Thomas François Raynal (1713-1796), French historian and philosopher and noted spokesman against slavery, writing some of the most devastating attacks on the institution.

64. Thomas Day (1748-1789), English author, whose *The Dying Negro* (1773) was effective in rousing antislavery opinion.

65. Jacques Necker (1732-1804), French financier and statesman.

66. Adam Smith (1723-1790), famous Scottish economist, author of *The Wealth of Nations*, who attacked slavery as both immoral and uneconomical.

67. George Fox (1624-1691), founder of the Religious Society of Friends, commonly called Quakers.

68. Although the men mentioned by Douglass were all important, he omits Thomas F. Buxton, Zachary Macaulay, Henry Brougham, Joseph Sturge and a number of others who rallied together to form the Anti-Slavery Society in England and developed the campaign to end slavery.

69. Illegible in original.

70. Illegible in original.

71. The Sommerset case occurred in 1772. James Sommerset was a Negro slave who was confined in irons on board a ship bound for Jamaica. Abolitionists obtained a writ of habeas corpus under which he was to be held in England while the case was disposed of. In his decision which abolished slavery in England, Lord Mansfield declared: "The state of slavery is of such a nature, that it is incapable of being introduced on any reasons, moral or political, but only by positive law, which preserves its force long after the reasons, occasion, and time itself from whence it was created, is erased from memory. It is so odious, that nothing can be suffered to support it, but positive law. Whatever inconveniences, therefore, may follow from the decision, I cannot say this case is allowed or approved by the law of England; and therefore the black must be discharged." Sommerset was thus freed and slavery declared illegal.

72. On February 23, 1807, the House of Commons passed the Act for the Abolition of the Slave Trade, already carried in the Lords. The African slave trade was ended about the same time in the United States by act of Congress.

73. The reference is to Hannah More (1745-1833), English woman of letters and foe of

the slave trade and slavery. She was a leading force in the "African Institution" founded in 1805 to abolish the slave trade.

74. Ten years later, Douglass delivered another West India Emancipation speech in Canandaigua, New York. But here, having broken with Garrisonian nonviolence ideology, he placed more emphasis on the role of the slaves themselves in ending slavery in the British West Indies. Thus he said: "What Wilberforce was endeavoring to win from the British Senate by his magic eloquence, the Slaves themselves were endeavoring to gain by outbreaks and violence. The combined action of one and the other wrought out the final result. While one showed that slavery was wrong, the other showed that it was dangerous as well as wrong. . . . There is no doubt that the fear of the consequences, acting with a sense of the moral evil of slavery, led to its abolition." For the text of this West India Emancipation speech, see *Life and Writings of Douglass*, vol. II, pp. 426-39.

75. Illegible in original.

76. Isaac T. Hopper (1771-1852), Pennsylvania Abolitionist, who led many runaway slaves to freedom on the Underground Railroad, and was frequently the target of proslavery mobs.

## PART TWO

1. The letter to Gay is written by Douglass underneath the Prospectus for *The North Star*.

2. However, the *Voice of Industry*, the labor paper published in Lowell, greeted *The North Star*. "It gleams and flashes all over with the light of genius," it editorialized on December 31, 1847. "It is such a paper as Frederick Douglass would be expected to edit. Unlike many of his friends, we are glad to see him where he is. We think he will be far more useful in his present relation to the anti-slavery cause, than in any other, devoted and eloquent as he has been as a lecturer. Mr. Douglass is in every sense a gentleman, and his large acquaintance with me, individually and socially, as a slave and as a hunted fugitive, in America, and in England, fit him, as no other among us is fitted, to conduct an anti-slavery journal. We cordially welcome him to the labors, so recently entered upon ourselves, and earnestly wish him the happiest success."

   On May 5, 1848, *The North Star* endorsed the ten hour bill sponsored by the *Voice of Industry* and others in the New England labor movement for the establishment of the ten-hour day.

3. Martin R. Delany (1812-1885), born free in Virginia, the grandson of an African chief, was active in the antislavery movement and editor of *The Mystery*, which he published in Pittsburgh from 1843 to 1847. Delany became an agent for *The North Star* in Pittsburgh and then was named co-editor with Douglass.

4. William Cooper Nell (1817-1874), born in Boston, had worked on *The Liberator* and was listed as publisher of *The North Star*.

5. *The North Star* of January 21, 1848, contained Delany's announcement that he had given up his connection with *The Mystery* with the completion of Volume IV. "We leave *The Mystery*," he wrote, "for a union with the far-famed and world-renowned FREDERICK DOUGLASS, as a co-laborer, in the cause of our oppressed bret-

hren, by the publication of a large and capacious paper, the *NORTH STAR* in Rochester, N.Y., in which our whole time, energy and services will be given, which cannot fail to be productive of signal benefit to the slave and our nominally free brethren when the head and heart of Douglass enters into the combination. We feel loath to leave our *Mystery* but duty calls and we must obey."

6. *See Life and Writings of Douglass*, vol. I, p. 291.

7. In February, 1842, Charles Lenox Remond testified before a legislative committee of the Massachusetts House of Representatives that was then holding hearings on the issue of abolishing segregation on the railroads of the state. His address helped win the battle against discrimination. Segregation was finally abolished in April, 1843. For Remond's speech, *see* Philip S. Foner, editor, *The Voice of Black America: Major Speeches of Negroes in the United States, 1797-1971*, New York, 1972, pp. 72-81.

8. The *People's Journal* of London had announced on July 24, 1847, that the fund raised in Great Britain as a testimonial for Frederick Douglass to be devoted to the purchase of a printing-press, amounting to $2,000, was to be used for other purposes, since Douglass, on the advice of his friends, had abandoned the idea of publishing his own paper. Douglass wrote this letter to clarify the issue.

9. Wendell Phillips (1811-1884), Boston-bred and Harvard-educated, was one of the greatest of the Abolitionist leaders associated with William Lloyd Garrison. Phillips accompanied Douglass on a number of his antislavery speaking tours and always fought discrimination against his black companion.

10. On April 15, 1848, the schooner *Pearl*, with 77 fugitive slaves aboard, was captured at the mouth of the Potomac River and was brought to Washington, D.C. The slaves and their white rescuers, Daniel Drayton, Capton Sayres, and Chester English, were imprisoned. The Negroes were turned over to slave-dealers to be sold in the lower South, and the white men were brought to trial. During the excitement of this event, a mob attempted to destroy the office of the *National Era* in Washington, and to force Dr. Bailey, its editor, to leave the district. Drayton and Sayres were found guilty of transporting slaves and were sentenced to life imprisonment.

11. On April 20, 1848, John P. Hale (1806-1873), Abolitionist Senator from New Hampshire, introduced a bill in the Senate, prompted by the mob attack on the *National Era*, which made the city liable for injuries inflicted by mobs on property in the District of Columbia. Douglass complained that the bill made no reference to injuries to blacks.

12. On February 24, 1848, the working class of Paris which had driven King Louis Philippe from the Tuileries, routed the Royalist deputies from the Chamber of the Palais Bourbon, and a Provisional Republican government was proclaimed by Alphonse Lamartine. The National Assembly instituted a number or reforms including the abolition of slavery in the French colonies.

13. Douglass was a bitter foe of the American Colonization Society formed in 1816, with impressive sponsorship which included Henry Clay and other persons of distinction, North and South, to remove free Negroes from the United States and colonize them in Africa. The Society established Liberia. For other examples of

Douglass' opposition to colonization, *see Life and Writings of Douglass*, vol. I, pp. 350-52, 387-99, 416-18.

14. The Wilmot Proviso was introduced into the House of Representatives in 1846 by Representative David Wilmot of Pennsylvania as an amendment to an appropriation bill. It provided that neither slavery nor involuntary servitude should ever exist in any part of the territory that might be acquired from Mexico as a result of the war then in progress. The House passed the resolution several times, but it was always defeated in the Senate.

15. Theodore Parker (1810-1860), Boston liberal and scholar who became a foremost opponent of slavery and advocated complete resistance to the Fugitive Slave Law.

16. The original seems to be printed incorrectly, for it reads: "He is now teaching the world, by French example, the folly of injustice, oppression and wrong, and of relying upon the sword for that which can only be accomplished by the foolishness of preaching."

17. Soon after the Provisional Government was formed, owing to the insistence of the unemployed, the government founded the National Workshops under the direction of Louis Blanc.

18. Samuel Ringgold Ward (1817-c. 1864) was brought to New York at the age of three by his parents, who escaped from slavery in Maryland. Ward received an education, taught school, became a preacher, and a leading antislavery agent.

19. In his "Address To the Four Thousand Voters of the State of New York," Ward began: "Fellow Citizens: You need no other apology for my addressing you, than the bare mention of the fact, that I am one of your oppressed, insulted, rejected, despised and downtrodden number. I beg to call your attention to what are my own humble views of the duties incumbent on us, as exhibited in the present aspect of political affairs."

20. At the Buffalo Convention of the Free Soil Party, Martin Van Buren was nominated for President of the United States. In the summer of 1848, Van Buren had declared that he opposed abolition of slavery in the District of Columbia, a cardinal point in the Abolitionist program.

21. John Adams Dix (1798-1879), Secretary of State of New York (1833-39) and United States Senator (1845-49).

22. Pre-emption was the practice of settling on the public lands in the pre-Civil War period before such land was purchased or surveyed, with the privilege of purchasing it afterward. The Pre-emption Act of 1841 was one of a series of such Acts between 1800 and 1841 providing legal title to the settled land. The Act of 1841, however, specifically provided for the grant of 160 acres of public lands to any squatter over 21 years of age who was a free white citizen, upon considerations of residence and improvements.

23. The "Barnburners," the name applied to the New York faction of the Democratic party in the late 1840's and early 1850's, were followers of Martin Van Buren who supported the Free Soil party when Van Buren was the candidate in the election of 1848, having been rejected by the Democrats. The name derived from the declaration of their enemies that they were acting like the Dutch farmer who burned his barn to rid it of rats.

24. In the early years of the American Colonization Society, Abolitionists like Wil-

liam Lloyd Garrison and Gerrit Smith supported colonization in the belief that if free Negroes were colonized, slaveowners might be inclined to manumit their slaves. Both Garrison and Smith became foes of colonization later.

25. "Doughface" was a term first used by John Randolph during the debate over Missouri in 1820, and then used later to designate Northerners with Southern principles.

26. It is interesting that while Douglass indicates he still clings to the Garrisonian non-voting doctrine, based on the proslavery interpretation of the Constitution, he leaves the door open to change his mind if "stronger reasons" should persuade him that he was incorrect.

27. The reference here is to the treaty signed by the United States and Great Britain on June 15, 1846, under which the territory north of the Columbia remained American while Britain retained Vancouver Island and navigation rights on the Columbia River. Just why this was a "free soil victory" is not clear.

28. Douglass never knew his father, but in his *Narrative*, he stated positively: "My father was a white man. He was admitted to be such by all I ever heard speak of my parentage." (Boston, 1845, p. 2.)

29. Between sixty and seventy delegates met in Cleveland and chose Douglass as president of the National Negro Convention. The delegates endorsed *The North Star* as answering the needs of the Negro people for a press and urged its support by all blacks. They also endorsed the Free Soil Party, but declared that they were "determined to maintain the higher stand and more liberal views which heretofore characterized us as *abolitionists.*" Committees were appointed in different states to organize vigilante groups, "so as to enable them to measure arms with assailants without and invaders within." (*The North Star*, Sept. 19, 1848; *The Liberator*, Oct. 20, 1848.) For a discussion of Douglass' role in the Negro Convention movement, *see* Philip S. Foner, *The Life and Writings of Frederick Douglass*, New York, 1950, vol. II, pp. 19-37.)

30. In an editorial entitled "Ohio Black Laws" (*The North Star*, March 10, 1848), Douglass wrote: "In no State of this Union are there to be found laws more cruel, unjust and atrocious, than those on the Statute Book of Ohio. An assembly of devils could not have enacted laws more infernal, and better fitted to promote crime, than that what are called the 'black laws' of that State." Among other provisions, the laws required Negroes entering the state to place a bond of five hundred dollars for good behavior with a state official. Ohio also excluded Negroes from public schools by law.

31. Delany's report from Philadelphia appeared in *The North Star* of October 6, 1848. In it Delaney was critical of the fact that not enough black young men of Philadelphia were going into business and trade.

32. Robert Purvis (1810-1898) was the son of a white South Carolina merchant and a Moorish-Jewish woman whose mother had been a slave. Independently wealthy and so light-skinned that he could have passed for white, he was educated in private schools in Philadelphia, and finished his education at Amherst College. But he left college to devote himself to the antislavery movement and at the age of seventeen made his first public speech against slavery. A founder of the American

Anti-Slavery Society, Purvis was a supporter of William Lloyd Garrison throughout the pre-Civil War era.

33. Henry Highland Garnet (1815-1881) was born a slave in Maryland, the son of an African chief who had been kidnapped and sold into slavery. He escaped with his parents in 1824 and settled in New York City. He was educated at New York's African Free School, Canaan Academy in New Hampshire (until local farmers destroyed the school), and Oneida Institute. Licensed to preach, he became one of the foremost ministers in New York City. At the National Negro Convention of 1843, he called for slave rebellions as the surest way to end slavery. In the 1850's Garnet was a leader in the African emigration movement.

34. William Whipper (1805-1885), the only delegate in attendance at all six of the early National Conventions, was the leading spokesman of the American Moral Reform Society and editor of its journal, the *National Reformer,* the first black monthly magazine, and an extremely successful business man. In Columbia, Pennsylvania, where he was engaged in the lumber business, Whipper was a conductor on the Underground Railroad.

35. Lucretia Mott (1793-1880), pioneer woman's rights advocate and reformer, Mrs. Mott was influential in movements advocating abolitionism, woman's rights, temperance, and liberal religion.

36. *Young America,* formerly the *Working Man's Advocate,* was the organ of the land reform movement headed by George Henry Evans, who argued that labor was enslaved by industrial capitalism and that its only hope of escape lay in breaking the monopoly in land and assuring to every man a homestead. Evans argued also that the black slaves were better off than the white wage slaves of the North, and that it would be pointless to end chattel slavery before wage slavery was first abolished.

37. Alexander von Humboldt (1769-1859), German naturalist, statesman, and explorer of South America and Asia.

38. "I am not a Philadelphian," wrote the female correspondent, "but feel as one. My native home is the fair and sunny South. Though cursed by the iron rule of slavery, as my home, I love it still." She objected strongly to the "language used by the Anti-slavery lecturers," and urged: "Let us pull together, every one feeling that he has something to do for the common good, and then as a well-organized family we must prosper."

39. *The North Star* of March 11, 1849, published part of the proceedings of the meeting under the heading, "Great Anti-Colonization Meeting in New York," and introduced it as follows: "A large and enthusiastic meeting of the colored citizens of New York was held on the evening of Monday April 23d, and continued on the following evening, for the purpose of expressing their views respecting the Colonization Society, and a Mr. Miller, an agent of that Society now in Great Britain. The Anti-Slavery Standard has a phonographic report of the Speeches delivered on that evening from which the following are extracts. We regret our inability to publish the proceedings entire."

40. Douglass heard Daniel O'Connell (1775-1847), the Irish liberator and abolitionist, speak when he was in Ireland and he sat enthralled by O'Connell's oratory.

41. In June, 1849, in a speech in Faneuil Hall, Douglass astonished the pro-Garrison Boston antislavery audience by using the almost identical language, saying: "I should welcome the intelligence tomorrow, should it come, that the slave had risen in the South, and that the sable arms which had been engaged in beautifying and adorning the South, were engaged in spreading death and devastation." *(Life and Writings of Douglass,* vol. II, p. 50.)

42. In October, 1841, the brig *Creole* sailed from Virginia for New Orleans, laden with over 100 slaves. During the voyage the slaves, led by Madison Washington, rose in revolt, killed one owner, overpowered the crew, and brought the vessel into the English port of Nassau. At the request of the American consul, the governor imprisoned nineteen involved in the mutiny, allowing the others to go free. Secretary of State Daniel Webster demanded the surrender of all the slaves, but the British refused. Finally, in 1853, an Anglo-American Commission awarded an indemnity of $110,330 to the United States.

    For Douglass' short story about Madison Washington, "The Heroic Slave," *see Appendix.*

43. In 1772, in the case of the Negro slave, James Sommerset, the British court, with Judge Mansfield reading the decision, abolished domestic slavery in England, using the argument that liberty was "commensurate with, and inseparable from British soil."

44. Edward Everett (1794-1865), Unitarian clergyman, orator, and statesman, member of Congress, United States Senator, and Secretary of State under President Fillmore.

45. George T. Downing of Rhode Island presented the preamble and resolutions which read:

    "Whereas, letters have been received in this country from the Rev. Alexander Crummell, now in England on a mission in behalf of his Church, informing us that the Rev. Mr. Miller, an agent of the American Colonization Society, is soliciting the aid of British Philanthropy, representing to the British public, that the colored people of these United States are beginning to favor the Colonization scheme. And whereas, this representation of said agent is false and unfounded, inasmuch as the people of color in these United States, having during the last thirty years, held many hundred meetings in public, on the subject of the American Colonization Society, and whereas at all these meetings they have uniformly protested against the doctrines, the designs, and influences of that Society, as evil doctrines, diabolical designs, and slave crushing influences, which views, we do still retain, therefore be it Resolved,

    "That the idea of the American Colonization Society when first conceived, was combinedly opposed and denounced by the people of color throughout the free States in 1817, and in the present moment, being identically the same, it has, and will continue to have as it always has had, the abhorrence and contempt of our people.

    "Resolved, That the testimony of our generation of the people of color is entirely, uniformly, and absolutely against the scheme of African Colonization, and that this solemn testimony—peculiar to the history of the people, should be abundant evidence to all men that we will not remove to Africa except by the exercise of force.

"Resolved, That as natives of the soil we feel an affinity, an attachment thereto, which neither injury, oppression nor insult in the form of American Colonization Society or any other similar wicked scheme, can destroy, and it is our solemn determination while life lasts to be neither seduced nor driven from our homes."

46. James Forten (1766-1842) was born free in Philadelphia, served as a powder boy aboard a privateer during the Revolution, and invented a device for handling sails which earned him a fortune. Forten devoted much of his wealth to the campaign against slavery and discrimination against free blacks. He was founder of the National Negro Convention movement. While at first inclined to favor African colonization, Forten became a leader of the opposition to the American Colonization Society.

47. Douglass is referring to the celebrated proclamations of General Jackson to the free colored inhabitants of Louisiana, first enrolling them in the ranks of his army during the Battle of New Orleans, and then praising them for their contributions to the victory over the British. Douglass reprinted the text of the declarations in the Address he wrote in 1853 for the National Negro Convention. *See Life and Writings of Douglass,* vol. II, pp. 264-65.

48. The Maryland Colonization Society, with headquarters in Baltimore, was a leading division of the American Colonization Society.

49. New York Central College was founded in 1849 at McGrawville, New York by the American Baptist Free Missionary Society. Pledged to the "morality of anti-slavery," the coeducational school welcomed Negroes as students and as teachers. During its twelve years of existence three Negroes served successively as professor of belles lettres—Charles L. Reason, William G. Allen, and George B. Vashon.

50. For an earlier discussion of the issue of Bible for Slaves, *see Life and Writings of Douglass,* vol. I, pp. 253-55.

51. In the August 17, 1849, issue of *The North Star,* Douglass reviewed *Narrative of the Life of Henry Bibb,* and called it "one of the most interesting and thrilling narratives of slavery ever laid before the American public. . . . We deem the work a most valuable acquisition to the anti-slavery cause, and we hope that it may be widely circulated throughout the country."

52. Stephen S. Foster, militant Abolitionist of New Hampshire, who favored revolutionary methods to overthrow slavery.

53. Zachary Taylor (1784-1850), twelfth President of the United States, defeated the Mexicans at Palto Alto (1846) and Buena Vista (1847). He was named commander of the United States army of the Rio Grande during the Mexican War.

54. The *Impartial Citizen* was published by Samuel Ringgold Ward.

55. Theodore Dwight Weld (1803-1895), one of the leading Abolitionists, organizer of the famous Lane Seminary Debate and leader of the "Lane Rebels" who founded Oberlin College. An excellent speaker, Weld had to abandon the antislavery platform when his voice gave out. He was the editor of the influential *American Slavery as It Is* (1839).

56. Delany's departure from *The North Star* as co-editor was one sign of his growing disenchantment with the integrationist viewpoint Douglass stressed in his weekly. More and more Delany opposed collaboration with whites in the struggle against slavery and for the full freedom of the "nominally free," and became a champion of emigration.

57. Free Produce was a movement sponsored especially by Quaker Abolitionists who hoped that if Northerners could be convinced to buy the products of the labor of free men, rather than that manufactured under a slave system, slavery could be made economically unprofitable and Southerners would be encouraged to turn away from the slave system. Free produce remained more a slogan than a viable antislavery weapon.

58. At the National Negro Convention in Buffalo, 1843, Garnet had stirred the assembly with a speech calling upon the slaves to revolt and urged the convention to go on record in favor of this principle. Douglass, still under the influence of the Garrisonian principle of moral suasion and nonviolence, took issue with Garnet. For several days, the convention debated Garnet's proposal, and finally, by the narrow majority of one vote, 18 in favor of Garnet's meaasure and 19 against it, Douglass' position was sustained.

Garnet's speech is reprinted in Foner, *The Voice of Black America,* pp. 82-89.

59. In a speech before a meeting of the American Anti-Slavery Society, following his return from England, Douglass took issue with Garrison's comment that (Douglass) really loved and was attached to his native land. "I cannot agree with my friend Mr. Garrison, in relation to my love and attachment to this land. I have no love for America, as such; I have no patriotism; I have no country. What country have I? The institutions of this country do not know me, do not recognize me as a man." *(National Anti-Slavery Standard,* May 20, 1847.)

60. While a slave in Baltimore, Douglass joined the Sharp Street Methodist Church. After fleeing to the North in 1838, he soon became a class leader and licensed preacher in the Negro New Bedford Zion Methodist Church. Nevertheless, his experiences as a slave had weakened his faith in the Church. He was disillusioned to an extent by the blatant hypocrisy exhibited by his two most avowedly Christian masters, Thomas Auld and Edward Covey. "If religion had any effect at all on him," Douglass wrote of Captain Auld, "it made him more cruel and hateful in all his ways." *(Life and Times of Frederick Douglass,* New York, 1962, p. 109.)

61. During his tour in the United States in 1849 Father Mathew was invited by Governor Lumpkin to visit Georgia in furtherance of the temperance cause. But when the Governor learned that his name had been associated with that of Daniel O'Connell in the famous Anti-Slavery Apeeal from Ireland to Irish in America, he wrote to Father Mathew asking him if he entertained the same sentiments on the subject of slavery. Father Mathew assured the Governor that he had come to America for the sole purpose of advocating "the high and holy cause of temperance . . . being firmly resolved not to interfere in the slightest degree with the institutions of this mighty republic." Even earlier Father Mathew had refused to speak with Garrison and Phillips at a West Indies Emancipation meeting. "I have as much as I can do," he wrote to Garrison, "to save men from the slavery of intemperance without attempting to overthrow any other kind of slavery." (Rev.

Patrick Rogers, *Father Theobold Mathew: Apostle of Temperance,* Dublin, 1943, pp. 126-28.) In *The Liberator* of November 28, 1845, Garrison had written: "The manner in which the great apostle of Temperance, Father Mathew, received him [Douglass], will exalt that great benefactor of the human race still more highly in the estimation of all those whose good opinion it is desirable to possess." Now Garrison joined Douglass in denouncing Father Mathew for his capitulation to the slavery forces.

62. The *Anti-Slavery Bugle,* published in Ohio, accused Garnet of having "done every-thing in his power to injure the reputation and destroy the influence of Frederick Douglass, by echoing the charges of 'Infidelity,' brought against him by a pro-slavery Church. . . . That he will misrepresent and malign Douglass in Great Britain we have no doubt, and therefore we anticipate that he will do vastly more harm than good." (Reprinted in *The North Star,* Aug. 31, 1849.)

63. In *The North Star* of October 12, 1849, Pliny Sexton deplored the disagreement among "talented ind influential colored men," and observed:

"You certainly ought not to let a disagreement as to a proposition to send Bibles to the Slaves divide you, any more than a proposition to send the Slaves to the Moon."

64. The Report of the Committee on Colored Schools, signed by Hiram F. Hatch, Samuel D. Porter, Edwin Pancost, and Hiram C. Smith, insisted that "the system of exclusive schools for colored children cannot be maintained upon the ground of economy nor utility," and proposed that the citizens of Rochester open the doors of their "Free Schools" to those "whose only impediment is their color." The Report concluded: "Your committee have searched in vain for a reason for continu-ing the barrier to our schools; none have been suggested worthy of the name of reason."

# PART THREE

1. Illegible in the original.
2. Illegible in the original.
3. George Bradburn was the editor of the *Pioneer and Herald of Freedom.* For an editorial by Douglass on that paper, *see The North Star,* January 5, 1849.
4. Douglass' criticism of Ward appeared in the editorial, "Shameful Abandonment of Principle." *The North Star,* May 30, 1850, and reprinted in the *Life and Writings of Douglass*, vol. II, pp. 121-25. Delany wrote to Ward deploring the bickering among blacks. He felt that "a people wholly oppressed, all making struggling efforts for liberty and elevation among their oppressors, have no time to spend in personal hostility towards each other, and especially among their leaders. *We cannot afford to be divided—it costs too* much."
5. The letter was drawn up by Douglass at the Meeting of Fugitives from Slavery and their Friends held in Cazenovia, New York, August 21-22, 1850. Douglass was president of the meeting.
6. Judge John McLean of Boston handed down several decisions upholding the Fugitive Slave Law of 1850 and ordering the return of fugitives to slavery.

Moses Stuart (1780-1852), a leading clergyman and Biblical scholar in New England, upheld the constitutionality of the Fugitive Slave Law.

The Fugitive Slave Law of 1850 provided for the appointment of special federal commissioners to facilitate the reclaiming of runaways. These commissioners could appoint marshals to arrest fugitives, and these marshals could, in turn, "call to their aid" any bystanders at the scene of an arrest, who were "commanded" to "assist in the prompt and efficient execution of the law. . . ." Slave owners could "pursue and reclaim" fugitives with or without a warrant; the commissioner would judge the case without a jury. In addition, "In no trial or hearing under this act shall the testimony of such alleged fugitive be admitted in evidence." Satisfactory" written or oral "proof" being offered that the person arrested was the sought-for fugitive, the commissioner would issue a certificate. The slave owner was authorized to use all "reasonable force" necessary to take a fugitive back to the place of his or her escape. If a slave owner feared "that such fugitive will be rescued by force" it was the duty of the officer involved to employ any number of persons necessary "to overcome such force," and deliver the fugitive back to the fugitive's owner. Any marshal who failed to properly execute the fugitive law was to be fined $100; the marshal was also liable for the full value of any fugitive escaping from his custody. Finally, an officer was "entitled to a fee of five dollars each" for every person he arrested; a commissioner was "entitled to a fee of ten dollars" if he delivered a fugitive to a slave owner, but only five dollars if he freed the Black claimed.

The new Fugitive Slave Law was approved by Congress on September 18, 1850.

7. The New York City Committee of Vigilance was established to guard Blacks from kidnappers who would return them to Southern bondage. Its secretary was the militant David Ruggles (1810-1849) who was jailed several times because of his frank criticism of the police who collaborated with slave hunters. *See* Dorothy Porter, "David M. Ruggles, An Apostle of Human Rights," *Journal of Negro History*, vol. XVIII, Jan. 1943, pp. 23-50.

8. In August 1850, William L. Chaplin and others were arrested by Washington police on Maryland soil, for taking part in the escape of two slaves, the property of Robert Toombs and Alexander H. Stephens. Chaplin was kept in jail at Rockville, Maryland, until December; was subsequently indicted in the District of Columbia on a charge of assault with intent to kill, and in Maryland he was indicted on seven counts: three for assault with intent to murder, two for assisting slaves to escape, and two for larceny of slaves. Bail was fixed at $6,000 in the District and $19,000 in Maryland.

In an appeal to the Liberty Party, the fugitive slaves, meeting in Cazenovia, New York, recommended that it nominate Chaplin for President of the United States. "He is emphatically a scholar, a statesman, a philanthropist, a gentleman, and a Christian Job, who was the supreme magistrate in the community, in which he dwelt, numbers among his own qualifications for office, 'I WAS A FATHER TO THE POOR.'—Beautiful, precious, indispensable qualification is this! and who had it more abundantly than William L. Chaplin." The fact that Chaplin was in prison for a worthy cause was another reason that merited his nomination. "It is true, that we would not, for this reason, ask for his nomination, were it not also, that he is fit for it. But, being fit for it, we find in the fact of his imprisonment, good cause why he, among all, who have such fitness, should be singled out for the nomination." *The North Star,* September 5, 1850.)

With the aid of Gerrit Smith, Lewis Tappan, William H. Seward and others, Chaplin's bail was secured and he was released from jail. Smith served as treasurer of the Chaplin fund, and contributed $10,000 to the movement to free Chaplin.

9. Douglass delivered a series of lectures on slavery in Rochester's Corinthian Hall. For Lectures No. 1 and No. 2, *see Life and Writings of Douglass,* vol. II, pp. 132-49.

10. Henry Long was a fugitive slave seized by the federal authorities in New York City to be returned to his owner in the South under the new Fugitive Slave Law. When the Anti-Slavery Society came to Long's defense, delaying the return and adding to the expense of the Southern claimant, the Union Safety Committee of New York City, composed of merchants and other businessmen (many in the Southern trade), raised a fund to hire a lawyer to aid in restoring Long to his owners. After an elaborate hearing, the court ruled that Long be delivered up to his owners.

11. James Hamlet, a fugitive slave in New York City, was arrested soon after the adoption of the Fugitive Slave Law, tried before the United States Commissioner, and ordered sent back to his former owner in Baltimore. He left behind him a wife and two children. His freedom was later purchased by a committee of New York businessmen and he was reunited with his family.

12. Isaiah Rynders was a leader of the extreme pro-Southern elements in New York City. He made a specialty of breaking up Abolitionist meetings by leading his mob of toughs into the gatherings. Douglass had a run-in with Rynders at one such meeting in New York City.

13. Washington Hunt was the Whig candidate and Horatio Seymour the Democratic candidate for Governor of New York.

14. On April 3, 1851 Thomas Sims, a fugitive from Georgia, was seized in Boston, rushed to the courthouse and imprisoned awaiting return to slavery. Legal efforts to free Sims were unsuccessful as were efforts to achieve his escape, organized by Lewis Hayden, a leader of the Boston black community. On April 13 Sims was marched to the Long Wharf in Boston and returned to slavery.

15. The union of papers was the amalgamation of *The North Star* with the *Liberty Party Paper,* a weekly journal edited and published by John Thomas in Syracuse. This paper had fewer than seven hundred subscribers and was in great financial distress. The merger resulted from a suggestion by Gerrit Smith, the financial backer of Thomas's paper. Douglass was to become the editor of the new publication, Thomas the assistant editor. A new printing office and a good press would result in a "good looking paper . . . free from all typographical, grammatical, orthographical, and rhetorical errors and blunders." Smith advanced two hundred dollars for the purchase of the press and type and promised to provide a monthly donation toward the paper's upkeep.

After considerable bickering with John Thomas over the salary of the assistant editor and the location of the paper, the merger became an accomplished fact. On June 30, 1851, the first issue of the new weekly, now named *Frederick Douglass' Paper,* appeared.

16. For Douglass' changing views on the Constitution and slavery, *see Life and Writings of Douglass,* vol. I, pp. 41, 44-45, 209, 210, 274-75, 328-29, 352-67, 374-79; vol. II, pp. 51-53, 75-76, 118-19, 149-51, 155-67, 174, 177-78, 201-03, 351-54, 368-79, 379-83, 418-21, 467-80.

17. Julia Griffiths, the daughter of a close friend of William Wilbeforce, came to the United States with her sister from England, moved into Douglass' home and helped him with his business problems in running *The North Star.* (She also assisted Douglass in perfecting his writing as editor.) When *The North Star* and the *Liberty Party Paper* merged, Miss Griffiths became business manager of the new paper.

    For a discussion of Miss Griffiths' role and her relationship with Douglass, *see Life and Writings of Douglass,* vol. I, pp. 87-92, 306-07; vol. II, 44-45, 47-48, 57-58, 62, 150, 155, 166-67, 174, 178, 205, 395, 547, 548.

18. This was the motto of *Frederick Douglass' Paper,* proposed by Gerrit Smith. It replaced the motto of *The North Star*—"Right is of no Sex—Truth is of no Color—God is the Father of us all, and we are all Brethren."

19. In the June 25, 1851 issue of *The North Star,* Douglass wrote: "We announced two weeks ago, that Mr. Ward would probably unite his *Impartial Citizen* with this paper. We now learn from him that he will not enter into a union at present, but he will be pleased to act as our New England correspondent. His racy letters will do much to impart interest to our new paper." (The June 11, 1851 issue of *The North Star,* with Prospectus, is no longer in existence.) On October 30, 1851, Douglass announced in *Frederick Douglass' Paper* that the *"Impartial Citizen* is discontinued. It has died for want of support. Mr. Samuel R. Ward, its editor and proprietor, a man of genius, an able writer, and an eloquent speaker, and withal, an unalloyed representative of our sable race, has bestowed upon it his best energies, during the last two years, with a view to its permanent establishment; but his hopes and labors have been disappointed, and he is left now to stagger under a heavy debt, incurred by its publication." Douglass was critical of the free black community in the North for not sufficiently supporting Ward financially.

20. George Thompson, the British Abolitionist, had previously visited the United States in the 1830's. During his visit in the early 1850's, he was repeatedly mobbed by pro-slavery groups.

21. James William Charles Pennington (1809-1870), an escaped slave who received an honorary degree of Doctor of Divinity in 1849 from the University of Heidelberg and became a minister in New York City.

    William Wells Brown (c. 1814-1884), the escaped slave who became America's first black man of letters, author of novels and plays.

    Alexander Crummell (1819-1898), granson of an African prince, was born free in New York where he attended the African Free School. After graduating from Oneida Intitute, he was refused admission to New Yorks General Theological Seminary because he was black. He completed his studies in Cambridge, England and afterwards spent twenty years in Africa as minister and teacher. On his return to the United States, he became a noted black scholar and founder of the American Negro Academy.

    Josiah Henson was the fugitive slave who helped many slaves escape from slavery, was the author of a famous autobiography, and helped Harriet Beecher Stowe with information about slavery when she was writing *Uncle Tom's Cabin.*

William and Ellen Craft were the famous young black couple from Georgia who escaped from slavery by the ingenious method of her assuming the role of a slaveowner and he serving as his slave. After their escape, they lectured widely in the North and England.

22. Amos G. Beman (1803-1874), born in Connecticut and tutored at Wesleyan University until students forced him to leave the campus. Beman taught school, became a minister and Underground Railroad stationmaster in New Haven. Beman contributed several letters to Douglass' paper as well as to the Abolitionist press. He was a specialist on the history of Africa.

23. In his speech, John Scoble defended the abolition of slavery in the British West Indies from criticism that it had resulted in the degradation of the free black population. He described a visit to the West Indies since emancipation, and told how in general, the conditions of the black population had improved. As for economic depression resulting from emancipation, Scoble insisted that "whatever of depression may exist in our West India Colonies, is not to be traced to emancipation, but to other causes, plain to the man of reflection and knowledge."

24. W.W. Anderson of Jamaica was the speaker referred to. Anderson spoke highly of conditions in Jamaica and recommended emigration of free blacks from the United States to the island.

25. An old study of the Christiana Riot is W. U. Hensel, *The Christiana Riot and the Treason Trials of 1851,* Lancaster, Pa., 1911. But it has been superseded by Jonathan Katz, *Resistance at Christiana: The Fugitive Slave Rebellion, Christiana, Pennsylvania, September 11, 1851: A Documentary Account,* New York, 1974.

For Douglass' role in the escape of William Parker, leader of the black resistance group, and his views on the Christiana Riot, *see Life and Writings of Douglass,* vol. II, pp. 44-46; Katz, *op. cit.,* 149-53, 242, 259-61.

26. The reference is to the capture by the Spanish of filibusters, led by Narciso López, who sought to end Spanish rule over Cuba and unite the island with the United States.(López was executed.) For Douglass' criticism of the filibusters, *see* his editorial, "Cuba and the United States," *Freerick Douglass' Paper,* September 4, 1851, reprinted in *Life and Writings of Douglass,* vol. II, pp. 159-63. For a discussion of the López filibustering expedition, *see* Philip S. Foner, *A History of Cuba and its Relations with the United States,* New York, 1963, vol. II, pp. 41-65.

27. Daniel Sharp (1783-1853), Baptist; Gardiner Spring (1785-1873), Presbyterian; Jesse Ames Spencer (1816-1898), Episcopalian; Nathan Lord (1792-1870) and Orville Dewey (1794-1882), Unitarians—all defended the Fugitive Slave Act in their sermons and urged obedience to the law.

28. Millard Fillmore (1800-1874), thirteenth president of the United States, signed the Fugitive Slave Act of 1850.

29. Popularized by William H. Seward in his Senate speech opposing the Compromise of 1850, the "Higher Law" doctrine held that there was a "Higher Law" than the Constitution, and the argument was advanced to justify resistance to the Fugitive Slave Act of 1850.

30. For William Parker, *see* William Parker, "The Freedman's Story," *Atlantic*

*Monthly,* vol. XVII, February and March, 1866, and Katz, *op. cit.,* pp. 6-21.

31. The Blacks and Castner Hanway, a white man, were tried for treason in Lancaster, Pennsylvania. Defended by Thaddeus Stevens, they were found not guilty by the jury. For the details of the trial, *see* Katz, *op. cit.,* pp. 177-243.

32. In his letter to Gerrit Smith, August 26, 1851, Henry C. Wright (1797-1870), radical Abolitionist and one of the founders of the Non-Resistant Society in 1838, wrote that he honored Smith's "purity and benevolence," but insisted that in seeking "a *righteous* Civil government," he was "aiming at an impossibility. You seek to make that just and righteous which ever has been, and ever must be, from its nature, unjust and unrighteous."

33. "Dr. McCune Smith."—footnote in original.

34. Four months after Douglass came to New Bedford, Massachusetts to live, after his escape from slavery on September 3, 1838, he obtained a copy of William Lloyd Garrison's *Liberator.* So deeply was he moved by the paper that despite his poverty he became a regular subscriber, and every week read the journal avidly, studying its principles and philosophy.

35. The Jerry Rescue occurred at Syracuse, New York, on October 1, 1851. Gerrit Smith and other Abolitionists forcibly rescued the fugitive slave Jerry McHenry, who had been seized and imprisoned by a deputy United States marshal, and helped him to escape to Canada and to freedom. A number of those involved in the Rescue were arrested and tried.

36. In the spring of 1852, Douglass visited Cincinnati to attend an antislavery convention, and while in Cincinnati, went on to address a church congregation in Harveysburg in Warren County, Ohio. A reporter from the Wilmington, Ohio, *Herald of Freedom* was present when Douglass spoke, and while he did not report the speech in full, inserting some paraphrases into the midst of verbatim quotation by Douglass and sometimes even substituting his own digests of the speaker's argumentation, he did report most of the address faithfully. (The sections which are not directly quoting Douglass are placed within parentheses in the text.) The reporter urged his readers to give Douglass' speech "a careful and candid reading," for it contained "many brilliant thoughts and important truths—truths which must be faithfully presented to this nation in order to effect its reformation."

37. Douglass frequently noted that one of the inevitable results of the industrial and communications revolutions was to be the end of slavery.

38. The reference is to the nomination of Zachary Taylor, a slaveholder and hero of the Mexican War, for the presidency in 1848.

39. Many Americans sympathized with both Ireland and Hungary in their battle for national self-determination. For the viewpoint of a black American, see the speech by George T. Downing, "May Hungary Be Free," December 9, 1851, in Foner, *Voice of Black America,* pp. 100-02.

40. Louis Kossuth (1802-1894), Hungarian patriot and leader of the unsuccessful national revolt of 1849. He disappointed American Abolitionists because of his avoidance of the slavery issue while on tour of the United States in order to get maximum support for the cause of Hungarian independence. For Douglass' criticism of Kossuth, *see* "Letter to Kossuth," *Frederick Douglass' Paper,* February 26, 1852, reprinted in *Life and Writings of Douglass,* vol. II, pp. 170-72.

41. Henry Wadsworth Longfellow (1807-1882), famous poet and Smith professor of modern languages at Harvard, did not respond to Douglass' entreaty. The "Autograph" referred to was *Autographs for Freedom*, a slim volume of writing with facsimile autographs of the authors, published by the Rochester Ladies' Anti-Slavery Society. The idea of the *Autographs* originated with Julia Griffiths as a means of helping Douglass' paper financially through sales of the volume. The first number published in December, 1852, contained 41 original articles, including contributions by John Greenleaf Whittier and Harriet Beecher Stowe, but nothing by Longfellow.
42. Henry Clay died on June 29, 1852.
43. Illegible in the original.
44. Alphonse Marie Louis de Prat de Lamartine (1790-1869), French poet and statesman, representative of the liberal bourgeosie of 1848, and author, among other works, of *Meditations poétique* (Paris, 1820) and *Politique rationelle* (Paris, 1831).
45. Douglass was travelling to Pittsburgh to attend the convention of the Free Soil Party. His reference to the "American demon" is to the discrimination against Blacks in Philadelphia which Douglass hated as the most racist city in the North. "There is not perhaps anywhere to be found a city in which prejudice against color is more rampant than in Philadelphia," he wrote early in 1862. (*Douglass' Monthly*, February, 1862.) For a discussion of racism in Philadelphia, *see* Philip S. Foner, "The Battle to end Discrimination Against Negroes on Philadelphia Street Cars, Part I," *Pennsylvania History*, vol. XL, July, 1973, pp. 261-67.
46. *Uncle Tom's Cabin*, the anti-slavery novel written by Harriet Beecher Stowe, first appeared serially in 1851-1852 in the Washington *National Era*, and was published in book-form in 1852.
47. William Allen, a graduate of Oneida Institute, was the first black college professor in the United States. After studying law in Boston, becoming co-editor of *The National Watchman*, a newspaper published in Troy, New York, he taught Greek and German at Central College in McGrawville, New York, until 1853. Following his marriage to a white student, he and his wife were forced to leave the country, and he continued to teach in England.
48. Jeremiah W. Loguen (1813-1872), a fugitive slave who settled in Syracuse, New York, Loguen became a prominent Abolitionist, leader of the Underground Railroad, and a bishop of the African Methodist Episcopal Zion Church.
49. Franklin Pierce was the Democratic candidate and General Winfield Scott, the Whig candidate for President in the election of 1852. Pierce easily defeated Scott by a popular plurality of 214,000 votes and a margin of 254 to 42 in the electoral college. John P. Hale, the Free Soil candidate, won only half as many votes as Van Buren in 1848, as many "Barnburners" returned to the Democratic Party.
50. Illegible in original.
51. Horace Greeley (1811-1872), founder of the New York *Tribune*, a successful and influential antislavery organ and later one of the foremost of Republican editors.
52. Cassius M. Clay (1810-1903), the son of a large slaveholder in Kentucky, was inspired by William Lloyd Garrison, whom he heard at Yale College, and became an Abolitionist. In June, 1845, he founded the newspaper *True American* in Lexington, which campaigned to rid Kentucky of slavery. Two months later a

committee of sixty prominent Lexingtonians visited his office while he was absent, boxed up his equipment and dispatched it to Cincinnati. Clay continued to publish his paper from the Ohio city, and later, changing its name to the *Examiner*, he moved it to Louisville.

53. The purchase of Louisiana from France in 1803 for $15,000,000 made available a vast territory for the expansion of slavery.

54. The Seminole Wars were really two wars between Seminole tribes in Florida and the United States lasting from 1815 to 1842. A motivating factor of importance in the drive against the Seminoles was that they offered a refuge for fugitive slaves from Georgia and South Carolina, and that indeed many Blacks intermarried and became Seminoles. After final defeat the Seminoles were removed west of the Mississippi.

55. In his March 7, 1850, speech, Daniel Webster called for concessions to the South as the sole means of preserving the Union, and supported adoption of the Compromise of 1850, including the infamous Fugitive Slave Act. Webster was denounced by the Abolitionists and burned in effigy all over Massachusetts.

56. Horace Mann (1796-1859), educator and antislavery Whig member of Congress, known as "Father of American Public School System" because of his work in reorganizing the entire public school system of Massachusetts.

57. George Washington Julian (1817-1899), antislavery Whig from Indiana who became a leader of the radical wing of the Republican Party. Julian was a member of Congress from 1849-52 and 1861-71.

58. Douglass was campaigning for Gerrit Smith, who had been nominated for Congress on the Liberty Party ticket.

59. Samuel Joseph May (1797-1871), noted antislavery figure of Syracuse, New York, also famous for favoring woman's rights and educational reform.

60. To everybody's surprise, including Douglass's, Gerrit Smith was elected to Congress by an overwhelming majority. However, he served only until August 7, 1854, when he resigned his seat in Congress. The only explanation Smith gave was the "pressure of my far too extensive business."

61. Serfdom was abolished in Russia in 1862.

62. The report referred to was from the *Daily State Register*, and it carried the proceedings of "The Jerry Rescue Trials, U.S. Circuit Court—Special Term—Albany, Jan. 26, Before the Hon. N.K. Hall, U.S. Circuit Judge: the People *vs.* Enoch Reed—Jerry Rescue Indictment." "The Defendants," the report also noted, "some fourteen in number—five or six of them colored—were all present, together with about fifty witnesses for Government and Defense."

63. The letter from H. O. Wagoner, Chicago, March 8, 1853, condemned "the hell-black and heaven-daring enactment *called* LAW, passed by the late general Assembly of Illinois, to prohibit the immigration of colored persons into the State. . . . It embraces all who may have one-fourth Afraican blood in their veins." Wagoner urged: "Now, friend Douglass, let me here say, that, I think the time has come when it is advisable to call, or rather to advise to be called, a North American Convention of colored men, to be held at some central point, which may be thought best, by friends generally, if approved of." A National Negro Convention did meet in Rochester in July, 1853.

H. O. Wagoner, a frequent correspondent of Douglass, moved to Denver, Colorado, from which city he continued to send letters to Douglass' papers.

64. For additional writings of Douglass on this theme, *see* his editorials "Learn Trades or Starve," *Frederick Douglass' Paper*, March 14, 1853, and "A Few More Words about Learning Trades," *ibid.*, March 11, 1853, both reprinted in *Life and Writings of Douglass*, vol. II, pp. 223-26, 236-38.

65. William Henry Seward (1801-1872), antislavery Whig governor of New York (1839-1843), U.S. Senator (1849-1861), and leading figure in the early Republican Party. Seward was Secretary of State under President Lincoln.

66. Douglass here seems to have envisaged Seward's role in the Republican Party even though that party did not come into existence until 1854.

67. This is the second of three letters Delany promised to send Douglass. *See, for example*, "Uncle Tom," *Frederick Douglass' Paper*, April 29, 1853.

68. "Is not Mrs. Stowe a colonizationist? having so avowed, or at least subscribed to, and recommended their principles in her great work of Uncle Tom," Delany wrote. In the concluding paragraphs of her novel, Mrs. Stowe envisaged African emigration as the solution for the problems facing Negroes in the United States.

69. *See* "The National League," *The North Star*, October 26, 1849, reprinted in *Life and Writings of Douglass*, vol. I, pp. 408-11.

70. *The Voice of the Fugitive* was published in Detroit and Canada by Henry Bibb.

71. "I say," Delany wrote, "that the benevolent, great and good, the Duchess of Sutherland, Mr. Gurney, their graces the Earl of Shaftesbury and the Earl of Carlisle had better retain their money in the Charity Fund in the Stafford House, or any other place, than to send it to the United States, if money is to be sent to aid the Colonization Society."

In the New York *Tribune* of February 9, 1853, Karl Marx referred to the Duchess of Sutherland angrily, writing: "the enemy of British Wage-Slavery has no right to condemn Negro-Slavery, a Duchess of Sutherland, a Duke of Atholl, a Manchester Cotton Lord—never."

72. Douglass spoke at meetings of both the American and American and Foreign Anti-Slavery Society in New York City.

73. The June 3, 1853 issue of *Frederick Douglass' Paper* carried the call for a "convention of Christians who are opposed to *Sectarianism*, and in favor of the Union of all who love God and man," to be held June 8-9, 1853. The call was signed by Gerrit Smith and six others.

74. The proceedings of the Woman's State Temperance Convention are published in the June 10, 1853, issue of *Frederick Douglass' Paper*.

75. The dispute over the boundary from the Rio Grande to the Colorado under the Treaty of Guadalupe Hidalgo ending the Mexican War was resolved by the Gadsden Treaty of December 30, 1853, which went into force on June 30, 1854.

76. The reference is to the letter of Horace Mann, May 29, 1853, to Garrison, published in *The Liberator* and reprinted in *Frederick Douglass' Paper* in which Mann defended himself in voting. "Repeatedly challenged, through your paper, to defend the grounds on which, as a moral and Christian man, I can vote or hold office under our governments, state and national," Mann informed Garrison, he had decided to send this letter.

77. The reference is to the editorial, "The Testimonial to Mrs. Stowe and What Shall be done with it," in the May 27, 1853, issue of *Frederick Douglass' Paper*. The issue dealt with the money given Mrs. Stowe while in England to be used for Blacks in the United States.

78. The material from the London *Anti-Slavery Advocate* following "sentence" is illegible in the original.

79. The Constitution of the American Anti-Slavery Society contained the provision: "This Society shall aim to elevate the character and conditions of the people of color, by encouraging their intellectual, moral and religious improvement, and by removing public prejudice, that thus they may, according to their intellectual and moral worth, share an equality with the whites of civil and religious privileges. . . ."

80. For further evidence on this point, *see* Douglass' editorial, "A Day and Night in 'Uncle Tom's Cabin,'" *Frederick Douglass' Paper*, March 4, 1853, reprinted in *Life and Writings of Douglass*, vol. II, pp. 226-29.

81. The Call for a National Emigration Convention of Colored Men opened: "*Men and Brethren*: The time has now fully come, when we, as an oppressed people, should do something effectively, and use those means adequate to the attainment of the great and long desired end—to do something to meet the actual demands of the present, and prospective necessities of the rising generation of our people in this country. To do this, we must occupy a position of entire equality of unrestricted rights, composed in fact, of an acknowledged necessary part of the ruling element of society, in which we live. The policy necessary to the preservation of this element must be in our favor, if ever we expect the enjoyment of freedom, sovereignty, and equality of rights anywhere.

    "For this purpose, and to this end, then, all colored men in favor of emigration out of the United States, and opposed to the American Colonization scheme of leaving the Western Hemisphere, are requested to meet in CLEVELAND, OHIO, on TUESDAY the 24th DAY OF AUGUST, 1854, in a great National Convention, then and there, to consider and decide upon the great and important subject of emigration from the United States."

82. James M. Whitfield, black poet and advocate of emigration of black Americans, was well known in antislavery circles for his odes read at August 1st celebrations.

83. Douglass is referring to his speech at the annual meeting of the American and Foreign Anti-Slavery Society, New York City. For the full text of the speech, *see Life and Writings of Douglass*, vol. II, pp. 243-54. An extract also appears in *Autographs For Freedom*, edited by Julia Griffiths, Auburn, N.Y., 1854, pp. 251-55, which is preceded by the note: "Dear Madam, If the enclosed paragraph from a speech of mine delivered in May last, at the anniversary meeting of the American and Foreign Anti-Slavery Society, shall be deemed suited to the pages of the forthcoming annual, please accept it as my contribution." This is followed by a facsimile autograph of Frederick Douglass, and the notice, Rochester, November, 1853.

## PART FOUR

1. In introducing the speech the *Manchester Democrat* wrote: "The eleventh lecture before the New Lyceum was delivered on Tuesday evening, Jan. 24, by Frederick Douglass of Rochester, N.Y. Subject—Slavery."
2. Calvin Ellis Stowe, religious scholar, was the husband of Harriet Beecher Stowe.
3. For the Address of the 1853 Rochester Convention, *see Life and Writings of Douglass*, vol. II, pp. 254-67.
4. George T. Downing (1819-1903), son of a well-known New York restaurateur. Downing became a successful caterer in Providence, Rhode Island and owned several summer hotels in Newport. Although a successful businessman, Downing was involved in the civil rights struggle throughout his entire life.
5. Mrs. Margaret Douglass, a white seamstress, ran a school for Negro children in Norfolk, Virginia. Brought to trial for violating the law which forbade teaching Negroes to read and write, she was sentenced to prison for one month. When Mrs. Douglass came out of prison, she moved to Philadelphia, "happy in the conscious- ness," as she put it, "that it is here no crime to teach a poor little child, of any color, to read the word of God." *See* Margaret Douglass, *Personnal Narrative*, Boston, 1854.
6. Seward favored compensated emancipation in the District of Columbia, the system by which slavery was ended in the District in 1862.
7. Seward's speech entitled, "Freedom and Public Faith," opposing the repeal of the Missouri Compromise in the Kansas-Nebraska bills, was published in *Frederick Douglass' Paper*, March 10, 1854.
8. The amendment barring blacks from participating in homestead benefits passed both the House and Senate.
9. The Industrial School, a favorite plan of Frederick Douglass, was proposed by him to the 1853 National Negro Convention. (*See* "The Industrial College," *Frederick Douglass' Paper*, January 2, 1854; reprinted in *Life and Writings of Douglass*, vol. II, pp. 272-75.) The Plan published in *Frederick Douglass' Paper* of March 24, 1854, was signed by Douglass, John D. Peck, Amos G. Beman, John Jones, J. D. Bonner, and J. McCune Smith, the Committee on Manual Labor School set up by the 1853 Convention. It called for the American Industrial School to be located within one hundred miles of the town of Erie, Pennsylvania, as soon as three thousand dollars had been paid in; the school building and workshop to be erected as soon as ten thousand dollars had paid in, and the school started as soon as fifteen thousand dollars had been paid in. In accordance with a vote of the 1853 conven- tion, the teachers were to be selected for, and pupils admitted into, the school, without reference to sex or complexion. Special provision was to be made for an industrial school for females, as well as males, and it was emphasized that "a prominent principle of conduct will be to aid in providing for the female sex, methods and means of enjoying an independent and honorable livelihood." The Industrial School's curriculum provided that for every branch of literature taught, there should be one branch of handicraft also taught, and that each pupil should occupy one-half his time when at school in work at some handicraft or on the farm.
10. Anthony Burns had escaped from Richmond in February, 1854, and was hiding in

Boston. He was arrested on May 24, 1854. The next morning he was about to be delivered to his master when black and white Abolitionists attacked the Court House to free Burns. During the attack, James Batchelder, a truckman serving as a United States marshal, was killed. President Pierce ordered out federal troops to force Burns' return to his master, and an army carried him down State Street and flung him, manacled, into the hold of a vessel bound for Virginia.

11. The speech, "First of August Address, at Canandaigua," was published in the *National Anti-Slavery Standard*, August 19, 1847.

12. Under the heading, "Spirit of the Press," *Frederick Douglass' Paper* reprinted editorials from the Massachusetts *Spy*, Cincinnati *Commercial*, Philadelphia *Argus*, Norfolk *Daily News*, Syracuse *Standard*, and Richmond *Daily Whig* on the suggestion of the New York *Tribune* that Douglass should succeed Gerrit Smith in Congress. Southern papers insisted that Southern Congressmen would have to be excused from going to Congress with a Negro.

13. For a study of the community where Douglass spoke, *see* John Kevin Anthony Farrell, "The History of the Negro Community in Chatham, Ontario 1787-1865," unpublished Ph.D. thesis, University of Ottawa, Canada, 1955.

14. Starting with a nucleus of his own ex-slaves, Reverend William King, a Scotch-Irish missionary and Louisiana slave-owner turned Canadian Abolitionist, founded the Buxton Mission and Elgin Association colony. "Perhaps," notes Jonathan Katz, "the relation between King and the black people of Buxton was not so idyllic as Douglass painted it. Present-day members of old Buxton families relate some critical and apparently traditional legends about the founding father." (*op. cit.,* p. 347.) For Douglass' picture of the community, *see* his editorial, "The Elgin Settlement at Buxton, Canada West," *Frederick Douglass' Paper*, August 25, 1854.

15. For further discussion of this issue, *see* Douglass' letter to Smith, August 22, 1854, *Life and Writings of Douglass*, vol. II, pp. 309-10.

16. Douglass had written, "Davis is a plain, not forcible speaker," when Smith had said that "Davis is a plain, but forcible speaker." (*Frederick Douglass' Paper*, September 1, 1854.) It was corrected in the following week's issue.

17. For the suffrage issue in Rhode Island and Douglass' role in the campaign, *see Life and Writings of Douglass*, vol. I, pp. 48-49.

18. William Wells Brown (1815-1884) was born a slave in Kentucky. He escaped to the North and became an effective antislavery speaker, novelist (author of *Clotel, or The President's Daughter*, the first novel published by an American Negro), playwright and historian. Brown worked as a lecturer for antislavery societies in the United States and Great Britain. In 1854, years after he had escaped from slavery, his English friends, worried for his safety under the Fugitive Slave Act of 1850, purchased Brown's freedom for three hundred dollars.

19. Brown's letter to Douglass was also published in the *National Anti-Slavery Standard* of March 10, 1855. For a defense of Brown's position, *see* William Edward Farrison, *William Wells Brown: Author & Reformer*, Chicago and London, 1969, pp. 262-65.

20. Douglass is probably referring to his speech, "The Anti-Slavery Movement," delivered before the Rochester Ladies' Anti-Slavery Society, January, 1855. It is reprinted in *Life and Writings of Douglass*, vol. II, pp. 333-59.

21. The Call for a Convention of Radical Political Abolitionists to be held in Syracuse, June 26-28, 1855, was signed by Lewis Tappan, William Goodell, Gerrit Smith, S. S. Jocelyn, W. E. Whiting, James McCune Smith, George Whipple, and Frederick Douglass. It is published in *Frederick Douglass' Paper*, April 20, 1855.

22. In 1838, despite the vigorous protest of 40,000 Negroes, written by the distinguished black Philadelphia Abolitionist Robert Purvis, the Pennsylvania state legislature adopted a new constitution which included a provision limiting the franchise to adult white men. Not until the Fifteenth Amendment was ratified in 1870 did black Pennsylvanians regain the right to vote.

23. Even Negroes outside of Massachusetts sent their children to these schools. Thus Charlotte Forten, granddaughter of James Forten, was educated in the integrated schools of Salem, Massachusetts so that she would not have to attend the segregated schools in Philadelphia. Miss Forten taught in the Salem schools in the 1850's.

24. Sumner was assisted by a young Negro lawyer, Robert Morris. Sumner argued that segregated schools were inherently inferior, anticipating the argument of the Supreme Court in its *Brown v. Board of Education* decision of 1954.

25. The report said in part: "All this evidence of the practical working of the truly 'common' school, established in the minds of your committee two points: First, that colored children can make less progress in a separate school; and, second, that no practical in convenience need follow the abolition."

   While the committee report failed to move the legislature, it did finally respond to a well-organized campaign by the black community of Boston set up by William C. Nell and supported by *The Liberator*. Under Nell's direction, Negroes in Boston deluged the Massachusetts legislature with petitions demanding the abolition of separate schools and had their children taught privately until in 1855 a law was enacted requiring public schools in the state to admit students without regard to color.

26. New York state law required that Negro citizens own real estate valued at two hundred and fifty dollars as a condition for voting. For Douglass' role in the campaign to abolish this discriminatory provision, see *Life and Writings of Douglass,* vol. II, pp. 98-99, 259-66, 369-74, 389-90, 518-20, 525, 530-32, 555, 566-67.

27. "Communipaw" argued that blacks were "come-outers" of the Church and acknowledgers of Woman's Rights "long before William Lloyd Garrison was born," and that the American Anti-Slavery Society had fallen down in fulfilling its pledge to advocate full equality for free Blacks. He insisted that the *National Anti-Slavery Standard* of January 13, 1853 lied when it charged that Blacks stayed out of anti-slavery societies because "many of them are either pro-slavery in feeling, or indifferent to the wrongs of the slave," "Had there dwelt in them the least recognition of the equal manhood of the black man," he wrote angrily, "they would not have printed it without the most searching examination into its truthfulness." (*Frederick Douglass' Paper*, May 11, 1855.)

   "Communipaw" was the pseudonym for James McCune Smith (1813-1865), a leading black physician, writer and Abolitionist, who was educated in the African Free School of New York City and entered the University of Glasgow in 1832, receiving the degrees of B.A. in 1835, M.A. in 1836, and M.D. in 1837. Following a short period in the clinics of Paris, he returned to New York City and for twenty-five years was a noted doctor and surgeon. But his fame rested largely on his activities in the struggle of the black community of New York for equality and on his battle against slavery.

28. James W. C. Pennington (1809-1870) was born in slavery on the Eastern Shore of Maryland, and was trained as a blacksmith, a trade he followed until he was about twenty-one, when he decided to run away. Befriended by a Pennsylvania Quaker, he stayed with him for six months and began what was to be an extensive education under his direction. After attending evening school in Long Island, he taught in colored schools, and, at the same time, studied theology. Pennington became a pastor in the African Congregational Church, held pastorates in Hartford, Connecticut, and represented that state at the World Anti-Slavery Convention in London in 1843. He was also a delegate to the World Peace Society in London that same year.

Following the brutal discriminatory treatment he received on the public car, together with Dr. James McCune Smith and the Reverend Highland Garnet, Pennington organized the Legal Rights Association for the purpose of establishing the rights of Negroes to the public conveyances in the city. The Association fought the cases for Negroes kept off the streetcars until such segregation practices were abolished during the Civil War.

29. Alexis de Tocqueville (1805-1859), French writer who toured the United States for his government on a special mission in 1831, and wrote *Democracy in America* (1835) which has become famous for its excellent picture of America at that time.

30. U.B.'s letter, "Dissolution of the Union—Its Probable, Almost Certain Results," insisted that dissolution would result in weakening the Slave Power, since it would no longer have the support of the population of the North; would hasten slave insurrections in the South, and that the "final and grand result would be, that slavery would be abolished—it would end sooner by the dissolution of the Union than it will if the Union continues." Later all the states where slavery now existed, "would come into the Union again, thus constituting one great and free Republic."

31. Passmore Williamson, a Quaker lawyer, was imprisoned by Pennsylvania officials on a charge of forcible abduction and assault when he sought to prevent the return to slavery of a Negro woman in Philadelphia. When Williamson refused to divulge the whereabouts of the slave woman, he was imprisoned for contempt of court for three months.

32. After the passage of the Kansas-Nebraska Act, settlers from the North and the South poured into Kansas. The slaveowners organized bands of ruffians recruited from the riff-raff elements of western Missouri to invade Kansas and assist in establishing slavery in the territory. In elections for a delegate to Congress in November, 1854, and for a territorial legislature in March, 1855, the pro-slavery forces, through the use of illegal voting and the terroristic tactics of the "Border Ruffians" from Missouri, carried both contests.

33. The rest of the sentence is illegible in the original.

34. The American (or Know-Nothing) Party was founded in 1849 as a secret patriotic

society known as the Order of the Star Spangled Banner. Members were sworn not to reveal its secrets, hence their answer to all questions concerning the movement was, "I know nothing about it," thus giving the organization its popular name, the Know-Nothing Party. Its members were pledged to vote only for native-born Americans, to agitate for a twenty-one-year probation period preceding naturalization and to combat the Catholic Church. The movement grew enormously after 1852, but declined a few years later.

35. The Republican Party was organized at Ripon, Wisconsin in 1854 following passage of the Kansas-Nebraska Act. It was an amalgamation of former Whigs and Free Soilers and raised as its key issue opposition to the further expansion of slavery in the territories.

36. Elizabeth Cady Stanton (1815-1902), Abolitionist and woman suffrage leader who was the organizer of the Seneca Falls Convention in 1848, the first woman's rights convention in history. For Douglass' relations with Mrs. Stanton and woman's rights in general, see Life and Writings of Douglass, vol. II, pp. 15-29, 541-42.

37. The National Anti-Slavery Standard of January 12, 1856 reprinted an article from The Empire, an anti-slavery paper published in London, which included a letter from Garrison, part of which was a criticism of The Empire's previous review of Douglass' second autobiography, My Bondage and My Freedom, published in 1855, with an introduction by Dr. James McCune Smith. Garrison wrote: that Douglass' book was "remarkable, it is true, for its thrilling sketches of a slave's life and experience, and for the ability displayed in its pages, but which, in its second portion, is reeking with the virus of personal malignity towards Wendell Phillips, myself and the old organizationists generally, and full of ingratitude and baseness towards as true and disinterested friends as any man yet had on earth, to give him aid and encouragement. The Empire speaks of the work as 'frank and ingenious'— when it is precisely the reverse of this. The preface by J. McCune Smith is, in its innuendoes, a very base production." The editor of The Empire thanked Garrison for setting him straight about Douglass' book, and explained that his friendly review was based on reviews in the American papers, and copious extracts from the work which had been circulated by the publishers. "It was not our intention or design to pronounce any opinion on the conduct of Mr. Douglass as an Abolitionist; still less to convey the impression that we approved of the course which, since 1851, he has pursued towards those whom we know to have been his truest friends, and whose only cause of offence to Mr. Douglass has been their steadfastness to principles, and their desires and efforts (alas! in vain) to save a brother from self-destruction."

Actually, the sections Garrison complained of were anything but "reeking with the virus of personal malignity." The earlier portion of the book, like the Narrative, is extremely appreciative of the influence of Garrison and Phillips on Douglass' dvelopment as an antislavery spokesman, and when he discusses his break with Garrison, he devotes only two pages to it (396-398) and treats the issues as one of honest disagreement without the slightest disparagement of either Garrison or Phillips.

In his preface, James McCune Smith does have some sharp words to say about Garrison and his associates. Thus he writes: ". . . these gentlemen, although proud of Frederick Douglass, failed to fathom, and bring out to the light of day, the highest qualities of his mind, the force of their own education stood in their own way, they did not delve into the mind of a colored man for capacities which the pride of race led them to believe to be restricted to their own Saxon blood. Bitter and vindictive sarcasm, irresistible mimicry, and a pathetic narrative of his own experiences of slavery, were the intellectual manifestations which they encouraged him to exhibit on the platform or in the lecture desk." (p. xxii).

There is no evidence that Garrison answered Douglass' letter. For a discussion of the split between Douglass and Garrison, see *Life and Writings of Douglass*, vol. II, pp. 48-65.

38. Illegible in original.

39. Lysander Spooner (1808-1887), Boston lawyer and exponent of individualism, author of *The Unconstitutionality of Slavery* (1845), which was widely quoted in the battle over the interpretation of the Constitution as a pro-slavery or anti-slavery document.

40. In his message to Congress, Pierce justified the repeal of the Missouri Compromise in the Kansas-Nebraska Act, blamed the North for any difficulties arising out of the Kansas situation, and praised the South for having made many concessions to the North in the interest of the Union. Referring to the danger of the disunion, he asked if the American people were ready to uphold the "interests of the relative few Africans in the United States as totally to abandon and disregard the interests of 25,000,000 Americans." Evidently, according to President Pierce, Negroes were not Americans.

41. William J. Watkins operated in Boston; Dr. Smith sent his contributions from New York City, Vashon from Pittsburgh, Langston from Ohio, and Gaines from Philadelphia.

42. Garrison's reply to the speech of Congressman A. P. Granger of New York in the House of Representatives appeared in *The Liberator* of April 25, 1856. In his speech, Granger contended that "slavery in the United States is unconstitutional, and therefore unlawful." Garrison attacked the concept, and concluded: "Away with such childish folly, and up with the banner whereupon is inscribed the motto, 'NO UNION WITH SLAVEHOLDERS!'"

The issue of *Frederick Douglass' Paper* containing Douglass' discussion of Garrison's editorial appears to be no longer in existence.

43. The "Address to the Abolitionists of the United States," reported to the Convention on May 28 by Gerrit Smith, was a long analysis of the shortcomings of the Republican Party as being, among other things, often motivated by an anti-Negro sentiment rather than opposition to slavery in opposing further extension of slavery in the territories. The full text of the "Address" is published in *Radical Abolitionist*, June 2, 1856, pp. 89-94.

44. Elihu Burritt (1811-1879), pacifist and founder of the League of Universal Brotherhood, in 1846 to lead the movement against war. Burritt advocated compensated emancipation as a means of ending slavery.

45. For a discussion of this aspect of the Republican Party, see Eric Foner, *Free Soil*,

*Free Labor, Free Men, The Ideology of the Republican Party before the Civil War,* New York, 1970.

46. Douglass may be referring here to the feeling of Anna Douglass over the scandal that erupted in connection with the relations of Douglass and Julia Griffiths. For a discussion of this issue, *see Life and Writings of Douglass,* vol. II, pp. 55-59.

47. Anna Douglass continued to suffer from rheumatism which confined her to the indoors until she died in August, 1882. "Mother was the post in the center of my house and held us together," Douglass wrote shortly after her death. (Douglass to Doctress S. M. Loguen, August 12, 1882, *Mss.* Howard University Library.)

The tribute to Anna Murray Douglass by her daughter Rosetta Douglass Sprague, *My Mother as I Recall Her,* makes it clear that Douglass was sincere, that he had been devoted to his wife, and appreciated the many contributions she made towards his progress from obscurity to fame:

"During her wedded life of forty-four years, whether in adversity or prosperity, she was the same faithful ally, guarding as best she could every interest connected with my father, his life-work and the home. Unfortunately an opportunity for knowledge of books had been denied to her, the lack of which she greatly deplored. Her increasing family and household duties prevented any great advancement, altho' she was able to read a little. By contact with people of culture and education, and they were her real friends, her improvement was marked. She took a lively interest in every phase of the Anti-Slavery movement, an interest that father took full pains to foster and to keep her intelligently informed. I was instructed to read to her. She was a good listener, making comments on passing events, which were well worth consideration, altho' the manner of presentation of them might provoke a smile. Her value was fully appreciated by my father, and in one of his letters to Thomas Auld (his former master), he says: 'Instead of finding my companion a burden she is truly a helpmeet.'" (Rosetta Douglass Sprague, *My Mother as I Recall Her. Delivered Before the Anna Murray Douglass Union W.C.T.U. Washington, D.C., 1900,* reprinted Washington, D.C., 1923, pp. 12-14.) For Douglass' letters to his former master, *see Life and Writings of Douglass,* vol. I, pp. 336-43, 403-06.

48. Douglass had four children: Rosetta, Lewis, Frederick Junior, and Charles Remond.

49. In 1836 James A. Thomas and Horace Kimbell were sent to the West Indies by the Americans Anti-Slavery Society to investigate and report on the results of the emancipation program. The resulting report, *Emancipation in the West Indies. A Six Months Tour in Antigua, Barbadoes, and Jamaica, in the Year 1837* (New York, 1838), emphasized the success of the program and was widely read, going through many editions.

50. This must be an error in reporting, for Douglass meant to say "caves of millions and mountains of gold."

51. Douglass refers to President James Buchanan, Democratic Senator Lewis Cass of Michigan, Democratic Senator Isaac Toucey of Connecticut, and Democratic Congressman Howell Cobb of Georgia.

52. Rufus Choate (1799-1859), famous as a trial lawyer and orator, member of the U.S. House of Representatives (1831-1834) and U.S. Senate (1841-1845).

53. Caleb Cushing (1800-1879), Whig member of U.S. House of Representatives (1835-1843), and U.S. Attorney General (1853-1857) under President Franklin Pierce.

54. Edward Everett (1794-1865), U.S. Secretary of State (1852-1853) under President Millard Fillmore and famous orator of the period.

55. All of these men were Massachusetts anti-slavery figures.

56. Douglass here quotes from Lincoln's famous "House Divided" speech delivered in Springfield, Illinois, June 16, 1858. (For the text of Lincoln's speech, *see* Roy P. Basler, editor, *The Collected Works of Abraham Lincoln*, New Brunswick, New Jersey, vol. II, pp. 461-69.)

   Douglass' attack on Stephen A. Douglass and his praise of Abraham Lincoln made his Poughkeepsie speech an issue in the famous Lincoln-Douglas debates. The editorial in the *Illinois State Register* of August 7, 1858 was entitled, "Another Ally of Lincoln—The N----r Chief Out for Him." *See also* Senator Douglas' speech in Charleston, Illinois, September 18, 1858, in Basler, *op. cit.*, vol. III, pp. 171-72.

57. The reference is to David R. Atchison, an ardently pro-slavery Missouri Democrat.

58. The speeches in the evening meeting were not reported. In its report of the whole proceeding, the *Times* reporter observed: "Never was the event more warmly welcomed or more pleasantly observed than in Poughkeepsie yesterday." (Aug. 3, 1858.)

59. Benjamin Coates of Philadelphia was a leading supporter of African emigration as the solution for the problems of black Americans. He helped finance Martin R. Delany's mission to Africa in 1858 to make a Topographical, Geological and Geographical Examination of the Valley of the River Niger. Delany dedicated his report to contributors in America and England, "but particularly to *Benjamin Coates* of Philadelphia, whose unremitting efforts contributed in no small degree to the success of the enterprise."

60. Dred Scott, a slave was brought by his master, Dr. Emerson, into the Louisiana Territory above the line where slavery was legally prohibited. Here he lived a number of years, married and raised a family. Eventually Dred Scott and his family were brought back to the slave state of Missouri. After Dr. Emerson's death, they were sold to a New Yorker, Sanford, whom they eventually sued for their freedom.

   The case was decided by the Supreme Court on March 6, 1857. Chief Justice Taney, writing the majority decision, held that the Missouri Circuit Court had no jurisdiction over the case since the Scotts were not and could never have been citizens within the meaning of the Constitution, and therefore, had no right to sue in a Federal Court. Indeed, the Negro "had no rights which the white man was bound to respect." Taney also upheld the right of slaveowners to take their slaves to any territory of the United Sates and to hold them there in bondage no matter what Congress or the territorial legislature said to the country. Congress, in short, had no constitutional power to enact the Missouri Compromise.

For Douglass' discussion of the Supreme Court opinion, *see* his speech "The Dred Scott Decision," *Life and Writings of Douglass*, vol. II. pp. 407-25.

61. Neither Haiti nor Liberia were recognized by the United States until 1862 during the Lincoln Administration.

62. The resolutions, drawn up by Douglass for a meeting to protest the execution of Ira Stout for the crime of murder, were never acted on at the meeting, which was broken up by a mob. "Our resolutions were now read by Mr. Douglass," wrote one of the women present, "but it was impossible to act upon them. The scene at this time beggars description; yells of the most hideous order, groans, hisses, stamping of feet, whistling, language too vile to pen, were the order of the hour." (Lucy N. Colman in *The Liberator*, October 22, 1858.)

63. H. Ford Douglass was a runaway slave who became a leading Abolitionist orator in the Midwest.

64. Frances Anne "Fanny" Kemble was a famous English actress. She came to the United States in 1833, toured the country, and married Pierce Butler, a member of an aristocratic Southern family. Before leaving for the South, she promised to write her friend Elizabeth Sedgwick, who was an opponent of slavery, of her experiences on Butler's cotton and rice plantations. In a series of letters Fanny Kemble described the conditions of the slaves and her reaction to slavery, and later she released her letters for book publication, hoping that her description of slavery would influence Great Britain to support the Union rather than the Confederacy. Her *Journal of a Residence on a Georgia Plantation* was published in New York, 1863.

65. The African Civilization Society, founded by Henry Highland Garnet, had as one of its aims opening up of commerce between Africa, the United States and Great Britain. Opponents of emigration were particularly critical of Garnet because the African Civilization Society accepted support from members of the Colonization Society. For Douglass' criticism of Garnet and the African Civilization Society, *see* "African Civilization Society," *Douglass, Monthly*, February, 1859, reprinted in *Life and Writings of Douglass*, vol. II, pp. 541-47.

66. The reference, of course, is to John Brown (1800-1859) who had been involved in the struggles in Kansas resulting from the passage of the Kansas-Nebraska Act, and had led the Pottawatomie massacre in Kansas in May, 1856.

67. *See* in this connection, Douglass' editorial after Harper's Ferry, "Capt. John Brown Not Insane," *Douglass' Monthly*, November, 1859, reprinted in *Life and Writings of Douglass*, vol. II, pp. 458-60.

68. On May 22, 1856, two days after Senator Sumner delivered his speech, "The Crime Against Kansas," he was accosted at his desk by Representative Preston S. Brooks (1819-1857) of South Carolina, who denounced him for having uttered "a libel on South Carolina, and Mr. Butler, who is a relative of mine." Brooks then struck Sumner a blow on the head with his heavy walking stick, and continued to beat him until he fell bleeding and unconscious to the floor. Three and a half years passed before Sumner was sufficiently recovered to return to the Senate. Meanwhile he had been re-elected by the almost unanimous vote of the Massachusetts legislature.

69. And first among these may be named, Arthur and Lewis Tappan, Rev. S. S.

Jocelyn, Rev. A. A. Phelps, Robert Vaux of Philadelphia, E. Wright, Jr., Joshua Leavitt, Samuel J. May, Reuben Crandell, Hon. James G. Birney, Theodore Sedgwick, Beriah Green, Gerrit Smith, John Scobie of England, Lydia Maria Child, Miss Grimke of South Carolina, Wm. Goodell, G. Bailey, Jr., Rev. Dr. Morrison of England, Gov. R. W. Haversham of Georgia, W. Anderson, Esq., of Jamaica, W.I., Joseph Sturge, Esq., of England, Hon Jabez D. Hammond, Geo. W. Alexander of England, Hon William Slade of Vermont, Hon. John Quincy Adams, Hon. Wm. H. Seward, Hon. S. P. Chase, Prof. C. C. Cleveland of Philadelphia, Thomas Clarkson of England, Sir W. Colebrook, Governor of New Brunswick, Hon. Charles Sumner, Chief Justice Hornblower of New Jersey, Hon. J. G. Palfrey, Hon. John P. Hale, besides more than a hundred others. —footnote in original.

70. When Oregon applied for admission as a state, its constitution barred Blacks from entering the state, and the few already there were forbidden to testify in court, make contracts or hold property. While about fifteen Republicans in the Senate did, as Douglass indicates, vote to admit Oregon with the proposed constitution, seventy-three were opposed.

71. This letter is interesting since it indicates quite clearly that Douglass planned to leave for Europe before he met John Brown at Chambersburg, Pennsylvania, on the eve of the raid in Harpers Ferry. For Douglass' relations to the raid, see *Life and Writings of Douglass*, vol. II, pp. 85-94.

72. Unable to use churches and halls for their meetings, the Abolitionists and other proponents of free discussion in Philadelphia erected in that city, at the cost of $40,000, Pennsylvania Hall. Dedicated on May 14, 1838, it was burned to the ground by a pro-slavery mob three days later.

73. This was the original plan Brown and Douglass had agreed to put into operation and which Douglass believed Brown was planning to undertake when he was summoned to meet him at Chambersburg.

74. Julia Griffiths had married Reverend H. O. Crofts.

75. The *Wakefield Express* noted that "he [Douglass] speaks the English language with great purity, and that as an orator he is most effective, being able to move the passions of men at will."

76. James Gillespie Birney (1792-1857), antislavery leader and advocate of colonization who was nominated for President in 1840 by the Liberty Party.

77. John C. Fremont (1813-1890) was the Republican candidate for president in the election of 1856.

78. Sarah P. Remond was the sister of Charles Lenox Remond and a noted antislavery speaker in her own right. She shared the platform with Douglass at the Wakefield meeting. For a discussion of her career, see Ruth Bogin's "Sarah Park Remond: Black Abolitionist From Salem," *Essex Institute Historical Collection*, April, 1974 pp. 120-150.

79. Douglass is undoubtedly referring to the visit of Brown to Rochester in the spring of 1859. *See above* pp. 000.

80. The convention held in Worcester was called by Stephen S. Foster and John Pierpont "to consider the propriety of organizing a *Political Party* upon an anti-

slavery interpretation of the U.S. Constitution, with the avowed purpose of abolishing slavery in the states, as well as the Territories of the Union."

81. The letter to Garrison, headed "The Political Anti-Slavery Convention At Worcester," generally heaped scorn on the gathering. In its comments on Douglass, "J. A. H." wrote: "Mr. Douglass seemed to come quite readily into the work of the annihilation of the American A.S. Society, and in his various speeches took frequent occasion to misrepresent its character, and with his inimitable powers of sarcasm to caricature its positions and measures. At one time, in urging the support of this new movement, he said that it was the only organization that proposed the abolition of slavery. Mr. Howland suggested the incorrectness of this assertion. In reply, Mr. Douglass said, I know that our friend thinks that the object of the American Anti-Slavery Society is the abolition of slavery, but he is mistaken, for the object of that Society is the dissolution of the American Union. To be sure, they hold that the abolition of slavery will follow the dissolution of the Union, but that is a matter of opinion. In my opinion it would not."

"J. A. H." called Douglass' remark, as he reported it, an "audacious libel," adding: "Had Mr. Douglass simply said that, in his opinion, the position or action of the American Anti-Slavery Society could not result in the abolition of slavery, or even explained that this was what he meant in what he did say, it would have clearly appeared to be his right to hold and express this opinion. . . . But he did no such thing. And it is to be hoped that whenever he utters so atrocious a slander, some one will have the manliness to rebuke him with as plain Anglo-Saxon speech as Mr. Howland did on this occasion." (*The Liberator*, September 28, 1860.)

82. The events at Tremont Temple grew out of a meeting in Boston on December 3, 1860, to commemorate the anniversary of John Brown's execution. Ruffians, hired by merchants engaged in the Southern trade, invaded the hall, disrupted the proceedings, and singled out Douglass for attack. For Douglass' reply to the disruption of the meeting, *see* his masterful, "A Plea for Free Speech in Boston," *Life and Writings of Douglass*, vol. II, pp. 538-40.

83. The *Boston Pilot* was a Catholic paper extremely hostile to the Abolitionists. For evidence that this is not entirely fair to Garrison, see *The Liberator*, December 14, 1860.

84. Douglass was referring to the fact that leading Republicans, like Thurlow Weed, were urging that concessions be granted to the South to keep the Southern states in the Union.

85. Early in April, 1861, however, Douglass made plans to visit Haiti so that he could investigate conditions for himself and report back on the value of emigration to that country. His steamer, chartered by the Haitian Bureau of Emigration at Boston, was scheduled to sail on April 25. But with the firing on Fort Sumter by the Confederates and the outbreak of the Civil War, Douglass cancelled the plans.

# Appendix

1. The *Creole* sailed from Hampton Roads, Virginia, for New Orleans in October 1841 with eight crew members, five sailors, a cargo of tobacco, 135 slaves, and six white passengers (three white men in charge of the slaves, together with the captain's wife, child, and niece). *See Senate Documents*, 27 Congress, 2nd Session, vol. II, No. 51, pp. 1-46. This is a fairly complete documentary collection on the *Creole* affair.

2. Only nineteen slaves, led by Madison Washington, participated in the slave uprising, but they quickly took control of the brig.

3. Only one white man died, John Hewell, owner of thirty-nine of the slaves. Two of the Blacks in the revolt were seriously wounded, one of them later dying.

4. Douglass' account here is basically correct, but he omits the fact that the slaves aboard the *Creole* were actually released by the Black islanders who surrounded the brig in boats, an action which led the authorities to release the slaves of the *Creole*. British officials in Nassau warned Americans of the *Creole* that resistance to the slaves' liberation would incite the Blacks on the island and cause bloodshed.

   In 1855 an Anglo-American Claims Commission awarded $110,330 to owners of the liberated slaves. The British government was required to compensate owners of the *Creole's* slaves on the ground that the brig had been on a lawful voyage, and had had the right to expect shelter from a friendly power when "unavoidable necessity" drove it into Nassau. *See* Howard Jones, "The Peculiar Institution and National Honor: The Case of the *Creole* Slave Revolt," *Civil War History*, March 1975, pp. 45-47.

5. Sections of the short story also appeared in *Frederick Douglass' Paper*, March 11, 1853.

# Index

## BY PHILIP S. FONER

History of the Labor Movement in the United States (4 vols.)

The Life and Writings of Frederick Douglass (4 vols.)

A History of Cuba and Its Relations with the United States (2 vols.)

The Complete Writings of Thomas Paine (2 vols.)

Business and Slavery: The New York Merchants and the Irrepressible Conflict

W.E.B. Du Bois Speaks (2 vols.)

The Fur and Leather Workers Union

Jack London: American Rebel

Mark Twain: Social Critic

The Jews in American History: 1654-1865

The Case of Joe Hill

The Letters of Joe Hill

The Bolshevik Revolution: Its Impact on American Radicals, Liberals, and Labor

American Labor and the War in Indochina

The Autobiographies of the Haymarket Martyrs

Helen Keller: Her Socialist Years

The Black Panthers Speak

The Basic Writings of Thomas Jefferson

The Selected Writings of George Washington

The Selected Writings of Franklin D. Roosevelt

The Selected Writings of Abraham Lincoln

The Voice of Black America: Major Speeches of Negroes in the United States, 1797-1971

Morale Education and the American Army: War for Independence, War of 1812, Civil War

The Spanish-Cuban-American War and the Birth of American Imperialism, 1895-1902 (2 vols.)

When Karl Marx Died: Comments in 1883

Organized Labor and the Black Worker, 1619-1973

American Labor Songs of the Nineteenth Century

History of Black Americans: From Africa to the Emergence of the Cotton Kingdom